THE BEST PLAYS OF 1988–1989

THE BEST PLAYS OF 1985-1986

THE

BURNS MANTLE

YEARBOOK

THE
BEST PLAYS
OF 1988–1989

EDITED BY OTIS L. GUERNSEY JR.
AND JEFFREY SWEET

*Illustrated with photographs and
with drawings by* HIRSCHFELD

APPLAUSE ❦
THEATRE BOOK PUBLISHERS
211 West 71 St. New York, N.Y. 10023

25th Street, New York, N.Y. 10010. All other inquiries should be addressed to: Jeannine Edmunds, c/o Curtis Brown Ltd., 10 Astor Place, New York, N.Y. 10003.

Al Hirschfeld is represented exclusively by The Margo Feiden Galleries, New York.

EDITOR'S NOTE

WITH THIS 70th *Best Plays* volume in the series of theater annuals started by Burns Mantle after the season of 1919–20, we take a promising and challenging new turn. Glenn Young's Applause Theatre Books has replaced Dodd, Mead & Company as the publisher of *Best Plays* on a rising note of service and interest for the reader. Specifically a publisher and purveyor of a large selection of theater scripts, critiques, essays, reminiscences, etc., Applause is wholly *theater*-oriented and already had an important relationship with the *Best Plays* series after publishing *Curtain Times: The New York Theater 1965–1987*, an anthology of all the Guernsey reviews of the New York theater in the *Best Plays* volumes of those years. Referencing every Broadway and off-Broadway title season by season, and reporting on most of them with allusions to all the major achievements of writing, acting, directing and design, *Curtain Times* is a compact "starter" volume for anyone wishing to begin a theater library of *Best Plays* annuals in the Applause era, rooting it back to 1964–65 across seasons whose individual *Best Plays* yearbooks have long been out of print.

The promise of this new Applause era is handsomely fulfilled here in *The Best Plays of 1988–89*. Henceforth we will consider for Best Play citation those off-off-Broadway scripts which have made their mark in national and/or world theater before arriving in New York and thus deserve special consideration among the works-in-progress, of which most of OOB consists. Such an exception is David Williamson's scintillating Australian comedy *Emerald City*, a Best Play in this volume. And Applause wishes to provide its *Best Plays* readers with the nugget of a *complete* playscript along with the usual synopses, certainly in this volume and, we hope, in each succeeding Applause volume—a script which has not previously and might not otherwise be published in the U.S. (and this year we choose and offer *Emerald City* in its entirety in these pages).

What of all the traditional departments of information that have made the *Best Plays* series a star of personal and public theater library shelves for lo these 70 years? *Best Plays* has grown steadily in scope and usefulness through six editors, and it never has and never will move backward. All the previous ingredients are abundantly present in *The Best Plays of 1988–89*, mixed by the same skillful and untiring hands. Jonathan Dodd is still supervising publication, now for Applause, and the editor-in-chief's indefatigable wife is still guarding and improving the accuracy of our coverage. Associate editor

Jeffrey Sweet, a successful playwright and screen writer as well as a supremely articulate critic, reviews Broadway and off Broadway in detail never before attempted by the *Best Plays* critic; and *his* indefatigable wife, Sheridan Sweet, compiles our broad-based listing of new plays produced in cross-country theater (and we are as proud as ever that the American Theater Critics Association annually announces and represents its choices of outstanding cross-country production in our yearbook, their committee headed this year by Dan Sullivan of the Los Angeles *Times* and their ATCA New Play Prize going to August Wilson's *The Piano Lesson*).

With our ever-closer look at off off Broadway, we offer the most comprehensive coverage of this vital and ever-expanding area of New York tributary theater: a survey of its season by Mel Gussow, distinguished theater critic of the New York *Times*, with his choices of the season's best work OOB, plus Camille Croce's annual record of the activities of 100 or more OOB groups. We cherish the continuing annual expertise of Rue E. Canvin (play publications and necrology), Stanley Green (reporting major cast replacements for his 20th *Best Plays* year), Sally Dixon Wiener (two Best Play synopses), William Schelble (Tony Awards), and many other enhancers of *The Best Plays of 1988–89*: Thomas T. Foose (historical footnotes), Henry Hewes (a previous *Best Plays* editor, helpful in many, many respects), Ossia Trilling (Our Man in London), Michael Kuchwara (Critics Circle voting), Gary Denys (for his layouts), Dorothy Swerdlove of the Lincoln Center Library, Robert Newman of the Drama Book Shop—and most particularly the men and women in the Broadway, off-Broadway, OOB and cross-country press offices without whose diligence, patience, generosity and know-how there could never be a *Best Plays* yearbook in its present form.

We don't know how to express fully our delight in and admiration for Al Hirschfeld's witty coverage of the New York stage, except to publish as many of his wonderful drawings as we can. We also extend our admiration and thanks to David Mitchell and Jane Greenwood for their permission to publish examples of their drawings for stage designs, among the best of the season. We greatly appreciate the handsome extra of photographs of the 1988–89 season in New York and across the country by Martha Swope (especially in our extended pictorial coverage of *Jerome Robbins' Broadway* as a Best Play citation) and her associates Carol Rosegg, Linda Alaniz and Rebecca Lesher, and Catherine Ashmore, Clive Barda, Chris Bennion, Eddie Birch, Tom Brazil, Susan Cook, Peter Cunningham, Alan David, T. Charles Erickson, Gerry Goodstein, Randall Hagadorn, Carol Halebian, Ken Howard, Paul Kolnik, Brigitte Lacombe, Tom Lawlor, Joan Marcus, Claudia Miller, Mark Navarro, Arlene Schulman, Anita and Steve Shevett, Diane Sobolewski and Jay Thompson.

It was a time of some stress for the *Best Plays* publishers, editors and contributors during the transition from Dodd, Mead to Glenn Young and

Applause, just as 1988–89 was a season of some discontent, as the lights seemed to be growing dimmer on musical stages. Our *Best Plays* series has emerged into the sunlight, however, and "bigger and better than ever" would not be an exaggeration when applied to it. The theater does not recover so quickly from an occasional malaise, but recover it always does. When the lights go down in one area, they invariably brighten in another, sustaining attention and excitement through any temporary adversity. Our dramatists see to that; whatever happens, ten best or also-ran, they never give up, and collectively they always come through—witness the amusing, trenchant, stimulating stuff of which this volume is made as it records the events of the 1988–89 season. Good luck to them now, and better luck to them next year, when *Best Plays* will be watching and applauding (Applausing?) for the 71st time.

OTIS L. GUERNSEY Jr.
Editor

September 1, 1989

CONTENTS

Drawings by HIRSCHFELD   55

THE BEST PLAYS OF 1988–1989

THE SEASON
ON AND OFF
BROADWAY

Characters
of the Season

Left, Kevin Conway as Garfinkle in *Other People's Money; above,* Pauline Collins as *Shirley Valentine; below left,* Joan Allen as Heidi in *The Heidi Chronicles; below right,* Philip Bosco as Saunders in *Lend Me a Tenor.*

BROADWAY AND OFF BROADWAY

By Jeffrey Sweet

IT TAKES no equestrian expertise to figure that a horse with only three legs will not do well in a race. Theatrically, the 1988–89 season was something of a three-legged horse. Yes, there were several strong new plays. Yes, there were a number of fine revivals. Yes, there were some marvelous special events. No, there was little of significance by way of new musicals.

The year's biggest attempt at a new musical, cabaret star Peter Allen's show about a gangster with a passion for singing and dancing, *Legs Diamond*, was widely viewed not merely as a failure but as an embarrassment. Other essays at the form on Broadway—*Starmites*, *Welcome to the Club* and *Chu Chem*—were of a smaller scale and, at best, amiably forgettable. Nor did off Broadway make significant contributions to the form, the only notable piece being writer-director-choreographer Kim Friedman's *The Middle of Nowhere*, which imaginatively employed a trunkful of Randy Newman's songs in the service of a small ensemble of characters of her own creation.

The smashing success of *Jerome Robbins' Broadway* underscored the drought. A spectacular sampling of high points from the master director-choreographer's theatrical work, dating from shows originally produced in the Forties, Fifties and early Sixties, it prompted the nearly universal reaction of, "Wow! Why can't anybody do work that good today?" I believe the answer to that question lies not so much in a lack of musical theater talent but in the economic climate which discourages that talent and offers little practical opportunity to gain the experience necessary to sharpen skills. Whatever the reason, however, clearly nobody currently on Broadway has filled the vacancy Robbins left when he turned away from the stage to devote the bulk of his energies to ballet roughly 25 years ago. Clearly, too, we are the poorer for it. It is sobering to watch a brilliant ensemble of dancers hurtle their way through a suite of breathtaking dances from 1957's *West Side Story* in one theater and to stroll down the street to another to watch a young man frolic wanly about the stage in a lizard's costume in 1989's *Starmites*. One can but hope that the

3

The 1988–89 Season on Broadway

PLAYS (8)

Checkmates
Spoils of War
Rumors
EASTERN STANDARD (transfer)
Hizzoner!
LEND ME A TENOR
Metamorphosis
THE HEIDI CHRONICLES (transfer)

MUSICALS (4)

Legs Diamond
Chu Chem
Welcome to the Club
Starmites

REVUES (3)

Canciones de Mi Padre
Black and Blue
JEROME ROBBINS' BROADWAY

FOREIGN PLAYS IN ENGLISH (3)

SHIRLEY VALENTINE
Run for Your Wife!
Ghetto

HOLDOVERS WHICH BECAME HITS IN 1988–89

M. Butterfly
The Phantom of the Opera
Sarafina!
Speed-the-Plow

REVIVALS (10)

Long Day's Journey Into Night
Juno and the Paycock
Ah, Wilderness!
The Night of the Iguana
Ain't Misbehavin'
Paul Robeson
The Devil's Disciple
Our Town
Born Yesterday
Cafe Crown (transfer)

SPECIALTIES (6)

Michael Feinstein in Concert
Kenny Loggins on Broadway
Christmas Spectacular
The Wizard of Oz
Barry Manilow at the Gershwin
Largely New York

Categorized above are all the new productions listed in the Plays Produced on Broadway section of this volume.
Plays listed in CAPITAL LETTERS have been designated Best Plays of 1988–89.
Plays listed in *italics* were still running June 1, 1989.
Plays listed in **bold face type** were classified as successes in *Variety's* annual estimate published May 31, 1989.

Robbins show will inspire younger artists and encourage producers to revitalize a form which used to be synonymous with the glory of Broadway.

All four of the Best Plays on Broadway this year were comedies: Wendy Wasserstein's *The Heidi Chronicles*, Richard Greenberg's *Eastern Standard*, Willy Russell's *Shirley Valentine* and Ken Ludwig's *Lend Me a Tenor*. Ludwig's was one of three new farces this year, the others being Ray Cooney's frantic *Run for Your Wife!* and *Rumors*, a rare fizzle from the prolific and usually proficient Neil Simon. The three dramas produced on Broadway—Michael Weller's *Spoils of War*, Joshua Sobol's *Ghetto* and Steven Berkoff's adaptation of Kafka's *Metamorphosis*—were more notable for ambition than achievement, though a substantial audience turned out to see ballet superstar Mikhail Baryshnikov make his dramatic debut playing one of literature's most famous bugs.

Away from Broadway, the business of dramatists was frequently business, the two most successful of these works being the Best Plays *Other People's Money* and *Emerald City*; the former, Jerry Sterner's tale of a hostile takeover, the latter, Australian playwright David Williamson's bruising view of show business down under. The season's two most distinguished imports, both Best Plays, dealt with ways of life transformed in the wake of financial depression: *Road*, Jim Cartwright's tour of a devastated town in Northern England, and *Aristocrats*, a group portrait of a once well-to-do Irish family on the verge of disintegration. Another well-to-do family, this one American, was the subject of A. R. Gurney's Best Play *The Cocktail Hour*, which dealt in a comic mode with their alternately bewildered, bemused and irritated reactions to an era in which they are viewed as anachronisms.

Gurney's play was an essentially cheerful one building to a reconciliation; and so, ultimately, was Lee Blessing's *Eleemosynary*, a piece about a grandmother, mother and daughter in conflict. Few other off-Broadway writers offered hopeful or comforting views of American family life, however. Bill Gunn's *The Forbidden City*, Susan Miller's *For Dear Life*, Paul Zindel's *Amulets Against the Dragon Forces*, Craig Lucas's *Reckless*, John Patrick Shanley's *Italian American Reconciliation* and Keith Curran's *Dalton's Back* all dealt with failed marriages and/or destructive parent-child relations.

As is now more the rule than the exception, most of the Broadway attractions originated elsewhere, usually in nonprofit arenas. *The Heidi Chronicles* was developed at Seattle Rep and was introduced to New York by Playwrights Horizons. *Eastern Standard* also began at Seattle and premiered in New York at the Manhattan Theater Club. *Lend Me a Tenor* (though written by an American) was first produced in London, as were *Shirley Valentine, Run for Your Wife!* and *Metamorphosis. Spoils of War* was first given off off Broadway at the Second Stage, *Rumors* at San Diego's Old Globe, Ron Milner's *Checkmates* at Los Angeles's Inner City Cultural Center, Paul Shyre's *Hizzoner!* at Albany's Empire State Institute for the Performing Arts,

OUTSTANDING STAGE DESIGNS OF THE SEASON—*Above,* examples of
the Claudio Segovia-Hector Orezzoli costumes for *Black and Blue* (with
Frederick J. Boothe and Kyme *in foreground*); *below,* a photo of David
Mitchell's model for a scene in the musical *Legs Diamond; above on opposite
page,* Jane Greenwood costume sketches for *Our Town*

Chu Chem at the Jewish Repertory Theater, a brace of O'Neill revivals at Yale Rep, a revival of *Juno and the Paycock* at Dublin's Gate Theater, a revival of *Paul Robeson* at New Jersey's Crossroads Theater Company, a revival of *Cafe Crown* at the New York Shakespeare Festival Public Theater, *Welcome to the Club* at Florida's Coconut Grove Playhouse, *Black and Blue* at the Théâtre Musical de Paris, *Ghetto* in Israel at the Haifa Municipal Theater and *Starmites* at the Ark Theater Company, Musical Theater Works and Milford, New Hampshire's American Stage Festival.

Off Broadway again the bulk of the plays began their lives off off Broadway, in regional theaters or on foreign stages. Among the producing organizations which premiered works which made their way to off Broadway this season were Boston's American Repertory Theater, the Hartford Stage, the Indiana University Department of Theater and Drama, the O'Neill Theater Center, St. Paul's Park Square Theater, the Philadelphia Festival Theater for New Plays, the American Theater Company in Aspen, Colorado, Los Angeles's Mark Taper Forum, the National Theater, the Royal Court Theater and the Hempstead Theater Club of London, Ireland's Field Day and, in New York, the American Jewish Theater, the Jewish Repertory Theater and the WPA.

Four companies stood out among New York's institutional theaters this season, presenting two or more memorable productions. In addition to *Eastern Standard* and *Aristocrats*, the Manhattan Theater Club produced a splendid revival of Joe Orton's *What the Butler Saw*. In addition to *The Heidi Chronicles*, Playwrights Horizons premiered another Best Play, Albert Innaurato's *Gus and Al*. Lincoln Center's presentation of *Road* was followed by a controversial staging of Samuel Beckett's *Waiting for Godot* and strong productions of *Measure for Measure* and *Our Town*. Joseph Papp's Public Theater had little success with the new works it premiered, but this season's batch of Shakespeare productions was of an unusually high order, capped by a magical *The Winter's Tale*.

The season's most potent concentration of star power had to be found in the company of the *Godot*, featuring as it did Robin Williams and Steve Martin as the two tramps, the Academy Award-winning F. Murray Abraham as Pozzo and Bill Irwin as Lucky. Among the other celebrated performers who commanded stages this season were Jason Robards, Colleen Dewhurst, Kevin Kline, Blythe Danner, Christopher Reeve, Joan Allen, Anne Meara, Jerry Stiller, Mandy Patinkin, Jane Alexander, Maria Tucci, Joseph Maher, Carole Shelley, Ruby Dee, Paul Winfield, Denzel Washington, Kevin Bacon, Edward Asner, Madeline Kahn, Kate Nelligan, Len Cariou, Jack Weston, Joan Rivers, Alfre Woodard, Christopher Walken, George Hearn, Eric Stoltz, Spalding Gray, Esther Rolle, Ken Howard, Nancy Marchand, Avery Brooks, Elizabeth Wilson, Nell Carter, Diane Venora, Philip Bosco, Joan Cusack, Victor Garber, Jessica Walter, Ron Leibman, Julie Wilson, Eileen Heckart, Joanna Gleason, Avery Schreiber, Keene Curtis and Marilyn Sokol.

Actors whose names may not be as familiar to those outside theatrical circles also enriched the year, notable among them John Kavanagh, Donal McCann, Kevin Spacey, Peter Friedman, Raphael Sbarge, Jamey Sheridan, Robin Bartlett, John Spencer, Deborah Hedwall, Peter Frechette, Boyd Gaines, Joanne Camp, Christine Baranski, Tovah Feldshuh, Ron Holgate, Paul Hecht, Kevin Conway, Mercedes Ruehl, Jay O. Sanders, Roger Robinson, Penelope Ann Miller, Roberta Maxwell, Paxton Whitehead, Gloria Foster, Richard Libertini, William Converse-Roberts, Larry Keith, Paul Provenza, Rocco Sisto, Frankie R. Faison, Christine Kellogg, Jimmy Slyde, Bunny Briggs, Jason Alexander, Scott Wise, Robert La Fosse, Faith Prince, Debbie Shapiro, Charlotte d'Amboise, John Turturro, John Pankow, Niall Buggy, Pauline Collins, and the comedy teams of Kathy (Najimy) and Mo (Gaffney), and (Linda) Wallem and (Peter) Tolan.

Several directors familiar from past seasons were represented this go-round, among them Gregory Mosher, Jerry Zaks, Norman Rene, Mike Nichols, Daniel Sullivan, James Lapine, John Tillinger, Arvin Brown, Jose Quintero, Stephen Porter, Jack O'Brien, Martin Charnin, Gene Saks and Gerald Freedman. Among directors less familiar to New York audiences who contributed impressive work were Robin Lefevre with *Aristocrats*, Joe Dowling with *Juno and the Paycock*, Gloria Muzio with *Other People's Money*, Mark Lamos with *Measure for Measure*, David Warren with *Gus and Al* and Michael Engler with *Eastern Standard*. (It should be noted that only one of this number is a woman. Similarly, though Wendy Wasserstein was the season's most highly-honored dramatist, only a handful of other female writers got to see their work on or off Broadway.)

Scenically there was nothing on the scale of knock-'em-dead spectacles like *The Phantom of the Opera* and *Les Misérables*. David Mitchell contributed some delightfully jazzy images of mythical New York for *Legs Diamond*, and Claudio Segovia and Hector Orezzoli served up some dazzling variations with curtains in concert with Neil Peter Jampolis and Jane Reisman's lights for *Black and Blue*. Among straight plays on Broadway, I was particularly taken by Philipp Jung's sets for *Eastern Standard*, Tony Walton's sets and William Ivey Long's costumes for *Lend Me a Tenor* and Santo Loquasto's evocation of Second Avenue night life for *Cafe Crown*. Thomas Lynch's sets, Jennifer von Mayrhauser's costumes and Pat Collins's lighting underscored the satiric tone of *The Heidi Chronicles*. *Our Town* benefitted from costumer Jane Greenwood's remarkable variations on small-town themes, as well as Kevin Rigdon's subtle lighting on Douglas Stein's necessarily minimal sets.

Off Broadway, the technical emphasis was on wit and delicacy, befitting the large number of pieces which were either comedies or fantasies. Among the more notable achievements were Ray Recht's nimble scenery and lighting for *Laughing Matters*, James Youman's sets, David C. Woolard's costumes and Robert Jared's lighting which created in Playwrights Horizons's tiny upstairs space the most delicate suggestion of gracious living in old Vienna for *Gus and Al*; the clash between American plastic and Asian elegance in Kent Dorsey's sets, Jess Goldstein's costumes and Dan Kotlowitz's lighting for *Yankee Dawg You Die*; and the storybook enchantment John Arnone's sets, Franne Lee's costumes and Beverly Emmons's lighting created for *The Winter's Tale*.

As admirable as much of the designing was, the focus of this volume is on the texts the editors believe defined the best work of contemporary dramatists represented in New York this season. To repeat the guidelines articulated by Otis L. Guernsey Jr. in past editions, "The choice is made without any regard whatever to the play's type—musical, comedy or drama—or origin on or off Broadway, or popularity at the box office or lack of same.

"We don't take the scripts of bygone eras into consideration for Best Play citation in this one, whatever their technical status as American or New York 'premieres' which didn't happen to have a previous production of record. We draw the line between adaptations and revivals, the former eligible for Best Play selection but the latter not, on a case-by-case basis.....If a script influences the character of a season, or by some function of concensus wins the Critics, Pulitzer or Tony Awards, we take into account its future historical as well as present esthetic importance. This is the only special consideration we give, and we don't always tilt in its direction, as the record shows."

Our choices for the Best Plays of 1988–89 are listed below in the order in which they opened in New York (a plus sign + with the performance number signifies that the play was still running on June 1, 1989).

Road
(Off B'way, 62 perfs.)

The Cocktail Hour
(Off B'way, 258+ perfs.)

Eastern Standard
(Off B'way, 46 perfs.;
B'way 92 perfs.)

Emerald City
(Off Off B'way, 17 perfs.)

The Heidi Chronicles
(Off B'way 81 perfs.;
B'way 96+ perfs.)

Other People's Money
(Off B'way, 121+ perfs.)

Shirley Valentine
(B'way, 136+ perfs.)

*Jerome Robbins' Broadway
(Special)*
(B'way, 109+ perfs.)

Gus and Al
(Off B'way, 25 perfs.)

Lend Me a Tenor
(B'way, 104+ perfs.)

Aristocrats
(Off B'way, 42+ perfs.)

RUMORS—Ken Howard, Ron Leibman, Mark Nelson and Andre Gregory in Neil Simon's comedy, directed by Gene Saks

New Plays

The Heidi of Wendy Wasserstein's *The Heidi Chronicles* is an art historian circling 40 with a special mission to bring recognition to overlooked women artists. We meet her giving a lecture on some of her favorite painters; then, in a series of flashbacks, we follow her from a high school dance forward to the present. The play pursues two tracks. Track one: her relationship with the community of what she would probably cringe to hear called her peers, from the early days of consciousness-raising groups to the packs of career women who have cashed in the opportunities the women's movement helped create for lives centered on money, power, fashion and status. Track two: Heidi's relationships with two men—the publisher of a trendy magazine called *Boomer* named Scoop Rosenbaum and a pediatrician named Peter Patrone. With Scoop, who embodies many of the most disagreeable masculine qualities and yet somehow remains stimulating and engaging, she has a long-term affair which, after his cynical marriage to another, evolves into an abrasive friendship. Peter, on the other hand, has the qualities Heidi finds most appealing, but his revelation of his homosexuality frustrates the hopes she had of a romantic relationship, and she resigns herself to the consolation prize of his sympathetic comradeship.

The first track reaches a climax when a successful Heidi accepts an invitation to give an address on the future of women to the students of her old high school. She arrives at the podium without a prepared speech, having little inspirational to say about the future of women, given what she sees of their—and her—present. In a stunning passage, she describes an exercise class she attended the day before. The competitiveness, materialism and trendiness of the "today" women around her in the changing room overwhelmed her, making her feel simultaneously "worthless and superior." Most crushing, in view of the model of sisterhood invoked in the huggy, consciousness-raising days, is her profound sense of isolation. Where is the mutually supportive, idealistic community of women which was the movement's objective?

Wasserstein is less successful with the two scenes following the speech in which Peter and Scoop appear for the last time. Line-by-line they are admirably written, but they seem conceptually forced, as if, because the two have maintained such high profiles earlier in the play, Wasserstein felt she had to pay them off but couldn't organically muster appropriate resolutions. At the end, Heidi has found regeneration through an adopted child; but, though a final picture of her and her baby standing under a sign proclaiming a retrospective of Georgia O'Keefe's work at Chicago's Art Institute charms, it struck me as overly neat and unpersuasive.

Such formal imperfections are offset by a wealth of wonderful scenes. At her best, Wasserstein is simultaneously satiric and compassionate, and she's at her best in a lot of this play. One of the purposes of art is to create structures through which our experience is made more understandable, and her work here accomplishes this with special distinction. What could have been an easy wallow in nostalgia is a genuinely valuable social document.

Wasserstein had the blessing of a nearly perfect production. Under Dan Sullivan's direction, the entire ensemble excelled. Joanne Camp offered a series of superb cameos as a variety of the women who trigger Heidi's disillusion, notably an over-hearty lesbian and a sharklike talk-show host. Boyd Gaines held a true course on Peter's balance of wit and decency. Peter

PLAYS (38)

Zero Positive
Right Behind the Flag
V & V Only
Green Card
Big Time
From the Mississippi Delta (return engagement)
Playwrights Horizons:
  Young Playwrights Festival
  Saved From Obscurity
THE HEIDI CHRONICLES
GUS AND AL
Yankee Dawg You Die
Circle Repertory:
  Reckless
  Brilliant Traces
  Dalton's Back
  Amulets Against the Dragon Forces
THE COCKTAIL HOUR
MTC:
  EASTERN STANDARD
  Italian American Reconciliation
  Eleemosynary
American Place:
  A Burning Beach
  The Unguided Missile
  The Blessing
  The Faithful Brethren of Pitt Street
EMERALD CITY
The Majestic Kid

Negro Ensemble:
  Sally
  Prince
N.Y. Shakespeare
  What Did He See?
  For Dear Life
  The Forbidden City
  Phantasie
  Bunnybear
Cantorial
OTHER PEOPLE'S MONEY
The Night Hank Williams Died
Only Kidding!
S.J. Perelman in Person
The Phantom Tollbooth

REVUES (6)

Urban Blight
Forbidden Broadway
Legends in Concert
Blame It on the Movies!
Laughing Matters
Showing Off

FOREIGN PLAYS IN ENGLISH (6)

Pavlovsky Marathon
The Death of Garcia Lorca
English Mint/L'Amante Anglaise
ROAD
Temptation
ARISTOCRATS

MUSICALS (7)

Blues in the Night
Suds
The Taffetas
The Hired Man
The Middle of Nowhere
N.Y. Shakespeare:
  Genesis
  Songs of Paradise

REVIVALS (19)

Godspell
Six Characters in Search of an Author
Shakespeare Marathon:
  Much Ado About Nothing
  King John
  Coriolanus
  Love's Labor's Lost
  The Winter's Tale
  Cymbeline
Roundabout:
  The Mistress of the Inn
  Ghosts
  Enrico IV
  The Member of the Wedding
  Arms and the Man
Cafe Crown
Lincoln Center:
  Waiting for Godot
  Measure for Measure
  What the Butler Saw
Acting Company:
  Love's Labor's Lost
  Boy Meets Girl

SPECIALTIES (7)

I'll Go On
Miracolo d'Amore
Stranger Here Myself
Sweethearts
The Kathy and Mo Show
Together Again for the First Time
Reno in Rage and Rehab

FOREIGN-LANGUAGE PLAY (1)

Stars in the Morning Sky

Categorized above are all the productions listed in the Plays Produced Off Broadway section of this volume. Plays listed in CAPITAL LETTERS have been designated Best Plays of 1988–89. Plays listed in *italics* were still running June 1, 1989.

Friedman played the womanizing opportunist Scoop with such relish that one could well understand how Heidi could find him both fascinating and appalling. Joan Allen, who won the Tony for her performance in 1987's *Burn This*, triumphed in the best role of her New York career. She did full justice to the ferocious high school speech, but as impressive was her work in a consciousness-raising scene in which she barely said a word but vividly registered her reaction to every syllable of the funny and unsettling things being said by the other proto-feminists in the room.

Technically, too, the production was a treat, featuring wittily precise costumes by Jennifer von Mayrhauser and an ingenious series of sets which brilliantly overcame the spacial constraints of the small Playwrights Horizons stage. The play subsequently moved to justifiable acclaim on Broadway.

Another play produced at Playwrights Horizons took its central character from despair to regeneration; but, whereas in interviews Wendy Wasserstein has emphasized the differences between herself and Heidi, in *Gus and Al*, playwright Albert Innaurato has put a character named Albert Innaurato onstage. Ordinarily, this would seem to be courting disaster, and one feels a bit queasy when the piece starts with Al, bitter over the lousy reviews his last play received, climbing into a time machine to escape. Time travel has been a much-used gimmick in film and TV and onstage over the past few years; but, in spite of the familiarity of the plotting device, the play's overtly autobiographical theme and some inevitable self-indulgence, *Gus and Al* is a genuinely winning work. Arriving in the Vienna of 1901 at a discouraging point in Gustav Mahler's career, the playwright becomes friends with the composer, and the two enter into witty and poignant discussions of art and sex and depression. At a time when playwrights (and indeed many artists) seem unaware that there is such a thing as the past, or use it mainly for frivolous exercises in nostalgia, it's particularly touching to encounter one who sees it as something which may teach one a little about how to live in the present. Innaurato was blessed with a wonderfully resourceful little production capped by engaging performances by Sam Tsoutsouvas and Mark Blum in the title roles.

A. R. Gurney's Best Play *The Cocktail Hour* was also founded in autobiographical impulse. John, a playwright in early middle age, is visiting his parents and sister in a W.A.S.P. enclave in upstate New York. He has written a comedy called, yes, *The Cocktail Hour* which includes characters based on them, and he wants their approval before he goes ahead with a projected production.

The premise of Gurney's play is wonderfully appealing to a dramatist: that the very act of writing a script should occasion deeper understanding and love between a writer and his family. The premise is all the more beguiling because the healing occurs even though neither of the parents actually gets around to *reading* the script in question. There is a good deal of delightful comedy here, Gurney peppering his first act with wry comments on two turfs of which he is an acknowledged expert: the politics of theater and the archaic rituals and beliefs of the socially and financially privileged. The second act, in which the obligatory family secrets come tumbling out, has less impact, the secrets themselves a little shy in emotional force and the tensions between the characters being resolved too conveniently. (I couldn't help wishing that some of the darker colors of Gurney's moving and under-appreciated play *Another Antigone* were more evident here.)

Under Jack O'Brien's trim direction, Bruce Davison, Keene Curtis and Holland Taylor gave elegant performances as the playwright, his autocratic father and miffed sister. As the mother, Nancy Marchand had the best developed role of the evening and responded with a stunningly precise performance of a woman who polices her emotional boundaries with the help of a few too many cocktails.

Michael Weller also had an autobiographical impulse and a fine idea for *Spoils of War*—to dramatize the fragmentation of the American left through the story of a marriage formed at the height of the left's pre-World War II activity and disintegrating during the Red scare of the 1950s. Unfortunately, he didn't develop the idea dramatically. There was little sense of the chemistry which had brought the couple together, and little of the role their divergent politics played in dooming the marriage. The source of Weller's problems in developing the play may lie in the autobiographic content; though he conscientiously wrote extended scenes for him, the playwright seems to have little sympathy for Andrew, the father to Martin, Weller's teen-aged stand-in, and Jeffrey De Munn seemed to have consequent difficulty building a full character. In contrast, Elisa, reportedly based on Weller's mother, appears to have engaged the author's full sympathy and registers as a vibrant figure—gallant, wry, manipulative, self-destructive and sexy. Kate Nelligan's rich, full-hearted performance went a long way toward offsetting the script's shortcomings.

Neil Simon, whose autobiographic impulses served him well with the trilogy of *Brighton Beach Memoirs, Biloxi Blues* and *Broadway Bound*, put aside the serious matters in favor of an attempt at farce entitled *Rumors*. Four couples arrive at the suburban house of friends celebrating a wedding anniversary to find the husband bleeding from a bullet wound in the earlobe and the wife missing. In the first act, fearing possible scandal, the early arrivals go through elaborate ruses to keep the news from the later ones. In the second, the eight try to keep the news from a pair of suspicious cops. In candor I must report the audience around me seemed to be having a wonderful time. But, despite the best efforts of a talented cast, including a hyper-tense Ron Leibman and a bristling Christine Baranski, I found little of this amusing. Too many of Simon's jokes rested on wisecracks about brand names and facile cultural references, and too much of the humor depended on the catalogue of physical problems distributed among the dramatis personae, the characters largely being identifiable by their disabilities.

Run for Your Wife! was another attempt at farce, a long-running British concoction featuring its author-director Ray Cooney in the leading role of a bigamous cab driver. The play concerns his attempts to keep his two wives and two remarkably dense policemen from learning about his double life. It is filled with demeaning jokes about gays and double entendres of primary school sophistication. But, like *Rumors*, it too kept the audience around me happy. The most appealing aspect of the evening was the performance of Paxton Whitehead as a neighbor who gets embroiled in the cabbie's lie-juggling. Whitehead is built like a giraffe, possesses flawless timing, near-acrobatic dexterity and a wry baritone voice which makes even a witless collection of words sound clever. How I wish that Circle in the Square, or anyone else who produces Shaw in New York, would offer him a leading role in a Shavian excursion.

The most satisfying sally at farce was Ken Ludwig's *Lend Me a Tenor*, the story of a meek would-be singer and how—made up to look like Otello—he comes to impersonate a famous Italian tenor onstage and off (including in bed). Spasms of unbridled hysteria, rage, and lust keep the action whizzing along with scarcely a moment's lapse, though Ludwig's verbal skills are not quite on a par with his considerable skills for plot construction. The production exemplified Broadway professionalism at its most polished. Under Jerry Zaks's endlessly-inventive direction, Victor Garber, Philip Bosco, Ron Holgate, J. Smith-Cameron and Tovah Feldshuh cut loose and gave gloriously outsized performances, dashing through the doors of Tony Walton's elegant art deco set and jumping in and out of William Ivey Long's opulent costumes.

John Patrick Shanley's *Italian American Reconciliation* returned to the milieu of New York Italian life he so engagingly portrayed in his Academy Award-winning screen play, *Moonstruck*. The story concerned a cocky, comical character named Aldo and how, in his attempts to help his best friend Huey make peace with his combative ex-wife Janice, he comes to a new understanding about his own troubled dealings with women. Shanley at his best has a bracing, boisterous way with colloquial speech, but here he lapses into extended patches of pseudo-poetry which seem to be saying, "Aren't these little people with hearts bigger than their vocabularies and their rough but honest folk wisdom endearing?" At the same time he tries to generate our affection for his characters, Shanley winks at us in the audience as if to tell us he knows we exist on a higher level of sophistication than they do. Shanley did a creditable job staging his play, getting a virtuoso performance from his frequent collaborator John Turturro as Aldo. That fine comic actor John Pankow had less scope to register as the smitten Huey.

SPOILS OF WAR—Kate Nelligan and Jeffrey De
Munn in a scene from the play by Michael Weller

Happily, late in the season Pankow had a role worthy of his talent in Brian
Friel's Best Play *Aristocrats*. In it, members of what had previously been a
well-off Irish family gather at their deteriorating estate to witness the wedding
of one of four sisters to a man she doesn't love. The death of their abusive and
unlovable father, a former judge in the district, postpones the wedding in favor
of a funeral. With the patriarch dead, three of his daughters (the fourth is in
Africa), their peculiar brother and a handful of others blink and look around at
their not very encouraging futures. Pankow, as the sardonic working-class
boy married to one of the judge's daughters, and Niall Buggy, as the odd son
convinced of the reality of a number of fanciful memories, gave subtle and
vivid performances. The play's many admirers in the press were right to
compare this accomplished work to Chekhov.

The first act of Richard Greenberg's *Eastern Standard* introduces a group of New Yorkers in their 30s, sitting in a trendy New York restaurant, commenting about the dissatisfactions of their prosperous lives. From their conversation, we get the impression of the city as an overheated Petrie dish cooking up a variety of social and spiritual malignancies. Architect Stephen Wheeler, despairing over having achieved success by having designed buildings he abominates, decides to go on retreat to his country house to rethink his life. We join him there in the second act, as do three others from the restaurant: his new girl friend, Phoebe Kidde, trying to recover from a bruising relationship with a Wall Street character under investigation for corporate malfeasance; Phoebe's gay brother Peter, whose withdrawal from the compromise-ridden world of television producing is being hastened by the news that he has AIDS; and Stephen's friend Drew Paley, a gay artist who, unaware of Peter's medical problems, has a crush on Peter and a habit of non-stop ironic commentary.

Featuring a cast of characters who philosophize in bucolic surroundings, this play also brings Chekhov to mind—but with a twist: whereas Chekhov's characters dream about escaping the backwaters in which they languish for the self-fulfillment they believe they'll find in the city, Greenberg's flee the city hoping to find realization in the country. The escape is far from complete, however. Stephen's sympathy for Ellen, a waitress at the restaurant of the first act, has led him to invite her to join them, and she in turn persuades the foursome to allow her to invite a bag lady named May Logan to sample gracious living in the country. May, whom the others met during a deranged episode in the restaurant, is now well-supplied with pills to keep her condition under control, and she offers them the opportunity to carry into action their yearnings to do something concrete for someone less privileged. Ultimately, May takes advantage of their generosity, disabusing them of some of their sentimentality about the underprivileged. But the end of the play finds them wiser from their experience and hearteningly resolved to return to the city and do good as well as doing well.

In a season populated by so many youngish smash-and-grabbers, Greenberg's play comes as encouraging news. Yes, he says, there are a lot of thirtyish people making an obscene amount of money in a society in which so many unlucky others suffer from poverty and homelessness. But these affluent ones are not all hopelessly acquisitive and insensitive. Some indeed are capable of responding to the prickings of conscience, of identifying with a larger vision of humanity and backing up their protestations of ideals with concrete action.

Michael Engler's production, supported by Philipp Jung's sets, Candice Donnelly's costumes and Dennis Parichy's lighting, served Greenberg's play well, and it featured an admirable ensemble. As Drew Paley, Peter Frechette delivered many of Greenberg's tartest witticisms with aplomb and simultaneously revealed Drew's more vulnerable side. Anne Meara was equally adept at presenting two faces of May, the out-of-control near-psychotic of the first act and the likeable but cunning survivor of the second.

Kevin Heelan's *Right Behind the Flag* and Jim Leonard's *V&V Only* both featured shopkeepers under pressure. In *Right Behind the Flag*, a sardonic, obsessed Vietnam vet tried to disrupt a barber shop owner-friend's dealings with a yuppie gangster. In *V&V Only*, the proprietor of an Italian coffee house battled unseen Asian real estate interests threatening to dislodge him from his establishment. Both playwrights had obvious fun writing verbal fantasias of hostility and profanity (in his play, Mr. Heelan went beyond the verbal, having the vet take out his penis and wield it as if it were a microphone in front of the yuppie's face), but neither play proved to be dramatically engaging.

V&V Only was followed at Circle Rep by *Reckless* by Craig Lucas (author of the popular *Blue Window* and the book to *Three Postcards*, a Best Play of the 1986–87 season) which began in the bedroom of a husband and wife on Christmas Eve. The wife chatters on brightly for several minutes about the meaning of Christmas and how happy she is in their cozy house. Finally her husband tells her that he has hired a hit man to kill her in a few minutes and that she should run. And run she does, out into the cold and snowy night and a series of absurd misadventures which take her through several more Christmases, assorted therapists, accidental deaths, murders and reunions. I thought the opening scene a delight, and every now and then Lucas would lob another grenade-like surprise into the proceedings which would startle a laugh out of me; but for my taste it was too haphazard and disjointed, riddled with arbitrary effects and, in the end, tried to claim an emotional response from the audience it hadn't earned. This said, it must be reported that the play was an enormous success for Circle, both with most of the critics and the audience. A major part of its success was due to Robin Bartlett's performance as the heroine.

Circle Rep followed this with simultaneous productions in two different spaces of two disappointing scripts. In *Dalton's Back*, author Keith Curran runs scenes about the title character's stormy relationship with a new girl friend in counterpoint with flashbacks of his childhood and his stormy relationship with his mother. Cause and effect are implied. But in production the audience was way ahead of the author, and much of the evening was devoted to playing out the *de rigueur* confrontations. The one brief vital scene concerns Dalton and his mother meeting in the present and his realization that she honestly has no idea that his problems are in any way related to how she treated him as a child.

Cindy Lou Johnson's *Brilliant Traces* concerns a young woman who, after walking out on her own wedding in Arizona, quite by happenstance several days later arrives on the doorstep of a young hermit in Alaska in the middle of a blinding snowstorm. It's a metaphoric snowstorm, of course, with the two injured souls reaching for a way out of their blinding isolation. This is accomplished with a lot of overheated poetic language. Underneath the affectations and the frequent detours into strained verbal arabesques is a slim and rather conventional one-act in which, as per formula, two misfits connect after a good deal of contrived sparring and misunderstanding capped off by the obligatory blurted-out secrets. The director, Terry Kinney, and the actor who played the hermit, Kevin Anderson, are members of Chicago's Steppenwolf Theater, and the production had the earmarks of such previous Steppenwolf stagings as *Orphans* and *True West*, with a lot of wall slamming and furniture abuse. Anderson and his co-star, Joan Cusack, gave the piece their energetic all, but the script refused to meet them half way.

Finally at Circle Rep, Paul Zindel's *Amulets Against the Dragon Forces,* set in the 1950s, begins with a nurse hired to attend the soon-to-expire mother of a brutal Staten Island shipyard worker named Dipardi. The nurse is given a room in the house, as is her awkward teenage son, and they and Dipardi instantly clash. The essence of the play is in the contrast between Dipardi and the son, Chris, both of whom are gay. Dipardi's homosexuality has led him to self-loathing, sadism and alcohol abuse. He brutalizes Chris because he sees in the boy what he hates in himself. But by play's end, it is evident that Chris, having freed himself from his alternately bullying and clinging mother, will come to terms with his sexual identity and live a constructive, self-respecting life, probably as a writer. The script is a verbal jungle, over-written, self-indulgent, littered with leaden symbolism and contrivance. But it refuses to be dismissed. The performances are too potent and disturbing, and for this Zindel deserves much credit. Deborah Hedwall, as the nurse-mother, and John Spencer, as Dipardi, managed to convey both the horror and the bruised hearts of these two monsters. Under B. Rodney Marriott's skillful direction, the scene in which these two bitter antagonists almost find comradeship in their mutual loathing played with a brilliance which offset the evening's flaws.

Over at New York Shakespeare, Bill Gunn's *The Forbidden City* also featured a sensitive son (again a nascent writer) in unequal combat with a monstrous parent. In this case, the setting is a house in a black neighborhood in 1936 Philadelphia. The mother, Molly, has dreams of mixing in cultured circles barred to her by her race. She takes her frustration out on her family, humiliating her cowering boy and treating her adoring, unsophisticated husband Nick with undisguised condescension. The first act is long, and at its end one still has no idea what its central question is. Suddenly, in the second act, when Nick discovers Molly has spent the evening in a hotel room with a rich white man, the play finds direction. Rather than respond with fury, Nick listens with genuine and touching sympathy as his wife explains the loneliness in her heart. Frankie R. Faison imbued Nick with an almost palpable natural decency, and Gloria Foster made Molly a compelling combination of the pitiable and the

THE FORBIDDEN CITY—Gloria Foster and
Akili Prince in the play by the late Bill Gunn at
the Public Theater, directed by Joseph Papp

appalling. Joseph Papp must be credited with getting uniformly fine performances out of his cast and must be charged with not having helped the playwright find the play's proper shape. Tragically, Gunn died the day before the
play opened.

Temptation is Czech playwright Vaclav Havel's retelling of the Faust
legend within a totalitarian society. Havel, who at the time of the production
was in a Czech prison for political activities, is dealing with the same central
motif here as in his earlier *Largo Desolato* (cited as a Best Play of the 1985–86
season)—the individual's struggle to hold onto his soul without incurring the
wrath of the state. Unfortunately, in this play Havel seems to articulate this
idea without developing it much. I write "seems" because director Jiri Zizka
covered the production with a blanket of irrelevant props and effects and
staged it at such a languid pace that the play's virtues were obscured.

A number of people with taste professed to see profound things in Richard
Foreman's theatrical construction *What Did He See?* in which three actors
ambled around a cluttered stage (which, for some reason, was separated from

the audience by sheets of clear plastic) in a series of bemused and symboli-
cally-intended dialogues. I can't pretend I got much out of the experience.

Green Card, another dramatic construction by a well-known avant-garde
director, took immigration as its theme. The work had its moments of visual
ingenuity, but writer-director JoAnne Akalaitis was heavy-handed in stating
her thesis that a nation developed by immigrants from oppression has become
a nation whose imperialism supports oppression in other countries, which in
turn creates more immigrants.

The thirtyish business-oriented go-getter was a common target of dramatists' contempt. The problem with a common target is that it tends to provoke
common attacks, which in turn tend to breed cliches. Such was the case with
Keith Reddin's *Big Time: Scenes from a Service Economy*. Chronicling the
professional and personal decline of a financial wheeler-dealer, the playwright
was content merely to point a finger at the superficial characteristics and
habits of the species rather than to explore his leading character's interior life
or how he came to be what he was. Ironically, Reddin's undeniable facility at
dialogue underscored the play's weaknesses, creating an effect analogous to
shellac on cardboard—shiny on the surface but with little substance
underneath.

Financial wheeling and dealing also held center stage in Jerry Sterner's
Other People's Money. A corporate raider named Lawrence Garfinkle takes
an interest in a New England-based wire and cable company, and the company's officers hire an attorney named Kate Sullivan to defend their interests.
The contest between the caustic but curiously charming Garfinkle and the
girlishly brash Sullivan is fought on both financial and romantic grounds. Even
as we deplore Garfinkle's moves to dismantle and sell off the assets of the
company—leaving the workers and the town to fend for themselves—we
(and Kate) ultimately are brought to the realization that Garfinkle's pursuit is
motivated not only by money but by sincerely-held beliefs. The play manages
to be simultaneously informative on the ways of Wall Street and raucously
entertaining. Sterner has supplied his two leads with the sort of dialogue
Spencer Tracy and Katharine Hepburn might have batted about if Tracy and
Hepburn had used four-letter words, and Kevin Conway as Garfinkle and
Mercedes Ruehl as Sullivan, under Gloria Muzio's slambang direction, played
it with gusto. If the odd line fell flat, stated the themes too explicitly or was
over-familiar ("He who has the most when he dies, wins" has been gracing T-
shirts for years), Sterner more than compensated for these lapses with that
rare thing—yards of old-fashioned plot offering old-fashioned satisfactions.

For the 1987 musical *Don't Get God Started*, Ron Milner wrote several
scenes juxtaposing older black characters, who have found contentment by
hewing to traditional family values, with several younger blacks, who have
lost their spiritual bearing in their pursuit of status and money. Milner's
Checkmates marked a return to this thematic territory, alternating between

scenes of a loving older black couple and the ambitious younger couple who rent an apartment from them. A series of flashbacks fills us in on how the older couple's faith and mutual support helped them overcome the trials they faced during and in the wake of World War II. Not having such faith, the highly competitive younger couple succumb to the problems and ultimately split up. The contrast between generations of the black middle class is relatively unexplored and promising territory, but Milner trivialized the issues he hoped to dramatize with a barrage of glib patter and easy (and, in the cases of some jibes about an offstage gay character, offensive) jokes. He also makes the mistake of recycling devices which hadn't served him well in earlier work; as in *Don't Get God Started*, female characters take their stands by threatening errant mates with weapons. The script was all the more disappointing given the extraordinary cast. Ruby Dee, Paul Winfield and Denzel Washington are among our finest actors, and one ached to see them employ their time and talent in work worthy of them.

Ira Levin is perhaps best known to general audiences for his thriller *Rosemary's Baby*, in which he posited the modern birth of an anti-Christ in an Upper West Side apartment. In *Cantorial*, he again mixes the religious and the supernatural, but to more serious purpose. A young unmarried couple has purchased an apartment on the Lower East Side, to discover that the place comes with a feature not mentioned by their real estate agent: the singing of a long-dead cantor. The apartment has been built on the site of what once had been a shul, and the cantor's ghost evidently sings to urge that it be returned to its former purpose.

Initially the couple investigate ways to exorcise the ghost; but gradually, though it threatens their relationship, the young man becomes obsessed with the project of restoring the shul. Adopted as a child by a gentile couple, he also becomes convinced that the mother he never knew was Jewish, and, under the guidance of a local deli owner named Morris Lipkind, he begins seriously to investigate what he believes to be his roots. Levin has employed this fanciful conceit to deal with the issue of the disintegration of culture in an assimilationist world, the cantor's singing serving as a poignant symbol of a voice which refuses to give way even to death. I wish Levin had gone further with the implications of his story. Here we have a young protagonist driven by something inside him to be a Jew; yet, aside from a minor incident involving some hooligans who toss rocks through a window, he is confronted with little of the pain of being a Jew, that pain being a necessary and determining part of the heritage he seeks to embrace. Nonetheless, adroitly directed by Charles Maryan, and featuring charming performances by Anthony Fusco and Woody Romoff as the young man and the deli owner, *Cantorial* was one of the mitzvahs of the season.

Mark Medoff's *The Majestic Kid* bore more than a passing resemblance to Woody Allen's *Play It Again, Sam*. In each, the leading man is an amiable

CANTORIAL—Woody Romoff, Lesly Kahn and
Anthony Fusco in a scene from the play by Ira Levin

nebbish who is given tips on manhood by a fantasy figure—in Allen's play, Humphrey Bogart; in Medoff's, a naive cowpoke out of B oaters named the Laredo Kid. Unfortunately, it takes but a few minutes for the audience to come to the understanding that the Laredo Kid's values are of little use in confronting contemporary controversies, but the play continues for the rest of two acts to demonstrate this self-evident conclusion—a curiously inconsequential play from the gifted writer of *Children of a Lesser God.*

Charles Fuller, the Pulitzer Prize-winning author of *A Soldier's Play,* stumbled on a more ambitious scale with *Sally* and *Prince,* the first two plays of a projected five-play cycle of black America titled *We.* Both of these plays centered around Prince, a former slave who, in the first play, is compelled to betray fellow blacks while a soldier in the Union Army; in the second, he confronts the hypocrisy and racism of Northern do-gooders on a farm run by missionaries. While both plays throw interesting light on lesser-known chapters of the black American experience, in production at The Negro Ensemble Company they seemed choppy and underdeveloped. Some of the sequences —a battle on a river bank, the announcement of the Emancipation Proclamation in front of black troups—would doubtless be effective onscreen with the scores of extras the movies can afford; but, even with a cast of 17, onstage they looked skimpy. The disappointment was all the greater, given Fuller's proven abilities and the paucity of drama of epic vision in contemporary American theater.

There were two new plays for solo actors on Broadway this season—one fictional, the other biographic. The fictional, Willy Russell's *Shirley Valentine,* is about an English housewife who one day decides that life with her clod of a husband is stifling her, so she takes off on a trip to a Greek island, where she has a restorative affair with a tavern owner and decides not to go back to England. In the first act, Shirley is in her kitchen describing the circumstances leading up to her departure. The second act catches up with Shirley in Greece giving us the rundown on what's happened to her during the intermission—a familiar story in outline, but old stories can charm if they have a bit of sparkle in their treatment. Unfortunately, most of the writing lacked such sparkle. There are several very good jokes and quite a few more painfully obvious ones. (There is an extended bit about the hypothetical use of Clitoris as a girl's name, most of it pretty labored, followed by a line in which she says that it should be considered because, after all, aren't a lot of men named Dick? This brought down the house around me.) The script gets particularly wearing when Russell indulges in moralizing about how to find the path to self-fulfill-ment. The point isn't whether one agrees with these sentiments or not (who is going to champion the virtues of leading an unfulfilled life, after all?), but whether they are embodied rather than articulated. The main pleasure of the evening, and it was a considerable one, was to watch Pauline Collins, a British actress mostly unknown to American audiences, managing by sheer convic-tion to kick some life into this mild stuff. (My opinion of the script is a minority one. In deference to the majority, it is included as a Best Play.)

The subject of the biographical solo show, *Hizzoner!* by Paul Shyre, was legendary New York Mayor Fiorello H. LaGuardia. LaGuardia was also the subject of the Pulitzer Prize-winning musical *Fiorello!*. That show managed to convey what was endearing about LaGuardia and still presented a convincing portrait of a talented politician. Shyre's LaGuardia comes across as naive and simple-minded. But surely a man who was elected to three terms and whose political legacy is still admired after 45 years must have been cannier than the figure presented here. Tony Lo Bianco is an actor of proven gifts, but in trying to recreate LaGuardia's piping voice and indulging in spurts of rudimentary slapstick, he made the late mayor look like fourth member of the Three Stooges.

Another one-man play, off Broadway's *S. J. Perelman in Person*, adapted by Bob Shanks from the humorist's writings, was also unsuccessful, despite a consummate performance by the excellent Lewis J. Stadlen. Perelman was a master of short pieces, but the range of his humor was a narrow one, and two insufficiently varied hours of it became repetitive. Joke after joke based on punnery and absurd juxtapositions at first entertained but then wearied.

Another work derived from a literary source demonstrated the difficulty of transferring a literary experience to the stage. Steven Berkoff's adaptation of Kafka's *Metamorphosis* struck me as a dated piece of expressionism. It was in fact created by Berkoff in the 1960s, and he apparently saw no reason to rethink the choices he made over 20 years ago. It seemed to me that the stylization undercut what potentially could have been most moving about the piece. This is the story of how a young man named Gregor Samsa is mysteriously transformed into a giant insect and how this transformation alienates him from that first ring of love and association, his family. For this to register, there should be some sense of the value he places on what he has been alienated from. But the flashbacks of his life with his family before the transformation are staged with such oversized and cartoony gestures that there is little sense that Gregor has much to lose. Ballet superstar Mikhail Baryshnikov's performance as Gregor was certainly a marvel of mimetic discipline, and he projected an affecting sense of vulnerability, if just because of our awareness of his vulnerability as an artist in a field different from the one which he has called home. But only Laura Esterman as Gregor's mother seemed to find heart under the outsized gestures.

The Lincoln Center production of Jim Cartwright's Best Play *Road* was not greeted in New York with anything like the chorus of critical enthusiasm which welcomed the play's debut in London in 1986. The script bears a structural resemblance to Thornton Wilder's *Our Town* (which, it will be remembered, Lincoln Center also produced this season and with which Cartwright reportedly had had no contact before composing his work). But instead of Wilder's genial stage manager to act as interlocutor, Cartwright introduces Scullery, an unemployed, alcoholic petty thief to lead us through a blighted, nameless trash-bestrewn town which typifies much of today's Northern England. Through a series of scenes and monologues featuring six actors in 14 roles, we get a remarkably comprehensive picture of life in a society in which hope has all but been extinguished. The scenes shift in tone from poignant cameos of older citizens stunned by the precipitous decline of the proud, purposeful Britain they hold in their memories, to comedy of grotesque scavengers picking through physical and spiritual wreckage, to graphic and obscenity-laden dialogues between young people filling the vacuum of their lives with drugs, booze, violence and impersonal sex.

That good actor Jack Wallace was too genial to realize Scullery fully; in London, Scullery was simultaneously entertaining and threatening (one got the impression that at any minute he might lift your wallet or throw up on you). But the six who played the town's repertory of characters—Betsy Aidem, Kevin Bacon, Gerry Bamman, Joan Cusack, Jayne Haynes and Michael

Wincott—were exemplary, offering one precisely-conceived portrait after another.

Given these excellences, why then did the play not succeed in New York? Here, as in London, director Simon Curtis gave it an environmental staging in which the audience followed the cast around the set. At the Royal Court the audience sensed that the actors were witnesses, reporting on directly-observed experience, but the New York edition felt a little like a theme park of poverty. It was hard simultaneously to accomodate Cartwright's unpleasant truths with the production's obvious desire to give the audience a good time. One doesn't feel comfortable with the idea of having fun watching a show in which two unbalanced young people lock themselves into a bedroom and purposely starve themselves to death. The miscalculations of the production should not be held against the text, however. I suspect that in other non-promenade stagings the play's considerable merits will become clearly apparent to American audiences.

The gifted Betsy Aidem was seen again some months later playing a troubled young woman in Larry L. King's play about small-town life in Texas in 1952, *The Night Hank Williams Died.* Structurally, King's script was a rickety affair, lurching from incident to incident and reaching its climax in a fairly arbitrary explosion of violence, but the sheer gusto of King's language and his simple but vibrant portraits of a handful of colorful types offered real rewards.

YANKEE DAWG YOU DIE—Stan Egi and Sab Shimono in a scene from the play by Philip Kan Gotanda

Joshua Sobol's *Ghetto* was welcome for its attempt to put a larger-scale vision onstage than is the norm these days. The play concerned the Jewish community in the Vilna ghetto in the days of the Holocaust. Aware that their culture is in danger of being decimated by the Nazis, residents accept the sadistic German commandant's odd offer to create a theater troupe. The action of the play concerns the participation in and reactions to this troupe on the part of a people facing doom. Unfortunately, the play was too diffuse. It introduced many characters and many issues, any one of which, if sufficiently explored, could well have made for a full and challenging evening of theater. For instance, Sobol introduces us to Gens, the Jewish head of the ghetto, who finds himself cooperating in the deportation and extermination of some under his authority so that others might have a better chance of living. Sobol gives Gens a monologue touching on the moral issues involved, but that's about the extent of his exploration of this fascinating dilemma.

Philip Kan Gotanda's *Yankee Dawg You Die* bore more than a passing resemblance to David Mamet's *A Life in the Theater*. Each features a younger actor and an older, more established one; and, in each, the play describes how the two come to change places. In *A Life in the Theater*, the switch is in status, the younger overtaking the older. In *Yankee Dawg*, Bradley, the younger, starts out by announcing his determination not to play the condescending, stereotypical roles usually allotted to Asian actors in film. The older, Vincent, has made a career of doing precisely the roles Bradley decries. Sure enough, by the end of the play, Bradley is rationalizing his acceptance of a humiliating job in some cheesy science-fiction movie, and Vincent is savoring the fact that he has turned down the role of Bradley's father in the same movie. Stan Egi as Bradley and Sab Shimono as Vincent gave accomplished and subtle performances; but, though showing a definite talent for bright dialogue, Gotunda seems to have very little new to say after the early scene in which he skillfully limns the characters' different styles and philosophies. This feels like a one-act that was forced into a full-length.

Show business again was the subject of Jim Geoghan's *Only Kidding!*, specifically the backstage life of stand-up comics. The central figures are an older comedian (whom we meet in Scene 1 of the first act) and a team of younger men (whom we meet in Scene 2), all dreaming of an appearance on "The Buddy King Show" which could catapult them into celebrity and big money in clubs. I found the script two-faced. On the one hand, it pretended to postures about morality in show business, giving lip service to disdaining ethnic jokes; on the other hand, it was saturated with the very kind of ethnic jokes of which it pretended to disapprove. The play's second act was based entirely on the improbable idea that all of the people we met in the first act would happen to be at "The Buddy King Show" on the same night. For all the crudeness of its execution, though, it was undeniably effective, making the audience howl with laughter almost continuously. Performances by Larry

Keith as the older comic, Paul Provenza as a particularly aggressive younger comic and Sam Zap as a Mafia figure dabbling in career management helped considerably.

Show business Australian-style was the subject of David Williamson's Best Play *Emerald City*, a dark comedy focussing on the relationship between a screen writer of serious aspirations and the hustling, semi-literate deal-maker who gloms onto him and uses the prestige of the association to climb to power in the film world. Williamson, himself a well-known screen writer of serious aspirations, writes with authority and bite about the politics of movie development and production, but there is more here than yet another story of the compromising of an individual's artistic principles. Williamson is also concerned about why the wave of compelling and idiosyncratic Australian movies of a decade or so ago was so brief. Just as his screen writer-hero loses his innocence when he moves to the rough-and-tumble world of Sydney showbiz, so, too, did Australian filmmakers lose much of what was distinctive about their work when they moved into the rough-and-tumble world of the international film market. He who homogenizes his art in the pursuit of a larger audience is likely to have little of distinction to say, once he is successful in corraling that audience.

Among the season's other offerings were disappointments by writers of exceptional talent. Lee Blessing's *Eleemosynary*, a brief, fluidly staged sketch of three generations of eccentric women, never quite congealed into a dramatic event, though one must be thankful for any play showing Eileen Heckart and Joanna Gleason to advantage. Susan Miller's *For Dear Life*, which toyed with a scrambled chronology, told of a marriage which disintegrates for no urgent reason and the effect on the couple's son. Unfortunately, rather than convey the characters' emotional life through behavior, Miller had them talk incessantly, albeit intelligently, but to little dramatic effect. A similar problem hobbled Clare Coss's *The Blessing*, a static piece about the relationship between an eccentric woman in a nursing home and her lesbian daughter.

Here's where we list the Best Plays choices for the outstanding straight-play achievements of 1988–89 in New York, on and off Broadway. In the acting categories, clear distinction among "starring," "featured" or "supporting" players can't be made on the basis of official billing, which is as much a matter of contracts as of esthetics. Here in these volumes we divide acting into "primary" or "secondary" roles, a primary role being one which might some day cause a star to inspire a revival in order to appear in that character. All others, be they vivid as Mercutio, are classed as secondary. Furthermore, our list of individual standouts makes room for more than a single choice when appropriate. We believe that no useful purpose is served by forcing ourselves into an arbitrary selection of a single best when we come upon multiple examples of equal distinction.

PLAYS

BEST PLAY: *The Heidi Chronicles* by Wendy Wasserstein; *Eastern Standard* by Richard Greenberg

BEST FOREIGN PLAY: *Aristocrats* by Brian Friel

BEST REVIVAL: *Juno and the Paycock*; *The Winter's Tale*

BEST ACTOR IN A PRIMARY ROLE: John Kavanagh as Joxer Daly in *Juno and the Paycock*; Kevin Kline as Benedick in *Much Ado About Nothing*; Mandy Patinkin as Leontes in *The Winter's Tale*

BEST ACTRESS IN A PRIMARY ROLE: Joan Allen as Heidi Holland in *The Heidi Chronicles*; Nancy Marchand as Ann in *The Cocktail Hour*; Maria Tucci as Hannah Jelkes in *The Night of the Iguana*

BEST ACTOR IN A SECONDARY ROLE: Niall Buggy as Casimir in *Aristocrats*; Peter Frechette as Drew Paley in *Eastern Standard*; Peter Friedman as Scoop Rosenbaum in *The Heidi Chronicles*; Bill Irwin as Lucky in *Waiting for Godot*

BEST ACTRESS IN A SECONDARY ROLE: Joanne Camp as Fran, Molly, Betsy and April in *The Heidi Chronicles*; Anne Meara as May Logan in *Eastern Standard*; Penelope Ann Miller as Emily Webb in *Our Town*

BEST DIRECTOR: Jerry Zaks for *Lend Me a Tenor*; James Lapine for *The Winter's Tale*

BEST SCENERY: Santo Loquasto for *Cafe Crown*

BEST COSTUMES: Jane Greenwood for *Our Town*

BEST LIGHTING: Beverly Emmons for *The Winter's Tale*

SPECIAL CITATIONS: Bill Irwin for creating and performing in *Largely New York*; William Finn and Michael Starobin for incidental music for *The Winter's Tale*

STARMITES—Brian Lane Green, Christopher Zelno, Bennett Cale and Victor Trent Cook in the Stuart Ross-Barry Keating musical

New Musicals

The eligibility committee for the Tony Awards chose to categorize *Jerome Robbins' Broadway* and *Black and Blue* as musicals. Well, they had their reasons, principal among them the fact that, without those two shows, there would have been nothing creditable to nominate in the "best musical" category.

But this volume has a more rigorous definition of the term. For our purposes, a musical must have more than singing (and possibly dancing) in it; it must also present characters involved in a sustained dramatic situation. Not fitting their description, *Jerome Robbins' Broadway* and *Black and Blue* must be considered revues and accordingly will be discussed in another section.

What's left to consider as bona fide musicals is a dispiriting group of efforts. Harvey Fierstein's name is attached as co-author (with Charles Suppon) of the book of *Legs Diamond*, but nothing in the script gave any indication of being the product of the same talent which gives us *Torch Song Trilogy*. Legs Diamond was a New York gangster of the 1920s, but the show makes no claim of appropriating anything from history but his name and the milieu. Fierstein and Suppon's conceit is that Legs only turns to crime in order to get a club in which he could sing and dance. This gave star Peter Allen license to sing and dance to a lot of his own songs. Were the songs wonderful, one might be inclined to complain less about the illogical and unfunny book, but the music is characterized more by energy than melody, and the lyrics, in addition to being ill-rhymed ("champagne" as a rhyme for "came"?), alternate between clumsy double entendres and mawkishness. Allen has a large following in cabarets and concert halls, but his performing gifts didn't transfer well to the stage. This may be owing partially to the charmless nature of the character he played, but then the show was Allen's idea to begin with, so he can hardly be seen as the victim of others' misconceptions. The only source of wit in the entire enterprise was David Mitchell's set designs, which adroitly invoked the glamor of the speakeasy life.

Some talents with significant Broadway credits behind them also stumbled this season. Mitch Leigh, the composer of *Man of La Mancha*, wrote the music and co-produced *Chu Chem*, a slight fable set several hundred years ago and concerning a Jewish father and daughter whose journeys take them to a Chinese kingdom. There the daughter falls in love with the local king, but being something of a suffragette (a Jewish sufragette in old China?—uh, O.K.), she refuses to consider marrying him unless he institutes the reforms she desires. The silly book was by Ted Allan, and the lyrics, which shifted between strained whimsey and attempts at poetry, were by Jim Haines and Jack Wohl. The music, however, when it wasn't toying with mock-Asian motifs a la "Chopsticks," featured some lovely ballads which were well sung by an attractive cast, notably Emily Zacharias as the daughter and Thom Sesma as the king.

Cy Coleman, best known for his sizzling score for *Sweet Charity*, weighed in with *Welcome to the Club,* co-written with A. E. Hotchner, about a group of men stuck in jail for non-payment of alimony. The childish book had little by way of plot, consisting mostly of the men either complaining or fantasizing about their exes. The level of the humor may be gauged by the fact that the zippiest song had as its refrain the line, "Don't fuck around/Don't fuck around/Don't fuck around with your mother-in-law." As distressing as much of this was, one looked forward to the songs because, if one could ignore the undistinguished Coleman-Hotchner lyrics, there were a number of catchy Coleman tunes sung by a cast with voices to put them over. Most notable were Scott Wentworth as an embittered writer and Sally Mayes, who showed real flair as a spunky country-Western star. Top-billed Avery Schreiber and Marilyn Sokol gave assured comic performances which would have been a lot funnier if the writers had given them much to work with.

Starmites was the last original musical to hit Broadway this season. Stuart Ross and Barry Keating's book told of a teenage girl named Eleanor who magically is transported into the fantasy world of the comic books she so avidly reads. Here she is no longer shy and nerdy but a superhero with a mission to save the universe, in which capacity she is joined by a hero named Spacepunk and a trio of his associates, the Starmites. Also in this alternate world, in the book's cleverest touch, are an Amazonian goddess named Diva, who looks a good deal like Eleanor's mother, and Diva's oddball daughter Bizarbara, who feels as out-of-step here as Eleanor did in the real world. (Eleanor and Bizarbara, of course, were played by the same person.) At best, the piece was sweet-natured and undemanding, something to which one could safely take youngsters. Liz Larsen, as Eleanor/Bizarbara, was the most impressive of the performers, singing with a strong, impassioned voice and finding moments of real heart under the campiness.

Off Broadway, *Genesis* featured some pleasing scenic conceits by John Conklin, but the power and poetry of the medieval mystery plays from which it was derived seemed diminished to moments of sporadic charm. Joseph Papp, who produced it, presented another show covering some of the same territory, *Songs of Paradise*. Based on the Biblical poetry of Itsik Manger, the piece alternated between English and Yiddish and shifted in tone from serious to broad vaudeville and back again at a second's notice. The most engaging moments invariably were provided by Rosalie Gerut's songs.

Two off-Broadway musicals featured pre-existent songs. *Suds* took place in a laundromat and purported to be about a severely depressed young woman who, when she contemplates ending it all because of love problems, is visited by guardian angels. The guardian angels offer her moral support through a series of songs made famous by the "girl groups" of the Fifties and Sixties. The result was loud, obvious and devoid of humor or poignancy.

The other musical without an original score was *The Middle of Nowhere*. In a prologue, writer-director Kim Friedman introduces a group of travelers trapped in the middle of the night in a Southern bus station in the 1960s with the station's black attendant. After a series of uneasy exchanges, a flash of lightning suddenly jolts them into a fantasy zone where the five find themselves participants in a surreal minstrel show in which they perform sardonic and melancholy songs by Randy Newman. Inventively staged and choreographed by Friedman, the songs cohere into a unified and unsettling vision of America. In an impressive cast, Roger Robinson was particularly strong as the attendant. Unfortunately, though it received some fine notices, the show didn't last long. Within weeks of its opening, it was gone. Only a handful of people had the pleasure of seeing this small-scale but rewarding work.

To sum up on the most positive note, here's where we list the *Best Plays* choices for the musical and musical revue bests of 1988–89.

Above, Tony Hoylen, Roger Robinson, Diana Castle, Vondie Curtis-Hall and Michael Arkin in *The Middle of Nowhere,* cited by *Best Plays* for its Kim Friedman book; *right,* Peter Tolan and Linda Wallem in *Laughing Matters,* cited for its Peter Tolan lyrics; *below,* Marcia Mitzman, Marilyn Sokol, Jodi Benson, Terri White and Avery Schreiber in a scene from *Welcome to the Club,* cited for Cy Coleman's music

MUSICALS AND REVUES

BEST MUSICAL OR REVUE: *Black and Blue*

SPECIAL CITATION: *Jerome Robbins' Broadway*

BEST BOOK: Kim Friedman for *The Middle of Nowhere*

BEST MUSIC: Cy Coleman for *Welcome to the Club*

BEST LYRICS: Peter Tolan for *Laughing Matters*

BEST ACTOR IN A PRIMARY ROLE: Jason Alexander as the Setter, Emcee, Pseudolus, Pa, Cigar, Floy and Tevye in *Jerome Robbins' Broadway*

BEST ACTRESS IN A PRIMARY ROLE: Ruth Brown and Linda Hopkins in *Black and Blue*

BEST ACTOR IN A SECONDARY ROLE: Scott Wise as Chip, 3d Protean, Riff, Papa Crook and member of ensemble in *Jerome Robbins' Broadway*; Bunny Briggs in *Black and Blue*

BEST ACTRESS IN A SECONDARY ROLE: Faith Prince as Ma and Tessie and member of the ensemble in *Jerome Robbins' Broadway*; Christine Kellogg for *Blame it on the Movies!*

BEST DIRECTOR: Jerome Robbins for *Jerome Robbins' Broadway*

BEST CHOREOGRAPHY: Cholly Atkins, Henry LeTang, Frankie Manning and Fayard Nicholas for *Black and Blue*

BEST SCENERY: David Mitchell for *Legs Diamond*

BEST LIGHTING: Neil Peter Jampolis and Jane Reisman for *Black and Blue*

BEST COSTUMES: Claudio Segovia and Hector Orezzoli for *Black and Blue*

Revues and Special Attractions

The brightest achievements in theater songwriting appeared not in musicals but revues. *Urban Blight* featured sketches of varying quality on life in the city by some of our most celebrated playwrights, but the most memorable offering was "Miss Byrd," a song by composer David Shire and lyricist Richard Maltby Jr. about the secret joy of an office worker at having found love, sung with infectious spirit by Nancy Giles. In *Forbidden Broadway*, director-parodist Gerard Alessandrini took some good-natured swipes at the current theatrical scene, including a riotous assault on *Les Misérables'* ever-spinning turntables and a sequence in which an actor playing Stephen Sondheim insisted that one of his convoluted tunes was catchy, and in order to prove his point, tried to get the audience to sing along. (Sondheim was in the audience the night I saw it, and he seemed to get a great kick out of the ribbing.)

An even sharper Sondheim satire was a high point of *Laughing Matters*, a revue by and starring Linda Wallem and Peter Tolan. A medley from a hypothetical Sondheim adaptation of the *Dick and Jane* reading primers, it not only registered with a well-executed passage of extended, densely-rhymed word-play and scored with some wonderful jokes (Dick calling for his dog—"Spot, Spot, Spot, Spot, Spot, Spot"—accompanied by a paraphrase of the pointillistic music Sondheim had George sputter as he peppered his canvas with dots in *Sunday in the Park with George*), it also caught Sondheim's plaintive quality as Dick sang, "See, Jane, see." Yes, one felt, Tolan (who wrote the songs) had got it *exactly* right. But Tolan gives signs of being not only a canny parodist but a fine lyricist in his own right. Two other songs, one echoing Lenny Bruce's observation that New York has a tendency to turn goyim into Jews and a second about a dog with unusual eating habits, demonstrated a level of craft absent from any of the new lyrics found in book musicals this year. Apart from the songs, Wallem and Tolan proved to be an adept comedy team. If their sketches were haphazardly structured, their moment-to-moment playing achieved a fine balance of precision and spontaneity. Reportedly, they were inspired by Nichols and May, and comparison to that peerless duo is valid. As did Elaine May, Linda Wallem demonstrates the ability to play a wide variety of characters; as did Mike Nichols, Peter Tolan has a narrower acting range but provides the solid grounding of understated wryness which makes his partner's flights possible. Now, if they could just find more adventurous targets for their humor ...

A. Whitney Brown had the opposite problem. He is a rare animal, a genuine social satirist; his material in *A. Whitney Brown's The Big Picture (In Words)* (presented in American Place's American Humorists series, recorded in our OOB listings) was pointed and full of surprising connections and fantastic arabesques in demented logic. But he is not yet an adept enough performer to serve his own work expertly. Either he needs to collaborate with a more rigorous director than Wynn Handman and hone his performance skills or he should consider writing for other actors. Another solo comic performer made a splash—an explosive woman named Reno who, in her show *Reno in Rage and Rehab*, railed at the top of her voice on a number of contemporary themes. Some of those themes, e.g. the blandness of life in the suburbs, are old and much picked-over, but in her best moments, such as her analysis of the values implicit in various slang words for "vagina," the outrageousness of her manner was perfectly married to the outrageousness of her matter.

More successful yet was the comedy team of Mo Gaffney and Kathy Najimy who, in *The Kathy and Mo Show: Parallel Lives*, presented a wide repertory of characters, male and female, in a variety of modes. The peak of the show came in a superb little playlet set in a Texas bar in which Najimy played a boorish but not entirely off-putting middle-aged drunk man flirting for the 150th time with a woman (played by Gaffney) who is another of the bar's regulars. "You're looking very, very pretty tonight," the drunk repeats endlessly as he presses the woman to accept another drink and jokes wistfully about the two of them running away together. The beauty of the scene lies in the delicacy with which the two convey the sadness of their lives, which generates this nightly ritual of mock courtship.

Barry McGovern held the stage solo in *I'll Go On*, a widely-acclaimed piece derived from novels by Samuel Beckett. The first act, adapted from *Molloy*, was particularly strong, including the famous passage of the stones and the pockets. I found the second act less successful, being less an acting piece and more in the nature of straight recitation. Another solo performer, Angelina Réaux, paid tribute to the songs of Kurt Weill in a Public Theater presentation called *Stranger Here Myself*. Accompanied by pianist Christopher Berg, she sang the songs well, but Christopher Alden's concept for the production—that Réaux was a woman alone in an unnamed room agonizing over her unhappy situation and toying with suicide—contributed little but arty attitudinizing. Better if Réaux had simply sung the remarkable songs rather than squirm around on the floor and stare moodily into a mirror. On Broadway, rock star Linda Ronstadt surrounded herself with other singers, instrumentalists and dancers for *Canciones de Mi Padre*, an evening invoking the romance of old Mexico. My only reservation was that the lighting equipment set up at the lip of the stage made it impossible for much of the audience in the front rows of the orchestra to see the dancers' feet.

One saw considerably more than feet in *Miracolo d'Amore*, a theater piece by choreographer-director Martha Clarke in which a number of undressed, vulnerable young women were pursued around the stage by a pack of leering grotesques with sexual mischief on their minds. Read by many as being a simplistic portrayal of the relations between the sexes, the disappointment was mitigated somewhat by Clarke's eye for arresting compositions.

Bill Irwin's *Largely New York* was the subject of much debate, one camp insisting that, because it had no dialogue, it could not be called a play, and the other countering that only a fuddy-duddy insists that the defining characteristic of a play is dialogue. I find myself leaning toward the latter view. To my mind, a play is a coherent and logical sequence of behavior performed by actors in front of an audience. The fact that most plays are filled with words does not invalidate a work that does not. This annual being devoted to the theater as represented by its texts, however, and there being no text for *Largely New York* (at least not in the sense that the editors of this volume

Bill Irwin in *Largely New York*

have come to use the term), for the purposes of this discussion we classify it as a special attraction. And a special attraction it was, Irwin playing a top-hatted, soft-shoeing innocent losing his heart to a beautiful modern dancer, finding unlikely camaraderie with a pair of remarkably lithe poppers (as the limber street performers who dance to rap music are now called), evading analysis by a group of mortar-boarded academics portrayed as intellectual piranhas, and resisting the cannibalistic propensities of video. The sight gags were intricate, ingenious and numerous, and the work as a whole was both a stimulating fable for adults and a romp for children—a delight.

Black and Blue, too, was a delight—a lavish revue saluting black entertainers and filling the stage with a series of all-stops-out songs and dances. Three wonderful singers were top-billed—Ruth Brown, Linda Hopkins and Carrie Smith—Brown wickedly funny belting out the song "If I Can't Sell It, I'll Keep Sittin' on It" and trading verses with Hopkins in a thrilling two-handed version of "T'Aint Nobody's Bizness If I Do." Though their billing wasn't as large, the impression hoofers Bunny Briggs and Jimmy Slyde made was every bit as big, demonstrating that age need not restrict a tap dancer's precision or expressiveness. I was also particularly taken with "I'm Confessin'" in which a feather-light lady known simply as Kyme floated through a routine supported by a quartet of elegant dancers and a sweet, swinging jazz fiddle. Cholly Atkins, Henry LeTang, Frankie Manning and Fayard Nicholas won a well-deserved Tony for their spectacular choreography. Though the show was generally well-received, some significant voices quarreled with the nature of the production designs conceived by co-directors Claudio Segovia and Hector Orezzoli, saying they violated the spirit of black American culture. (Such quarreling amused many because these self-appointed guardians of black American culture were white critics.) I had no such problems and, in fact, was charmed by the surprising and imaginative ways in which the designers combined a variety of drapes with the almost sculptural use of light by Neil Peter Jampolis and Jane Reisman.

Across the street from the Minskoff, where *Black and Blue* opened, the cabaret space in the Criterion Center played host to *Blame It on the Movies!*, the New York transfer of a long-running Los Angeles revue, the score of which was made up of material originally written for films. Hampered by woefully engineered sound and cheesy arrangements, the show didn't come to life until the second act with a steamy *pas de deux* to the accompaniment of Franz Waxman's music for *A Place in the Sun*. In this and in another number set on a spiral staircase, singer-dancer Christine Kellogg invited flattering comparison to Cyd Charisse.

Which brings us to *Jerome Robbins' Broadway*. What began as an archival project for Robbins to preserve on videotape numbers he had choreographed over his career in musical theater turned into a theatrical retrospective. The format of the show was reminiscent of a television special, with Jason Alexander acting as host, giving the audience the information it needed to appreciate each number's place in the work from which it was excerpted. If the structure of the show was necessarily choppy, the vast majority of the excerpts were wonderful. I have never been particularly fond of the arch "The Small House of Uncle Thomas" ballet from *The King and I*, and "Mr. Monotony," a "lost" song by Irving Berlin, is not one of that great songwriter's better efforts, but virtually everything else scored. What particularly impressed, from the exuberant sailors' dances from *On the Town* through the sensational suite from *West Side Story* to the bottle dance from *Fiddler on the Roof*, was the marriage of athleticism and grace. And the humor! The shameless vaudeville shenanigans of "Comedy Tonight," *A Funny Thing Happened on the Way to the Forum*'s opening number, were a reminder that once the form was called "musical comedy," and the comedy could be genuinely funny. There were opportunities enough for a large number of the company's gifted performers to stand out—Scott Wise, Faith Prince, Debbie Shapiro, Robert La Fosse, Charlotte d'Amboise, Jane Lanier—and, of course, Jason Alexander, who often stepped into the frames of the pictures he introduced, most notably as Pseudolus and Tevye. And yes, as widely observed, there was something bittersweet about the evening. The show closes with the lovely Comden-Green-Bernstein song "Some Other Time" from *On the Town*, and one could not help reflecting that it was indeed "some other time" when American musical theater regularly offered such deep pleasures.

Revivals

Some plays are considered classics primarily because of the formal or thematic ground they broke. Unfortunately, many of these no longer hold the stage well today. The Roundabout Theater produced more than its share of such plays this year. With its frank discussion of venereal disease, in its day Ibsen's *Ghosts* caused a sensation. Today, what with its torturous exposition, contrivances, coincidences and Oswald's conveniently-timed madness at the end, the play requires the extreme indulgence of the audience even in the best of productions, and this was not the best of productions. Fionnula Flanagan has proved herself elsewhere to be a fine actress, but matched with a miscast Pastor Manders and Oswald, under Stuart Vaughan's stodgy direction, she seemed lost.

Tovah Feldshuh infused Robert Kalfin's production of Goldoni's *The Mistress of the Inn* at the Roundabout with as much energy as she could muster, but the play stayed resolutely unfunny. (What a relief to see her later in the season sail triumphantly through another farce, *Lend Me a Tenor*.) Despite Harold Scott's earnest and intelligent work, his revival of Carson McCullers's *The Member of the Wedding* seemed endless, and J Ranelli's production of Pirandello's *Enrico IV*, even given a strong performance by Paul Hecht in the title role, gave little indication of why this play has been called one of the masterworks of 20th century theater. (As part of the Joyce Theater's American Theater Exchange series, the visiting American Repertory Theater production of Pirandello's *Six Characters in Search of an Author*, in an adaptation by producer-director Robert Brustein, was significantly better. The staging may have been riddled with gimmickry, but at least the play had some vitality.)

Two of the hottest tickets of the season were revivals of other 20th century classics. There was little doubt that the reason so many people wanted to see Mike Nichols's production of Samuel Beckett's *Waiting for Godot* had more to do with the cast including Steve Martin and Robin Williams than the appeal of the play itself, but the production had its strengths. Bill Irwin was a fierce and brilliant Lucky, and Steve Martin gave a very strong account of himself as Vladimir. F. Murray Abraham was a surprising disappointment; this unusually fine actor seemed to substitute a general blustery attitude for a real understanding of Pozzo. As for Robin Williams as Estragon, in his best moments he

Above, George Ede and Tovah Feldshuh in Goldoni's
The Mistress of the Inn; right, Amelia Campbell and
Esther Rolle in McCullers's *The Member of the
Wedding; below foreground,* Paul Hecht and Lazaro
Perez in Pirandello's *Enrico IV*

achieved a marvelous comic balance with Martin, acting the child, all appetite and impulse, to Martin's wryer, more philosophical bent. But, like a child, Williams sometimes went too far and crayoned outside the lines (for example, tossing a mock Oscar acceptance speech into a passage calling for general alarums).

The other sold-out revival had no superstars to attract its enthusiastic audience. The Gate Theater of Dublin's production of Sean O'Casey's *Juno and the Paycock*, presented as part of the First New York International Festival of the Arts, was tough and, as many critics pointed out, very Beckett-like. (Reportedly, Beckett himself had seen and admired it.) Certainly Donal McCann and John Kavanagh, as the Captain and Joxer, achieved a sense of symbiotic desperation not unlike that of Vladimir and Estragon. Kavanagh's was one of the commanding performances of the season, giving the impression of a pair of vulture-like eyes hovering above a clattering collection of animated bones. There was nothing cozy or sentimental here. Joe Dowling's production seemed designed to underscore Juno's comments on the sorrows Ireland's men have inflicted on the women unlucky enough to have their company. The production was an enormous critical success, but scheduling considerations kept it from receiving the long run it surely would have received otherwise.

In the opinion of our historian, Thomas T. Foose, this was "the best stage work of the season. Documentation may be helpful since, for whatever reason, interest in the O'Casey plays has cooled in recent years. In fact, the last production of Broadway calibre seen here was a 1976 visit of the Dublin Abbey to the Brooklyn Academy with *The Plough and the Stars* (the late Siobhan McKenna played Bessie). Aside from off-off stagings, *Juno and the Paycock* has not been seen here in any form since the 1958-59 Broadway musical *Juno* which lasted only two weeks (music and lyrics by Marc Blitzstein, direction by Jose Ferrer, Captain Jack and Juno played by Melvyn Douglas and Shirley Booth).

"The American premiere of *Juno and the Paycock* was on March 15, 1926 at the Mayfair Theater, and it ran for 74 performances. Aside from the Blitzstein musical, this is the only major production of this play in New York with an American cast. Back to 1927, most stagings were with Abbey Theater actors. The last was not an official Abbey production, but it was Abbey-inspired, produced by Edward Choate and Arthur Shields (who also played Joxer). It opened at the Mansfield on January 16, 1940 and ran for 105 performances. Captain Jack and Juno were Barry Fitzgerald (Arthur Shields's brother) and Sara Allgood, who had originated these same roles at the Abbey premiere in 1924."

Also presented as part of the Festival were two Yale-sponsored productions of O'Neill plays. Jason Robards was more successful in this attempt at playing James Tyrone than in the production at the Brooklyn Academy some years back, but I am still not convinced this is his role, and for reasons similar to those I expressed about Jack Lemmon when he undertook the part two years ago—James Tyrone must be a convincing classical tragic actor for the frittering away of his talent to be affecting. There is no question that Robards is one of our finest actors; but, as was true with Lemmon, it is impossible to see him as having once triumphed as Othello. Colleen Dewhurst summoned up a rarely-seen fragility for Mary Tyrone, and Jamey Sheridan and Campbell Scott were solid as the sons, but Jose Quintero's production as a whole fell short of the necessary urgency.

In contrast, Arvin Brown's production of *Ah, Wilderness!* was an almost constant joy. Robards gave an assured, expansive performance as Nat Miller, even making the over-familiar scene in which he attempted to explain the facts of life to his son fresh and moving. The son, Richard, was played with a great gallumphing, wide-eyed passion by Raphael Sbarge that stopped within inches of being too much. Dewhurst as his mother, George Hearn as the unreformable Sid and Elizabeth Wilson as the disappointed aunt offered beautifully-modulated support.

Another classic play of American small town life received a nearly exemplary production. Under the meticulous direction of Gregory Mosher, *Our Town* was divested of the cutesy touches which have so often made past productions nigh unto insufferable. Penelope Ann Miller was an achingly fine Emily Webb, well partnered with Eric Stoltz as George Gibbs. Their soda fountain scene played as if it were freshly written and newly discovered. Mosher was wise in almost all of his other casting, from Frances Conroy and Roberta Maxwell as George and Emily's mothers to Bill Alton's Professor Maloney and Jeff Weiss's dour Simon Stimson. My one reservation: Spalding Gray as the Stage Manager. Gray has made his reputation with acerbic monologues in which he has attacked the small town values Wilder celebrated in this play; and, try as he evidently did, he was not able to suppress his evident desire to put distance between himself and the people and rituals he was introducing. It was if the play he was doing were called *Their Town*. Nonetheless, this was easily one of the season's handful of truly distinguished revivals. It was particularly good to see that Gregory Mosher, who till now has directed in New York only chamber-sized pieces, can indeed do assured work on a larger scale.

There were six other revivals on Broadway. Hy Kraft's *Cafe Crown*, transferred from off-Broadway's Public Theater, offered Santo Loquasto the opportunity to design a gorgeous set; but, even under Martin Charnin's direction and with a cast including such notables as Eli Wallach, Anne Jackson and Bob Dishy, the play resolutely refused to be more than mildly amusing. Madeline Kahn's performance as Billie Dawn in a revival of Garson Kanin's *Born Yesterday* was exquisitely calibrated but cold as ice. Something is wrong when you like the brutal Harry Brock (given an assured, engaged interpretation by Edward Asner) better than Billie. James Earl Jones played the title role in the premiere of Phillip Hayes Dean's *Paul Robeson* a decade ago. Jones was powerful as the legendary actor-activist, but he didn't have the vocal equipment to be convincing as the singer. Avery Brooks being a fine singer as well as an accomplished actor, this season's revival included a good deal more music than did the original production, thus presenting a more complete picture than previously of this complex man. *Ain't Misbehavin'* reassembled its original cast for a high-spirited reminder as to why the show had been successful in the first place. As for the Circle in the Square production of *The Devil's Disciple*, except for the celebrated scenes with General Burgoyne (played with his usual authority by Philip Bosco), the script played as if were a musical from which all the songs had been excised. More successful was Circle in the Square's production of Tennessee Williams's *The Night of the Iguana* in which Maria Tucci gave one of the best performances of her career as an intense and infinitely compassionate Hannah Jelkes.

A couple of years back, I expressed disappointment that the passing of time had made Joe Orton's script for *Loot* seem tame, despite an immaculate production at Manhattan Theater Club featuring Joseph Maher under the direction of John Tillinger. The good news this season was that, in contrast to *Loot*, Orton's *What the Butler Saw*, a farce about lust, madness and a missing phallus from a statue of Winston Churchill, proved itself to be as pointedly outrageous and stageworthy as ever. Maher and Tillinger were again in collaboration at Manhattan Theater Club, with Charles Keating, Bruce Norris, Carole Shelley, Patrick Tull and Joanne Whalley-Kilmer making up the rest of this nearly ideal complement of Ortonites.

At Lincoln Center, Mark Lamos, who has earned a considerable reputation staging classics at the Hartford Stage (where he is artistic director), directed a modern-dress version of *Measure for Measure*. There was much critical quibbling over the casting of an actor of Campbell Scott's youth as Angelo, but I thought it one of the production's strengths. In my experience, it is the young ideologues who are particularly likely to have untempered theories to impose upon the world. In a sense, Angelo is as ideologically rigid as Isabella is, and their confrontation has added resonance when they are of equivalent ages and intransigence. As the New York *Post's* Clive Barnes observed, this production was also distinguished by the fact that it prepared the audience for the eventual marriage between the Duke and Isabella, here played with intelligence by Len Cariou and Kate Burton. Jack Weston's full-throttle performance as Pompey was a welcome lagniappe.

Mention Shakespeare in New York, and the name of Joseph Papp must arise. Last season, I had little good to say about the first entries in Joseph Papp's Shakespeare Marathon. This season saw a remarkable improvement in the level of the work, only *Cymbeline* being generally considered a failure.

(I'm one of those nay-sayers who think that any production of *Cymbeline* is doomed by virtue of the text; but then there are many who swear by the text who swore *at* JoAnne Akalaitis's eclectic production.)

One of my favorite black sheep in the Shakespeare canon is *King John*. Long badmouthed by critics as having a title character too devoid of nobility to sustain a play, it is John's very lack of nobility I find of interest. He is king, but he hasn't the character to go with the title. Self-pitying, with paranoid tendencies and a habit of cutting sharp political deals and indulging in unsavory behind-the-scenes manipulations, he anticipates the character and habits of a President of recent memory. Some day I should like to see a *King John* which embraces the black satiric comedy which I think makes the play unique among Shakespeare's histories, a true medieval Watergate. Stuart Vaughan's was not such a production, being staged in a very stolid, conventional way. But he had a first-rate John in Kevin Conway, who gave a vivid portrayal of a man haunted by his own inadequacy. Conway received fine support from Jay O. Sanders, as the sardonic Bastard who ironically comes to embody the honor of England, and Mariette Hartley, who gave full expression to both Constance's combativeness and her grief.

"*King John* has rarely been staged recently in New York," our Mr. Foose observes, the last having been at the Delacorte in 1967. "This was Joseph Papp's first offering of the play, and he staged it himself, with Harris Yulin in the title role. Before 1967, one must go back to 1908–09 when this play was presented in repertory by Robert B. Mantell, and before that to 1874 at Booth's Theater, where King John was played by the elder brother of Edwin and John Wilkes Booth, Junius Brutus Booth Jr. In the first half of the 19th century, however, *King John* had many stagings in New York."

Gerald Freedman directed two excellent productions for the Shakespeare series. A summer production in Central Park of *Much Ado About Nothing* featured the always alluring Blythe Danner as Beatrice and Kevin Kline as a marvelously physical yet sensitive Benedick. Had Joseph Papp fulfilled his announced desire to transfer this production to Broadway, I have no doubt that the Tony nominations, and perhaps the awards themselves, would have been very different. Later in the season, Freedman guided a remarkable *Love's Labor's Lost*. This is hardly one of the most satisfying of Shakespeare's texts. There is barely a half hour's worth of dramatic action to spread over nearly three hours of playing time, and the four young ladies whom the four students pursue are given very little definition in the text. Somehow, Freedman transformed this recalcitrant stuff into a vacation of carefree youth, made all the more poignant by its abrupt end when a sudden offstage death yanks the lovers out of their bubble of romance. William Converse-Roberts as Berowne and Richard Libertini as the woebegone Don Armado headed the gifted ensemble.

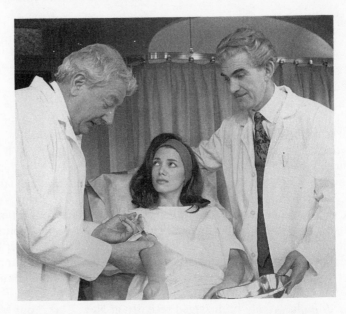

WHAT THE BUTLER SAW—Joseph Maher, Joanne Whalley-Kilmer and Charles Keating in the revival of Joe Orton's play

In an election year, *Coriolanus* had special meaning. Shakespeare is dealing here with contrasting ideals of leadership. The same qualities which make Coriolanus a brilliant military leader make him a disastrous politician, leadership in one arena not necessarily being transferable to another. Steven Berkoff's staging received widespread praise for the tautness of its ensemble work and the sheer, brutal muscularity of the conception. The transitions between scenes were accompanied by a percussive martial score by Larry Spivak. For my taste, the score and the marching about lost their effectiveness with overuse, but Christopher Walken's Coriolanus was an arresting characterization. His relationship with the rest of the ensemble seemed to mirror his character's relationship with Rome—determinedly emphasizing rhythms in conflict with everyone else. One might disagree with particular choices at particular moments, but Walken's was an original and distinctly American interpretation. Irene Worth, who has previously played Volumnia in very different productions with Ian McKellen and Alan Howard, successfully accomodated herself to Berkoff's harsh interpretation.

"A decade earlier, Joseph Papp had offered an all-black-actor production of *Coriolanus*," Mr. Foose reminds us, "staged at the Public Theater in March 1979 and then moved to the Delacorte in June. Morgan Freeman was Caius Marcius and Gloria Foster was Volumnia. In his long production history, it has been very unusual for Papp to move a production from the Public to the Delacorte. Incidentally, *Coriolanus* was adapted as a rock opera, *Marcius*, given in London in 1976 at the Round House, and there have been several other opera versions, most notably Jan Cikker's 1974 Czech opera."

The high point of the Shakespeare Festival's distinguished year was *The Winter's Tale*. James Lapine, who last season directed and co-wrote with Stephen Sondheim *Into the Woods*, through this play continued to explore the world of the fairy tale. He was blessed with a marvelous cast. Mandy Patinkin made Leontes's sudden insane jealousy horrifyingly real and his restoration to sanity and realization of loss soul-wrenching. Diane Venora's dignity and intensity made her a perfectly matched Hermione. In supporting roles, James Olson was stalwart without being stuffy as Camillo, and Rocco Sisto's Autolycus was a rogue who unapologetically relished his own bad behavior.

This production was also technically accomplished, John Arnone's multi-levelled set making the best use of the pillar-ridden Anspacher Theater I can recall, Franne Lee's costumes reinforcing the brooding qualities of the first half and the festivities of the second, and Beverly Emmons's lighting helping to create the illusion of a world in which the air is pregnant with magic. Special praise, too, is due to William Finn and Michael Starobin for a score of extraordinary delicacy, the most impressive new music of any show—musical or straight play—this season. I wish I could convey the visual beauty of the production's final moments, but in the wake of the statue scene I could barely see for my tears. All in all, this was the best production of Shakespeare I have seen under Papp's sponsorship.

Offstage

According to the press release from the League of American Theaters and Producers, in terms of raw dollars, at least, it was a terrific year. For the second straight season, Broadway set a box office record with approximately $262 million in ticket sales, as opposed to last season's $253,471,282. Though there was an increase in new Broadway plays, 11 this season (8 American, 3 foreign), the number of musicals (even if one chooses to place *Black and Blue* and *Jerome Robbins' Broadway* in this category), declined from 7 to 6. Touring income rose, too, going from $223 million last season to $255 million this. Off Broadway, by our count, production held fairly steady with 38 plays, 7 musicals and 6 revues (compared with 37-6-7 last year, with a dropoff of 4 shows in the foreign-play category).

A good deal of Broadway's income was a reflection of holdover successes from past seasons—primarily the British-originated *Cats, Me and My Girl, Les Misérables* and *The Phantom of the Opera*. The only show to enter those blockbusters' company this season was the Robbins evening.

Jerome Robbins' Broadway was also the year's most expensive production. What with a 22-week rehearsal period, a cast of 53 (plus assorted swing dancers), and dozens of stagehands, musicians and costume personnel (not to mention authors' royalties distributed 21 ways), capitalization came to $8.8 million (breaking *Phantom's* record $8 million). Even with a $55 top ticket price (up $5 from the previous Broadway top), the show is projected to require nearly two capacity years to recoup (in contrast to the 60 weeks it took for *Phantom* to recoup). The initial signs looked promising. In the wake of near-unanimous rave reviews, on opening day the box office took in $535,000 in advance sales and soon had racked up a more than $10 million advance. (Even so, it would have to go a long way to overtake *Cats*, which *Variety* pronounced the most profitable theatrical production in history, having netted in excess of $44 million in North America alone.)

Another pricey show was *Legs Diamond*, which reportedly lost $7 million before its collapse, about equal to the record loss *Carrie* posted last season. Among the non-musicals, Bill Irwin's *Largely New York* was capitalized at $750,000, *Metamorphosis* at $460,000, and *Rumors* at $688,540. At season's end, *Variety* reported that *Rumors* and the return engagements of *Ain't Misbehavin'* and Michael Feinstein's concert program had made their money back. Eventual profit seemed certain for *The Heidi Chronicles* and likely for *Largely New York, Metamorphosis, Shirley Valentine, Black and Blue,* and *Lend Me a Tenor.* Off Broadway, where there was relatively little commercial activity, *Suds* cost $500,000 to mount, and *The Taffetas* cost $250,000.

Talk of the business side inevitably leads to talk of theatrical real estate, which just as inevitably summons up this year's catalogue of births, deaths and hoped-for resurrections. The most ambitious of the last, the 42d Street Redevelopment Project, continued with plans designed to revitalize the seamy block on 42d Street between Seventh and Eighth Avenues. Once home to nine functioning legitimate theaters, none of which is currently operating as a stage venue, the street's revitalization would not only provide Broadway with more houses but also serve as a potent symbol to those who view the block's woebegone state as representing the worst of New York. Of the nine theaters, two have already been spoken for by the Nederlander organization, and one is to be converted to retail space. The other six have been put up for bids. Two are designated for nonprofit companies, and 30 organizations have expressed active interest in acquiring them as home bases, not surprising given the fact that the cost for renovating the houses will not be borne by the companies selected (though they will be responsible for covering operating costs). The other four are intended for commercial use.

A few blocks north, the Minskoff Rehearsal Studios closed up shop at the end of the season because their proprietors reportedly could not meet the 250 percent rent increase demanded by the Astor Plaza building's owners, the Tishman Speyer real estate firm. With the Minskoff Studios gone, the New

York theater community faces a paucity of spaces appropriate for rehearsing big musicals, not to mention large-scale auditions.

Further north, the landmark-designated 958-seat Biltmore Theater, which during its glory days housed the long run of *Hair*, was reported by *Variety* to be in a state of "terminal deterioration." The theater preservationist group, Save Our Theaters, attempted to compel the owner to protect the house from further destruction. The owner, in the meantime, was trying to find a buyer to offer something in excess of $5 million to take it off his hands.

Further north yet, the Mark Hellinger Theater, most famous as the home of the original run of *My Fair Lady*, was leased by the Nederlander organization to a nondemoninational church for $1 million a year for five years, precluding its use as a theater for that time. This deal was commonly read as the Nederlanders' resignation to the improbability of finding for a tenant a musical of sufficient size, quality and profitability. The Nederlanders were also reportedly exploring the idea of converting the Lunt-Fontanne to a movie theater.

Off Broadway, there was more grim news. The Second Avenue Theater, a 499-seat house which was the original home of *Grease*, was sold by M Square Entertainment to City Cinemas, which plans to chop it up into a complex of small movie houses.

Two theaters were gained under one roof at the southeast corner of Broadway and 45th Street. The larger is the Criterion Stage Right which, at 499 seats, qualifies as a Broadway house and looks to be a valuable addition to the neighborhood. The other, the 399-seat Stage Left, is a cabaret which might be suitable for well-amplified pop performers, but its lack of intimacy, at least in its current configuration, makes it a less appealing venue for theatrical pieces.

On the labor front, the year proved to be fairly quiet. Broadway box office personnel, stagehands, press agents and managers won wage increases of 5, 4 and 5 percent over the next three years in their new contracts with the League of American Theaters and Producers, and Equity negotiated a new three-year contract with the League of Resident Theaters under which members will ultimately receive 16 to 19 percent increases keyed to the size of the theaters. The quietude may not last, however. At season's end, Equity was about to go into negotiations with producers for the new three-year contract covering actors' salaries on Broadway, and the Society of Stage Directors and Choreographers was openly discussing the possibility of a strike against the LORT theaters to protest what they saw as insultingly low compensation for their efforts, particularly in view of the large salaries (some in six figures) many in LORT companies' management are receiving.

Those looking for drama were not dependent only on what was presented onstage this season. There was plenty of pulse-quickening conflict to be found in the periodicals' arts pages, what with one showdown after another erupting between various leading figures in the community.

Lincoln Center was the subject of frequent debate. For years, the question hovering over the Lincoln Center Theater Company was whether producing at the Vivian Beaumont and Mitzi Newhouse Theaters was viable at all. For most of the houses' first two decades, they had played host to a series of producing teams which had either abandoned the task in frustration or been jettisoned by unhappy boards. The fortunes of the company changed with the installation in the 1985–86 season of company director Gregory Mosher and executive producer Bernard Gersten. In four seasons at the helm, their productions of an enviable string of genuinely attractive attractions laid to rest the question of the institution's viability. But this season, their very success generated controversies.

One of these centered on the revival of *Waiting for Godot*. Director Mike Nichols and his stellar cast decided that they wanted to play the 299-seat Mitzi Newhouse. The problem was that the cast's other commitments permitted only a seven-week run which would accommodate only about half of Lincoln Center's membership. Mosher and Gersten employed a lottery system to determine which of the membership would be granted tickets. The unlucky half were understandably miffed, complaining that such practices made a mockery of their membership. Mosher and Gersten responded by saying that, even given their inability to share this production with all of their members, the opportunity to present a work featuring such distinguished collaborators could not be responsibly bypassed.

Mosher and Gersten also decided to keep the hit production of *Anything Goes* running at the Vivian Beaumont rather than go to the expense of transferring it to a Broadway house. With the Beaumont thus indefinitely occupied, the pair had to find another theater in which to produce part of their 1988–89 season. They selected the Lyceum, a Broadway venue which has had little luck housing plays in recent years (though evenings with Whoopi Goldberg and Michael Feinstein have done well there). To facilitate production of the large-cast *Our Town*, they sought and received a special salary concession from Equity under which actors were paid $600 a week rather than the standard Broadway minimum of $775. Some members of the commercial theater community cried foul, saying that by agreeing to this arrangement, Equity was in effect subsidizing Lincoln Center's hits, creating unfair competition for commercial projects.

Rocco Landesman, president of the Jujamcyn organization, heated things up with a broadside in the New York *Times* in which he wrote that Mosher and Gersten were pursuing a commercial agenda under the guise of a nonprofit theater, citing as examples the production of "safe" classics like *Anything Goes* and *Our Town* and the casting of stars such as Madonna, Robin Williams and Steve Martin in chancier plays. While Landesman raised some valid issues regarding the contrasting mandates of commercial and noncommercial producers, he neglected to mention sizeable chunks of the

AIN'T MISBEHAVIN'—Armelia McQueen, Ken Page, Charlaine Woodard, Andre De Shields and Nell Carter in the Broadway return engagement of the Fats Waller revue

Lincoln Center record which did not support his charges. Yes, *Sarafina!* turned out to be a Broadway hit, but it was hardly on the top of anyone's list of hot prospects when it was announced for the 1987–88 season, nor were Wole Soyinka's *Death and the King's Horseman* or *A Boy's Life* calculated and predestined crowd-pleasers. A review of this regime's record reveals that the clear majority of their productions have been projects in which few commercial producers would have invested, except with 20-20 hindsight.

Joseph Papp got into his usual quota of scuffles. When *Times* critic Frank Rich wrote a piece critical of Papp's ongoing project to produce all of Shakespeare's plays, Papp responded with a long riposte in which he made plain he took great umbrage at Rich's speculation as to the psychological forces motivating the undertaking, particularly at the idea that this was Papp's way of compensating for cultural deprivation in his boyhood. His family may not have been wealthy, the producer wrote with some heat, but he remembered his childhood as being a wonderfully rich one. So there!

John Simon's review of *The Winter's Tale* provoked an even sharper response. Simon, critic for *New York Magazine*, doesn't believe in color-and-ethnic-blind casting in general and specifically objects to it in Shakespeare.

The production in question gave him occasion to rail in particular against Mandy Patinkin as Leontes and Alfre Woodard as Paulina. He claimed Patinkin's gestures, posture and intonation reminded him of a caricature of a Jew such as might be found in an anti-Semitic publication of the Third Reich, and he wrote that Woodard reminded him of "visually a cross between Topsy and Medusa, aurally (at any rate in the first half) a pretty fair impersonation of Butterfly McQueen. If Miss Woodard weren't black," Simon continued, "one might suspect her of racism." Papp called Simon's review "the most scurrilous I have ever read." Colleen Dewhurst agreed. In a letter to Edward Kosner, the publisher and editor of *New York Magazine*, she averred that Simon's writing had the effect of unwittingly condoning bigotry and racism. "Mr. Simon has irresponsibly attacked and defamed the theater, a producer, and a cast committed to presenting on the stage the face of our nation, on the basis of race and national origin. This is completely unwarranted and unacceptable. And therefore, as president of Actors Equity, I call upon you to remove him from his present position." Though some others in the community found Simon's remarks distasteful, they saw calls for his firing as a threat to the First Amendment. Still others didn't see the remarks as offensive but as the statement of a conscientious critic bravely stating an unpopular truth. At any rate, *The Winter's Tale* proved to be an enormous success, and Kosner did not fire Simon.

The Tony Awards were at the center of even more scuffling, as one divisive issue after another provoked public argument and private rancor. The perennial question "What to do about off Broadway?" arose yet again. Organized to recognize achievements in theaters designated as Broadway houses, the Tony categories are closed to all work done in the smaller venues, though that work is generally on a par with and frequently superior to what is offered on Broadway. The Tony Administration Committee has so far resisted making off-Broadway plays eligible. Several members of the committee are Broadway producers who presumably wouldn't relish the prospect of an off-Broadway play capitalized at $200,000 competing against and beating one of their $1 million-plus offerings. There is also speculation that CBS, which broadcasts the annual ceremonies, would not be happy to devote national prime-time attention to productions in small theaters. Also, were off-Broadway plays to be eligible, according to the rules the entire list of Tony voters would have to be invited to see those plays free. As the list comprises about 740 voters, and off-Broadway houses usually hold between 199 and 499 seats, making pairs of tickets available to all voters could take a big bite out of such shows' income.

Frank Rich stirred matters up some more by implying in a radio broadcast that theater artists who disagree with the Tonys' ignoring of off Broadway should consider refraining from participating in the award ceremonies. The *Times* executive editor, Max Frankel, made more Tony news by decreeing that no *Times* employees should participate in the Tony or any other consensual process. Accordingly, 13 *Times* employees withdrew from the list of Tony voters, and the paper's television reporter, Jeremy Gerard, was compelled to leave the Nominating Committee. (Two other members of the Nominating Committee, Second Stage's co-artistic director, Robyn Goodman and lyricist Sheldon Harnick, withdrew to avoid conflicts of interest; each was associated with a Tony-eligible work.)

Still more controversy arose over matters of Tony eligibility. The celebrated production of *Juno and the Paycock* had not invited Tony voters and consequently was not allowed to compete for "best revival." In special sessions, the Administration Committee decided to make Bill Irwin's non-verbal *Largely New York* eligible for "best play" and *Jerome Robbins' Broadway* eligible for "best musical" rather than "best revival," even though the bulk of the Robbins show was made up of elements already seen on Broadway. Of course, neither the Robbins show nor *Black and Blue*, the other well-received musical entertainment of the year, had anything to offer in the categories of best book or best score. The paucity of creditable candidates led the Tony Administration Committee to eliminate those categories this season. The Administration Committee also gave a nod to reality by allowing the Nominating Committee to name only three candidates for "best musical" rather than the usual four.

When the nominations were announced, there were more howls. Clive Barnes of the New York *Post* vehemently protested the nomination of *Largely New York* as a play and proclaimed his decision to boycott the proceedings. Others noted with jaundiced eyes the multiple nominations *Starmites* received, including one for "best musical."

The final awards were no surprise. *The Heidi Chronicles*, which had already picked up the Pulitzer Prize, the Hull-Warriner Award and prizes from the New York Drama Critics Circle, the Drama Desk and the Outer Critics Circle, took "best Play" as expected. *Jerome Robbins' Broadway* danced off with "best musical," having also collected the Outer Critics Circle Award (the New York Drama Critics Circle and the Drama Desk gave no "best musical" award this year).

On the subject of awards, the *Times's* decision to prohibit employees from participating in the Tony Awards applied to other awards as well. Accordingly, Frank Rich and Mel Gussow resigned from the New York Drama Critics Circle, of which Gussow had been president. Presumably, the *Times's* policy will also preclude future participation by staffers in judging the Pulitzer Prize for drama.

All in all, though some moments linger in the memory, as a whole 1988–89 was not a season that will be remembered with much warmth. In the hopes of planting seeds for happier seasons to come, Jujamcyn Theaters, in partnership with producers James B. Freydberg, Max Weitzenhoffer and Stephen

Graham, announced the American Playwrights Project under the auspices of which a group of well-regarded playwrights were to be given commissions to write new works for the stage. Rocco Landesman, president of Jujamcyn, was quoted in *Variety* as saying, "There are no strictures for the writers. Basically we're just saying, 'Here's some dough, go write a play, and when it's finished it will be developed as you see fit.'" At the end of the 1988–89 season, three playwrights had been commissioned, and Freydberg expected more to be joining the program as they discharged other obligations. Freydberg believes it will take three years for a complete cycle of the program—one year for the writing, a second for development in a collaborative nonprofit theater and a third for the final move to New York. One wishes the writers and producers luck and hopes to see the fruits of their work represented in subsequent editions of this annual.

A GRAPHIC GLANCE

Campbell Scott, Jamey Sheridan, Colleen Dewhurst and Jason Robards in *Long Day's Journey Into Night*

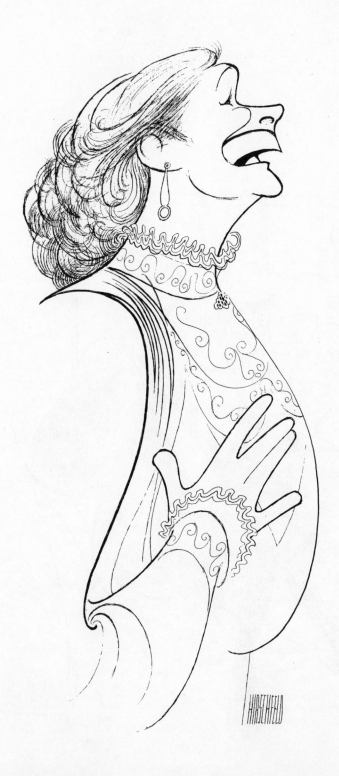

Colleen Dewhurst in *Long Day's Journey Into Night* and *Ah, Wilderness!*

Raphael Sbarge in *Ah, Wilderness!*

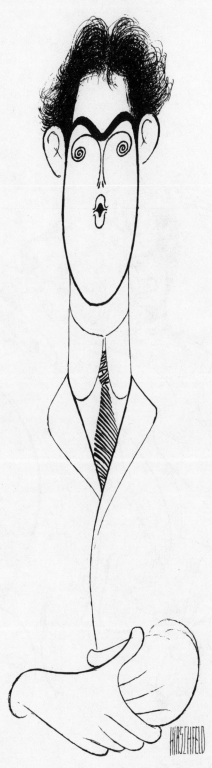

Charlaine Woodard, Andre De Shields, Nell Carter, Ken Page and Armelia McQueen in *Ain't Misbehavin'*

Nell Carter and Ken Page in *Ain't Misbehavin'*

(*Clockwise from top*) Denzel Washington, Marsha Jackson, Ruby Dee and Paul Winfield in
Checkmates

Marita Geraghty, Jeffrey De Munn, Kate Nelligan, Christopher Collet, Alice Playten and Kevin O'Rourke in *Spoils of War*

Jarlath Conroy, Helen Schneider, Stephen McHattie, Donal Donnelly, George Hearn, Avner Eisenberg and Gordon Joseph Weiss in *Ghetto*

Christine Baranski in *Rumors*

Ron Leibman, Jessica Walter, Lisa Banes, Ken Howard, Andre Gregory, Joyce Van Patten, Christine Baranski and Mark Nelson in *Rumors*

James Rebhorn, Frances Conroy, Eric Stoltz, Peter Maloney, Roberta Maxwell, Penelope Ann Miller and Spalding Gray in *Our Town*

Frances Conroy in *Our Town*

Randall Edwards, Jim Fyfe, Christian Kauffmann, Joe Silver, Peter Allen, Julie Wilson and Raymond Serra in *Legs Diamond*

(*Top left to right*) Jazz musicians: Roland Hanna, Claude Williams and Grady Tate and (*bottom left to right*), Ruth Brown, Bunny Briggs, Linda Hopkins, Jimmy Slyde and Carrie Smith in *Black and Blue*

Bunny Briggs and Ruth Brown in *Black and Blue*

Athol Fugard in *The Road to Mecca*

Daniel Hugh Kelly, Edward Asner and Madeline Kahn in *Born Yesterday*

Jane Connell, Victor Garber, Tovah
Feldshuh, Philip Bosco and Ron
Holgate in *Lend Me a Tenor*

Ron Holgate

Philip Bosco

(*Clockwise from lower left*) Ellen Parker, Joanne Camp, Drew
McVety, Boyd Gaines, Peter Friedman, Sarah Jessica Parker and
Anne Lange surround Joan Allen (*center*) in *The Heidi Chronicles*

Boyd Gaines and Joanna Camp
in *The Heidi Chronicles*

Jeff Gordon, Bill Irwin, Leon Chesney, Steve Clemente and Margaret Eginton in *Largely New York*

Mikhail Baryshnikov in *Metamorphosis*

(*Clockwise from lower left*) Jerry Stiller, Richard Woods, Kevin Kline, Blythe Danner, Don Reilly and Phoebe Cates in *Much Ado About Nothing*

Christopher Walken, Moses Gunn, Paul Hecht, Keith David and Irene Worth in *Coriolanus*

Christopher Walken in *Coriolanus*

Diane Venora, Christopher Reeve and Mandy Patinkin in *The Winter's Tale*

Robin Williams, Steve Martin, Lukas Haas, F. Murray Abraham and Bill Irwin in *Waiting for Godot*

Jerome Robbins directs numbers from eight of the musicals represented in *Jerome Robbins' Broadway*

B. D. Wong (*above*) and
David Dukes (*right*) in *M. Butterfly*

Howard McGillin and Leslie Uggams in *Anything Goes*

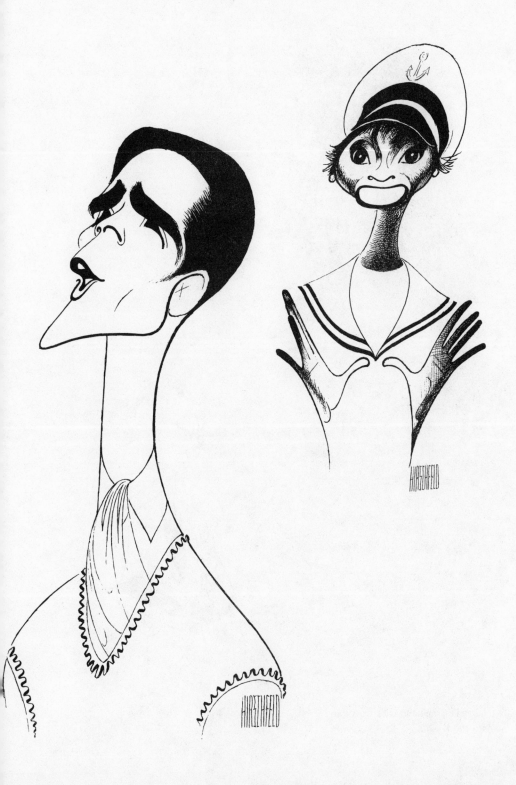

Nancy Dussault and Dick Cavett in
Into the Woods

Sharon McNight in *Starmites*

Michael Feinstein

Sandra Bernhard in *Without You I'm Nothing*

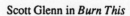
Scott Glenn in *Burn This*

Rudy Caporaso in *Brimstone and Treacle*

Nancy Cassaro in *Tony 'n' Tina's Wedding*

Frances Sternhagen in *Driving Miss Daisy*

Rebecca Luker in *The Phantom of the Opera*

Mary Murfitt in *Oil City Symphony*

Alison Fraser in *Romance Romance*

Ellen Foley in *Me and My Girl*

Joan Rivers in *Broadway Bound*

Eli Wallach in *Cafe Crown*

Pauline Collins in *Shirley Valentine*

Sean O'Casey

Linda Ronstadt in *Canciones de Mi Padre*

Debbie Shapiro in *Jerome Robbins' Broadway*

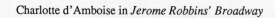
Charlotte d'Amboise in *Jerome Robbins' Broadway*

Maria Tucci in *The Night of the Iguana*

Victor Garber in *The Devil's Disciple*

Kevin Anderson in *Brilliant Traces*

John Pankow in *Aristocrats*

Kevin Conway in *Other People's Money*

Robin Bartlett in *Reckless*

Carole Shelley in *What the Butler Saw*

Anne Meara in *Eastern Standard*

Woody Romoff in *Cantorial*

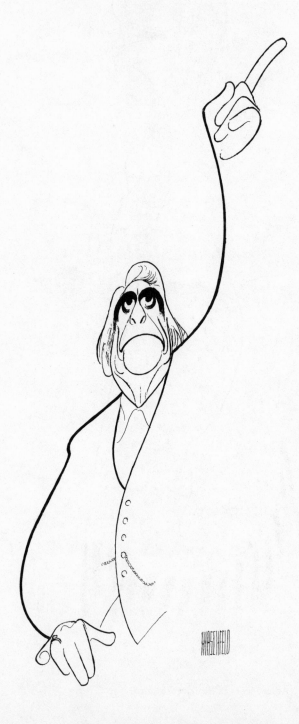

Mark Blum in *Gus and Al*

Roxie Lucas (*above*) and Toni DiBuono in *Forbidden Broadway*

Matt McGrath in *Amulets Against the Dragon Forces*

Keene Curtis (*below*), Nancy Marchand (*right*) and Holland Taylor (*opposite page*) in *The Cocktail Hour*

Martha Graham

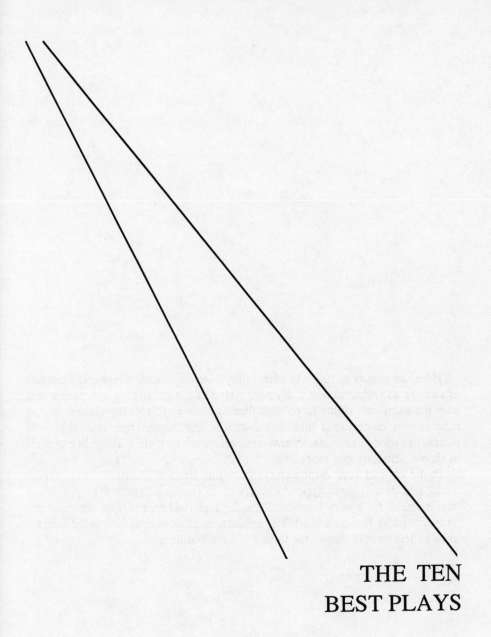

THE TEN
BEST PLAYS

Here are details of 1988–89's Best Plays—synopses, biographical sketches of authors and other material. By permission of the publishing companies that own the exclusive rights to publish these scripts in full in the United States, most of our continuities include substantial quotations from crucial/pivotal scenes in order to provide a permanent reference to style and quality as well as theme, structure and story line.

In the case of such quotations, scenes and lines of dialogue, stage directions and descriptions appear *exactly* as in the stage version or published script unless (in a very few instances, for technical reasons) an abridgement is indicated by five dots (.....). The appearance of three dots (...) is the script's own punctuation to denote the timing of a spoken line.

ROAD

A Play in Two Acts

BY JIM CARTWRIGHT

Cast and credits appear on pages 424–425

JIM CARTWRIGHT was born in 1958 in Farnsworth, near Manchester, into a typical English North-country working-class family. After attending local schools he continued his education at the Royal Academy of Dramatic Art and then set forth on an acting career, in the course of which he wrote his first play, Road. *He submitted it to the Royal Court Theater; they accepted it for production March 22, 1986 at their Theater Upstairs and then transferred it to their mainstage June 9. The BBC aired a TV version of it the following year, and the worldwide series of stage productions of* Road *now includes off Broadway under the joint sponsorship of Lincoln Center and La Mama E.T.C., winning a Best Play citation.*

In England, Road *won for Cartwright the George Devine (Arts Council) playwriting prize, plus many accolades as the 1986 season's best, including those of Drama Magazine and Plays and Players. Both his first movie,* Vroom, *and his second play,* Bed, *appeared in early 1989, the latter at London's National Theater. Cartwright is married and lives in Bolton, Lancashire, where for a six-month period he is serving as playwright-in-residence at the Octagon Theater.*

Road *isn't a conventional theatrical experience. As staged in London and in New York, the audience shared the playing area with the actors.*

At the beginning of the play, we are welcomed by a high-spirited, scruffy, semi-intoxicated character of indeterminate age named Scullery. He introduces us to the road. The name of the road isn't mentioned, and the implication is that it could be any of hundreds of roads in northern England where poverty and redundancy (their word for unemployment) are rife. Scullery tells us he will act as our guide, introducing us to the various characters who people the neighborhood.

The body of the play consists of a series of vignettes and monologues dramatizing the ways in which the people of the road manage to get through the night. The operative word is escape, and the methods include sex, violence, religion, nostalgia, suicide and, almost always, drink.

Given the episodic nature of the script, rather than present a synopsis of the action, we present three self-contained excerpts of the text.

Time: Tonight

Place: A road in a small Lancashire Town

ACT I

Lights come up on a young man, Skin-lad, sitting on a wooden chair. A bare light bulb is dangling.

SKIN-LAD: Om. He opens his eyes. He sees you. He wants to tell you the story. He feels the need to drift back on the tide of his memory, back, back, back. And I'm the lonely skinhead again. Jogging away, every day, to be the best, to be the best. And the press-ups. And the sit-ups. And the 1-2-3, 1-2-3, 1-2-3, 1-2-3. And you've gotta be fit to fight, and I do, every Saturday night, with my friends at weekends, fight. Do you know about fighting? No. I'll tell you in my story. And I want to be the best skinhead, and I want to give everything, every single thing, to the experience of the tingle. I'll tell you about the tingle later. And you've got to be fit to fight and practice tactics every night.

He practices with an imaginary opponent.

Do you? I do.

Practices.

Do you work in the asbestos factory? I did.

Practices. Stops.

I'll explain.

He indicates the imaginary opponent.
My opponent! Anyone you like! City fan, the cunt that shagged Ricky's bird,
Ted the foreman, you choose. Targets!
Goes down on imaginary body.
Face, neck, beerbag, dick, top of the foot. Today I want the neck, this vein
here. I don't want to fuck Christine Dawson, I don't want my mother's love, I
don't want to work at the engineering firm, I want the neck, this vein here.
Practices.
Tactics, new techniques. What does he think? What do you think?
Strikes.
You thought, he thought, the neck and that's that. The neck and that is that.
Now I've told you about the three things you need to get the experience of the
tingle. One, fitness, told you. Two, tactics, told you. Three, new techniques, I
told you. Now I'll tell you about the tingle.
*He comes off the stage into the audience. This next bit should be
improvised.*
Well it's ... you can't say it, can you ... ? It'll come when you're fighting.
Sometimes in the middle, sometime beginning, sometime end, but it won't stay
... it's like you are there, you are fighting, but "you" are not there ...
Pause.
You don't understand.
Pause.
Anyway, once you've had it you need it, and I thought that's all there was until
that night, right, should I tell you about that night? No. I'll show you.
He leaps back on stage.
I came out the disco, last man to leave, all my lads had gone. I'd been talking
to Mickey Isherwood the bouncer:
    "See you Jim."
    "Aye, see you Ishey."
Then I saw them. Skins. Bolton boot-boys. Skinheads. Some sitting on the
wall, some standing. I moved off to the right.
    "Eh, Cunty."
    "Eh, git head."
    "Come 'ere."
I looked at the moon. I heard the crack of denim, the scuffle down the wall,
the pad and fall of the Dr. Martins, pad, pad, pad. I closed my eyes. Pad, pad.
As they moved in, pad, pad, I moved out. Pad, pad. I felt their breath ... lifted
one man by the chin ... can you imagine it? Magnificent ... they were
scattering. Caught one man between thigh and calf, took him round to the
ground, fingers up the nose, dragged a pace, nutted, lifted my fingers to pierce
out his eyes when, to my surprise, I saw a figure watching, like a ghost, all
pale in the night. Seemed like I'd known him all my life. He was laughing at
me. Mocking my whole fucking life. I sprang; when I arrived, he'd gone. Too

quick for me? No, I saw him disappear down a blind alley. I had him now. I had him now!

He was facing the wall in a sort of peeing position. I moved in to strike, my fist was like a golden orb in the wet night, I said it was night, I struck deep and dangerous and beautiful with a twist of the fist on the out. But he was only smiling, and he opened his eyes to me like two diamonds in the night. I said it was night and said, "Over to you, Buddha."

> *Pause.*

So now I just read the dharma. And when men at work pass the pornography, I pass it on and continue with the dharma. And when my mother makes egg and bacon and chips for me I push it away towards the salt cellar and read of the dharma. And when the man on the bus pushes I continue with the dharma. Om.

ACT II

> *Darkness except for a spotlight on an armchair center stage. A young soldier is sitting in it, very drunk, staring out front. The spotlight breaks out over the stage. He turns to see the door open. An Alsatian dog crosses the room and goes out through the opposite door. Then a middle-aged woman, Helen, backs in with two plates. One has chips, pudding and peas on it, one fish and chips. She shuts the door with her bum and goes over to him.*

HELEN: Here they are, love. I've put 'em on plates. Now, which is which? Hang on. You're pudding, that means I'm fish. Watch the gravy, love, it's dripping off one side.

> *She gives him it, lays it on his knees. She drags a poufah, in the shape of a tortoise, over to the side of the armchair and sits by him. Her suspenders show.*

They make a nice chip at the Chinky, don't they? Bit greasy. Bet you miss this in the mess? Where's your camp anyway? You never said. You don't say much, do you? Take your boots off if you like. Do you want the telly on ... ? Well yes or no? Oooooh, you're the real quiet type, aren't you? Still waters run deep, or what? The Clint Eastwood type. Little mini Clint. Eh, I like him though, do you? I like loners. That's why I sent Maureen to fetch you over tonight. That uniform. Dead romantic. It's ages since I've seen a soldier. You just sort of stood out in the crowd. Would you kill somebody if you had to? Say they provoked you. That's your duty, though, int it? This is what you get paid for. License to kill. You must have a laugh, though. All this one-armed combat and what not.

> *She sees something in her meal.*

What the bloody hell's this? It's either mine or that bloody dog's. I'll skin the beast. Kojak! Kojak! Come 'ere. Look at that.

She holds up in front of his face a chip dangling on a long hair. He throws up into his meal. She gets up.

Oh bloody hell. Oh heck.

She puts her chips down and goes off into the kitchen. The dog comes back on and starts eating her chips and fish. She comes back with an old dirty towel.

Kojak you bastard! Get out of it!

She shoos the dog off with the towel.

You bloody dirty git.

The soldier looks up at her, all lost and bleary.

Not you, cocker, him, that hound.

She looks at him and the mess.

Oh dear. Not to worry.

She gets down and starts padding up the sick with a towel. Then she goes back in the kitchen. The soldier passes out, leaning right back in the chair with his eyes closed. She comes in again with a flannel.

I've got a flannel here, cock. Let's just wipe your chops off.

She wipes his face like a baby. He fights a bit in his drunken stupor like a baby might. She pauses a moment in her wiping.

Aaaaw.

She looks again, wipes on. She starts to loosen his tie.

Look, it's all over your shirt and down your nice smart jacket. We can't have that, can we now. Eh? No, we cannot.

She starts to unbutton his jacket. At first she's brisk and fast. Then she slows down, almost enjoying it. She pauses in thought. She gets up and goes over to the record player by the bed. It's on the floor, an old-fashioned mono-portable with a heavy arm. She picks a record up. The records are without sleeves, just in a pile on the floor, some in an old wire record rack. She squats as she puts it on. As she gets it on and the automatic begins and drops, she falls over.

Oh bloody hell.

She giggles. As she lies there, she looks up at him. The music starts, she gets up and walks over to him. The music is Barry Manilow. Now as she undresses him, the music has affected her. And she does it seductively. She gets the jacket and shirt off, then goes off into the kitchen. She comes in with an unfolding clothes-horse; puts it up; puts his clothes over it. She looks again at the soldier. A new record starts. She goes over and kisses him: very sloppy and round.

Oh you are naughty. And so young as well. So young and full of it. I bet you've had loads of girls already, 'ant you, eh?

She kisses him again.

Why should you choose me, eh?

She gets his cheeks in her hands.

Eh? Why? What have I got?

She puts her tongue in his ear.

Oh you sexy bugger. Watch it. You really know what to do, don't you? Not like most blokes. I bet you're the type that knows how to cherish a girl.

She hugs him and puts her head on his chest.

So firm. I imagine you've got the girls running around you like flies on muck. Why me? You could have your pick any time.

She touches his mouth with her fingers.

You could have your pick even of the famous stars.

She kisses him again, she shifts position, she kneels in her plate of chips.

Oh. (*She looks at him.*) Oh, I am sorry, I've kneeled in my chips. Forgive me.

She stands up, picks them off her tights and drops them on the plate. She picks the plate up and goes over to put it on the sideboard. She sees the bed. She lies back on it in a sexy pose, looking at him.

Come on then. Oh you, you do play it cool. You know how to hold back and get a woman sexed. (*She looks at him.*) I know what we'll do.

She rolls over and changes the record.

I know. Just the job this one. Just the blinking job.

It starts blurring out. It's James Brown's "Sex Machine." She turns it up even louder. She rolls about a bit.

Wheeeeeeeee. (*She goes over to him, arms outstretched.*) What, you're gonna tak' me now. Just like that, out the blue. Bloody soldiers.

She grabs him up off the chair and holds him close.

Oh. Oh. What you doing? Oh, oh, lover boy, soldier of love. (*They wobble back over to the bed.*) Wow, you've been overseas, haven't you. What a touch, boy. Wowie.

She flops back on the bed, letting him go: he just falls on top of her. She wraps her legs around him quick.

Oh. Oh.

He slides off her into the record player and out on the floor. The music stops. She leans off the bed and over him.

Are you all right?

She comes out of it a bit. She runs her finger over his face.

You're like a little boy. (*She starts crying.*) I'm sorry. Oh dear.

She cries more. She gets up and puts him on the bed. Takes his shoes off. Puts him under the blankets. She goes out of the room

and comes back in with a piece of toilet roll. She sits on the armchair drying her eyes.
I don't know what they think you are. They treat you like last week's muck. *(She looks like she's going to cry again. She closes her eyes and gently shakes her head.)* I feel right ashamed now. And so sad. *(She whispers it.)* So sad. *(She says it voiceless. She closes her eyes and puts her head back.)*
        Blackout.

        Brink's place. A long settee, two chairs, a massive stereo speaker like bands have, in the corner; by it, a flat record deck; on the wall, hung by a gold nail, is a single record. Eddie enters first, he has five bottles of wine in his arms. He unloads them all on the end of the long settee. Brink enters. Then Carol and Louise come in together, giggling.
EDDIE: Take a seat girls, I'll get some glasses.
CAROL: Why can you not see?
        The girls both giggle.
EDDIE: Eh?
        They giggle again. Eddie shrugs, smiles and goes into the kitchen.
BRINK: Come on, have a seat.
        Brink goes off into the kitchen. The two girls walk around the settee together to front center. They stand looking around. They look at each other and start giggling again.
EDDIE *(from the kitchen)*: Just tryin' to find a corkscrew.
CAROL: That's nice.
        They both laugh. Carol starts throwing things off the couch onto one of the chairs, one at a time.
Lovely place you've got here. *(She pulls a face at Louise.)*
        They both sit down really close to each other, up one end of the settee. Eddie comes in with glasses and a corkscrew and puts them down.
EDDIE: Here we are.
CAROL *(looking behind)*: Where's whatsisname then?
EDDIE: Oh, he's just coming.
        The sound of a toilet flush rattling loud. Carol and Louise both burst out laughing. Eddie just hands out the glasses. Brink enters. He goes and sits on an armchair.
CAROL: Hiya.
        Brink smiles. Louise titters. Eddie is getting the corkscrew in a bottle. He opens two bottles.
CAROL: Is he t'waiter then?
BRINK: No, he's just better at it than me.
CAROL: What a confession.

Louise laughs. Carol stays straightfaced.

BRINK: What? Oh yeah. Ha.

Both girls crack up laughing.

EDDIE: Here we go.

He gets up, starts pouring the wine, to Carol first.

CAROL: Hang on, is that white?

EDDIE: Yeah.

CAROL: Aw, I wanted red.

EDDIE: Oh.

He goes back and gets red. He pours hers; goes on to pour Louise's.

CAROL: Er no, go on I'll have white.

Eddie comes back toward her with the bottle.

Oh I don't know though, red's good, int it.

EDDIE (*laughing*): I'll pour it over your head in a minute.

CAROL: Oh God, Louise, int he masterful?

She puts her glass down, picks up an empty one.

Go on then, pour.

He does. He passes one to Louise.

Er, waiter, what's your name again?

EDDIE: Eddie.

CAROL: Eh, Eddie, you know what they say, don't you?

EDDIE: What?

CAROL: White and they're up all night. (*She drinks.*) Red they're straight to bed.

Louise splutters.

EDDIE: Oh aye, an' who told you that?

CAROL (*sips*): She did.

LOUISE: I never!

CAROL: Did you not, well I thought you did. Never mind. Carry on. Carry on.

Eddie pours some for Brink and himself. They all drink.

BRINK: So what do you do?

CAROL: What do you fancy?

Louise tuts.

EDDIE: What do you mean?

CAROL (*pretending to change the subject*): Er, nice wine, in' it?

LOUISE: No.

They both laugh.

EDDIE (*tries again*): So what do you do?

BRINK (*quickly*): To live.

CAROL: Well, I breathe, I can't speak for her like.

Louise splutters.

Michael Wincott (Eddie), Joan Cusack (Louise), Betsy Aidem
(Carol) and Kevin Bacon (Brink) in a scene from *Road*

EDDIE: I don't know, you're quick you two, aren't you?

CAROL: No. You two are slow.

Louise spills her drink on herself, drops glass, it breaks.

LOUISE: Oh look!

EDDIE: I'll get you a cloth.

He goes off into the kitchen. Brink gets up and goes too.

CAROL (*shouts*): God, how big is this cloth? Take two corners each, then just walk in with it!

LOUISE: Oh Carol. Do you not like 'em?

CAROL: They're O.K. But they just think they're great.

LOUISE: Eh? They're a bit of all right though, aren't they?

CAROL: Did you not see 'em at the bar posing off?

LOUISE: I know, but you fancied 'em when you saw 'em.

CAROL: Maybe I did. Maybe I did. But I'm not letting 'em get away with nowt. And the way they chatted us up.

LOUISE: I know, but it were good, though, weren't it? Very different.

CAROL: You could say that. They just think too much of themselves for my liking.

LOUISE: I think they're all right.

CAROL: Oh. Really, they just think we're pains in the arse, you know. But they're being all patient and nice with us cause they want a screw.

LOUISE: Carol!

CAROL: Well it is. They make me sick. They'll be talking about us now in there. Weighing up how it's going and what's the best next move. Well, no ways are they gettin' the better of me.

> *Eddie comes back in. He goes to Louise and gives her a cloth. He gets down and starts picking up bits of glass. Carol looks round.*

Where's he gone again? Is there summat wrong with his bowels, or what?

EDDIE (*laughs*): He's just looking for another glass for Louise.

> *Louise gives him back the cloth. He starts mopping up the couch arm and floor with it. Brink appears in the doorway.*

BRINK: There's not another one. You can have mine.

LOUISE: No, it's all right.

EDDIE (*passing it to her*): You're all right, here you are.

LOUISE: Oh I don't want to take your glass. What'll you have?

CAROL (*grabs it out of Eddie's hand*): Here get it. Sap.

> *Brink goes into the kitchen. Eddie gets up and goes into the kitchen. Carol gets the bottle and pours more wine.*

Here, and top it up.

LOUISE: Carol!

> *She puts the bottle down as they re-enter. Brink has a mug with him. Eddie sits on the couch with the girls. Brink sits on the arm of the armchair.*

CAROL (*looks at Eddie, then looks at Brink*): Eh what's this? Manoeuvers. We're being surrounded, Louise cock.

BRINK (*to Louise*): Is she always like this?

LOUISE: Yes.

CAROL: Hang on a minute. Like what?

BRINK: Like …

CAROL: What?!

BRINK: Aggressive.

CAROL: In what way? What's that s'pose to mean?!

BRINK: I don't know.

EDDIE: He's sorry he spoke.

CAROL: Sorry he spoke. I should think so. I'm not aggressive.

> *She grabs Louise, mock nuts her.*

Am I not, Louise love?

LOUISE (*laughs*): I'm saying nowt!

CAROL: Anyway, what does it mean, aggressive? I'm just having a bit of fun. If you can't take that there's summat wrong with you.

BRINK: We can take it.

CAROL: I s'pose you're not used to this, you're used to women just fallin' all over you, aren't you?

BRINK: Not really, no.

CAROL: Just fallin' all under you then.

> *Brink smiles.*

Dick.

BRINK: She's mad.

EDDIE: She's not.

CAROL: I am.

LOUISE: She is.

> *They all laugh. Pause.*

EDDIE (*holding up a bottle high*): Anybody want some more?

CAROL (*holding up her glass high*): Not yet. (*Pause.*) How long you lived here?

> *Brink shrugs.*

Well, it's certainly a … certainly a … What's that word I'm looking for?

EDDIE: Tip?

CAROL: No. Slag heap.

LOUISE (*laughs*): That's it.

EDDIE: Eh, well feel free, girls, to put it in order.

CAROL: You must be a joke.

LOUISE: You must be joking. You want to see the state of her room at home.

CAROL: Louise, shut up givin' away my personals. You'll be telling 'em what color knickers I've got on next. (*She looks at them.*) Go on say it. "If you had any on" or "See-through."

BRINK: I'm saying nothing.

CAROL: Oh what gentlemen. Or are you just puffs?

LOUISE: Carol, you're terrible.

CAROL: Eh eh, Louise, don't desert the ranks now. Especially when they're just coming on so strong. Eh lads?

> *They just smile.*

So now we're round to it. When are you going to move in then, lads? When should we expect the first move?

> *Brink leans right over and starts kissing her.*

Get off.

> *He stops, and stands.*

Get off.

He goes back to the chair, unaffected.

BRINK (*hands up*): I'm off.

CAROL (*a bit stunned; to compose herself*): Oh, is it you? I thought I could smell summat.

No one laughs. Brink sits away in the chair. Eddie drinks.

LOUISE: It's nice this place, really.

EDDIE: Really?

LOUISE (*laughs*): I mean underneath it all. If it was tidied up.

EDDIE: I s'pose it's not bad, it's …

CAROL (*to Brink*): So are you not speaking now? (*Not giving him time to answer, to Eddie.*) Is he sulking now?

BRINK: No. Not at all. Nothing like that.

CAROL (*looking from one to the other*): I don't know where I am with you two.

EDDIE: What do you mean?

LOUISE (*excited*): You're right different.

EDDIE: Than what?

CAROL (*quick*): Watch it, Louise, they'll get all big-headed. Well, bigger-headed. (*She scrutinizes them both.*) What is it with you two?

Brink reaches out and takes Louise's hand. He leads her over toward him, stands up and kisses her. Carol looks, gets up, goes into the kitchen.

(*Shouts from the kitchen.*) Is it through here?

EDDIE: What? (*No reply; he realizes she means the toilet.*) Oh yeah, yeah. Straight through.

Louise separates from Brink, though still in his arms.

BRINK: What is it?

LOUISE: Carol.

Brink looks at her.

She's gone off 'cause she likes you really.

BRINK (*recognizing something in her*): And what about you? Who do you like?

She looks down, a bit embarrassed.

You like Eddie really, don't you?

She looks a bit more embarrassed.

It's all right. Eddie.

Eddie stands up and takes Louise onto his knee in one single movement. Brink goes off through the kitchen. Eddie kisses Louise very gently, and again. She puts her hand in his hair.

CAROL (*from the kitchen*): What's this? Hey. You soon change your tune.

Then movement is heard as he kisses her. The kitchen light goes off. Then they enter, him with his arm around her, she looking a

*bit embarrassed. He turns the light off. The stage is in darkness.
Black. Sounds of kissing and movement.*

(*Shuffling*): No. (*Movement.*) Get off. (*Shuffling; turns the light on.*) That's
enough of that.

> *Carol is standing at the light switch. Louise has moved away from
> Eddie.*

What do you think we are? (*Brink shrugs.*) What do you think we are, slags?

EDDIE: Nooo.

BRINK: Why did you come back?

CAROL: Just for something to do.

BRINK: What about all the lead ons, lead ins?

LOUISE: Don't he talk funny. You were like that in the pub. Lead ons, lead
ins.

EDDIE (*changing the subject*): Anyway.

LOUISE (*turning on him, realizing she should be mad*): Anyway what?

EDDIE: Eh eh. Don't be bad-tempered. Anyway, more drinks?

> *He lifts the bottle.*

CAROL: You can't get us drunk then start again, you know.

BRINK: Forget it.

CAROL: Listen to him now. Typical. They're all the same. Can't get their
end away, they don't wanna know. Do get their end away, they don't wanna
know.

EDDIE: Oh come on.

CAROL: No. I want somethin' else to happen for a change. It's the same
every time. Every time some smart-arse spends time and money on you with
one thing only in mind. Then upsets you. It's boring and upsetting. I'm sick of
it. You think you're just wanted for use. You two seemed a bit interesting, a bit
unusual like. I thought I might find something else here. But not so. You're
always wrong, aren't you? Nowt's ever the way you wanted. You always
have to make do. Every single thing's a disappointment.

LOUISE: Carol.

> *Carol stops.*

CAROL: Come on then, Louise.

> *She gets her bag. Louise gets hers. They start leaving.*

EDDIE: Come on, have another.

> *They go for the door. Brink suddenly jumps up really quick, the
> fastest thing he's done all night, and stands in front of the door.*

BRINK: Stay, and I promise you something different. Let's see how much
difference you can take.

> *Carol stops in her tracks. So does Louise.*

You want something different? Stay, I mean it.

> *He guides them back to the settee, sits.*

You know what we do for it. To really get a change. We have a something that
we always do when outside gets to you. Eddie, shall we show them.
>*Eddie looks.*
Come on, let's show them. Let's have it out of them.
>*The girls sit, mystified.*
Do you like good music?
>CAROL: Yeah, like what?
>BRINK: Like soul. Real down there soul.
>CAROL: Don't know what you mean.
>>*While he's talking, Eddie is pouring wine in the glasses.*
>BRINK: What about you, Louise?
>LOUISE: Well, I like hot chocolate.
>>*Brink shakes his head. Eddie is passing round glasses.*
Drink.
>*They hesitate.*
>BRINK: Drink, don't worry. Go on.
>EDDIE: Go.
>*They do.*
Fast, though, fast!
>*They do.*
>BRINK: Good.
>*Eddie quickly fills up the glasses again.*
>CAROL: Eh, hang on.
>*Brink grabs one and drinks it.*
>EDDIE: Do. Another?
>BRINK: Another.
>CAROL: What you doing?
>*The lads are laughing. Eddie fills up again.*
>BRINK: It's all part of it. You'll see after.
>EDDIE (*lifts glass*): Brink old drink.
>>*They cheer and clink glasses, then drink. Louise laughs. Carol*
>>*does a bit.*
>BRINK: Come on Eddie, steady.
>>*They lift the glasses and down them. Eddie lets himself fall back.*
>>*Carol suddenly laughs too.*
Come on in. Join us.
>*He touches her chin. She knocks his hand away.*
>CAROL: All right, set 'em up.
>LOUISE: Carol.
>CAROL: Oh, what the hell.
>>*Eddie has already set them up. They get a glass each.*
>BRINK: Down.

He opens his mouth wide first. Eddie too. They pour it down in one. Carol and Louise laugh and giggle, try it too, can't get it down so fast but manage to shift it. Eddie is opening another two bottles.

CAROL: What about some music then?

BRINK: Some will be coming soon and ...

CAROL: And what?

BRINK: Wait for it, love.

LOUISE: Ooooh.

They drink again.

CAROL: Come on, put summat on now, what you got? Let's see.

Eddie, drinking, points to the single on the wall.

Eh just that one!

EDDIE: Aye, that's it.

BRINK: One more drink then it's on.

EDDIE: Up up.

The glasses are raised.

CAROL: This is mad.

LOUISE (*laughing*): It is, int it?

They drink them down.

CAROL: Music!

BRINK: Put it on.

LOUISE: Put it on.

Eddie gets up and puts it on.

CAROL: Bloody hell, I hope I like it.

Silence. In the silence begins the slow crackling you always get with old records. The record is Otis Redding, "Try a Little Tenderness." The volume is up very loud. There is a screaming climax in the record. Brink stops it. Eddie takes off from there.

EDDIE: Bzzzzzzzzzzzzzzzzzzz Raaaaaaaaaaaaaaaaaa. Blast off! Wyatt Earp, Wild Bill Hickock, Jessie James, Buffalo Bill, Billy the Kid, Maverick, Jim Bowie, Geronimo, Butch Cassidy, Davy Crockett, Doc Holliday, Eddie, Eddie, Eddie the hero. This is it, you let owt out, show what's below, let go, throw, glow, burn your Giro. I got me suit, I got me image, suit, image. (*Sings.*) "Who could ask for anything more?" Me! England's in pieces. England's an old twat in the sea. England's cruel. My town's scuffed out. My people's pale. Pale face. (*He pulls a pretend gun.*) Bang Bang Bang. It's a shoot-out with the sheriff. EDDIE, EDDIE, EDDIE the hero. Don't weaken, or you're Dole and Done, Dole and Done, never weaken, show yoursel' sharp, so sharp you cut. Head up. Eyes hard. Walk like Robert Mitchum. (*He draws and shoots.*) Bang, Bang, Bang, Bang, Bang, Bang, Bang. I'm going to lie out now and burn for all I'm worth.

He stops, lies down. Silence. The girls' faces are wide open, stunned, and drunk.

BRINK: That's what you do, you drink, you listen to Otis, you get to the bottom of things and let rip.

LOUISE (*in wonder*): What for?

BRINK: To stop going mad.

LOUISE: Oh.

Carol is quiet, swigging from the bottle. Hiccups.

CAROL: Does he have to shout?

LOUISE (*drunk*): Give us a swig on that.

BRINK: I'm full of something nasty tonight. A smelly memory I can't wipe off. I'm s'pose to be the strong, silent type, me, but I'm not. It's just a casing, in case I get it again. Once I fucked an older woman, hated and fucked her hard on the kitchen floor, knees hitting the fridge, dog bowl in her hair, handfuls of old white skin in my mitt. After she'd gone, I sat on the lino and cried. My first scricke since "No Mummy left." I always keep tight in front of people, me, I don't want them in, they stink. HANDS OFF FOREVER! I want to be free. I want to be a cowboy, those dream fellows who died for us. Guns and smoke, one more dead, a mouthful of saloon dust. I want cowboy, but I'm just cattle, herded, helpless, waiting, aching to be killed, at the mercy of my CUNT-TRAY. Oh God, on I crow. Down I go. I lie to myself, I lie to the Pope. I lie on the rug. I lie with my bedtime cheese. I must stop now because I'm crying real tears, but inside. A man cry. I cry through the Dole, hole, times in which we live. Them slag's hands I still feel and I don't know why.

CAROL (*stands*): Can I say anything? Can I? I'll say this then. BIG BUST. BIG BUST ON ME BODY. BIG BRA BURSTING BUST. MEN LOOK. How's that? CRACK CRACK CRACK the whip on 'em. Crackoh crack, cut men for their sins. POVERTY. Poverty wants me. He's in my hair and clothes. He comes dust on me knickers. I can't scrape him off. Everythin's soiled you know, our house, me mum, the bath. I'm sick. Nowt's nice around me. Nowt's nice. NOWT'S NICE. Where's finery? Fucked off! Where's soft? Gone hard! I want a walk on the mild side. I want to be clean. Cleaned. Spray me wi' somethin' sweet, spray me away. (*Stated.*) Carol has nowt. (*Sits, falls over to one side, curls up on couch.*)

LOUISE: It's all gambling this, int it? Gambling with gabble to see what come out. That record, it's so about pure things it make you want to cry. Why's the world so tough? It's like walking through meat in high heels. Nothing's shared out right, money or love. I'm a quiet person, me. People think I'm deaf and dumb. I want to say things, but it hard. I have big wishes, you know. I want my life to be all shined-up. It's so dull. Everything's so dulled. When that man sings on that record there, you put the flags up. Because he reminds you of them feelings you keep forgetting. The important ones. Once you wrap 'em up and put 'em away, there's nothing left but profit and loss and who shot who? But it's so hard, life. So hard. Nothing's interesting. Everything's been made ordinary in our eyes. I want magic and miracles. I want a Jesus to come and change things again and show the invisible. And not let us keep forgetting, forge-netting everything, kickin' everyone. I want the surface up and off and all the gold and jewels and light out on the pavements. Anyway, I never spoke such speech in my life and I'm glad I have. If I keep shouting somehow a somehow I might escape.

EDDIE (*drunk*): Somehow a somehow, might escape. (*Pause.*) Somehow a somehow, might escape.

BRINK: Somehow a somehow, might escape.

EDDIE and BRINK: Somehow a somehow, might escape.

LOUISE: Somehow a somehow, might escape.

EDDIE, BRINK and LOUISE: Somehow a somehow, might escape.

CAROL (*comes up*): Somehow.

ALL: Somehow a somehow a somehow, might escape. (*They all move in together.*) Somehow a somehow— (*Snatched.*) Might escape!

All pressed together, arms and legs round each other.

Somehow a somehow a somehow—might escape! (*Out to the audience. A chant now.*)

Somehow a somehow a somehow—might escape!
Somehow a somehow a somehow—might escape!
Somehow a somehow a somehow—might escape!

Faster.

Somehow a somehow a somehow—might escape!
Somehow a somehow a somehow—might escape!
Somehow a somehow a somehow—might escape!

Very fast and loud.

SOMEHOW A SOMEHOW A SOMEHOW—MIGHT ESCAPE!
SOMEHOW A SOMEHOW A SOMEHOW—MIGHT ESCAPE!
SOMEHOW A SOMEHOW A SOMEHOW—MIGHT ESCAPE!

Loud and massive.

SOMEHOOOOOOOOOOO—

Blackout.

OOOOOOOOW

Silence.

THE COCKTAIL HOUR

A Comedy in Two Acts

BY A. R. GURNEY

Cast and credits appear on pages 442–443

A. R. GURNEY (who recently dropped "Jr." from his byline) was born Nov. 1, 1930 in Buffalo, N.Y., the son of a realtor. He was educated at St. Paul's School and Williams College, where he received his B.A. in 1952. After a stint in the Navy, he entered Yale Drama School in 1956 and emerged with an M.F.A. after studying playwriting in seminars conducted by Lemist Esler, Robert Penn Warren and John Gassner. His first production, the musical Love in Buffalo, *took place at Yale in 1958.*

"Pete" Gurney's first New York production of record was the short-lived The David Show *off Broadway in 1968, repeated in an off-Broadway program with his* The Golden Fleece *the following season. His* Scenes From American Life *premiered in Buffalo in 1970, then was produced by Repertory Theater of Lincoln Center for 30 performances in 1971, winning its author*

148

Drama Desk and Variety poll citations as a most promising playwright and achieving many subsequent productions at home and abroad.

Gurney next made the off-Broadway scene with Who Killed Richard Corey? *for 31 performances at Circle Repertory in 1976, the same year that his* Children *premiered in Richmond, Va. and his* The Rape of Bunny Stunte *was done OOB. The next year,* Children *appeared at Manhattan Theater Club,* The Love Course *was produced OOB and* The Middle Ages *had its premiere at the Mark Taper Forum in Los Angeles. Gurney's* The Problem *and* The Wayside Motor Inn *were done OOB in the 1977-78 season. In 1981-82* The Middle Ages *came to New York OOB and Circle Rep workshopped* What I Did Last Summer.

In that same season, Gurney's first Best Play, The Dining Room, *began a 583-performance run at Playwrights Horizons on Feb. 24. His second Best Play,* The Perfect Party, *opened a 238-performance run April 2, 1986, also at Playwrights Horizons. His third Best Play,* The Cocktail Hour, *reached independent off-Broadway production this season as of Oct. 20. New York has also seen Gurney's* What I Did Last Summer *for 31 performances in full production at Circle Rep and* The Middle Ages *for 110 off-Broadway performances, both in 1983;* The Golden Age, *suggested by Henry James's* The Aspern Papers, *on Broadway April 12, 1984 for 29 performances;* Sweet Sue *on Broadway January 8, 1987 for 164 performances; and* Another Antigone *at Playwrights Horizons Jan. 11, 1988 for 30 performances. Another Gurney playscript,* Love Letters, *was receiving special performances this season at the theater housing his* The Cocktail Hour.

Gurney is also the author of the TV adaptation from John Cheever's O Youth and Beauty! *and of three novels:* The Gospel According to Joe, *Entertaining Strangers and* The Snow Ball. *He has been the recipient of Rockefeller and National Endowment Awards, an Old Dominion Fellowship, an honorary degree from Williams, a New England Theater Conference citation for outstanding creative achievement and an Award of Merit from the American Academy and Institute of Arts and Letters. He has taught literature at M.I.T. for 25 years. He is married, with four children, and lives in New York City, where he serves on the artistic board of Playwrights Horizons and as secretary and council member of the Dramatists Guild.*

The following synopsis of The Cocktail Hour *was prepared by Sally Dixon Wiener.*

Time: An early evening in early fall in the mid-1970s

Place: A city in upstate New York

ACT I

SYNOPSIS: The play takes place in a comfortable living room decorated in traditional conservative good taste. There's a fireplace, a bookcase, a grand piano with suitably framed family photographs ranged over it, an antique desk, several chairs and tables and, downstage, the inevitable large couch with the coffee table in front of it, upon which rests a large manuscript with a black cover. Upstage left, a step leads up through an archway to the hall, where the early evening light can also be seen coming through a fanlight over the front door. *"The set is basically realistic, but.....vaguely theatrical, reminding us subliminally of those photographs of sets of American drawing room comedies in the 1930s or 40s, designed by Donald Oenslager or Oliver Smith."*

Bradley (*"in his 70s and very well dressed"*) comes on with a tray with bottles and glasses. Following him on, with the silver ice bucket, is John, his son (*"in his early 40s and more informally dressed"*). Things weren't always this way, Bradley reminds John. Maids used to bring things and hand around the cheese.

BRADLEY: Let's see ... What are we missing? ... Have we got the lemon for your mother's martini?

JOHN: It's right there, Pop.

BRADLEY: Your mother likes a small twist of lemon in her martini.

JOHN: I know.

BRADLEY: And my Cutty Sark scotch.

JOHN: Oh yes.

BRADLEY (*looking at the label*): It's a good scotch. Not a great scotch, but a good one. I always enjoy the picture on the label. The American clipper ships were the fastest in the world. Magnificent vessels. Beautifully built. Made our country great.

JOHN: The *Cutty Sark* was English, Pop.

BRADLEY: I know that. I'm speaking generally.

JOHN: Actually, the clipper ships only lasted a few years.

BRADLEY: Not true.

JOHN: Only a few—before steam.
BRADLEY: Not true at all.
JOHN: I think so, Pop.
BRADLEY: I wish your brother were here. He'd know. He knows all there is to know about boats.
JOHN (*going to bookcase*): I'll look it up.
BRADLEY: Never mind. I said, *never mind.* We are not going to waste the evening in pedantic arguments.

Bradley has tried unsuccessfully to get John's brother Jigger to join them for the evening, even offering to pay the expenses if he'd want to bring his wife and children as well. John remarks that it is a difficult trip for Jigger, and that he's working weekends.

His father is surprised that John only wants a glass of soda water, but John reassures him that he just wants to "keep a lid on" himself and not say or do anything he'd be sorry about afterward. Bradley comments that people don't drink as much these days, even younger people, he says, recalling remarking to a girl who was drinking Lemon Squirt at a recent wedding that she ought to be having champagne. She walked away. He guesses he's "becoming a tiresome old fool," but John claims not. Bradley rallies, admitting that he's still asked to be master of ceremonies at the annual Art Gallery fund raiser.

Eventually Bradley settles in to deal with the subject at hand—John's new play—another play, yes, and John believes it will be produced. Bradley understands that it's hard to get a play done, but he also is convinced that "nobody goes to the theater any more." A friend of Bradley's, a former theater enthusiast, only recently told him that "all they do these days in the theater is stand around and shout obscenities at each other. And then take off their clothes." Bradley admits to having liked the play of John's they saw in Boston, and also a play of his they saw in New York—"Miserable little theater. Impossible seats. Impossible bathrooms"—but it was charming, or, in any event, the actress was.

In Bradley's opinion, the new play looks too long, and people don't like plays that are long. John explains that he will be made to cut it. Bradley hopes the same actress will be in the new play, but John doesn't think so—the new play isn't "as light as the others." It's about their family. Bradley concedes that when he's toastmaster he sometimes uses family stories. John further admits that the play is centered around Bradley, and that people who know them will recognize them in the play, even though the names are different.

Bradley doesn't believe John's ever written anything without wise cracks about the family and their lifestyle. He asks John if he recalls what a critic said about his last play, and John admits the critic said "we weren't worth writing about." Bradley sees this as a case in point, that no one does care about their way of life.

JOHN: I care, Pop.

BRADLEY: You? You've never cared in your life. You've gone out of your way *not* to care. Where were you for our fortieth anniversary? Where were you for my seventy-fifth birthday?

JOHN: You said not to come.

BRADLEY: I didn't want you snickering in the corner, making snide re-marks. Oh, God, I should have known. I should have known that's why you came up here this weekend. Not to visit your parents in their waning years. Not to touch base with the city that nourished you half your life. Oh no. Nothing like that. Simply to announce that you plan to humiliate us all in front of a lot of strangers in New York City.

JOHN: I came home to get your permission, Pop.

BRADLEY: My permission?

JOHN: I haven't signed any contract yet.

BRADLEY: Then don't.

JOHN: All right, I won't.

BRADLEY: How can I give my permission for a thing like that?

JOHN: All right, Pop.

BRADLEY: How can I approve of someone fouling his own nest?

JOHN: I don't foul—

BRADLEY: How can I possibly seal my own doom?

JOHN: Oh, come on, Pop.

BRADLEY: I suppose I have no legal recourse.

JOHN: The play's *off*, Pop.

BRADLEY: I mean, you don't need to write plays anyway. You have a per-fectly good job in publishing.

JOHN: That just keeps me going, Pop.

BRADLEY: It's a fine job. It's a solid, dependable, respectable job.

JOHN: It's not what I really want to do.

BRADLEY: Well, do it anyway. Most men in this world spend a lifetime do-ing what they don't want to do. And they work harder at it than you do.

JOHN: Come on, Pop …

BRADLEY: After I'm dead, after your mother's dead, after everyone you can possibly hurt has long since gone, then you can write your plays. And you can put them on wherever you want—New York, Hollywood, right here in Memorial Auditorium, I don't care. But now now. Please.

John assures him the case is closed, and Bradley thanks him. He is tired and unwell, he wants John to know. They both stand as Ann comes on, a handsome woman, nicely dressed, her eyeglasses on a chain, wearing the ubiquitous string of pearls. She puts the cheese and crackers on the coffee table and sits down, ready for a drink. Although she and Bradley have been married for nearly 50 years and he knows what she would like, it is part of the ritual that he ask. As for dinner, she's not sure when they'll eat, because she doubts the current incumbent in the kitchen has ever made gravy. But the sanctity of the cocktail hour, which she cherishes, makes Ann believe in paying someone to cook dinner—even if it's someone named Cheryl Marie. Bradley agrees, remembering how the bishop used to remark that "the cocktail hour took the place of evening prayers."

They've been discussing the theater, Bradley tells her. Ann passes the cheese and recalls how the theater was such a part of their lives when all the plays came here.

ANN: Such wonderful plays. With such wonderful plots. They were always about these attractive couples …

BRADLEY: And the husband would have committed some minor indiscretion …

ANN: Normally the wife did, darling.

BRADLEY: No, no. I think it was he …

ANN: She did it more, sweetie. The *wife* was normally the naughty one.

BRADLEY: Well, whoever it was, they were all very attractive about it. And they'd have these attractive leading ladies …

ANN: Gertrude Lawrence, Ina Claire, Katharine Hepburn …

BRADLEY: They'd all come here …

JOHN: I remember your talking about them …

BRADLEY: Your mother played tennis with Hepburn at the Tennis Club.

ANN: Oh, I think we hit a ball or two …..

BRADLEY: And we met the Lunts.

ANN: Oh, the Lunts, the Lunts …

BRADLEY: They were friends of Bill Hart's. So we all met at the Statler for a cocktail. After a matinee.

ANN: They were terribly amusing.

JOHN: I remember your telling me about the Lunts.

BRADLEY: They could both talk at exactly the same time …

ANN: Without interrupting each other … ·

BRADLEY: It was uncanny …

Bruce Davison as John with Keene Curtis as Bradley, his father (*above*),
and Nancy Marchand as Ann, his mother (*below*), in *The Cocktail Hour*

ANN: They'd say the wittiest things …
BRADLEY: Simultaneously …
ANN: And you'd understand both …
BRADLEY: It was absolutely uncanny.
ANN: Of course, they'd been married so long …
BRADLEY: Knew each other so well …
ANN: They made you feel very sophisticated.
BRADLEY (*touching her hand*): They made you feel proud to be married.
ANN: Absolutely. I totally agree.....

Ann wishes John would write that kind of play. He won't, Bradley states, and furthermore he does not like the title of the new play, *The Cocktail Hour*—"To begin with, it's been used." John assumes he's referring to T.S. Eliot's *The Cocktail Party*. "Even worse," his father complains, recalling walking out on the Eliot play. The difference, Ann points out, is that a cocktail party is public, something to which people are invited, and a cocktail hour is for the family, private and personal. Bradley's convinced the title will confuse people, they'll think it's Eliot and get John—"Either way, they'll want their money back." In any event, John's new play is going on the shelf. They have agreed on that, Bradley informs Ann.

Ann changes the subject to inquire about John's wife (unable to come because she had a conference) and children (one will be going out West to college). Bradley sees it all as couples leading separate lives and children scattering, the old way of life vanished. Ann wishes they all could have come, John's family and Jigger and his family as well. Bradley wonders why John doesn't write a play about his wife and children instead of his parents. And Ann proposes John turn the new play into a book, which isn't as public.

Nina, John's sister, is expected but late (Ann believes it has something to do with Nina's dog). Ann would like another drink, and Bradley refuses John's offer to fix it for her. When he has some trouble bending over to take her glass, John asks him about his back. Ann and the doctor think it's a pinched nerve. Bradley thinks it's something worse. When he had double pneumonia Ann said "it was just a cold." When he's being lowered into his grave, she will tell his friends "it's hay fever." In any event, he's convinced he's not long for this world.

Ann looks at the manuscript and supposes she should read it, but reading John's plays is "so painful." Seeing them is worse, with everyone "*watching*," but it ought to be produced, because it's John's career. It's his hobby, Bradley insists, "an amusing little hobby which probably costs more than it brings in." Bradley is curious about how much John might lose by not putting on the play.

John wouldn't know. Bradley, disgusted at John's lack of business acumen, proceeds to write him a $20,000 check as a reward for not putting on his play John refuses to take it. If John doesn't want it for himself, he should give it to his children, his father urges and he hopes John's children will be more respectful of him in his old age than John has ever been of him. If he doesn't take it, Bradley will leave him that much extra in his will.

They are interrupted as Nina (*"well-dressed, attractive, mid-40s"*) arrives, sorry to be late—but Portia, their new dog, is in some trouble. Nina will have white wine, with ice and soda—"My stomach is in absolute knots." John would get it, but Bradley takes umbrage, insisting he can still officiate. Ann sympathizes about Nina's nervous stomach, but Nina wants to talk about John and the new play. Apprised of the fact that John has come to seek his father's permission to have it put on and been refused, she's really more interested in who else besides her father is in the play and especially wants to know if she is in it.

Nina's parents want to know about her husband and their grandchildren, but once John tells her she is in the play, her mind is only on the play and whether or not she's "the wicked older sister" or "the uptight, frustrated, bossy bitch." She has a minor role, she learns. "Do I get a *name*, at least?" she asks. It's the name she'd wished she'd had, Diana, for the goddess protectress of wild animals. Ann doesn't like the name Diana—she knew a Diana who climbed down drainpipes and hung around drugstores—but Nina likes it better than her own name, a diminutive of her mother's name. Nina's thumbing through the script, looking at the role of Diana and finding it to be not very substantial.

Impatiently, Bradley goes to the bookshelf and selects a large volume, announcing his intention to "exercise his mind" until the discussion is broadened. But Nina is not to be diverted. She always plays a minor role in the family, she complains, even when the others remind her she was the one who always had dogs, who had a coming-out party, a trip to Europe, a beautiful wedding—and his mother's tea set when she died, Bradley points out. He and Jigger used to call her the Gravy Train Girl, John recalls. Nina continues with her list of complaints—how everyone must be at their beck and call when John and Jigger deign to come home once a year or so, how she has had to attend to her parents, having them for holidays, helping them out with medical problems and getting a new cleaning woman, and still being told "I play a goddam minor role!" She'd like another drink, and if she gets ulcers, they will be minor ulcers. If she dies, it will be a minor death.

John attempts to assuage her. He tried to make her part larger, but failed. "I never could get your number," he tells her, because she'd appeared to be so content. Ann believes he's complimenting Nina, but Nina thinks otherwise. John doesn't know anything about her life and has never bothered to find out.

NINA: Did you know that I am interested in seeing-eye *dogs*, John? Did you know that? I am profoundly interested in them. I'm good with dogs, I'm the best, everyone says that, and what I want to do more than anything else in the world is go to this two-year school in Cleveland where you do nothing but work with seeing-eye dogs.

ANN: You can't just commute to Cleveland, darling.

NINA: I know that, Mother.

JOHN: Why can't you?

NINA: Because I have a husband, John. Because I have a—*life*!

BRADLEY: And a very good life it is, Pookins.

NINA: I mean, what am I supposed to *do*, John? Start subsidizing Eastern Airlines every other *day*? Live in some mo*tel*? Rattle around some strange city where I don't know a *soul*? Just because I want to work with ... because I happen to feel an attachment to ... oh God. (*She starts to cry.*)

BRADLEY (*going to her*): Oh now, Pookins ... Now stop, sweetie pie ...

ANN: I didn't realize people could get quite so upset about dogs.

BRADLEY: It's not dogs, it's John. (*Wheeling on John.*) You see what happens? You arrive here, and within half an hour you've thrown the whole family into disarray. It's happened all your life. Par for the course, my friend. Par for the course. (*Comforting Nina.*) Now calm down, sweetheart. He's not going to do the play, anyway.

NINA (*breaking away*): Well, he should! He should do one about *me*! You've never written about me, John. Ever. Why don't you, some time? Why don't you write about a woman who went to the right schools, and married the right man, and lived on the right street all the days of her life, and ended up feeling perfectly terrible! (*She runs from the room.*)

As Bradley follows Nina off, calling to her, Ann holds out her glass to John—"Just a splash. I'm serious." She remarks on the fact that John is not drinking. He gets angry if he does, he explains. "I guess I'm sore about something." He asks his mother if his father is as sick as he says.

JOHN: He keeps saying he's dying.

ANN: He's been saying that for years. He announced it on his fortieth birthday. He reminds us of it whenever he gets a cold. Lately, when we go to bed, he doesn't say "goodnight" any more. He says "goodbye" because he thinks he won't last till morning.

JOHN: But you think he's O.K.?

ANN: I think ... No, I *know*, we all know, that he has a blood problem, a kind of leukemia, which seems to be in remission now. Somehow I don't think that will kill him. Something else will.

JOHN: You think my play will?

ANN: *He* seems to think it will.

JOHN: Oh God ...

ANN: And *you* must think it might, John. Otherwise you never would have bothered to clear it with him.

JOHN: I almost wish I hadn't.

ANN: I'm glad you did. It shows you have strong family feelings.

JOHN: Family feelings, family feelings! The story of my life! The bane of my existence! Family feelings. Dear Mother, Dear Pop. May I have your permission to cross the street? May I have permission to buy a car? Would you mind very much if I screwed my girl?

ANN: Now that's enough of that, please.

JOHN: Well, it's true! Family feelings. May I have your approval to put on a play? Oh God, why did I come here? Why did I bother? Most playwrights dish out the most brutal diatribes against their parents, who sit proudly in the front row and applaud every insult that comes along. Me? Finally—after twenty-five years of beating around the bush—I come up with something which is—all right, maybe a little on the nose, maybe a little frank, maybe a little satiric at times—but still clearly infused with warmth, respect, and an abiding affection, and what happens? I'm being censored, banned, bribed not to produce.

If he would only make it into a book, Ann argues, because plays make so much noise and cause attention, not just for them, but for him also, and the bad reviews must hurt him very much. Book reviewers, she believes, seem to be kinder than theater critics, who don't seem to understand what he's writing: "They don't like us, John. They resent us. They think we're all Republicans, and all trivial, and all alcoholics. .....Only the latter is true."

In a book it would be different, Ann believes. But all he can write is plays, John insists. He's caught in this old-fashioned medium and feels "like some medieval stone cutter, hacking away in the dark corner of an abandoned monastery, while everyone else is outside, having fun in the Renaissance." He doesn't know why it's the only thing he wants to do or why he's always written plays. Even before he could write he was putting on plays down in the playroom that his mother and father had to sit through, that made them late going out for dinner. John wishes Ann could remember something about them. His psychiatrist wants to know, but John can't recall. Ann struggles to remember: John always played a foundling, an outsider, an adopted child. In one in particular, he wore his "little wool bathing trunks from Best & Co., and Nina's red bathing cap." John recalls the title of the play—*The Red-Headed Dummy*—and realizes that he now knows what the play was about and believes his psychiatrist would agree. John was showing off his penis in front of his father and mother. He was doing a phallic dance, he announces.

ANN: I think it's time to turn to another topic.

JOHN: No, but wait. Listen, Mother. I'll put it in a historical context. What I was doing was acting out a basic, primitive impulse which goes back to the Greeks. That's how comedy *originated*, Mother! The phallic dance! These peasants would do these gross dances in front of their overlords to see what they could get away with! And that's what I was doing, too, at three years old! Me! The Red-Headed Dummy! Dancing under the noses of my parents, before they went out to dinner! Saying, "Hey, you guys. Look. Look over here. I'm here, I'm alive, I'm wild, I have this penis with a mind of its own!" That's what I was doing then! That's what I've always done! That's what I'm doing right now, right in this room! And that's why I have to write plays, Mother. I have to keep doing it.

Long pause.

ANN: Are you finished, John?

JOHN: For now, at least.

ANN: All right, then, I want to say this: I don't like all this psychological talk, John. I never have. I think it's cheap and self-indulgent. I've never liked the fact that you've consulted a psychiatrist, and your father agrees with me. It upsets us very much to think that the money we give you at Christmas goes for paying that person rather than for taking your children to Aspen or somewhere. I don't like psychiatrists in general. Celia Underwood went to one, and now she bursts into tears whenever she plays bridge. Psychiatrists make you think about yourself too much. And about the bedroom too much. There's no need. So if this is what your play's about, people sitting around making remarks about their own anatomy, then I'm afraid I'm much more on your father's side than I thought I was.

JOHN: Mother—

ANN: No, please let me finish. Now I want you to write, John. I think sometimes you write quite well, and I think it's a healthy enterprise. But I think you should write *books*. In books, you can talk the way you've just talked, and it's not embarrassing. In books, you can go into people's minds, you can excuse things, you can argue things *out*. Now we all have things in our lives which we've done, or haven't done, which a book could make clear. I mean, I myself could tell you … I could tell you … I could tell you lots of things if I knew you would write them down quietly and carefully and sympathetically in a good, long book …

Bradley returns to report that Nina is fine. She's out in the kitchen coping with, among other things, the underdone roast—the oven had been turned off. Ann, upset, rushes off to the kitchen. Bradley tells John, a bit smugly, that he has talked to the maid in the kitchen, and the dinner will be the better for his time and trouble in doing so. John bets he gave her a ten-dollar tip as well. Bradley has—"because I firmly believe good service is important" he pontificates. Civilization is dependent upon it.

Bradley's also phoned Jigger, and his wife told him that Jigger would return his call as soon as he gets home. Bradley very much wants John to have a drink with him as they wait, and John concedes. His father also wants to know more about the play, about the plot, for instance. John confesses that it doesn't have much of one. Bradley's concerned, too, as to whether or not John has included anything about the family having Indian blood, because they don't, although John's great uncle might have had something to do with an Indian princess. John seems not to have been aware of this, but his father is disturbed because someone down at the club frequently mentions it, claiming it explains "our affinity for alcohol." And another thing that concerns his father is if John has mentioned in the play anything about the death of his grandfather. John *has* mentioned it in the play: "It helps to say who we are." But Bradley wants him to be specific about what he's written.

JOHN: I say he was a good man, a kind man, one of the best lawyers in town …

BRADLEY: True enough …

JOHN: A leader in the community. A pillar of the church …

BRADLEY: True … All true …

JOHN: Who, one day, for no discernible reason, strolled down to the edge of the Niagara River, hung his hat, his coat, and his cane on a wooden piling, and then walked into the water and drowned himself.

Pause.

BRADLEY: That's what you say in your play?

JOHN: That's what I say, Pop.

BRADLEY: He left a note.

JOHN: I didn't know that, Pop.

BRADLEY: Oh, yes. There was a note in his breast pocket. Addressed to me and my mother. I have it in my safe deposit box.

JOHN: I didn't know he left a note.

BRADLEY: You can have it when I die.

>   *Pause.*

He says there will be enough money to support my mother and to send me through college.

>   *Pause.*

Which there was.

>   *Pause.*

Then he says he's terribly, terribly sorry, but he's come to the conclusion that life isn't worth living any more.

>   *Pause. He takes out a handkerchief and dries his eyes.*

JOHN: Oh, Pop.

BRADLEY: Churchill suffered from my father's affliction.

JOHN: So does my son Jack.

BRADLEY: Jack too? That sweet Jack?

JOHN: He gets it in spades.

BRADLEY: Of course, it's just ... life, isn't it? It's part of the equation. The point is, we don't complain, we deal with it. We divert ourselves. We play golf, we have a drink occasionally.

JOHN: We write plays.

BRADLEY: Well, we do *some*thing. What does that sweet Jack do?

JOHN: Builds model airplanes.

BRADLEY: Oh that poor boy. That poor, poor boy.

Bradley feels the play might be depressing, as well as short on plot, and ought to have an element of surprise. John says there's one, and Bradley insists on hearing it, despite John's reluctance to tell him.

JOHN: All right. At the end of the first act, I have this older man ...

BRADLEY: Me. I'm sure it's me.

JOHN: It's you and it's not you, Pop.

BRADLEY: What does this fellow do?

JOHN: He tells his older son ...

BRADLEY: You.

JOHN: *Partly* me, Pop. Just *partly*.

BRADLEY: Tells his son what?

JOHN: The father tells his son that he doesn't believe ...

>   *Pause.*

BRADLEY: Doesn't believe what?

JOHN: Doesn't believe his son is his true son.

BRADLEY: WHAT?

JOHN: He says he thinks his wife once had an affair, and the son is the result.

Pause.

BRADLEY: That is the most ridiculous thing I ever heard in my life!

JOHN: I knew you'd get sore.

BRADLEY: Of course I'm sore. Who wouldn't get sore? Where in God's name did you get such a ridiculous idea?

JOHN: I don't know. It just happened. As I was writing.

BRADLEY: Thank God this play is not going on! It's demeaning to me and insulting to your mother! Why in heaven's name would you ever want to write a thing like that?

JOHN: Because I don't think you ever loved me, Pop.

The telephone is ringing offstage. Bradley goes to answer it, assuming it's Jigger. John pours himself another drink. *Curtain.*

ACT II

While their parents are offstage talking to Jigger on the telephone, Nina and John are in the living room. It's all too familiar a scene to John, waiting for dinner. Jigger was always late, and Nina would be reading an Albert Payson Terhune dog book, and he'd be sitting there while their parents had another drink and talked about their day, and the maids would have to hold up dinner again. Nina recalls the wonderful three-course meals, but the wonder of it to John is how the maids put up with them. Nina remembers they were always kind to the maids, but John disagrees: "We still built our life on their backs..... Every dinner party, every cocktail hour, good Lord, every civilized endeavor in this world is based on exploiting the labor of other people." The one in the kitchen at the moment is exploiting them, according to Nina, "probably getting fifty bucks for three hours' work," and she and her mother have done most of it.

And Nina castigates John for coming and upsetting their parents with his play. He claims he was doing a decent thing, but Nina goes into a tirade. John has always caused trouble and always will. He's never been able to let anyone alone, he was always teasing, causing arguments, starting fights, and when he'd finished with the members of the family he'd start on the servants. He teased his teachers; and since starting playwriting, he's been teasing the critics. "Why are you so passionately concerned with disturbing the peace?" she wonders.

Bruce Davison (John), Holland Taylor (Nina), Keene Curtis (Bradley)
and Nancy Marchand (Ann) in a scene from *The Cocktail Hour*

JOHN: Because there's a hell of a lot of horseshit around, and I think I've known it from the beginning.

NINA: Would you care to cite chapter and verse?

JOHN (*indicating his father's chair*): Sure. Horseshit begins at home.

NINA: He's a wonderful man.

JOHN: He's a hypocrite, kiddo. He's a fake. Talk about civilization. All that jazz about manners and class and social obligation. He's a poor boy who married a rich girl and doesn't want to be called on it.

NINA: That's a lie! He was only poor after his father died!

JOHN: Yes, well, all that crap about hard work and nose to the grindstone and burning the midnight oil. What is all that crap? Have you ever seen it in operation? Whenever I tried to call him at the office, he was out playing golf. Have you ever *seen* him *work*? Has he ever brought any work *home*? Have you ever heard him even talk on the *telephone* about work? Have you ever seen him spade the garden or rake a leaf or change a light bulb? I remember one time when I wrote that paper defending the New Deal, he gave me a long lecture about how nobody wants to work in this country, and all the while he was practicing his putting on the back lawn!

NINA: He's done extremely well in business. He sent us to private schools and first-rate colleges.

JOHN: Oh, I know he's done well—on charm, affability, and Mother's money—and a little help from his friends. His friends have carried him all his life. They're the ones who have thrown the deals his way. You ask him a financial question, he'll say, "Wait a minute, I'll call Bill or Bob or Ted."

NINA: Because that's *life*, John! That's what business *is*! The golf course, the backgammon table at the Mid-Day Club, the Saturn Club grill at six— that's where he *works*, you jerk!

JOHN: Well then that's where his family is, not here. Did he ever show you how to throw a ball or dive into a pool? Not him. Mother did all that, while he was off chumming it up with his pals. All he ever taught me was how to hold a fork or answer an invitation or cut in on a pretty girl. He's never been my father and I've never been his son, and he and I have known that for a long time.

NINA: Well, he's been a wonderful father to me.

JOHN: Maybe so. And maybe to Jigger. I guess that's why I've teased both of you all my life. And why I tease everybody else, for that matter. I'm jealous. I'm jealous of anyone who seems to have a leg up on life, anyone who seems to have a father in the background helping them out. Hell, I even tease my own children. I've bent over backwards to be to them what my father never was to me, and then out of some deep-grained jealousy that they have it too good, I tease the pants off them.

Nina has the feeling John will go ahead with the play, despite his promise that he isn't going to. She wants him to take his father's check, which her mother has told her about, so that Nina can be sure he won't go on with it. John takes it, but says he won't cash it. Even so, it's his, and, she insists, the play is to stay in the drawer until their parents are dead—unless his father changes his mind, John counters and then admits to being relieved the play isn't going to be done. He hasn't found the secret of what went wrong, and when, between his father and himself. Did he wake him with his crying as a baby, did he embarrass him in front of someone, or maybe "I made the unpardonable mistake of contradicting him—of looking something *up* in the Book of Knowledge, and proving him wrong—no, not wrong, that makes no difference, right or wrong—what I did was destroy the 'rhythm of the conversation.'" John believes his father's always been saying to him, "I don't know this boy. This is not my son," and he wants to know what he did to cause it.

It's Nina's opinion that if their father should say to John that he loves him, John would immediately irritate him to the point that he'd deny it. John may not have her number, but she's got his, and she knows why he's written the play. It's because his father is dying, and John loves him, and he's been writing the play "to hold onto him after he's gone."

Ann returns, and John goes off to speak to Jigger on the telephone. Ann asks for "a splash more" in her glass. She seems troubled. The trouble is Jigger, who wants to move to California to work for a man building wooden boats, and for half the money he has been making. Bradley is on the telephone attempting to talk Jigger out of it.

Nina recalls that Jigger felt a sense of freedom on the water and wishes she felt that way about something. Maybe she should go to the dog school in Cleveland. Ann thinks she should consider her husband. Nina has; she and her husband have talked it over, and his encouragement is making it harder for her.

ANN: Horses I can understand. The thrill of riding. The excitement of the hunt. The men.

NINA: The men?

ANN: There used to be a lot of attractive men around stables.

NINA: Mother!

ANN: Just as there are around garages today.

NINA: Are you serious?

ANN: But I don't think they hang around kennels.

NINA: I'm interested in *dogs*, Mother.

ANN: I know you are, darling, and I don't think that's any reason to change your life. I mean if you had met some man ...

NINA: Mother, have you ever watched any of those Nature things on TV?

ANN: I love them. Every Sunday night ...

NINA: I mean, you see animals, birds, even insects operating under these incredibly complicated instincts. Courting, building their nests, rearing their young in the most amazing complex way ...

ANN: Amazing behavior ...

NINA: Well, I think people have these instincts, too.

ANN: Well, I'm sure we do, darling, but ...

NINA: No, but I mean many more than we realize. I think they're built into our blood, and I think we're most alive when we feel them happening to us.

ANN: Oh well now, I don't know ...

NINA: I feel most alive when I'm with animals, Mother. Really. I feel some instinctive connection. Put me with a dog, a cat, anything, and I feel I'm in touch with a whole different dimension ... It's as if both of us ... me and the animal ... were reaching back across hundreds of thousands of years to a place where we both knew each other much better. There's something there, Mother. I know there's something there.

Bradley returns, announcing that they have lost Jigger, he won't ever see Jigger again, only with luck will Jigger even come to his funeral. Ann is convinced dinner will make them all feel better, but Bradley needs another drink. Some men's sons are near them throughout their lives, some even work with them. As for him, one son is attacking him and the other is deserting him.

John comes back to report that he's told Jigger he ought to go; that not many people have the opportunity to do what they really like. Jigger's current job is a fine one, Bradley insists, and it's a job that he got for him. This leads to John admitting to his father that he was responsible for getting Jigger the new job, "because he was miserable where he was." That wasn't John's business, Bradley believes, John may be his brother, but he's his father. John is glad, however, that Jigger is going; and furthermore, he thinks Nina should go to Cleveland. Bradley turns on John.

BRADLEY: You kind of like playing God around here, don't you?

ANN: Yes, John, I really think you should stop managing other people's lives.

BRADLEY: Yes. Do that in your plays if you have to, not in real life.

JOHN: Oh yeah? Well, I'm glad we're talking about real life now, Pop. Because that's something we could use a little more *of*, around here. Hey. Know what? The cocktail hour is over, Pop. It's dead. It's gone. I think Jigger sensed it thirty years ago, and now Nina knows it too, and they're both trying to put something back into the world after all these years of a free ride.

BRADLEY: And you? What are you putting back into the world?

JOHN: Me?

BRADLEY: You.

Pause.

JOHN: I'm writing about it. At least I have the balls to do that.

Bradley is incensed. He doesn't allow vulgarities, bodily references, spoken under his roof, and he demands that John leave the room. If balls are vulgar, John wonders if it means his father doesn't have any; and are they supposed to "just sit around on our ass and watch the world go by?" Vulgar people resort to vulgar language, and he will not tolerate the destruction of the "civilization in this wilderness" that John's ancestors on both sides of the family have tried to establish since the 17th century, Bradley rages before storming off.

Ann, meanwhile, has been trying to get everyone to go to the dining room. John was right about the fact that the cocktail hour is over, she concedes, but Nina reports that it isn't exactly over. There's more trouble in the kitchen. The maid mistook the microwave for a warming oven, and the roast is ruined. Nina's substituting some lamb chops, and she'll bring some cheese upstairs to Bradley to tide him over.

Ann bemoans the loss of the roast, but she is angry at John and not sure why she's talking to him after all the trouble he's caused. It's the story of his life, John shrugs, and he wishes he knew why. She wants to go see to the chops, but John detains her. He's realized that a big problem with his play is that he's missing an obligatory scene; not a confrontation with his father, as Ann assumes, but a scene with her—because she's never wanted it to happen, he believes. All Ann wants to have happen is everyone sitting down to have a meal together, but he insists she tell him about whatever it was that went wrong when he was small. She claims she doesn't know what he's talking about. She refuses to "rake over a lot of old coals" and goes out of the room. He calls off to her, and she comes back.

ANN: You got lost in the shuffle, John. That's what went wrong. I mean, there you were, born in the heart of the Depression, your father frantic about money, nurses and maids leaving every other day—nobody paid much attention to you, I'm afraid. When Nina was born, we were all dancing around thinking we were the Great Gatsby, and when Jigger came along, we began to settle down. But you, poor soul, were caught in the middle. You lay in your crib screaming for attention, and I'm afraid you've been doing it ever since.

JOHN: That's it?

ANN: That's it. In a nutshell. Now I feel very badly about it, John. I always have. That's why I've found it hard to talk about. I've worked hard to make it up, I promise, but sometimes, no matter how hard you work, you just can't hammer out all the dents.

She turns to leave again.

JOHN: Exit my mother, after a brief, unsatisfactory exchange …

ANN: That's right. Because your mother is now responsible for a meal.
JOHN: I can see the scene going on just a tad longer, Mother.
ANN: How?
JOHN: I think there's more to be said.
ANN: About what?
JOHN: About you, Mother.
ANN: Me?
JOHN: You. I think there's much more to be said about you.
ANN: Such as?
JOHN: Such as, where were you while the king was in the counting house
and the kid was in the cradle?
ANN: I was … here, of course.
JOHN: Didn't you pick me up, if I was screaming in my crib?
ANN: Yes. Sometimes. Yes.
JOHN: But not enough?
ANN: No. Not enough.
JOHN: Why not?
    Pause.
ANN: Because … because at that point I was a little preoccupied.
JOHN: With what?
ANN: Oh, John.
JOHN: With what?
ANN: I don't have to say.
JOHN: With *what*, Mother?
    Pause.
ANN: I was writing a book.

She sat at the desk every day writing a book that took an inordinate
amount of her time and thoughts, and she's sorry if it resulted in her neglecting
him. She has never mentioned the book to anyone, and she burned it, "all six
hundred and twenty-two pages," in the fireplace when his father was out
golfing, because she felt she hadn't gotten it right. Then they had Jigger, and
that took her mind off the book.

John wants to know what the book was about. She agrees to tell him, but
first she'd like "a splash more" in her glass. Ann's book was about a gov-
erness who works for a man to oversee the rearing of his children. Like Jane
Eyre, John comments. No, she doesn't fall in love with him. She falls in love
with a groom, and "has a brief, tempestuous affair with the man who saddles
her horse." It does not work out, and she ends the affair. The groom is upset

and sets fire to the stable. "The fire symbolizes his tempestuous passion," Ann tells John. She hurries in to save the horses, and her face is horribly burned. "Punished, in other words, for her indiscretion," John concludes. But, Ann continues, when her wounds have healed and the bandages have come off she is more beautiful than before. The children gather around, and her employer, who has always loved her, marries her: "Her experience has helped her. In the long run." It's corny, Ann finishes, almost shyly, but John finds it very touching.

It still seems to bother Ann that she couldn't get the passionate emotions right. John admits he's not been able to in a play, either. Ann thinks it's not possible in a play, and that's why John ought to write a book. She starts to leave again, but John wants to know something else—what happened to the groom? Ann supposes she must have had him (in the book) go "off to Venezuela or somewhere." But John wants to know what *really* happened: "Where did he go? Who was he?" Ann shies off, she hadn't said he was real. John surmises that he was, that his mother met him before he was born, and that he left, at which point she began to write the book. She must have based him on someone, he's convinced. Ann claims not to know. Maybe it's that she is getting older, maybe it's the cocktails, but she has begun to think she based him on John's father.

When Ann goes off, Bradley has returned. He and John apologize to each other. Bradley also informs John that when he was upstairs he called Jigger back and gave him his blessing: "The old oak must bend with the wind." John is pleased.

BRADLEY: Maybe I've loved him too much. Maybe I've loved him at your expense. Do you think that's true?

JOHN: I don't know ...

BRADLEY: Maybe he's trying to get away from me. What do you think?

JOHN: I think ... (*Pause*.) I think maybe he's trying to get away from all of us. I think maybe I got him to go because I was jealous of him. And I think we've done enough psychologizing for one day. He likes boats, Pop. He likes working with wood. Maybe he'll build a new clipper ship.

BRADLEY: Well, the point is, he'll be happy there. Sailing. He's a magnificent sailor. Remember right here on Lake Erie?

JOHN: I remember ...

BRADLEY: I could sit in my office and look out on the lake, and sometimes I think I could actually see his sails ...

JOHN: Yes ...

BRADLEY: Of course, that friend of yours is hardly paying him a nickel out there. Hardly a plug nickel.....Even after he sells his house here, he'll need a considerable amount of additional cash. So I told him I'd send him a check.

Bradley looks around—or rather, tries to look around—for the check he's given to John.

And I told him the cupboard was a little bare, at the moment. A little bare. I'm no longer collecting a salary, as you know, and I do need to keep a little cash on hand these days. Doctors ... Pills ... If I should have to go into the hospital ...

John takes the check out of his wallet, hands it to Bradley.

JOHN: Here you go, Pop.

Pause. Then Bradley takes it.

BRADLEY: Thank you, John. (*Pause.*) I mean, I refuse to sell stock. I can't do that. When I die, I want your mother to have ... I want all of you to have ... I've got to leave something.

They've been discussing the national debt, John tells Nina, as she comes to take the hors d'oeuvre plate away. Nina confesses she'd like to borrow money from her father for Cleveland, money which she'll pay back when she gets a job. Bradley will work something out, and she goes off, gratefully, after kissing him.

"It's only fair," Bradley comments, but he won't touch capital. And John will get twenty extra in Bradley's will, and the play can open the day after his funeral. But he hopes John will put some of the good things into the play, like their singing at the piano, and the skiing. They're both mentioned in the play, John assures him.

Ann calls from off that she's going to light the candles. Bradley asks for a couple more minutes. He wants to know what happens at the end of John's play. If John doesn't kill him off, how will he end it? John's still working on that. His father suggests some references to his charities also, as well as his feelings for Ann over their long years together, but he realizes that John needs something else. He probably needs a kicker. When Bradley gives a speech, he tries to end it with a kicker—"some final point which pulls everything together," to make people applaud.

JOHN: You can't *make* people applaud, Pop ...

BRADLEY: You can create congenial circumstances. You can generate an appreciative mood. I mean, isn't that what we want, really? Both of us? In the end? Isn't that why I make speeches and you write plays? Isn't that why people go to the theater? Don't we all, all of us, want to get together and celebrate something at the end of the day?

JOHN (*looking at him as if for the first time*): I guess we do.

BRADLEY: Of course we do. In spite of all our difficulties, surely we can agree on that. So find a good kicker for the end of your play.

JOHN: Kicker, kicker, who's got the kicker?

BRADLEY (*picking up the script, handing it to him*): Meanwhile, here. Put it away somewhere, so it doesn't dominate the rest of our lives.

JOHN (*taking it*): O.K., Pop.

BRADLEY (*turning off lights*): Because there are other things in the world besides plays ...

JOHN: Pop ...

BRADLEY: The company of women ... good food ... congenial conversation ...

John's thought of a kicker: "Suppose, in the end, he (the older son) discovers he's the true son of his father, after all." It might do, Bradley thinks. Ann comes in and takes Bradley's arm to go in to dinner, but Bradley looks back at John. He still doesn't like the name of the play and asks him to think about calling it *Cocktail Time* or *The Family Hour*. "Or why not *The Good Father* ..."

John stands, holding his play, watching his parents go off, arm in arm. Curtain.

EASTERN STANDARD

A Play in Two Acts

BY RICHARD GREENBERG

Cast and credits appear on pages 401 & 443

RICHARD GREENBERG was born in 1958 in East Meadow, Long Island, the son of an executive of a film theater chain. He was educated in local schools and went to college at all of the Big Three: Princeton (B.A. 1980), Harvard (in a Ph.D. course in English literature, abandoned after less than a year) and Yale (M.F.A. from the Drama School in 1985). He began writing fiction at Princeton, including a novel for his thesis; but it was his first play, started after the Harvard experience and later submitted to Yale that won him a place in the latter's playwriting program under Oscar Brownstein.

Greenberg's first New York production took place while he was at Yale: The Bloodletters off off Broadway November 27, 1984 at Ensemble Studio Theater. It won him the 1985 Oppenheimer Award for best new playwright. His one-acter Life Under Water was produced by the same OOB group later that season and was published in The Best Short Plays of 1987. Ensemble also mounted his one-acters Vanishing Act (1986) and The Author's Voice (1987, another Best Short Plays selection). Also in 1987, his adaptation of a Martha Clarke performance work based on Kafka writings appeared OOB as a Music-Theater Group/Lenox Arts Center showcase.

172

Greenberg's first full off-Broadway production was The Maderati *at Playwrights Horizons February 19, 1987 for 12 performances. His first Best Play,* Eastern Standard, *opened October 27 at Manhattan Theater Club after a run last season at Seattle Repertory Theater. Greenberg is a member of Ensemble Studio Theater and the Dramatists Guild, lives in New York City and almost always starts a new play while in rehearsal for the previous one.*

Time: Spring and summer, 1987

Place: Act I—A restaurant, midtown Manhattan, late May
Act II—Stephen's summer house

ACT I

SYNOPSIS: In a corner of a restaurant, the left one of two tables is occupied by Drew Paley (late 20s) and Stephen Wheeler (30), friends since college, the former an artist who doesn't often venture this far uptown and the latter an architect with a major firm. Drew is complaining that his closest friendship has been with his housemaid who, he has discovered, is stealing from him. Stephen had introduced Drew to a man in his office, hoping they would get on, but they didn't.

DREW: Really, Stephen. He's not handsome, he's not charming, he's not even rich, which at least would be *something*. He has many finer qualities, which doesn't interest me at *all*. I sit there thinking, "Has Stephen lost his mind?"
STEPHEN: I just thought—
DREW: I could not figure out *what* you were thinking. Suddenly, he leans over to me—we're in this bar, the God-help-me *Upper* East Side—he leans over to me and says, "I don't know if Stephen told you; I've never ... blush, sigh, harrumph ... *been* with a man before." All of a sudden, I uncover your hidden agenda: this is a match made in hygene! Stephen, please, you're very sweet, but—
STEPHEN: He seemed like your type.
DREW: Catatonic has never been my type, Stephen. The truth is, you think that when I broke up with Eric I embarked on a sexual rout of Manhattan Island. Well, I haven't, so why not give me a break? I wasn't having fun, so we broke up, big deal.
STEPHEN: You made no effort.

DREW: I don't *want* to make an effort! Why should everything be an effort? God. He was … depressed. He was depressing. He put a damper on everything. I saw no utility in spending the charred remains of my youth on a bad time. Why am I justifying myself to you? You've been rebounded on more often than a basketball court, you're hardly the one to dispense advice on how to—oh, look, look, I'm getting all riled, I'm not going into this. So tell me—how are *you*?

    Beat.

STEPHEN: Fine.

DREW: Really?

    Beat.

STEPHEN: Well … fair …

DREW: What have you been doing?

    Beat.

STEPHEN: Nothing much. (*Beat.*) I swallowed a bottle of pills last night.

At this moment the waitress (Ellen, late 20s) arrives with their lunch, so Drew suppresses his violent reaction until she departs. Stephen tries to gloss it over as a mere whim (he put his fingers down his throat in plenty of time). As to why he did it, he hates his job; his architectural firm is blighting the Manhattan neighborhoods, throwing welfare families into the street to clear areas for development. A developer tells the architect, "Make me a building. I don't care what it looks like as long as people notice it." When Stephen is assigned to the design and tries to produce something tasteful and harmonious, his firm inevitably expands it into a monstrosity. And, Stephen tells Drew, "I say to myself, 'Stephen, you have labored mightily and brought forth an abortion. But don't despair! For with any luck, this building will some day be demolished.' Which means that everything I do is pardonable only insofar as it is potentially *reversible*."

Having not even a girl friend, only his hated job, Stephen impulsively swallowed the pills in the middle of the night but decided not to let himself die because his parents would disapprove: "I'm thirty, and I still have parents. If that isn't an admission of failure....."

Strident cursing in a woman's voice offstage cuts across their conversation. Stephen picks it up again by telling Drew he is waiting for a woman to appear at the empty table, a woman he's seen lunching there every day for three weeks. Stephen is obsessed with her but has never spoken. He is letting himself get all worked up because she seems to be late in arriving today. Just as he is getting desperate, she (Phoebe Kidde, late 20s) appears, smiles at Stephen's back (just before Stephen quickly turns to glance at her and more quickly turns back), sits at the vacant table at right and is brought a glass of white wine by the waitress. Drew comments, "I have never seen anyone so ambient of Wall Street in my life. She looks as if she breakfasts on ticker tape and the Dow rises with her hemline," but he finishes, "I absolutely approve."

> *Peter Kidde (late 20s) enters, kisses Phoebe on the cheek, sits by her; they begin to talk, inaudible to us.*

DREW (*rises, stares at Peter*): Oh my God!

STEPHEN: What?

DREW: Oh my God!

STEPHEN: Would you please sit down.

DREW: God, that's beautiful.

> *Phoebe notices Drew staring, looks at him, says something to Peter, who glances at Drew briefly, then turns around. Drew sits.*

STEPHEN: What are you talking about?

DREW: It's what the Garden of Eden must have looked like.

STEPHEN: What?

DREW: The two of them together.

STEPHEN: There's a man with her?

DREW: Yes. A beautiful one.

Drew upsets Stephen by suggesting that these two will have beautiful children; then calms him down by reminding him that summer is soon coming, and they'll go out to Stephen's Long Island place and forget all their city problems.

The scene blacks out as the offstage voice screams an obscenity, then when the lights come up it is the conversation at Phoebe and Peter's table that is heard, while that at the other table is inaudible. The action is repeated from Peter's entrance, and Phoebe tells Peter that she is not here to discuss someone named Loomis, she doesn't want even to mention his name.

> *Phoebe notices Drew.*

PHOEBE: I think you have an admirer.

PETER (*looks over his shoulder, turns back*): Fine, that's all I need—

PHOEBE: You don't think he's cute?

PETER: I'm finding that all very irrelevant these days—

PHOEBE: His friend is stuck on me.

PETER: What?

PHOEBE: For weeks now it's the strangest thing. We've sat at these two tables every lunch hour. He may be marital timber.

PETER: Oh, just your type.

PHOEBE: I think he follows me.

PETER: What?

PHOEBE: I'm not sure. Sometimes I'll be walking and I'll turn, and out of the corner of my eye—if he didn't look so blandly respectable, I might worry. Or is it the blandly respectable ones you're supposed to worry about? Don't they end up having hostages in their basements, and—oh, well, even that would probably be an improvement over—but I'm *not* talking about it, *don't* ask.....

Phoebe changes the subject, and Peter describes a problem he's having developing a script for CBS. Phoebe notices that Drew is still looking at Peter, but Peter isn't interested.

The cursing starts again offstage. Peter and Phoebe look over and can see from their vantage point that "She's just some poor, demented street woman."

Phoebe can't resist coming back to the subject of Loomis. Some sort of financial scandal in which Loomis is involved is spread all over today's papers. Even Phoebe's mother has called her about it and incidentally asked how Peter is doing. And Phoebe broke up with Loomis yesterday, telling him, "For five years you've cast your shadow over every crevice and corner of my life. And for some reason, I looked at that shadow and thought it was the sun.....For the first time I realize I didn't fall in love, I was *seduced*.....What you have done is despicable. Through your actions, you have torn to tatters the basic integrity of our profession. 'Our profession doesn't have any basic integrity,' he said. Well, I didn't have a reply to that, of course, so I turned on my heels and walked out."

Unfortunately, she had to return to get her purse, and the argument continued with her calling Loomis a sleazebag. His reply was, "Maybe, but if you *weren't* a sleazebag, you'd stick by me even though I am one."

Peter considers Phoebe well rid of Loomis. Phoebe unburdens herself to Peter of a nightmare about dancing on the rim of a champagne glass and having the bubbles turn into huge faces of all the people she knows. Phoebe realizes that Peter also has something he wants to get off his chest, and she asks him what it is.

PETER: I'm going to be dead soon.
Long pause. The waitress approaches them.
ELLEN (*waitress*): Are you ready to order?
PETER: No, I think we need a few minutes.
ELLEN: All right. (*Exits.*)
PHOEBE: Oh God, Peter ...
PETER: Really, don't cry, this is a restaurant—
PHOEBE: Peter—!
PETER: I found out the other day. I was sweating at night and had this sore throat that just seemed to last. Well, that's all gone now. I feel fine. I think I'm behaving beautifully, don't you?
Drew and Stephen start looking over, discreetly curious.
PHOEBE: Oh, God ...
PETER: It can't be that surprising; you knew my life—

PHOEBE: Who have you told?

PETER: No one.

PHOEBE: You'll have to—

PETER: No! I don't want anyone to know until it's absolutely necessary. I almost didn't tell you, except that I thought I'd go crazy if I didn't—

PHOEBE: At least, Mother.

PETER: You can't be serious. She knows less about my life than strangers passing me on the street, this is hardly—

PHOEBE: It's not fair not to—

PETER: What, the double whammy? "Mom—there's something I have to tell you. I'm gay; but it's all right, I'm dying!"

Peter wants things to go on as usual, except that he will cease his romantic adventuring. At this moment, a Perrier bottle crashes against the wall, hurled from offstage, and a woman shouts as the lights black out.

When the lights come up, the scene begins some time before the throwing of the bottle. May Logan (50 to 60, a bag lady) is seated at a table at right. Phoebe and Peter are at their table at left, but the table of Stephen and Drew is now offstage left. May shouts to someone at a nearby table, "And what are you lookin' at, lardass? What the *fuck* you think you're doin' here, huh, you look like a RHINOCEROS! Can't a woman just drink a Perrier in *peace*, Goddamnit!"

Ellen comes in to try to keep May quiet and is regaled by one of May's obscenities. The manager has sent Ellen over to ask May to stop disturbing the other customers and leave the restaurant.

MAY: Yeah? Well, why'n't he say so himself?

ELLEN: The manager, who is a chickenshit, would like you to leave and has delegated the responsibility for getting rid of you to me.

MAY: Honey, there's somethin' I gotta tell you—

ELLEN: Yes?

MAY: You're oppressed.

ELLEN: Thank you, I know.

MAY: We got that in common.

ELLEN: Yes, well—to tell the truth, I'd probably have a greater feeling of—soli*dar*ity if you hadn't stolen my tip ...

MAY: Are you accusin' me of somethin'?

ELLEN: The guy who was sitting there before you? He comes every day, orders the same thing, leaves the same tip. Twenty-two percent.

MAY: Today he stiffed you, sweetheart.....

ELLEN (*a little gingerly*): The manager would like you to leave.

MAY: Goddamnit, wherever I go it's the same thing—!

ELLEN: —I—

Anne Meara as May Logan and Barbara Garrick as Ellen in a scene from *Eastern Standard*

MAY: I'm on a grate, I'm in an alley, I'm in a hallway—train tracks, benches, vestibules, islands in the middle a' Broadway—I'm tryin' to sleep, I'm nursin' a cold, I'm tryin' to look like somethin' ya might possibly not wanna kill—somebody always comes along and says, "Move on." Well, where, where—where should I go? Tell me where to go, and I'll go there. No, no, that's right, it's always, "Move on. Outta my sight. Wherever's not here." Trouble is, every place I get to's just another *here*. Well, I only got so much movin' in me. Somewhere along the line, somebody's gotta say, "Rest."

Ellen must deliver menus to Peter and Phoebe, and she moves back and forth taking care of her customers while at the same time trying to learn more about May (who discloses that she used to be a waitress herself). Ellen, who has ambitions to become an actress, has thought about spending a night sleeping in the street, to see how it feels. May offers to tell Ellen her entire life story if Ellen will pay her for it.

ELLEN: I'm not paying for some talk—

MAY: This is not *talk*, Cookie—this is the story of my life. 'fI give that away, what've I got to sell?

ELLEN (*starting to leave*): All right, forget it, I have customers anyway—

MAY: *Wait one Goddamn minute—!*

ELLEN: ... What?

MAY: Now, let me get this straight—you are seriously suggestin' that I tell you intimate secrets about myself—

ELLEN: I'm going—

MAY: Which you will use as the basis for charmin' conversation with eligible bachelors who are supposed to marvel at your sensitivity and buy you *presents*?

ELLEN: Goodbye.

MAY: And out of this whole profit-makin' situation, I get *nothin'*?

ELLEN: The manager would like you to leave—

MAY: Screw the manager—

ELLEN: Listen—

MAY: Yeah, yeah, yeah, why'n't you just go and wait on those faggots at the next table—that whore and that fag—give them the gift of your presence—

ELLEN: Go—

MAY: Goddamn fuckin' Bloomingdale *faggots*—

ELLEN: I'm getting the manager—

MAY (*yelling at Peter and Phoebe*): *You stinkin' pigs!*
    She hurls her Perrier at them.

This action creates pandemonium. May overturns her table and knocks Peter down when he tries to intervene. Stephen and Drew join the fray; Stephen manages to restrain May and take her off, while Drew helps Peter into a chair. Phoebe, feeling ill, goes off to the ladies' room, leaving Drew and Peter to become acquainted; Drew learning that Phoebe and Peter aren't man and wife but brother and sister, Peter learning that Drew is a well-known painter whose work he has seen and appreciated. But when Drew comments that he "feels this instant simpatico," Peter immediately backs off.

Phoebe and Stephen return. Peter leaves, heading for a taxi that will take him uptown. Drew leaves with him to share the cab, pretending that he is also going in that —for him—unlikely direction.

Awkwardly, Stephen and Phoebe introduce themselves to each other. Phoebe informs him that she knows he's been looking at her—and she's been looking back. The emotional strains of the day are affecting Phoebe, and to Stephen's dismay she starts to cry.

STEPHEN: Phoebe—

PHOEBE: Oh, listen, I'm not hysterical ... you don't know, you really don't know what's happened, but could you ... please ...

STEPHEN: Sure ... sure ...

PHOEBE: Take me somewhere ... anywhere ... take me to your house ... take me ... I'm not like this, but I do sort of know you, don't I? We do know each other. And you have a nice face—

STEPHEN: Whatever you want—God, I—!

PHOEBE: I'm really not like this ... but could you, please ... before we go anywhere ... could you please ... could you hold me?

STEPHEN: Here in the restaurant?

PHOEBE: We've already been a spectacle, what could it hurt?

STEPHEN (*draws up a chair beside her*): Sure.

He holds her.

PHOEBE: Thank you.

They sit embracing. After a long moment, Ellen enters.

ELLEN: Excuse me. The manager has instructed me to give you anything on the house. Anything you want.

STEPHEN (*softly*): No ... no. I think we're fine.

Slow fade. Curtain.

ACT II

Scene 1: A month later

On the broad porch of the summer house which Stephen designed, built and owns, overlooking beach and sea, Stephen and Phoebe lie in each other's arms. Despite their idyllic situation, Phoebe can't help thinking about the stock market from time to time, with thoughts of stock option indices intruding on her bucolic contentment. Stephen in his turn is thinking of twin Gothic towers to be included, senselessly, in the design of a new midtown Manhattan building. Stephen's firm seduced him with expanding opportunity, and "My work got cleverer and cleverer.....But talent becomes a nightmare when you hate what you're doing with it." They have given him as much time off as he wants for this seaside sojourn, provided he comes back to them when he's ready.

Phoebe admits loving her job, "somewhere in between" a mogul and a peon: "I loved crossing my legs in a swivel chair.....And I loved turning on my computer and sipping coffee from a styrofoam cup and phoning strangers and telling them what to do with their money and having them *believe* me." Phoebe's company is also generously allowing her to take this time off: "It's amazing how generous they can be when you're the moll of one of the criminals who brought disgrace upon them. They'd probably give me the rest of my life off."

They should both consider that they're on sabbatical, Stephen declares. It's only the phone calls that bother him.

PHOEBE: The phone calls?
STEPHEN: Forget it.
PHOEBE: What are you talking about?
STEPHEN: Nothing ...
PHOEBE: Stephen ...
STEPHEN: The ones you take and never tell me about; the ones I intercept—
PHOEBE: They're nothing—
STEPHEN: This vague male voice. "Is, uh, Phoebe there?" "No." "Thank you very much." Click. No identification so that I don't start making connections. Of course, that sends my head spinning in a thousand different directions, why the secrecy, why the clandestine—
PHOEBE: It's hardly clandestine—
STEPHEN: It's Loomis, of course, I know that, but why can't you tell me?
PHOEBE: Yes, of course it's Loomis. I hate him.

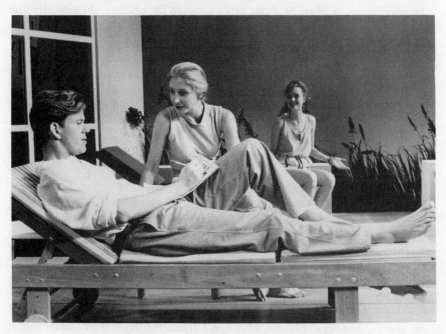

Dylan Baker (Stephen Wheeler), Patricia Clarkson (Phoebe Kidde) and Barbara Garrick (Ellen) in *Eastern Standard*

STEPHEN: How did he get this number?
PHOEBE: He's not without resources. (*Beat.*) I gave him the number.

Phoebe has been letting him talk to her on the phone out of a kind of sympathy for a has-been lover, but she promises to do so no more—"Nothing but us and this beach."

Peter joins them. When Phoebe asks him how he's feeling he answers facetiously, in a clear warning to her not to raise the subject of his health.

Drew rides in on a bicycle with Ellen on the handlebars. Ellen exclaims that she feels reborn here under the country sun. She was invited by Stephen, after Stephen found he'd left his wallet in the restaurant, went back to fetch it, got talking to Ellen and found that she had severe housing problems. It seemed only natural to ask her to join them here, and now Ellen is asking herself, "Why not just get some little job and lie here forever?"

Drew remembers to tell them that he took a phone call from Phoebe and Peter's mother while they were out.

PETER: Damn! What did you say?
DREW: I said, "I'm sorry, Peter can't come to the phone right now. He and I are engaged in a sex act. You've interrupted our coitus—"
PETER: Not even in jest—
DREW: I said you were out.
PHOEBE: It's probably because you haven't spoken to her in a month—
DREW: Why not even in jest?
PETER: She wouldn't understand; our mother is not a worldly woman—
DREW: But still, you have to—
PHOEBE: She's a tad ... would you say, conservative?
PETER: Oh, please. There's not a revolution in history that would have failed to execute her.
DREW: Peter—
PETER: My mother has a certain way of seeing me. I don't want her to lose it. I rely on it—
DREW: But it's a lie—
PETER: No. Just a provisional truth.

Ellen comments that they owe this new-found friendship with each other to May, the bag lady, and admits she's become friends with her since the unfortunate incident in the restaurant, which Ellen attributes to some physical cause like the *petit mal*, because May can't afford medicine. Her family threw her out of their home in Kansas City because they couldn't afford it either, but apparently May is O.K. when she can get it. Ellen permits herself to wallow in pity for May, as she imagines what it must have been like to make her way from Kansas City to New York in a hostile and uncaring environment "sleeping in depots, raped a couple of times, beaten." Ellen bursts into tears and runs off, followed by Stephen and Phoebe.

Drew and Peter pass from a discussion of Peter's script problems to a discussion of each other. Peter admits he finds Drew very attractive.

DREW: Then why won't you give me a tumble?
PETER: Go away.
DREW: Have you been listening to Stephen?
PETER: Stephen?
DREW: Stephen thinks I've slept with the entire homosexual population of the East Village—
PETER: No, I'm not listening to—
DREW: I haven't! That's a complete misconception! I was with Eric for four years, and during that time we had an entirely, unswervingly, absolutely, ninety-eight percent monogamous relationship. And since then, I've been practically a *monk*—
PETER: That's not the reason—
DREW: So, as risks go, I'm minimal!
PETER: Drew—
DREW: And you're all right, aren't you?
PETER: Yes, of course, but that doesn't mean I'm going to have an affair with every—
DREW: I don't mind taking things slow, I can stand it, as long as I know that there's a chance—
PETER: Would you just—
DREW: Because in four years with him, I never felt anything like what I'm feeling now—
PETER: Just shut up, O.K.?

But Drew doesn't shut up. He compares his strong feelings for Peter to the bright colors he'd use to paint the idea of him, finishing, "And it's not just that you're a beauty. I've forgotten beauties by the time the traffic light changed. It's you—all of you—the thing entire." Peter insists, "Nothing will ever come of it," but Drew dares to keep on hoping.

Scene 2: Two weeks later

Phoebe joins Peter, who is husking corn, on the porch. Phoebe has been receiving phone calls from Loomis, who is now going to stay out of jail because he is turning state's evidence. All their friends think Phoebe was in on the illegal deal, and, Phoebe assumes, "All think I'm letting him take the fall for me.....That sort of rumor never fades. And it couldn't matter less that it isn't true."

Stephen and Drew cross and re-cross the porch, carrying packages, while Phoebe confesses to Peter that she loves Stephen: "He wants to be *good* ... Have we ever known anyone who even *thought* that way? It's driving him crazy, lying around here, doing nothing. I see him late at night, making lists, thinking things through, scouting for a way to make himself useful. And he looks at me and I realize that what he wants is to be good enough for *me*—which is completely absurd—but it touches me and it makes me happy and I think, 'Life can be something completely different from anything I'd planned.' Things can be calm and simple and complete—except Loomis is there."

Phoebe also senses that Peter is similarly attached to Drew, which he does not deny but insists that nothing will come of it. He has quit work, he will finish the summer here, and then he plans simply to disappear. Phoebe protests, but he asks her, "Then what do you want me to do instead? Watch while people turn subtly away? Calculate how much I'm ceasing to exist by how little they're able to look me in the eye? No, I've made a decision, I am going to diminish without witnesses."

Drew and Stephen have finally finished bringing in the groceries, Drew complaining about Stephen's plan to entertain Ellen's friend for the weekend.

DREW: In the city, we devote ourselves to blocking out the ugly. Now here we are in Paradise, and we *import* gritty reality?

STEPHEN: You're just bantering—

PETER: But you don't devote yourself to blocking out the ugly, do you? I thought your reputation was based on wallowing in it.

DREW: That's *painting*.

STEPHEN: Ah, I see, then you have a double-pronged mission—to challenge complacency in your art and embody it in your life.

DREW: I mean, what has possessed you, Stephen? Having Ellen here forever and ever and ever is one thing, but now you're playing host to her peer group?

STEPHEN: Just because it's her idea doesn't mean it's a bad one.

DREW: It's not bad, it's preposterous—

STEPHEN: Well, I thought that too, at first, but we do have all these rooms, and it's just for a weekend. Ellen says she's under control these days, and actually very sweet. The only thing I had against it was that it wasn't like anything I'd ever done before. But I've spent my whole life doing things that are like the things I've done before, and I haven't been all that happy, so I said, "Why not?"

DREW: I hope we've all hidden our valuables.

PETER: Drew darling, why don't you just knock it off?

Peter's comment triggers Drew's anger at such "trashy little faggot endearments" thrown at him, and he exits in a huff. Phoebe follows to calm him down. Left alone with Stephen, Peter suggests that since Stephen is in love with Phoebe, he should marry her. Stephen fears that Loomis is in the way, especially now that he's not going to jail.

Phoebe has told Stephen that Peter has "slept with the entire free world." Stephen, who has always believed in "slow and difficult and ultimately fruitless" affairs, wonders if it was fun for Peter living like that.

PETER: ... Not really.
STEPHEN: No?
PETER: No, not really.
STEPHEN: Is that the truth?
  Beat.
PETER: No.
STEPHEN: I didn't think so.
PETER: It's not remotely the truth; it's a great, fat lie ...
STEPHEN: I thought so.
PETER: It was ... wonderfully fun, it was ...
STEPHEN: I'd imagined—
PETER: ... Those *years* ... Clicking onto people like little magnets—
STEPHEN: Huh—
PETER: That's how it was, entering a room ... Lovers everywhere. People you'd had, people you might soon have. Oh God, and the way you stared, and the way you were stared at. You could fall in love with anything—a jawline, a chin—because it didn't have to last beyond the half-hour. And everything was understood; no negotiations that made you lose your appetite for the prize. You'd see someone, you'd find him early; and you didn't think—is he going to like me, is he smart, will we have anything to talk about? "No," you thought, "there's my evening." And the glitter in his eyes, taking you in as if you were a newly-discovered continent. And it might last an hour; or sometimes a day, or some amazing times a month, but it never got stale, because the minute you felt yourself start to become boring, you'd just click away—scarcely even saying goodbye. And never—never—any regret, because there was always someone else who'd fall in love with you a few minutes away.
  Pause.
STEPHEN: I'm sorry—but it sounds awful.
PETER: Once in a while it was.

Drew and Phoebe return, Drew apologizing. In a moment, Ellen is heard shouting offstage, "Hey! We're here!," and she enters with May Logan, the bag lady who created the disturbance in the restaurant.

For a moment the two of them just stand looking at the other four, who look back at them. Everyone smiles. May takes a step for-

ward to greet them. Involuntarily, Stephen, Phoebe, Drew and
Peter jerk defensively back. An awkward recovery from this.
MAY: Hi. I'm sorry about the way I'm dressed. I forgot to pack my sportin'
togs.
PHOEBE: Don't be silly. Welcome.
STEPHEN: There's food and wine—
PETER: Eventually, *corn*—
STEPHEN: We've set up a nice bed, and we've filled your prescription for
you—
PHOEBE: There's sunshine, there's the beach—
PETER: We're very glad you're here.
DREW: When do you think you'll be leaving?
Blackout.

Scene 3: Two weeks later

At dusk, May dominates the festive scene on the porch, "serving food, re-
plenishing drinks, holding forth" to Peter, Phoebe and Drew. She shouts culi-
nary orders to Stephen and Ellen offstage—she is obviously a gifted cook, and
the others have become accustomed to enjoying her gifts. She sympathizes
with Drew, who is having trouble getting started on a sketch. Ellen enters with
table settings and salad and announces her intention of having her room re-
painted. It's late in the season to start such embellishments, but obviously
Ellen and May have long-range plans—and May prevents Ellen from telling
the others about them at this time.

Peter congratulates May on fitting so well into their lives here. May attributes this to her special ability to adapt.

MAY: Ya see, the way I look at it, ya can't weigh yourself down with
backward philosophies. Ya just gotta assess the situation and *travel!*—
PETER: I suppose that's really—
MAY: Even though that gets to be a real heart-tearin' situation sometimes.
Pardon me for talkin' on like this, but I got to be starved for an attentive
crowd—
ELLEN: Oh, sure, that's—
MAY: Ya see, in the street ya can talk an' talk for weeks an' never get a
reply. So ya shout—an' the nobody answerin' gets to be loud as a marchin'
band. That's what makes ya loco. 'Cause pretty soon, the words are throwin'
themselves around inside your head, an' ya start puttin' pretend people in
there to catch 'em. An' before ya know it you're talkin' to these people, an'
this is what is known as the birth of a bad reputation in the neighborhood.
PHOEBE (*fondly, just saying the name*): May ...

MAY: An' whatever ya know about yourself just starts driftin' away. You're not pretty any more or a good dancer. Ya never cook or tell jokes an' have people laugh at them. I once cooked for a livin', ya know, my best job. In a house with nice people. Before my troubles started, an' I kinda lost myself. An' it got to be like there was nothin' hingin' me to the earth—so sick at heart, so *scared*—
PETER: May ...
MAY: But now—now it feels like I'm livin' inside the person I useta be again—'Cause you people, ya give me a place to stay, ya fill my prescription for me, ya let me cook—now *this* is a different story—
PHOEBE: Well, you make it easy for us—
ELLEN: Yes—
PETER: You take care of us.

Stephen comes on in a state of high excitement over the fact that he has just quit his job in a phone conversation with his boss in Houston. He has been drinking to celebrate and means to keep on doing so. When he sobers up, he'll devote himself to something important. Drew guesses correctly what this is: housing for the homeless, inspired by May's presence among them, and he comments sarcastically, "What a wonderful idea.....You can build housing for the homeless, Stephen ... and Phoebe, you can counsel them on their investments. Peter can option their stories for a mini-series. And I'll supply the postmodern art for the living rooms. It's perfect, I can't imagine when four people have been so uniquely equipped to deal with a problem."
Stephen won't be put off, though, and Ellen takes this opportunity to reveal her plan: her acting career has never gotten off the ground, and May needs a place to stay, so why don't they both just stay here all winter as caretakers? "You said you wanted to make a home for May," Ellen reminds an obviously reluctant Stephen, and Drew explains, "Not a home, *housing*, that's a very different concept." Ellen adds that when she went into the city to pick up May she found her own apartment padlocked.

ELLEN: .....It was bound to happen, and it's not so bad. I mean, it's not like May's situation or anything. It's not like I'm *homeless*—I just don't have any place to *live*—
STEPHEN: Ellen—
ELLEN: But I have plenty of places to *crash* ... The thing is, when I went back and saw that padlock, it was like this sign or something—like this incredible omen. It was like the city was saying to me, "Go away—you're not wanted here."
STEPHEN: Oh, well, that's—
ELLEN: And I realized I didn't want to be there anyway! Everywhere I go, someone's rejecting me back there—agents and apartment buildings, my boy

friend—I lose a *job* every six months—but here—here you can just lie on the beach and look at the water, and you're not spending every second of every day just trying to survive ten more minutes—You can lie there and figure out who you really want to be—

STEPHEN: Well, yes, I understand, but it's really not *feasible*—

ELLEN: Why not?

STEPHEN: It's just that—there's so much expense entailed in keeping the house open through the winter ... heating and ...

ELLEN: I can pay for that with what I make—

STEPHEN: It's not just the expense, it's—

PHOEBE: Well ... you know ... it's ...

STEPHEN: There are all sorts of ... things ... involved in running a house like this; in living alone in a town like this, and ... well, you really wouldn't know anything about them—

PETER: *I* would!

STEPHEN: What?

PHOEBE: What?

DREW: *What?*

PETER: I know everything about living in a house like this in a town like this; it's exactly what I was raised to do.

Peter offers to stay here with the women in a cozy trio of country dwellers. Phoebe protests, but Stephen, a bit in his cups, begins to think that giving away his house might be consistent with his master plan. Drew tries to pull him back to reality, but Stephen is floating on euphoria, considering "bringing in busloads of the disenfranchised" and lowering real estate values. But when Phoebe threatens Peter with disclosure of his condition, Peter is forced to take back his offer to stay with the women.

Stephen is disappointed at Peter's abrupt and apparently unmotivated about-face. There is no question of the two women staying on by themselves, and Ellen is concerned about what is then going to happen to May. She and Stephen go into the house, and Phoebe, echoing Ellen's concern, reassures May that the decision not to make the house available had nothing to do with her. May bears her own disappointment gallantly.

PHOEBE: We've loved having you here. We've all felt ... renewed ...

MAY: Let's get the dinner. O.K.?

PHOEBE (*somehow unable to stop confiding in her*): Life becomes overwhelming sometimes, doesn't it?

MAY: What's that, doll?

PHOEBE: ... You manage for days at a time to forget that anything's wrong and then suddenly ... and it can be at the very nicest time of all ... I don't know why I keep talking like this to you ... but then, who else? ... It does, though, doesn't it? It gets to be much more than we should ever have to handle, doesn't it?

MAY: I wouldn't know.

> *They start in.*

PHOEBE: Peter—?

PETER: What?

PHOEBE: Do you want to help get the things?

PETER: In a bit ...

PHOEBE: ... Peter ...

> *He turns, just looks at her; she looks away, slowly.*

Where's Stephen? Oh, he must have gone in with Ellen ... Oh, God ... (*She starts laughing unaccountably.*)

MAY: Whaddaya laughin'?

PHOEBE: I don't know ... I don't know ... What do you want, May?

MAY: What do I *want*?

PHOEBE: Out of life?

MAY: Money. (*Beat.*) What do you want?

PHOEBE: I don't know ... I guess I just want to be happy.

> *May pauses, looks at her, bursts out laughing. The two of them walk offstage, May trailing laughter behind her. Peter remains for a long moment, staring out. Suddenly, he shivers. He looks around, then, panicky, lost, he grabs himself, quells the shivers. The lights fade.*

Scene 4: The next morning

Vestiges of last night's intensive partying are strewn over the porch, including Drew, who slept outdoors and is just beginning to wake up as Stephen enters and surveys the mess. Ellen comes in and out, looking for May. Peter comes in, searching for a wallet he thought he had with him last night, and when Ellen comes back she reveals that she is missing a pair of earrings. And Stephen can't find his watch this morning.

STEPHEN: I could have lost it, or—

DREW: Or we all could have collected our valuables, thrown them on the hibachi and had a cookout—

STEPHEN: I'm always losing my wa—

DREW: She stole your watch, Stephen.

STEPHEN: I knew it.

DREW: And Peter's wallet and Ellen's earrings—

PETER: You don't know that—

DREW: And Phoebe's bracelet and Peter's watch, too; if you check, Peter, you'll see that it's missing—

ELLEN: How the hell do you—

DREW: —and my camera and my watch; God, all these watches, I hope nobody's running on a schedule—

ELLEN: How the hell do you know all this?

DREW: I saw her.

STEPHEN: *What?*

DREW: The whole operation.

PETER: You—? And you didn't do anything?

DREW: I was stunned. I was amused.

STEPHEN: *Amused?*

DREW: I was drunk on my feet; I thought it was a riot.

STEPHEN: Jesus, Drew, she took all our things!

DREW: And absconded with them on a bus in the middle of the night. I know, it's shocking.

PETER: This is really *past* the limit—

ELLEN: In the middle of the night—?

DREW: You were all passed out; you looked like carnage—

STEPHEN: How the hell did she get to the bus, anyway?

DREW: I drove her.

PETER: You *drove* her?

STEPHEN: Drunk?

DREW: Thank God I'm alive.

After all, Drew points out, they all wanted him to be nice to May. Peter thinks Drew's behavior is a sign of his contempt for them all. Drew believes May's behavior "incredibly just," in view of the fact that they had clearly decided not to keep her sheltered here but were sending her back to the street.

Phoebe comes in and hears what has happened, but she is thinking only of getting to the city via a bus that leaves in 20 minutes. Apparently Loomis tried to kill himself last night. The others agree with Stephen that Phoebe's place is here in the crisis over May's departure, not with Loomis—but Ellen inadvertently mentions that Phoebe has been having long and intense conversations with Loomis on the phone daily, an activity which was unknown to Stephen until now and visibly hurts him. All refuse to give Phoebe a ride to the bus, and Stephen adds, "Or even take you back, necessarily, if you go." Phoebe exits, leaving them in confusion.

Stephen announces that he's decided to close the house and it's time for them all to leave, then exits followed by Ellen. Alone with Peter, Drew accuses Peter of avoiding him, and at the same time behaving in a way that seems to belie his statement that nothing would ever come of their relationship.

Kevin Conroy (Peter Kidde) and Peter Frechette
(Drew Paley) in a scene from *Eastern Standard*

DREW: You tantalize! You make people fall in love with you without the remotest intention of returning it. And you couldn't care less, because they're not people to you. They're just mirrors for you to see yourself in.

PETER: Not you.

DREW: How do you measure your success—by the amount of pain you cause? Well, in that case, I'm your masterpiece, your triumph! I am in absolute pain—

PETER: I don't want to hear this—

DREW: I can't work, I can't eat, I can't sleep, I squeeze paint onto a palette every morning, and by the time I can rouse myself enough to get any of it on canvas, I've lost my light.

PETER: Drew, I never meant to—

DREW: All I ever see is you. You come between me and everything else in the world—

PETER: Drew, listen to me—
DREW: And you know it and you let it happen. God, you're—
PETER: Stop it, just—
DREW: You're a monster.
PETER: *Listen, I'm sick!*
      Pause.
DREW: Oh, my God—Oh, Jesus, I thought if it was that—I thought if it was that, you would have told me—Jesus ...
      He embraces Peter.
PETER: The funny part is, you probably would have been the love of my life.
      Fade out.

Scene 5: The next morning

Drew is alone, sketching, when Stephen enters looking for a broom—he is readying the house for closing. Peter comes in as Stephen exits and notices that Drew has started a sort of happy painting, the kind that will cause him to be condemned by the entire avant garde—but he can't help himself.

Ellen has already packed and gone, reluctantly, though she has arranged shelter with a cousin when she gets to the city. Peter observes that this sojourn has failed Ellen's and everyone else's expectations: "She came here thinking maybe she'd get Stephen and who knows what else. Stephen and Phoebe just wanted each other. I was looking for an escape. And you'd sort of hoped for a lover without complications."

Peter and Drew decide that today is a day for taking off in a boat and enjoying the water and each other's company. Even so, Peter's illness isn't far from the front of his mind.

PETER: When are you going to leave me?
DREW (*turns to him; simply*): When you aren't there any more.
      Beat. They look at each other .....
PETER: Oh, Drew, it's going to get so much worse.
DREW: I know.
PETER: Today I feel fine, most days I do, but that won't last. And I'm going to panic and wake up screaming—
DREW: I know.
PETER: And I'm going to look like hell.
DREW: I'm planning not to notice.
PETER: I've got a lot of things to take care of.
DREW: Yes, yes, yes—we'll tell your mother—
PETER: My mother!
DREW: —and your bank and your landlord; we'll auction your clothes and give away your after-shave collection, but today we're sailing!

Drew mounts a bicycle and challenges Peter to race him to the boathouse. Peter runs off after him, watched by Stephen who has entered a beat previously. He is standing looking off when, to his surprise, Phoebe comes in, returning from her trip to the city. Even their small talk is awkward and hesitant, as they try to rearrange their reactions to each other in the new light of recent events. Finally Phoebe admits that Loomis's "suicide attempt" was nonexistent, merely a ruse to get her to come see him. For a moment Phoebe was charmed by this gesture, but finally she was relieved: "Because for the first time I looked at him, and I knew that there wasn't anything worthwhile about him. I'd been so afraid that if I went back I'd have to stay. I was so sure that I didn't have enough will to leave him twice, but I did! I did!" She spent the evening alone in her apartment listening to the phone ring and not answering it, and now she's rid of Loomis for good and all. "I don't know why Loomis expected me to be charmed by a compulsive liar *or* an attempted suicide. I've come to realize neither interests me."

Stephen feels he must confess to Phoebe that he himself comes under this general heading, having attempted suicide himself, just before he met her.

PHOEBE: So this is what my life comes down to? Two men who flirt with self-extinction, like it's going to the movies?
STEPHEN: I guess so. What are you going to do about it?
    She goes to him, starts to kiss him; he pulls away.
I'm sorry, I can't accept your terms!
PHOEBE: What?
STEPHEN: It's impossible. I mean, you lie to me all summer, and you leave, and you come back the next day, and in between you say you've had this huge revelation. But how do I know it's going to stick? Any minute you could run out on me, and then where would I be?
PHOEBE: That's true.
STEPHEN: You could run back to Loomis—
PHOEBE: Easily. Or I could just get tired of you.
STEPHEN: Yes, sure—
PHOEBE: Or I could become sick and die—
STEPHEN: No, don't say that—
PHOEBE: That happens all the time, believe me. Or you could fall out of love with me. Or we could be murdered in the street. Or we could just discover we're not who we think we are and go numb—
STEPHEN: Any of this—
PHOEBE: Drastic things will happen to us, so why not marry me?
    Beat.
STEPHEN: What?
PHOEBE: I'd like to have you around for a while.

STEPHEN: You're really ... something, you know that?

Stephen tells Phoebe about Ellen's effort to capture his fancy the night before by saying wonderful things about him. Stephen turned her down, even though he thought Phoebe had left him permanently for Loomis. Phoebe repeats her invitation for Stephen to marry her, to which Stephen hasn't yet replied when Drew comes back on his bicycle. Stephen informs Drew that he's getting married, thus discovering that his answer to Phoebe is yes.

Peter staggers in, having pursued Drew for several laps around the house but feeling very fit. Their unusually boisterous behavior prompts Stephen to ask, "Drew, are you two an item?," to which Drew replies, "After a fashion" and promises Phoebe he'll take care of Peter from now on.

Stephen declares that he's going through with his plan to organize a group to build low-cost housing, even though the May episode was a flop.

STEPHEN: .....This is a good idea, no matter what anyone says. It's worked before, and I've got the resources, and, oh, you know, we're just too *old* to keep giving things up because our feelings have been hurt.

DREW: Stephen, that's—

STEPHEN: Don't start.

DREW: I wouldn't think of it. After all, it's what I was advocating all along.

STEPHEN: What!

PETER (*overlapping*): My God!

PHOEBE (*simultaneous with above*): The gall ...

DREW: Well, it was my *subtext*. If you were all too obtuse to see that, don't blame—

STEPHEN: You are an incredible hypocrite.

DREW (*loftily*): I never pretended to be anything else.

> *This is Drew's version of a concession. Stephen looks at him, taking him in lovingly.*

STEPHEN: Is there any wine? We need to drink a toast!

PHOEBE: Stephen, it's morning—

STEPHEN: That's all right, it's bad wine—

DREW (*getting glasses*): These glasses have sand in them—

STEPHEN: It's probably better than the wine.

PETER (*getting a bottle*): These have been lying here uncollected for the last two days—

> *Drew starts pouring.*

PHOEBE: What do we toast?

DREW: ... Yes, what?

STEPHEN: To coupling!

PETER: Well, to couples, anyway.

PHOEBE: And to going back to the city!

DREW: A horrifying concept, but inevitable, it seems.

STEPHEN: And to—O.K.—and to all the disappointments, which are inevitable, and compromises, which are legion, and lies, which are our daily bread ... And to the sadly infrequent—accidental—happinesses of all the rest of our lives.

PETER: Skol.

> *They all clink glasses and drink. The wine has turned. The glasses have sand in them. They grimace or gag a little or spit the wine out. Then they catch sight of one another, and as they laugh we fade to black. Curtain.*

EMERALD CITY

A Play in Two Acts

BY DAVID WILLIAMSON

Cast and credits appear on page 449

DAVID WILLIAMSON is Australia's most widely produced playwright and its leader of playwrights as president of its Writers Guild. He was born in Melbourne Feb. 24, 1942 and raised in Bairnsdale in Victoria. At Monash University he graduated in mechanical engineering and then lectured in thermodynamics and social psychology at Swinburn Institute of Technology until 1973. The attraction of script writing overcame him before he was out of his 20s, however, with his scientific background, he believes, helping him develop special powers of observation of detail. His first play, The Coming of the Stork *(1970), was produced at the La Mama Theater in Carlton. His next two,* Don's Party *and* The Removalists *(1971) were performed throughout Australia, the latter premiering at the Nimrod Theater in Sydney Oct. 13, 1971 (winning Britain's George Devine and Australia's Awgie Awards) and then moving on to the Royal Court in London (1973) and to New York as a New Phoenix Theater Side Show and later a Manhattan Theater Club OOB offering in 1974. His first Best Play,* Emerald City, *has followed much the same route. After its premiere by the Sydney Theater Company at the Sydney Opera House's Drama Theater Jan. 1, 1987 (and citation by that city's Critics Circle as the best play of the year), Emerald City moved on to productions in London's West End and off off Broadway by the New York Theater Workshop at the Perry Street Theater Nov. 30, 1988 for a limited 17-performance engagement.*

In accordance with our stated intention of widening Best Play eligibility to include special cases of OOB production (i.e.: modern scripts which have already made their esthetic mark outside New York but for commercial reasons appear outside the defined limits of Broadway and off-Broadway production), we enthusiastically cite Emerald City as a 1988–89 Best Play. And in accordance with our publisher's determination to enhance these volumes by including a complete script which won't otherwise be in general American publication, we proudly present David Williamson's Emerald City in its entirety herewith.

Between The Removalists *and* Emerald City, *the only Williamson play to reach New York was* The Club *(1977), produced on Broadway under the title* Players, *but his works have blossomed elsewhere. The plays are* Jugglers Three *(1972),* What If You Died Tomorrow *(1973),* The Department *(1975),* A Handful of Friends *(1976),* Traveling North *(1979),* Celluloid Heroes *(1980),* The Perfectionist *(1982) and* Sons of Cain *(1985). His work for the large and small screen has included the originals* Libido, Petersen *(Australian Film Institute script award),* Eliza Fraser, Duet for Four, Gallipoli, Phar Lap, The Year of Living Dangerously *and* The Last Bastion, *plus several adaptations of his own stage plays. He has served as visiting professor of dramatic writing at the University of Aarhus, Denmark. His stage direction credits include the State Theater Company of South Australia. He is an officer of the Order of Australia and a director of the Sydney Theater Company.*

Like the leading characters of his Emerald City, *Williamson moved from Melbourne to Sydney, where he has lived since 1979. He is married (his wife Kristin is a journalist), with four children.*

ACT I

Colin stands by a window, gazing out. He is a handsome, engaging man in his late 30s whose natural disposition is warm and open, though when he feels uncertain or under attack he's capable of an aloof, almost arrogant air and of sharp retaliation. He is watched by Elaine Ross, a shrewd, capable woman in her 50s.

COLIN (*turning away from the window*): What other city in the world could offer a view like this?

ELAINE: Rio. But I'm prepared to believe it's the second most beautiful city in the world.

COLIN: I used to come here when I was a kid and go back with my head full of images of lushness. Green leaves spilling over sandstone walls, blue water lapping at the sides of ferries. Flame trees, jacaranda, heavy rain, bright sun.

ELAINE (*drily*): Yes, there's no lack of color.

COLIN: Everything in Melbourne is flat, grey, parched and angular. And everything is controlled and *moderate*. It never rains in buckets like it does here in Sydney, it drizzles. The wind never gusts, it creeps along the streets like a wizened old mugger and slips a blade into your kidneys. Sydney has always felt like a city of sub-tropical abundance.

ELAINE: Abundance. (*Nodding.*) Yes. There's abundance. Sometimes I'm not sure of what.

COLIN: There's a hint of decadence too, but to someone from the puritan south, even that's appealing.

ELAINE: I didn't drag you up here, then?

COLIN: No, I would've come years ago, but I couldn't persuade Kate. She's convinced Sydney is full of con men, crooks and hustlers.

ELAINE: She's right.

COLIN: Melbourne has its quota of shysters.

ELAINE: Sydney is different. Money *is* more important here.

COLIN: Why more so than Melbourne?

ELAINE: To edge yourself closer to a view. In Melbourne all views are equally depressing, so there's no point.

COLIN (*laughing*): I'm not convinced.

ELAINE: It's true. No one in Sydney ever wastes time debating the meaning of life—it's getting yourself a water frontage. People devote a lifetime to the quest. You've come to a city that knows what it's about, so be warned. The only ethic is that there are no ethics, loyalties rearrange themselves daily, treachery is called acumen and honest men are called fools.

COLIN: I thought you liked the place?

ELAINE: I do. It's my city and I accept it for what it is. Just don't behave as if you're still in Melbourne, because if you do you'll get done like a dinner.

> *Elaine exits. Colin moves thoughtfully to center stage. Kate walks on. She's Colin's wife. An attractive, vivacious and intelligent woman in her 30s. Her frowning earnestness often makes her funny when she's not trying to be.*

COLIN: This is an amazing city.

KATE (*bluntly*): I hate it.

COLIN (*suddenly angry*): Christ, Kate! If you're going to be this negative right from the start, let's just cancel everything and go back south.

KATE: We can't. You insulted everybody as soon as you knew we were going.

COLIN: It's a stunning city, Kate. You should see the view that Elaine's got.

KATE: To judge a city by the views it offers is the height of superficiality. This city is *dreadful*. The afternoon paper had three words on the cover: "Eel Gets Chop," and no matter how much I juggle that around in my mind I can't find a meaning that justifies the whole front page of a newspaper.

COLIN: To judge a city by *one* afternoon newspaper is also the height of superficiality.

KATE: *All* the media here is devoted to trivia. The places to be seen dining in, the clothes to be seen wearing, the films to be seen seeing—it's all glitter and image and style. New York without the intellect.

COLIN: What's Melbourne? Perth without the sunshine?

KATE: People in Melbourne care about more than the image they project.

COLIN: They seem just as eager for money and fame as anyone is.

KATE: My friends don't care about money and fame. Terri works her guts out in the Western suburbs helping kids fight their way out of intellectual and physical poverty. Sonia tries to repair the psyches of wives whose husbands beat the Christ out of them, and Steve uses his legal skills to try and stop the powerless being ripped off by the powerful—

COLIN (*interrupting*): Have you ever seen any of them laugh? Wait, I'm wrong. I have. When one of Sonia's battered wives sliced off her husband's member. She had quite a chuckle over that one. And she didn't want the wife to go to prison because it was only a "one off" act.

KATE: They might have tunnel vision in some areas—

COLIN (*interrupting*): Some areas? That lot are so paranoid they blame the C.I.A. if the weather turns cloudy!

KATE: At least they don't live their lives totally for themselves.

COLIN: You know what I couldn't stand about them? Their smug self-righteousness. They were all earning salaries five times the size of any of the poor bastards they were supposed to be helping.

KATE: All right. You didn't like them. I did.

COLIN: I have heard Terri laugh too, come to think of it. When I fractured my elbow tripping over that clump of wheezing fur she claims is a cat.

KATE: They used to laugh a lot. Just not when you were around.

COLIN: What's that meant to mean?

KATE: You picked a fight with them every time they opened their mouths.

COLIN: Can you blame me? They made it quite clear they despised the films I'd written.

KATE: Colin, you're paranoid.

COLIN: They despised them. My scripts were about the lives of middle-class trendies. The truth was *they* were the biggest middle-class trendies of the lot. Steve managed to hate my films without ever *seeing* one.

KATE (*laughing*): Colin, you're totally paranoid.

COLIN (*agitated that she won't believe him, impassioned*): He told me with immense pride that he's never seen an Australian film in his life, and that in the last ten years he'd never seen a film that didn't have subtitles. How trendy can you get? How many working-class Australians drink vintage wine every night of the week like that lot did? How many working-class Australians go to listen to Hungarian string quarters? How many working-class Australians find the neo-realist fabulism of the South American novel "sadly passe." Those friends of yours were right on the cutting edge of middle-class trendiness, yet they kept telling me—not directly and honestly like their beloved working-class would—but subtly and snidely, that if I was a *real* writer I'd be tackling the problems of the real people in our society. The poor, the maimed, the halt and the blind. I must never, never write about the lifestyles *they* themselves were leading. *Pricks!* Loathsome, do-gooding, trendy pricks! Stuff them!

KATE: Perhaps they felt it was a little self-indulgent to concentrate on the problems of the middle-class when the problems of the disadvantaged are so much more acute.

COLIN: I see. The middle-class have no *real* problems. So how is it they manage to pack so many traumas and breakdowns into their sunny middle-class lives? How is it that they unerringly turn every relationship they embark on into the story line of a soap opera?

KATE: I don't think that comment's justified, Colin. Teresa's been married for eighteen years.

COLIN: Yes, but has anyone ever *seen* Gavin in the last fifteen? I know he's supposed to be writing poetry upstairs, but my guess is that he's been in Katmandu since the early seventies.

KATE (*finding his histrionics amusing*): Colin.

COLIN: I know the middle class shouldn't have emotional problems—they're infinitely better off in a material sense than your average third world villager—but for some perverse reason they successfully screw up their lives with great flair, and I find that interesting, and I'm going to keep charting their perturbations and try and make some sense of it all, and those Chardonnay socialists of Melbourne aren't going to stop me!

KATE (*to the audience*): If I hated Sydney that much, why did I agree to come? In hindsight I suspect that there was something in me that responded to that odd, pulsing, garish city to the north. A reckless streak, a habit of getting quickly bored—I think that deep down I felt something might *happen* up here. And until it did I was in the happy position of having Colin to blame for all the misfortunes that befell us.

COLIN (*to the audience*): I shouldn't've been so bloody reckless. What kind of idiot uproots himself from a lifetime of connections for childhood memories of flame trees and jacarandas? Lunatic. But *was* it just that? Wasn't there a little grub in my soul hungry for the lionizing and celebrity mania that grips the harbor city? Devouring my integrity until I drifted towards the sun and journalists who asked me what I'd like to see in my Christmas stocking and did I sleep nude?

> *Kate exits. Colin stands by himself. We hear the noise of cocktail party chatter. Mike McCord approaches him. Mike is a smartly-dressed man about the same age as Colin. His hair is carefully swept up over his brow in a stylish sweep. His manner is abrupt, authoratitive and conspiratorial, conveying the impression that he knows far more than anybody about everything.*

MIKE: Colin Rogers?

COLIN (*awkwardly*): That's right.

MIKE: Mike McCord. Welcome to Sydney.

COLIN: Thanks.

MIKE: Seen any of his films?

COLIN (*not understanding*): Sorry?

MIKE (*inclining his head*): Our guest. The Hun.

COLIN: No.

MIKE: Don't rush. Best he's ever done is win a jury prize at the Dublin film festival, which places his talent pretty exactly.

COLIN (*smiles and shakes his head*): Dublin.

MIKE: None of his films have ever made a cent, so what does our Film Commission do? Throws a cocktail party for him.

COLIN: I don't usually go to these things. Hate 'em.

MIKE: Go to all the cocktail parties. Golden rule of Sydney life. Only time you ever learn anything. There are the McElroy brothers over there. Only non-identical twins you can't tell apart. Saw one of your old movies on video last weekend.

COLIN (*steeling himself against possible criticism*): Ah. Which one?

MIKE: *Days of Wine and Whitlam.*

COLIN: Ah.

MIKE: Enjoyed it. Can't work out why the critics were so savage.

COLIN (*tense*): Most of the crits were very good.

MIKE (*shrugging*): Must have read one of the bad ones. No, I enjoyed it. Good entertainment.

COLIN (*bristling*): A little more than that, I hope.

MIKE: End was a bit of a worry. I would've been inclined to tie up the loose ends.

COLIN (*curtly*): Loose ends were symptomatic of the times. You write yourself do you?

MIKE: Got some projects on the boil. Yep.

COLIN: What sort of projects?

MIKE: Contemporary action-adventure. Right for today's market.

COLIN (*tight lipped*): That's what we all should be writing then is it? Contemporary action-adventure.

MIKE (*misses the sarcasm; nodding*): Look around you. Yesterday's men. Cranking out pictures that nobody wants to see any more. Slow pans over the vast outback. Pretty pictures. No action. No drama. It's about time we woke up to the fact that the little bit of history we've had has been so bloody dull there's no point trying to mythologize it. We've got to start making films that are hard-hitting, contemporary and international. Movies that'll work all over the world. What are you working on?

COLIN (*reluctantly*): Another script.

MIKE: Is it going to be contemporary?

COLIN: Recent history.

MIKE: Given up on the middle classes?

COLIN (*defensively*): I feel like a change.

MIKE: Elaine Ross producing?

COLIN: I imagine so.

MIKE: Haven't asked her yet?

COLIN: Not yet. No.

MIKE: Ever thought of producing your own scripts?

COLIN: It's hard enough to write them.

MIKE: Worth considering. More money, greater artistic control.

COLIN: Elaine's always done my scripts well.

> *Mike rocks his head backwards and forwards, indicating that he's not sure he agrees.*

You don't think so?

MIKE: If you're happy, fine. Got a project I'd like to talk to you about. Got an hour or so next week?

COLIN (*to the audience*): What I should have said was, "No." Not this week, next week or any other week. The man was patently a hustler and a spectacularly insensitive human being. It was the confidence and assurance that made me hesitate. In my defense, it's an industry in which today's joke is tomorrow's genius. Lucas, Spielberg—laughed at by the studios when they first did the rounds. Who knows where the next hot project is going to emerge from? And it was only a few minutes of my time. (*To Mike*) Sure.

MIKE (*fishing for a notebook*): I'll get your number.

> *Mike takes the number and exits. Colin stands staring ahead, deep in thought. Kate enters.*

KATE: How was the cocktail party?

COLIN: Appalling. Last time I go to one of those. Everyone in the room knew who I was, but not *one* of them came across to say hello. I don't expect anyone to genuflect, but I do happen to be the screenwriter with the best track record in the country, and not one of them came and said hello.

KATE: You can look a bit ... unapproachable. Why didn't you walk up and introduce yourself?

COLIN: I hate *imposing* myself. I hate the humiliation of having to *loom*.

Colin acts himself looming. Kate smiles.

Standing there with your facial muscles going rigid around a forced smile, blood freezing in your veins as you wait at the edge of a conversation for the circle to widen—until finally you croak, "Mind if I join you," and everybody looks at you as if you'd just farted. Why are Australians so bloody graceless? Why can't we *occasionally* show a little social tact and flair?

KATE: You're too sensitive, Colin. A dozen people probably wanted to talk to you, but were just as nervous about approaching you as you were about them.

COLIN (*gloomily*): If you do make the effort and approach someone, it inevitably turns out to be the most boring person in the room, and you're stuck. If you leave too soon they'll know you think they're boring, and if you stay, they catch you glancing desperately over their shoulder and say, "I'm boring you aren't I?," and you shriek "No!," and you're stuck for another hour. I find mass social intercourse a total mystery. Nobody likes it but it keeps on happening.

KATE (*smiling*): Colin, you're so *inept*. All you've got to do is say, "Ah, there's Dennis: catch up with you later." Being scrupulously polite to all people at all times makes you just as many enemies as being rude.

COLIN: The only guy that did come and talk to me was some aging shyster who script edits soap operas.

KATE: What did he want?

COLIN: He's trying to get a project up.

KATE: And he wants you to write it?

COLIN: I expect so.

KATE: You're not going to talk to him about it?

COLIN: Won't do any harm. There's just an odd chance it might be brilliant.

KATE (*reprovingly*): Colin!

COLIN (*irritated*): There's no harm in *talking* to the man. Don't you think I can look after myself?

KATE (*to the audience*): Frankly, no. Colin does his best to appear confident, but just under that prickly surface is a monumental insecurity and an almost childlike desire to please. If I hadn't been round to rescue him from the hucksters and operators, his career up to now would've been a disaster.

They exit. Mike enters with his girl friend Helen. She's a lot younger than he and is smart, engaging, buoyant and very sexy.

MIKE: Met Colin Rogers today.

HELEN (*impressed*): Really?

MIKE: Had a long chat.

HELEN: Where'd you meet him?

MIKE: Film Commission.

HELEN: Did you just walk up to him?

MIKE: What am I supposed to do? Crawl on my hands and knees?

HELEN (*shrugging*): I would've been a bit nervous.

MIKE: He's just a working writer like I am.

HELEN: You haven't had eight of your screen plays shot.

MIKE: His era's over. The public wants *excitement* when they go to the cinema. Action, adventure—not a bunch of middle-class wankers chatting about their problems.

HELEN: Hate action flicks.

MIKE: Hate action flicks? Cinema *is* action.

HELEN: I occasionally like to exercise my mind.

MIKE: You want to exercise your mind—go and read philosophy. (*To the audience.*) Apart from a tendency to worship anything that smelt of culture with a capital C, who could fault her? I still look at her and can't believe it's me who gets into bed with her every night. I get erections when I hear her on the phone. I watch her talking to other men and wonder how they can keep their hands off her. And she's funny. And she's smart. And when we screw she goes "Mmm, mmm, mmm," like she's eating zabaglione, and when she comes she shakes like a jet hitting turbulence. (*Pauses slightly and gives a worried frown.*) I'm not putting this all that sensitively. What I'm trying to say is that if what I feel for her isn't love, then it's pretty bloody close.

HELEN: What was he like?

MIKE: Boring.

HELEN: I'd like to meet him.

MIKE: He's boring.

HELEN: I'd still like to meet him.

MIKE (*shaking his head in disgust*): The power of the media. Just because you've read in some women's magazine that he sleeps in red pyjamas—

HELEN (*interrupting*): In the nude. He sleeps in the nude.

MIKE: So do I, but it never seems to get you excited.

HELEN: You're not famous.

MIKE: I'll be more famous one day than he is.

HELEN: You get famous, I'll get excited.

MIKE: People come from nowhere in this industry. You can make it on the basis of a three line synopsis written on the back of a coffee chit.

HELEN (*mischievously rather than cuttingly*): If that's all it takes, why has it taken you so long?

MIKE: Because everyone wants tomorrow's projects, but they won't look at anything unless it's got one of yesterday's names attached.

> *Mike stares across at Colin as he walks onstage. He leaves the stage with Helen as Colin paces up and down waiting for the phone to ring.*

COLIN (*to the audience*): I gave Elaine the best outline I'd ever written. Three weeks later she still hadn't phoned. For the first week I put it down to the fact that her five-hour lunches didn't leave her with much time, or in any condition to absorb new material. The sheer rudeness of her silence was unforgivable.

> *Colin paces up and down, makes a decision, reaches for his coat and storms out the door. He arrives at Elaine's office. He appears outwardly calm but clenches his right fist and taps his right foot, his characteristic sign that he's distressed. Elaine looks up.*

ELAINE: Colin.

COLIN: Just passing by. Thought I'd drop in and say hello.

ELAINE: How nice.

> *She knows what he's here for, but pretends she doesn't. There's an awkward pause.*

COLIN: Busy?

ELAINE: Yes, I am.

COLIN: Money'll be hard to find this year.

ELAINE: Good projects always find their money.

> *Elaine wants to avoid discussing the outline. She tries to look as if she's desperate to start work again, but Colin stands there shuffling, clenching and looking agitated and uncomfortable.*

ELAINE (*with noticeable reluctance*): Would you like some coffee?

COLIN: No, I'd better go.

> *He's extremely reluctant to go, but having said it he has to finally turn and make for the door. He summons up his courage and turns back.*

(*Tensely*): Oh, by the way. Did you get a chance to glance at my outline?

ELAINE: You're outline. Yes. Just a quick glance.

COLIN (*quickly*): It's very rough.

ELAINE (*nodding*): It's interesting. I was expecting something contemporary.

COLIN (*quickly*): Were you? Why was that?

ELAINE: Everything else you've done has been contemporary, so I didn't think the assumption was unreasonable.

COLIN: I wanted to move away from contemporary. People have been suggesting that it's all I can do.

ELAINE: What people?

COLIN: Critics, friends.

ELAINE: *Never* let critics force you into areas you don't want to go.

COLIN: I did want to go. It's a story that's important to me.

ELAINE: Coastwatchers?

COLIN: My uncle was one during the war.

ELAINE: My Aunt wrapped Red Cross parcels, but cinema hasn't suffered irreparably because her story remains untold.

COLIN (*upset*): They were incredibly brave. They saved this country from invasion.

ELAINE: Do you think it'll have wide appeal?

COLIN: Absolutely.

ELAINE (*with a false smile*): Let's have lunch next week and talk about it.

COLIN: You don't think it'll have wide appeal?

ELAINE: Let's have lunch and talk about it next week.

COLIN (*in an impassioned outburst*): Elaine, these men were incredibly brave. Didn't you feel at least slightly moved by what you read in that outline? When's the last time you saw anyone in today's society risking their lives for their fellow countrymen? These men were heroes. Old fashioned, genuine heroes. Can't we make films about heroes any more?

> *The phone rings. Elaine looks immensely grateful. She picks it up, puts her hand over the mouthpiece and turns to him.*

ELAINE: I'll read it again and ring you. (*Turns her attention to the phone.*) Ross productions. Carmel. I'm so sorry, I've been meaning to call.

> *Colin clenches his fist. Now he's finally burst forth he wants to continue the debate, but as he watches Elaine nod and smile into the phone, he realizes he's not going to have a chance. He turns and leaves. Mike walks onstage. Colin picks up an outline and reads to himself.*

MIKE (*addressing the audience*): I had to pitch and hook him. No second chance. Deep down I knew he was yesterday's man and I was the future, but not so deep down, all that media hype about him over the years impressed me against my will. He was such an arrogant prick he'd make anyone nervous. He stood staring at me as if I'm a wood grub and he's a red gum. I took three indigestion tablets, and it still didn't stop the flames in my gullet and the fire in my gut. I remember thinking as I swallowed them, "Why are you doing this? What are you trying to prove?" I knew the answer before I'd finished asking the question. I was trying to prove to every bastard who's ever laughed at me behind my back, sneered at the mention of my name, or sacked me, that despite a less than glorious career in insurance, real estate, sales, advertising, burglar alarms and pigs, I was a top talent waiting for the right time and the right game and I'd found it. And every time I thought of Helen, it made me even more desperate to succeed. I won her on a promise of future greatness, and time was running out. I couldn't exist without her. No way. So there I was, wood grub to the red gum, needing him to say yes, because none of those miserable merchant bankers are ever going to trust a script with my name on the front even if they love it, their wives love it, their secretaries love it and it gives off the odor of dollars. With Colin Rogers's name on it, my career is launched.

> *Mike turns to Colin. Colin puts down the outline of Mike's and regards him with bemused disdain. Not quite red gum to the wood grub, but Colin's manner does indicate that he feels comfortably superior to him.*

COLIN: Certainly full of action.

MIKE: Based on fact.

COLIN: Really?

MIKE: Absolutely.

COLIN: Shoot-outs?

MIKE: Anything goes up in the gulf. It's like the wild west.

COLIN: Next time I eat a prawn I'll appreciate the drama behind it.

MIKE: Structure's neat. Notice how when the seventeen-year-old spunk is hired as cook, she focuses all the tensions?

COLIN: Yes. What are you going to call it? Prawn Wars?

MIKE (*with a forced laugh*): *Night Boats.*

COLIN: *Night Boats.*

MIKE: Nothing's set in concrete. The girl doesn't have to be swallowed by the crocodile.

COLIN: Saves her having to choose between the men.

MIKE: How do you feel about the overall concept?

COLIN: Sounds highly commercial.

MIKE: Absolutely. Would you like to co-write it? You'd get first credit of course, and we'd produce it ourselves so that we make some money, and keep control. No slow pans over gulf sunsets, and no Jack Thompson and Bryan Brown. The only bit of decent casting in an Australian movie was the horse in *Phar Lap.*

COLIN (*bristling*): I think the casting in my movies has been quite good.

MIKE: Who thought of Stewart Egan as the lead in *Days of Wine and Whitlam?*

COLIN: Elaine Ross.

MIKE (*nodding knowingly*): Stewart Egan looks O.K. on rock clips, but he was a disaster on film.

COLIN (*coldly*): I didn't think he was bad.

MIKE: Producers who cast *names* instead of good *actors* and think it'll earn them megabucks don't know the business they're in. Egan might've been a big rock star, but the public know he can't *act*, so they stayed away in droves.

COLIN (*coldly*): Stayed away in droves?

MIKE: I know it made its money back.

COLIN: It made a healthy profit.

MIKE: It could've made a *massive* profit. It was a great screen play. Didn't it win the best screen play at ...

COLIN: Berlin.

MIKE (*nodding*): Not best actor. Not best director. Best screen play. One of the best that's ever been written in this country, but the public stayed away in droves because Elaine Knucklehead Ross cast a lead actor who'd make your average corpse look as if it was tap dancing. And why the hell did she let Scranton direct it?

COLIN (*defensively*): He's not my favourite director but he did a competent enough job.

MIKE: Scranton can barely direct shit from his arsehole. Your script *made* him, if you call success screwing up historical epics in Hollywood. Your scripts have *made* Elaine Ross too.

COLIN: I wouldn't say that.

MIKE: She's the one living in splendor in Darling Point. You're stuck here in a terrace in Paddington. Why should she have the harbor views? You're the one with the talent. *Night Boats*. What do you think?

COLIN: I'm not sure it's my type of project.

MIKE: I don't need an answer straight away. Sleep on it. It's got color, action, tension, pathos, romance. What were you working on again? Recent history wasn't it?

COLIN: Yes.

MIKE: Second World War?

COLIN (*looking up sharply*): Why?

MIKE: You know Gary McBride at Channel Ten?

COLIN: No.

MIKE: Gary's a mate of mine. Says Second World War always rates. What angle are you taking?

COLIN (*reluctantly*): Coastwatchers.

MIKE: Coastwatchers?

COLIN: The men who stayed behind on Jap occupied islands and reported Jap ship movements by radio. They saved us from a full-scale invasion.

MIKE: We could get this one up, mate. Gary said that if I ever had anything Second World War to come straight to him.

COLIN: I'm developing it for film.

MIKE (*shaking his head*): Second World War doesn't rate on the big screen, mate. This is television. Six-hour, eight-hour mini-series. I could get a pre-sale from Gary within a week, go straight to a merchant bank for underwriting, and we'd be shooting by August.

COLIN: I'd rather see it as a movie.

MIKE: It's an epic story, mate. How could you tell it in two hours?

Mike exits. Colin crosses to discuss his future with Elaine.

ELAINE: Television?

COLIN: A six-hour or eight-hour mini-series.

ELAINE: Colin, I know how passionate you are about this, and I truly want to believe, but I keep on stumbling over the fact that Coastwatchers basically watched coasts. I can't see eight hours of television.

COLIN (*passionately*): They fought guerilla actions, they were always on the run—they ran incredible risks! My uncle used to tell me the stories when I was a kid.

ELAINE: Colin, the impact an uncle can have on a young kid is one thing. If we go the television route I've got to sell the concept to network executives with sloping foreheads and Neanderthal brows who are living proof that we share ninety-nine percent of our D.N.A. with the higher apes, and they only ever ask one question: "Why in the hell would Mr. and Mrs. Western Suburbs want to watch that shit?" Which is an odd questions when the opposition channel is featuring a wrestling bout between King Kong Bundy and Junkyard Dog, but they still ask it.

COLIN: Surely you can sell them quality occasionally?

ELAINE: There are executives in our networks who, if asked to name an American intellectual, would answer, "Sylvester Stallone." Colin, if you want to go in a new direction, I've got the perfect project for you. Have you heard the name Tony Sanzari?

COLIN: Yes, but I can't remember the context.

ELAINE: He's the father of the two boys killed in that fun park accident.

COLIN (*nods without enthusiasm*): Ah. Yes.

ELAINE: He's waged an incredible one-man war against the authorities to prove it wasn't an accident.

COLIN (*bored*): He's a bit of a nut case, isn't he?

ELAINE (*quietly angry*): I think he's anything but a nut case. He's got very convincing proof that the so called "accident" was organized by one of the country's biggest crims so he could get the park condemned and buy it up cheap for development. And there've been two serious attempts on his life while he was getting that proof.

COLIN: If he's got proof, why don't the authorities do something?

ELAINE: Because a lot of money has been spread around to make sure that they don't.

COLIN: I can't get excited by corruption, Elaine, it's so bloody sordid.

ELAINE: Can you get excited by the story of a father who's so shattered by the loss of his sons that he'd risk his own life to get the man responsible? You've got kids. Imagine how you'd feel?

COLIN: Elaine!

ELAINE (*with a tough glint in her eye*): It's a powerful story, and it should be told, and I want you to tell it.

COLIN: I'm sorry. It doesn't appeal.

ELAINE: Colin, I've paid a fortune for the rights.

COLIN: I want to do *Coastwatchers*.

ELAINE: *Coastwatchers* is a turkey!

COLIN (*angrily*): How can you say that? It hasn't been written yet!

ELAINE: Colin, it's a turkey!

COLIN: All right. I'll do it myself.

ELAINE: Produce it?

COLIN: Yes!

ELAINE: Don't be ridiculous, Colin. What experience have you ever had in production?

COLIN: It's about time I learned.

ELAINE: Have you any idea what's involved?

COLIN: Nothing that any intelligent person couldn't handle.

ELAINE: Is that so?

COLIN: It's time I started taking more responsibility for the key creative decisions.

ELAINE: Are there any creative decisions *I've* taken that you've been unhappy with?

COLIN (*averting his eyes*): One or two.

ELAINE: Which ones?

COLIN: Casting Stewart Egan in *Days of Wine and Whitlam.*

ELAINE (*incensed*): Egan was wonderful.

COLIN: I felt he was wooden.

ELAINE: Wooden?

COLIN: Mahogony, Teak. Possibly even Jarrah.

ELAINE: I'm sorry you didn't mention your doubts about him when I showed you the screen tests—you didn't seem to have any of these polished wood anxieties then. In fact you told me he was the only possible choice.

COLIN (*averting his eyes*): I didn't want to rock the boat.

ELAINE: You told me you couldn't believe it was the same man who did the rock clips.

COLIN (*embarrassed*): I can't remember saying that.

ELAINE: You did.

COLIN: Everybody gets a bit over-optimistic when a film is coming together.

ELAINE (*coldly furious*): Are there any other mistakes you think I've made?

COLIN (*backing off*): This isn't the time to nit-pick over old grievances.

ELAINE: What are the others?

COLIN: I don't think this is the time—

ELAINE (*interrupting*): Richard Scranton as director? I suppose I made a mistake there too?

COLIN: I wasn't entirely happy—

ELAINE (*interrupting*): I don't believe it. The man is now a top Hollywood talent. Has Hollywood been over here begging you to get on the plane?

COLIN (*stung*): If I was prepared to write mindless genre pieces they probably would be.

ELAINE (*with Arctic coldness*): I'm sorry you won't do the Sanzari story, Colin. I think it's going to make the writer who does do it very famous.

COLIN (*to the audience*): That's a threat that chills any writer to the marrow of their bones. A dozen other writers I'd hate to see collecting a bronze statuette flashed before my eyes, but for once in my life I stuck to my guns. Why was I so obsessed with *Coastwatchers?* Dogged loyalty to the memory of Uncle Jimmy. I was a lonely kid whose own parents devoted all their energies to bitter marital warfare, and Jimmy, whose own marriage had been a childless disaster, made me the son he was never going to have. I idolized him. His Coastwatcher stories became sagas of infinite importance to me, and I questioned him about every rock, every tree, every close encounter and every death. I wanted answers to the most urgent, chilling and unsettling questions in my young mind. How does one face death, and how can one man kill another? Jimmy told me something he'd never told anyone else. He'd killed a Japanese soldier who'd come to the edge of a clearing in the moonlight. At first he couldn't shoot, then the soldier began to urinate and Jimmy felt a wave of disgust and pulled the trigger and had had nightmares ever since. How could he kill a man for urinating in the open when he himself had done it half an hour before? *Coastwatchers* had to answer that question. It was a shrine I was building to the memory of Uncle Jimmy.

 Mike enters.

MIKE (*to the audience*): *Coastwatchers?* I hated every minute of it, but the writing was the worst. The status difference between us stood out like a hooker in the lobby of the Hyatt Hilton. I sat there, grublike, over the typewriter while Red Gum strode up and down dictating the thing word for word. When I got so pissed off I couldn't stand it any longer I'd throw in a suggestion, and there'd be a frozen silence, and he'd look up at the ceiling and say, (*Imitating Colin.*) "Nooo, I don't think so." Then he'd stare at me. We'd eyeball to eyeball for about a sixteenth of a second, and I'd go back to my typing. And the subject? *Coastwatchers*, quite frankly, interested me about as much as going to bed with a six-foot, fourteen-stone lesbian, which I have done under odd circumstances I won't bore you with. But an odd thing happened. I started reading the words I was typing out of sheer boredom, and found that this arrogant prick, striding up and down like Napoleon plus growth hormones, was telling a story that was getting me in. Guys taking incredible risks under appalling conditions so that fat little babies like myself slept on undisturbed. In the world I see around me where everyone is out for number one, this sort of behavior gives you an odd jolt. The turd had the odd knack of making his characters live. He didn't have my visual sense, though, and towards the end I started sneaking in some of my images.

 Mike exits. Colin strides up and down the room gesticulating. He's acting out some of the crucial scenes he's about to write the next day. He doesn't speak the lines out loud but emits a curious, high speed mumble, rather like a tape recorder being played backwards at triple speed. Kate watches him. She's used to it, but is still irritated by his total absorption in his work.

KATE: Penny lied about where she was last weekend.

COLIN: Penny? She's never lied in her life.

KATE: Well, she just started.

COLIN: Wasn't she here last weekend?

KATE: Colin, as a father you're a joke.

COLIN: As a wife you don't give me many laughs.

KATE: If you ever give another interview in which you claim to do fifty percent of the household chores and put the responsibilities of fatherhood before your work I'll ring the bloody journalist and demand the right of reply.

COLIN: I do the shopping.

KATE: I pin a series of lists headed "butcher," "greengrocer," "delicatessen" to your jumper which you usually manage to leave at the right shop and which you often remember to collect. I'm the one who does all the thinking.

COLIN: *I'll* do the thinking, *you* spend an hour a day behaving like a fork lift truck. Have you ever had to have a prolonged conversation with Doug the butcher? He's a great guy, but after the weather it can get tricky. Especially when the only reason he can think of as to why I do the shopping at ten every morning and why I don't speak like an outback Queenslander, is that I'm the boyfriend of a Qantas flight director.

KATE: Let him think it.

COLIN: I don't want him to think it. I'm not.

KATE: There's nothing wrong with being gay.

COLIN: Nothing wrong at all, except that I'm not. And while we're on this, will you stop all this nauseating stuff with young Sam about, "No one knows what one's sexual preferences will be until one grows up, but if one's sexual preferences *do* turn out to be minority preferences, one must *never* be ashamed of it."

KATE: You're just prejudiced against gays.

COLIN: I am not in the *least* prejudiced against gays. I just want the kid not to feel guilty if by some odd chance he grows up hetero.

KATE: You *are* prejudiced.

COLIN: It took fifteen million years of evolution for my genes to get to me, I'd just like to see them go a bit further. Where *was* Penny?

KATE: At a disco called Downmarket. She was supposed to be studying at her friend's place.

COLIN: Disco? When she was in Melbourne the only thing she'd listen to was Mozart.

KATE: I'd be surprised if Downmarket is noted for its Mozart.

COLIN: How did you find out?

KATE: A twenty-three-year-old German tourist turned up on our doorstep looking for our daughter.

COLIN: What did he want?

KATE: It wasn't Mozart. Apparently he felt an offer had been made on the dance floor.

COLIN (*shocked*): That's terrible. She's only thirteen.

KATE: Fifteen, but it's still a worry.

COLIN: Those discos are where the pushers operate.

KATE: Our daughter says it isn't a problem. If you stay out on the dance floor they soon stop bothering you.

COLIN: We'll have to do something.

KATE: I've stopped this week's pocket money.

COLIN (*agitated*): That'll really strike terror into her.

KATE: What do you want me to do? Lock her in a dark cupboard for a month?

COLIN: This is serious. She's rubbing shoulders—and God knows what else—with pushers and pimps. What's made her interested in discos, for God's sake?

KATE: This is a very cosmopolitan city.

COLIN: Discos aren't cosmopolitan, they're tawdry.

KATE: I was going to say tawdry, but I didn't want to be rude about your chosen city.

COLIN: Don't sit there being smug. This is serious. We've got to take firm action.

KATE: What do you suggest?

COLIN: If we let her keep on going like this she'll end up in William street hopping into passing Jaguars.

KATE: If you're so worried, you take over the problem. And you can handle Sam and Hannah as well.

COLIN: What's wrong with Sam and Hannah?

KATE: Sam's apparently running a protection racket in his sixth grade—

COLIN (*interrupting*): Protection racket? In Melbourne we couldn't get him away from his computer.

KATE: New city, new skills. And Hannah's teachers say she's depressed.

COLIN: Who wouldn't be in this family?

KATE: How about taking some of the blame for that yourself? You can go to the schools and hear the bad news next time! I'm sick to death of organizing this menagerie. I've got problems of my own.

COLIN: Such as?

KATE: Such as going quietly crazy because my idiot boss refuses to publish the first manuscript in years that's got me excited.

COLIN: That black woman's novel?

KATE: I wish you wouldn't keep calling her "that black woman."

COLIN: What am I expected to call her? "That woman whose complexion is not as ours?"

KATE: Call her by her *name*.

COLIN: I forget it.

KATE: Take the trouble to *learn*. You've heard it often enough. Her name is Kath Mitchell, and her book is called—

COLIN (*interrupting*): I know the name of her book. Who could forget it? *Black Rage*.

KATE: See?

COLIN: See what?

KATE: The tone of contempt.

COLIN: It's a terrible title.

KATE: Just because she's a member of a minority who've been made marginal in a land they owned for forty thousand years, and a member of another minority who've been made marginal by the post agricultural patriarchy for eight thousand years, doesn't entitle you to dismiss *her* or her *work*.

COLIN: I haven't.

KATE: You'd better not. It gives her work a lot of power.

COLIN: Whereas mine, being pale and male, is limp?

KATE: You're work hasn't got her power. No.

COLIN (*hurt*): Thank you.

KATE (*attempting tact, which she's not very good at*): But yours has got certain qualities hers hasn't.

COLIN: Of course. It's more frivolous, less passionate, less committed. You know, I've got a certain sympathy for your boss. Why *shouldn't* he publish stuff people want to read, instead of yet another frothing-mouthed cry of rage from yet another disadvantaged minority? I *hated* those bleak Melbourne bookshops full of surly, pinched-faced zealots shuffling down corridors stacked with envy, anger and hate.

KATE: You prefer Sydney bookshops? Filled with cookbooks.

COLIN: If people want cookbooks, let them have cookbooks.

KATE: I'm not devoting my life to improving the North Shore souffle!

COLIN: Of course not. You're going to keep trying to publish stuff that nobody wants to read.

KATE: I'm going to keep trying to publish books which prick the consciences of a few thousand people out there and make them aware that under the gloss of affluence there is *real* suffering. Did you know that rents are so high in this subtropical lotus land that all the women's hostels are overflowing, and five hundred women and their kids are being turned away every week? Families are out there sleeping on golf courses and in car wrecks?

COLIN: What do you want me to do? Go to my nearest golf course and redirect them here? What do your two thousand pricked consciences actually go and *do* when they've put down the book?

KATE: Eventually they change the consciousness of this nation. They make it a fairer place for everyone.

COLIN: Kate, the country isn't going to become fair because someone in a book says it should be. The unpalatable truth is that we're an egocentric species who care a lot about ourselves and our children, a little bit for our tribe, and not much at all for anyone else.

KATE: Where did you pick up that right-wing drivel?

COLIN: Kate, can you be honest with yourself for a change without *posing?* Whenever one of those ads comes on urging us to save starving children, we're shocked by the images of the emaciated kids, we look at each other and murmur "Must do something," but we don't even *note down the number.* But if our young Sam so much as whimpers in the night, we're instantly awake, bolt upright, staring at each other with fear in our eyes. Face up to this awful equation: one cut finger of Sam's equals more anguish than a thousand deaths in Ethiopia!

> *The logic hits home.*

KATE: All right. Most of us *are* selfish. We're taught to be.

COLIN: We aren't taught! No parent is *taught* to care more about their child than someone else's!

KATE: All right. We *are* selfish, but we can be taught to change. We can be taught to *care* about others. Sometimes the process is slow, and you don't think it's happening at all, but it is. We don't have eight-year-olds working in mine pits any more. Perhaps you hadn't noticed?

COLIN (*suddenly reflective*): No, we don't.

KATE: Things *can* change for the better, but I'm sure you're not convinced.

COLIN: I want to be convinced. I *hate* the thought that humanity is grasping and egocentric, but the evidence often seems overwhelming, and some of it comes from pretty close to home.

KATE: You mean me?

COLIN: No, I mean *me.*

> *Pause.*

KATE: I *am* getting tired of organizing this family, Colin. You're too self-obsessed to ever do your share, and I'm starting to feel very, very trapped. (*Exits.*)

COLIN (*to the audience*): That wasn't exactly music to my ears. I knew the dream behind that threat. A room in Glebe where she'd write short stories for women's anthologies published by McPhee Gribble. And they'd be about leaving a husband who was so thick he had to have shopping lists pinned to his jumpers and so right-wing he voted Labor. If our domestic harmony was precarious, it became even more so after Kate met Mike.

> *Mike enters the kitchen and reads the morning paper. He's wearing nothing except a towel around his waist. Kate enters wearing a dressing-gown and stares at him.*

KATE: Good morning. I'm Kate.

MIKE (*looks up and then down*): Hi.

KATE: I was going to pop my head in and say hello when I got home last night, but I thought I wouldn't interrupt. You, er, stayed overnight?

MIKE (*not looking up*): Raining. Couldn't get a cab.

KATE: You're both working here again today?

MIKE (*not looking up*): Going to work here from now on. Much more room.

KATE: Ah.

> *Kate looks at the paper Mike is reading. She has come downstairs to collect it.*

KATE: Anything interesting?

> *Mike looks up, puzzled.*

Anything interesting happen in the world overnight?

MIKE (*looking down*): No. Same old shit. Makes you wonder why you keep reading it.

> *Kate hopes this means he'll stop reading it, but it doesn't.*

KATE: Could you possibly leave the paper there when you've finished? I like to glance at the headlines before the children get up.

MIKE (*still reading*): Right.

> *Kate gets visibly irritated. She takes an electric jug and plugs it in, banging it down noisily.*

MIKE: Making coffee?

KATE: Yes.

MIKE: Could you pour me a weak one with no sugar?

KATE (*tersely*): Are you married, Mike?

MIKE: Have been. Twice.

KATE: But not now?

MIKE (*still reading*): Right. (*Pause.*) Present lady won't marry me.

> *Kate's look indicates that she finds this far from surprising.*

MIKE (*still reading*): *Richard Mahony's* collapsed.

KATE: Sorry?

MIKE: The movie Tony Klineberg's supposed to be directing. He's talking here as if it's all happening, but the money fell through three days ago.

KATE: Was it a film of the novel?

MIKE (*nodding*): Thought it would fold.

KATE: Wonderful novel.

MIKE: Screen play was shithouse. Actor mate of mine got me a copy.

KATE: The novel was wonderful.

MIKE: Screen play was shithouse. Doctor's marriage goes bad, he goes to the goldfields, gets gangrene and dies. Can't see the crowds queuing in Pitt street for that little number.

KATE: I don't think your synopsis quite does the book justice.

MIKE (*shrugging*): Screen play was a real downer.

KATE: What does your friend do?

MIKE (*looking up, puzzled*): What friend?

KATE: The woman you live with.

MIKE (*going back to the paper*): Not nearly enough.

KATE (*getting really irritated*): She's not working?

MIKE: Freelance P.R. Gets about one good job a month and usually stuffs it up.

KATE: Lacks experience?

MIKE: Lacks grey matter.

KATE: Does she mind you having such a low opinion of her?

MIKE: She's got her good points.

KATE: I'm glad to hear it.

MIKE: She's a woman, which is more than you can say for half the dragons around this town.

KATE: What exactly do you mean, Mike—"She's a woman?"

MIKE: Looks good. Wears nice clothes. Doesn't screech at you like a white cockatoo. Funny. Has the occasional tantrum, and she's so sexy she's dangerous.

KATE: That's your definition of a woman?

MIKE: Yep. And I'm sticking with it.

KATE: Don't you think it's a little bit limited?

MIKE: If some women want to be pile drivers, that's fine. As long as they don't expect me to get under 'em.

      Mike exits. Colin enters. Kate is not happy.

KATE: He's awful! I didn't believe that men like that still existed. What kind of woman would tolerate him?

COLIN: I can't begin to imagine. Some anemic little scrubber who enjoys being booted around, I suppose.

KATE: Why are you working with the man?

COLIN: I'm going to produce this script myself, and I need some help.

KATE: You're letting him *co-write* this script with you? What's he done?

COLIN: He's not co-writing. He's sitting there typing what I tell him.

KATE: His name will be on it as co-writer.

COLIN (*cutting in*): Everybody's going to know he didn't do anything. All he's done up to now is script-edit soapies.

KATE: So why are you working with him?

COLIN: He knows where to look for finance.

KATE: You said you were going to approach Malcolm Bennett. You've known Malcolm for years.

COLIN (*uneasy*): Mike gave me the confidence to realize I could produce my own scripts.

KATE: You've never had any complaints about Elaine up to now.

COLIN: Elaine *hated* this idea. Right?

KATE: She still would have done it.

COLIN: I don't want to work with someone who doesn't believe in what I'm doing. She can find someone else to make her rich.

KATE: Make her rich?

COLIN: Who's got that stunning harbor view? She has. Not me.

KATE: This city's getting to you already.

COLIN: I wouldn't mind a nice view. Is that so decadent?

KATE: You're working with Mike so you can buy yourself a nice view?

COLIN (*tensely*): I am perfectly aware of the fact that Mike is a buffoon, but he obeys orders, does what he's told and he's helping me get what I want.

KATE (*nodding*): A stunning harbor view.

COLIN: Creative control! Deciding who's cast. Deciding who directs. Making sure the script is shot as I wrote it. And if there *is* some money to be made, making sure I'm the one who gets it.

KATE: He's using you, Colin. Getting co-authorship of one of your scripts means he's going from nothing to something in one huge jump.

COLIN: Everyone in the business will know I wrote it all.

KATE: You think you're using him, but he's using you.

COLIN (*irritated*): I can look after myself.

> *Kate exits. Colin sits in an armchair and thinks. Mike enters and sits poised at the typewriter. Suddenly Colin bounds up out of his chair and starts pacing around waving a clenched fist as if he is threatening the gods of creativity with physical violence if they don't start the ideas flowing.*

COLIN: The trouble with this scene is that there's nothing at *stake*! Unless something's at stake you have no emotional undercurrent, and all you're left with is two people chatting. What's at *stake*?

MIKE (*dutifully repeating the magic litany*): What's at stake?

COLIN: Hold it a minute while I think this one through.

> *Colin returns to his armchair and to deep thought. Mike looks to the heavens as if to say, "How much more of this do I have to put up with?"*

MIKE (*to the audience*): I began to think I wasn't going to last the distance. My stomach was giving me hell. Every morning it'd flicker from yesterday's embers and by the end of the day I'd have your full fireball. I was taking three times as many tablets a day as I should've been but it had as much effect as pissing on a bushfire. (*To Colin.*) Just make a quick call.

> *Mike picks up the phone and dials.*

MIKE (*into the phone*) Bob? How about a drink? Six-thirty at the Admiral's Cup Bar. Heard about Terry's film? *Disaster*. Absolute disaster. Only took three thousand over the long weekend. (*He nods.*) Disaster. See you at six-thirty.

COLIN: Terry's film not doing well?

MIKE: Disaster.

Daniel Gerroll (Colin) and Dan Butler (Mike) in *Emerald City*

COLIN: Do you know what really amazes me about this industry, Mike? I've got the best track record on script in the country, and that phone never rings. Terry could've asked me to write that script, and I could've made it work. But he didn't. They never do.

MIKE (*to the audience*): If I'd've heard him whinge once more about why producers weren't lining up to plead for his services, I'd've perforated. The thing that amazed me about him was that he knew nothing about how the real world operated. The reason producers weren't flocking to him was that they had egos almost as big as his, and who would enjoy crawling on their bellies like I had to do? (*To Colin.*) I'll get some coffee. (*Leaves.*)

COLIN (*to the audience*): I watched Mike with the fascination of a zoologist who's found a new species. Port Jackson huckster. He kept ringing around an endless list of contacts, all male, and arranged meetings. The currency being exchanged at the meetings was failure. Other people's. It seemed crucial to Mike that everything failed. If there was a film due for release that seemed in any danger of being declared a success, Mike and his drinking mates would expend enormous amounts of mental energy cracking its pretentions like a walnut. I had an image of Mike as a kind of filmic gridiron player, waiting with the ball until all of his opponents were lying bloody and prostrate so that he could wend his way through them to the touchline. I found this behavior amusing and reassuring. Other people's failures are always re-assuring, but the frantic energy and effort he put into his networking of failure was worrying.

> *Kate comes home looking upset.*

What's wrong?

KATE: I'm so angry I can't even talk about it. The children are all scream-ing for food, I suppose?

COLIN: Don't worry about that. We'll phone up for some pizzas. He's not going to publish?

KATE: I just wanted to grab that hollow little man by his collar and hurl him down that sparkling blue harbor he's paid seventy thousand dollars a year to gaze at. I know you can't understand my passion about that book—

COLIN (*interrupting*): I can. I'm not totally insensitive.

KATE: I was nearly in tears today. I'm going to have to resign.

COLIN: Don't do that. He'll change his mind.

KATE: No, he won't. He's gutless. And he just doesn't care.

> *Kate moves across and flops into a chair. There's a pause.*

I didn't mean to hurt you about your work. You write beautifully. You can't be expected to write with her power and passion when you've led such a cos-seted life. (*Sees Colin's look.*) What's wrong?

COLIN: That's a bit like saying, "I'm sorry I said you were indescribably ugly. I've just seen your parents and I understand why."

> *Mike returns with the coffee. Kate see him, gives a frozen smile, and leaves.*

MIKE: What's wrong with Kate?

COLIN: Her boss won't let her publish a book she thinks is crucial.

MIKE: Making things a bit difficult domestically?

COLIN: I agree with her. I think it should be published too.

MIKE: What's it about?

COLIN: A black girl trying to break out of the urban poverty cycle.

> *Colin picks up some pages Mike has typed and walks away from the desk as he scrutinizes them.*

MIKE: What's the name of Kate's boss?

COLIN: Ian Wall. He reckons, "blacks don't sell books."

> *Mike searches through the teledex and locates the name. Colin engrossed in the script, doesn't notice.*

MIKE: What's the writer's name?

COLIN: Kathy Mitchell.

> *Mike starts dialing. Colin barely notices.*

MIKE: Ian?

> *Colin looks up, frowning, but still isn't sure what Mike's doing.*

Ian, there's a rumour going around that you won't publish Kathy's book? (*Pause.*) Kathy Mitchell. (*Pause.*) Don't worry about who's speaking, mate, just listen to what I'm telling you. A lot of people reckon it's one of the most important books ever written on the black people's problems, and they're bloody mad. They've heard the reason you won't print it is that you said, "blacks don't sell books"—and they reckon that's a pretty racist statement. (*Pause.*) Well, that's how they feel it comes across, and they're so bloody mad that they're going to give you twenty-four hours, and then they're going to start putting up tents around your building and calling the media in. (*Hangs up.*)

COLIN (*frowning*): Jesus, Mike! What in the hell do you think you're doing?

MIKE (*reassuringly*): Blow torch to the belly.

> Colin looks anything but reassured. He sits there wondering how in the hell he is going to explain this to Kate. Mike exits. Later: Colin still sits in an armchair. Kate enters, smiling and excited.

KATE: You won't believe what happened.

COLIN (*tensely*): What?

KATE: Ian got a call from some black guerrilla group who threatened to bomb the building unless he published. Should have seen the panic. It was wonderful.

COLIN (*worriedly*): Did he call the police?

KATE: God, no. He's *terrified* of bad publicity.

COLIN: He's going to publish?

KATE (*nodding*): Three thousand copies. What's your news?

COLIN: I forgot the dishwashing powder and the broccoli.

KATE: I'm sorry I've been so rotten lately. I just started feeling that nothing was ever going to go right again.

COLIN: And the dried apricots. They were on the list, but I made that fatal mistake of going straight to the breakfast foods. Even when I was doing it I kept saying to myself, "Remember the apricots, remember the apricots," but I didn't.

KATE: Stop it. Sorry I've been so down on the kids. When you're having a bad time at work everything can seem pretty black.

COLIN: No, you're quite right. The kids are appalling. I tried to talk to Penny about her disco going and the like, but the look of pity and contempt on her face at my presumption that I might have any wisdom to offer her stopped me right in my tracks.

KATE: Depressing, isn't it?

COLIN: I spend most of my time taking messages from girls with names like Manon, Melissa and Foxglove. They chat on for hours with each other about which boys are likely to be at what bars when, who's been dumped by who and who's therefore available, who got with who at which party and who doesn't know about it yet, and won't there be hell to pay when they do. What does "getting with" mean?

KATE: Why?

COLIN: Our daughter seems to be one of the most frequent "getters with" in town.

KATE: It's just petting. Surprising as it may seem, they're all still virgins.

COLIN: They're the most sophisticated bunch of virgins I've ever heard.

KATE: It's all very innocent. Don't get depressed.

COLIN: The only thing I'm depressed about is that it all sounds so bloody interesting. When's the last time we leapt to the phone to hear who had just got with what? We're totally irrelevant to our daughter's life because as far as she's concerned we're middle-aged stodges whose life is effectively over. And maybe she's right. Maybe all the excitement happens up front.

KATE: You're morbid tonight.

COLIN: Well don't you ever get struck with a sense of *unfairness*? We're supposed to be professionals at the peak of our powers leading highly interesting lives, and our daughter is having all the fun!

KATE (*wistfully*): Yes. We can have sex every night, but she gets ten times the excitement we do thinking about a session of heavy petting with some spotted adolescent.

COLIN (*hurt*): I didn't realise it was that bad.

KATE: It happens in every marriage.

COLIN (*defensively*): It's not exactly cosmic for me either. I watched a re-run of *Ryan's Daughter* the other night and had to search my memory to work out what was happening when Sarah Miles got under the stiff-legged Englishman and started making those plaintive little yelps.

KATE: She was acting. I can't.

   Kate exits. Mike enters and they have a strategy session.

COLIN: He's a typical merchant banker. On the one hand he's urbane, arrogant, cynical, vain and ruthlessly determined to screw you for the last quarter of one percent ...

MIKE: And on the other hand?

COLIN (*thinking*): I don't think there is another hand.

MIKE: Can't wait to meet him.

COLIN: Are you O.K.?

MIKE (*swallowing pills*): Stomach's playing up a bit.

COLIN: Don't worry. It's a good project, and he'll go for it. Don't show him you're nervous. Speak to him as if he's a drinking mate.

   As he enters, Colin and Mike confront Malcolm, an impeccably dressed, urbane, arrogant, cynical and vain merchant banker. Mike is nervous and out of his class.

COLIN: Congratulations on your election.

MALCOLM: You read that embarrassing little item did you? I've no idea how the press picked it up. (*Turns to Mike.*) For my sins I was elected President of The Friends of the Opera.

MIKE: Needs all the friends it can get.

MALCOLM (*generously trying to cover for Mike's gaffe*): Don't be too harsh. At its best moments it can be sublime.

MIKE: I could bore people for a fraction of the cost, but every man to his poison.

COLIN (*trying to recover the situation*): Have you had time to read the script, Malcolm?

MALCOLM: I read the synopsis. Colin, I've got to be honest with you. I don't think it's our sort of project.

COLIN (*stunned*): How can you say that when you've only read the synopsis?

MALCOLM: Colin, how do you expect me to get my investors excited about men who sat and watched coasts?

COLIN (*coldly*): If you read the script, I think you'll find they did a lot more than that.

MALCOLM: Colin, I need a concept that's exciting. Exciting enough to hook investors and convince them that the project will sell here and overseas.

COLIN: This *is* exciting. How a handful of men saved Australia!

MALCOLM: Colin, no one under fifty knows Australia was even threatened, and the rest of the world hardly knows Australia exists. Believe me, after spending half my life boarding and leaving international flights I've come to the conclusion that the only thing the nations of the world have in common is a profound indifference to anything that's ever happened here.

COLIN: So you're saying you'll only underwrite projects that have nothing to do with this country or its history?

MALCOLM: I've got to be absolutely honest. I can't even *think* the word "Coastwatchers" without yawning.

COLIN (*angrily, passionately*): This is a *real* story about *real* people who risked their necks for years at a time so that you and I could be here in this room today! You can't dismiss it without reading the script.

MALCOLM: Look, Colin, it could be the best-written script in the world, but unless it smells exciting it's no use to us.

COLIN: Malcolm, all my scripts have made money for you in the past. You owe it to me to *read* it.

MALCOLM: All right, I'll read it.

COLIN: Sit down and read it now.

MALCOLM: Colin, I've got appointments all afternoon.

COLIN: Malcolm, I spent six months of my life writing this. The least you can do is spend two hours reading it!

MALCOLM: I'll read it. I'll read it tonight and phone you in the morning. (*Exits.*)

MIKE (*to the audience*): Malcolm was right. The only people who would ever find the concept wildly exciting were the surviving Coastwatchers, which gave us a guaranteed audience of three, but we finally got the money. It was the only way Malcolm could get Colin off his back.

COLIN (*to the audience*): The production and shoot were hellish. Mike was useless. He talked big but knew *nothing*. In a single day we lost our director, art director and cinematographer when he insisted that the opening sequence feature a slow-motion close-up of a Caucasian head being severed by a Samurai sword, leaving newly exposed arteries to pump red blood into white titles. We had to get a line producer in to pick up the pieces two days before the cameras rolled. I turned grey, Mike threw up a lot, but finally, miraculously, it was in the can.

MIKE (*to the audience*): The shoot went well. Our director walked out on us, but it was just as well. He had no visual flair. Colin panicked every time there was the slightest hiccup, but I held things together, and we finished right on schedule.

COLIN (*to the audience*): We finished the mix and sent out the tapes to the critics.

MIKE (*to the audience*): The critics loved it. I knew we had a disaster on our hands. When critics say "sensitive" and "lyrical," the public reads "slow" and "arty." Colin ran around with the crits in his hands beaming at everyone. I nodded politely and waited for the ratings.

> *Kate enters, and they wait for the ratings at Mike's place. It's evening, and there's been some drinking. Kate, in particular, is showing the effects.*

COLIN (*tensely*): Ring them again.

MIKE: They said they'd ring as soon as the figures came through.

KATE: I don't know what you're worried about. It was *wonderful*. Everyone in the country would've been watching. I cried.

COLIN: You always cry.

KATE: When that young boy—that *beautiful* young boy—What was his name?

COLIN: Gary Denton.

KATE: *Gary Denton*. Beautiful golden hair. I would like a *very* deep conversation with that young man.

COLIN: He can barely talk.

KATE: When he died, the tears just flowed. (*She looks around.*) How long have you had this place, Mike?

MIKE: Too long.

KATE (*condescending*): It's charming. Little stairways here and little alcoves there. It's remarkable how *little* space you really need. When we were in China we saw whole families of peasants living in a place *half* the size of this, didn't we, Colin? (*Looking up.*) I don't know whether khaki's right for the ceiling, though.

MIKE: It used to be white, but we left the window open.

KATE (*laughs loudly*): You're very funny, Mike.

COLIN: Helen says I'm a walking joke.

> *The phone rings. Mike darts across to it. He listens. He nods. His face shows no emotion. He puts down the phone.*

MIKE: Thirteen.

COLIN (*alarmed*): That can't be right. Are you sure they didn't say thirty?

MIKE: Thirteen. Fourteen in Melbourne.

KATE: Thirteen?

COLIN (*tersely, to Kate*): Thirteen percent of sets tuned to us.

MIKE: Disaster.

COLIN: It has to be wrong. They only sample a few hundred.

MIKE: A few thousand.

COLIN: The promotion was hopeless.

KATE: To hell with the ratings. We all know what gets ratings. Trash.

COLIN (*irritated*): Kate, in this business if you don't get ratings you're dead. You can't sell your next project.

MIKE: We'll sell it.

KATE (*to Colin*): What next project?

COLIN: I don't want to talk about it.

KATE: You said you were going to do the Sanzari film with Elaine.

COLIN: Kate, I've started producing my own work, and I'm not about to take three steps back!

KATE: What's this next project?

COLIN (*gesticulating*): For Christ's sake, we've just had a catastrophic failure. I'm not in the mood to talk about what I might or might not be doing next!

KATE: It's not a failure. It was excellent.

COLIN: Nobody watched!

KATE: What's this next project?

COLIN: Kate, we've just scored a thirteen! I don't want to talk about it.

> *He turns away. Kate glares at him. Mike tries to defuse the tension.*

MIKE (*to Kate*): Colin and I have been knocking around some pretty exciting ideas.

KATE: Such as?

COLIN (*agitated*): I don't want to discuss it. I don't even know if I'll be doing anything at all after this. I might pack the whole game in and go back to teaching!

KATE (*to Mike*): Ideas for what? More mini-series?

MIKE: Long-running series.

KATE (*frowning*): What do you mean? Something like *Dallas*?

MIKE: Field's wide open for a big international hit. Could make millions.

KATE: Television series are trash!

COLIN: It's barely got to discussion stage!

KATE: You're going to spend the rest of your life writing soap opera?

COLIN: Not writing, producing! And it wouldn't be trash!

KATE: Name me the series that isn't.

MIKE: If we get a U.S. sale we could make millions.

KATE (*to Colin*): Since when have you been interested in making millions?

COLIN: What's wrong with making money?

KATE: I think it's very sad.

COLIN: What?

KATE: You came to Sydney an artist, and you're turning into a businessman.

COLIN: We just made art and nobody watched.

KATE: I think it's very sad.

COLIN: If being an artist means that you have to starve, then I don't want to be an artist!

> *He walks away, and there's an awkward silence. Helen enters the room behind them.*

HELEN: Hi there. Sorry I'm late.

MIKE: Hi, honey. This is Colin and Kate.

HELEN: Hi. Doesn't exactly seem to be a celebration going on in here. What were the figures?

MIKE: Thirteen.

HELEN: Oh migod. The series wasn't *that* bad?

KATE (*incensed*): The series was *good. Too* good.

HELEN (*embarrassed*): I meant in commercial terms. It wasn't very commercial.

KATE: Who cares? *I* am publishing a book that will be lucky to sell a few thousand copies, but it's an important and passionate book, and its long term influence will be enormous!

HELEN (*not aggressively*): You're lucky. You still get your weekly pay check no matter how many it sells. Mike and Colin only get paid if they get results.

KATE: Colin *has* been getting results. Not enough to make him a millionaire, but until *very* recently he never wanted that. What good is money? What can you do with it? Buy a house with a better view? Go for another trip to Venice?

HELEN (*without malice*): I'd like to go on my first trip to Venice. I wouldn't say no to a house with a better view, either. All we see out of our bedroom window is a twenty-foot-high baby wearing Dri Tots.

KATE (*to the audience*): She was *exactly* what I expected. A carefully packaged and presented material girl of the eighties. A blow-waved, brittle dolly bird. Totally self-obsessed and convinced that the trinkets of affluence were the ultimate prizes of life.

COLIN (*to the audience*): My first reaction was that this couldn't be right. This vision—this ravishing, mind-scrambling beauty can't belong to Mike. The gods are unjust, but surely not *that* unjust. I flattered myself that I was a progressive male, totally opposed to reducing women to sex objects, but Helen was a walking male fantasy. I focused all my powers of imagination on what she'd look like without clothes on, felt ashamed of myself and by way of compensation fell desperately in love.

KATE (*to Colin*): Well, you're going to have to decide.

COLIN (*snapping out of it*): Decide what?

KATE: Between art and money.

COLIN: Surely they're not always mutually excited—sorry, mutually exclusive. Why did I say excited?

HELEN (*to the audience*): Because he was. By me. I liked that, and I liked the fact that he was subtle about it too. He didn't stare at my tits as if they were choc chip ice creams like most of them do. I found him very attractive and thought that if I could ever shake myself free of brainless for a weekend or two it could be exciting. I wouldn't've felt the least bit guilty about his wife either. What a dragon. I thought that if that's what Melbourne does to you, thank God I've never been there. (*To Colin*) Shakespeare.

KATE: Shakespeare what?

HELEN: He was an artist who made money.

KATE: Shakespeare made money? Surely not.

HELEN: He owned five houses. He died a wealthy man.

MIKE (*to the audience*): The only trouble with that broad of mine is that she never knows when to shut up. That bloody wife of Colin's was going to put the hard word on Colin to ditch me as soon as possible, and Helen makes the situation worse by starting to pick a fight. After putting all that hard slog into the *Coastwatcher* fiasco, there was no way I was going to let go until we got ourselves a smash hit. After that he could write art until his balls dropped off.

KATE: If Shakespeare were alive today, I'm sure he wouldn't be writing *Dallas*.

Mike goes into contortions and belches.

Is something wrong?

MIKE: Stomach's playing up again.

COLIN: We'd better go.

MIKE: Sorry about this. Like a tame tiger snake. Never know when it's going to strike.

COLIN: Thanks for your hospitality.

MIKE: Only wish the news had've been better.

HELEN: Bye, Kate. Bye, Colin.

COLIN (*to the audience*): I felt the deft touch of her fingers and the breath of her voice in my ear. I felt chemistry between us that would make Sarah Miles and her stiff-legged lover look jaded.

> *Mike and Helen exit. Colin and Kate stand outside the house. Colin tries to hail a cab.*

KATE: I hope I never have to meet those two socially again.

COLIN: They're not that bad.

> *Colin looks at Kate, grits his teeth, misses another taxi and stares straight ahead.*

KATE: Colin, I'm shocked. Really shocked.

COLIN (*truculently*): At what?

KATE: I'm shocked that you're going into a continuing relationship with that man and talking seriously about producing soap opera.

COLIN: We're not going to produce soap opera.

KATE: Colin, what's happening to you?

COLIN (*suddenly passionate*): What's happening is that I'm getting older and I'm starting to have the nightmare that every writer gets: ending my life as a deadbeat, flogging scripts to producers who don't want 'em. And it's not paranoia. It happens. Henry Lawson was sent to gaol because he couldn't pay his debts. Ended his life begging in the streets of Sydney and did anyone care? Not one. He'd be really amused today if he could see his head on our ten dollar note. Cultural hero—kids study him in schools—ended his life as a joke and nobody cared! It's not going to happen to me. I'm sick of sending scripts off and waiting patiently for the call that never comes and ringing back and ringing back and finally getting someone on the other end of the phone who says, "Sorry," they haven't had time to read it yet. Being a writer is one of the most humiliating professions on earth, and I'm sick to death of it. I want to be a producer, and I want to have money, and I want to have power. I want to sit in my office with people phoning *me*. I want to sit back and tell my secretary that I'm in conference and can't be disturbed and that I'll ring back, then make sure I never do. I want scripts to come to *me*, and *I'll* make the judgements about whether they're good, bad or indifferent. *I'll* be the one with the blue pencil who rips other people's scripts apart, complains about the banality and predictability, groans at the cliched dialogue, mutters, "There must be some good writers *somewhere*." Why *shouldn't* I have money and power? Why *shouldn't* I have a great big house on the waterfront like all the rest of the coked-out mumblers out there masquerading as producers? I want *you* to stop telling people what *I* want out of *my* life, because you are *wrong*! I don't want to make art films or films with a message, I want to produce a product that entertains, and I want it to make me awesomely powerful and fabulously rich!

> *Curtain.*

ACT II

Kate and Colin arrive home.

KATE: Awesomely powerful and fabulously rich?

COLIN: Yes.

KATE: Colin, I can understand your anxieties, but this isn't the way to handle them. You mustn't compromise your integrity.

COLIN: Of course, you've never compromised your integrity, have you?

KATE: No.

COLIN: No. Your boss told me he was enormously pleased with the ethnic cookbook series you've initiated.

KATE (*embarrassed*): That's just to give me commercial credibility, so I can do the books I really want to, like *Black Rage*.

COLIN: He told me that the Southeast Asian section breaks new ground. What have you got? Fretilin-style snacks for eating on the run? And which one of us insisted on ferreting our daughter through a seventy-year waiting list into the most exclusive girls school in Sydney? Where all her friends live within half a mile of each other in Bellevue Hill, and where she's already planning to graduate at twenty-one, marry at twenty-seven, have two daughters named Francesca and Chloe, divorce her husband at thirty-two and recommence her stockbroking career.

KATE: We couldn't send her to a state school. They're appalling. The system has almost broken down.

COLIN: The state school system is not *nearly* as appalling as guilty socialist mothers who know they shouldn't be stuffing their kids into top private schools would like to believe.

KATE: You went along with it. You came and grovelled in front of the headmistress.

COLIN: I wasn't as low on my belly as you were. (*Imitating Kate.*) "I've been *amazed*, simply *amazed* at how *many* people have told me how *excellent* this school is." Grovel, grovel. "I'd be so *happy* if I thought my daughter was being educated in such a *stimulating* intellectual environment."

KATE: That's really unfair, Colin. It *is* an excellent school academically, and if it has got her thinking in terms of career independence—

COLIN (*interrupting*): Career independence? It's turning her into a predatory neo-feminist socialite. She and her friends know the name of every eligible private school boy in Sydney. They swap descriptions and wealth assessments of ones they've never even met. Australia a classless society? There's selective breeding out there in the Eastern suburbs that would make our pedigree stud farms look like amateurs, and our daughter is in the thick of it. Do you know that she hasn't met one boy who goes to a state school since she came to Sydney? I said to her, "Do you realize that *I* went to a state school? If I was your age you would never have met me." She said, "Good."

KATE: If you feel so strongly about it, take her out of there.

COLIN: She's settled in. She likes it.

KATE: And you like it too, if the truth be known. State school boy's daughter gets to top private school.

COLIN: I am *riddled* with compromise and ambivalence. At least I admit it.

KATE: My primary purpose in sending her there was to give her a good education!

COLIN: You rage at the fact that thousands in this city are homeless, yet you send your daughter to be educated in an atmosphere that'll teach her not to give a damn!

KATE (*angrily, defensively*): Take her out of there, then.

COLIN: *You* take her out. You're supposed to be the one with the social conscience!

KATE: She'll see through all that phony Bellevue Hill stuff.

COLIN: You want her there because it's a top private school too. You're one of that vast army of fake altruists who condemn the filthy rich and mouth platitudes about the sufferings of the underprivileged, then go along and collect their fat paychecks every week and never do a damn thing about it. Well, I've stopped pretending. I'm going to be a producer and become enormously powerful and *disgustingly* rich!

KATE: If I wasn't so appalled, I'd laugh.

COLIN: Would you? Why?

KATE: You can't even do the shopping without forgetting half of it.

COLIN: What's that got to do with it?

KATE: You forget my birthday, the kids' birthdays and every second appointment you make.

COLIN: Producing involves more than attention to petty detail.

KATE: That's got to be *part* of it, surely?

COLIN: It's picking the right projects. Knowing scripts.

KATE: The kids have got to repeat every question they ask you because you're off in another world. Our credit cards are always bouncing, and we're always about to lose either the telephone, electricity or the gas because you never remember to pay. You had to hire a line producer on *Coastwatchers* to get you out of the mess.

COLIN: It was just inexperience.

KATE: That fiasco over the extras—

COLIN (*interrupting*): I wrote "*Forty* Japanese burst from the clearing." Mike got it wrong.

KATE: Most producers would have spotted the error before a chartered Jumbo with four hundred extras arrived from Tokyo. Colin, you just haven't got the right temperament to be a producer. You turned grey during

Coastwatchers and I couldn't sleep at night because you were rotating like a corkscrew, shouting abuse at Mike in your sleep.

COLIN: *He's* the reason we had to get a line producer. Never did a bloody thing.

KATE: And you're going to work with him again?

COLIN: He'd better shape up this time, and he knows it.

KATE: You've spoken to him?

COLIN: He knows it. He knows I'm not happy.

KATE: Colin, *I* know when you're not happy. You tap your right foot and clench your right fist, but it's taken eighteen years of marriage to spot the signals. Mike is so insensitive he'd be hard-put to spot the irritation on the face of a charging tiger.

COLIN: He *knows* I'm not happy.

KATE: Colin, I wish you'd look at the situation honestly. Mike's a down-market hustler, and you're a writer. You might end up begging on the streets of Sydney, but it's a chance you're going to have to take. You're absent-minded and vague because your brain's always away somewhere else working on plotlines and dialogue. You wake up at night and tell me stories you've dreamt. You mustn't try and be what you're not.

COLIN: Stick in the same old rut. Let yourself be kicked from pillar to post.

KATE: You can't do something that's not in your nature.

COLIN: I'll decide what my nature is, not you.

KATE: A producer has to be ruthless.

COLIN: I can be ruthless. I'm going to be the most ruthless bastard in this city.

KATE: Colin, you're about as ruthless as a toothless old pussycat.

COLIN: You're wrong. I'm going to be so ruthless you wouldn't believe.

> *Kate exits and Mike enters. Colin sits and listens to Mike. They're at Mike's place.*

MIKE: Right. There's these two undercover cops in Darlinghurst. Prositutes, drugs—all of that sort of stuff going on around them. These aren't your typical cops. These guys are young, spunky, wear the latest fashions, and the art direction gives us everything in pastel shades, and there's a lot of action and car chases and a rock soundtrack.

COLIN: You're three years too late. That's *Miami Vice*.

MIKE: No, it's different.

COLIN: How's it different?

> *Pause.*

MIKE: Right. There's this career woman divorced with a young kid. She gets someone in to housekeep and he's a guy and *he's* got a kid—

COLIN (*interrupting*): Where'd that come from?

MIKE: There's a show a bit similar in the States, but this'll be set in Australia.

COLIN: Mike, we have to do something *original*.

MIKE: There's nothing new under the sun, mate. All we can do is add a new twist.

COLIN: I don't believe that.

MIKE: A series about a D.J.

COLIN: Sitting there playing records?

MIKE: Things are always happening. A gang of Arab terrorists fly in and take over the station.

COLIN: Why would Arab terrorists endure the horrors of a twenty-four-hour Qantas flight to take over 2GB?

MIKE (*ignoring the jibe*): They take the D.J. hostage and start making demands.

COLIN: No more talk back? Get rid of John Laws?

MIKE (*tensely, under pressure*): Release of Arab prisoners.

COLIN: Why are we holding Arab prisoners?

MIKE: We can plug the holes in the plot later. It's the concept.

COLIN: The concept's lousy. We've got to come up with an idea that's brilliantly original and commercial. We can't afford another lemon like *Coastwatchers*.

> *Helen enters the room looking tantalizingly sexy. Colin tries to disguise his interest, but finds it hard not to stare at her.*

HELEN: Working late?

MIKE: Two coffees, love.

HELEN (*to Colin*): Black with one sugar?

COLIN: Please.

HELEN: No, it's not. It's black with *no* sugar isn't it?

COLIN: It is, actually. I wasn't thinking.

HELEN: Head like a sieve. I can never remember things like that.

COLIN: Neither can I.

HELEN: Names too. I'm hopeless with names.

COLIN: So am I. Introductions are a nightmare.

HELEN: Really? You always look so assured and confident.

COLIN: Me?

HELEN: When you get one of your awards or something on T.V.

COLIN: Shaking like a jelly.

HELEN: There's hope for me.

MIKE: How'd it go today?

HELEN: Disaster.

> *She turns to Colin to explain. During the explanation Colin doesn't take in one word. He watches the expressions on her face, transfixed.*

I was hired to organize the publicity for Rod Miki—heard of him?

> *Colin shakes his head.*

Neither had anyone else. He's a new-wave comedian from L.A. who's about as funny as a funeral.

COLIN: You had a problem.

HELEN: Did I ever. By the time I picked him up he'd finished his first bottle of whiskey; he tried to get my top off, I hit the car in front, and when we got to the first interview he lay on the floor and screamed at the journo to jump on him.

COLIN: Jump on him?

HELEN: He said she'd only come to put the boot in—why didn't she do the job properly?

COLIN: Jesus!

HELEN: What was I supposed to do? He was uncontrollable.

MIKE: You should have told him that the journo thought he was a genius.

HELEN: It's a bit hard to spread disinformation when you're being raped in peak-hour traffic in George Street.

MIKE: If you didn't wear gear that opened you for public inspection, you wouldn't have that sort of problem. Two coffees! Do you think you can do that without getting yourself raped?

> Helen glares, turns and goes.

COLIN (*to the audience*): Why did she put up with it? She deserved someone sensitive, intelligent—someone who sat and marvelled as the passions passed like summer storms across the face of her beauty. She deserved me, but I didn't know how to make the offer. In the past I'd been so inept and shy that I always waited for the woman to give the first sign in case I made a fool of myself, but this time it was too urgent for that. I didn't want to wreck my marriage, I just wanted a heady, passionate affair, but if I made an approach and she refused, she'd be sure to tell Mike, and if she accepted, knowing my luck, Kate would find out and be off to her room in Glebe like a flash. I didn't know what to do, but I knew I had to do something. Every time she spoke, every time she did *anything* including standing stock still, I was overpoweringly attracted.

> Colin exits. Elaine enters at a cocktail party. Chatter and the clinking of glasses can be heard. Elaine stands by herself with a glass in her hand. Mike approaches her.

MIKE: Mike McCord.

ELAINE (*frostily*): Oh, yes. You're working with Colin.

MIKE (*nodding*): Getting a few projects together.

ELAINE: Good.

MIKE: You?

ELAINE: Getting a few projects together too.

MIKE: Good.

> There is an awkward pause. Elaine doesn't want to continue the conversation, but Mike stands there doggedly.

MIKE: Ned Wiseman's film's a disaster.

ELAINE (*interested despite herself*): Really?

MIKE: They put it in the third house at the Hoyts complex and it only did seven thousand.

ELAINE: The first day?

MIKE: The first week.

ELAINE: That's a disaster.

MIKE: Total. Have you seen it?

ELAINE: Bad?

MIKE: A character says, "I don't know why we're doing this," and the audience yells, "Neither do we."

ELAINE (*trying to hide her glee*): How sad for Ned. I quite liked *Coastwatchers*.

MIKE: Could have been better.

ELAINE: It lacked momentum.

MIKE (*nodding*): Right.

ELAINE: Second half was a little better.

MIKE (*nodding*): A lot of that was mine.

ELAINE: You wrote the second half?

MIKE: We were both still in on it, but Colin ran out of steam.

ELAINE: The second half was quite strong. Emotionally.

MIKE: Had to fight for that. Emotion embarrasses Colin.

ELAINE: Yes, it does, doesn't it?

MIKE: Prefers things clinical and distant. With me it's emotion, emotion, emotion all the way. Colin's a bit cold.

ELAINE: As a person?

MIKE (*nodding*): Never seems to get stirred up by anything.

ELAINE: No, he doesn't.

MIKE: Shows up in his writing.

ELAINE: I've never thought of it like that, but you could be right. The second half was a lot stronger emotionally.

MIKE (*shrugging, taking credit*): Well, if you don't know when to put the accelerator down, you shouldn't be driving the car. Whenever I write a scene I ask myself one simple question: "What's at stake? Who stands to lose, who stands to gain?" Unless something's at stake, all you've got is two people chatting.

ELAINE: That makes a lot of sense, Ian.

MIKE: Mike.

ELAINE: Sorry. Mike.

MIKE: Those films you made with Colin. How much of the horsepower and the emotion came from you?

ELAINE: An enormous amount. An enormous amount. You can't skirt around anguish and you can't skirt around pain, and I made him take back those scripts and rewrite and rewrite until we got it.

MIKE: It shows.

ELAINE: Not that he's ever thanked me for it. I'm not denying that he's a very talented writer, but I had to ride shotgun over him to ensure we felt something.

MIKE: It shows.

ELAINE: Not that he ever thanked me for it. Did you ever see *Days of Wine and Whitlam*?

MIKE (*nodding*): Good movie.

ELAINE: Do you remember how big Stewart Egan was then? International rock star—every producer in the country offering him roles and every one of them being turned down flat. I was with him *seventeen* times before he agreed to do it. *Seventeen* times, and he finally signed. It *made* that film and it *made* Colin. Now, can you believe this? Without a word of warning, Colin turned on me last year and launched an *incredible* tirade about how I'd compromised the film because Egan was a rock star. Can you believe that? Can you believe that?

MIKE (*shifting uneasily*): Turned on you?

ELAINE (*gritting her teeth*): I said to myself, "You ungrateful *swine*. You ungrateful bloody *swine*." And then he had the gall to tell me Scranton was the wrong choice of director.

MIKE (*uneasily*): Really.

ELAINE (*gritting her teeth*): I thought to myself, "You conceited young swine. You were damn lucky to get him. Damn lucky to get him."

MIKE: Scranton names his own price in Hollywood these days.

ELAINE: I thought to myself, "Let's see you have the guts to land in Los Angeles without a penny and make it to the top like Scranton." It took years to talk Colin into coming as far as Sydney.

MIKE: Perhaps he knows he wouldn't make it over there.

ELAINE: Exactly.

MIKE: If there's one thing Hollywood demands, it's emotion.

ELAINE (*grudgingly*): He's got talent.

MIKE: Sure.

ELAINE: But severe limitations.

MIKE: Yep.

ELAINE (*looks slightly ashamed of herself for having said so much*): Must go and meet this director. What is he, Yugoslav?

MIKE: Pole. Don't bother.

ELAINE: You've seen his film?

Mike nods.

A little slow?

MIKE (*nodding*): Starts at a crawl and gallops to a standstill.

ELAINE (*smiles, turns to go away, then turns back*): Are you and Colin working on your projects full-time, or do you have some time to spare?

MIKE: Always got time to spare if the project's good.

ELAINE: I've got a *very* good project. I should talk to you about it.

MIKE: I'll give you a ring.

Elaine exits.

(*To the audience*): I'd worked out by this time that collaborating with Colin was leading nowhere. He didn't have a gut feel for the commercial and never would. I had my doubts about Elaine too. Pompous old chook, with more venom than the reptile house at the zoo, but she still had a reputation around the traps, and when the word got round that I was working on one of her projects, the *real* offers would start coming in.

Mike exits. Colin speaks to Helen in another corner of the room. He's consumed with desire and trying desperately to conceal it.

Gates McFadden (Kate), Daniel Gerroll (Colin), Dan Butler (Mike, holding glass) and Alice Haining (Helen) in a scene from *Emerald City*

COLIN: I don't normally come to these things.

HELEN: I have to. I'm organizing the P.R. for this guy.

COLIN: Must be difficult to crank yourself up into a state of enthusiasm if you don't really feel it.

HELEN: Can be, but this guy's really nice. Have you met him?

COLIN: I haven't seen his film yet, so I'm too embarrassed.

HELEN: It's really good. I know I'm being paid to say that, but it really is.

COLIN: I must see it.

HELEN (*nodding*): It's about this guy who loves his wife like crazy—even though she's a bit off, behaviorwise. Manic depressive or something. She falls in love with a truck driver and goes off with him and feels really guilty about it, but it's compulsive, and she can't really help herself—you know?

COLIN (*nodding*): Right.

HELEN: The husband is *absolutely* devastated. There's this one scene that would have to be one of the most moving scenes I've ever seen on film.

    Colin nods.

The husband just sits there crying for two minutes, and the camera doesn't move. I sat there bawling my eyes out. Can you imagine an Australian writer or director having the guts to do anything as sensitive as that?

COLIN (*melancholy*): If an Australian writer scripted something like that it just wouldn't get made. The distributors and merchant bankers and network execs who run this industry wouldn't bother to read the script. All they want is money, lust, power, crime, fashion, intrigue, murder, jewelry and crocodiles.

HELEN: I know. I feel disloyal saying it, but I hate some of the Australian product I've had to promote.

COLIN: I hate it too, but Mike and I are writing one to exactly the same formula. It's fine for the Poles. They don't have to face commercial pressures.

HELEN: They have to face other kinds. The Ministry of Culture watches this guy like a hawk. He nearly went to prison after his last film because his main character was a corrupt party official.

COLIN: Really?

HELEN: Colin, I'm going to say something to you I shouldn't say.

COLIN: Please do.

HELEN: I don't think your partnership with Mike is good for either of you.

COLIN: Why not?

HELEN: Mike's at home with power, lust, murder and crocodiles and I'm not knocking him for it. We all have to earn a living. People in glass houses. But occasionally, when I've seen a film like that, I wish I lived in a better world where I could say what I felt and mean what I say, and you can write films like that, and I think you should.

COLIN: Yes, I should. And you should be doing something better than selling people and products you don't believe in.

HELEN: Yes, I should.

COLIN: I have to say this, and I don't care how corny it sounds. You are one of the most beautiful women I have ever seen.

Helen looks into his eyes. Colin becomes nervous, manic.

(*Talking rapidly*): When you first walked into the room, I just stood there dumbstruck. Absolutely dumbstruck. You must have noticed.

HELEN: I did sense there was an extraordinary affinity between us. Right from the start.

COLIN: There was. An *extraordinary* affinity. And all I did was stand there, mouth agape. Instead of trusting the feeling that you were feeling what I was feeling, I began feeling that I might be wrong. Why is it that at the moment we should throw caution to the wind, we're struck deaf mute with panic?

HELEN: Do you want to stay here long?

COLIN: I suppose you have to stick around here until the end?

HELEN: I should, but to hell with it. Let's go and book into a hotel.

COLIN: Hotel? Yes. Hotel. What's a good hotel on this side of the city?

HELEN: We'll find one.

COLIN: Helen, this is crazy. This is really crazy.

HELEN: Crazy, but right.

COLIN: Did I bring the car? Yes, of course I did. Hotels. Where are we? North Sydney. Hotel. Jesus, my mind is a total blank. God, I *didn't* bring the car. We'll get a cab. There is quite a nice hotel somewhere over in Manly. God, no, that's miles away. Artarmon! On the highway just down the road. Do you know the one I mean?

HELEN: No.

COLIN: No. It's actually pretty appalling. No, there's no way we're going to go there.

HELEN: There must be dozens of places within a few miles of here. Let's just get a cab and cruise.

COLIN (*suddenly pulling a set of car keys out of his pocket*): Jesus, I *did* bring the car. *I am going crazy.* Can you believe that? I *did* bring the car.

HELEN: Great. Let's go then.

COLIN: What about Mike?

HELEN: You go down first. I'll think of an excuse then follow.

Colin hesitates.

Do you want to go, or don't you?

COLIN (*to the audience*): I couldn't do it. In the seventies you could wreck marriages and traumatize kids and call it personal growth. In the eighties we realized that personal growth was a polite term for self-indulgence.

HELEN (*to the audience*): What a bummer. Still, you can't win 'em all.

COLIN (*to the audience, berating himself*): Gutless, pathetic, pathologically timid! But it probably was just as well.

They stare at each other in the moonlight, nod, and finally part. They exit. Some time later Colin walks into his living room. Kate

sits there with an inscrutable look on her face. Colin looks agi-
tated and annoyed. As always, when worked up about something,
Colin patrols up and down gesticulating as he speaks.

KATE: What's wrong.

COLIN: Kate, what am I doing with my life? I've just been to a film commission cocktail party and met a Polish director who works under daily threat,
and yet he makes masterpieces! I have every freedom in the world, and I'm
writing shit!

KATE: Not quite *every* freedom. The money men won't look at anything
that's not sex, sadism or sensation.

COLIN (*at a peak of gesticulation*): That's the *excuse* I use to justify what
I'm doing, but honestly, isn't it just that? An excuse? A justification? Couldn't I
fight harder? Couldn't I batter at the walls? Couldn't I keep going back, bloody
and wounded until I found *someone* in this merciless money maze who asked
what *sort* of film he was putting his money into, rather than the rate of return
he thinks he'll get? There must be rich men with the souls of artists out there,
and it's my responsibility to find them. Why don't I? Why don't I try?

KATE: Apparently because you want money and power.

COLIN: I don't want money and power!

KATE: You did yesterday.

COLIN: I don't any longer.

KATE: Good. Want to know my news?

COLIN: What?

KATE: *Black Rage's* been selected as a finalist in the Booker prize.

COLIN: The Booker?

KATE (*nodding*): Everyone in the office went berserk, and guess who was
the first to congratulate me? Ian. The man who opposed it all the way.

COLIN (*dully*): That's great.

KATE: I'm being flown over there.

COLIN: To London?

KATE (*nodding*): We've got to be represented in case we win.

COLIN: What about the author?

KATE: She'll be there too. They're flying us first class.

COLIN: First class? I've never flown anywhere first class in my life.

KATE: The Booker is big time, my dear. Big time. Just in being *nominated*
will double our sales, and there'll be *huge* sales in the States if we win. *Huge*
sales. When Tom Keneally won the Booker, Stephen Spielberg bought the film
rights.

COLIN (*moral outrage sparked*): Wait a minute? Hang on there! Wasn't
Black Rage going to be the book that was only going to sell a thousand or two
but seep slowly into our consciousness? Stephen Spielberg? What kind of film
will Stephen Spielberg make? Aliens descending in spaceships to take our

downtrodden aboriginals off to a loving, more equitable planet? Where are your ideals, woman? What's happened to your ideals?

KATE (*defensively*): Nothing!

Colin picks up a brochure Kate has brought in with her. He reads it.

COLIN: Thai Airways? You're going to be met at the doorway by an "elegant and courteous stewardess attired in traditional Thai dress and offered your choice of French champagne or orange juice and delicious satay beef cubes and crab claws to nibble on." How wonderful for you.

KATE: For once in my life I'm going to have a little bit of luxury and enjoy it.

COLIN: You're living in a city in which thousands are homeless!

KATE: I can't do anything about it in the short term, can I?

COLIN: Not when you're thirty thousand feet up nibbling crab claws, no.

KATE: I voted for the government that should be doing something about it. It's not my fault that they aren't.

COLIN: You found out that Sue Michaelis had flown first class and asked her how she could ever justify the fact that the extra ten cubic feet of body space she had bought herself for twenty-four hours, would have kept eight families in Bangladesh alive for a year.

KATE: I was a little fanatical in those days.

COLIN: That was just last year.

KATE: Colin, whether I travel first class or not, the families in Bangladesh aren't going to get any extra money.

COLIN: They would if you cashed in your first class ticket, went tourist, and sent Freedom from Hunger the difference.

KATE: Colin, I'm feeling guilty enough already. Don't make me feel any worse. The minute I have any success in my career you get nasty.

COLIN: I'm not getting nasty. I'm just pointing out that it only takes one first class ticket, and your ferocious moral standards take a nosedive.

KATE: Colin, this book has been one of my great triumphs. Can't you be a little bit generous?

COLIN: Triumph? A mouldy little book in an overrated competition? I'm just about to become the first foreign producer ever to sell a series to prime time television in the United States.

KATE: What kind of an achievement is that? Prime time television in America is to art what McDonald's is to cooking.

COLIN: Which would you rather have a percentage of? Maxim's or McDonald's?

KATE: Colin, I think you're coming apart at the seams. You came in here ranting with Polish-fired zeal, determined to make films of quality, and now you're bursting with pride because you're about to sell schlock to NBC. What's going on in your head?

COLIN (*gesticulating wildly*): I wish I knew! One minute I want to make a film that's so beautiful and truthful and angry and funny that people in this country who still *care* about justice and truth and compassion will leave the cinema weeping, and the next minute my head is full of images of mansions on the waterfront. I know what I *should* do! Reject the false gods—but it's not that easy! We live in a culture that *worships* wealth and *worships* power and gives artistic success no recognition or honor of any kind!

KATE: Colin, you're being a *little* bit overdramatic.

COLIN (*overdramatically*): Am I? Am I? What do you have at the end of your life to show for your artistic success? An old age pension, a one-bar radiator—if you can afford the fuel bills—and a few yellowing crits in a dusty scrapbook. It's too demeaning, Kate. It's too bloody demeaning! If I've got to choose between money and oblivion, I'll take the money!

> *Kate exits. Colin sits at Mike's place. He dictates, or attempts to dictate, the script to Mike as of old, but there's a subtle change. Mike is offering resistance.*

Let's have a close-up of him kick-starting the bike.

MIKE: Kick-start shots went out with *Easy Rider*.

> *Mike taps out a few lines rapidly.*

COLIN (*tersely*): What was that you wrote?

MIKE: Just a thought I had.

COLIN: What?

MIKE: Catch up with it later.

COLIN (*quietly fuming*): If kick shots went out with *Easy Rider*, what do you suggest?

MIKE: Zoom in on the helmet going on with a snap and pan down across his body to the exhaust pipe belching fumes.

COLIN (*considering this reluctantly*): All right. Write it.

MIKE: I've written it.

COLIN (*trying to regain control*): Right, now before Grant rides off he should turn and say—

MIKE (*interrupting*): Don't need any dialogue. The intention's clear.

COLIN (*clenched teeth*): I'd like him to make the point—

MIKE (*interrupting*): You wouldn't hear what he was saying in any case over the exhaust and the rock track.

COLIN: What are we making here? A cartoon? We're twenty minutes into the episode, and only twelve words have been spoken.

MIKE: This is an eighties series in a visual medium, mate. If you can't tell your story in images, don't tell it at all.

COLIN: Mike, we share ninety-nine percent of our D.N.A. with the chimpanzee. The bonus of that extra one percent is language. An astonishing facility for language. There are sixteen distinct meanings for the word "beat," but we can instantly recognise which of the sixteen is intended by context. When the most advanced language computer tried to translate "The spirit is willing but the flesh is weak" into Russian, it came out "The vodka's strong, but the veal is pallid."

MIKE: What point are you trying to make?

COLIN: How can we ever know our characters if they're never allowed to speak? We're writing a series about chimpanzees! Before you can be interested in a character, you've got to know how they speak and think, how they justify what they're doing, to themselves and to each other, how they cope with the big questions: life, death and meaning; how they view the tragic irony of being transient specks of living matter in an infinite and incomprehensible universe!

MIKE: O.K. What do you want him to say?

COLIN (*thinks*): "We'd better check this one out, Zac."

> *Mike hesitates, then taps it out. Colin frowns and stares at Mike. He doesn't understand the new assertiveness. Malcolm, the merchant banker, enters some weeks later. Colin and Mike stand in front of him. Malcolm has a thick script in his hand.*

MALCOLM (*indicating the script*): You really think this is going to sell to the U.S. network?

COLIN: Yes.

MALCOLM: You've sent the script across?

COLIN: Yes.

MALCOLM: You've had some response?

COLIN: Nothing definite, but a high level of interest.

MALCOLM: From who?

COLIN: The reader at NBC said she found the concept intriguing.

MALCOLM: The concept is five years too late. It's *Miami Vice* down under.

COLIN: On the surface it's a little similar—

MALCOLM (*interrupting*): Colin, this is the seventh *Miami Vice* I've been given in the last six months.

COLIN: There are a lot of novel twists. One of the cops, Zac, is a Ph.D.

MALCOLM: In astrophysics? A cop in Darlinghurst? And the other's an ex-world surfing champion and cordon bleu cook? Colin, this is *shit*.

COLIN: So is *Miami Vice*.

MALCOLM: That's classy shit. This is *absolute* shit.

COLIN: I can't see the difference.

MALCOLM: Which is exactly why the chances of you getting a network sale are about the same as the monkey accidently typing *Hamlet*. The writers of *Miami Vice* don't sit down and say to themselves, "I am going to write shit." They write at the highest level they're capable of, and when they finish they think they've written a masterpiece. When someone who can write at a higher level tries to imitate them it's a disaster.

COLIN (*taking the script*): I hope you're big enough to admit that you were wrong.

MALCOLM: I'll be delighted to admit I was wrong. You get a pre-sale from the Americans, we'll finance.

> *Colin glowers and moves towards the door. Mike turns to follow.*

(*To Mike*) That project you're working on with Elaine Ross sounds like something we'd be interested in, Mike.

MIKE (*embarrassed*): Oh. Right.

MALCOLM: Send me a script when it's done.

> *Malcolm exits. Colin and Mike stand outside the office.*

COLIN: What's the script you're doing for Elaine?

MIKE (*embarrassed*): It's about a guy whose kids die in a fun park accident. Said she offered it to you and you turned it down.

COLIN: I couldn't see a film in it. Seemed like a worn-out theme to me.

MIKE: I think it's strong. I think it's a winner.

COLIN (*waving the script*): We'll get *this* one up. He's not the only merchant banker in town.

MIKE: That's the game we're in. When it's hot, run with it, when it's cold, bail out.

COLIN: We've spent months on it. We're not giving up yet.

MIKE: It's dead, mate.

> *Mike exits. Kate enters. Colin paces up and down. Kate watches him.*

COLIN: I can't believe it. He's never written anything and Elaine's got him working on a script she really cares about.

KATE: It's exactly what I told you would happen.

COLIN: He's never written a thing in his life!

KATE: He's the co-writer of *Coastwatchers*.

COLIN: Everyone knows he couldn't have written any of that.

KATE: Do they? How?

COLIN: They know *my* record. They know *his*.

KATE: What do you think Mike's been doing out there since *Coastwatchers*, Colin? Going around the cocktail circuit admitting that he didn't write a word?

COLIN: I'm the only writer in the country who could do that script of Elaine's. It's got to have characters that are *individual* and who *live*. Elaine must be off her head.

KATE: You can't expect her to wait around forever when you turn her down flat.

COLIN: I would have done it eventually.

KATE: You're *impossibly* arrogant sometimes, Colin. She's expected to wait round forever on the off-chance?

COLIN: If I can't get this series into production I'll have no money coming in all next year.

KATE: Not to worry.

COLIN: Not to worry? Do you know how much Penny's school fees are now?

> *Kate nods. Colin examines her narrowly.*

COLIN: Have you been drinking?

KATE: I've had a few glasses of champagne. I've just got a forty percent rise.

COLIN: Forty percent?

KATE: It won't be that much after tax.

COLIN: Forty percent?

KATE: I've been promoted.

COLIN: To what? You're only two rungs under God now.

KATE: Ian's become national manager. I've got his job.

COLIN (*choking on the words*): Congratulations. That's wonderful.

KATE: I get his old office on the seventeenth floor. You see the whole harbor.

COLIN: Really.

KATE: You must come up and have a look. On a sunny day when the eighteen footers are out, the combination of striped spinnaker, sparkling blue water and sky is *absolutely* overwhelming. I don't know how I'm ever going to get any work done.

COLIN: That's wonderful.

KATE: You were right about Sydney. It's the most exciting city in the *world*. I couldn't live anywhere else. (*To the audience.*) I've got to be honest. I loved that moment. Deep at the heart of every marriage between professionals there's a struggle for supremacy, and if one partner gets too far ahead for too long, the marriage goes sour. Colin had had his years of being lionized. It was my turn.

COLIN (*dully*): Will you still be going to London?

KATE: Oh, yes. And the promotion means my living expenses go up by seventy dollars a day. I'll be able to have a ball.

COLIN (*dully*): Great.

KATE (*To the audience*): Marriages can be awful. Right when your partner's at his lowest ebb, you sink in the boot. I'm not proud in retrospect, but at the time I *loved* it.

> *Kate and Colin exit. Mike and Helen enter. Mike talks on the telephone. Helen watches him.*

MIKE (*into the phone*): Sounds great. Why don't I come around and we'll talk about it? (*Pause.*) Yep. That's fine. See you then.

> *He hangs up and notes down the time and place in his diary.*

(*Exultantly*): Terry Severino wants me to write a movie for him.

HELEN: Mike, you can't take on any more work. You're doing five already.

MIKE: When you're hot, you run with it. Next week you might be colder than Melbourne in May.

HELEN: How are you going to finish any of them?

MIKE: I'll manage.

HELEN: You'll kill yourself.

MIKE: Honey, it's make-or-break time. They've thrown me the ball, and I've got to run with it.

HELEN: Look at your hand shaking.

MIKE (*taking tablets*): You want to live in this dump all your life?

HELEN: Don't take any more of those tablets, Mike. Your stomach'll dissolve.

MIKE: Add up the numbers in the contracts I've signed in the last two months and it comes to more than I've earned in the last ten years.

HELEN: Look, I know I give you a hard time about this house, but—

MIKE (*interrupting*): Honey, you are "*un poule superieux.*"

HELEN: A what?

MIKE: A top chook. You could've had any guy in this city, and don't think I don't know it. I am going to put you in a mansion on the waterfront with a boat moored outside, because anything less is an insult.

HELEN: Mike—

MIKE (*interrupting*): Honey, there are women out there with a tenth of what you've got who've treated me like shit. How do you say thank you to someone who's given you more than you ever hoped for and much more than you deserve? This is the only way I know how.

HELEN: Mike, I'm really moved, and I am, believe me, but I'd much rather be living here with you, than sitting in a waterfront while you're in intensive care.

MIKE: Honey, for the first time in my life I've found a game I might win. Suddenly, there's a doorway, and I've got a foot in, and I can see myself through and on the other side and nobody's putting me down any more, and do you know what that's like to me? That's like being in heaven. Bliss.

> *Helen exits.*

(*To the audience*): Problem is, when you take on half a dozen big jobs at once, you do eventually have to deliver. I started living on a diet of milk and indigestion tablets, and as the telephone calls started coming in my brain log-jammed with fear and dread. No shortage of ideas. Brilliant ideas. But between the idea and the typewriter something happened. There was some freak circuit in my brain that, right at the last moment, in the instant before the idea hit the paper, turned gold into shit. I was in a waking nightmare. I was a grand opera singer who hears the nightingale inside her head, opens her mouth, and out comes the croak of a frog. The phone kept ringing, and I extended the dates again and again. My brain was on the point of exploding. My stomach already had. I looked down, teetering on the brink of the success I'd always dreamed of and saw the crocodiles below. There *had* to be a way out. *Had* to.

> *Malcolm enters.*

MALCOLM: I raise finance, Mike. I don't want to get involved in production.

MIKE: Malcolm, listen. Let's have a long hard look at this industry of ours. Over four hundred films in the last ten years, and only *one* has done big business where it counts: in the U.S.

MALCOLM: It's a hard market to crack.

MIKE: It shouldn't be, Malcolm. We've been failing because we've been going about it in a half-arsed way. We bring over a few faded American stars and plonk them in a cliche-ridden Australian wank and think we've made something international. We'll *never* make true international product that way. We have to go the whole hog. A big production house with ten or twelve projects going at once and *everything* international. International scripts, international stars, international directors. Malcolm, there's no reason why Australia couldn't become one of the world's great production houses. Climate's better than California, technicians are much cheaper. Got good local actors for the supporting roles.

MALCOLM: The Americans can't understand their accents.

MIKE: Bring out tutors. Voice coaches. It can be done, Malcolm. I swear to you, it can be done. The Canadians make better American movies than the Americans, and the reason they succeed is that they don't feel they have to make pissant little movies about the Canadian way of life. We'll have all the Advance Aussie patriots having hernias because we put American number-plates on Aussie cars, but stuff 'em, Malcolm. Stuff 'em. If we'd just be honest with ourselves for a change, we'd admit that our accent *is* bloody awful for the simple reason that we never open our bloody mouths. It was good enough in the old days when Grandad was out in the bush and had to keep the flies out, but it's *death* to the international saleability of our product.

MALCOLM: What's the precise deal you're suggesting, Mike?

MIKE: You pay expenses to get me to L.A. so I can line up the talent and do the deals. Every project I get up we split the profits fifty-fifty. If I don't get anything up, all you've lost is a few plane fares.

MALCOLM: You're convinced it could work?

MIKE: The world's a global village, Malcolm. A merchant banker in New York has got far more in common with you than a sheep farmer from Walgett, right?

MALCOLM (*nodding*): It's high time we stopped being so bloody parochial.

MIKE (*nodding*): Stuff the gumnut clique. Let's start making hard-headed, rational business decisions for a change. The North American market is three hundred million, ours is fifteen. Where does the future lie?

> *Mike and Malcolm exit. Colin and Kate enter. Colin reads a newspaper. He puts it down like a man who's been hit in the solar plexus.*

COLIN (*in a strangled voice*): Kate, this is like a nightmare.

KATE: What?

COLIN: Malcolm Bennett and Mike McCord have just floated a joint production company with a hundred million dollars worth of projects slated for the coming year.

KATE: Is there some other Mike McCord?

COLIN: God forbid.

KATE: Why would Bennett go into partnership with—

COLIN (*interrupting*): Why did I go into partnership with him? He's Mephistopheles doing the rounds of the industry.

KATE (*reading the paper*): They will make films that will "compete on the international market without sacrificing their essential Australianness."

COLIN: I feel devastated.

KATE: I don't wonder.

COLIN: I feel as if, suddenly, I don't know how the world works any more. There are producers all over the city screaming for scripts he hasn't finished, and the reason he didn't finish them, I suspect, is that if he ever did, he'd be revealed as a total charlatan. He's risen to the top on the basis of *Coastwatchers*, in which he hardly wrote a line, and six scripts that no one has ever seen! In the sort of world I can comprehend, a man like that wouldn't be up there deciding our futures.

KATE: He has to be found out eventually.

COLIN: This is the first time in my life I've actually felt I could kill.

KATE: He has to be found out.

COLIN: I don't think he will. Anyone who can rise so far on the basis of so little has to be some kind of ... genius.

> *Kate exits. Elaine enters at a cocktail party. A background of chatter. Elaine stands by herself. Colin walks in and practically bumps into her. He looks confused and searches for something to say.*

COLIN: Ah. Elaine. How are things?

ELAINE (*cuttingly*): Things are fine. I've just taken a third mortgage out on my house, my bank manager's given me thirty days to reduce my overdraft by twenty thousand ... life is very full and very exciting.

COLIN (*embarrassed*): Ah. (*Struggling.*) Script progressing?

ELAINE (*with a deadly edge*): Script progressing? Script? You would possibly be referring to the Sanzari script?

COLIN: Yes.

ELAINE: No.

COLIN: Did Mike finish it?

ELAINE (*coldly*): Thank you for warning me against him, Colin.

COLIN: It's not my place—

ELAINE: If you see an old friend about to cast twenty thousand dollars to the wind, don't you have a slight obligation to speak a few words of caution? Do you think I enjoy taking out mortgages?

COLIN: The script was bad?

ELAINE: Script? I got fourteen pages and had to go around to his flat and *demand* it!

COLIN: Elaine, I couldn't warn you. I've never seen a word that he's written!

ELAINE: I've seen several, and they're etched on my brain. "O.K. Rogan, this time the game is up." "I've got news for you, Mason: the game has barely begun." "I thought you might say that, Rogan, but there's something I think you ought to know: I shuffled the deck. I hold the trumps."

COLIN: I'm relieved.

ELAINE: I imagine that anyone who didn't have to pay five hundred dollars for that little exchange would be.

COLIN: I started having nightmares that the man actually had talent. I couldn't find any other explanation for his meteoric rise to the top.

ELAINE: He won't last. (*Reassessing.*) He probably will.

COLIN: I'd like to write the Sanzari story, if you're still interested.

ELAINE: I sold the rights.

COLIN: To who?

ELAINE: To Mike McCord.

COLIN: Elaine, you're joking.

ELAINE: I wish I was.

COLIN: You can't be serious. Have you heard about some of the projects they're doing? A fifteen million dollar drama about Lesbian Nuns set in Cincinnati.

ELAINE: Starring Brooke Shields.

COLIN: Why did you sell Sanzari to McCord?

ELAINE: It was the only way I could get my twenty thousand back.

COLIN: Why did I ever come to this city? The water in the harbor's not blue, it's cold and hard and green!

ELAINE: Emerald. The Emerald City of Oz. Everyone comes here along their yellow brick roads looking for the answers to their problems, and all they find are the demons within themselves. This city lets 'em out and lets 'em rip.

COLIN: You can't let it off that easily. This city is evil! Glitter, money, fashion, fads, corruption, compromise—

ELAINE (*interrupting*): Intelligence, professionalism, hard work, standards, flexibility, dedication. It's got the best and the worst, and if you choose the worst, you've only got yourself to blame.

COLIN (*gesticulating*): There's no forgiveness here. No compassion! If there isn't a dollar in it, it just doesn't happen.

ELAINE: My daughter teaches handicapped kids on a wage marginally higher than the dole. I keep telling her she's exploited and overworked, but she doesn't want to do anything else. She was born and raised here.

COLIN: Elaine, it's a city that walks over its fallen heroes and picks their pockets on the way!

ELAINE (*running out of patience*): Go back to Melbourne then, you whinger! Your inner demons won't get you into trouble down there. They couldn't think of anything to suggest! (*Shaking her head.*) Brisbane boys are rough as guts, Adelaide's a shade on the prissy side. Perth persons are a worry, but you Melbournians—you're so stuffed full of moral rectitude, the only time you open your mouths is to lecture. (*Turns to go away, then turns back.*) If you're going to stay here, for God's sake go away and write me a screen play or we'll both be on the dole!

    Elaine goes.

COLIN (*to the audience*): Go and write me a screen play. About what? Critical patience for my observations of middle-class life was running thin. Corruption was passe. The boom area was the underprivileged, the unemployed and exploited minorities. Did I have the depth to identify with their anguish and pain? Did I have the soul? Did I have any alternative?

    Kate storms in, slamming things around and looking furious. She sees a newspaper Colin has been reading and hurls it in a waste paper basket.

COLIN: Something upsetting you?

KATE: Bloody journalists! Have you read it?

COLIN: Certainly have.

KATE (*staring at him*): Do you agree with her?

COLIN: I think she's got a case.

KATE: She's being totally hysterical!

COLIN: If she doesn't want to sell the film rights, why should she?

KATE: A film will triple the sales of the book.

COLIN: Did you describe the film as being Australia's *The Color Purple?*

KATE: No! I said that *The Color Purple* had shown that films about the mistreatment of minorities could make powerful movies and attract large audiences! She's the one who'll be getting most of the money. We only take twenty percent.

COLIN: She said she had written the book to help her people, not to gain personal fortune or fame.

KATE: She'll just have to cry all the way to the bank.

COLIN: You're going to go ahead and sell the film rights?

KATE: We've sold them.

COLIN: Without her consent?

KATE: Her contract gives us the right to act as her agents. Colin, she's just being hysterical.

COLIN: She says she's scared the film will sensationalize and cheapen what she's written.

KATE: It's sure to be less subtle than the book. Films always are, but it will triple the sales of her novel!

COLIN: Wouldn't it have been smarter to wait and see if she won the Booker? If you're determined to make money with film rights, they'll be worth much more if she wins.

KATE: She's not going to win the Booker. Ian felt it was best to take the offer we had.

COLIN: Who did you sell the rights to?

KATE (*full of guilt*): I'm sure the film will be hideous, but it will triple the sales of the book, and the book is what is going to have the lasting impact.

COLIN: You didn't sell it to—

KATE: They offered twice as much as anyone else. (*She sees the look on Colin's face and gets even more defensive.*) You can't live in a dream world! You've got to take profits into account.

COLIN: Kate, can you imagine what someone with the sensitivity of a Mike McCord will do with *Black Rage*?

KATE: They've got international connections. If the film works in the States, the book will sell in hundreds of thousands. (*She sees Colin's look.*) Colin, when you're in a top-level executive position the pressures are enormous. Ian and I have a board of directors to answer to. How am I supposed to explain to them that we turned down a prime international marketing opportunity because I don't like Mike McCord?

COLIN: I presume you won't be going to London now?

KATE (*puzzled, defensive*): Why?

COLIN: Now that you know you're not going to win the Booker.

KATE: We're not absolutely certain.

COLIN: And now that your author is refusing to go.

KATE: That's her decision.

COLIN: Your boss's secretary phoned.

KATE: What about?

COLIN: She said the Dorchester was confirmed for both of you.

KATE (*embarrassed*): Ian's decided to come, now that Kath has pulled out.

COLIN (*tersely*): Great.

KATE (*defensively*): Surely you haven't got any worries on that score.

COLIN (*tersely*): Why shouldn't I have?

KATE: You've seen him.

COLIN: Yes. He looks like the young Richard Burton.

KATE: He looks like a garden gnome. Colin, grow up. Ours is a strictly business relationship. (*To the audience.*) He did look more like the young Richard Burton than a garden gnome, and there had been certain indications of interest. I had no intention of taking them up. (*To Colin.*) Colin, I feel just as badly as you do about a philistine like Mike getting the film rights, but unfortunately that's how the commercial world works.

COLIN: I suppose there is a certain justice. Without Mike the book would never have been published.

Kate exits.

(*To the audience.*) At least I was able to play that one last trump card on that desolate afternoon. When Kate had left for London I got a phone call from the person I least expected.

Mike enters and Colin sits in front of him.

MIKE: Busy?

COLIN: Not particularly.

MIKE: Done a script for Elaine, I hear.

COLIN (*nodding*): First draft.

MIKE: What's it about?

COLIN: The victims of corporate greed.

MIKE: Got the money?

COLIN: No.

MIKE: Subject like that might be difficult to raise money on.

COLIN: It will. It's set in Australia, it's saying something important and has characters who spend part of their time outside cars and who occasionally talk.

MIKE: Got something you might be interested in.

COLIN: Really.

MIKE: The Yanks have really gone for *Black Rage*.

COLIN: I'm surprised.

MIKE: Colin, I've got to be honest with you. We've already had a writer working on it, but the script's got a fair way to go.

COLIN: You'd like me to do the changes?

MIKE: There's eighty grand in it for you if you see it through to final draft. It's going to be a big film, Colin. First writer was a hot shot young American, and he couldn't come up with the goods. If you can bring it off, it'll make your reputation over there.

COLIN: Why are the Americans interested in the plight of our aboriginals?

MIKE: It's been relocated.

COLIN: Relocated?

MIKE: It's been reset in Tennessee. The characters are black Americans. Richard Pryor is very interested in playing the lead.

COLIN: Mike, do you have the faintest idea why I might not want to take this job?

MIKE: The story is universal. Poverty-stricken black girl grows up to be a human rights lawyer. Could happen anywhere.

COLIN: Mike, there are vast differences between our aborigines and the American blacks.

MIKE: People are people wherever they live, Colin. This is the era of the global village.

COLIN: Not quite. Hundreds of years of separate histories and environments aren't swept away because *Sesame Street* teaches our kids to say "Have a nice day."

MIKE: Colin, nationalism is one of the most destructive of all human forces. Caused countless wars. Billions of deaths.

COLIN: Where are you resetting the Sanzari story? Wyoming?

MIKE: Nebraska, and there might be some work for you on that one too.

COLIN: You're a harlot, mate. You've sold your soul to the highest bidder, and you can stick your eighty grand up your arse!

MIKE (*puzzled, hurt*): We can't go backwards, mate. I'm flogging myself to within a scalpel's width of major surgery to keep our industry afloat. Trying to generate a hundred million dollars' worth of film making—a fair proportion of which will stay in Australian pockets. How does that make me a harlot? I don't understand your point.

COLIN (*to the audience*): I wasn't sure I did either. I've always hated flag-waving chauvinism. What's so special about being Australian? What's to rejoice in that I'm a member of this polyglot lot of pale-skinned usurpers who treated their predecessors abominably and resent giving them back some tracts of arid desert and one big rock? Why bother whether we have our own stories or not? My only answer to that is that we have a *right* to them. We are human beings with our own feelings, strengths and weaknesses, and we need to know what we are like, and we need to know that we are important enough to have fictions written about us or we will always feel that real life happens somewhere else and is spoken in accents other than our own. But then again, that might be a rationalization. If there are no Australian stories told, I'd be out of a job. If my version of *Miami Vice* had sold to a U.S. network, would I be so virtuous today? Who was I to be judgmental? I thought seriously about relocating *Black Rage* to Tennessee, and it started to make a certain amount of sense. Eighty thousand dollars worth of sense. But by the faintest whisker some residual integrity, some deep rooted sense of patriotism, or just the ignominy of having to work for Mike, prevented me doing it.

MIKE (*to the audience*): The bastard walked out of here and made me feel like a grubby little louse. I sat at my desk and stared into darkness for hours. I finally got up from behind my desk and shouted, "All right! I'm a harlot! Some of us don't have any choice!"

Helen enters.

HELEN: I don't think I'll ever get tired of this view. Come and have a look. The eighteen footers have got their spinnakers out.

MIKE: Colin turned down eighty grand today.

HELEN: Colin?

MIKE: I've been hearing stories that he's really down on his luck. Nothing's been happening for him. I get on the phone to L.A. and convince them he's a top writer, which is bloody hard, given his current track record. I call him in, offer him the job, and he calls me a harlot.

HELEN: Why?

MIKE: Because the story's being relocated to Tennessee.

HELEN: A story's a story wherever it's set.

MIKE: Exactly.

HELEN: I can understand why he might be a bit ...

MIKE: What?

HELEN: Reluctant to work for you.

MIKE: I can't.

HELEN: Now your roles are reversed. It would be a bit hard.

MIKE: So he throws away eighty grand just to spite me? It's insane.

HELEN: Any luck with *Lesbian Nuns*?

MIKE: Got it through last week.

HELEN: You didn't tell me. Did you have to change the script much?

MIKE: A bit. Only one of the nuns is allowed to be lesbian, and it's got to be a tendency. Not consummated.

HELEN: Mike, that's crazy. Isn't the whole point of the story that there are a *lot* of lesbian nuns, and they're suffering a hell of a lot of guilt?

MIKE: Honey, you sit at my desk day after day and try and get any film through the American system, and you'll realize that what I've done is a bloody miracle.

HELEN: Can't they show the *truth* of anything just for once?

MIKE: Jesus, honey. We get enough truth in our lives. We don't want it up there again on our screens.

HELEN: I know the commercial logic, but occasionally I'd like to see the truth!

MIKE: The only truth that matters in this situation is that they have the money, and if they ask me to change nuns into astronauts and lesbians into doughnuts, I will make them a movie about astronauts eating doughnuts. They ask. I give. It's called commerce; it's grubby, and it's how I paid for this view. If you don't like it, we'll go back to Dri-Tot Manor.

HELEN: I just can't believe people wouldn't be interested in a movie about the *real* situation.

MIKE: They probably would, but the men who have the money don't *believe* they would, and that, I'm afraid, is an end to it.

> *Mike and Helen exit. Colin enters and sits reading. The doorbell rings. Colin frowns and goes to get it. It's Kate with a suitcase. Colin embraces her with passion.*

KATE: Kids in bed?

COLIN (*nodding*): Even Penny. Sorry you didn't win.

KATE: I knew we wouldn't. Still. (*She shrugs.*) That was a warm welcome. I'm surprised.

COLIN: So am I. I was planning to be cold and distant.

KATE: Bad time while I was gone?

COLIN: Awful. Shopping without lists is a major trauma, and our daughter's been a monster.

KATE: You said on the phone she had a new boy friend.

COLIN: Yes.

KATE: He goes to an ordinary high school?

COLIN: Yes.

KATE: That should make you pleased.

COLIN: He was kicked out of his private school for selling dope in the toilets.

KATE: She told you this?

COLIN: No, I listen to the phone calls on the extension. How was the Dorchester?

KATE: Overrated.

COLIN: And the garden gnome?

KATE (*embarrassed*): Oh, I, er, didn't see much of him. He found himself a native.

COLIN: Black lady?

KATE: English rose. How's work?

COLIN: On to the second draft of the screen play. No money in sight.

KATE: Tell me something cheerful.

COLIN: I'm very glad to see you home.

KATE (*to the audience*): And I was very glad to be home. Ian didn't find an English rose. He found me, but what Colin doesn't know won't hurt him. I'd been promoted, I'd been unfaithful, and the marriage was back on an even keel.

COLIN: I did some thinking about the future while you were away. Did you?

KATE (*guiltily*): Ah. No. It was all a bit frantic.

COLIN: I thought we should go back to Melbourne.

KATE: Melbourne? But Colin—

COLIN (*interrupting*): But then I changed my mind. Do you know what made me change my mind?

KATE: What?

COLIN: I was waiting for a taxi in the city, and there were two derelicts asleep on benches. A City Mission van drove up, and a young guy went across and talked to them without any hint of judgement and took them somewhere safe and warm.

KATE: How does that relate to Melbourne?

COLIN: That young guy doesn't dream of waterfront mansions. He gets a couple of hundred dollars a week, a handful of people know that he's a good human being, and as far as he's concerned, that's enough.

KATE: What are you telling me, Colin? You're going to work for the City Mission.

COLIN: No. I'm not as good a human being as he is, and after the film deal you did on *Black Rage*, neither are you. The incident reminded me of something Elaine said. Don't blame the city. The demons are in *us*.

KATE: So we're going to stay in Sydney?

COLIN: Yes.

KATE (*drily*): Good. Now that we've settled our future, and you've established that we're both evil, do you think we could go to bed?

> *Kate exits. Colin stands by himself. Cocktail chatter is heard in the background. Mike enters and walks up to him.*

MIKE: Finally got that film of yours up.

COLIN: Yes, we did.

MIKE: How were the reviews?

COLIN: Very good. Excellent.

MIKE: I only saw the one in the Herald.

COLIN: That was the only bad one.

MIKE: Pity. That would've been the most important one for you.

COLIN: Not really.

MIKE: Meant to catch it. Didn't seem to be around long.

COLIN: It did eight weeks.

MIKE: Eight?

COLIN: If I'd wanted to run for a year I'd've written *E.T.*

MIKE: Won't be much return for the investors.

COLIN: We're hoping for an overseas sale.

MIKE: Wish you luck.

COLIN: The American reviewers seemed a bit cool to *Sister Nun*.

MIKE: Crying all the way to the bank. Had a six million U.S. presale.

COLIN: I read that you're cutting back on production.

MIKE (*swallowing a tablet*): It's been tougher than we expected, but we're getting there.

COLIN: No plans for *Black Rage*?

MIKE: We've put that one on the back burner. Poor black kid making it is big news here, but it happens every day over there. Be hard for you to get a new movie up now, I suppose?

COLIN: It's always hard. Having problems with Equity I hear?

MIKE: Storm in a teacup.

COLIN: I heard they were axing your next movie unless at least one Australian got a lead role.

MIKE: They've got their head in the sand. How can I pre-sell our movies to the States with unknown actors in the lead? (*To the audience.*) Why does the Film Commission invite him? Everyone in the industry knows his last film was a disaster. Eleven thousand in its first week, and it went down from there.

He'll be lucky if he ever gets another film up in his life, poor bastard. Can't help feeling sorry for him. I just wish the papers would start employing critics who like what the public likes for a change, instead of giving losers like that the good crits.

COLIN (*to the audience*): Why does the Commission keep inviting him? If he knew the contempt he was held in by all the people in this room, he'd never show his face around here again. I can't bring myself to hate him any more. He's a figure of great pathos. The only thing that makes me angry is the money he makes. I don't want to be rich, but it's sad to see the dollars go to turds like that, while *serious* film makers beg and scrape.

MIKE: Take care.

COLIN: You too.

> *Mike and Colin nod at each other and turn away to face the audience. They stand there shaking their heads, assuming with never a doubt that the audience is on their side. As they share this certainty with the audience, the lights fade. Curtain.*

THE HEIDI CHRONICLES

A Play in Two Acts

BY WENDY WASSERSTEIN

Cast and credits appear on pages 410 & 431–433

WENDY WASSERSTEIN was born in Brooklyn in 1950. Her father was a textile manufacturer, and her mother saw to it that her daughter developed an enthusiasm for theater at an early age, combining classes at a dancing school in the Broadway area with visits to matinee performances. Wasserstein received her formal education at Calhoun School in Manhattan and Mount Holyoke College and by 1973 was testing her mettle as a playwright with a staged reading of Any Woman Can't *at Playwrights Horizons. In 1976 she graduated from the Yale Drama School.* Uncommon Women and Others *was first staged at the Yale Drama School (1976), followed by readings at Playwrights Horizons and the Eugene O'Neill Theater Center (1977), and finally—her first produced play—off Broadway by the Phoenix Theater Nov. 17, 1977 for 22 performances. The Phoenix also presented Wasserstein's* Isn't It Romantic *in 1981 for 37 performances; and on Dec. 15, 1983 Playwrights Horizons produced a revised version of* Isn't It Romantic *which ran for 733 performances. Her one-acter* The Man in a Case, *based on a Chekov story, appeared off Broadway in 1986 on an Acting Company program entitled* Orchards. *Her first Best Play,* The Heidi Chronicles, *was written in 1987 with a National Theater British American Arts Association grant. It was produced in a Seattle Repertory workshop in association with Playwrights Horizons, who later presented it off Broadway Dec. 11 for 81 performances, after which it moved to Broadway on March 9 and was awarded the Pulitzer Prize and the Critics and Tony best-play awards.*

Among other Wasserstein play titles appearing as experimental stagings in New York and other venues are When Dinah Shore Ruled the Earth *(written with Christopher Durang),* Hard Sell *(a musical to which she supplied additional material),* Tender Offer *and* Miami *(a musical book, with music and lyrics by Bruce Sussman and Jack Feldman). She has received NEA and Guggenheim grants and is a member of the Dramatists Guild Council and has served as one of the dramaturges for the Guild's Young People's Festival of plays by teen-agers, presented annually in New York, where she now lives.*

ACT 1

Prologue: A lecture hall, New York, 1988

SYNOPSIS: Heidi Holland, mature (late 30s), poised, informed, is lecturing on the work of unrecognized women painters from the 16th to the 19th century. A woman in one of the paintings, projected on a screen as examples of her talk, looks a bit like Heidi herself. She observes, "Frankly this painting has always reminded me of me at one of those horrible high school dances. And you sort of want to dance, and you sort of want to go home, and you sort of don't know what you want. So you hang around, a fading rose in an exquisitely detailed dress, waiting to see what might happen."

Scene 1: Chicago, 1965

The scene changes to a corner of a high school dance with folding chairs and streamers. Offstage, the orchestra is playing "The Shoop Shoop Song." Heidi and her friend Susan Johnston—two 17-year-olds—survey the scene and notice particularly a boy who "can twist and smoke at the same time." Susan warns Heidi that they must move around separately, not huddle together, in order to attract boys. One of them comes over to meet Heidi (who is the editor of her school paper), but Heidi drives him away by insisting that she and Susan are together.

The next dance is a Ladies Choice, and Susan decides to approach the twister-smoker, leaving Heidi alone to sit with a book on her lap, as the orchestra plays "Play With Fire."

> *Peter Patrone, a young man in a St. Mark's School blazer, sits next to her. He looks at her. She smiles and looks down.*

PETER: You must be very bright.

HEIDI: Excuse me?

PETER: You look so bored you must be very bright.

HEIDI: I'm sorry?

PETER: Don't be sorry. I appreciate bored people. Bored, depressed, anxious. These are the qualities I look for in a woman. Your lady friend is dancing with the gentleman who looks like Bobby Kennedy. I find men who smoke and twist at the same time so dreary.

HEIDI: Not worth the coordination, really.

PETER: Do you have any?

HEIDI: I can sit and read at the same time.

PETER: What book is that?

HEIDI: *Death, Be Not Proud.*

PETER: Of course.

HEIDI: A favorite of mine at dances.

They pretend that they are meeting on a cruise on the Queen Mary and facing tragic futures in sanatoriums (actually, he is headed for Williams and she for Vassar). To his proposal of marriage she replies that she wants to remain independent, and he urges, "If we can't marry, let's be great friends." Once again the orchestra plays "The Shoop Shoop Song." It's the last dance, and Peter and Heidi get up to dance and sing the lyrics to each other as the lights fade.

Scene 2: Manchester, New Hampshire, 1967

At another dance, the decorative sign reads "Eugene McCarthy for President," and the music is provided by Janis Joplin and Big Brother and the Holding Company. Heidi is standing by the food table, when "*Scoop Rosenbaum, slightly intense but charismatic in blue jeans and workshirt,*" comes over to her. Sarcasm seems to be his long suit. He belittles her effort to come all this way from Vassar to New Hampshire to be "neat and clean for Eugene" in support of his bid for the Presidency. When Scoop asks her name, Heidi tells him it's Susan. She reminds Scoop, a Princeton dropout, that he too seems to be part of this McCarthy drive.

SCOOP: I came with a friend. Susan, don't you know this is just the tip of the iceberg? McCarthy is irrelevant. He's a C-plus Adlai Stevenson. The changes in this country could be enormous. Beyond anything your sister mind can imagine.

HEIDI: Are you a real life radical?

SCOOP: You mean, do I make bombs in my parents' West Hartford basement? Susan, how could I be a radical? I played lacrosse at Exeter, and

Joan Allen as Heidi Holland with Peter Friedman (*left*) as Scoop Rosenbaum and Boyd Gaines (*right*) as Peter Patrone in *The Heidi Chronicles*

I'm a Jew whose first name is Scoop. You're not very good at nuance. And you're too eager to categorize. I'm a journalist. I'm just here to have a look around.

HEIDI: Do you work for a paper?

SCOOP: Did they teach you at Vassar to ask so many inane questions in order to keep a conversation going?

HEIDI: Well, like I said. I have to meet my friend.

SCOOP: Me, too. I have to meet Paul Newman.

HEIDI: Please tell him Susan says "Hi."

SCOOP: You don't believe I have to meet Paul Newman.

HEIDI: I'm sure you do.

SCOOP: I'm picking him up at the airport and taking him and Mr. McCarthy to a press conference. Paul's a great guy. Why don't you come drinking with us? We can rap over a few brews.

HEIDI: I'm sorry. I can't.

SCOOP: Why not?

HEIDI: I just can't.

SCOOP: Susan, let me get this straight. You would rather drive back to Poughkeepsie with five virgins in a Volkswagen discussing Norman Mailer and birth control on dangerous frozen roads than go drinking with Eugene McCarthy, Paul Newman and Scoop Rosenbaum? You're cute, Susan. Very cute.

HEIDI: And you are really irritating!!.....

SCOOP: I like you, Susan. You're prissy, but I like you a lot.

HEIDI: Well, I don't know if I like you.

SCOOP: Why should you like me? I'm arrogant and difficult. But I'm very smart. So you'll put up with me. What?

HEIDI: What what?

SCOOP: You're thinking something.

HEIDI: Actually, I was wondering what mothers teach their sons that they never bother to tell their daughters.

SCOOP: What do you mean?

HEIDI: I mean, why the fuck are you so confident?

Heidi tells Scoop of her plan to have a career as an art historian. Scoop calls her "Heidi," which startles her. He explains that as editor-in-chief of the tiny *Liberated Earth News* he knows all (actually, she's forgotten that she's wearing a name tag). Scoop reminds her that she's the one with the most at stake in this push for political and social change.

SCOOP: .....You're the one this is all going to affect. You're the one whose life this will all change significantly. Has to. You're a very serious person. In fact, you're the unfortunate contradiction in terms—a serious good person. And I envy you that.

HEIDI: Thank you. I guess.

SCOOP: Yup. You'll be one of those true believers who didn't understand it was just a phase. The Trotskyite during Lenin's New Economic Policy. The worshipper of fallen images in Christian Judea.

HEIDI: And you?

SCOOP: Me? I told you. I'm just here to have a look around.

HEIDI: What if you get left behind?

SCOOP: You mean, if after all the politics you girls decide to go "hog wild," demanding equal pay, equal rights, equal orgasms?

HEIDI: All people deserve to fulfill their potential.

SCOOP: Absolutely.

HEIDI: I mean, why should some well-educated woman waste her life making you and your children tuna fish sandwiches?

SCOOP: She shouldn't. And for that matter, neither should a badly educated woman. Heidella, I'm on your side.

HEIDI: Don't call me "Heidella." It's diminutive.

SCOOP: You mean "demeaning," and it's not. It's endearing.

Scoop takes a direct approach—"I'm subtly asking you to go to bed with me"—and adds, "I can't guarantee absolute equality of experience." Scoop goes on: "You're a serious good person. And I'm honored. Maybe you'll think fondly of all this in some Proustian haze when you're thirty-five and picking your daughter up from the Ethical Culture school to escort her to cello class before dinner with Dad, the noted psychiatrist and Miro poster collector.....maybe I'll remember it one day when I'm thirty-five and watching my son's performance as Johnny Appleseed. Maybe I'll look at my wife who puts up with me and flash on when I was editor of a crackpot liberal newspaper and thought I could fall in love with Heidi Holland, the canvassing art historian."

He kisses her, and they exit, as the scene ends.

Scene 3: Ann Arbor, Michigan, 1970

In a church basement, "*Jill, 40, immaculate in a whale turtleneck and pleated skirt and Fran, 30, in army fatigues*" are setting things up for a women's rap session. Jill is organizing, Fran is dancing to "Respect" and making blunt four-letter-word comments. Becky, 17, "*in blue jeans and a poncho*" enters, shyly introduces herself and is made welcome by Jill. Then Heidi and Susan come in, both dressed in "*blue jeans, hiking boots and down jackets.*" Susan is greeted as a member of the group and introduces Heidi as a visiting friend.

Jill calls the consciousness-raising group to order. They all sit while she confesses that she used to be "a fuckin' Hostess cupcake," taking care of everybody in her life but forgetting to take care of herself.

BECKY: I feel that way sometimes.
SUSAN: We all feel that way sometimes.
BECKY: You do?
FRAN: No, we grow up on fuckin' *Father Knows Best* and we think we have rights! You think Jane Wyatt demanded clitoral satisfaction from Robert Young? No fuckin' way.
SUSAN: I love you, Fran.
JILL: I love you too, Fran.
FRAN (*primping*): Maybe I should dress for combat more often.
SUSAN: Fran, sometimes I think you let your defensiveness overwhelm your tremendous vulnerability.
JILL: Becky, Heidi, you should know that Fran is a gifted physicist, and a lesbian, and we support her choice to sleep with women.
BECKY: Sure.

FRAN: Do you support my choice, Heidi?

HEIDI: I'm just visiting.

FRAN: I have to say right now that I don't feel comfortable with a "just visiting" in the room. I need to be able to come here and reach out to you as my sisters. Okay, Heidi-ho?

HEIDI: Okay.

FRAN: Just don't judge us. Christ, we spend our lives having men judge us. All right, let the good times roll!

Susan reports that she's decided to work "within the male establishment power system" and accept a position on a Law Review. Fran throws her weight around almost reflexively, and Becky tells of problems with her family and boy friend. Asked to tell about herself, Heidi informs them that she is at Yale in the Art History graduate program.

HEIDI: My interest is in images of women from the Renaissance Madonna to the present.

FRAN: A feminist interpretation?

HEIDI: Humanist.

FRAN: Heidi, either you shave your legs or you don't.

HEIDI: I'm afraid I think body hair is in the realm of the personal.

FRAN: What *is* your problem, woman?

HEIDI: I don't really want to share that with you. I'm stingy that way.....

FRAN: Heidi, every woman in this room has been taught that the desires and dreams of her husband, her son or her boss are much more important than her own. And the only way to turn that around is for us, right here, to try to make what *we* want, what we desire, to be as vital to us as it would unquestionably be to any man. And then we can go out there and really make a difference!

SUSAN: I'm so happy I'm living at this time.

FRAN: Heidi, nothing's going to change until we really start talking to each other.

Heidi confesses that she is obsessed with Scoop Rosenbaum, "a charismatic creep" now a teaching fellow at Yale Law School. She knows that her old friend Peter Patrone would be a better choice, but she can't help herself. She allows Scoop to "account for so much of what I think of myself. I allow him to make me feel valuable. And the bottom line is, I know that's wrong. I would tell any friend of mine that's wrong. You either shave your legs or you don't."

The meeting is now a love feast all around. The women come together with their arms around each other and sway to the rhythm of a summer camp song sung by Jill, which Fran interrupts to play "Respect" again. They all dance as the scene ends.

Scene 4: Chicago, 1974

Outside the Chicago Art Institute, Heidi is leading a demonstration and protesting, via a bullhorn, that the Institute displays the work of too few women painters. She is holding an umbrella, and so is Peter when he comes in and joins the protest. The plan is to march on the curator's office to demand more attention to women artists, but there are only a couple of other women in the group, and they go off to see whether others have gone to the wrong place for the rendezvous.

Heidi intends to be in Chicago only four hours, so Peter has taken this slim opportunity to see her. He tells her he has become dyspeptic as part of the advance guard moving into a decade of self-obsession. He asks after Scoop. Heidi says he's clerking for the Supreme Court in Washington, "But I'm not involved with him any more. I just like sleeping with him."

Peter and Heidi have not seen each other for eight months while Heidi was writing her dissertation. She decides what Peter needs is a girl friend, and she's determined to help find him one. Peter asks her not to.

HEIDI: You've never liked my girl friends.
PETER: *Women* friends, and I like Fran, the furry physicist from Ann Arbor.
HEIDI: Fran is unavailable. I promise I'll find someone.
PETER (*earnestly*): Heidi, I don't play on your team.
HEIDI: So what? Susan says no man really plays on our team. And no man isn't threatened by our potential. Trust me, you're a lot more secure than most.
PETER: Is Susan the one who used to roll up her skirts with straight pins? She was always giving herself stigmatas in the waist.
HEIDI: She's become a radical shepherdess/counselor.
PETER: Good for her. I've become a liberal homosexual pediatrician.
HEIDI: Well, what I mean is, she lives on a woman's health and legal collective in Montana. Susan was clerking for the Supreme Court with Scoop, but, uh, uh … she realized she prefers, uh, uh …
PETER: Sheep. She realized she prefers sheep. And I prefer Stanley.
HEIDI: Who?
PETER: My friend's name is Stanley Zinc. He's a child psychiatrist from Johns Hopkins. But he's thinking of quitting in order to study with Merce Cunningham.....Anyway, I'm thinking of replacing him with a waiter I met last week.

Heidi is irritated with Peter for changing the subject from politics to sexual preference, but Peter insists that his pursuit of happiness merits as much of Heidi's attention and concern as women's painting. The other demonstrators return, but Heidi decides she can't leave Peter as they march off crying "Women in Art!" on the bullhorn.

PETER: Heidi, I know that somewhere you think my world view is small and personal and that yours resonates for generations to come.
HEIDI: I'm going to hit you.
PETER: I dare you. C'mon, put up your dukes.
He takes her hand and punches it against his arm.
That's for my having distorted sexual politics.
HEIDI: Correct.
Peter punches himself with her hand again.
PETER: And that's because your liberation is better than mine.
HEIDI: Correct again.
PETER (*punches himself with her hand again*): And that's for my decision to treat sick children rather than shepherd radical sheep. (*He hits himself.*) And that's for being paternal. And caustic.
HEIDI: Correct.
She begins hitting him on her own.
And that's for being so goddamned ...
PETER: Narcissistic? Supercilious?
HEIDI: No. Um ...
PETER: Sounds like?
HEIDI: Oh, I give up.
Suddenly she hits him again.
And that's for liking to sleep with men more than women.
She hits him again.
And that's for not being desperately and hopelessly in love with me.
PETER: That hurts!
HEIDI: Suffer.

Peter reassures Heidi that the future looks brighter than ever and advises her neither to lose her sense of humor nor to marry Scoop. Peter's new friend, the waiter, shows up and is persuaded to march off with them shouting "Women in Art!" as the scene ends.

Scene 5: New York, 1977

An anteroom of the Hotel Pierre ballroom is furnished with a couple of chairs and a table, on which flowers and a tray of champagne symbolize the party that can be heard through the door upstage. It's Scoop and Lisa Friedlander's wedding reception. Peter and Heidi join Susan and her friend Molly from Montana in the anteroom, and Peter is soon characterizing the bride as "went to good schools.....is not particularly threatening.....from the best Jewish family in Memphis." Susan comments, "I'm surprised he married someone so bland," but Heidi feels Lisa will be perfect for Scoop.

Scoop comes into the room, meets Peter for the first time and urges this jolly group to join the rest of the celebrity-filled party. After Susan and Molly go off into the ballroom, Scoop admits that Susan might have interested him if she were less of a fanatic and commited to women's causes. Scoop predicts that Susan will eventually give it all up and go to business school.

Staring at Scoop, Peter challenges him with "Are you in love?" and pretends that he and Heidi are also a romantic item. "Sure, why not?" Scoop replies as his bride Lisa comes into the room.

LISA (*with a very slight Southern accent*): Sweetie, they're about to play our first dance.

SCOOP: Sweetie, this is Peter Patrone and his fiancee, Heidi. Peter is a pediatrics resident at Bellevue.

LISA (*takes Peter's arm*): Hey there. How nice to see you.

SCOOP: I was just telling Peter that we're hoping for a large family.

PETER: Not common these days.

LISA: I've always known I wanted to be a mom. I guess that's pretty embarrassing.

PETER (*to Heidi*): Sweetie, do you think that's embarrassing?

HEIDI: No, sweetie, of course not. Not at all.

LISA: Well, I am going to keep up my illustration work.

SCOOP: Lisa's books are very popular.

PETER: Wait a second. Are you Lisa Friedlander, the illustrator of *King Ginger, the Lion*?

LISA: You know *King Ginger*?

PETER: The best medical text in the country is *King Ginger Goes to the Hospital*.

SCOOP (*puts his arm around Lisa*): She's terrific. Isn't she?

PETER: There'll be a riot in my waiting room if you stop working.

Lisa invites Peter to have the first dance with her, and they exit. Scoop accuses Heidi of letting him marry Lisa and wants to know if Heidi means to marry Peter. "Maybe," she says, though she knows Peter is gay; but she is now living with someone else, a writer of essays on art (Heidi nervously shreds a paper napkin as she tells Scoop all this). Scoop is planning to go back into journalism by starting a magazine. Heidi has applied for a Fulbright to write her next book in England. Finally they get around to the subject that interests both of them the most—Heidi and Scoop—and Heidi explains her presence here: "Peter wanted to meet you. That's why we came. He said if I witnessed your ritual it would put an end to an era." Scoop in his turn explains what he's doing here.

SCOOP: .....Let's say we married and I asked you to devote the, say, next ten years of your life to me. To making me a home and a family and a life so secure that I could with some confidence go out into the world each day and attempt to get an A. You'd say no. You'd say, "Why can't we be partners? Why can't we both go out in the world and get an A?" And you'd be absolutely valid and correct.

HEIDI: But Lisa ...

SCOOP: "Do I love her?" as your nice friend asked me. She's the best that I can do. Is she an A-plus like you? No. But I don't want to come home to an A-plus. A-minus maybe, but not A-plus.

HEIDI: Scoop, we're out of school. We're in life. You don't need to grade everything.

SCOOP: I'm sorry, Heidella. But I couldn't dangle you any more. And that's why I got married today. So.

HEIDI: So. So now it's all my fault.

SCOOP: Sure it is. You want other things in life than I do.

HEIDI: Really? Like what?

SCOOP: Self-fulfillment. Self-determination. Self-exaggeration.

HEIDI: That's exactly what you want.

SCOOP: Right. Then you'd be competing with me.....On a scale from one to ten, if you aim for six and get six, everything will work out nicely. But if you aim for ten in all things and get six, you're going to be very disappointed. And unfortunately, that's why you "quality time" girls are going to be one generation of disappointed women. Interesting, exemplary, even sexy, but basically unhappy. The ones who open doors usually are.

So Scoop will settle for a secure six and concentrate on his magazine. Heidi claims she hasn't made such life choices yet, but Scoop tells her, "Yes you have, or we'd be getting married today."

In the ballroom, a drum-roll is followed by an announcement that Scoop and Lisa have requested the song "You Send Me." But it is Heidi with whom Scoop dances the number, after kissing her, taking her in his arms and declaring, "I love you, Heidi, I'll always love you." He sings the lyric to her, while *"Lights fade as she looks at him, puts her head on his shoulder, and they slow dance."*

ACT II

All Act II scenes take place in New York
Prologue: A lecture hall, 1988

Lecturing on works of female painters, Heidi concludes, "There is something uniquely female about these paintings. And I'm not referring to their lovely qualities, delicate techniques or overall charm. Oh, please! What strikes me is, both ladies seem slightly removed from the occasions at hand. They appear to watch closely and ease the way for others to join in. I suppose it's really not unlike being an art historian. In other words, being neither the painter, nor the casual observer, but a highly informed spectator."

Scene 1: An apartment, 1980

At Lisa and Scoop's apartment a gathering of women includes Susan and Betsy (managing editor of Scoop's new magazine, *Boomer*). They are playing records and opening presents of baby clothes (Lisa is obviously pregnant). Heidi comes in, having attended the memorial for John Lennon in Central Park. Susan, it seems has left Montana, gone through business school and accepted an executive job with a new production company in Los Angeles. Lisa's younger sister, Denise, reassures them all that Ronald Reagan is going to be very good for the ecomony, and the 1980s are "going to be great." She plans to have all her children before she's 30, "once my career's in place."

Heidi admits she too would like to have a family—she almost got married in England, but her prospective spouse wouldn't move to the U.S. when Heidi got a job at Columbia. Betsy wishes she could make a match for all her single friends like Heidi, but apparently "There's absolutely no one." She admires Heidi's latest book, *And the Light Floods in From the Left*. So does Denise, who's a TV production assistant, and she thinks maybe they could do a "Women in the 80s" show on Heidi.

Denise goes to answer the phone—it's Scoop, who is apparently at Princeton taking part in a symposium. Lisa exits to talk to Scoop on the phone.

BETSY (*quietly*): I honestly don't think she knows.
DENISE: Oh, Lisa knows. She was being really cheerful. That means she knows.
BETSY: Honestly, you should see his little friend. She's a graphics assistant on the magazine. And now she runs around New York in leather miniskirts and fishnet stockings. And she's not very bright. She's like that entire generation. Except for you, Denise. They have opinions on everything and have done nothing. I'm sorry, Heidi. It's just someone we both don't care for very much.

HEIDI: You mean the woman Scoop's seeing?

SUSAN: What?

HEIDI: Susie, this morning I was with the best pediatrician under forty at the John Lennon memorial in Central Park, and Scoop was not at Princeton. Scoop was with the graphics assistant, also in Central Park.

SUSAN: Maybe it wasn't him.

HEIDI: Oh, it was him. He embraced me, shook hands with Peter and said it was very important we were all there. He said this was for our generation.

Lisa comes back and wonders what the others were "huddling about." They had just finished making a party hat for her out of wrapping paper, Betsy says. This token of their friendship—their concern for her—makes Lisa weep, evidently not only because of the paper hat. She pulls herself together. They all stand to toast the Beatles as the scene ends.

Scene 2: A TV studio, 1982

Steve (a studio hand) and Denise (visibly very pregnant) are setting up a program about the baby boom generation with Heidi, Scoop (whose second child has just been born) and Peter. On the air, they are introduced by the show's hostess, April. Peter immediately starts putting April on with mild sarcasm, but she is unflappable. Scoop tries to answer her questions seriously ("I think we're a generation that is still idealistic, and idealists wonder what they're going to do when they grow up" or "Having my own family has certainly pulled me out of any 'Me Generation' residue"). As for Heidi, she can hardly get a word in edgewise.

APRIL: .....Heidi, a lot of women are beginning to feel you can't have it all. Do you think it's time to compromise?

HEIDI: Well, I think that depends on ...

SCOOP: Can I interrupt and say that I think if we're asking women to compromise, then we also have to ask men to compromise. This year, my wife Lisa won the Widener Prize for her illustrations of *King Ginger Goes to Summer Camp*. I'm every bit as proud of that as I am of *Boomer* magazine.

APRIL: But Scoop, everyone isn't as capable as Lisa. For instance, a lot of my single women friends are panicked now about their biological clocks winding down. Do you find that's true, Heidi?

HEIDI: If you look ...

PETER (*cuts her off*): April, can I still call you "April?"

APRIL: You have the sweetest face. Can we get a closeup of this face?

PETER: I run one of the largest pediatric units in this country. And I am here to tell you that most women can have healthy and happy children till well after forty-two.

APRIL: Well, my friends will certainly be happy to hear that. Peter, so far you've chosen not to have children.

PETER (*after a pause*): I think, April, what distinguishes our generation from the previous one is our belief that any individual has a right to pursue his or her particular lifestyle. In other words, say you want to dress up as a Tylenol capsule to host "Hello New York" tomorrow … (*In outrageous mock-camp.*) I'd say there's no need, but why not? Go for it!

APRIL (*looks at him and back at her card; to Heidi*): So what's next? After the kids and the country house? Once we're settled, Heidi, do you think we'll see a resurgence of a social conscience?

HEIDI: Uh …

PETER: Yes, Betsy Bloomingdale will be at the barricades.

APRIL: Heidi …

SCOOP: There's a line in a Ferlinghetti poem. "And I am awaiting the rebirth of wonder." I think we're all awaiting a rebirth of wonder.

PETER (*sharp*): What does that mean exactly? I wonder.

APRIL: I'm afraid we only have a minute left. Scoop, *Boomer* magazine was an immediate success. Something very rare in the magazine business. Why?

SCOOP: Well, as you've seen this morning, we're serious people with a sense of humor. We're not young professionals, and we're not old lefties or righties. We're unique. We're powerful, but not bullies. We're rich, but not ostentatious. We're parents, but we're not parental. And I think we had the left magazines in college, we had the music magazines in the seventies, and now we deserve what I call a "power" magazine in the eighties. We're opinion and trend-setters, and I hope *Boomer* is our chronicle.

APRIL: It certainly looks like it's heading in that direction. The baby boom generation, are they all grown up now? Well, they're rich, powerful, famous and even parents. But who knows what we'd do if Peter Pan came through our bedroom windows? Thank you, Scoop Rosenbaum, editor of *Boomer* magazine, Heidi Holland, essayist, curator, feminist, and Dr. Peter Patrone, chief of pediatrics at New York Hospital.

PETER: Thank you, April. Goodbye, New York.

Off the air, April sums up Peter, "That face is so sweet and that mind is so savage." Scoop invites April and her husband to lunch at Le Cirque. She wonders who else will be there, and when she hears that Scoop's friend Paul Newman is joining them, she accepts. After April exits, Scoop confides to the others that she is "irrelevant," but her husband owns an enormous amount of Manhattan real estate. Scoop found Peter's on-air comments "hilarious." Peter suggests that Heidi won the conversation because she didn't say anything. "How could I say anything when both of you were so eager and willing to say it for me? You two should become regulars here, the cynic and the idealist," Heidi replies and exits frostily despite the others' attempt to soothe her.

SCOOP (*to Peter*): I didn't mean to upset her. We were once very close.

PETER: Yup.

SCOOP: You and she are still very close.

PETER: Yup.

SCOOP: That's nice. You know, I'm sorry I never really got to know you. You seem like a very nice man.

PETER: Are you having a sentimental spasm? You seem to be sorry, moved and touched at the drop of a hat. It's sort of manic.

SCOOP: Fatherhood changes people.

PETER: Oh, please ...

SCOOP: Heidi says that. "Oh, please." You and Heidi have managed to maintain a friendship. I envy you that. How do you do it?

PETER: Scoop, I'd like to leave before April comes back.

SCOOP: Peter, do people like you ever wonder what it's all for?

PETER: People like you run the world. You decide what it's all for.

SCOOP: You know what genuinely surprises me? You're a far more arrogant man than I am.

PETER: Scoop, I'm just a simple man of medicine. And now I leave you to await the rebirth of wonder.

He exits. Scoop stares out, as the scene ends.

Ellen Parker (Susan), Sarah Jessica Parker (Denise) and
Joan Allen (Heidi) in a scene from *The Heidi Chronicles*

Scene 3: A restaurant, 1984

Susan joins Heidi at a table in a fashionable restaurant ("There must be no one in L.A. Everybody's here"), and they start catching up. Heidi is putting on art exhibitions, writing, seeing something of a lawyer who calls her "angel." Susan, a producer, has hired Denise as an assistant and has asked her to join them here, though Heidi had hoped to see Susan alone.

SUSAN: .....For a while now I've been wanting to put together a half-hour show about three women turning thirty in a large urban center. It can be New York, Chicago, Houston. I want to really get into the issues—dating, careers, marriage. There are at least ten other single-women series currently being developed. But your history with women and art could make us a little different.

DENISE: They've already done doctors, lawyers, nurses and detectives. But when you called, we realized that no one has touched the art world.

SUSAN: What we're interested in is, say, a way-out painter, an uptight curator and a dilettante heiress in a loft.

HEIDI: In Houston?

SUSAN: Wherever. You don't have to write. We'll hire a writer. It's a package, and we want you as our consultant.

HEIDI: Susie, I'm an art historian and essayist. I'm very flattered, but ...

SUSAN: Maybe some network executive who actually read a book five years ago will recognize your name and buy the pilot.....Heidi, this is something we can really care about. You and I are people who need to commit. I'm not political any more. I mean, equal rights is one thing, equal pay is one thing, but blaming everything on being a woman is just passe.

DENISE: Really.

SUSAN: Okay, three gals on the town in an apartment. Curators, painters, sculptors, what have you.

DENISE: All we need is three pages. Who these people are. Why they're funny.

HEIDI: But I have no idea who these people are. Or why they're funny.

DENISE: They're ambitious, they're professional, and they're on their way to being successful.

SUSAN: And they don't want to make the same mistakes we did.

HEIDI: I don't want to make the same mistakes we did. What exactly were they?

DENISE: Well, like, a lot of women your age are very unhappy. Unfulfilled, frightened of growing old alone.

HEIDI: It's a good thing we're not doing a sitcom about them.

DENISE: Oh, I know. I can't imagine life without my husband or little Max.

Our girls want to get married in their twenties, have their first baby by thirty and make a pot of money. It's just much more together than your generation.

SUSAN: Is that Diane Keaton? I think that's Diane Keaton. Heidi, you'll come to L.A. next week. We'll meet with the network and get going on this. Diane looks terrific! I'd love to get her into a series. But until Meryl does a series, none of them will do a series.

HEIDI: Susie, I can't do it either.

DENISE: Why not?

HEIDI: Because I don't think we made such big mistakes. And I don't want to see three gals on the town who do.

If Heidi doesn't like that idea, they'll come up with another one—but Heidi isn't interested in TV. Susan and Denise make their cordial goodbyes and exit in the direction of Diane Keaton, as the scene ends.

Scene 4: The Plaza Hotel, 1986

Heidi is giving an address on the chosen topic "Women—Where Are We Going?" to a reunion of her classmates of the school from which she graduated in 1965. She tells them she doesn't lead anywhere nearly as scheduled a "quality time" life as they probably imagine. She goes into what she did yesterday, lecturing at Columbia on Alexander Pope, then going on to an exercise class of women, attended by many different types, from a woman "who has perfect red nails and confessed to anyone who would listen the hardship of throwing her dinner party on the same night as a benefit at the Met" to a pair of "twenty-seven-year-old hot shots" dressed in purple leather and carrying alligator datebooks.

Heidi felt awkward and alienated in the midst of these women, she tells her audience. She decided not to take the class after all, the reason being that she was just not happy—"I'm afraid I haven't been happy for some time." She finishes by explaining to her audience, "I don't blame the ladies in the locker room for how I feel. I don't blame any of us. We're all concerned, intelligent, good women. (*Pause.*) It's just that I feel stranded. And I thought the whole point was that we wouldn't feel stranded. I thought the point was, we were all in this together. Thank you." Heidi walks off as the scene ends.

Scene 5: A pediatrics ward, 1987

It is midnight, the ward is closed to visitors, but Heidi is carrying in boxes of toys and records as a donation, under the eye of Ray, "*a young man in a doctor's uniform sitting on a child's desk and smoking.*" Peter comes in, angry at this intrusion. Both of them apologize to Ray, who merely wishes them Merry Christmas and departs.

Heidi brought the boxes because she's been packing her belongings prior to a move to the Midwest to teach and finish her new book. She's also come to say goodbye to Peter. She's upset because Peter seems to be unusually cool toward her.

HEIDI (*softly*): Peter, sweetie, what is it?

PETER (*moves away*): Nothing. So you're going to Northfield, Minnesota to start again. Goodbye, New York. Goodbye, mistakes. Make new friends. Give donations to the old.

HEIDI: I hate it when you're like this.

PETER: Heidi, you arrived at midnight and promptly announced you're leaving tomorrow. I'm just feeling my way through here.

HEIDI: I thought you would be the person who would completely understand.

PETER (*quite angry*): Understand what? Looking back at your life and regretting your choices? Deciding your work, your friends, your history are totally expendable.

HEIDI: You have a life here that works for you, I don't.

PETER: Right. So I am expendable, too.

HEIDI: Peter, stop it!

PETER (*very distant*): I'm not doing anything. I was going to spend a quiet Christmas here with the Hardy Boys.

HEIDI: The Hardy Boys?

PETER: For our last midnight donation, we received my sister-in-law Paula Patrone's complete childhood collection of Nancy Drew, the Bobbsey twins, the Hardy Boys, Honey Bunch and *Heidi*, which I actually perused last night in your honor.

He picks up a book from the floor.

Did you know that the first section is Heidi's year of travel and learning, and the second is Heidi uses what she knows? (*Softly.*) How will you use what you know, Heidi?

HEIDI: I've been sad for a long time. I don't want to be sad any more.

Peter tries to stay cheerful (though he mistrusts forced cheerfulness), and his present mood was probably brought on because he just received bad news about his friend Stanley's health. With this, and with Heidi's imminent departure, his world is becoming uncomfortably narrow. Heidi offers to postpone her trip West for a year: "I promise you won't lose this member of your family." Echoing the night they met at the high school dance (Peter is in tears), Heidi picks up a couple of dixie cups and pretends that they have just met on a cruise, repeating the line, "I want to know you all my life. If we can't marry, let's be great friends." They sing the words to "The Shoop Shoop

Song" to each other very softly, then embrace, then wish each other Merry Christmas as the scene ends.

Scene 6: An apartment, 1988

In an almost empty room with a fireplace in the background, Heidi is seated in a rocking chair checking some papers, when Scoop enters. They go through their usual friendly banter, including the information that Heidi is seeing an editor she rather likes. Scoop has sold *Boomer* magazine (Heidi is the first to know) and says he plans to collect maritime art. Heidi can't understand why Scoop sold his magazine, when he liked editing it and was good at his job.

SCOOP: .....I helped get a few people elected, and a few people investigated, and a single man who likes oral sex when he reads the Talmud placed an ad and married a woman who doesn't. I did all that. Now what?

HEIDI: What do you mean?

SCOOP: Now what? What do I show my children and say, "See, kids, Daddy did that?" Do I say, "See that restaurant, Maggie? Daddy started going there, and suddenly everybody was going there until they started going somewhere else?" Do I say, "Pierre, your father was known as an arbiter of good taste in a decade defined as sexy and greedy?" Or is my greatest legacy to them buying a farm in Litchfield County before the land value went soaring? Will my kids say, "My dad was basically a lazy man and a philanderer, but he had a nose for Connecticut real estate, and we love him because he didn't make us weekend in the Hamptons?"

HEIDI: I didn't know you worried so much about your children.

SCOOP: I'm sorry. I mean, we hardly know each other any more. (*He looks at her.*) I'm being very self-indulgent. Yes?

HEIDI: Yes.

SCOOP: I'm a spoiled man with superficial values. Yes?

HEIDI: Don't look at me like that.

SCOOP: Like what?

HEIDI: Don't look at me with those doe eyes and tell me how spoiled you are. Next thing I know, you'll tell me you never meant to hurt me.

SCOOP: Maybe we should try again.

HEIDI: Why?

SCOOP: You're lonely and I'm lost.

HEIDI: Oh, please.

　　　　Pause.

SCOOP (*smiles*): I thought you might enjoy that.

HEIDI: I did. A lot.

SCOOP: How much?

HEIDI: A lot.

SCOOP: So as my old friend and long time observer, what do you think I should do now?

HEIDI: I'd say hold on to the land in Litchfield County.

Scoop kisses Heidi on the cheek, as she observes that they might have married but wouldn't have stayed married. They reminisce a bit, and Scoop asks after Peter—he's moved in with Ray, and they have a house in Bucks County.

And Scoop has heard from Susan Heidi's news: Heidi has adopted a baby. The baby, a girl named Judy, is asleep in the next room. It's not impossible — Heidi insists—that some day Judy Holland will meet Pierre Rosenbaum, maybe in a plane over Chicago: "And he'll never tell her it's either/or, baby. And she'll never think she's worthless unless he lets her have it all. And maybe, just maybe, things will be a little better. And yes, that does make me happy."

Scoop has brought a silver spoon as a present for the baby. Heidi goes into the other room, as Scoop calls to her that he's dating an actress. Heidi comes back wheeling a baby carriage. Scoop greets the infant and comments, "They all look like Winston Churchill. A-plus intelligence, B-minus vocabulary." Scoop prepares to leave, and Heidi sees him to the entry way.

SCOOP: Hey, Heidella. If I do something crazy like announce I'm running for Congress next week, will you and Peter be there? Gay men and single mothers for Rosenbaum. Grass roots movements. A man for all genders.

HEIDI: So that's why you sold your magazine. Are you putting together a crackpot coalition?

SCOOP: Why not? It's time we had equal representation. All people deserve to fulfill their potential. Judy, that's what your mother told me in 1967 on the first snowy night in Manchester, New Hampshire. America needs heroes.

HEIDI: Scoop, you are many things, but ...

Scoop takes Heidi's hand.

SCOOP: What do you think, Judy? A mother for the nineties and a hero for the nineties. 'Bye, Heidella.

He kisses her on the cheek, exits.....Heidi takes Judy out of the stroller and lifts her up.

HEIDI: A heroine for the twenty-first! (*She sits in the rocker and begins to sing softly, adding her own spirited high and low harmonies.*)

"Darling, you send me.

Darling, you send me.

Honest you do, honest you do, honest you do."

Lights fade as Heidi rocks. Curtain.

OTHER PEOPLE'S MONEY

A Play in Two Acts

BY JERRY STERNER

Cast and credits appear on page 452

JERRY STERNER was born in The Bronx in 1938. His mother loved the theater and took him there frequently, and in his teens Inherit the Wind *so impressed him that he determined to try writing plays himself. He was educated in New York City public schools and CCNY, which he attended for six years without graduating, working during the day to earn the money for college at night. In 1965, still with an eye on the theater, he landed a job working in a subway toll booth (tokens were then 15 cents) on the night shift, 11 p.m. to 7 a.m., giving him the means and, in the slow hours, the time to write plays. Finally he submitted a script to Edward Albee's aspiring young playwrights' group, was rejected, attended the performance of the winners and was so disappointed in what he saw that he decided, finally, that this kind of theater wasn't for him.*

In 1970, Sterner went into the real estate business, succeeded handsomely ("writing a lease can be as creative as writing a play") and retired as president of David Gold and Company in 1984 with the means to concentrate

277

on his writing and at the same time support his family. His Be Happy for Me *was produced off off Broadway at the Judith Anderson Theater May 15, 1985 and then off Broadway Jan. 7, 1986 for only one performance. His second produced play,* Other People's Money, *appeared in a reading at Los Angeles Theater Works and production in Teaneck, N.J. before opening off Broadway Feb. 16 and collecting his first Best Play citation. Sterner is married, with two daughters, and lives in Brooklyn.*

Time: The present

Place: New York and Rhode Island

ACT I

SYNOPSIS: Most of the setting represents the Rhode Island factory complex of New England Wire and Cable and its executive offices. Downstage a walkway circles the playing area and ends down right in the New York office of Lawrence Garfinkle, *"an obese, elegant, cunning New York 'takeover artist,' about 40."*

William Coles ("mid–40s, attractive, polished"), president of New England Wire and Cable, appears in a spotlight at center and promises to tell an important story "about loyalty, tradition, friendship and, of course, money." The story starts several years before, on a day when Coles and the company chairman, Andrew Jorgenson ("*68, a good looking man in good physical condition.....a 'hands-on' type, more comfortable with his sleeves rolled up tinkering with a machine than sitting in a board room*"), are nervously expecting a visit from the abovementioned Lawrence Garfinkle from New York, at a time when more company shares have been traded in the last month than in the past year, and the stock has just risen two points.

Bea Sullivan ("*longtime assistant and friend of Jorgenson, an attractive woman in her early 60s*") enters and calls their attention to the window where Garfinkle can be seen emerging from his stretch limo. After a moment or two, Garfinkle enters ("*He is an immense man of 40, though he looks older. He is always elegantly dressed, surprisingly graceful for his bulk. He is in some way larger than life. His deep, rich voice fills the stage*"). He declines an invitation to have his chauffeur come inside ("He's a 'yard' chauffeur. Bring him inside and you'll spoil him"). After introductions, he sits, and when offered coffee asks for Dunkin' Donuts. They don't have any, so Garfinkle takes out a roll of bills, hands it to Bea and sends her off in his limousine to fetch a dozen of any kind of local donuts she can find.

James Murtaugh as William Coles in *Other People's Money*

JORGENSON: Larry, you made her day. Last limo we saw up here was in '48 when Harry Truman was running for President. Came right here to the plant. Come, I'll show you.

Takes him to window.

Stood right out there. Right there. Gave a speech. Just after the war. It was the golden age, rebuilding America and all. Had thirty-five hundred men working right here. Right at this plant. Going twenty-four hours a day, seven days a week. Truman gave a fine talk. Very impressive. Only Democrat I ever voted for.

COLES: What can we do for you, Mr. Garfinkle? What brings a busy man like you up this way?

GARFINKLE: Harry Truman stories don't grab you, huh?

COLES: We're all busy.

GARFINKLE: You're right. Let's do business. I got a computer back in New York. Call her Carmen. Every morning when I wake up—before I even brush my teeth, I punch out, "Carmen computer on the wall, who's the fairest of them all?" You'll forgive me—my programmer isn't Shakespeare.

COLES: Go on.

GARFINKLE: Most mornings she spits out, "You are, Garfinkle, you're the fairest of them all." But once in a while, maybe two, three times a year, she says something else. Six weeks ago she said: "Garfinkle, Garfinkle, scratch your balls, New England Wire and Cable is the fairest of them all."

Jorgenson laughs.

I thought it was funny too. "Wire and Cable—gross me out," I yell back to Carmen. And I do it again. "Carmen computer on the wall, who's the fairest of them all?" She responds, "Don't be a schmuck, Garfinkle—do the numbers!"

COLES: I'm interested. Do the numbers.

GARFINKLE: Get a paper and pencil. Carmen will educate you.

Coles takes a pad and pencil from Jorgenson's desk.

The wire and cable business is a little soft. Has been for the last ten years. What's it worth?

JORGENSON: This would not be a good time to—

GARFINKLE: I know. I'm not blaming you. You've done a hell of a job. You've kept it alive. That's an accomplishment. Carmen agrees. I'll bet she thinks it's worth more than you do. She says you got equipment up here that cost a hundred and twenty million. Worth, even at salvage, thirty, thirty-five million. Write down thirty million. How many acres you got here?

COLES: One hundred ten.

GARFINKLE: What's that worth?

JORGENSON: It would depend on what it's used for.

GARFINKLE: Worst case basis. Grazing land. Ten million fair?

Coles nods.

Good. Write down ten million. Put it underneath the thirty.

As they continue figuring the company's assets, Jorgenson reminds Garfinkle that Coles has helped them to diversify and they have other more profitable businesses which offset the wire and cable losses: "We haven't paid taxes in years." And they haven't shown a profit in years, either, Garfinkle observes. He estimates that the rest of the assets amount to about six times its $10 million annual cash flow, plus $25 million in working capital. Added to the other figures, this makes the company worth about $125 million, or, conservatively (as Garfinkle likes to figure it), at least $100 million. The company has no debt or other liabilities. Its four million shares divided into its $100 million assets make the shares worth $25 each—and they were selling at $10 before Garfinkle started buying. He's now acquired just under 5 per

cent of New England Wire and Cable (at 5 per cent he would have to file a
13–D form with the Securities and Exchange Commission). "Plan on buying
more?" Coles inquires, but Garfinkle doesn't commit himself either way.

Bea returns with the donuts (healthful, rustic honey and whole wheat,
Garfinkle doesn't want any part of them), much impressed with the amenities
of the limo. After being welcomed by Jorgenson as a stockholder and assured
that none of the stockholders' investment is wasted here in the operations of
the company Jorgenson's father founded, Garfinkle takes his leave.

The lights come up on Garfinkle in his New York office with desk and
computer downstage center. Coles enters and tries to open with polite small
talk, but Garfinkle urges him to get to the point of his visit. Garfinkle now owns
10 percent of the company and still buying (Coles observes), and Coles wants
to know how much farther Garfinkle intends to go with his purchase of its
stock. "That's none of your business," Garfinkle declares and brusquely
pushes Coles into revealing frankly the self interest behind this visit. Coles
wants two years of grace for the status quo. Jorgenson is 68, will retire at 70,
and has promised Coles that "it'd be my company to run when he steps
down." Coles can cause the profitable sections of the company to grow by 20
percent annually, so that the package will be worth a good deal more two
years from now.

GARFINKLE: Billy boy, look at me. I weigh a ton. I smoke three packs a
day. I walk from here to there, I'm out of breath. I can't even steal life insurance. Two years for me is forever. Do what you have to do now. I'm not a
long-term player.

COLES: I can't do it now, I can't do it till he leaves. If I try, I'm out on my
ear.

GARFINKLE (*handing Coles his briefcase*): That's the problem with working for a living.

COLES: Two years is not a long time. I have waited a lifetime for the
opportunity.

GARFINKLE (*puts his arm around Coles's shoulder*): You got stock, don't
you?

COLES: Yes.

GARFINKLE: Fifty, seventy-five thousand, right?

COLES: Sixty.

GARFINKLE: Well, shit, look—want to feel better?

Garfinkle taps out stock on his quote machine.

Before you heard my name your stock was ten. Now it's fourteen and a half.
In two months I made you a quarter of a million dollars. Billy boy, the least you
can do is smile.....

The lighting changes the scene to Jorgenson's office, where Coles is arriving back from his trip to New York. Coles informs his boss that Garfinkle, now the owner of 11 percent of the stock, means to take over this company. Jorgenson reminds Coles that "I have a million shares—that's twenty-five percent," and he doesn't believe that the stock is rising in price only because Garfinkle is buying it.

"You don't understand," Coles says, "He's well known. What he does is not a secret. He's called 'Larry the Liquidator' on Wall Street. He finds companies worth more dead than alive, gains control and kills them. Then he pockets the proceeds and goes on to the next one. He spelled it out for us right here in this office."

Coles suggests they protect themselves by changing the bylaws to require a two-thirds majority for control—but they'd have to move the incorporation from Rhode Island to Delaware. Jorgenson won't have it, though such a move would show fight. The boss believes they've survived in Rhode Island and will continue to survive in Rhode Island. With Jorgenson's 25 percent, the Board's 10 percent and employees' 5 percent, they'll be able to ward off predators. Those owning the remaining 60 percent, Jorgenson believes, are "long-term holders. If they were looking to sell they would've sold when the stock was sixty.....You are paid to manage this company. Manage it. It's my company. I'll see to it that it stays that way, thank you."

The lights and scene change to a conversation between Coles and Garfinkle, who now owns half a million shares, which are now over 15. Garfinkle demands that Coles raise the subject of restructuring the company with Jorgenson. Coles can't do this in the short time Garfinkle grants him— two weeks—so Garfinkle is soon on his way back to Rhode Island to handle the situation himself.

When Garfinkle arrives, New England Wire and Cable is ready for him in one sense: they have designed and built a special trolley filled with many different kids of donuts, and Bea wheels it in. The trolley is a homemade product, but the donuts are Dunkin'—Bea went to Providence to obtain them. Jorgenson suggests that Garfinkle take the trolley home with him and set it up in his office, and Garfinkle comments, "With all the pricks in the world I got to do business with a nice guy."

When they get down to business, Garfinkle asks that they sell the Wire and Cable division, which is a cancer "starving out all the other boring things Billy boy runs." Garfinkle will find them "some paper-shuffling Wall Street types" who will buy the division and profit from the tax advantages of selling off its assets.

JORGENSON: And what happens to the plant?
GARFINKLE: Gets sold for scrap.
JORGENSON: And the men? And the town?

GARFINKLE: Not your problem. You're not the mayor. You're not a missionary.

JORGENSON: So that's what they mean when they talk about restructuring—maximizing shareholder values?

GARFINKLE: That's what they mean.

JORGENSON: Nice turn of phrase. We used to call it "going out of business."

GARFINKLE: Welcome to the wonderful world of Wall Street.

JORGENSON: Shouldn't surprise me. Those boys down there can't charge millions by going out of business. First they become lawyers and investment bankers—then they restructure.

GARFINKLE: On Wall Street, "Restructuring means never having to say you're sorry." Got it?

JORGENSON: I got it. Now you get it. I understand what you want. Thank you for coming.

GARFINKLE: Yorgy, are you dismissing me?

JORGENSON: I have no time for this. I have a company to run.....

GARFINKLE: Don't get your bowels in an uproar. We're just doing business.

JORGENSON: Do it somewhere else. You're not welcome here.

GARFINKLE: Now I'm going to tell you something. I don't like the way my company is being run. There is a God damned fire raging here, and this whole industry is up in flames. And you call the Fire Department, and who shows up? Nobody. Because they're all in Japan and Singapore and Malaysia and Taiwan and every other shithole place where they're crazy about pollution. And they build factories over there, and they stuff them with little dedicated people who work for twelve cents an hour, ten hours a day, six days a week, and then they go home at night and pray for their health so they can come back and do it again tomorrow. And while that God damned inferno is raging, you're out front tidying up, mowing the lawn, playing with your putz on my money.

JORGENSON: Now you listen to me. This plant was here before you were born, and I promise you—will be here long after you're gone. Its products helped build the roads, bridges and buildings throughout the face of New England. And I will not—do you understand me—will not have it commit suicide and kill these people and this town so you and your cronies can pocket the insurance money.

GARFINKLE: Don't think of it as suicide. Think of it as euthenasia.

JORGENSON: Go back to those other parasites on Wall Street. Tell them to restructure somewhere else.

Bea and Jorgenson express their anger by throwing a donut at Garfinkle and kicking over the trolley. The lights go down in the Jorgenson office and come up on Kate Sullivan, Bea's daughter, "*an attractive, sexy Wall Street attorney, about 35,*" alone onstage talking to her mother on the phone. Kate is hearing about the intended takeover of Wire and Cable, considers it about as attractive as "taking over the psychiatric ward at Bellevue." Bea asks her daughter to come to the plant to advise them. Kate agrees to take a day off from Morgan, Stanley next month. "Tomorrow," Bea tells her, "the early flight." Kate has no alternative but to yield to her mother.

Lights up in the office where Kate, carrying her briefcase, arrives to confer with Bea, Coles and Jorgenson. Kate suggests a possible "greenmail" deal to pay off Garfinkle and get rid of him. Jorgenson will make no deal with the predator. As Kate begins to explain what other options may be available to them, "*lights up on Garfinkle as he views, unseen by them, their meeting,*" and the scene is played imagining that Garfinkle can see and hear what is going on and comment upon it.

Kate suggests the possibility of hiring an investigator to look for dirt in Garfinkle's background. "Investigated?" Garfinkle scoffs, "I get sued or subpoenaed every week." Coles likes the idea, but Jorgenson vetoes it.

JORGENSON: .....We have better things to do with our money.

GARFINKLE: The man's got class ... or he's cheaper than shit.

KATE: Get the Board to authorize a search for a "white knight."

BEA: White knight?

KATE: A protector. A larger company that will buy you out and allow you to do business the way you want. You know, someone to rescue the damsel in distress ... a white knight.

JORGENSON: I don't know anyone like that.

BEA (*to Kate*): Do you?

GARFINKLE: Of course she doesn't. (*Smiles, pats his middle.*) You got to have the stomach for it.

JORGENSON: Next.

KATE: We can formulate a "shark repellent."

BEA: Come again?

KATE: The purpose of a shark repellent is to make yourself undesirable to an unwanted suitor, i.e., shark.

BEA: How would that work?

GARFINKLE: Listen close. It's an education.

KATE: Take the most attractive part of the company—in this case I assume it's the non-wire and cable divisions—give someone, anyone, the option to buy that part of the business for a song. The option only gets triggered if and when anyone not presently on the Board acquires thirty percent or more of the company's stock. Garfinkle buys more shares, the option gets triggered. He now owns a lot of shares that are worth considerably less than he paid for them.

JORGENSON: So do we. So do all stockholders.

KATE: That's the risk. The hope is that the shark will go elsewhere to feed.

GARFINKLE: Ingenious, isn't it? Next.

JORGENSON: Next.

GARFINKLE: Mah man.

KATE: We could create a "poison pill." It's a form of shark repellent, but one you might find more acceptable. Get the Board to authorize three million shares of preferred stock, one share for each share held by all but Garfinkle. If he gains control of thirty percent or more, issue them for say—a dollar a share.

JORGENSON: A dollar a share!

COLES: What a great idea. We'd make Garfinkle's shares worth less. We'd dilute them.

JORGENSON: We would be diluting ours as well. Book value and earnings per share would be halved.

KATE: Exactly. Once you swallow the poison pill you're no longer desirable. But you can still keep your businesses. To most everyone, nothing has changed.

GARFINKLE: Except the "stuckholder." People get paid big money—honored people—pillars of the community—to sit and dream this shit up. You know what I said when I first heard it?

JORGENSON: That's legal?

GARFINKLE: That's what I said.

Kate further informs Jorgenson that if her firm took on New England Wire and Cable as a client in these matters, it might cost $1 or $2 million—or many times that if it went into litigation. Jorgenson voices his dismay that the daughter of his best friend and assistant would outline the situation in such harsh terms. "Don't blame the messenger for the message," is Kate's reply, and she will send no bill either from her company or herself for this visit. But she explains, before leaving, that speculators all over the country have noticed that this company stock has suddenly begun to rise, and that Garfinkle—whose interest is now public knowledge via the form he had to file—is responsible: "They know Garfinkle and they ride the coattails. Congratulations. You're now 'in play' in the big leagues where the game is called hardball and the winner takes all.....And the shame of it is, I would be perfect for this deal. Garfinkle is a blatant sexist. I love blatant sexists. They're my meat. But I wouldn't work for you if you begged me. I like being associated with winners."

The lights change and come up on Bea and Kate, with Bea reproaching her daughter for talking that way to Jorgenson. Kate expresses her concern that her mother has devoted her life to this company and will be left with nothing if it folds. Bea assures her daughter she's well provided for, and it is obvious that

Bea's attachment to Jorgenson is more than merely a business relationship—and everybody knows it. "Why in God's name did you ever marry Dad?" Kate wants to know. "I was nineteen. He asked. I thought I loved him," Bea replies and goes on, "Until one day, thank God, I walked through that door. And there stood the most beautiful, scared young man I had ever seen. Had on blue jeans and a red flannel shirt with the sleeves rolled up. Said he just became president. I remember thinking, 'How peculiar for a president. This company'll never last.' And then the magic words: 'How about it, Miss? I'm ready to take a chance with you. Ready to take one with me?'"

Bea begs Kate to take their case. Kate cannot deny her mother, and besides, she sees it as a career opportunity. She agrees. Bea's parting shot is, "And you'll do something about those fees. They're horrendous."

Lights up on Garfinkle's office where he is reflecting on the unattractiveness of the arbitrageurs with whom he customarily deals. When attractive Kate enters and introduces herself as the lawyer for New England Wire and Cable, Garfinkle is delighted. He has a stable of lawyers in the outer office, but he never talks to them, he sends them terse orders in writing. Garfinkle offers Kate a donut. She refuses.

GARFINKLE: Why not—you a health food freak?
KATE: No. Just not hungry.
GARFINKLE (*incredulous*): You have to be hungry to have a donut?

Kevin Conway as Lawrence Garfinkle and Mercedes Ruehl
as Kate Sullivan in a scene from *Other People's Money*

KATE: ... you don't?

GARFINKLE: Are you shitting me? In all my life I never heard of such a thing. Have to be hungry? Why? It don't taste better that way.

KATE: How would you know?

GARFINKLE: My luck. A broad with a mouth.

KATE: Show me a broad worth knowing who doesn't have one.

GARFINKLE (*laughs*): I like you. Can you tell?

KATE: Not yet.

GARFINKLE: Hang in. You will.

Kate has come to ask for a month's time in which to get New England Wire and Cable's act together, or she'll tie him up in court with injunctions and other lawyer's tricks. Garfinkle gives her two weeks in which he promises to hold off, buy no more stock. She thanks him and prepares to exit, but he has something else on his mind.

KATE: What's that?

GARFINKLE: You're legs ... your ass ... your tits ...

KATE (*leaning forward, her face close to his*): Garfinkle, *sit.* (*He does.*) Listen close. I don't want to repeat this. You listening? Now take your right hand out of that donut drawer and put it between your legs. (*He looks at her, uncertain.*) Come on. They visit each other all the time.

GARFINKLE (*laughs ... a little nervously*): ... Can't

KATE: Why?

GARFINKLE: I'm a lefty. (*Switches hands. Fumbles a bit.*)

KATE: Good. Now look directly down at the little guy and say—"You must behave yourself when you're in the presence of a lady." (*Garfinkle sits motionless, transfixed.*) Garfinkle, if you don't say exactly that, right now, I'm resigning from this case. You'll deal with the Morgan, Stanley B team. They think arbitrageurs are fun.

Garfinkle does as ordered and throws Kate a donut as a peace offering. She leaves, as Garfinkle comments, "I think I'm falling in love." Munching her donut as she goes, Kate admits to herself, "The man does have ... a certain undeniable ... charm."

In Jorgenson's office, Kate reports that they have been allowed two weeks to get organized. She advises them to start buying as much stock as they can, either with company reserves or with borrowed money, to make fewer shares available on the market and push the price higher, discouraging Garfinkle. Jorgenson is proud of his debt-free balance sheet, but it makes the company all that more attractive to raiders.

Kate also advises them to get in touch with the major stockholders emphasizing the company's ever-brighter future; also, to try to get the politicians interested in the company as a community asset.

Coles brings up the subject of "golden parachutes." It's too soon to discuss this, Kate believes, the important thing is to start pushing the stock up right away. Jorgenson is wondering what this two weeks' respite has cost (only a donut, Kate tells him), as the lights fade.

In the darkness, Kate is screaming in anger at Garfinkle. The lights come up in his office with Kate accusing Garfinkle of going back on his word, of setting up a group called OPM to buy New England Wire and Cable stock during the presumed truce period. "You think I'm a fool," Garfinkle counters, "I sit here and twiddle my thumbs while you drive the price of the stock up.....All the buying was coming from this cock-a-mamy little brokerage firm in Rhode Island." Kate pretends ignorance of this, but he is not deceived.

GARFINKLE: .....You want to play the game—let's play. Only I don't watch while you do "holier than thou." That's not the way this game is gonna get played.

KATE: Game, huh?

GARFINKLE: God damned right. The best game in the world.

KATE: You're playing Monopoly with people's lives here.

GARFINKLE: I'm doing them a favor. I'm making them money. I thought that's what they were in the business for.

KATE: I know this might be difficult for you to believe—for some people business means more than making money. They don't know how to play your game.

GARFINKLE: I'll teach them. It's easy. You make as much as you can for as long as you can.

KATE: And then what?

GARFINKLE: And then what? Whoever has the most when he dies—wins.

KATE: Goodbye, Garfinkle.

GARFINKLE: Aw, Katie, don't leave so soon. We haven't spoken about your thighs, your nipples, your—

KATE: See you in court.

GARFINKLE: At least have a donut.

KATE: Stuff it.

GARFINKLE: You didn't have to leave. I'm not mad at you. Lying to protect your client is just doing your job good.

KATE: Round One to the fat man. It ain't over till it's over, fat man.

GARFINKLE: And you didn't even ask me what OPM stands for. (*With a big smile.*) "Other People's Money."

Curtain.

ACT II

Jorgenson, Coles and Bea watch Kate give a champagne toast to the judge who has granted an injunction against Garfinkle buying any more shares of New England Wire and Cable, an injunction good at least for the five weeks until the annual meeting. In the meantime, they intend to keep up political pressure at the state level and local demonstrations against takeover.

Kate is loving this, but as the lights go down in the factory office and up in New York, Garfinkle is hating it, ranting at his unseen legal staff which has let "some broad wet behind the ears" get the better of them. Kate comes in to gloat, accepts a donut. Garfinkle launches into sexual innuendo until she finally gets down to business: "What number do we buy you out at?" Garfinkle feigns shock at what he characterizes as an offer of greenmail. Garfinkle sums up the situation: if he accepts greenmail and backs off, Jorgenson is happy, the employees are happy, everybody is happy "except the 'stuckholders.' Their stock falls out of bed."

Kate concentrates on the numbers, offering to buy Garfinkle's million shares at 18; perhaps they could even go as high as 20, a handsome profit for someone who started buying them at 13. But Garfinkle knows the full reconstruction value of New England Wire and Cable and demands 25. Kate calls that figure impossible, but for Garfinkle this offer is final: 25.

KATE: I can't deliver that.

GARFINKLE: I know. Let's talk about something nice. Let's talk about your eyes.

KATE (*getting up to leave*): I really thought we could work something out.

GARFINKLE: We can't. You're too far away.

KATE: You could lose it all.

GARFINKLE: I could. That's why so few of us have the balls to play the game.

KATE: Thanks for the donut.

GARFINKLE: Don't be depressed. You're in a tough place. Go fight your fight. It's not personal—it's principle. Hey, no matter what—it's better than working at the Post Office.

KATE (*softly*): Oh yeah … it's better than the Post Office.

She smiles sadly and exits. He is alone.

GARFINKLE: A lot better than working at the Post Office. It's the best there is. Like in the old Western, didn't everyone want to be the gunslinger? Didn't everyone want to be Butch Cassidy and the James boys? There's just a few of us—us modern-day gunslingers. There's T. Boone and the Bass brothers out of Texas. Irwin Jacobs out of Minneapolis. Would you believe a gunslinger named Irwin Jacobs? The Belzberg boys up north in Canada. And here in New York we got Saul Steinberg and Ronald Perlman and Carl Icahn. (*Places his hand on his heart.*) Out of respect for the stupid, a moment of silence for our gunned-down colleague Ivan Boesky. (*With a big smile.*) It's assholes like him that give assholes like us a bad name. And last but not least, Garfinkle from the wilds of the Bronx. But instead of galloping in with a six-gun a-blazing in each hand, we're driven in, escorted by a herd of lawyers and investment bankers, waving our limited partnerships in one hand and our 13–D filings in the other. But they quake just as hard. And they wind up just dead. And it's legal. And it's exciting. And it's fun. (*Moves to desk.*) And the money ain't bad either. (*Sits at desk.*) And every so often, every once in a while, we even wind up with the girl.

Garfinkle is looking over some papers when Kate comes in to listen to a couple of propositions Garfinkle thinks might make her feel better. Number one, they go to Garfinkle's place and make passionate love, and the first one who comes sells out all shares at the other's price. Kate doesn't take this history-making offer seriously. His second, though, she takes back to Jorgenson's office: Garfinkle will swap the million shares he now owns for the wire and cable division. This will eliminate the company's losses and materially increase the price of the stock they all own; and Jorgenson, with two million shares, will be in absolute control of what's left.

"You've given me nothing but different ways to kill myself," Jorgenson comments, angering Kate by rejecting this latest offer. Bea takes her daughter to task for refusing to understand the emotional and ethical consequences of such a deal. Jorgenson puts his arm around Bea, comforting her and leading her off before turning to confront Kate: "What do you want of me, Kate? Want me to say 'I'm sorry?' For what? For loving your mother?" He isn't sorry. Kate, angry because Bea lectured her and because of Jorgenson's stubbornness, threatens to walk out on the whole situation.

JORGENSON: Well go ahead then and leave. You're a lousy lawyer anyway.
KATE: Lousy lawyer? I want to tell you something. I'm a God damned good lawyer. You are a lousy client. You say "No" to everything. You say "No" to what ninety-nine percent of other corporations say "Yes" to. If this was any other outfit they'd put a statue out there in the yard of the woman that saved this company.
JORGENSON: Saved this company? You're not looking to save this company. You're looking to save your own ass.
KATE: ... What?

JORGENSON: Being beaten by Garfinkle wouldn't look so good on your resume, would it? Damn it, Kate—you want to win so badly, you don't even know what this fight is all about!

KATE: Oh yes I do. It's about your incredible—pigheadedness.

JORGENSON: O.K. Sure it is. But it's more than that. It's also about the twelve hundred men who work here and their families—and their future. Let's ask them if you're trying to "save this company."

KATE: Why ask them? They're not stockholders.

JORGENSON: Does that mean they don't matter?

KATE: ... O.K. ... Look. They matter. Nothing gets resolved, but everything matters.

Jorgenson tells her he's decided to leave the matter up to the stockholders. If he can count on the faithful 40 percent, Kate believes, this might work; he might prevail.

Scotty Bloch (Bea Sullivan) and Arch Johnson
(Andrew Jorgenson) in *Other People's Money*

Kate and Jorgenson move into the latter's office, leaving Coles alone to speculate, "It didn't seem the appropriate time to ask, 'And what happens to me if we lose?' It never seemed the appropriate time to ask that.....I deserve a golden parachute." He exits with this on his mind.

Kate and Jorgenson return, discussing Kate's assignment to sweet-talk Garfinkle and put him as much off guard as possible. The scene changes to Garfinkle's office, where she challenges him with a proposition: "Let's leave it up to the stockholders. Run your own slate of directors at the annual meeting. You get fifty-one percent of the votes, it's your company. You buy everybody out at twenty. You don't get the votes, you sell us back your shares at thirteen. You slink away, never to be seen or heard from again." Garfinkle knows that the others have the advantage of 40 percent of the votes going in. It's going to be close, he guesses, but he agrees.

Kate goes back to Rhode Island to report to Jorgenson and Bea, who are delighted. Jorgenson figures, "We have forty percent. He has twenty-five. We would only need ten of the remaining thirty-five. That's less than one in three." Their tactic will be simply to tell the stockholders the truth, the way Harry Truman always did with the voters.

In Garfinkle's office, Coles shows up to bargain for his "golden parachute." Coles now owns 100 thousand shares of New England Wire and Cable and will sell him the right to vote this stock for $1 million. Not knowing whether they'll make a critical difference to him or not, Garfinkle offers Coles half a million if they turn out not to make the difference, one million only if they do. Coles accepts. He has brought over the necessary papers and will come around for the check tomorrow.

Lights out in Garfinkle's office, leaving Coles onstage alone and making his explanation to the audience: "Don't look at me like that. Everybody looks out after their own self-interest. 'What's in it for me?' Isn't that, ultimately, what it's all about? Jorgenson looks out for his monument. Garfinkle for his money. Bea for her man. Kate for her career. The employees for their paycheck. I kept this company alive. I helped make it all possible. Who looks out for me?"

Coles exits as the lights come up on Garfinkle's office, where Bea arrives, not as an emissary from Kate but on her own, to offer Garfinkle $1 million—a trust fund she owns, in treasury notes—to withdraw and permit the others to buy back his shares at 13. "Go home," Garfinkle tells her, "I don't want your money."

BEA: I know a million dollars is not a great deal of money to you. It's all I have. If I had more I'd give you more. I had really hoped to appeal to whatever decent instincts you have left. I'm here to plead for my company.
GARFINKLE: Go home.
BEA: Please, Mr. Garfinkle.

OTHER PEOPLE'S MONEY 293

GARFINKLE: I don't take money from widows and orphans. I make them money.

BEA: Before or after you put them out of business?

GARFINKLE: You're getting on my nerves. Go home.

BEA: I intend to. Before I go, I'd like to know—I'd like you to tell me—how you can live with yourself?

GARFINKLE: I have no choice. No one else will.

BEA: How? How can you destroy a company ... its people ... for the sake of dollars you don't even need?

GARFINKLE: Because it's there.

BEA: ... Because it's there?

GARFINKLE: What? People climb mountains—swim oceans—walk through fire—'cause it's there. This way is better. You don't get all sweated up.

BEA: There are people there. There are dreams there—

GARFINKLE: Do you want to give a speech, or do you want an answer? 'Cause the answer is not complicated. It's simple. I do it for the money. I don't need the money. I want the money. Shouldn't surprise you. Since when do needs and wants have anything to do with one another? If they did, I'd be back in the Bronx and you'd be getting Yorgy his coffee up in Grimetown. You don't need the job. You need the million dollars. But you're prepared to give up what you need—a million dollars—for what you want—a stinking job. You're fucked up, lady. You're sick. Go see a psychiatrist.

Garfinkle loves money more than the things it can buy, he asserts. "I hope you choke on your money and die," Bea declares and exits.

In a meeting in his office with Kate, Garfinkle complains about the public outcry she's mounted against him—unions, churches, even the governor's office. She warns him that some day there will be laws against him and what he does. Garfinkle pooh-poohs this as changing the rules but not stopping the game.

GARFINKLE: .....We've come from "Ask not what your country can do for you" to "What's in it for me?" to "What's in it for me—today!" all in one short generation. That's why those "stuckholders" all love me, and that's why you guys all work for me. Nobody's putting a gun to anyone's head. Everybody's got their hand out.

KATE: Not everybody. Not me. Not them.

GARFINKLE: Forget them. It's about you and me now, Kate. I'm the last thought you have when you fall asleep at night and the first when you wake in the morning. I make your juices flow, and you know it.

KATE: Garfinkle, if you knew what you do to me, you wouldn't brag about it.

GARFINKLE: Bullshit. And you know what makes the two of us so special? What sets us apart? We care more about the game than we do the players. That's not bad. That's smart.

KATE: That's grotesque. Garfinkle, you don't know me at all. You're not capable of knowing me. You can't see beyond your appetite.

GARFINKLE: Then what the fuck are you doing here? You can't keep away. You don't want to keep away. Come play with me, Kate. Be a player— not a technician. Feel the power. This is where you belong, Kate. With me. I know you. I know who you are. I like who you are. I want you, Kate.

KATE: I'm going to nail you, Garfinkle. I'm going to send you back to Wall Street with donuts up your ass, and everyone's going to know how some broad wet behind the ears did you. And whatever happens from this day forward, whatever successes I achieve, none—none will be sweeter than this one!

Kate exits with Garfinkle's admiring comments ringing in her ears.

In his office, Jorgenson is going over his speech and admits to Bea that he's a bit scared of the new environment he finds himself in. Bea is proud of him and encourages him: "If what we are counts for nothing any more, that won't be our failing—it'll be theirs."

At the annual meeting, "*played as if the audience were the stockholders*," Bea orders the election ballots distributed. Jorgenson goes to the rostrum, greets the stockholders as friends and tells them of the company's increase in market share. He warns them that Garfinkle is "playing God with other people's money," making no product, creating no railroad or bank like a robber baron of old but merely preying on a paper situation. The cable and wire business is bound to pick up, Jorgenson assures them, when America starts to rebuild its infrastructure in earnest; in the meantime, if they accept Garfinkle's offer, if he is truly "the wave of the future," Jorgenson continues, "we will then have become a nation that makes nothing but hamburgers, creates nothing but lawyers and sells nothing but tax shelters. And if we have come to the point in this country where we kill something because at the moment it's worth more dead than alive, then turn around and take a good look at your neighbor. You won't kill him because it's called 'murder' and it's illegal. This too is murder, on a mass scale, only on Wall Street they call it 'maximizing shareholder values,' and they call it legal, and they substitute dollar bills where a conscience should be.

"Damn it. A business is more than the price of its stock. It is the place where we make our living, meet our friends and dream our dreams. It is, in every sense, the fabric that binds our society together. Let us, right now, at this meeting, say to every Garfinkle in this land, that here we build things, we don't destroy them. Here, we care for more than the price of our stock. Here ... we care about people."

After applause, Garfinkle takes Jorgenson's place on the rostrum and characterizes the chairman's speech as "A prayer for the dead." Whatever anyone does, this company is dead, not because of Garfinkle's raid, but because of obsolescence. "An increasing share of a shrinking market" is a sure sign that the end is inevitably near. The stockholders should take whatever money can now be realized and "invest the money in something with a future." And as for employees, "They sucked you dry. You have no responsibility to them," Garfinkle assures his listeners.

Garfinkle continues: "For the last ten years this company has bled your money. Did the community care? Did they ever say, 'I know things are tough. We'll lower our taxes, reduce water and sewer?' Check it out. We're paying twice what we paid ten years ago. And the mayor is making twice what he made ten years ago. AND our devoted employees, after taking no increases for three years, are still making twice what they made ten years ago. And our stock is one-sixth what it was ten years ago.

"Who cares? I'll tell you—me! I'm not your best friend—I'm your only friend. I care about you in the only way that matters in business. I don't make anything? I'm making you money. And, lest we forget, that's the only reason any of you became stockholders in the first place. To make money. You don't care if they manufacture wire and cable, fry chicken or grow tangerines. You want to make money. I'm making you money. I'm the only friend you got.

"Take that money. Invest it somewhere else. Maybe—maybe you'll get lucky and it will be used productively—and if it is—you'll create more jobs and provide a service for the economy and—God forbid—even make a few bucks for yourself. Let the government and the mayor and the unions worry about what you paid them to worry about. And if anyone asks, tell them you gave at the plant."

The lights dim, and Coles steps forward to tell the ending of his story: the stockholders' vote was 2.7 million to 1.7 million shares in favor of Garfinkle, who didn't even need to vote Coles's shares in order to win. Coles was asked to stay on, with a raise, but refused and took a job down in Florida. Jorgenson "didn't take it well" but stayed there in town and died two years later, leaving $30 million with Bea as executor. Bea bought the land after the plant was razed, opened a retraining center for the employees and replaced a few in new jobs.

Lights up on Garfinkle. He speaks to an unseen Kate.
GARFINKLE: I'm sorry, Kate. I'm surprised myself. See, you do bring out the best in me … Come— (*He laughs.*) Ride back to New York with me … You worried it wouldn't look right? Don't. It's the perfect ending … Come.
　　　She enters the playing area. Stops. Looks at him. He extends his arms to her, beckoning.
Come. (*She doesn't move.*) I got donuts in the car.

COLES: Kate and Garfinkle? Well, three months later, which is as soon as she could work things out at Morgan, Stanley, she went to work for him.

Kate moves next to a seated Garfinkle.

She was very good. Three months after that she became his partner ...

Her arm moves to the back of Garfinkle's chair.

... then his wife.

Her arm is around his shoulder. Garfinkle beams.

They have two kids. Set of twins. Call them their "little bull and little bear." Friend of mine saw them the other day ... (*Moves to exit.*) Said he never saw them happier.

Exit. Curtain.

SHIRLEY VALENTINE

A Play in Two Acts

BY WILLY RUSSELL

Cast and credits appear on pages 403–404

WILLY RUSSELL was born in 1947 in Whiston, near Liverpool, and left school at 15 to take a series of jobs leading to becoming a teacher, at 20, and finally to playwriting after seeing an Everyman Theater, Liverpool, performance of Unruly Elements *by John McGrath. Russell's first works for the theater included* Blind Scouse *(Edinburgh Festival, 1972),* When the Reds *(an adaptation of* The Tigers Are Coming O.K. *by Alan Plater, Liverpool, 1973), the musical* John, Paul, George, Ringo ... and Bert *(which moved from the Everyman Theater to the West End and won the Evening Standard and Theater Critics Awards for best musical, 1974),* Breezeblock Park *(Liverpool-to-London, 1975),* One for the Road *(Manchester, 1976, revised for London, 1988) and* Stags and Hens *(Liverpool, 1978).*

Russell was then commissioned to write a play for the Royal Shakespeare company and came up with Educating Rita *(1980), a best comedy award-winner in London and later an Academy Award nominee for Russell's screen play. He wrote book, music and lyrics for* Blood Brothers, *a successful Liverpool-to-London production in 1983 and currently in revival in the latter city. His* Shirley Valentine *went from Liverpool (1986) to London (1988),*

297

winning the Olivier Award for best comedy on its way to New York, making its author's Broadway debut Feb. 16 and cited as his first Best Play.

Russell, author of numerous TV productions and the screen play for Shirley Valentine, *was writer-in-residence at C.F. Mott College, Liverpool, in 1976; a fellow in creative writing at Manchester Polytechnic, 1977-79; and received an honorary M.A. from Open University in 1983, in recognition of his playwriting career. He is married and resides in Liverpool.*

Shirley Valentine *is a one-character play performed in monologue, so that we have prepared the synopsis of its unusual structure and content somewhat differently from those of the other Best Plays. Instead of a series of short excerpts from the script connected by a detailed description of events, we offer two lengthy excerpts and one final shorter one, with the narrative merely sketched in between. In total length our quotations from* Shirley Valentine *are in about the same proportion to the length of its script as in the other synopses, but here we present them in bulk to fully illustrate and exemplify its style and personality. Spelling and punctuation are as in the published version, but we added some paragraphing to make the monologue stream easier to follow on the printed page.*

ACT I

Scene 1: The kitchen of a semi-detached house

SYNOPSIS: As is her habit, Shirley Valentine—a middle-aged housewife and mother of two grown children, a boy (Brian) and a girl (Millandra)—is talking to the kitchen wall as she prepares chips and egg for her husband Joe's dinner. She is sipping wine, considering how humdrum their marriage has become, sexually and otherwise, and trying to decide whether to accept her best friend Jane's invitation, including free airline ticket, for a two-week holiday in Greece, without asking her husband's permission. Jane is an ardent feminist who divorced her husband after finding him in bed with the milkman. Joe is set in his ways and will be furious to find he's not having the usual Thursday mincemeat tonight; and he'd never agree to go away on a trip anywhere.

Shirley's son Brian, himself an impulsive type, has seen the ticket and urged his mother to go. When she was of school age, all Shirley wanted to do was travel, possibly as an air hostess, but she was continually denigrated by the headmistress until she became hostile to everything and everybody, particularly one Marjorie Majors who took private elocution lessons.

SHIRLEY: .....But I didn't hate anythin' y' know. The only thing I hated was me. I didn't want to be a rebel. I wanted to be nice. I wanted to be like Marjorie Majors. I used to pick on her somethin' rotten an' I really wanted to be like her. Can't y' be evil when you're a kid? I saw her a few weeks ago, Marjorie Majors. Didn't I wall? I hadn' even heard of her for years. I'm in town, loaded down with shoppin' an' what's the first thing that always happens when y' in town loaded down with shoppin'? Right. The heavens opened. An' it's funny the way all these things are linked but they are; once you're in town, loaded with shoppin' bags, caught in a deluge—it always follows that every bus ever made disappears off the face of the earth.

Well I'm standin' there, like a drowned rat, me hair's in ruins and I've got mascara lines runnin' from me face to me feet, so I thought I might as well trudge up to the Adelphi an' get a taxi. Course when I got there the taxis had gone into hidin' along with the buses. Well I'm just rootin' in me bag, lookin' for somethin' to slash me wrists with when this big white car pulls up to the hotel an' of course I'm standin' right by a puddle an' as the wheels go through it, half the puddle ends up over me an' the other half in me shoppin' bags.

Well all I wanted to do by this time was scream. So I did. I just opened me mouth, standin' there in front of the hotel an' let out this scream. I could've been arrested but I didn't care. Well I was in mid-scream when I noticed this woman get out the white car an' start comin' towards me. An' she's dead elegant. Y' know she's walkin' through this torrential rain an' I guarantee not one drop of it was landin' on her. But the second she opened her mouth I knew who she was. I'd recognize those elocution lessons anywhere.

"Forgive me for asking," she said, "but didn't you used to be Shirley Valentine?"

I just stood there starin'. And drippin'. "It is," she said, "it's Shirley," an' the next thing, she's apologizin' for half drownin' me an' she's pullin' me into the hotel an' across the lobby an' into this lounge that's the size of two football pitches. Well, she's ordered tea an' I'm sittin' there, rain water drippin' down me neck an' plastic carrier bags round me feet an' I'm thinkin', "Well Marjorie, you've waited a long time for your revenge but you've got me good style now, haven't y'? Well go on, spare me the torture, just put the knife in quick an' let's get it over with; come on tell me about your bein' an air hostess on Concorde."

But she didn't say anythin'. She just sat there, lookin' at me, y' know really lookin' at me. I thought I'm not gonna let her milk it so I said, "You're an air hostess these days are y' Marjorie? Oh yes, I hear it's marvellous. You travel all over the world don't you?" But she still just kept lookin' at me. The waitress was just puttin' the tea an' cakes on the table in front of us. I said to her, "This is my friend Marjorie. We were at school together. Marjorie's an air hostess."

"An air hostess?" Marjorie suddenly said. "Darling whatever gave you that idea? I certainly travel widely but I'm not an air hostess. Shirley, I'm a hooker. A whore."

Marjorie Majors—a high class hooker! "Oh really Marjorie," I said, "an' all that money your mother spent on elocution lessons." By this time the waitress was pourin' the tea into the cream buns! Well me an' Marjorie—God, we had a great afternoon together. She didn't come lordin' it over me at all. Y' know she told me about all the places she works—Bahrain, New York, Munich. An' d' y' know what she told me? When we were at school ... she wanted to be like me. The two of us, sittin' there at the Adelphi, one's like somethin' out of *Dynasty*, one's like somethin' out of the bagwash an' we're havin' a great time confessin' that all those years ago, we each wanted to be the other. I was sad when I thought about it. Like the two of us could have been great mates—y' know real close. We didn't half get on well together, that afternoon, in the Adelphi. We were rememberin' all kinds. I could've sat there forever—neither of us wanted to leave. But then the time caught up with us an' Marjorie had to get her plane. An' y' know somethin'—she didn't want to go. Paris she had to go to, Paris France, an' she didn't want to. An' an' on the way out ... d' y' know what she did? She leaned forward an' just kissed me—there on the cheek—an' there was real affection in that kiss. It was the sweetest kiss I'd known in years. An' then she, she held my shoulders an' looked at me and said, "Goodbye Shirley. Goodbye, Shirley Valentine."

   Pause.

On the way home, on the bus, I was cryin'. I don't know why. I'm starin' out the window, tears trippin' down me cheeks. An' in me head there's this voice that keeps sayin', "I used to be Shirley Valentine. I used to be Shirley Valentine ... I used to be Shirley ..."

   She is crying.

What happened? Who turned me into this? I don't want this. Do you remember her wall? Remember Shirley Valentine? She got married to a boy called Joe an' one day she came to live here. An' an' even though her name was changed to Bradshaw she was still Shirley Valentine. For a while. She still ... knew who she was. She used to ... laugh. A lot. Didn't she? She used to laugh with Joe—when the pair of them did things together, when they made this kitchen together an' painted it together. Remember wall? Remember when they first painted you an' an' the silly buggers painted each other as well. Stood here, the pair of them, havin' a paint fight, coverin' each other from head to foot in yellow paint. An' then the two of them, thinkin' they're dead darin', gettin' in the bath—together. And the water was so yellow that he said it was like gettin' a bath in vanilla ice cream. And Shirley Valentine washed his hair ... and kissed his wet head ... and knew what happiness meant.

What happened wall? What happened to the pair of them—to Joe, to Shirley Valentine. Did somethin' happen or was it just that nothin' happened?

It would be … easier to understand if somethin' had happened, if I'd found him in bed with the milkman, if, if there was somethin' to blame. But there's nothin'. They got married, they made a home, they had kids and brought them up. And somewhere along the way the boy called Joe turned into "him" and Shirley Valentine turned into this and what I can't remember is the day or the week or the month or the … when it happened. When it stopped bein' good. When Shirley Valentine disappeared, became just another name on the missin' persons list.

Her friend Jane keeps telling her she can't understand why Shirley doesn't leave her dull husband. Shirley admits to herself that she may be a bit frightened of life these days, though as a child she would jump off the roof of her house for the thrill of it. She considers drinking another bottle of wine and imagining she's in Greece, when the back door opens.

Scene 2: The kitchen, three weeks later

Shirley is in a state of nervous excitement, bags packed, passport, tickets and money in hand, ready to go on the trip to Greece with Jane. She hasn't told Joe she's going, and she plans to leave him a curt note. Joe behaved so badly over the chips and egg on that Thursday night three weeks ago that Shirley left the house for a long walk and decided then and there to accept Jane's invitation.

Pauline Collins as Shirley Valentine

Shirley's daughter Millandra, fed up with her roommate, came home to Mother with all her possessions (Shirley tells her wall) but quarreled and left almost immediately after learning that Shirley intended going to Greece without consulting Joe—asking her mother "What for?" as though Shirley was past all possibility of adventure and romance. Millandra's comment made Shirley unhappily aware that she is 42 years old, with stretch marks from having borne two children. She made up her mind to be "Shirley the Brave," however, and, having checked her documents, sits on her suitcase waiting for Jane to come and fetch her. *Blackout.*

ACT II

Scene 1: A secluded section of shore

The blue of the Greek sky dominates the scene, with "*a hint of the village and taverna*" in the background. Shirley has found a place on the beach where a large rock offers shelter from the sun—and this is a rock she can talk to, as she talked to her kitchen wall.

It seems that Jane met a man on the plane, "all groin and Adidas labels," and has gone off with him for a few days, leaving Shirley to take care of herself. Jeanette and Dougie—a boring and intrusive British couple—tried to attach themselves to Shirley, but she managed to get away from them.

After dinner, she went for a walk which led to an adventure she later described to Jane as "point nine on the Richter scale," with a man she called Christopher Columbus because he helped her discover clitoral satisfaction and actually admired her stretch marks. His real name was Costas, and he ran the taverna to which Shirley wandered on her walk. There were tables and parasols outside, and—Shirley confides to her rock—she asked Costas to move one of them to the edge of the sea.

SHIRLEY: .....Well he looked at me for a minute. "You want," he said, "you want move table and chair to the sea? What for? You don't like here at my bar?" "Oh yeh," I said, "yeh, it's a lovely bar but, but I've just got this soft little dream about sittin' at a table by the sea." "Agh," he said an' he smiled. "A dream, a dream. We move this table to the edge of the sea, it make your dream come true?" "Erm, yeh," I said, "I think so." "Then is no problem, I move the table for you. And tonight when I serve in my bar, I say to customer —tonight, tonight, I make someone's dream come true."

Well I thought for a second he was bein' sarcastic—'cos in England it would have been. But no, he carries the table and chair over here an' he brings me out this glass of wine I've ordered. Well I paid him and thanked him but he said to me, "No, I thank you. Enjoy your dream," then gave a little bow an' he was gone, back to the taverna, leavin' me alone with the sea and the sky an' me soft little dream. Well it's funny isn't it, but y' know if you've pictured somethin', you know if you've imagined how somethin's gonna be, made a picture of it in your mind, well it never works out does it? I mean for weeks I'd had this picture of meself, sittin' here, sittin' here, drinkin' wine by the sea; I even knew exactly how I was gonna feel. But when it got to it, it wasn't a bit like that. Because when it got to it I didn't feel at all lovely an' serene. I felt pretty daft actually. A bit stupid an' an' awfully, awfully old.

What I kept thinkin' about was how I'd lived such a little life. An' one way or another even that would be over pretty soon. I thought to meself, my life has been a crime really—a crime against God, because ... I didn't live it fully. I'd allowed myself to live this little life when inside me there was so much. So much more that I could have lived a bigger life with—but it had all gone unused, an' now it would never be. Why ... why do y' get ... all this life, when it can't be used? Why ... why do y' get ... all these ... feelin's an' dreams an' hopes if they can't ever be used? That's where Shirley Valentine disappeared to. She got lost in all this unused life.

An' that's what I was thinkin', sittin' there on me own, starin' out at the sea, me eyes open wide an' big tears splashin' down from them. I must've sat there for ages because the noise from the hotel bar had died away an' even the feller from the taverna was lockin' up for the night. He came to collect me glass. It was still full. I hadn't even taken a sip. He saw that I was cryin' but he didn't say anythin'. He just sat down there, on the sand and stared out at the sea. An' when I'd got over it, when it was all right to talk, he said, "Dreams are never in the places we expect them to be." I just smiled at him. "Come," he said, "I escort you back to your hotel." An' he did. An' he told me his name was Costas an' I told him my name was Shirley. An' when we got to the front door of the hotel he said to me, "Tomorrow, you want, to come with me? I take my brother's boat. We go all round the island?"

I just shook me head. "No," I said, "It's all right. You've been dead kind as it is. Thank you." "Is no problem, I come for you early." "No," I'm goin', "Thanks but ..."

"You afraid?" he suddenly said, "No," I said, "but ..." "You afraid," he said, nodding, "You afraid I make try to foak with you." I didn't know where to put meself, but he just laughed. "Of course I like to foak with you. You are lovely woman. Any man be crazy not to want to foak with you. But I don't ask to foak. I ask you want to come my brother's boat—is different thing. Foak is foak, boat is boat. I come fetch you tomorrow. I bring wine, I bring food and we go. Tomorrow I just make you happy. No need to be sad, no need to be afraid. I give my word of honor I don't make try to foak with you."

Well what could I say? "Well I'll erm, I'll see y' in the mornin' then." Course the next mornin' I've just got dressed. I'm sittin' in me room, there's this knockin' on the door, I thought, "Oh Christ, he's come up to me room."

Well, I opened the door, an' guess what? Jane's back! "Shirley, please forgive me. I know I shouldn't have left you. Shirley, I know I've been awful but please, please forgive me. I'll make it up to you. Come on, it's still early, let's go and hire a car and drive around the island."

Well what could I do? I mean she had paid for me to be there. If it hadn't been for Jane I would never have been in Greece in the first place. She keeps askin' me if I forgive her. "Of course I forgive y'," I said, an' she threw her arms around me then. "Come on," she said, "Let's put it all behind us now. Let's make today the real start of our holiday. I know you've had an awful time and Shirley I'm sorry. Have you just been sitting here in your room the past few days? I know you. Without me being here I suppose you've just been sitting here talking to the wall, haven't you?" Well I thought to meself, "How does she see me? Does she think I'm an old-age pensioner or a five-year-old child?" "I'll only be a few minutes," she's sayin', "I'll just pick up a few things from my room."

Well it was just as she got to the door that there was a knock on it. She pulled it open an' Costas was there. She took one look at him an' said—"What is it, room service? Did you order anything Shirley?" But Costas just walked straight past her an' into the room. "Shirley, Shirley, you come, you come. You late. I wait for you on the quay. I already put the wine, the food on the boat. I stand I wait an' then I think, 'Ah, Shirley and me, we get to bed so late last night, Shirley she must have oversleep.'"

Well the look on Jane's face could've turned the milk. "Quickly now you get ready. Don't bring much clothing. I wait on quay for you. Hurry." An' as he passes Jane he just goes, "Apology for interrupting you. Now you continue cleaning the room." Well if Jane had kept her mouth shut, if she hadn't tried to treat me like a child, I might have run after Costas an' said I couldn't go, or could me friend come as well. But she said, "Shirley. What do you think you're playing at?" I didn't say a word. I just looked at her. She was goin' on about how I'd never been abroad before. When she got to the bit about "men like that, these Greek islanders who are just waiting for bored middle-aged women to fall into their ..." I just stormed straight past her and out.

I steered the boat y' know. See me on that bridge—natural. I mean, I knew I wasn't the first woman on that boat an' I certainly wouldn't be the last. But I knew I was with a good man. I knew that whatever happened he wouldn't take anythin' from me. We sailed for miles an' miles. An' we talked. Properly. An' we didn't half laugh. We liked each other. An' isn't it funny, but if you're with someone who likes y', who sort of approves of y'—well y' like, like start to grow again. Y' move in the right way, say the right thing at the right time. An' you're not eighteen or forty-two or sixty-four. You're just alive. An' I know if I could have seen myself that day I would have said, "Look at that lovely woman—riding on the sea. Look at the lovely woman, swimming." Well I know I'd left me swimmin' costume in the hotel. So what? We'd parked the boat an' was lookin' over the side. I said, "How deep do you think it is here, Costas?" "Mm. Maybe a thousand meters—maybe ten thousand meters, who knows. Maybe so deep it goes on forever." An' when I stood there, on the edge of the boat, naked as the day I was born, about to jump into this water that was as deep as forever I felt as strong an' as excited an' as bloody mad as I did when I jumped off our roof. The two of us just splashed and laughed an' swam in the water an' I knew Costas would keep his promise but I didn't want him to because it was the most natural thing in the world. So I swam up to him. An' I put me arms around him an' kissed him. An' that's when I nicknamed him Christopher Columbus. Mind you, I could just as easily have named him Andre Previn—I don't know where this orchestra came from.

Later on, just lyin' there on the boat, with the sun beginnin' to dip towards the evenin', that's when the thought came to me.

The thought was that it would hurt no one if she stayed in Greece instead of going home to a husband and two children who wouldn't miss her. She kept telling herself she wasn't going back (though she wasn't in love with Costas). In line at the airport for the flight home, she watched her suitcase disappear on the conveyor belt and realized she would leave her life unused if she followed it. Despite Jane's loud remonstrances, she walked away, back to Costas, not for romance but for a job in the taverna. At the end of her third week in the job, she finds that she gets on well with the customers, even the "Dougies an' Jeanettes."

SHIRLEY: .....I've got the night off tonight though. Well Joe's arrivin' tonight. The first time he phoned, y' know after Jane had got back, he screamed at me. He said I must have finally gone mad. He said I was a disgrace—to the kids, to him, to meself. It was the easiest thing in the world to just put the phone down on him. The second time he phoned he said you can't run away from life. I said I agreed with him an' now I'd found some life I had no intention of runnin' away from it. He started to scream an' shout again then; he said he knew all about me "holiday romance," an' how I'd made a fool of meself but, but if I stopped all this arsin' round, if I got meself home, where I belonged, he said, he'd promise never to mention it. I said ... said ... "The only holiday romance I've had, is with meself Joe. An' ... an' I think ... I've come to like meself, really." I said to him, I said, "I think I'm all right Joe. I think that if ... if I saw me, I'd say, that woman's O.K. ... she's alive. She's not remarkable, she's not gonna ... gonna be there in the history books. But she's ... she's there in the time she's livin' in. An' certainly she's got her wounds ... an' her battle scars but maybe, maybe ... a little bit of the bullshit is true an' an' the wounds shouldn't be hidden away—because, because even the wounds an' the scars are about bein' alive."

There was a long pause. I thought he'd gone off the phone. An' then I heard this voice, "I knew it," he was sayin', "I knew it, it's the bleedin' change of life isn't it?"

"That's right Joe," I said, "that's right, it's a change of life. An' that's why you're wastin' your money phonin' me to try an' get me back. I'm not comin' back."

The last time he phoned he said our Brian had been arrested—buskin' without a license. An' our Millandra was frettin' for me. An' that he loved me an' the only thing he wanted in the world was for me to come back. I explained to him that it was impossible because the woman he wanted to go back didn't exist any more. An' then I got this letter sayin' he was comin' to get me. To take me back home. Agh God love him, he must've been watchin' Rambo. He'll be here soon. I hope he stays for a while. He needs a holiday. He needs to feel the sun on his skin an' to be in water that's as deep as forever, an' to have his wet head kissed. He needs to stare out at the sea. And to understand.

Pause.

I asked Costas if he'd put the table out for me again. He said to me, "You look for you dream again?" "No, Costas," I said. "No dream. But I'm gonna sit here an' watch for Joe an' as he walks down the esplanade, an' keeps walkin', because he doesn't recognize me any more, I'll call out to him. An' as he walks back, an' looks at me, all puzzled an' quizzical, I'll say to him— "Hello. I used to be the mother. I used to be your wife. But now, I'm Shirley Valentine again. Would you like to join me for a drink?"

Blackout.

GUS AND AL

A Play in Two Acts

BY ALBERT INNAURATO

Cast and credits appear on pages 431–433

ALBERT INNAURATO was born June 2, 1947 in Philadelphia. He received his college degrees at the California Institute of the Arts (B.F.A.) in the early 1970s and Yale Drama School (M.F.A.) in 1974, where his playwriting career began to develop with contributions to Yale Cabaret (also presented off off Broadway in 1972), The Transfiguration of Benno Blimpie *(1973) and* The Idiots Karamazov *(written with Christopher Durang and produced at Yale Rep, post-graduation, in the fall of 1974). It was* Benno Blimpie *that made Innaurato's reputation in the professional theater, going from the O'Neill in 1973 to OOB stagings at Ensemble Studio and Direct Theaters to a full 61-performance off-Broadway production March 10, 1977, winning its author an Obie for distinguished playwriting. That same season Innaurato's* Gemini *moved up from an OOB presentation at Playwrights Horizons to off-Broadway production by Circle Rep March 15, 1977 for 63 performances (and another distinguished-playwriting Obie), then to Broadway May 21, beginning a tremendous run of 1,788 performances.*

Other Innaurato scripts have included Earth Worms *(shown at the O'Neill in 1974),* Urlicht *(OOB, 1974),* Ulysses in Traction *(off Broadway*

December 8, 1977 for 47 performances), Passione *(Broadway September 23, 1980 for 16 performances),* Coming of Age in Soho *(produced off Broadway by New York Shakespeare Festival February 3, 1985 for 65 performances, after a staging at Seattle Rep) and now* Gus and Al, *put on at Denver Center Theater Company in 1987 and brought to off Broadway by Playwrights Horizons February 27, 1989 for 25 performances, its author's first Best Play. The recipient of Guggenheim, Rockefeller and two National Endowment Grants (in 1986 and 1989), Innaurato now lives in Manhattan.*

Time and Place: Manhattan in 1989, then Vienna in 1901

Scene 1

SYNOPSIS: In Al's Manhattan apartment, Kafka, *"a gorilla who can talk,"* is tinkering with a complex Rube Goldberg electronic contraption tied in with a stereo system, when Al enters. *"He is a fat man in his late 30s in an ill-fitting, too tight, cheap raincoat."* He is carrying a bundle of newspapers hot off the press and is clearly in despair. As he disappears into the bathroom, possibly to slash his wrists (but the gorilla has dulled all the razor blades), the landlady, Mrs. Briggs (*"a tough though well-meaning paraplegic"*) enters in her wheelchair and demands the rent, two months in arrears.

KAFKA: It's no use. He's in despair.
MRS. BRIGGS: Oh, I see. He was out getting the reviews of his play. This was the one that was going to save him. I knew it was a bomb. He's a has-been. There's nothing wrong with failing, it's persevering after failing which is dumb!
KAFKA: Not being able to support yourself in Manhattan doesn't make you a failure.
MRS. BRIGGS: It does in 1989. (*Seeing the machine.*) What's that?
KAFKA: My new time machine. It's very crude.
MRS. BRIGGS: You and your blasted inventing. I thought apes picked nits and ate bananas. Leave it to Al to come up with an ape that invents. There's something ungodly about him.
KAFKA: On the contrary. He recognizes and promotes talent where he sees it.
MRS. BRIGGS: You think it'll actually transport people backwards?
KAFKA: I doubt it. I think it'll affect mental processes only, like a surround sound apparatus; plug it in, put it on, and I hope it'll send images of the distant past into one's mind in conjunction with the music one might be listening to.

MRS. BRIGGS: You're trying to make a monkey out of me. (*She cackles.*) Tell Al if he can't come up with the back rent in a week I'm starting eviction proceedings.

After which, Mrs. Briggs declares, she'll let the gorilla have the apartment. She exits, as Al comes out of the bathroom. He's read all the reviews of his play, and they are devastating—all, that is, except for the *Times*, which he hasn't read because he didn't dare. Kafka tries to comfort Al and goes to make some tea, while Al puts Gustav Mahler's Fifth Symphony on the player. "I wonder where he was living right as he composed it," Al muses and looks up the address: Mahler's workplace was 60 Ringstrasse, Vienna, on the second floor.

Instead of just listening to the music, however, Al turns on Kafka's contraption, licks four dangling wires and puts them in his mouth. *"There is a flash of light and billowing smoke, and Al disappears." Blackout.*

Scene 2

In the darkness the music changes from orchestral to a single piano and then the lights come up on Gustav "Gus" Mahler's house in Vienna in 1901, a well-appointed room with a large window upstage center. Mahler (*"41, short, wiry, Jewish looking.....The director of the Vienna Royal Opera, he has adopted a severe air, but there is still something vigorous and boyish about him"*) is playing the first movement of his Fifth Symphony on the piano, with Natalie Bauer Lechner (*"middle 40s, a devotee of Mahler"*) at his side. Her slavishness *"both pleases and embarrasses Mahler."* She writes every word he says into her notebook.

Gus complains that he can't seem to get beyond the first movement of his symphony, also that his Fourth Symphony received a bad review in Hamburg. He hears a tapping at the window, goes to see what it is, but there is nothing there.

Justine (*"Mahler's younger sister, mid-30s.....but rather matronly"*) enters with a tray of pastries and chocolate. She notices that Mahler's leg is twitching, which always happens when things are going badly for him in some way. Justine exits, but not before reminding the other two that their rooms are next to each other, implying that Gus and Natalie are courting, which irritates the former and pleases the latter. *"Suddenly, with a crash, the windows open wide and Al comes floating in, propelled from the 1980s to the year 1901. Al is struggling as though he is trying to free himself from some sort of wire. He is still carrying the sheaf of bad reviews."*

Gus and Natalie are astonished but polite. Al breaks free of his attachment and, also confused, tries to sort out the situation. He is offered chocolate and pastry, and it slowly dawns on him that he has actually time-traveled. He ex-

plains that he is an American, from New York, from the future. He also needs
to relieve himself. He's offered a chamber pot, offstage, and comes back to
empty it out of the window, at the same time considering the possibility of
throwing himself out too.

GUS: I am the director of the Royal Opera, we can't have an incident here.
You seem harmless enough, but an uninvited madman in my house?
NATALIE: A scandal!
Peeks out the window, then closes it.
AL: I'm not a madman!
GUS: But time-travel? How can we believe you?
AL (*suddenly realizes he still has his sheaf of bad reviews in his hand*):
Here, these are from my time ... newspaper articles ...
Gus and Natalie look at them.
NATALIE: Indeed, these are in English, which we don't read ...
GUS: But I see the dates. If you are from the future, it would seem to me
your first concern would be getting back.
AL: Oh no. I don't want to go back. I suffered a terrible blow, I wanted to
die. But since I'm here, anything has to be better than my life there. Am I
making sense? I doubt it. There is probably nothing more disorienting than the
future's despair. What year is it?
NATALIE: 1901.
AL: 1901! I couldn't even time-travel right. (*To Gus and Natalie, who look
puzzled.*) I aimed for 1900.
NATALIE: Master, what asylum do you think he escaped from?
GUS: If the future is a madhouse, that's the asylum he's from. I sense it.

Al admits to Gus that in his own time, 1989, he is a failed artist. Gus is curious about his own future reputation and is assured that he is "worshipped," his
music has even outstripped Strauss's in the opinion of the cognoscenti.
Justine comes in to complain angrily about the chamber pot emptied out of
the window—onto the head of a servant. Inquiring about Al, she is informed
by Gus that Al is from the future and is to stay here with them even though he
might be mistaken for a Jew because he is circumsized and the Mahlers become subject to arrest for harboring him. Al explains that he's a failed playwright, "Alone save for a gorilla" and has no reason to want to go back to
1989, even if he could. "Well, at least he doesn't look Jewish," Natalie comments. Al informs them he's of Italian descent. Gus decides that they should
hide Al in the attic until they can obtain official papers for him and take him
with them to Maiernigg for the summer. Al explains that he is "not a man for
the women," and "sex is dangerous" in the future for such as him. Gus un

derstands. For some mystical or scientific reason, Al and the Mahler contingent can understand each other perfectly, even though they don't speak each other's language.

The women go to prepare a place for Al in the attic, and Gus inquires of Al how the work he is now composing—his Fifth Symphony—will be received in future.

AL: It will not be one of my personal favorites, this Fifth Symphony, but it will become one of your more popular works.

GUS: Which of my works do you love?

AL: You haven't written them yet. So far I love most of the songs, the last movement of the Third and all the Fourth. I used to think the Fourth didn't have enough pain it in, but now I understand it better and am in awe of the variations in the third movement.

GUS: The Fourth! It has been reviled all over Germany. The reviews have been devastating.

AL: I doubt they were worse than those for my new play.

GUS: Indeed? Well, look here!
   Runs to his desk and retrieves a sheaf of reviews, shoving them in Al's face.
Read!

AL (*looking at the reviews*): I can't read German.

GUS: Well, how about this for excoriation—I will choose at random. (*Reads.*) "This latest dropping of Kappelmeister Mahler smells far worse than the last; and that, dear reader, almost surpasses belief. In fact, it might pass as a miracle of odification"—I believe "odification" is a coinage of disgust.

AL: So you think that's bad. Well, listen to this. (*Reads from one of the reviews in his sheaf of reviews.*) "I never thought Albert Innaurato had any talent, but *Coming of Age in Soho* proves it!"

GUS: Oh, come, come, that's nothing. This is much worse. (*Reads.*) "So to have avoided hearing this preposterous excrescence I would have willed myself deaf. Kappelmeister Mahler cannot be said to lack an ear, he has an ear of slime!"

AL: But that is palpably untrue, simply an idiot's shot in the dark. Now this is devastating: "Albert Innaurato ... " Innaurato is my last name.

GUS: I gathered. Rather hard to pronounce, isn't it?

AL: A nightmare. But listen! (*Reads.*) "Albert Innaurato is a vile, narcissistic writer whose only talent is getting his work on ... "

GUS: Oh, you're a crybaby! I wouldn't flinch if they stopped at that. Listen: "Gustav Mahler brings disgrace on our German public, intruding his alien nose into our pure atmosphere ... " That's because I was born a Jew.

Sam Tsoutsouvas as Gustav Mahler and Mark Blum
as Albert Innaurato in a scene from *Gus and Al*

AL (*reading*): "Albert Innaurato is a preposterous homosexual fat man with nothing to offer, not even self-pity and titillation. There is only this feeble drivel, the sad, thin slobber of a pitiable idiot who gives himself airs. Someone should do him the favor of ending his life, or at least offering a lobotomy gratis … "

Gus decides it might be fun to express themselves in dancing, and they are leaping about in abandon when the women return to take Al up to his quarters. Natalie leads Al off, explaining that since she writes down everything Mahler says, Al must tell her about their conversation while she was out of the room.

The walls of the room disappear, and the scene changes to the back of the summer villa at Maiernigg, with a porch overlooking a lake, an outdoor staircase to the upper part of the building and a table for outdoor dining. Gunshots are heard (Al and Gus are off shooting at birds), as Justine wonders what progress Natalie is making in her wooing of Gus. Justine can't leave Gus to pursue her own romantic interests until her brother is settled in marriage.

Natalie has been trying to snare her adored Gus for 15 years, and now Al is providing a new distraction.

Camillo, an Italian boy of about 18, comes running in looking for two errant children of the professor who employs him as an assistant gardener. He is soon followed onstage by the boys' father: Doctor Sigmund Freud, 44, dressed in hiking lederhosen. Camillo runs off after the children, and Justine goes into the house to fetch Freud a glass of water. Natalie's full name is Natalie Bauer Lechner, and it seems Freud knew her former husband Bauer in Trieste. As Justine comes on with the water and a bowl of fruit, Freud, looking off, wonders who Mahler's companion may be.

JUSTINE: A fat charity case my brother has taken in for reasons of his own.

FREUD: Oh yes? It seems succoring the overupholstered, underprivileged is a habit we Jews have inherited from our forefathers. Oh, I am sorry, I had forgotten. Mister Director Mahler has converted, hasn't he? Given way to the Christian Masses, so to speak?

JUSTINE: Can you blame him, Professor? If bowing to a man in a dress and chattering some Latin mumbo jumbo can forestall our being slaughtered by the Cossacks, so be it.

NATALIE: Justine, I am shocked by your cynicism. Opportunism was not even the slightest consideration for Mahler.

FREUD: I don't mean to sound censorious, but after all ... what other reason could there be?

NATALIE: The man, Jesus!

FREUD (*his professional interest piqued*): Really?

NATALIE: The suffering Saviour of unspeakable beauty and goodness. The Redeemer; the incarnation of all that is good in befouled mankind. Glorious proof that shining purity is innate in humans, not only possible but inevitable as the dark ages give way to the light. We are seeing this new age begin in our time, Professor, and Jesus prophesied this centuries ago.

Camillo enters and interrupts with the news that he has found the children and they have caught an enormous frog. Freud empties the fruit bowl, takes a penknife from his pocket and goes off determined to give his sons a lesson in biology. Camillo follows.

Justine calls to Gus and Al that it's nearly time for dinner. She repeats to Natalie her urgent desire to leave Gus and go off with her beloved Arnold, a violinist—but she won't leave Gus untended.

The men enter—they are dressed in bathing costume and show off a brace of birds, dripping blood, which they have just shot. This seems a cruel act to Natalie, but Gus explains, "In the mornings when I try to work, their singing maddens me!" Natalie exits in tears. Justine carries the birds off but returns to reproach Gus for spending so much time with Al this summer that he's neglecting his devoted Natalie. Gus vows to be attentive to Natalie at dinner, and the men go off to change.

Natalie returns and remarks wistfully to Justine, "I know the Master needs me, and sometimes in life need equals love, don't you find?" She has heard Gus speak of her as "Old Natalie." Al returns, dressed for dinner, as the sound of music and womens' voices singing is heard from the direction of the river. When Gus enters and goes onto the porch, the unseen women react with cheers—they are serenading him. One of them (in a bathing suit, soaking wet, after having swum ashore) comes onto the porch. She is Alma Schindler, "*a beautiful, voluptuous young woman of 22,*" a music student who composed the serenade her companions just sang. Gus, enchanted with Alma, touches her hair. Alma is angry—not because Gus touched her, but because he was sent a new ballet composed by her teacher and has been holding it without comment.

Alma is introduced to the others and identifies Al as "a fat Italian, just like a bad tenor," and tells him, "You do look rather like Dr. Freud's gardener's young assistant, he might be your younger brother or son, even; he's much thinner but there's something similar in the shape of the head." Natalie makes an acid comment, and Alma turns on her with, "So it's true, grey hair is associated with a nasty tongue." Natalie suggests that Alma's teacher, Zemlinsky, has put her up to this adventure (Alma denies this vigorously), and she is shocked when Alma addresses Mahler as "Mister Gustav."

GUS (*enraptured with Alma*): .....I am pleased for Zemlinsky that he has attracted so radiant a disciple.

JUSTINE: The tea will be bitter. We must all drink it now.

ALMA (*to Gus, oblivious to them*): I am so glad to hear you say it. But how dare you ignore his ballet, leave it moldering on your desk for a year?

GUS (*sterner*): My dear Miss Schindler, I am impressed with your abandon but think, please, before you defend too strenuously such outright trash!

NATALIE: The tea isn't that bitter, Justine.

    She sips.

ALMA: Trash? Outright trash? You of all people are that censorious of new work?! You who write such, shall we say, disputed musïc yourself?

NATALIE (*pleased at this turn of events*): In fact, though I adore sugar, this once it is sweet enough!

ALMA: And it is hardly as if you have looked at it. I wager it has sat on your desk this entire year, while you go on to produce bourgeois grotesqueries such as *The Korean Bride*!

NATALIE: Some more tea, Justine, please. And perhaps we should send Al to trundle after a carriage to ferry our wet guest into obscurity or wherever she lives.

GUS: Out of the question. Miss Schindler is too wet to travel. (*To Alma.*) You must join us for dinner. It is quite true that *The Korean Bride* is bourgeois trash, but I run a theater in the real world ...

ALMA: A theater subsidized by His Majesty ...

GUS: Even he likes to turn a profit. And it is true I cannot speak with authority about Mister Zemlinsky's ballet, I've only skimmed it. Well, in fact, I haven't opened it, but I know just where it is. I'll send for it forthwith. Meanwhile, I am famished, and you must certainly be after your impromptu swim.

    Natalie throws her cup down, breaking it.

Alma agrees to remain for dinner (though she is staying with her family only a half mile or so away), and Justine suggests that Natalie lend her a dress. Alma asks Natalie pointedly, "Won't you make a respectable matron of me with one of your frocks?" and Natalie exits in a huff. Gus exits to send a messenger to Alma's family, after being instructed by Alma, "Tell him to say I'm at our friends the Burckhards—I'm afraid my people despise you, Mister Mahler. You are a Semite, you see, and while they believe in religious tolerance during the winter, they like to take a vacation from it while on holiday."

Justine goes to see about dinner, leaving Alma to Al. Alma wonders if they've met before, but Al assures her, no, they're *going* to meet many years from now. Al knows that Alma's family isn't anti-Semitic, and Alma admits she sometimes tells a deliberate lie in order to polish her skill at deceit.

Natalie comes in with a somewhat soiled dress, which Alma goes to put on. Gus returns, and when Alma re-enters the dress looks attractive on her, despite its shortcomings. Gus regards her as Cinderella and has done her every bidding: the messenger is dispatched, and Natalie will be asked to send a telegram to the Opera House asking for the ballet score immediately. Justine announces dinner, and the scene blacks out.

At night in Gus' bedroom at the villa, with a big window outside of which there is a tree, Gus is looking over sketches while Al, to whom sweets are an obsession, is turning the handle of an ice cream freezer with one hand while making notes for a play with the other. Mahler wonders why his music seems controversial, and Al guesses it's because it anticipates the disturbed world to come.

GUS: The world is and always has been the same, essentially. And man, god and pig, has always been master.

AL: Not so. I'm thinking of the far past when men were rodents living in the shadow of a superior race of giants—the dinosaur.

GUS (*laughs*): The dinosaur? Those hideous, lumbering creatures ...

AL: In my time it is thought they were warm-blooded, fast, intelligent. The little furry rat-like creatures, our ancestors, envied and feared and hated them. What grand trumpeting noises the dinosaurs must have made—look at their facial and chest cavities—their mating calls and fighting sounds and death cries must have been Wagnerian. They've been banded reptiles because they remind humans of how puny we are ...

GUS: But there is nothing greater than the human. No dinosaur composed the late Quartets of Beethoven, or *Tristan*, or the plays of Shakespeare ...

AL: No dinosaur did these things, but after all, they are small things, when you think about it.

GUS: Small things! I thought you said you were an artist? You must worship the immense achievements of those who are dead and strive to match them. And you must believe in the beauty of people, hard as that can be. The dinosaur, indeed!

AL: True, I loathe people; if that's not an illness, it's inconvenient, as I'm surrounded by them. Maybe I'd be better off believing in their beauty as you seem to. But I need think only of my century, a century of plagues and wars and technology gone mad, to wonder why it is the dinosaurs lasted for millions of years and speaking people for barely ten thousand. And I wonder if the dinosaurs tolerated suffering as easily as we do. When I walk the streets of Manhattan and see people with no recourse but starvation and indignity, and hear those people blamed for their sufferings, or when I see young men better than me by far die of an imaginably horrible disease, and I hear a Jesus-shrieking Southern Senator call them perverts on the floor of the Senate ... ! Forgive me, but could the ugliest, bloodthirstiest dinosaur have matched that? The great works you and I know of between us, perhaps they are lucky accidents and rare; but the viciousness is inevitable and everywhere!

GUS: Suddenly, my friend, for the first time I can't understand you. Dinosaurs! They were on the earth for millions and millions of years, but they never evolved a civilization, a culture. After all, even in Vienna today, there is terrible poverty and injustice.....Isn't it truer to say these are the noxious waste products of great civilizations? To be hated and fought, certainly, but far from the only achievements of mankind?

AL: I am sorry, Gus. I am just a self-indulgent fat man. I have suffered very little, really. And still I complain. I have never loved anyone, and I have failed at everything I've tried. But perhaps it is because I have been so comfortable in my life that I have the time to fear this way.

Al tastes the ice cream and finds it good. Gus mentions Jesus as a palliative for life, and they discuss modern Fundamentalism and the scant historical evidence of Jesus's existence. "He's another myth we clever humans dream up to deodorize ourselves," Al declares, "because we live in shit. What are we really but bigger baboons with speech and technology who love to fuck? We need Jesus to justify our bringing children into this world so that they may know the exquisite pleasure of dying."

Gus counters, "I prefer a sweeter view, for example, the Heaven in the last movement of my Fourth." He goes on to explain what Jesus means to him: "The sudden rush of illumination, the terror we humans feel in confronting our beauty and ugliness." Since Al by his own confession has never loved, he is only what Gus calls an "apprentice human," his insights are bound to be faulty, where Gus has both loved and suffered greatly—he adored the brother who died in his arms at 13.

As they prepare to take to their beds, Gus confesses that Alma attracts him strongly: "Her rudeness is like an aphrodisiac." They open the window to hear the rustling tree and settle down. The lights out, Alma creeps into the room via tree and window and, nearly naked, joins Gus in his bed, ignoring the presence of Al, who is quiet and must be supposed to be asleep. Gus and Alma each admit to inexperience in love, and their affair goes badly. Gus's leg begins twitching, and then he prematurely spends himself, much to Alma's amusement.

At this moment Natalie intrudes, candle in hand, determined to "be a brave soldier in the lists of love." Alma hides herself in Al's bed. Notebook and all, Natalie enters Gus's bed, as both men snore loudly, pretending to be asleep. But Alma cannot bear being crushed by Al and leaps from his bed. Natalie jumps from Gus's bed, notebook at the ready.

NATALIE (*writing in her book*): Now let me see, how did you get in, Miss Schindler? Can you vaporize yourself like a noxious gas? Or do you fly, like a bat?

ALMA: What? Do you think your scribbling in that silly book gives you power? You pathetic creature! It is only your ugliness of spirit, very well mirrored in your flesh, that prevents my pitying you ...

GUS: Enough!

NATALIE (*sarcastic, to Alma*): But why are you so bitter, Almschi? You can have the Master if he desires you, and Al too. Though I recommend the Master send you to the doctor first. As he must remember from his student days, whores distribute syphilis more truly than love!

ALMA: You bitch!

    She hurls herself on Natalie. They fight, screaming.

GUS: My God! Stop! (*Not wishing to intervene, he cries out.*) Help!

    Justine, alerted by the noise the two women are making, comes running into the room.

JUSTINE: What's the trouble here? My God!

    She hurls herself into the fray and separates the two women, who are panting and still enraged.

Miss Schindler, how irregular. Natalie, I am appalled! Gustaverl, shame! Come Natalie, to bed. Miss Schindler, you had best stay here in the guest room ... really, what will the servants say?! And you Al, you immoral pervert, this is all your fault!

With considerable dispatch she hustles Natalie and Alma out of the room, holding each at arm's length from the other.

GUS: Oh, God, Al, I am so ashamed! I spent myself at the first touch, like a fool, a buffoon! Look, my stupid leg is still going! I must have her or my life is over!

AL: Poor Natalie ...

GUS: Damn Natalie!

AL: And poor Gus!

Blackout. Curtain.

ACT II

In the villa's garden, around the table, Gus, Al, Natalie and Justine are celebrating Gus's birthday—his 40th, July 7, 1901. Al—who turned 40 June 2—hands Gus the first act of his new play. Skimming it, Gus decries the careless grammar and the despicable characters, commenting, "If you weren't so jaded and cynical you'd be a better writer."

Justine brings in a number of congratulatory telegrams (but none from Alma). They open a bottle of champagne and toast Gus. Justine goes to answer the bell and returns with a telegram. It's from her suitor, Arnold Rose, whom Gus calls "an opportunist looking for preferment" but who Justine hopes may be "an aging bachelor looking for a wife!"

Alma enters, running, *"beautiful in a well chosen and very sexy summer outfit,"* bearing a collection of her own compositions and a large jar filled with cockroaches. The compositions are a birthday present for Gus and the cockroaches (Alma is studying biology) a lesson for the others: "These middle-sized monsters have a lot to teach us about endurance, reproduction and digestion."

Gus is captivated by Alma as she discusses the future with Al, and finally Gus can't resist blurting out what is very much on his mind.

GUS: Are you engaged to be married, Miss Schindler?

ALMA: Of course not.

GUS: I may woo you, then?

ALMA: Publicly and proudly!

JUSTINE (*suddenly seeing Alma and not Natalie as her own salvation*): Please join us, Miss Schindler. I'm glad to see you. We are about to have a birthday lunch, it will be no trouble for the servants to make something for you.

ALMA: Thank you. Now, my music, Gustav.

They go slightly apart with the sheaf of music. Natalie, agitated, grabs Justine.

NATALIE: Justine, you traitor. Encouraging her!

JUSTINE: I must save myself, and I will be as ruthless as Gustaverl. This telegram from Arnold, read it. It's an ultimatum—yes or no. And I intend on saying yes!

Natalie and Justine go in to arrange the lunch, leaving Al to chaperone the lovers. Gus sends Al a comfortable distance away to open the telegrams, then he gets directly to the point with Alma: "What if I never could complete the act with you?" Alma replies, "You'll soon be bored enough, and then you'll complete it," suggesting that he should a) marry her and b) consult Dr. Freud down the road if he's worried about this problem. Al, across the stage, assures Gus that in the future Dr. Freud's assistance will be highly valued.

Gus sends Al for coffee, and then he and Alma turn their attention to the music she has brought to show him.

GUS (*suddenly tense*): That damned Zemlinsky circle!

ALMA (*equally tense*): Zemlinsky is a great artist.

GUS (*sarcastically*): Indeed! His ballet score is crabbed and silly; no humanity, no depth of feeling, only a stilted obsession with form!

ALMA (*also sarcastic*): An obsession you don't share, perhaps?

GUS: And then, he throws all his work over for a stupid tune!

ALMA: Perhaps, had you the same courage, your symphonies would be more bearable!

AL (*enters with coffee*): Here's the coffee.

GUS (*waving him away*): Not now, man!

> *Al shrugs and drinks the coffee. Gus looks at one of Alma's scores.*

(*Not pleasant.*) Aha! A sonata movement! Let us see how this intellectual giant and physical dwarf has taught his favorite student!

ALMA (*snatching the music out of his hands*): I am not his favorite; he is no shorter than you, Mister Opera Director. It was a mistake for me to come ...

As Natalie enters with a plate of hors d'oeuvres, Gus and Alma decide that they'd better leave off arguing about music and enjoy the glories of nature in a walk along the lake shore. Alma takes the plate of food and dumps it into the cockroach jar, then walks off with Gus. Natalie looks at the music Alma has left behind, curses because it's good, then asks Al, "Does she have a great career?" Al tells her, "In a manner of speaking," so she throws the pages of music over the yard. But when Al starts picking them up, she helps him and confides to him, "I am childish. I have started to age. For age isn't chronology, is it? It is seeing the young suck up one's own future and start to matter more than one matters, to seem realer than one seems. I have flesh too, and breasts and a womb, and that young creature, ravenous for life, has begun to eat into them, like an acid. Soon, too soon, Natalie outside will start to wave and dissolve like a desert mirage, while Natalie inside still feels this horrid longing too concretely."

Again, Natalie looks over Alma's music and praises it in detail. Al hugs her comfortingly, as Justine enters with more food. Gus and Alma return and see Natalie still in Al's arms. They pretend they are dancing a waltz. Alma, looking on, comments, "Oh, the future isn't that arthritic! The future is lively!" and impulsively knocks over the jar of cockroaches, sending the insects scattering and the people panicking. *Blackout.*

In a shallow, curtained area at center, Gus is lying on a cot dreaming of Alma, while Al tears up what he has just written of his play. "I suppose any play I'd write here now would really be ahead of its time," Al comments and admits to Gus that in his own time Al is irrelevant. In Al's time, people are not hungry for new work and ideas, as they are in Gus's time. They respect only the long-dead like Shakespeare. He tries to describe TV and break dancing and rock 'n' roll to an amused and skeptical Gus.

AL: .....And there are many now who think rock music is magnificent. It has become the Plain Chant of the twenty-first century—and the basis for what we call Minimalism—the true music of the future—endlessly repeated, mostly major chords in a diatonic harmony with lots of rhythmical manipulation.

GUS: I don't believe you. Who would want to live in your time if it truly is as you say it is?

AL: Please understand me. I am part of that culture, and I think it's fun, but I worry that it simply reflects a drying up of the human spirit, whatever gave us civilization ...

GUS: Impossible!

AL: But what if I am telling the truth?

GUS: What truth? That art doesn't matter?

AL: Does it?

GUS: You aren't an artist if you must ask.

AL: All right. But then prove to me it matters somehow.

GUS: It won't save a life or fill a belly, perhaps, but we must believe that there is some concrete beauty somewhere which artists bring to a suffering world ...

AL: Perhaps you wouldn't be so sure if you knew that the most original art of the new twentieth century would be exquisitely efficient death machines—

GUS: Death machines?

AL: Some of them ovens for people, constructed by the very Germans you are hoping will swoon to your music. If only I could spread my flab into a magic cloak, I would give you a guided tour of the truly important museums of my time—missile silos, launching pads, atomic reactors. (*He laughs.*) But at least you will be dead. If I get back, I'm afraid I will be forced to watch the collapse of all you and I worship.

GUS: You have a disease, and it is catching, the disease of despair.

AL: Can you reassure me?

GUS: When I rehearse my music I have to fight to continue when I see the indifference, the hostility and confusion of the orchestra. I laughed with you when we read our reviews, but they hurt me, not all those Mahler-haters are stupid or merely anti-Semitic. What I try to do is so hard; after a day of composing my muscles ache, my bones quiver as though I were trying to build a pyramid according to a sadistic madman's time schedule. I won't let you infect me! Yours are a fat schoolboy's complaints, a failed scholar's insights. Finally, you're lazy and perhaps untalented.

AL: That's fame talking, that's ease and acclaim and a steady job talking; that's 1901 talking ...

GUS: That is a man who creates talking, who works and compromises and schemes and fights so he can create. You're an empty shell, that's why you talk this way! I am a man, I struggle, that is a man's destiny, while you ...

AL: Yes, I am not a man. Maybe you'd be right at home in my time ...

GUS: You must try and find love. Even the scent of it is enough to change some of this fury you feel. What I felt for my brother, and now Alma ...

As for Natalie, Gus is fond of her, but love is not in question. If Freud will reassure him about his physical performance, he means to marry Alma. Al accuses him of failing to appreciate Natalie's long and loyal attachment and calls him an "opportunist," a "survivor" who will accommodate any hostility in order to keep writing his "endless symphonies." Stung by this last comment, Gus demands an apology and finally gets one, grudgingly. But his feelings about Al have changed. He no longer wishes to support or share a room with someone who contends that "love is impossible or a dirty joke, that art is a delusion."

The curtained area opens out, as the scene changes to the garden of Freud's villa, where Camillo is sweeping up around the outdoor chairs and tables. Freud and Gus stroll onstage, soon followed by Al, who stares at Camillo while the other two stroll off. Camillo is a bit flustered by Al's attention. Al tells the lad how striking-looking he is, and somehow familiar, as though Al has seen a face like Camillo's in a Renaissance painting.

CAMILLO: Oh? You ... you like young men?

AL: In a sense.

CAMILLO: I see. Are you English?

AL: No. Why?

CAMILLO: This English gentleman, very nice, talked to me very pleasantly over a week's time, then kissed me and asked me to live with him in London. I said no. Then he went and told the Professor I had cheated him at cards. I didn't hate the Englishman for doing that, but I am a man now and don't want to be kept and fondled like a girl. I was willing to give him a few names of young Italians in the village who might be interested, but he said only I would do. These English, not very flexible.

AL: Well, I suppose I was flirting a little. I sounded smarmy, didn't I? (*Mocking himself.*) "Probably I've seen your face peeking out of a painting or two!" Pardon me while I shudder. I thought I had gotten over all that even before I time-traveled—that is, came here. I was really looking for sex but liked to pretend I was looking for love. Who could love me? Who could I love? But do you think queenly insinuation is a reflex, a habit that comes back to you like riding a bicycle? There is something grotesque about a fat man flirting.

Camillo feels comfortable with Al, and he shares some wine from a bottle he has hidden. When he hears that Al is an American, he tells Al of his older brother Luca, a tailor, who lives there and wants Camillo to join him as soon as he can.

Charles Janasz (Sigmund Freud), Jennifer Van Dyck (Alma Schindler), Sam Tsoutsouvas (Gustav Mahler), Cara Duff-MacCormick (Natalie Bauer Lechner) and Mark Blum (Albert Innaurato) in a scene from *Gus and Al*

Al remembers that he himself had a Great Uncle Luca whose younger brother, Camillo, founded the South Philadelphia Innauratos. And Camillo's tale of running away from Italy when he was 15, stowing away on a German vessel and gambling for his life with the Captain, is also familiar to Al—he's heard his own grandfather tell it. When the Captain found out Camillo was cheating, instead of taking revenge he put him to playing cards with the passengers. Camillo left the ship because he was afraid he'd be exposed eventually, and he could never remember the false name the Captain had given him.

CAMILLO: .....He would say that my real name was so hard to learn that it had used up all my brain power. Will the Americans find it hard? Listen carefully, sir. I'll pronounce it slowly—is it hard? Innaurato!
> *Al has caught on by now but is still moved to meet his grandfather like this. He reacts, but then hides his face for fear of frightening Camillo away.*
Sir? (*Interprets Al's reaction as reflecting the extreme difficulty of the name.*) It is hard.
AL (*finds it hard to speak*): ... Yes ...
CAMILLO: I'll never change it, never! I don't know why. They called me "head like a stone" in my family—you know, stubborn.
AL: You used to call me that ... I mean, I've been called that, too. I'm sorry if I get past and future mixed up.
CAMILLO: There's nothing wrong with being crazy, though I admit it's hard to be crazy and fat and poor.
AL: But if it's such a hard name ... Maybe you could change it to something else. Mamet, maybe.....

But Camillo holds to his name as an anchor in a stormy world. He looks off, sees that Gus and Dr. Freud are deep in conversation, has another swig of wine and promises himself a garden like this some day if he manages to get to America. Al assures him he will have it and, in tears, tries to tell his grandfather that he loved him, which he never told him during his childhood. He remembers kind things his grandfather did for him, but Camillo, appalled that this grown man should be weeping openly in front of a boy, slaps him and admonishes him, "Grab life, sir, love it, hug it to you, fuck it, dance with it and use it to wipe your tears, or kill yourself and be done with it. This weeping is not suitable for an Italian or even an American of Italian descent!"
Gus and Freud return. Al explains the goings-on by claiming to be an hysteric. The Professor seems interested in treating him until Al reveals his shortage of funds. Gus and Freud go to pay their respects to Freud's wife. Camillo brings Al a fig to settle his nerves, but at that moment Alma runs in distraught, grabs the fig and devours it. She is worried because she knows her future with

Mahler hangs in the balance at this interview with Freud, and she blames her own forwardness for Mahler's problem.

Gus comes back to the garden and is surprised to see Alma, who throws herself at his feet. They rush off to make love (Freud's garden seems a likely place for this), and soon Natalie enters in disarray, having seen the lovers in action. She has been climbing trees and wriggling through grass in pursuit of Gus, and she has heard—and written down—his conversation with Freud: "All about his mother. That's all the Doctor was interested in. Mother this and mother that. If that's true, why is the Master indifferent to me? I could play his mother better than that slut!"

Then, after writing down a description of Gus and Alma's love play, Natalie must admit to herself, "I have been vanquished." Reading about it in her journal in future may provide some sort of comfort: "Maybe I can laugh at how ugly their coupling was."

It is obviously going to rain, and Camillo and Al busy themselves with raising a tent to protect Natalie—and Freud, who has just joined her. Gus comes in, and in a few moments so does Alma; both are radiant. Natalie feels cold and runs in to the house to get a wrap but leaves her notebook behind. Alma picks up the notebook, realizes what it is, begins to read, then sends Gus for a glass of water. When he comes back with it, she pretends to spill it inadvertently over Natalie's notebook, then rips out the pages from Al's arrival onward and waves them, pretending to dry them.

Natalie returns with Justine who has come over bringing word of an impromptu party this evening (all of this reminds Al of the Hamptons). Natalie finds her notebook mutilated. Gus reassures her that "Nothing astonishing has happened this summer" worth preserving on the record, as the storm threatens with thunder and lightening.

All except Al and Natalie depart, Freud after assuring her that he'd like to consult about her problem at a later date. Camillo runs back to kiss Al "just in case you were telling the truth" and then runs off. Alone with Natalie, Al expresses sympathy for her.

NATALIE: I have lost him, my beloved.
There is more thunder. The light changes slightly.
An eerie sunset, tonight. You know, I am ruined. My husband took all my money. I've been living on the capital left me by my parents, and that is about gone. I have no livelihood. What can I do? She will have me thrown out of his house. Even Justine has turned against me, and it was I who introduced her to her Arnold. I am facing poverty and the worst kind of loneliness ... (*She has an idea.*) Take me with you!
AL: What do you mean?
NATALIE: You will leave us, I'm positive. She'll destroy you too. The spell you are under will fade. You will find your way home. Take me with you. I

derive my own purpose from serving artists. You are an artist. I will serve you. I could learn to love you.

AL: Come on, Natalie, you couldn't learn to love me.

NATALIE: What will I do? Should I try to die?

AL: Maybe we should both try to die. But you know, we don't want to. I don't know why we hug life, you and I. That's a mystery to me. In living we must both face the likelihood that life will be painful for us, perhaps more so than for most people. So be it.

More thunder. A strange lightening.

Natalie comes to the conclusion that they must both go on. She tells Al, "You are a better person than you think. And I will struggle on too. Let's go then; let's walk into the forest blessing life," which they do.

On a mound in a beautiful, densely wooded area, Alma, Gus, Justine and Camillo are watching a fine sunset, lit occasionally by lightning. Justine is impatient—she wants to get to the party and join Arnold. Alma and Gus confirm that they are now engaged to be married. Al and Natalie enter, and at Gus's suggestion they all join hands to affirm their allegiance to and affection for one another. Gus puts their feelings into words: "We are part of a tribe whose efforts, even when frustrated, or frail, have forced the expansion of that complex tapestry called human being. Through history we join hands in spirit and now, since you're from the future, Al, this once in the flesh. We join hands, I tell you, the greatly gifted, the merely hopeful, the dreamers, the doers, and we climb up on one another's shoulders, draw on one another's blood until we become all together, this beautiful earth, the heart of the universe. We here are brothers, and I tell you Al, whatever happens, we must all swear to keep fighting, to offer up our sufferings and work and work until we are spent, regardless of what the world thinks."

Al is agreeing with Gus that to have lived once is enough, when *"There is a burst of thunder, lightning flashes. All but Al freeze in place. Kafka and Mrs. Briggs come crashing down."* Kafka is glad they have found Al; Mrs. Briggs just wants to get home in time to see the next episode of *Dynasty*. Kafka reassures Al that the reviews weren't all bad and urges him to get aboard Mrs. Briggs's wheelchair because they have very little time to spare before having to return to 1989. But Al wants to say goodbye to his 1901 friends who are frozen in a state of suspended animation for the moment, as is the setting sun.

AL: Can they see me, hear me?

KAFKA: For what I know, if they remember you it'll be as a dream or hallucination, they'll forget you as an actual person.

AL: Good. (*He turns to the others, who are still holding hands and still bathed in the setting sun.*) Thank you all, and goodbye ... I'm so glad my last sight of you living is in this beautiful sunset. Goodbye, Gus. Goodbye, Natalie, maybe in your later years when you are poor and alone you'll remember a fat man far, far away in a strange land and hard time, who thinks of you fondly. Goodbye, Justine, I wish you happiness with your Arnold, and I know for a fact you'll find it. And Alma—my God, how you'll rule and ruin Gus's life and the lives of all these people, except for my grandfather here. But, you know, Alma, I've got a crush on you. And guess what? We'll meet again, when I'm a fat boy of fourteen and you're a very old lady, much married, world famous for your husbands. It'll be in the lobby of the old Met during an intermission of *Otello* in 1961, and you'll refer to me as a "klein grosser spaghetti fresser"—a little fat spaghetti eater, even as a girl I see you were just like that, Alma. But I love you for it. And remember these names: Kokoschka, Gropius and Werfel. Grandpop, I'm glad you'll be meeting me again. Come, Kafka and Mrs. Briggs. I hope I wasn't too long ...

KAFKA: We'll just make it .....

AL: I hope I don't break this thing.

MRS. BRIGGS: Trust me. Obesity runs in my family so I had it made at Hearty Prosthetics ...

KAFKA: We turn in this direction ... and let's go!

Just as they are about to take off, Alma becomes unfrozen and grabs onto the wheelchair.

ALMA: Wait for me ...

KAFKA: We can't!

The wheelchair rises. Alma tries to get on but is pushed off.

ALMA: All right for you, Albert, when I meet you at the old Met, whatever that is, in 1961, I am going to kick you in your barely pubescent balls!

She runs back to Natalie and grabs the pages she ripped out of her notebook and waves them at the disappearing wheelchair.

As for now, this is the only record of your visit, and I'm ripping it up!

Laughing wildly as she rips the pages. Blackout. Curtain.

LEND ME A TENOR

A Comedy in Two Acts

BY KEN LUDWIG

Cast and credits appear on page 408

KEN LUDWIG was born in York, Pa., March 15, 1950. "I was your typical stagestruck, starstruck kid," he remembers, going to the theater whenever possible—A Visit to a Small Planet *was a particular favorite—and experimenting with writing plays as early as high school days. He was pointed firmly in the direction of college and law school, however, getting his B.A. from Haverford in 1972, his Ll.M. from Trinity College, Cambridge, England and finally his J.D. from Harvard in 1976. He kept at his playwriting too and arrived on Theater Row off off Broadway with* Divine Fire *in the early 1980s, and then with* Postmortem, *both also produced in regional theater.*

OOB saw a production of Ludwig's Sullivan and Gilbert *in December 1984. This script was later co-produced by the Kennedy Center for the Performing Arts and the National Arts Center of Canada and was named the year's best play by the Ottawa critics. His* Lend Me a Tenor *premiered in London at the Globe Theater on June 3, 1986; was nominated for the Olivier Award for comedy of the year; was subsequently produced in Europe in eight languages including French in a Pierre Barillet and Jean-Pierre Gredy translation in Paris; opened on Broadway February 27, and is cited as its author's first Best Play.*

Ludwig has recently finished his first screen play, Heartbreaker. *He combines his theatrical and legal expertise as secretary of the board and general counsel for the Shakespeare Theater at the Folger. He is married and lives in Washington, D.C.*

The following synopsis of Lend Me a Tenor *was prepared by Jeffrey Sweet.*

Time: 1934

Place: A hotel suite in Cleveland, Ohio

ACT I

Scene 1: An early afternoon on a Saturday in September

SYNOPSIS: We are in an elegant suite of a first-rate hotel. Visible are two rooms connected by a door—a sitting room and a bedroom. Other doors: in the sitting room, one to a kitchenette, one to the outside corridor; in the bedroom, one to a bathroom, one to a closet and another to the corridor.

At rise, a pretty young woman named Maggie is alone in the sitting room listening to a radio playing a recording of an aria from Verdi's *Rigoletto* sung by a brilliant tenor. Max, a nervous man in his 30s, enters the sitting room from the corridor. He has to wait until the aria ends to get Maggie's attention.

It turns out that the singer on the radio, a famous Italian tenor named Tito Merelli, is Max's concern at the moment. Max is assistant to the general manager of the Cleveland Grand Opera Company, and he has been assigned to keep watch over Merelli, who should have checked into this suite some time ago. Merelli has been engaged to appear with the Cleveland Opera in the title role of *Otello* tonight, and everybody is in a high state of agitated anticipation about having a world-class star among them. Maggie has no news for Max, who has just returned from the train station where Tito (also known by the nickname "Il Stupendo") and his wife have not arrived.

The phone rings, and Max answers it. It's Saunders, the general manager, who also happens to be Maggie's father. Through the earpiece of the phone we can hear Saunders roaring with irritation over Tito's non-appearance. Max's lack of news doesn't make Saunders any happier, and Saunders's unhappiness doesn't help Max's nerves. The call over, Maggie chides Max mildly for taking her father's abuse so docilely. This upsets Max.

Max is further upset by Maggie's being so ga-ga over Merelli's voice. "I can sing, too, you know," says Max. But Maggie is dismissive of Max's talent. How can he possibly compare himself to Merelli, a man who is not only an international star but very sensitive? Max asks how she knows he's sensitive, and, in as casual a tone as she can muster, she tells him that she met Merelli with her father last year in Italy. They went backstage to see him after *Aida*. Merelli was in a loincloth, covered with sweat, and he kissed Maggie's palms—such a romantic gesture. She swooned. This upsets Max further— that his fiancee fainted when kissed by "this sweaty Italian guy."

Maggie instantly corrects him: she is not his fiancee. Saying "I'll think about it" to a proposal does not constitute a state of engagement. She wants to experience something "wonderful and romantic" first, and none of the moments with Max have yet measured up. She hasn't had any flings yet either.

MAX: I've been asking you to fling with me for three years! I begged you.
MAGGIE: I don't mean that! I feel that I need some … wider experience.
MAX: Oh. Sure. I get it. You mean like Diana.
MAGGIE: Diana?
MAX: Desdemona. Soprano.
MAGGIE: Oh, her.
MAX: She's flinging her way through the whole cast. All the men are getting flung out. You should see the guy who plays Iago. He's supposed to be evil. He can hardly walk.
MAGGIE: Max—
MAX: He's limping now—
MAGGIE: Max, listen. Let's be honest. When you kiss me, do you hear anything? Special?
MAX: Like what?
MAGGIE: Like … bells.
MAX: You wanna hear bells?
MAGGIE: I guess it sounds stupid, doesn't it?
MAX: Yeah. It does.
MAGGIE: Just forget it.

Saunders, Maggie's authoritarian father, now knocks at the door. Max opens it. Saunders snaps at his daughter that she shouldn't be there, and he continues to snap at Max about Tito Merelli's tardiness. The rehearsal is going to begin in minutes, and the lead still hasn't arrived. In his agitation, Saunders pops a grape from a fruit bowl into his mouth—unaware, until Max informs him, that it's wax. Saunders spits the grape out in fury.

While Max calls the train station again, Maggie asks her father if he has taken his pills. He says he has, but she knows better. She pulls a bottle out of her handbag and, over his protestations ("Where would Lauritz Melchior be today if he'd taken phenobarbital?"), makes him take his medicine.

The phone rings. Saunders anticipates that Tito has met with some disaster that will prevent him from appearing tonight. But it's Julia, the head of the Opera Guild's Collation Committee with her own emergency. The Committee "has decided to serve shrimp mayonnaise at the intermission, the refrigerator has broken down, and the temperature backstage is a hundred degrees." But Saunders knows how to deal with this. "If the shrimp stays pink, the audience gets it. If it turns green, we feed it to the stagehands."

The call over, Saunders tells Maggie to leave. But Maggie wants to stay and meet Merelli again. She asks Max to intercede with Saunders for her. Max meekly tries, but Saunders stands firm: she must go. She does, but in the process she manages to grab a copy of the room key unnoticed. Saunders continues to rant.

SAUNDERS: I've got a thousand of Cleveland's so-called cognoscenti arriving at the theater in six hours in black tie, a thirty-piece orchestra, twenty-four chorus, fifteen stagehands and eight principals … Backstage, I have approximately fifty pounds of rotting shrimp mayonnaise, which, if consumed, could turn the Gala Be-A-Sponsor Buffet into a mass murder … All I don't have is a tenor. Time?

Victor Garber as Max and Philip Bosco as Saunders in a scene from *Lend Me a Tenor*

MAX: One-fifteen. (*Pause.*) I'm—I'm really sorry, sir. I wish there was something I could do to help.

SAUNDERS: It's not your fault, Max. I wish it was. The question now is what to do if that irresponsible Italian jackass doesn't arrive.

MAX: I ... I have an idea about that, actually.

SAUNDERS: You do?

MAX: Yeah. I mean, sort of.

SAUNDERS: Well, spit it out, Max.

MAX: The thing is ... I mean, I was just—just thinking that ... well ... I mean ... I could do it.

SAUNDERS: Do what?

MAX: Sing it. Otello. Sort of ... step in. You see, I—I've been to all the rehearsals, and I know the part and I—I mean, I could do it. I know I could.

SAUNDERS: Otello? Big black fellow.

MAX: Yes, sir.

SAUNDERS: Otello, Max. He's huge. He's larger than life. He loves with a passion that rocks the heavens. His jealousy is so terrible that we tremble with irrational fear for our very lives. His tragedy is the fate of tortured greatness, facing the black and gaping abyss of insensible nothingness. It isn't you, Max.

MAX: It—it could be, I mean, if I had the chance.

SAUNDERS (*turning directly front, addressing the audience*): "Ladies and gentlemen. May I have your attention, please. I regret to inform you that Mr. Tito Merelli, the greatest tenor of our generation, scheduled to make his American debut with the Cleveland Grand Opera Company in honor of our tenth anniversary season, is regrettably indisposed this evening, but ... BUT! ... I have the privilege to announce that the role of Otello will be sung tonight by a somewhat gifted amateur making his very first appearance on this, or indeed any other stage, our company's own factotum, gofer and all-purpose dogsbody ... Max!" Do you see the problem?

MAX: I guess so.

SAUNDERS: Old women would be trampled to death in the stampede up the aisles.

MAX: I see what you mean.

SAUNDERS: Time?

MAX: One-twenty.

> A depressed silence. Saunders picks up a grape and starts chewing. Then he realizes and spits it out and starts stamping on it in his fury.

The phone again, this time with good news: Tito is in the lobby. Saunders warmly greets the tenor on the phone, says he'll be right down and hangs up. He turns to Max and goes over his assistant's key responsibilities for the day: he is to stay with Tito constantly and supply him with whatever he wants except liquor and women and, after the performance, deliver him sober to the reception. After that, Tito is free to "drop dead" as far as Saunders is concerned. This established, and with a final injunction that Max dispose of the bowl containing the bogus fruit, Saunders hurries out the door.

As he does, Maggie, using her purloined key, sneaks into the bedroom from the corridor and dashes into the bathroom. Max, having heard her move around, goes into the bedroom to investigate and discovers her in the bathroom. He is horrified to see her, but he hasn't managed to persuade her to leave by the time Saunders returns and pounds on the sitting-room door for Max to let him and their guests in. Max hands the fruit bowl to Maggie (who thanks him for it). She disappears into the bathroom again, and Max hustles into the next room, opening the door for the impatient Saunders.

Saunders escorts the Merellis in. Tito is "imposing." His wife, Maria, is "busty, proud and excitable." They speak with thick Italian accents. Saunders introduces Max to the Merellis. Tito is most interested in finding the bathroom, however. He isn't feeling well. Max, remembering Maggie is in there, tries to persuade him to use the bathroom in the lobby. Saunders doesn't understand what Max is doing, of course. In the meantime, Maggie has figured out what is up and has transferred herself to the closet. Saunders now leads Tito to the bathroom.

Back in the sitting room, Maria apologizes to Max for her husband. He has a tendency to overindulge in food. On the train, he kept ordering because he liked the view down the waitress's dress when she leaned over to serve him. Saunders has returned to the sitting room for the last part of this and so is there when the bellhop arrives with the luggage, singing an aria. Saunders shuts the bellhop up and has Max escort him with his load into the bedroom. Saunders apologizes to Maria, but she's used to this kind of behavior. People are always popping out of the woodwork to sing opera at her and Tito.

In a moment, Saunders is again stuck on the phone dealing with an emergency. In the meantime, in the bedroom, "As Max lays the fur stole and Tito's hat and coat on the bed, the bellhop opens the closet door, revealing Maggie standing in the doorway. He doesn't see her, however, having turned away to get the suitcases. Max, however, sees her and reacts. Beat. Max slams the door.

"The bellhop looks up, sees that Max has slammed the door and sighs at Max with annoyance. He returns to the closet door and opens it again—again turning away without seeing Maggie. As he picks up the two suitcases, Maggie runs out of the closet and hides behind the closet door.

"As the bellhop enters the closet with the suitcases, Max opens the bedroom corridor door and motions to Maggie to leave. She sticks her head out from behind the closet door and shakes it 'No.' As the bellhop re-enters from the closet, she disappears again.

"The bellhop goes to the bed and gathers up the stole, coat and hat—at which point, Maggie runs around the closet door and back into the closet, slamming the door behind her. This is followed immediately by Max slamming the corridor door. The bellhop looks at one door, then the other, then at Max, who feigns innocence, as though nothing has happened.

"The bellhop shrugs and walks to the closet with the wraps. He opens the door, and Maggie is standing there. He stares at her for a moment; then wordlessly, he hands her the hat, coat and fur. She nods as if to say 'Thank you' and smiles wanly. The bellhop closes the door on Maggie. He turns front, dazed; then shrugs and heads for the sitting room. Before leaving the bedroom, however, he stops and gives Max the 'thumbs up' and hits him on the arm as if to say 'way to go.' Then he goes into the sitting room, followed by Max, who closes the connecting door behind him."

Finished, the bellhop comments on the paltry tip he has received from Saunders. Saunders demands the bellhop apologize to Maria, which the bellhop does, with a flourish, in Italian, then exits.

Max expresses concern for Tito's well-being, as Tito emerges from the bathroom holding the fruit bowl and looking ill and a little puzzled. Maria assures Saunders and Max that, as long as there are women in the opera, Tito will make the performance.

Tito enters the sitting room. His wife comments that he looks like a sick dog, but Tito insists that he is in the pink. And no, he doesn't want the pills Maria is trying to force on him. This escalates into a major squabble, Tito calling her a crazy woman, Maria raging about his stupidity. Maria slams into the bedroom to cool off with a copy of *Vogue*.

Saunders suggests it's time for Tito to head for the rehearsal, but Tito says he's in no shape to rehearse. Saunders shouldn't worry, he's done the part 50 times, he'll be fine. Nor does he need to be seen for the costume fitting, as he's brought his own Otello costume along with him.

News of another emergency reaches Saunders (they've lost the music), and, having accommodated himself to Tito's desires, he dashes off, leaving Max to take care of the star. Max expresses concern over Tito's health, but Tito assures him that he'll be O.K.: "In my village, they got a saying— 'Nobody ever dies from a-gas.' And believe me, they know." What he needs is to relax. But this life of rushing from city to city, hotel to hotel, doesn't help much. Tension is the enemy of singing. "You get a-tense, you finished."

His doctor keeps trying to get him to take the pills he prescribes. Phenobarbital. "It makes-a you sleep. I'm-a Merelli. I done take pills." Mention of phenobarbital gets Max thinking, and he picks up the bottle of Saunders's pills Maggie left behind earlier. Tito proposes they have a drink of wine. Seeing an opportunity, Max agrees, and Tito goes to the bedroom to fetch some Chianti.

Tito finds Maria lying on the bed, still reading her magazine. She is in a sulky mood. Tito apologizes for his behavior. He promises that soon they'll take a vacation. She warms considerably, begins to kiss his neck. She is interested in acting on her passion, but Tito begs off on account of his stomach. Maria instantly flies into a jealous rage. He hasn't tended to her needs in three weeks, so she figures he must have a girl. He protests this isn't so. He's just not feeling well. If that's the case, she snaps, he should take his pills. Angrily, he pulls out the pills and knocks some down. He hopes she's satisfied now. She flares, he flares some more. Maria stomps into the bathroom and Tito, a bottle of Chianti in his hands, stomps back into the sitting room, where Max is just returning from fetching a pair of glasses from the kitchenette.

Tito hands the bottle of Chianti to Max and returns to the bedroom to fetch the corkscrew he forgot. In the meantime, Max puts several of Saunders's phenobarbital pills into one of the glasses. Tito returns with the corkscrew and opens the bottle, which Max takes, filling the glass with the pills. He hands the glass to Tito, who insists that Max join him in a drink. They drink their wine. Max expresses confidence that soon Tito will be good and relaxed and ready for a nap.

Feeling expansive, Tito, having learned in passing that Max sings, asks Max to sing for him now. He'll give Max a free lesson. Tentatively Max begins to sing from Verdi's *Don Carlo*. Tito stops him. He's too tense. He leads Max in some exercises to loosen up, and soon Max is indeed loose and in the mood. Tito now tells him one of his secrets: "You gotta hear the music. Before you sing. You gotta hear everything. The orchestra, the chorus—" Max understands. And the two of them, in a shared trance, hear the introductory notes to the duet from *Don Carlo*. (Through the magic of the theater's speakers, we, too, hear the notes.) And now, together, they sing the duet. They sing gloriously together, with confidence and friendship.

While they sing, Maria, in the bedroom, is finishing a goodbye note to her husband. She is going to leave him. She heads for the door, then remembers her fur stole is in the closet. She goes to retrieve it. She opens the closet door and Maggie tumbles out. Maggie tries to explain that there is an entirely innocent explanation for her presence, but Maria growls her skepticism, grabs her fur and charges out of the room into the corridor, Maggie running after her (not forgetting to close the door behind her).

In the sitting room, Max and Tito finish their duet triumphantly. Tito compliments Max on his voice. Max is ecstatic. Tito tells him that he's feeling tired all of a sudden. He wants to sleep. Max should wake him at 6:30 so he'll make the performance on time. Tito goes into the bedroom. He's about to conk out when he sees the note Maria has left behind. He howls with dismay.

Max tears into the bedroom. Tito tells him Maria has left him for good. Proof? Her fur is gone. And Tito begins to cry. He can't bear it. He wants to kill himself. He races around the apartment looking for something with which to end his life. He grabs a fork from the kitchenette and threatens to perforate himself with it. Max commandingly orders him to put it down, booming, "Tito!

This is not an opera!" This has the desired effect: Tito drops the fork. But he is still despondent at Maria's flight. Max assures him that she will return, and he pulls Tito into the bedroom, removes the singer's shoes and aims him at the bed. Tito is now feeling the full force of the phenobarbital. He asks Max to stay and sing him to sleep. Max obliges, and Tito begins to drift off.

Scene 2: Four hours later

Max is asleep on the sofa in the sitting room, Tito under covers on the bed. A wake-up call from the bellhop rouses Max, who agrees to allow the bellhop to meet Tito if he'll bring up some coffee. No sooner has he hung up the phone, than Diana, the sexy soprano who is to play Desdemona, arrives also hoping to meet Tito: "I thought it might be preferable to meeting him onstage." Max explains that Tito is napping, but Diana is determined to stay. She's hoping that Tito will be so impressed with her that he'll recommend her to the Met.

It is apparent that Diana is willing to demonstrate talents other than her singing to win Tito's good will. To get rid of her, Max promises to arrange for her to spend some time alone with Tito. Before allowing herself to be shooed away, she asks Max if he'll deliver a message to Tito from her. Max agrees and asks what the message is. In the next second, he finds himself in the middle of a long and steamy kiss. Recovering, Max promises to tell Tito. "Of course he might misunderstand," he adds. Diana leaves.

Realizing the time, Max calls to Tito to wake up. He busies himself with various tasks under the assumption that Tito is getting up. But Tito is not moving a muscle. Max, getting no response to any of his questions, goes to check on him. He shakes Tito in an effort to wake him, but Tito remains dead to the world. Max now sees the note Maria left behind and reads it. "By the time you get this, I'll be gone forever. After what has happened, it's just not worth to me the pain and unhappiness of staying around any more. The fun is gone, and now, so am I. Ciao." He instantly assumes that this is a suicide note from the unconscious tenor. The empty bottle of pills nearby confirms the impression. Frantically, he tries to shake Tito back to life, but to no avail.

Now comes heavy-handed knocking from the sitting-room door. It's Saunders yelling for Max. Max says a quiet goodbye to his newfound-and-lost friend and goes into the sitting room to admit Saunders. Saunders, elegantly dressed for the evening's events, initially misunderstands Max's report that Tito is dead. But Max finally gets him to realize he is not using the word "dead" in a figurative sense.

Saunders goes to see for himself, poking at Tito, opening one of his eyes, etc. He reads the presumed suicide note and explodes in a frenzy of rage. The audience will want their money back! Livid, Saunders jumps onto the bed and begins shaking the singer's body violently, yelling, "ARE YOU PROUD OF YOURSELF!!?? FEEL BETTER NOW!!?? *AHHHHHHH*!!" Max tries to calm him down. Saunders ruminates bitterly on Tito's lack of consideration: "He could have waited until tomorrow, he could have jumped out of the window after breakfast." And Saunders attacks Tito again.

Max calms Saunders down again and covers Tito's face with the blanket. He follows Saunders into the sitting room. The opera manager is trying to figure out how to manage the crisis. Max suggests they give the performance with Albert Rupp, the understudy, but Saunders bitterly expresses his doubt that the audience will accept a substitute. Frenzy gives way to gloom now. Saunders is certain he's looking at the end of his career. Then he begins to laugh ironically.

MAX: What's so funny? ... Sir? ...

SAUNDERS: Ohhh! ... I was just thinking. They probably wouldn't know the difference. Albert Rupp. Black his face. Huge wig, lots of padding. If we didn't tell the audience, they'd think that it was Tito Merelli.

MAX: Think so? (*He thinks about it. Then chuckles.*) I think you're right. (*He starts to laugh, in spite of himself—which sets Saunders off again.*) They ... they probably wouldn't know—

SAUNDERS: They'd give him a standing ovation!

MAX: Bring down the house! (*They both laugh uproariously, out of control. They can't stop. Finally:*) Oh ...

SAUNDERS: Oh ...

MAX: It wouldn't work.

SAUNDERS: I know.

MAX: I mean, the company would know it was him—

SAUNDERS: Of course.

MAX: And the story would leak out—

SAUNDERS: And then the audience would hang me. Yes, I realize that.

MAX: If he wasn't in the company, I bet it would work.

SAUNDERS: But he is.

MAX: Yeah. Too bad.

> Long pause. Slowly, a light dawns in Saunders's brain. He rolls it over in his mind, then turns his head and looks at Max. Max sees him and smiles amiably. He doesn't realize what Saunders is thinking. Then he sees the stony, maniacal look in Saunders's eyes ... and suddenly Max looks nervous.

SAUNDERS (*quietly*): Max.

MAX: Forget it. It wouldn't work. They'd spot me in ten seconds.

SAUNDERS: No they wouldn't.

MAX: Hey, stop it. The answer's no.

SAUNDERS: Max ...

MAX: You're out of your mind. I don't even look like him.

SAUNDERS: Black face. Lots of hair ...

MAX: Hey. We were joking. This is life. It's called reality. Remember that?

SAUNDERS: You could do it, Max. I know you could.

MAX (*starting to panic*): Hey. Look. Just—just one second, O.K.? I don't speak Italian. I—I—I—I—I hardly speak English.

SAUNDERS: You wouldn't have to speak Italian. Just sing it.

MAX: Look—look—just—just—O.K.? They'd know. They would know. It's me. Max.

SAUNDERS: No they wouldn't! That's the point! They've never seen him before. They're expecting *him*, not *you*.

MAX: Yeah, but—but—but—but …

SAUNDERS: They want to see him, Max. They want to say they've seen him.

MAX: But it's an opera! Four acts!

SAUNDERS: You know the part. You admitted it.

MAX: I can hum it! In the bathtub!

Saunders gets down on his knees and begins to beg the reluctant Max to undertake the impersonation. The sight of his boss weeping on his socks does the trick. Max agrees to do it.

Saunders has got it planned. Max will change and make up here, arrive just in time to play the first act, retreat into the dressing room between acts and disappear immediately thereafter. The next day, they'll break the news that, in his despair at having been ditched by Maria, Tito took his life.

They are pulling the costume out of a suitcase, when there is a knock at the door. Saunders dispatches Max to change in the bathroom and admits Julia, the Opera Guild chairman, to the sitting room. "*She's about 60 and wears a silver dress covered in sequins.*" She asks Saunders how she looks. "Like the Chrysler Building," he replies. She takes this for a compliment. She has come to cheer up Tito with "the woman's touch." Saunders tries to hustle her out, but she won't budge.

And now the bellhop appears with the coffee and a camera. The bellhop pours some coffee and generally makes it known that he intends to stay and collect on Max's promise to introduce him to Tito. Saunders is about to physically throw the bellhop out of the room, when Maggie appears at the door. She too wants to meet Tito. The bellhop promises to leave as soon as he's had a chance to take a picture, which prompts Saunders to make a grab for the camera. A chase ensues, Saunders pursuing the bellhop, Maggie and Julia pursuing Saunders.

In the meantime, Max emerges from the bathroom, in blackface and wearing Otello's costume and a large black wig. He is terrified. Saunders has just grabbed the bellhop, when Max knocks on the door connecting the bedroom to the sitting room. Everything stops in the sitting room. "Mr. Merelli? Is that you?" Julia asks. The only response Max can muster is "Ciao." Then, with a heavy accent, he asks Saunders to come in and see him. Saunders makes one last futile stab at chasing the visitors out of the sitting room, then ventures into the bedroom, closing the connecting door behind him.

Saunders is delighted at Max's appearance: "You'll get a curtain call just for the costume." But Max's reservations have returned. He can't do it. Saunders's pleas are of no avail. Max simply can't go through with it.

Saunders finally gives up. He goes into the other room to announce to Maggie, Julia and the bellhop that the famed tenor will not be appearing tonight after all. Maggie, believing Maria's fury and flight to be her fault, dashes past her father to the connecting door to talk to Tito. Max, afraid she'll see Tito's body, enters the sitting room, closing the door after him.

Maggie tells Tito-Max that she understands how bad a day it has been for him, but everybody in town has been so looking forward to hearing him. She speaks with such passion that Max cannot refuse her.

At the announcement that he will sing after all, everyone explodes with excitement. Saunders interrupts their celebrating with the reminder that the curtain will be going up shortly. Saunders, Julia and the bellhop pour out of the suite. Maggie stays behind. She has something to confess to Tito.

MAGGIE: It's about your wife. I did something terrible!
MAX: Maggie. Please. (*Pause.*) There are some, few moments when we done look back, and we done look ahead. And for that a-one moment, we have a-music, we have a-happiness, we have a-hope. Eh? That's all.
MAGGIE (*handing him the rose she brought with her*): This is for you.
MAX (*accepting it*): Grazie.
> *She extends her hand, and they shake. But Max doesn't let go. He turns her hand over and gives her a lingering kiss on the palm. She stares at him, speechless; looks at her hand; then reels out of the room, light-headed. Max watches her exit. He's stunned. Long pause. Then he falls to his knees, sobbing with fear. In the process, he drops the rose. After a moment, he hears (and we hear) two voices—his own and Tito's—singing the final moments of the* Don Carlo *duet that they sang in Scene 1. The music grows louder and swells in beauty. Max listens to it; then sees the rose and picks it up and smells it. His courage grows. He gets to his feet and stands up straight and tall. As the music continues, Max turns majestically, and at the threshold he pauses and turns back. He comes to the footlights, acknowledges the thundering applause in his head, throws a kiss to the audience and then turns again and hurries out of the door to his debut.*
> *At this moment—in the bedroom—the covers on the bed move, and Tito sits up with an effort, pulling the covers from his face.*

Groggy and heavily drugged, he looks around as ... the curtain falls.

ACT II

Scene 1: That night, about 11 o'clock

Our first view of the apartment reveals that Tito is gone. Maggie and Julia, having just returned from the opera house, let themselves into the sitting room, still enthusiastic about the magnificent performance they have witnessed.

The phone rings, and Julia answers. It's the police. Hanging up, she tells Maggie, "Apparently some lunatic dressed as Otello tried to get into the theater tonight. He said he was Tito Merelli.....When they wouldn't let him in, he started screaming in Italian, so the stage manager called the police." The "imposter" was arrested but managed to get away. The police are going to dispatch a couple of men to keep an eye out in case he shows up at the reception in the hotel and threatens to disrupt the evening any further.

Julia leaves for the reception. Maggie intends to wait for Tito to tell him that Julia's looking for him, of course. "I mean, I just want to be helpful." Julia teases that she won't mention anything to Max. Maggie is miffed at Max. Why, he didn't even show up for the performance! Julia exits, and Maggie swiftly picks up the phone to call backstage and see if anybody has seen anything of Max. The negative answer obviously disappoints her.

The door opens behind Maggie, and Max enters, still in full Otello get-up. Initially he doesn't see her, but she sees and greets him. Instantly he assumes his Tito impersonation. Nervous about being alone with what she thinks is the opera star, Maggie babbles a bit about how everyone's hoping he'll make an appearance at the reception and say a few words. Having exhausted her excuse for being there, she is about to leave, when Max indicates he'd like her to stay. Employing his Italian accent, he tells her that when he was singing his love song to Desdemona, it was her he was thinking of. *"He kisses her on the lips. She responds. Bells start to ring—all kinds of bells in a long peal of ecstasy. Maggie breaks and looks up, acknowledging them, then grabs Max in a kiss of passion. They both feel breathless and hot ..."* She exclaims, "I want to bear your children!" "Me too!" says Max. She asks about his wife. Improvising, Max tells her that Maria only *thinks* she's his wife: "Its a-very sad."

Another embrace, this one interrupted by a knock at the door. It's Saunders. Running to the mirror to check her appearance, she is startled to see that in their osculation she has gotten her face smudged with Max's black makeup. While Max stalls Saunders, she hurriedly corrects the damage. Now Max lets Saunders in, carrying Max's formal wear. Initially he speaks to him as Max but, seeing his daughter is there, reverts to proper deference for Mr.

Merelli. Saunders starts to hustle his daughter out of the room. Before she leaves, Maggie indicates her desire to have a return engagement with Tito-Max as soon as possible, broadly hinting that he should leave his door unlocked so she can come back later. He doesn't understand this last. Under the mistaken assumption that their rendezvous has been arranged, she exits.

Alone, Saunders congratulates Max on his triumph: "They floated, they suffered, they cried their eyes out." Saunders acknowledges that he owes Max. Max knows how to collect: he reels off a list of the parts he wants to sing next season. Saunders says he has something for him to sing before then: the tenor part in the performance of Verdi's *Requiem* they're going to give in Tito's memory. Saunders is already basking in the anticipated national publicity this will generate for the company and for him. Now, all that they have to do is make an appearance at the reception, announce that Tito's not able to attend and wait till next morning for Tito's body to be discovered.

In the middle of Saunders's euphoria, Max takes a second to remember how much he liked Tito and how sad his death is. Saunders gives lip service to the tragedy, but his eyes are still on the prestige he envisions. The hard part of the evening is over. "If it's any comfort to you, Max," says Saunders, "just remember—from here on out, it's clear sailing. Absolutely nothing can go wrong."

> *Saunders exits, closing the door behind him. Simultaneously, the bedroom corridor door bursts open, and Tito enters. He too is dressed as Otello, in exactly the same costume and makeup that Max is wearing. Tito is in a state of panic. Exhausted and bedraggled, he pants heavily from running. His eyes dart madly in every direction as he leans against the door, gasping for air. Also simultaneously, a siren wails from the street below as though a police car is pulling up at the hotel. Max walks to the window and looks down. Tito hears the siren and dives into the closet, closing the door behind him. Max shrugs and heads for the bedroom. As he reaches the connecting door, he hesitates and braces himself.*

MAX: Poor Tito.

> *He sighs, covers his eyes and enters the room, heading for the bathroom. Max doesn't want to see Tito's body—he couldn't bear it. And yet, he can't help himself. He separates his fingers and glances at the bed; then covers his eyes and turns away. Poor Tito! ... He continues into the bathroom and closes the door.*

Oh my God!

> *Max runs out of the bathroom—without the white tie and tails and closing the door behind him—and stares at the bed, dumbfounded. He tears away the covers, looks under the bed and around the room. No Tito!*

J. Smith-Cameron (Maggie), Jeff Brooks (Bellhop), Philip Bosco (Saunders), Jane Connell (Julia), Caroline Lagerfelt (Diana), Victor Garber (Max), Tovah Feldshuh (Maria) and Ron Holgate (Tito) in *Lend Me a Tenor*

Oh my God!!
> *He hesitates for a split second—then runs out of the bedroom and into the corridor, closing the door behind him.*

MISTER SAUNDERS!!
> *Pause. Slowly the closet door opens and Tito emerges. He looks around and listens. Not a sound. He sighs heavily, then totters cautiously through the bedroom and into the sitting room. He looks around the room. He feels certain now that he's safe at last and sinks on to the sofa and closes his eyes, at which point Julia enters through the sitting room corridor door and sees Tito from the back, sitting quietly on the sofa. She smiles; then walks silently into the room and covers his eyes with her hands.*

JULIA: Guess who?
TITO: YIY!! (*He bounds to his feet and stares at her.*)
JULIA: Now aren't you ashamed of yourself. Sitting here quietly enjoying yourself, while everyone downstairs is simply dying to meet you.
TITO: Excuse me please, but who are you?
JULIA: You're angry with me, aren't you?
TITO: Angry?

JULIA: Here I am, haranguing you about the reception when I haven't even told you how magnificent you were tonight. Tito. My dear man. (*Sitting and leaning back seductively, lowering her voice to the bass range.*) How can I ever thank you?

TITO: For what?

JULIA: For what? For what you did this evening!

TITO: I didn't do nothing! It wasn't me!

JULIA: No it wasn't you. You're right. It was Otello. There, onstage, in flesh and blood. It was beauty, and it was life. It was love, and it was pain. And as I sat there in the theater, watching you tonight, hanging on your every note, I thought to myself: Now, at this moment, I am hearing the greatest performance of any opera star that has ever lived!

TITO: ... I was good, eh?

JULIA: Words cannot express it.

TITO: I think I'm a-gonna siddown, O.K.? (*He does.*)

JULIA: You poor thing. You've had a bad day, haven't you?

TITO: Yeah.

Julia is sympathetic, but she insists that he come down and make his appearance at the reception. Tito is reluctant, but under pressure from her agrees to do so. She is delighted and, in her most suggestive tone, asks if there is anything she can do for him to show her gratitude. "Yeah," he says. "Go." He shows her to the door, closes it behind her and makes plans for an immediate and speedy exit from Cleveland.

He is looking through the phone book for the number of the train station when Diana, wearing a dress designed to accentuate her assets, enters. She reminds Tito (who of course has no memory of what she imagines passed between them) that she had mentioned the possibility of dropping by. Tito may be bewildered, but the condition doesn't retard his libidinous impulses. She calls room service to have a bottle of champagne sent up to complement the mood, then turns to him. She wants to ask a question.

DIANA: Was I good tonight?

TITO: ... Good?

DIANA: I'm sure it's difficult to make any lasting judgments, after having done it with me only once. But would you say I was ... exciting tonight?

TITO (*trying to work it out*): We spent a-some time together, eh?

DIANA: We certainly did.

TITO: Yeah ...

DIANA: Now I want the truth. Just take the big moment at the end. Would you say it was something special? (*No answer.*) I can take it, believe me, Tito. I'm a professional.

TITO: A pro ... ? Oh my God. A *professional*!

DIANA (*hurt*): You don't think so?

TITO: No, I do! I promise!

DIANA: Well then? How was I? (*Pause.*) Tito?

TITO: I'm trying to remember!

DIANA (*bitterly*): I suppose you're telling me I was no good.

TITO: No! Hey! You—you were great! You were fantastic!

DIANA: You're only saying that— .

TITO: No, I swear! You—you were unbelievable! It went a-by so fast, I can hardly remember.

DIANA: Oh, Tito. Do you mean it?

TITO: Yeah. Sure.

DIANA: Thank God. I'm so relieved.

TITO: Heh. This uh, profession. You take it a-pretty serious, eh?

DIANA: It's all I've ever wanted to be since I was a little girl. Isn't that awful?

TITO: It's terrible.

DIANA: Of course, my mother was in the business.

TITO: Ah.

DIANA: And my father was too.

TITO: You father?

DIANA: They started out in a little Gospel church, and here I am.

TITO: Oh my God.

DIANA: And you thought I was good tonight. I mean really, really good?

TITO: Oh yeah. Great.

DIANA: You have no idea what this means to me, Tito. Coming from you.

TITO: Heh … Thanks.

DIANA: I was so afraid you were disappointed. I mean, it's just so hard to tell with all those people there.

TITO (*after a slight pause*): People?!.....

DIANA: Tito.

TITO: Eh?

DIANA: Now, Tito, just supposing that I really am as good as you think. And supposing that I have the confidence and the stamina to make it in the big time, in New York …

TITO: Yeah?

DIANA: I was wondering if, perhaps, you'd like to introduce me to some of your friends. Is that possible, Tito?

TITO: Hey. I'm not so sure, eh?

DIANA: Producers. Directors. The ones that matter. What about your agent?

TITO: My agent, she's a woman.

DIANA: So? That's all right with me.

TITO: It is?

DIANA: Of course! I wouldn't care if she was a kangaroo! The important thing is whether she's good or not. Right!?

TITO: I guess.

DIANA: All I'd need with her is five minutes. And if she doesn't think I'm special, at least I tried. I had a chance! ... Tito?

TITO: Hey. I do my best, O.K.?

DIANA: You will?

TITO: If that's a-what you want.

DIANA: Tito. How can I ever thank you?

TITO: My pleasure, eh?

DIANA: It will be. I promise.

They are in the middle of a passionate kiss, when Maggie knocks at the door. Diana tells him to get rid of Maggie as soon as possible. In the meantime, she'll change into something more comfortable. Tito approves of the plan. Diana heads for the bathroom. Tito goes to the sitting room, closing the connecting door to the bedroom behind him. He lets Maggie in. She has slipped away from the reception to finish the business she thought she arranged earlier with Tito-Max. He, on the other hand, is under the impression she wants his autograph. They talk at cross-purposes for awhile, she in anticipation of the love-making she thinks is in the offing, he about how pleased he is to sign a picture for her. He begins to get the idea he has misunderstood the purpose of her visit when he looks up from the picture he has signed to see Maggie standing in her underwear saying, "I'm yours. All yours." He has no chance to sort the confusion out, for she is all over him in a second.

And then there's another knock at the door—Saunders again. Maggie panics. If her father finds her like this ... She must hide. She dashes into the bedroom. "Closet or bathroom!?" she asks. Remembering the waiting Diana in the bathroom, Tito directs her to the closet. No sooner has he closed that door behind her than Diana, wearing a towel, appears from the bathroom. In response to her question, he says he still hasn't managed to get rid of Maggie. Diana tells him that the sooner he does, the sooner he can join her in a bubble bath. And she disappears.

Tito returns to the sitting room and opens the door on a glowering Saunders, who obviously mistakes him for Max. Sanders tells Tito to drop the phony accent and change. People are waiting. Tito, of course, has no idea to what Saunders is referring. Then Saunders notices Maggie's dress on the floor. Now he thinks he understands—Max is still pretending to be Tito so he can get an opera groupie into bed.

Saunders sidles over to the kitchenette.

SAUNDERS (*whispering*): Is she in there?

TITO: No.

SAUNDERS (*looking around the room*): Well where is she?

TITO: The bathroom.

SAUNDERS: The bathroom! Are you crazy!? What about the body!?

TITO: The body?

SAUNDERS: The body!

TITO: Like I said, she's in the bathroom.

SAUNDERS: Not that body. The other body.

TITO: Oh. (*Resigned.*) The closet.

SAUNDERS: The closet? You stuffed the body in the closet?

TITO: Is a big closet.

SAUNDERS: Look. I would be the first to admit that you deserve a little reward for all you've been through.

TITO: Thanks.

SAUNDERS: But it's not the time!

TITO: O.K.

SAUNDERS: Now first of all, I want you to get rid of the girl—

TITO: Which one?

SAUNDERS: … There's more than one?

TITO (*sheepishly*): Two.

SAUNDERS: You've got two girls in there?

TITO: Yeah.

SAUNDERS: I knew you had potential, but this is incredible.

TITO: Thanks.

SAUNDERS: Look. I'm impressed. All right? I'm very impressed. But get them the hell out of here! Do you have any idea who's downstairs right now?

TITO: No.

SAUNDERS: The police! And they're asking questions!

TITO (*croaking*): Police?

SAUNDERS: That's what I came up to tell you. They're looking for some madman who tried to break into the theater tonight. In costume!

TITO: Police?

A knock at the sitting room corridor door.

SAUNDERS: Oh hell. That could be them. (*Lowering his voice.*) All right. Here's the story. You're still Tito. You came back from the theater and straight to your room … (*During the following, Saunders leads Tito to the connecting door, to hide him in the bedroom.*) You haven't seen anything unusual whatsoever. And whatever we do, we keep them away from the closet! (*He closes the connecting door, leaving Tito in the bedroom. Another knock at the door.*) Coming!

He opens the door. Max, still dressed as Otello, rushes in.

MAX: I've got to talk to you.

He closes the door. Saunders is speechless and reels backwards. Meanwhile, Tito, still in the bedroom, leans his arm against the connecting wall; and Max does the same in the sitting room. They unknowingly create a mirror image.

SAUNDERS: This is no time for jokes, you idiot!!!

MAX: Jokes?

SAUNDERS: Are you out of your mind!? What's the matter with you!?

MAX: What did *I* do?!

Saunders, of course, believes that it was Max he was talking to a moment before. Max insists it wasn't. In fact, he was out looking for Saunders to tell him that Tito's body was gone. Some more confusion ensues, and then Saunders gets it: Tito is alive. They rush in to confirm this; but in the meantime, Tito has left the bedroom through the door to the corridor. Max is delighted to learn that Tito didn't expire. Saunders, though, is afraid it will ruin everything. A knock at the sitting room door—Saunders is convinced it's either Tito or the police. "Whatever I say, just play along," he tells Max.

It's the bellhop, carrying the champagne Diana ordered and bursting with compliments for the man he believes to be Tito about how wonderful his performance was tonight. Max, of course, is delighted to hear the bellhop praise his singing. Saunders, as usual, is in a hurry to chase the bellhop out. The bellhop aims a few sarcastic remarks in Saunders's direction, tells Tito-Max that he'd be happy to do anything else he might ask, and exits.

Saunders has another plan. Max is to change. Saunders is going to try to find Tito, explain and, if necessary, pay him off.

Saunders exits. Max walks into the bedroom, leaving the connecting door open, and heads straight for the bathroom. He walks into the bathroom and closes the door. Pause. A cry from Max, as the door swings open, Max holding the handle for dear life. Diana yanks him back in, and the door slams. Repeat. Bubbles each time. Silence for a moment; then the closet door opens and Maggie cautiously emerges. She wears Tito's trenchcoat over her underwear.

MAGGIE (*in a whisper*): Tito?

There's a yelp from the bathroom, and Maggie is startled by it. Then she realizes he must be using the bathroom.

Oh. (*She calls quietly.*) Sorry.

She sighs with relief and goes into the sitting room, smiling happily. Then she notices the champagne.

Oh, Tito! Champagne!

She picks up one of the glasses admiringly. She notices a speck of dirt on it. She picks up the other glass, decides that both glasses need washing, and walks into the kitchenette, happily humming a popular tune. As Maggie exits, the bathroom door crashes open, and Max reels out, breathing heavily. Diana follows him out, still wearing her towel.

DIANA: Now don't go 'way, I have a little surprise for you. I'll be right back.
She exits into the bathroom and closes the door. Max catches his breath, then staggers into the sitting room, closing the connecting door behind him. Maggie, who's heard the door, enters from the kitchenette—without the glasses.

MAGGIE: Darling.
She shrugs the trenchcoat off her shoulders, and it falls to the floor.

Alone at last.
Max falls to his knees, speechless and exhausted.

You poor thing, you look tired. You've had a rough day, haven't you?
Max shakes his head "yes." Maggie goes to him.

Now, don't you worry. I'm going to make it all better.
She leads him to the sofa and pushes him on to it.

You'll see.
Max is flat on his back. Maggie's on top him, kissing him passionately, which is when the bedroom corridor door opens and Tito rushes in, closing the door quickly but quietly. He's on the lam and breathing heavily. Silently, he runs to his suitcase, grabs it and turns to go ... when Diana enters from the bathroom. She wears a nightie which is extremely sexy. Tito sees her, freezes, and drops the suitcase.

DIANA: Well? Do you like it?
Tito shakes his head "yes."

I thought you might.

TITO: Hey ...

DIANA: You poor thing, you look tired. You've had a rough day, haven't you?
Tito shakes his head "yes." Diana goes to him.

Now, don't you worry. I'm going to make it all better. You'll see.
She pushes him on to the bed and climbs on top of him, kissing him passionately.

MAX (*in the sitting room*): Shall we turn off a-the lights?

DIANA (*in the bedroom*): I like it with the lights on.

MAGGIE (*in the sitting room*): If that's all right with you.

TITO (*in the bedroom*): It's a-fine with me.

As music from a passionate duet from Donizetti's *Linda di Chamounix* fills the theater, the two couples begin activities which necessitate the lights fading to black.

Scene 2: Fifteen minutes later

The two couples have finished coupling. Maggie is ecstatic. "It was even better than I thought it would be. I guess that's because you're Italian," she says. Max doesn't argue. In the bedroom, Tito is exhausted from the paces Diana has put him through. Diana heads for the bathroom. Maggie, wanting champagne, goes offstage to the kitchenette to fetch glasses.

Now Max and Tito are alone onstage. A happy Max begins to open the champagne, singing the "Toreador Song" from *Carmen*. Tito hears this and opens the connecting door. Max's back is turned, so he can't see Tito. "*Tito takes a step into the sitting room and sees Max—or rather, he sees himself opening a bottle of champagne and singing. He freezes, speechless. He looks down at himself, then back at Max. He now realizes there's a fair possibility that he's lost his mind. And if he hasn't lost his mind, he doesn't want an explanation; he just wants out. Tito steps back into the bedroom, leaving the connecting door open. Then he runs to his suitcase, grabs it and runs from the room, out of the corridor door, closing it behind him.*"

Diana now emerges from the bathroom, still in her nightie, and goes into the sitting room where she sees Max opening the champagne. She, of course, assumes Max is Tito. As she enters, Maggie returns from the kitchenette with the glasses. The two women see each other. Max can come up with no explanation. Maggie assumes he had Diana on deck for the second half of a double feature. Diana figures something similar. They unite in their hostility to Tito-Max. He rushes through the connecting door into the bathroom and locks the door before the two women can grab him.

Maggie and Diana figure there is nothing to be done now but to get dressed. Diana remembers that she left her dress in the bathroom. A tartly-phrased threat prompts Max to toss it quickly out of the bathroom, whereupon he slams the door shut again. The two women dress in the bedroom. Maggie is bitter, but Diana is philosophical: "I've been two-timed before, but never with quite so much flair."

Now Maria enters the sitting room. She's decided to give Tito another chance. "Oh my God, he's got another one!" says Diana, and she goes through the connecting door to face Maria.

MARIA: Who are you?
DIANA: A friend of the family. Who are you?
MARIA: The family.
DIANA: ... Tito's wife?
MARIA: That's a-right.
DIANA (*calling*): Maggie, dear. Guess who's here.
MARIA: I'm gonna keel 'im.
DIANA: We know just how you feel.

MAGGIE (*as she enters the sitting room*): Hi.

MARIA: You again.

DIANA: You've met before?

MAGGIE: Just once. In the closet.

DIANA: You realize, of course, that she's Tito's wife.

MAGGIE: Yeah. Only she isn't really his wife. Tito told me. She likes to pretend she is, and he plays along because he doesn't want to hurt her feelings.

MARIA: Tito tell you this?

MAGGIE: Of course.

MARIA: I'm gonna keel 'im. I swear before God, on everything that's a-holy, I'm gonna strangle him!

DIANA: She sounds like his wife.

MARIA: With my bare hands!

DIANA: She's his wife.

MAGGIE: But he *said* … (*She realizes.*) Oh my God.

MARIA: Where is he? (*Maggie and Diana look at each other.*) Where is he!!?

MAGGIE and DIANA (*together*): The bathroom.

They proceed to the bathroom door. Maria, threatening murder, bangs on the door, ordering Tito to come out. Meanwhile, the real Tito dashes into the sitting room from the corridor, followed by Saunders, Julia and the bellhop. Maria, Maggie and Diana, attracted by the commotion, go to the sitting room. Tito, relieved to see his wife, pleads with her to take him away from this chaos. Saunders demands to know what Maggie and Diana are doing here. Maggie says she was only trying to get an autograph. "Did you get it?" asks the bellhop. "We sure did," Maggie replies dryly.

But a lot of questions remain—such as who is in the bathroom? It's certainly someone who *looks* like Tito. Julia knows: it must be the lunatic who's been running around town pretending to be Tito. Led by Maria, and oblivious to Saunders's suggestions not to bother pursuing the matter, the ensemble marches on the bathroom and demands that whoever it is open the door and reveal himself.

And he does. Max, minus the blackface and the wig, dressed in his formal wear, emerges and casually asks if he has missed something. Except for Saunders, the reaction is unanimous: this couldn't have been the imposter. "He doesn't even look a-like Tito!" says Maria. Max and Tito are pleased to see each other again. Maria takes matters into hand, bullying all but Max out of the bedroom and into the sitting room.

Tito thanks Max for everything he's done and tells him to keep his confidence high. "You gotta say, 'I'm a-the best. I'm a-Max.'" The moment of fellowship is interrupted by Maria, who demands that Tito follow her this instant.

And Tito does, promising a romantic vacation as he exits the suite with her, Julia tagging after them.

Saunders figures everything's in order now. In the meantime, Maggie has realized that it was Max with whom she slept. Max enjoys the realization. Saunders now realizes the dress he saw on the floor before—when Tito confessed he had two girls in the other room—is now on his daughter's body. He voices his suspicions about her story about the autograph. At this point, the bellhop finds the picture Tito signed, and it is indeed autographed to Maggie. Saunders looks at it. Maggie takes it from him. The bellhop, on an impulse, runs out of the room hoping to catch up with Tito and get his own autograph.

DIANA: Henry, is there any food left downstairs?

SAUNDERS: I should think so.

DIANA: Good. Let's go. For some reason (*Looking at Max.*) I'm very hungry. (*She takes Saunders's arm. He beams.*)

SAUNDERS: Oh. Well, what a lovely idea. (*They head for the door.*)

MAX: Sir? Shall we say tomorrow morning? Ten o'clock. Your office.

SAUNDERS: Max—

MAX: You see, I've got some new ideas for next season—

SAUNDERS: Max!

MAX: *Carmen, La Boheme.* Then finish off with something lighter—

SAUNDERS: Like *Die Fledermaus*?

MAX: Good idea.

SAUNDERS: I'll see you in the morning. Ten-thirty.

MAX: Sir.

SAUNDERS: Max?!

MAX: Don't be late!

> Beat. Saunders is stunned. He exits, dazed. Diana pauses in the doorway, gives Max a look, then follows Saunders, closing the door behind her. Max and Maggie are alone. Pause.

MAGGIE: Well … at least I had a fling.

MAX: Yeah.

MAGGIE: Max. I … I really liked it.

MAX: Me too.

MAGGIE: And I'm really glad it was with you.

MAX: Me too.

MAGGIE: But you really took an awful chance, you know, wearing his costume, and making all that fuss at the stage door. And hitting a policeman! If you hadn't gotten away, you might be in prison!

MAX: Maggie—

MAGGIE: The worst part is, you didn't even get to hear him sing. And he was so wonderful.

MAX: Was he?

MAGGIE: Oh, Max, he was unbelievable. When he first came out, a ... a shock went through the audience. And then he sang and ... I know it sounds silly, but I started to cry. I couldn't help it. I guess that's why he's Tito Merelli.

MAX: Yeah.

> *Music begins playing: the final orchestral moment from Act I of Otello. Max hears it; Maggie doesn't.*

MAGGIE: And even then I was thinking, God, where's Max? I want him to hear this. You know? I want to share this with him, and—

> *Max kisses Maggie's palm and starts to sing. She is lulled by the music and closes her eyes.*

MAX (*singing*): *"Gia le pleiade ardente al mar discende. Vien ... Venere splende."*

> *As Max holds the final note, Maggie's eyes snap open and her jaw drops. She realizes at last.*

MAGGIE: Oh, *Max!!*

> *She throws her arms around him and they kiss. Bells peal out loudly through the final orchestral swell as ... the curtain falls.*

ARISTOCRATS

A Play in Three Acts

BY BRIAN FRIEL

Cast and credits appear on pages 443–444

BRIAN FRIEL was born Jan. 9, 1929 in Derry City, Northern Ireland. Educated at St. Patrick's, Maynouth, he became a schoolteacher but since 1960 has devoted himself entirely to writing. His short stories have appeared in The New Yorker *and have been collected in volumes entitled* The Saucer of Larks *and* The Gold in the Sea.

Friel's first produced play was The Francophile *in 1958 in Belfast, followed by* This Doubtful Paradise, The Enemy Within *and* The Blind Mice *in Dublin, Belfast and London. His first far-flung international hit was* Philadelphia, Here I Come!, *produced in Dublin in September 1964, on Broadway Feb. 16, 1966 for 326 performances and a citation as Friel's first Best Play, and since then in every major theater center in Europe and America. A program of two Friel one-acts,* Lovers, *was named his second Best Play at the time of its Lincoln Center engagement July 25, 1978 for 148 performances, and his third was* Translations, *produced off Broadway for 48 performances by Manhattan Theater Club April 7, 1981 after its premiere in Derry at the Field Day Theater Company, of which Friel was a co-founder with Stephen Rea.* Aristocrats, *his fourth Best Play, was written in 1979 but did not reach New York until this season's production April 25, also by MTC.*

The succession of Friel's distinguished plays produced over the decades in Europe and America has included The Loves of Cass McGuire *(1967),*

Crystal and Fox *(1969, reaching Los Angeles in 1970 and off Broadway in 1973)*, The Mundy Scheme *(1969, reaching Broadway for 4 performances after a Dublin production)*, The Gentle Island *(1972)*, The Freedom of the City *(which premiered simultaneously at the Royal Court and Abbey Theaters and was produced by the Goodman Theater in Chicago and on Broadway Feb. 17, 1974 for 9 performances)*, Volunteers *(1975)*, Living Quarters *(1977, OOB 1983) and* Faith Healer *(world premiere on Broadway for 20 performances April 5, 1979), and in the 1980s* Fathers and Sons *and* Making History.

Friel was the recipient of the Irish-American Cultural Institute's 1980 award for his work on the Irish stage, an honor bestowed annually but seldom to a dramatist. He lives in Ireland and is married, with four daughters.

The following synopsis of Aristocrats was prepared by Sally Dixon Wiener.

Time: Summer, mid-1970s

Place: Ballybeg Hall, the home of District Judge
         O'Donnell, overlooking the village of Ballybeg,
         County Donegal, Ireland

ACT 1

SYNOPSIS: The setting for the play is the south side of a Georgian mansion which has seen better days, but it is lush now with the greenery of the Irish summer. The house itself fills the entire upstage area as well as the area downstage left which is the study, exposed except for the upstage and stage left walls. The study, through which other areas of the house may be entered, has wall-coverings with a look of green brocade, and there is a large chandelier, a marble fireplace, and antique furniture, including a writing table. Upstage center we see another part of the house through long uncurtained windows, and above there are also high uncurtained windows.

At stage right there is another entrance to the house and a dilapidated gazebo. Downstage, where most of the action takes place, is what remains of the uncared-for lawn that was once a tennis court, and before that, a croquet lawn. Offstage, there is, at the rise and frequently throughout the play, the pervasive sound of Chopin piano music being played inside the house (or sometimes on a cassette), a sort of leitmotif of the family. With the exception of one daughter, a nun, the whole family has gathered at Ballybeg for the wedding of the youngest daughter, set for two days hence.

As the play begins in early afternoon of a warm summer day, Tom Hoffnung is at the table in the study, jotting down book titles in a notebook. *"He is a quiet, calm, measured American academic in his mid-50s."* Nearby is Willie Diver. *"He is in his mid-30s and is from the village."* Willie, who stands on his jacket to keep from soiling the chair he's using in lieu of a stepladder, is hanging a speaker from the frame of a door. Both are busy at their tasks-at-hand when Uncle George comes into the study. He seems rather possessed and has a strange sense of urgency about him. He is the brother of the head of the family, the Judge, who lies ill in an upstairs bedroom. Uncle George, *"in his late 70s....Panama hat, walking stick, very old and creased off-white linen suit with an enormous red silk handkerchief spilling out of the breast pocket....is halfway across the study before he realizes that there are other people in the room."* Both Tom and Willie greet him, but he turns and goes off without speaking.

Tom wonders if he ever speaks. Willie says they claim he does, but Willie's never heard him speak. It seems Uncle George was a "fierce man for the booze when he was only a young fella—drunk himself half-crazy. Then all of a sudden packed it in. And stopped speaking." The locals believe that if he wasn't going to ask for a drink, he didn't think it worthwhile to say anything, but it's generally conceded that his brains were the best of the whole family.

Tom gives Willie a hand with putting up the speaker and believes that Judith, the daughter who's stayed at home to care for her failing father, will be appreciative of this new system, referred to later as "the baby alarm," and Willie agrees. It will save her a lot of going up and downstairs to and from the sickroom.

Tom is alone when Casimir, in his 30s, the only son of the family, comes on with some deck chairs and speaks to Tom from the step that leads into the study. *"One immediately gets a sense that there is something different about him—as he says himself, 'peculiar.' But what it is is elusive: partly his shyness, partly his physical movements, particularly the way he walks—rapid, jerky, without ease or grace—partly his erratic enthusiasm, partly his habit of suddenly grinning and giving a mirthless 'ha-ha' at unlikely times, usually when he is distressed. But he is not a buffoon nor is he 'disturbed.'"*

CASIMIR: Claire.
TOM: Yeah.
CASIMIR: Playing the piano.
TOM: Sure.
CASIMIR: My sister Claire.
TOM: I know.
CASIMIR: Welcome home recital for me.
TOM: Some welcome.
CASIMIR: Dexterity—simplicity—passion—Claire has everything.

TOM: She certainly—
> *But Casimir has gone and now stands in the middle of the lawn.*

CASIMIR: Claire!

CLAIRE: Yes?

CASIMIR: Play the G minor ballade.
> *The music stops.*

CLAIRE: Which?

CASIMIR: The G minor.

CLAIRE: I'm not in the mood for that, Casimir.

CASIMIR: Special request. Please.

CLAIRE: Just a bit of it, then.
> *He stands listening. She begins in the middle of the G minor bal-*
> *lade, Op. 23, just immediately before the molto crescendo, after 3*
> *FZ bars.*

CASIMIR: Yes-yes-yes-yes-yes!
> *He sings a few bars with the piano, conducting at the same time—*
> *he is radiant with delight. Then he returns to the step.*

The G minor. Wonderful, isn't it?

TOM: Yeah.
> *Casimir sings a few more bars.*

CASIMIR: When I think of Ballybeg Hall it's always like this: the sun shining; the doors and windows all open; the place filled with music.

As Casimir disappears to fetch more deck chairs, Tom overhears, on the newly-installed speaker, the conversation, off, from upstairs.

JUDITH: Oh, Father, You've soiled your pajamas again! Why didn't you tell me?

FATHER: Judith?

JUDITH: Come on. Let's get them changed.

FATHER: Where's Judith?

JUDITH: I'm Judith.

FATHER: Where's Judith?

JUDITH: I'm here beside you, Father.

FATHER: Where's Claire?

JUDITH: In the drawing room.

FATHER: Where's Claire?

JUDITH: Can't you hear her? She's playing the piano for you. Lift your leg, Father.

FATHER: Where's Alice?

JUDITH: Everybody's here.

FATHER: Where's Casimir?

JUDITH: Everybody's at home. They're all downstairs.

FATHER: Where's Anna?

JUDITH: Anna's in Africa—you know that. Now—the other leg. Father please, I can't get them off unless you help me.

FATHER: Where's Judith? Where's Claire? Where's Casimir? Where's Alice? Where's—

JUDITH: They're all here. They're all downstairs.

FATHER: Let me tell you something in confidence: Judith betrayed the family.

JUDITH: Did she?

FATHER: I don't wish to make an issue of it. But I can tell you confidentially—Judith betrayed us.

JUDITH: That's better. Now you're more comfortable.

FATHER: Great betrayal; enormous betrayal.

JUDITH: Let me feel those tops. Are they wet, too?

FATHER: But Anna's praying for her. Did you know that?

JUDITH: Yes, I know, Father.

FATHER: Anna has the whole convent praying for her.

JUDITH: Now let's get these clean ones on. Lift this leg again.

FATHER: Where's Judith? Where's Alice? Where's Casimir? Where's Claire?

When Willie returns with whiskey and groceries he has brought for Judith he is happy to hear the Judge over the speaker, now imagining himself to be back on the bench and authoritatively dismissing a case, though he hasn't been downstairs since his stroke.

Casimir has come on again, with more chairs, and re-enters the study, talking about Claire and her great love for Chopin, and how she had been offered a scholarship at 16 to study in Paris, but their father would have none of it—"Naughty of him," according to Casimir. He notices Willie, who expects Casimir to recognize him. It is painful to Willie to have to remind Casimir at some length of their childhood relationship, particularly when Willie recalls a near-accident when they were in a punt carried out by the tide. Casimir's response is merely to ask if they were drowned. Casimir claims he's pleased to see him, remarking that it's been 11 years since he's been home, but he must excuse himself because he's acting as chef for the day. "Same aul' Casimir," Willie comments, remembering how he and other village boys would follow him down the street "acting the maggot, you know, imitating him."

Tom is curious about what Willie meant when he'd told Casimir he's "taken the land from Judith." Willie explains, before going off, that she lets it, and he's taken it off her hands, despite the fact that it's "all hill and bog."

Casimir is arranging the chairs on the lawn when Claire stops playing and calls to him to identify the piece—an old game of theirs, it seems. It's the G sharp major, but they call it the McCormack Waltz because of the tenor whom his father had somehow assisted in getting a papal knighthood, as a result of which they became friends. Tom, interested, wants to take notes on this.

CASIMIR: Anyhow, McCormack was staying here one night, and Mother was in one of her down periods, and my goodness when she was like that— oh, my goodness, poor Mother—for weeks on end, how unhappy she'd be.

TOM: She was forty-seven when she died?

CASIMIR: Forty-six.

TOM: Had she been ill for long? Was it sudden?

> *Pause.*

CASIMIR: Anyhow, this night Claire played that waltz, the G sharp major, and McCormack asked Mother to dance, and she refused but he insisted, he insisted, and finally he got her to the middle of the floor, and he put his arm around her, and then she began to laugh, and he danced her up and down the hall and then in here and then out to the tennis court, and you could hear their laughing over the whole house, and finally the pair of them collapsed in the gazebo out there. Yes—marvelous! The McCormack Waltz!

TOM: Approximately what year was—

CASIMIR: A great big heavy man—oh, yes, I remember McCormack—I remember his enormous jowls trembling—but Mother said he danced like Nijinsky. *(Suddenly aware.)* I'm disturbing your studies, amn't I?

TOM: Actually you're—

CASIMIR: Of course I am. Give me five minutes to make a call, and then I'll leave you absolutely in peace.

> *As he goes to the phone (an old style phone, with a handle at the side) below the fireplace, he picks up a cassette player from the mantelpiece.*

Do you know what I did last night even before I unpacked? I made two secret tapes of her to bring back to Helga and the children, just to prove to them how splendid a pianist she really is.

TOM: Have they never been to Ireland?

> *Momentary pause.*

CASIMIR: And I'm going to play them this afternoon while we're having the picnic. And I've another little surprise up my sleeve too: *after* we've eaten, I've got a tape that Anna sent me last Christmas!

TOM: Very nice.

CASIMIR: A really tremendous person, Anna. Actually her name in religion is Sister John Henry, and she chose that name because John Henry Newman— you know?—the cardinal?—Cardinal Newman?—of course you do—well, he married Grandfather and Grandmother O'Donnell—in this very room as a matter of fact—special dispensation from Rome. But of course we think of her as Anna. And the tape she sent me has a message for every member of the family. And it'll be so appropriate now that we're all gathered together again.

>   *As he is saying the last few words he is also turning the handle on the phone.*
>
> FATHER: Don't touch that!
>   *Casimir drops the phone in panic and terror.*
> CASIMIR: Christ! Ha-ha. O my God! That's—that—that's—
> TOM: It's only the baby-alarm.
> CASIMIR: I thought for a moment Father was—was—was—

When the phone rings, Casimir panics again. It's Mrs. Moore, the Ballybeg postmistress, whom he asks to try Helga's Hamburg number again. She'll worry if she doesn't know he's arrived. Yes, he's here for the wedding, to give his sister away, and then leaving again, he tells Mrs. Moore.

Alice comes on and greets them. *"In her mid-30s. She is hung over after last night. As she enters she touches her cheek, which has a bruise mark on it."* Eamon, her husband, has gotten up much earlier and gone to visit his grandmother in the village. Alice is concerned that she was misbehaving the night before, but Tom claims she was just sitting by herself, singing nursery rhymes. She goes to sit on top of the step to the study, and Tom questions Casimir about where Gerard Manley Hopkins used to sit. "Look at the arm-rest, and you'll see a stain on it," Casimir points out. Hopkins had always set his teacup there. Casimir asks to be reminded of the title of Tom's research. It's "Recurring cultural, political and social modes in the upper strata of Roman Catholic society in rural Ireland since the act of Catholic Emancipation." "Awful," Tom apologizes.

Casimir also wants to be sure Judith has let Tom see the family records, the estate papers and the old diaries in the library. All covered, but now what Tom is after is family lore and reminiscences—the crucifix, for instance? Present from Cardinal O'Donnell: "No relation, just a great family friend." "Remember him, Alice?" Casimir asks. Alice claims he must have been dead for 70 years, and Casimir is surprised but assumes she's right.

"Everything has some association," Casimir tells Tom, who is noting it all down. G. K. Chesterton's is a footstool (he was imitating Lloyd George giving a speech and fell from it). Casimir's father had wanted him to be christened Gilbert Keith, but his mother preferred the name of a Polish prince. The chaise longue is Daniel O'Connell's ("See the mark of his riding boots"); the candlestick is George Moore's; a book is Tom Moore's ("Byron's friend"); a Bible is Hilaire Belloc's (wedding present to the parents); a cushion is Yeats's ("Oh, he was—he was just tremendous, Yeats, with those cold, cold eyes of his. Oh, yes, I remember Yeats vividly").

Claire has begun another piece, known to the family as the favorite Bedtime Waltz. Casimir goes outside to where Alice is now seated, and they sing a bit of it. "The E sharp major actually," Casimir explains. When their mother would play it, they would rush upstairs, wash and say their prayers and get into bed before the end of it.

They all listen to the music for a few moments.

CASIMIR: My God, isn't she playing well? The impending marriage—that's what it is: the concentration of delight and fear and expectation. And Judith tells me she's been in really bubbling humor for months and months—not one day of depression. Not even one; maybe she's grown out of it. Isn't it marvelous? May I tell you something, Tom? We always said among ourselves, Judith and Alice and I, isn't this true, Alice?

ALICE: Isn't what true?

CASIMIR: We always said—well, no, it was never quite expressed; but we always, you know, we always suspected—amn't I right, Alice?

ALICE: What are you saying, Casimir?

CASIMIR: Just that we always thought that perhaps Claire darling was the type of girl, you know, the kind of girl—we always had the idea that our little Claire was one of those highly sensitive, highly intelligent young girls who might choose—who might elect to remain single in life. Ha-ha. That's what we thought. Isn't that true, Alice?

ALICE: And we were wrong.

CASIMIR: Indeed we were wrong! Thank goodness we were wrong! Not that she isn't an attractive girl, a *very* attractive girl—isn't she attractive, Tom?—don't you find Claire attractive?

ALICE: For God's sake, Casimir—

CASIMIR: What's wrong with that? Tom finds little Claire attractive, or he doesn't find her attractive?

TOM: She's a very personable young lady.

CASIMIR: Personable—that's the word—an excellent word—personable. Of course she is. And such a sweet nature. And her young man, I gather, is an exceptionally fine type. You've met him, Tom, have you?

TOM: Just once—briefly.

CASIMIR: I'm really looking forward to meeting him. Aren't you, Alice? A mature man who neither smokes nor drinks and—

ALICE: A middle-aged widower with four young children.

CASIMIR: That's fine—that's fine. Claire is exceptionally good with children. Judith told me that when she was giving those piano lessons to the children in the village—

ALICE: What lessons? What children?

CASIMIR: All last winter she went every evening to five or six houses until —you know—poor old Claire—the old trouble—over anxiety, that's all it is basically, I'm sure that's all it is—and when she had to give it up, I'm sure she missed the pin-money—I mean she must have—what was I talking about? Yes, all those children. Judith wrote and told me they were devoted to her—

Margaret Colin as Alice and Niall
Buggy as Casimir in *Aristocrats*

Judith told me that. And her young man, Jerry, runs a very successful green-grocer's business and he has a great white lorry with an enormous plastic banana on top of the cab and he supplies wonderful fresh vegetables to all the hotels within a twenty-mile radius and he's also an accomplished trumpet player and they play duets together. Good. Good. It all sounds just—just—just so splendid and so—so appropriate. Everything's in hand. Everything's under control. I'm so happy, so happy for her. Ha-ha.

His head rotates between Alice and Tom in very rapid movements, staring at them with his fixed, anguished smile....

When the music changes, Casimir persuades the reluctant Alice to dance with him. He sings along so loudly he doesn't hear the telephone until Tom tells him it's ringing, and he goes to answer it. Alice would like some whiskey, so Tom brings out the drinks tray. Tom is curious as to whether or not, when she was a girl, she mixed with the local people. "We're 'local people,'" she retorts. Tom means the villagers, not the gentry. Alice points out that her husband Eamon is from the village. Actually, she and her siblings were sent to boarding school at 7 or 8, indeed Casimir was sent to the Benedictines at age 6. Later the sisters all attended a finishing school at a convent in Carcassone, and Casimir "began law" but then left to go to England where he met Helga, with whom he went to Germany. Alice thinks he has a part-time job in a food-processing factory in Hamburg, but claims Helga, a bowling alley cashier, is the real breadwinner. Tom wants to know more about Eamon, too.

> *She rises and fills her glass again.*
ALICE: Didn't we talk about that last night?
TOM: Briefly.
ALICE: What did I tell you?
> *He consults his notebook.*
TOM: "Poised for a brilliant career in the diplomatic service when—"
ALICE: "Poised for a—" I never said that!
TOM: I'm quoting you.
ALICE: I *must* have been drunk.
TOM: Then the civil rights movement began in the North in '68. The Dublin government sent him to Belfast as an observer, and after a few months observing and reporting he joined the movement. Was sacked, of course. Moved to England and is now a probation officer with the Greater London Council. Right?
ALICE: Listen—Claire's tired at last.
TOM: What was your father's attitude?
ALICE: To Eamon?
TOM: To the civil rights campaign.
ALICE: He opposed it. No, that's not accurate. He was indifferent: that was across the Border—away in the North.
TOM: Only twenty miles away.
ALICE: Politics never interested him. Politics are vulgar.
TOM: And Judith? What was her attitude? Was she engaged?
ALICE: She took part in the Battle of the Bogside. Left Father and Uncle George and Claire alone here and joined the people in the streets fighting the police. That's an attitude, isn't it? That's when Father had his first stroke. And seven months later she had a baby by a Dutch reporter. Does that constitute sufficient engagement?

Their conversation is ended by the sound of Eamon and Claire laughing as they come pell-mell into the study, Eamon with the headdress of Claire's wedding outfit on his head, and Claire trying to rescue it. *"Eamon is in his 30s. Claire, the youngest daughter, is in her 20s. At this moment she is in one of her high moods: talkative, playful, energetic. On other occasions she is soli-*

tary and silent and withdrawn." Claire agrees with Eamon that the headdress suits him, but insists on his giving it to her. Casimir reminds them he's on the telephone, and Eamon leans over to make a fresh remark into the telephone to Mrs. Moore, and then bumps into the furniture and apologizes to it—"Like walking through Madam Tussaud's, isn't it, Professor?"—until Claire gets him outside at last and retrieves her headdress. Judith made it, and the dress—as well as her own outfit—for reasons of economy. Claire recalls hearing that when her Grandmother O'Donnell married there was a gold sovereign for each child under 12, and when Claire's mother married, roses were given to everybody in the chapel. She wonders what she might do—"What about a plastic bag of vegetables to every old-age pensioner?"

Tom compliments Claire on her playing—"Really great"—but Claire forthrightly claims that she's only good, not great as she once thought.

Claire and Alice are conferring as to whether or not the net of the headdress needs shortening, when Eamon reports to Alice that his grandmother has sent her love. His grandmother, he explains to Tom, raised him from the age of 3, when he was left with her when the family emigrated to Scotland to find work. She's sending a present to Claire. Claire is disappointed she won't come to the wedding, but Eamon assures her that what she had wanted was just to be asked.

Eamon is told that Willie put up the baby-alarm. "Of course. Willie Slooghter, the ardent suitor" Eamon comments. Claire admits that Willie "haunts the place" and that he is a help to Judith. Eamon agrees he's a decent type. He'd heard only this morning in the village that Willie has 500 slot machines located in arcades all over the country, and that he'd be "worth a fortune if he looked after them," but he doesn't. He offers Claire a drink, but she's not allowed because she's taking sedatives. He turns to Tom.

EAMON: My grandmother. You'd find her interesting. Worked all her life as a maid here in the Hall.

TOM: In the Hall? Here?

EAMON: Didn't you know that? Oh, yes, yes. Something like fifty-seven years continuous service with the district Justice and his wife, Lord have mercy on her; and away back to the earlier generation, with his father, the high court Judge and his family. Oh, you should meet her if he looked after them, but he never goes near them!

TOM: She sounds—

EAMON: Carriages, balls, receptions, weddings, christenings, feasts, deaths, trips to Rome, musical evenings, tennis—that's the mythology I was nurtured on all my life, day after day, year after year—the life of the "quality"—that's how she pronounces it, with a flat "a." A strange and marvelous education for a wee country boy, wasn't it? No, not an education—a permanent pigmentation. I'll tell you something, Professor: I know more about this place, infinitely more, here and here ... *(Head and heart.)* ... than they know. Sure? *(Drink.)* You'll enjoy this. *(Now to Alice up in the gazebo.)* Telling the professor about the night I told Granny you and I were getting married. *(To Tom.)* Not a notion in the world we were going out, of course. My God, Miss Alice and her grandson! Anyhow. "Granny," I said this night, "Alice and I are going to get married." "Alice? Who's Alice? Alice Devenny? Alice Byrne? Not Alice Smith!" "Alice O'Donnell." "What Alice O'Donnell's that?" "Alice O'Donnell of the Hall." A long silence. Then: "May God and his holy mother forgive you, you dirty-mouthed upstart!" *(Laughs.)* Wasn't that an interesting response? As we say about here: Now you're an educated man, Professor—what do you make of that response?

TOM: Oh boy.

EAMON: "Oh boy?"

TOM: What do *you* make of it?

Casimir, his call still not having gotten through, announces that he'll be bringing out the picnic lunch shortly. Claire asks if he needs help, but he implies he doesn't—his sons call him "The kinder mädchen" ("children's maid"). Casimir claims it's a term of affection: his sons like to tease him, and the German temperament is "very, *very* affectionate." When he goes off, Eamon tells Tom the whole thing is fictitious. Casimir's pretending to call "Helga the Hun." Nobody's ever seen her. Casimir's invented her along with the three sons, a dachshund and the job.

The baby-alarm puts Eamon in mind of "the peep-hole in a prison door," the Judas hole, and maybe that would be a more suitable name for it. "But then we'd have to decide who's spying on whom, wouldn't we?" he goes on. He admits he's talking too much, as usual, perhaps because he still finds it intimidating here. He gets himself another drink and recalls being best man at 17 when Willie, at 18, got married to Nora Sheridan ("known locally as Nora the Nun— for reasons of Irish irony"), but Nora, "thirty if she was a day," went off five months later with a British soldier, and "Willie was back with the rest of us."

They are still waiting for lunch. Eamon pumps Tom on his research on the subject of what Tom calls the Roman Catholic aristocracy: "What political clout did they wield, what economic contribution did they make to the status of their co-religionists, what cultural effect did they have on the local peasantry?" Eamon repeats each question and to each shakes his head. "Sorry, Professor. Bogus thesis. No book." But he assumes Tom will go on with it anyway. "I may well be so obtuse," Tom admits.

At last Casimir appears with a huge tray, announcing "a magnificent lunch ... prepared especially and with meticulous care by—" but as he's preparing to set the tray down on the lawn, the voice of his father, imperious, is heard over the speaker: "Casimir!" Struck with terror, Casimir comes to attention as his father demands he appear in the library, as he wants to speak to him.

Casimir recognizes that the sound is from the speaker but still cannot cope with the situation. He lowers the tray to the lawn and ends up kneeling beside it, as Judith comes on with the teapot. *"The eldest of the O'Donnell family: almost 40. She is dressed in old working clothes."* And again we hear the father's voice demanding that Casimir bring with him his headmaster's report. Casimir calls out to Judith, and she gets down close enough to put her arms around him to reassure him. He's in tears, and apologizing, over and over, but he doesn't think it was fair—"That's the second time I was caught by it." *"She rocks him in her arms as if he were a baby. The others look away."* Curtain.

ACT II

About an hour later, lunch is over but the remains are still in evidence, including empty wine bottles. Casimir, on his hands and knees, is slowly, and with infinite patience, feeling about for the holes once made by the croquet hoops. Alice proposes that after the wedding the rest of them "head off somewhere and have some fun ourselves," but Judith is preoccupied with working out the details of the wedding, with Willie's cooperation. Alice, getting nowhere with her suggestions, subsides. Claire, queried by Judith about the arrival of the flowers for the wedding, seems uncertain about the arrangements, and uninterested. Nor has she arranged anything with Miss Quirk. "All she said was, 'I play the harmonium at every wedding in Ballybeg'," Claire reports.

Eamon meanwhile has switched on a Chopin cassette and has been singing along to the music *"in a parody of the Crosby style of the late forties."* Eamon reminds Willie how they used to dance to that at the Corinthian in Derry. "Every Friday night," Willie recalls. "And the big silver ball going round and round up on the ceiling. Jaysus."

When Willie goes for a cup of coffee for Judith, Eamon asks Judith if she recalls sneaking off to the Corinthian with him on a motor bike, and how they were sitting in the gazebo when morning came. She'd been wearing her mother's silver tiara. And a hedgehog had gotten caught in the tennis net and was rolled up in a ball, his spikes up against danger. Like Judith, he said. Judith admits she does remember. And he'd asked her then to marry him and she'd said yes, he reminds her, but Judith cuts off the conversation by calling out to Willie to ask him about the taxis for the wedding party, as he returns with the coffee. "They were good times, Eamon, eh?, them nights in the Corinthian," Willie reminisces. "Plebian past times," Eamon remarks for Tom's benefit. "Before we were educated out of our emotions."

Suddenly the father's voice is heard again briefly over the speaker, and then he calls for Judith. Alice offers to go, but Judith insists on going herself:

"He's very restless today." Casimir is pleased that he wasn't surprised that time by the sound of the voice, and he goes on looking for the holes, two of which he's already found.

Alice speaks of how shocked she was to see the difference in her father, once so strong, "and then to see him lying there, so flat under the clothes, with his mouth open." Casimir was there with her when she'd put her hands on his face. "I must never have touched his face before—is that possible never to have touched my father's face?" But he didn't recognize her, or Casimir, either, and she'd wept. Refusing the coffee Eamon offers her, she admits to being "slightly drunk" but insists on going to make herself another drink, and Casimir goes back to searching the lawn for the one remaining hole he still hasn't found.

Eamon admires the gold watch Claire is fingering: "Present from Jerry?" For her birthday, Claire says, and he's going to give her a car for Christmas; plus, the house where they will live with his children and his unmarried sister has been redone with new carpeting she'd helped Jerry's sister pick out.

As they are speaking we hear the voices of Judith and her father over the speaker.

> *Without any change in her tone, and smiling as if she were chatting casually, Claire continues.*

CLAIRE: I'm in a mess, Eamon
JUDITH: You're upset today.
CLAIRE: I don't know if I can go on with it.
JUDITH: You got your pills, didn't you?
FATHER: Judith betrayed the family—did you know that?
JUDITH: Yes. Now—that's better.
FATHER: Great betrayal; enormous betrayal.
JUDITH: Let me feel those tops.
FATHER: But Anna's praying for her. Did you know that?
JUDITH: Yes, I know that, Father.
CLAIRE: Listen to them! *(Short laugh.)* It goes on like that all the time, all the time. I don't know how Judith stands it. She's lucky to be so ... so strong-minded. Sometimes I think it's driving me mad. Mustn't it have been something trivial like that that finally drove Mother to despair? And then sometimes I think: I'm going to miss it so much. I'm so confused, Eamon.
EAMON: Aren't we all confused?
CLAIRE: But if you really loved someone the way you're supposed to love someone you're about to marry, you shouldn't be confused, should you? Everything should be absorbed in that love, shouldn't it? There'd be no reservations, would there? I'd love his children and his sister and his lorry and his vegetables and his carpets and everything, wouldn't I? And I'd love all of him, too, wouldn't I?

Eamon puts his arm around her.
That's one of the last nocturnes he wrote.

EAMON: Is it?

CLAIRE: Why does he not see that I'm in a mess, Eamon?

EAMON: You don't have to go on with it, you know.

Casimir is triumphant. "Number four! There you are! The complete croquet court!" *"Claire jumps up. She is suddenly vigorous, buoyant, excited. Her speech is rapid."* Nothing will do but that she and Casimir must play, and she demands a mallet. The two of them enthusiastically, with imaginary mallets, hoops, peg and balls, mime the game, down to and including pretending a ball has hit Casimir in the leg, much to Alice's disgust.

Uncle George makes one of his usual brief appearances. Eamon recalls that on the day of his wedding Uncle George had shaken his hand and spoken seven words to him: "There's going to be a great revolution." Eamon had believed it to be a profound observation. He is wiser now, Eamon tells Tom, and he claims he's solved the problem of Tom's book—"It has to be a fiction—a romantic fiction—like Helga the Hun." Tom should call it "Ballybeg Hall— From Supreme Court to Sausage Factory." It would cover four generations of the family, "a family without passion, without loyalty, without commitments....existing only in its own concept of itself....and with one enormous talent for—no, a *greed* for survival—that's the family motto, isn't it?—Semper Permanemus." And for "romantic possibilities," Eamon suggests, "Make Mother central." Alice is outraged and insists her mother be left out. It seems her mother had been an actress, unbeknownst to Tom, on the road with an acting company when the Judge saw her in the lounge of the Railway Hotel "and within five days wed and ensconced (her) in the Hall here."

EAMON: ....And a raving beauty by all accounts. No sooner did Yeats clap eyes on her than a sonnet burst from him—"That I may know the beauty of that form"—Alice'll rattle it off for you there. Oh, terrific stuff. And O'Casey —haven't they told you that one?—poor O'Casey out here one day ploughterin' after tennis balls and spoutin' about the workin'-man when she appeared in the doorway in there and the poor creatur' made such a ramstam to get to her that he tripped over the Pope or Plato or Shirley Temple or somebody and smashed his bloody glasses! The more you think of it—all those calamities—Chesterton's ribs, Hopkins's hand, O'Casey's aul' specs—the county council should put up a sign outside that room—Accident Black Spot —shouldn't they? Between ourselves, it's a very dangerous house, Professor.

TOM: What have you got against me, Eamon?

EAMON: And of course you'll have chapters on each of the O'Donnell forebears: Great Grandfather—Lord Chief Justice; Grandfather—Circuit Court Judge; Father—simple district Justice; Casimir—failed solicitor. A fairly rapid descent; but no matter; good for the book; failure's more lovable than success. D'you know, Professor, I've often wondered: if we had children and they wanted to be part of the family legal tradition, the only option open to them would have been as criminals, wouldn't it?

Offering the bottle.

There's enough here for both of us. No?

He pours a drink for himself.

After we went upstairs last night, Alice and I, we had words, as they say. She threw a book at me. And I struck her. You've noticed her cheek, haven't you? No one else here would dream of commenting on it; but you did, didn't you? And she didn't tell you, did she? Of course she didn't. That's why she's freezing me. But she'll come round. It'll be absorbed. Duty'll conquer.

TOM: I don't want to hear about your—

EAMON: What have I got against you?

TOM: Yes. You're the only member of the family who has been ... less then courteous to me since I came here. I don't know why that is. I guess you resent me for some reason.

Eamon considers this. He is not smiling now.

EAMON: Nervous: that's all. In case—you'll forgive me—in case you're not equal to your task. In case you'll loot and run. Nervous that all you'll see is— *(Indicates the croquet game.)*—the make-believe.

John Pankow (Eamon) and Kaiulani Lee (Judith) in a scene from *Aristocrats*

Casimir is called to the phone when it rings by Judith, who has come downstairs. Claire insists that Willie take his place in the croquet game. He demurs for a bit, feeling foolish about it, but Eamon encourages him, and he takes it up with a will. "Give us a mallet—out of my road—where do I begin?"

Judith remarks to Eamon that Alice looks older, and he agrees. Alice had stopped drinking for a year and a half, but since November she'd been in hospital twice, and Eamon knew the trip to Ballybeg would be disastrous. Judith has suggested to Alice that she take a job, but Alice's excuse was that "none of us was trained to do anything." "And she's right—we're not," Judith concedes. It's lonely for Alice in London, Eamon admits. Their basement flat is small and damp, and he's gone all day and many nights.

Eamon reminds Judith again that she'd said that morning long ago she would marry him and wants to know why she changed her mind. But Judith won't discuss it. She just goes on about how she manages to get the household by because they live so frugally. "There's Father's pension," she lets the land and grows vegetables and bakes, and now she's considering having the phone taken out.

JUDITH: And I have Willie. I don't think I could manage without Willie's help. Yes, I probably could. Yes, of course I would. But he's the most undemanding person I know. Some intuitive sense he has: he's always there when I want him. And everything he does is done so simply, so easily, that I almost take him for granted.

EAMON: Judith, I—

She closes her eyes, and her speech becomes tense and deliberate, almost as if she were talking to herself.

JUDITH: Listen to me, Eamon. I get up every morning at 7:30 and make breakfast. I bring Father his up first. Very often the bed's soiled, so I change him and sponge him and bring the clothes downstairs and wash them and hang them out. Then I get Uncle George his breakfast. Then I let the hens out and dig the potatoes for the lunch. By that time Claire's usually up, so I get her something to eat, and if she's in one of her down times I invent some light work for her to do, just to jolly her along, and if she's in one of her high times I've got to stop her from scrubbing down the house from top to bottom. Then I do out the fire, bring in the turf, make the beds, wash the dishes. Then it's time to bring Father up his egg-flip and shave him and maybe change his clothes again. Then I begin the lunch. And so it goes on and on, day after day, week after week, month after month. I'm not complaining, Eamon. I'm just telling you my routine. I don't even think of it as burdensome. But it occupies every waking moment of every day and every thought of every day. And I know I can carry on—happily almost, yes almost happily—I know I can keep going as long as I'm not diverted from that routine, as long as there are no intrusions on it. Maybe it's an unnatural existence. I don't know. But it's my existence—here—now. And there is no end in sight. So please don't intrude on it. Keep out of it. Now. Altogether. Please.

> *She lights a cigarette. Pause.*

EAMON: Whatever the lady wants.

Tom has gone off to do some packing, and Willie is ebullient, almost blooming at having "won" the game with Claire. Casimir comes out, relieved that his phone call is over. He'd spoken with his youngest son, he tells Judith, because Helga was at a meeting of her spiritualist group. Judith is all for clearing up, but Casimir insists that they must all listen to the tape Anna sent last Christmas, with messages on it for everyone. Willie feels it's his place to leave now, but Casimir persuades him to stay and arranges the chairs. Everybody is ready to hear the tape, but Casimir feels he must explain to Willie about Anna, who joined the convent 20 years ago at 17 (she was 18, Alice insists) and, except for one trip home, has been in Africa. Judith hushes everyone for a moment, thinking she'd heard her father, but decides she was mistaken and tells Casimir to go ahead.

> *He places the cassette on the lawn and switches it on. Anna's voice is a child's voice. She speaks slowly and distinctly, as if she were reading from a school book.*

ANNA: Hello Daddy and Judith and Alice and Casimir and little Claire.

ALICE: Hello, Anna.

ANNA: This is Anna speaking to you all the way from St. Joseph's mission in Kuala in Zambia. I hope you are all together when this is being played because I am imagining you all sitting before a big log fire in the drawing room—Daddy spread out and enjoying his well-earned relaxation after his strenuous day in court and the rest of you sitting on the rug or around the Christmas tree in the north window.

> *Alice has been trying to attract Claire's attention—she wants her glass refilled. But Claire does not notice her. Finally she has to whisper.*

ALICE: Claire.

CASIMIR: Shhh.

ALICE: Just a drop.

> *Claire fills the glass.*

ANNA: How are you all? May I wish each and every one of you—and you, too, dear Nanny—are you there, Nanny?

ALICE: Sorry, sister.

ANNA: May I wish you all a holy and a happy Christmas and all of God's peace and content for the new year.

ALICE: Amen.

ANNA: Later in the tape, Reverend Mother who is here beside me will say a few words to you, and after that you will hear my school choir singing some Irish songs that I have taught them—

ALICE: God!

ANNA: —and some African songs they have taught me.

ALICE: Good God!

ANNA: I hope you will enjoy them. But first I wish to speak to my own dear daddy. How are you, Daddy? I ought to be cross with you for never writing to me, but I know how busy you always are providing for us, and Judith tells me in her letters that you are in very good health. So thank God for that.

> *Father enters the study. An emaciated man; eyes distraught; one arm limp; his mouth pulled down at one corner. A grotesque and frightening figure. He is dressed only in pajamas. The tops are buttoned wrongly and hang off his shoulders; the bottoms are about to slip off his waist. He moves very slowly—one step at a time—through the study. He is trying to locate where Anna's voice is coming from—his distraught eyes are rolling round the room. When he speaks his voice is barely audible.*

FATHER: Anna?

ANNA: But before I go any further, I'm going to play the violin for you—a little piece you always liked me to play for you: The Gartan Mother's Lullaby. Do you remember it?

FATHER (*slightly louder*): Anna?

ANNA: So this is my Christmas present to you, my dear Daddy. I hope you like it.

> *She plays a few bars of the music—the playing of a child. Now Father is almost at the study door. He raises his head and emits an almost-animal roar.*

FATHER: Annaaaaaaaaaaa?

For a moment no one reacts. Then panic ensues. Trying to turn the cassette off, Alice accidentally turns the volume up and the sounds on the tape of the violin-playing overlap with the father's roar. Chairs are upset. Casimir, on his knees, cannot move, and Claire is on the verge of hysterics. The roaring stops, and the father is sinking toward the ground as Eamon rushes to him to try to catch him before he collapses, and they fall together. *"Eamon screams at the others—screams as if his own life depended on it:* Doctor! Call the doctor! For Christ's sake, will someone call the doctor!" *Curtain.*

ACT III

Early afternoon two days later, Claire can be heard at the piano playing a sonata. They have come back from the Judge's funeral, and Casimir, Eamon and Tom are onstage. Casimir is walking off the boundary lines of the one-time tennis court and remembering playing tennis with Alice and his father, who made a great ritual of putting his toe on the line before serving, adjusting it at such length that Casimir and Alice would get into "fits of secret giggling" and couldn't return the ball, thereby convincing their father he played better than he actually did.

Casimir checks his watch, noting that it's around the time they would have been having the reception after the wedding (now postponed for three months, out of respect). Claire's playing the B minor sonata, Grandfather O'Donnell's favorite, according to Casimir. "Probably because he actually heard Chopin play it." Tom is intrigued. He hasn't heard this story about the party in Vienna. "....a birthday party for Balzac. Everybody was there: Liszt and George Sand and Turgenev and Mendelssohn and the young Wagner and Berlioz and Delacroix and Verdi—and of course Balzac." Tom suggests Casimir's grandfather would not have been a contemporary of this group, that it must have been his great-grandfather. Casimir consents to the correction but points out that the expression, "a party in Vienna," has become a family saying for events of a romantic or exciting nature that have happened or could happen. He asks Tom if he saw how Claire went to the piano as soon as they'd gotten home and regrets again how his father thwarted her musical career.

Tom has questions for Casimir. He understands from something Judith has said that Casimir's mother did not play the piano, but Casimir insists she did, and that she also sang: "Her favorite piece was a song called 'Sweet Alice.' And Father hated it—hated it. 'Rubbish' he called it." Eamon begins to sing it, and Casimir joins in, remembering how his mother seemed to become young and beautiful again when she sang it.

Tom's other question is about Casimir's recollections of Yeats, who died two months before Casimir's birth on All Fools Day in 1939. Casimir seems taken aback. Seemingly to assuage him, Tom admits to having made similar mistakes himself, that it's natural enough. He goes off, leaving Casimir with Eamon.

CASIMIR: Ha-ha. It was very kind of Tom to stay over. I appreciate that very much. *(Begins pacing again.)* Father would have been so pleased by that funeral today—no, not pleased—gratified, immensely gratified. The packed chapel; the music; that young curate's fine, generous panegyric and he didn't know Father at all, Judith says. Then down through the village street—his village, his Ballybeg—that's how he thought of it, you know, and in a sense it was his village. Did you know that it used to be called O'Donnellstown? Yes, years and years ago. How simple it all was this time, wasn't it? You remember Mother's funeral, don't you?—all that furtiveness, all that whispering, all those half-truths. We didn't know until the very last minute would they allow her a Christian burial at all because of the circumstances—remember? But today it was—today was almost … festive by comparison, wasn't it? Every shop shut and every blind drawn; and men kneeling on their caps as the hearse passed; and Nanny sobbing her heart out when the coffin was being lowered—did you see her?—of course you did—you were beside her. All that happened, didn't it, Eamon? All that happened? Oh, yes, he would have been so gratified.

EAMON: There are certain things, certain truths, Casimir, that are beyond Tom's kind of scrutiny.

The same sonata music begins again.

CASIMIR: Oh, there are. Oh, yes, there are—aren't there? Yes—yes. I discovered a great truth when I was nine. No, not a great truth; but I made a great discovery when I was nine—not even a great discovery but an important, a very important discovery for me. I suddenly realized I was different from other boys. When I say I was different I don't mean—you know—good Lord I don't for a second mean I was—you know—as they say nowadays "homosexual"—good heavens I must admit, if anything, Eamon, if anything I'm—*(Looks around.)*—I'm vigorously heterosexual, ha-ha. But of course I don't mean that either. No, no. But anyway. What I discovered was that for some reason people found me … peculiar. Of course I sensed it first from the boys at boarding school. But it was Father with his usual—his usual directness and honesty who made me face it. I remember the day he said to me: "Had you been born down there"—we were in the library and he pointed down to Ballybeg—"Had you been born down there, you'd have become the village idiot. Fortunately for you, you were born here, and we can absorb you." Ha-ha. So at nine years of age I knew certain things: that certain kinds of people laughed at me; that the easy relationships that other men enjoy would always elude me; that—that—that I would never succeed in life, whatever—you know—whatever "succeed" means—

EAMON: Casimir—

CASIMIR: No, no, please. That was a very important and a very difficult discovery for me, as you can imagine. But it brought certain recognitions, certain compensatory recognitions. Because once I recognized—once I acknowledged that the larger areas were not accessible to me, I discovered—I had to discover smaller, much smaller areas that were. Yes indeed. And I discovered that if I conduct myself with some circumspection, I find that I can live within these smaller, perhaps very confined territories without exposure to too much hurt. Indeed, I find that I can experience some happiness and perhaps give a measure of happiness, too. My great discovery....

He and Eamon have never really talked, Casimir realizes, and he would like to talk to Eamon because he believes Eamon understands ... *("He gestures toward the house.")* ... what it's done to all of them.

Judith and Alice come on with Alice's suitcase. Mrs. Moore has arranged for Casimir's flight, and he's sent Helga a telegram: he'll be home that night. Willie is due soon to take them all to the bus. Tom is checking dates in the library and may stay over until the next morning, Judith reports. Eamon thinks he shouldn't have been allowed to come there to pry, but Judith gave Tom her permission. "Is there something to hide?" she asks Eamon. And besides, it is her home.

Alice is a little disparaging about the size of the funeral, but Casimir disagrees and found the mass moving. "Until Miss Quirk cut loose," Alice comments. (It seems Miss Quirk played "This Is My Lovely Day," possibly under the impression it was the wedding.) And Alice wants to know who the man was—"pasty-looking, plump, bald"—at the service. She's shocked when she learns it was Jerry McLaughlin, Claire's fiance. He's old enough to be her father, Alice insists. (He is 59, it is revealed.) Alice is glad the wedding's been postponed and hopes Claire will reconsider.

Judith calls Claire to come out to join them. She has to discuss what will happen now that their father has died. The house, the furnishings and the land have been left to the four of them, and what are they going to do? she asks. Alice points out that she lives in London, Casimir lives in Hamburg, so the house is Judith's and Claire's. Casimir agrees. Both he and Alice would like to come for visits, but the house should be Judith's and Claire's. Casimir would, however, like to take a small silver-framed picture of his mother as a keepsake, if he may. The sooner the better as far as getting the place in the two sisters' names, Alice sums up, and that's settled—but Eamon suggests Judith has other ideas about it.

The fact is, owning the house and continuing to live there is not possible, Judith explains: "We can't afford it." Their father's modest pension is gone now, and Willie's leasing the land cannot go on. The house is a liability, the bank manager told her last fall when she tried for, and failed to get, an overdraft because a storm caused roof damage. She and Willie nailed plastic to the rafters, but they need 17 buckets to catch the water in the upstairs rooms when it rains heavily. Dry rot has collapsed the morning room floor, and only the father's bedroom was heated during the winter. She's also had a Dublin dealer evaluate the library and some furniture and was offered 70 pounds for a grandmother clock and 90 for the books.

They hadn't suspected, and they could all help, Alice sympathizes, but Judith claims it's pointless to sign the place over to her, as she's not going to go on staying here. Claire is getting married and will be leaving too.

ALICE (*to Judith*): Where will you go? What will you do?

JUDITH: The first thing I'm going to do is take the baby out of the orphanage.

ALICE: Of course. Yes.

JUDITH: "The baby"—he's seven now. (*To Casimir.*) Do you know he's two days younger than your Heinrich? Where I'll go I haven't made up my mind yet. Willie has a mobile home just outside Bundoran. He has a lot of slot machines around that area, and he wants me to go there with him.

ALICE: That would be—

JUDITH: But he doesn't want the baby. So that settles that. Anyhow, I've got to earn a living somehow. But the only reason I brought all this up is— what's to become of Uncle George?

EAMON: What you're saying is that after Claire's wedding—if you can wait that length—you're going to turn the key in the door and abandon Ballybeg Hall?

JUDITH: I'm asking—

EAMON: You know what will happen, don't you? The moment you've left the thugs from the village will move in and loot and ravage the place within a couple of hours. Is that what you're proposing? Oh, your piety is admirable.

JUDITH: I'm asking what's to become of Uncle George.

EAMON: Judith's like her American friend: the Hall can be assessed in terms of roofs and floors and overdrafts.

ALICE: Eamon—

EAMON: No, no; that's all it means to her. Well I know its real worth—in this area, in this county, in this country. And Alice knows. And Casimir knows. And Claire knows. And somehow we'll keep it going. Somehow we'll keep it going. Somehow we'll—

ALICE: Please, Eamon.

Judith breaks down. Pause.

EAMON: Sorry … sorry … sorry again … Seems to be a day of public contrition. What the hell is it but crumbling masonry. Sorry. (*Short laugh.*) Don't you know that all that is fawning and forelock-touching and Paddy and shabby and greasy peasant in the Irish character finds a house like this irresistible? That's why we were ideal for colonizing. Something in us needs this … aspiration. Don't despise us—we're only hedgehogs, Judith. Sorry.

He goes to the gazebo.

ALICE: He hates going back to London. He hates the job. (*Pause.*) What is there to say? There's nothing to say, is there?

JUDITH: No.

Judith reminds them that it has not yet been decided what to do with Uncle George, and Alice asks Eamon if they can take him to London with them to live. Eamon doubts he would come; but when Uncle George appears, Alice approaches him on the subject. If he comes with them, even if he didn't speak, he would be company for her, she tells him. Uncle George considers the proposition at some length, and then announces that he hasn't been to London since 1910. "Another visit's about due, I suppose. I'll pack," he says before going off. Alice is delighted. She hopes Eamon won't mind. "He'll be *my* keepsake," Eamon comments. "Jaysus, he'll fair keep London in chat," Willie remarks to Judith when he arrives and is apprised of Uncle George's decision.

There isn't time for anything to eat or for a cup of tea, Willie points out, but he can't seem to hurry up their departure for the bus. *"There is an unspoken wish to protract time, to postpone the final breaking up."*

"They gave him a nice enough wee sendoff, didn't they?" Willie comments to Judith about the funeral. He was up before her father in court once, he remembers. It was to do with a car he'd had—"No tax, no insurance, no license, no brakes, no nothing—buck all except that the damn thing kind of went." He'd told her father a lot of lies, and her father had pretended to believe him and had let him off. "Jaysus, he was a strange bird."

Claire wants Casimir, who is playing a cassette again, to come back for the wedding. She wishes it were going to be the next day, but Casimir says the time will fly and promises to return.

Alice and Eamon are talking between themselves.

ALICE: What are you thinking?
EAMON: That in a way it's as difficult for me as it is for you.
ALICE: What is?
EAMON: Leaving; leaving for good. I know it's your home. But in a sense it has always been my home, too, because of Granny and then because of you.
ALICE: I don't know what I feel. Maybe a sense of release; of not being pursued; of the possibility of—*(Short pause.)*—of "fulfilment." No. Just emptiness. Perhaps maybe a new start. Yes, I'll manage.
EAMON: Because you're of that tradition.
ALICE: What tradition?
EAMON: Of discipline; of self-discipline—residual aristocratic instincts.
ALICE: I'm the alcoholic, remember.
EAMON: So was Uncle George—once.
ALICE: You and Judith always fight.
EAMON: No, we don't. When did you discover that?
ALICE: I've always known it. And I think it's because you love her. I think it's because you think you love her; and that's the same thing. No, it's even more disturbing for you. And that's why I'm not unhappy that this is all over—

because love is possible only in certain contexts. And now that this is finished, you may become less unhappy in time.

EAMON: Have we a context?

ALICE: Let's wait and see.

Casimir invites all the family to come for a holiday in Hamburg next summer. "A party in Vienna," Eamon says. "Exactly!" Casimir agrees.

Claire turns off the cassette and states very matter-of-factly that she's suddenly gone off Chopin: "I don't think I'll ever play Chopin again."

Eamon starts to sing "Sweet Alice," and Alice joins in. Then Casimir joins in, and Claire begins to hum. Uncle George has come into the study with his small suitcase and sits patiently awaiting departure. *"One has the impression that this afternoon, easy, relaxed, relaxing—may go on indefinitely."* Willie is sure they're going to miss the bus, but Judith insists they won't, and the singing continues. Before the end of the song the lights are brought down *"slowly to dark." Curtain.*

Special Citation for Choreography

JEROME ROBBINS' BROADWAY

A Musical in Two Acts

CONCEIVED, DIRECTED AND CHOREOGRAPHED BY
JEROME ROBBINS

Cast and credits appear on pages 404–408

JEROME ROBBINS was born in New York City Oct. 11, 1918, and by the time he reached his teens in the mid-1930s he was studying ballet, modern, Spanish and Oriental dancing at N.Y.U. He made his debut as a performer at the Sandor-Sorel Dance Center in 1937. He worked as a chorus dancer in Broadway musicals including The Straw Hat Revue *(1939) until joining the American Ballet Theater company in 1940. From 1941 to 1944 he danced the works of Fokine, Tudor, Massine, Balanchine, Lichine and de Mille as a soloist with that group. His choreography for his first ballet for American Ballet Theater,* Fancy Free *(1944) was a tremendous hit, and he continued as a choreographer for that company until 1949, when he joined the New York City Ballet as choreographer and associate artistic director (with George Balanchine), becoming ballet master in 1969 and co-ballet master in chief (with Peter Martins) from 1983 to the present. He has created more than 50 ballets celebrated in performance by the world's major dance companies; included among these are* Interplay *(1945),* Afternoon of a Faun *(1953),* The Concert *(1956),* Dances at a Gathering *(1969) and* Glass Pieces *(1983).*

The first Robbins-choreographed Broadway musical was On the Town *(1945) based on his own* Fancy Free. *There followed* Billion Dollar Baby *(1946),* High Button Shoes *(1947),* Miss Liberty *(1949),* Call Me Madam *(1950),* The King and I *(1951) and* Two's Company *(1952). Robbins directed as well as choreographed* Peter Pan *in 1954 and subsequently performed both artistic functions as one of Broadway's great director-choreographers for* Bells Are Ringing *(1956),* West Side Story *(1957),* Gypsy *(1959)*

377

and finally Fiddler on the Roof *(1964), the fifth-longest running Broadway show of all time with 3,242 performances.*

These Robbins musicals have won a long list of awards in all categories. For Robbins individually they have brought four Tonys, five Donaldson Awards, two Academy Awards (for co-directing and choreographing the movie West Side Story*), a Drama Critics Award, an Emmy, New York City's Handel Medallion, a Screen Directors Guild Award, Kennedy Center Honors (in 1981), an Astaire Lifetime Achievement Award, the French Chevalier des Arts and a National Medal of Art (conferred by President Ronald Reagan). He is an honorary member of the American Academy and Institute of Arts and Letters, the recipient of honorary degrees from Ohio University and CUNY and has been a panel member of the New York Council on the Arts, the National Council on the Arts and the National Endowment for the Arts. The wide-ranging Robbins credits in other areas of show business have included co-direction of* The Pajama Game *(with George Abbott) in 1952, production supervisor for* Funny Girl *(1964), director of the plays* Oh Dad, Poor Dad *(1963) and* Mother Courage and Her Children *and TV credits for the choreography of* Two Duets *(1980) and* Live From Studio 8H *(1980), a program of Robbins ballets. At present, he and his activities are based at the New York State Theater in Lincoln Center, New York City.*

All but two of the Robbins-choreographed musicals are represented in Jerome Robbins' Broadway *by one or more dance numbers from each. We likewise include a photo of each of the dozen restaged Robbins dances in the new show as a special Best Play citation of this glorious choreography. These photographs of* Jerome Robbins' Broadway *depict the scenes as produced Feb. 26, 1989 at the Imperial Theater by The Shubert Organization, Roger Berlind, Suntory International Corp., Byron Goldman and Emanuel Azenberg, as directed and choreographed by Jerome Robbins, with scenery by Robin Wagner (and Boris Aronson, Jo Mielziner, Oliver Smith and Tony Walton), costumes by Joseph G. Aulisi (and Alvin Colt, Raoul Pène du Bois, Irene Sharaff, Tony Walton, Miles White and Patricia Zipprodt) and lighting by Jennifer Tipton.*

Our special thanks are tendered to the producers and their press representatives, the Fred Nathan Company, Bert Fink and Merle Frimark, for making available these selections from the excellent photographs of the show by Martha Swope.

ACT I

Above, Michael Kubala holding Robert La Fosse (*center*) as "Sailors on the Town," and (*below*) Scott Wise, Mary Ellen Stuart, Michael Kubala, Debbie Shapiro and Robert La Fosse in "Ya Got Me," both numbers from Jerome Robbins's first Broadway musical, *On the Town*

Above, Mary Ann Lamb, Barbara Yeager and JoAnn M. Hunter as flappers, and *right,* Joey McKneely and Michael Scott Gregory as gangsters in "The Charleston Ballet" from *Billion Dollar Baby*

Below, Jason Alexander as Pseudolus and Michael Kubala, Joey McKneely and Scott Wise as the Proteans in "Comedy Tonight," from *A Funny Thing Happened on the Way to the Forum*

The company in "Suite of Dances" from *West Side Story*, the
"Somewhere" ballet (*above*) and as the Jets in "Cool" (*below*)

ACT II

Right, Susan Kikuchi (*kneeling*) as Eliza and Irene Cho as The Angel in the ballet "The Small House of Uncle Thomas" from *The King and I; below,* Susann Fletcher (Electra), Faith Prince (Tessie), Debbie Shapiro (Mazeppa) and Mary Ann Lamb (Louise) in the "You Gotta Have a Gimmick" number from *Gypsy*

Above, Charlotte d'Amboise (Peter), Donna Di Meo (Wendy), Linda Talcott (Michael) and Steve Ochoa (John) in "I'm Flying" from *Peter Pan; below,* Angelo H. Fraboni, Michael Scott Gregory, Mary Ann Lamb and Greg Schanuel in the Sennett-like "On a Sunday by the Sea" from *High Button Shoes*

Debbie Shapiro (Singer, *right*) and Robert La Fosse (*above*) and with Janie Lanier (*below*) in "Mr. Monotony" cut from *Call Me Madam* and *Miss Liberty* during out-of-town tryout, making its New York debut here

Dances from *Fiddler on the Roof: above*, Mark Esposito, Scott Jovovich, Greg Schanuel and Christophe Caballero perform "The Bottle Dance"; *below*, the Mamas in "Tradition"

FINALE

The full company in a tribute to Jerome Robbins including "Some Other Time" and "New York, New York" from *On the Town*, with a setting depicting "Broadway at Night," designed for this production by Robin Wagner

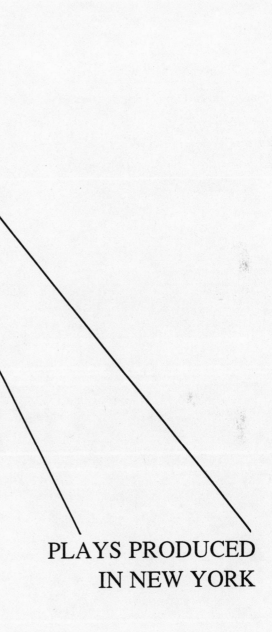

PLAYS PRODUCED
IN NEW YORK

PLAYS PRODUCED ON BROADWAY

Figures in parentheses following a play's title give number of performances. These figures are acquired directly from the production offices and do not include previews or extra non-profit performances. In the case of a transfer, the off-Broadway run is noted but not added to the figure in parentheses.

Plays marked with an asterisk (*) were still running on June 1, 1989. Their number of performances is figured through May 31, 1989.

In a listing of a show's numbers—dances, sketches, musical scenes, etc.—the titles of songs are identified wherever possible by their appearance in quotation marks (").

HOLDOVERS FROM PREVIOUS SEASONS

Plays which were running on June 1, 1988 are listed below. More detailed information about them appears in previous *Best Plays* volumes of appropriate years. Important cast changes since opening night are recorded in the Cast Replacements section of this volume.

*A Chorus Line (5,756; longest regular run in Broadway history). Transfer from off Broadway of the musical conceived by Michael Bennett; book by James Kirkwood and Nicholas Dante; music by Marvin Hamlisch; lyrics by Edward Kleban. Opened April 15, 1975 off Broadway where it played 101 performances through July 13, 1975; transferred to Broadway July 25, 1975.

*Oh! Calcutta! (5,856; playing 10 performances weekly, 2 more than regular Broadway productions, under a special "middle" contract). Revival of the musical devised by Kenneth Tynan; with contributions (in this version) by Jules Feiffer, Dan Greenberg, Lenore Kandel, John Lennon, Jacques Levy, Leonard Melfi, David Newman & Robert Benton, Sam Shepard, Clovis Trouille, Kenneth Tynan and Sherman Yellen; music and lyrics (in this version) by Robert Dennis, Peter Schickele and Stanley Walden; additional music by Stanley Walden and Jacques Levy. Opened September 24, 1976 in alternating performances with *Me and Bessie* through December 7, 1976, continuing alone thereafter.

42nd Street (3,486). Musical based on the novel by Bradford Ropes; book by Michael Stewart and Mark Bramble; music and lyrics by Harry Warren and Al Dubin; other lyrics by Johnny Mercer and Mort Dixon. Opened August 25, 1980. (Closed January 8, 1989)

*Cats (2,777). Musical based on *Old Possum's Book of Practical Cats* by T. S. Eliot; music by Andrew Lloyd Webber; additional lyrics by Trevor Nunn and Richard Stilgoe. Opened October 7, 1982.

*Me and My Girl (1,595). Revival of the musical with book and lyrics by L. Arthur Rose and Douglas Furber; music by Noel Gay; book revised by Stephen Fry; contributions to revisions by Mike Okrent. Opened August 10, 1986.

Broadway Bound (756). By Neil Simon. Opened December 4, 1986. (Closed September 25, 1988)

*Les Misérables (868). Musical based on the novel by Victor Hugo; book by Alain Boublil and Claude-Michel Schönberg; music by Claude-Michel Schönberg; lyrics by Herbert Kretzmer; original French text by Alain Boublil and Jean-Marc Natel; additional material by James Fenton. Opened March 12, 1987.

Starlight Express (761). Musical with music by Andrew Lloyd Webber; lyrics by Richard Stilgoe. Opened March 15, 1987. (Closed January 8, 1989)

Fences (526). By August Wilson. Opened March 26, 1987. (Closed June 26, 1988)

Burn This (437). By Lanford Wilson. Opened October 14, 1987. (Closed October 29, 1988)

*Lincoln Center Theater. *Anything Goes (675). Revival of the musical with original book by Guy Bolton & P. G. Wodehouse and Howard Lindsay & Russel Crouse; new book by Timothy Crouse and John Weidman; music and lyrics by Cole Porter. Opened October 19, 1987. Speed-the-Plow (278). By David Mamet. Opened May 3, 1988. (Closed December 31, 1988)

Cabaret (262). Revival of the musical with book by Joe Masteroff; music by John Kander; lyrics by Fred Ebb; based on the play by John van Druten and stories by Christopher Isherwood. Opened October 22, 1987. (Closed June 4, 1988)

*Into the Woods (655). Musical with book by James Lapine; music and lyrics by Stephen Sondheim. Opened November 5, 1987.

*The Phantom of the Opera (563). Musical with book by Richard Stilgoe and Andrew Lloyd Webber; music by Andrew Lloyd Webber; lyrics by Charles Hart; additional lyrics by Richard Stilgoe; adapted from the novel by Gaston Leroux. Opened January 26, 1988.

*Sarafina! (560). Transfer from off Broadway of the musical conceived and written by Mbongeni Ngema; music by Mbongeni Ngema and Hugh Masekela. Opened October 25, 1987 off Broadway where it played 81 performances through January 3, 1988; transferred to Broadway January 28, 1988.

A Walk in the Woods (136). By Lee Blessing. Opened February 28, 1988. (Closed June 26, 1988)

*M. Butterfly (491). By David Henry Hwang. Opened March 20, 1988.

Joe Turner's Come and Gone (105). By August Wilson. Opened March 27, 1988. (Closed June 26, 1988)

Michael Feinstein in Concert (62). One-man performance by Michael Feinstein; conceived by Michael Feinstein and Christopher Chadman. Opened April 19, 1988. (Closed June 12, 1988)

Macbeth (77). Revival of the play by William Shakespeare. Opened April 21, 1988. (Closed June 26, 1988)

Chess (68). Musical based on an idea by Tim Rice; book by Richard Nelson; music by Benny Andersson and Bjorn Ulvaeus; lyrics by Tim Rice. Opened April 28, 1988. (Closed June 25, 1988)

Romance Romance (297). Program of two one-act musicals with book and lyrics by Barry Harman; music by Keith Herrmann: *The Little Comedy* based on a short story by Arthur Schnitzler and *Summer Share* based on the play *Pain de Menage* by Jules Renard. Opened May 1, 1988. (Closed January 14, 1989)

Jackie Mason's "The World According to Me" (203). Return engagement of the one-man show created, written and performed by Jackie Mason. Opened May 2, 1988. (Closed December 31, 1988)

PLAYS PRODUCED JUNE 1, 1988—MAY 31, 1989

O'Neill Plays. Revival of two plays by Eugene O'Neill in repertory. **Long Day's Journey Into Night** (28). Opened June 14, 1988. **Ah, Wilderness!** (12). Opened June 23, 1988. Produced by Ken Marsolais, Alexander H. Cohen and The Kennedy Center for the Performing Arts in association with Yale Repertory Theater, Richard Norton, Irma Ostreicher and Elizabeth D. White at the Neil Simon Theater as part of the First New York International Festival of the Arts. (Repertory closed July 23, 1988)

PERFORMER	"LONG DAY'S JOURNEY INTO NIGHT"	"AH, WILDERNESS!"
William Cain		David McComber
Colleen Dewhurst	Mary Cavan Tyrone	Essie Miller
Jennifer Dundas		Mildred Miller
Annie Golden		Belle
George Hearn		Sid Davis
Jane Macfie	Cathleen	Norah
Jason Robards	James Tyrone	Nat Miller
Raphael Sbarge		Richard Miller
Campbell Scott	Edmund Tyrone	Arthur Miller
Kyra Sedgwick		Muriel McComber
Jamey Sheridan	James Tyrone Jr.	Bartender
Steven Skybell		Wint Selby
Nicholas Tamarkin		Tommy Miller
Elizabeth Wilson		Lily Miller
William Wise		Salesman

BOTH PLAYS: Costumes, Jane Greenwood; lighting, Jennifer Tipton; sound, Alan Stieb; production stage managers, Mitchell Erickson, John Handy; press, Burnham-Callaghan Associates, Edward Callaghan, Jacqueline Burnham, Owen Levy.

LONG DAY'S JOURNEY INTO NIGHT: Understudies: Mr. Robards—William Cain; Mr. Sheridan—Jeff Hayenga; Miss Macfie—Louise Roberts.

Directed by José Quintero; scenery, Ben Edwards.

Directed by José Quintero; scenery, Ben Edwards.

Time: A day in August 1912. Place: Living room of the Tyrones' summer home. Act I: 8:30 a.m. Act II, Scene 1: Around 12:45. Scene 2: About half an hour later. Act III: Around 6:30 that evening. Act IV: The same, around midnight. The play was presented in two parts.

The last major New York revival of *Long Day's Journey Into Night* took place on Broadway 4/28/86 for 54 performances. This production was originally mounted at the Yale Repertory Theater, Lloyd Richards artistic director.

AH, WILDERNESS!: Standbys: Mr. Robards—William Cain; Mr. Tamarkin—Robbie Dekelbaum; Messrs. Sheridan, Wise—Jeff Hayenga; Miss Golden—Jane Macfie; Misses Dundas, Sedgwick, Macfie— Louise Roberts; Messrs. Hearn, Cain—William Wise.

Directed by Arvin Brown; scenery, Michael H. Yeargan.

Act I, Scene 1: Sitting room of the Miller home in a large smalltown in Connecticut, early morning, July 4, 1906. Scene 2: Dining room of the Miller home, evening of the same day. Act II, Scene 1: Back room of a bar, 10 o'clock that night. Scene 2: Sitting room of the Miller home, after 10. Act III, Scene 1: Sitting room of the Miller home, about 1 o'clock the following afternoon. Scene 2: The strip of beach along the harbor, about 9 o'clock that night. Scene 3: The Miller sitting room, 10 o'clock that night. The play was presented in three parts.

The last major New York revival of *Ah, Wilderness!* took place in the musical version *Take Me Along* 4/14/85 for 1 performance; and in straight play version off Broadway 6/14/83 for 48 performances. This production was originally mounted at Yale Repertory Theater, Lloyd Richards artistic director.

Circle in the Square. 1987–88 season continued with **Juno and the Paycock** (17). Revival of the play by Sean O'Casey in the Gate Theater Dublin production, Michael Colgan director. Opened June 21, 1988. (Closed July 2, 1988) **The Night of the Iguana** (81). Revival of the play by Tennessee Williams. Opened June 26, 1988. (Closed September 4, 1988) Produced by Circle in the Square Theater, Theodore Mann artistic director, Paul Libin producing director (*Juno and the Paycock* at the John Golden Theater, *The Night of the Iguana* at the Circle in the Square Theater) as part of the First New York International Festival of the Arts.

JUNO AND THE PAYCOCK—John Kavanagh and Donal McCann in the Gate Theater Dublin production of Sean O'Casey's play

JUNO AND THE PAYCOCK

Mary Boyle	Rosemary Fine	Mrs. Tancred	Stella McCusker
June Boyle	Geraldine Plunkett	Needle Nugent	Seamus Forde
Johnny Boyle	Joe Savino	Irregular Mobilizer	Anto Nolan
Jerry Devine	Tony Coleman	Irregular; Coal-Block Vendor	Brendan Laird
Capt. Jack Boyle	Donal McCann	Irregular; Sewing Machine Man	Michael Egan
Joxer Daly	John Kavanagh	Furniture Removal Men	Enda Oates,
Charles Bentham	Garrett Keogh		Donagh Deeney
Maisie Madigan	Maureen Potter	Neighbor	Eithne Dempsey

Directed by Joe Dowling; scenery, Frank Hallinan Flood; costumes, Consolata Boyle; lighting, Rupert Murray; production stage manager, Bill McComb; press, Merle Debuskey, Leo Stern.

Time: 1922. Place: The living apartment of a two-roomed tenancy of the Boyle family, in a tenement house in Dublin. The play was presented in three parts.

Juno and the Paycock was first produced on Broadway 3/15/26. It has been revived in Broadway production 12/19/27; the 1932–33 season (in repertory); 11/23/34 and 12/6/37 by the Abbey Theater Players; 1/16/40; and as *Juno*, a musical version, 3/9/59. It has been revived in off-Broadway production in the seasons of 1935–36, 1946–47, 1947–48 and 1954–55.

THE NIGHT OF THE IGUANA

Pancho	Mateo Gomez	Wolfgang	Peter Lang
Maxine Faulk	Jane Alexander	Frau Fahrenkopf	Kathleen Marsh
Pedro	Mark Damon	Miss Judith Fellowes	Pamela Payton-Wright
Rev. T. Lawrence Shannon	Nicholas Surovy	Hannah Jelkes	Maria Tucci
Hank	Jonathan Mann	Charlotte Goodall	Marita Geraghty
Herr Fahrenkopf	Christopher Martin	Nonno (Jonathan Coffin)	William LeMassena
Hilda	Chandra Lee	Jake Latta	Tom Brennan

Understudies: Messrs. Brennan, Mann, Surovy, Martin, Lang—Robert Emmet; Misses Marsh, Geraghty—Chandra Lee; Messrs. Gomez, Damon—Jonathan Mann; Misses Alexander, Tucci, Payton-Wright, Lee—Kathleen Marsh.

Directed by Theodore Mann; scenery, Zack Brown; costumes, Jennifer von Mayrhauser; lighting, Richard Nelson; production stage manager, Michael F. Ritchie; stage manager, William Hare.

Time: Summer of 1940. Place: The Costa Verde Hotel in Puerto Barrio on the west coast of Mexico. Act I, Scene 1: Afternoon. Scene 2: Later that afternoon. Act II: That night.

The Night of the Iguana was originally produced on Broadway 12/28/61 for 316 performances and was named a Best Play of its season and won the New York Drama Critics Award for best American play. A previous attempt to revive it in a Broadway production closed out of town 11/9/85.

Canciones de Mi Padre (Songs of My Father) (18). Revue of Mexican musical numbers. Produced by James M. Nederlander and Jerome Minskoff at the Minskoff Theater. Opened July 12, 1988. (Closed July 30, 1988)

Cast: Linda Ronstadt, Mariachi Vargas De Tecalitlan (mariachi musicians), Danny Valdez, Gilberto Puente (guitarist), Ballet Folklorico de La Fonda, Sal Lopez & Urbanie Lucero (folkloric dancers).

Dancers: Mary Louise Diaz, Elsa Estrada, Luis Valdez, Lalo Garcia.

Musicians: Ruben Fuentes conductor; Jose Martinez, Mario A. de Santiago, Juan Manuel Biurquix, Daniel Martinez, Ildefonso Moya, Francisco Gonzalez violin; Rigoberto Mercado, Federico Torres trumpet; Arturo Mendoza harp; Nati Santiago, Rafael Palomar guitar; Victor Cardenas vihuela.

Directed and choreographed by Michael Smuin; scenery, Tony Walton; lighting, Jules Fisher; produced by Ira Koslow for Asher/Krost Management; stage manager, Randy Post; press, Peter Cromarty.

Subtitled "A Romantic Evening in Old Mexico," a collection of songs in the Mexican language, Mexican dances and instrumentals. Previously produced at New York City Center 2/88.

ACT I

Scene 1—First mariachi section: Fanfarria—Mariachi Vargas; Los Laureles; Por un Amor; La Cigarra; Tu Solo Tu—Linda Ronstadt, Ildefonso Moya (violin solo—Jose Martinez, Juan Manuel Biurquix); Cancion Mexicana.

Scene 2—Traditional dances, Jalisco costumes: La Negra—Mary Louise Diaz, Elsa Estrada, Urbanie Lucero, Lalo Garcia, Sal Lopez, Luis Valdez; El Gusto—Diaz, Estrada, Lucero, Garcia, Lopez, Valdez; El Caballito—Lopez, Diaz.

Scene 3—Revolutionary section: El Tren—Mariachi Vargas; La Rielera; Corrido de Cananea; Adios del Soldado—Ronstadt, Danny Valdez (Chorus—Mario A. de Santiago, Moya; violin solos—Martinez, Biurquix); Yo Soy el Corrido—Rondstadt, Valdez; El Sol Que Tu Eres—Rondstadt, Valdez, La Rielera (mini reprise); Viva Mexico—Company.

ACT II

Scene 1—Mariachi Vargas: Fiesta en Jalisco, Las Bodas de Luis Alonso.

Scene 2—Ballad section: Hay Unos Ojos—violin solos, Martinez, Biurquix; Rogaciano el Huapanguero—Ronstadt, Martinez, Moya; Dos Arbolitos—Ronstadt, Martinez, Moya with Lopez & Lucero; Violin solos—Martinez, Biurquix; La Barca de Guaymas—Ronstadt, Moya, Rafael Palomar with Diaz, Estrada, Lucero, Garcia, Lopez & Valdez; Violin solos—Martinez, Biurquix; Amorcita Corazon—Valdez.

Scene 3—Traditional dances: La Bamba—Dance Company (Vera Cruz costumes); Malaguena Salerosa—Gilberto Puente; Jarabe Tapatio—Dance Company (China Poblana costumes); El Cascabel—Mariachi Vargas.

Scene 4—Town courtyard: Y Andale—Ronstadt, Martinez; Crucifijo de Piedra; La Calandria—Ronstadt, Martinez, Moya; La Charreada; Cancio Mexteca; Volver—Company.

Checkmates (177). By Ron Milner. Produced by James M. and James L. Nederlander, Philip Rose, Michael Harris and Hayward Collins at the 46th Street Theater. Opened August 4, 1988. (Closed January 1, 1989)

Sylvester Williams	Denzel Washington	Frank Cooper	Paul Winfield
Mattie Cooper	Ruby Dee	Laura McClellan-Williams	Marsha Jackson

Standbys: Mr. Winfield—Gilbert Lewis; Miss Dee—Yvette Hawkins; Mr. Washington—Darnell Williams; Miss Jackson—Elizabeth Van Dyke.

Directed by Woodie King Jr.; scenery, Edward Burbridge; costumes, Judy Dearing; lighting, Ronald Wallace; stage manager, Ed DeShae; press, the Joshua Ellis Office, Adrian Bryan-Brown, Chris Boneau.

Place: Detroit, or just about any other American metropolis. Act I: The present. Act II: Three weeks later.

Comedy, a younger couple and an older couple share a duplex and the problems of modern living. Previously produced in regional theater in Los Angeles and Washington, D.C.

Ain't Misbehavin' (176). Revival of the musical revue with music by Fats Waller; based on an idea by Murray Horwitz and Richard Maltby Jr. Produced by The Shubert Organization, Emanuel Azenberg, Dasha Epstein and Roger Berlind at the Ambasador Theater. Opened August 15, 1988. (Closed January 15, 1989)

Nell Carter
Andre De Shields
Armelia McQueen

Ken Page
Charlaine Woodard

Standbys: Misses Carter, McQueen—Kecia Lewis-Evans; Miss Woodard—Jackie Lowe; Mr. De Shields—Eric Riley; Mr. Page—Ken Prymus.

Conceived and directed by Richard Maltby Jr.; musical staging and choreography, Arthur Faria; musical supervision, arrangements, conductor and pianist, Luther Henderson; scenery, John Lee Beatty; costumes, Randy Barcelo; lighting, Pat Collins; sound, Tom Morse; associate director, Murray Horwitz; vocal and musical concepts, Jeffrey Gutcheon; vocal arrangements, William Elliott, Jeffrey Gutcheon; production stage manager, Scott Glenn; stage managers, Tracy Crum, Peter Lawrence; press, Bill Evans & Associates, Sandy Manley, Jim Randolph.

Ain't Misbehavin' was orginally produced on Broadway 5/9/78 for 1,604 performances and won both the Critics and Tony Awards for the best musical of its season.

CHECKMATES—Paul Winfield and Ruby Dee in the play by Ron Milner

The list of musical numbers and authors of *Ain't Misbehavin'* appears on pages 372–373 of *The Best Plays of 1977–78*. The song "This Is So Nice" (music by Fats Waller, lyrics by George Marion Jr.) was added to this production and was sung by Nell Carter.

Terri White replaced Nell Carter, Patti Austin replaced Armelia McQueen, Ken Prymus replaced Ken Page, Jackie Lowe replaced Charlaine Woodard 12/20/88.

Paul Robeson (11). Revival of the play by Phillip Hayes Dean. Produced by Eric Krebs in association with South Street Theater at the John Golden Theater. Opened September 28, 1988. (Closed October 9, 1988)

Paul Robeson...................................Avery Brooks   Lawrence Brown..................................Ernie Scott
Paul Robeson
(Wed. & Sat. matinees)................... Herb Downer

Directed by Harold Scott; musical direction, Ernie Scott; scenery and costumes, Michael Massee; lighting, Shirley Prendergast; original choreography, Dianne McIntyre; special arrangements and orchestration, Eva C. Brooks; stage manager, Doug Hosney; press, Shirley Herz Associates, David Roggensack.

This account of Robeson's life, with piano accompaniment for the singing, was first produced on Broadway 1/19/78 for 77 performances. The present revival was tranferred from South Street Theater after previous production at Crossroads Theater, New Brunswick, N.J. and Peterborough, N.H. Players. The play was presented in two parts.

The list of scenes and multiple characters appears on pages 361–362 of *The Best Plays of 1977–78*.

Michael Feinstein in Concert: Isn't It Romantic (38). Return engagement of the one-man performance by Michael Feinstein; conceived by Michael Feinstein and Christopher

Chadman. Produced by Ron Delsener and Jonathan Scharer at the Booth Theater. Opened October 5, 1988. (Closed November 6, 1988)

Musicians: Joel Silberman pianist, conductor; David Finck bass; Ian Finkel xylophone; Dave Ratajczak drums; John Basile guitar; Ralph Olsen woodwinds.

Production staged and supervised by Christopher Chadman; musical direction, Joel Silberman; scenery, Andrew Jackness; lighting, Beverly Emmons; sound, Daryl Bornstein; orchestration, Ian Finkel; special material, Bruce Vilanch; additional orchestrations, Joseph Gianono, Larry Hochman, Pete Levin, Johnny Mandel, John Oddo; special arrangements, Stan Freeman, Joel Silberman; production stage manager, Kenneth Cox; press, the Joshua Ellis Office, Adrian Bryan-Brown, Jackie Green.

This Michael Feinstein concert of piano pieces and songs, some from Broadway shows, was previously produced on Broadway 4/19/88 for 62 performances. The show was presented in two parts.

Kenny Loggins on Broadway (8). One-man performance by and with Kenny Loggins. Produced by James M. Nederlander, James L. Nederlander and Arthur Rubin at the Neil Simon Theater. Opened November 1, 1988. (Closed November 6, 1988)

Special Guest: Craig Shoemaker. Band: Steve Wood keyboards, vocals; Guy Thomas lead guitar, vocals; Tris Imboden drums; Cornelius Mims bass, vocals; Marc Russo saxophone, keyboards.

Scenery and lighting, Michael Ledesma; Back to Avalon Tour manager, Denny Jones; press, Peter Cromarty, David Gersten, Jim Baldassare.

Concert performance by the singer-composer in various styles including folk and rock.

Spoils of War (36). By Michael Weller. Produced by Ed and David Mirvish in association with the Second Stage Theater, Robyn Goodman and Carole Rothman artistic directors, at the Music Box. Opened November 10, 1988. (Closed December 10, 1988)

Martin	Christopher Collet	Penny	Marita Geraghty
Andrew	Jeffrey De Munn	Emma	Alice Playten
Elise	Kate Nelligan	Lew	Kevin O'Rourke

Standbys: Miss Nelligan—Laurie Kennedy; Messrs. De Munn, O'Rourke—Stephen Rowe; Mr. Collet—Jonathan Del Arco; Misses Geraghty, Playten—Gloria Biegler.

Directed by Austin Pendleton; scenery, Andrew Jackness; costumes, Ruth Morley; lighting, Paul Gallo; sound, Gary and Timmy Harris; production stage manager, Pamela Edington; stage manager, James Harker; press, the Joshua Ellis Office, Adrian Bryan-Brown, Susanne Tighe.

Time: The 1950s. Place: New York City. The play was presented in two parts.

The impact of his parents' divorce upon a young boy. Previously produced in Toronto and off off Broadway at the Second Stage.

Christmas Spectacular (166). Return engagement of the spectacle conceived by Robert F. Jani. Produced by Radio City Music Hall Productions, Robert F. Jani producer, at Radio City Music Hall. Opened November 11, 1988. (Closed January 4, 1989)

Narrator; Scrooge; Santa	Charles Edward Hall	Belinda	Roie Ward
Mr. Cratchit	Steven Edward Moore	Martha	Andrea-Leigh Smith
Mrs. Cratchit	Ann-Marie Blake	Coachman	Marty McDonough
Sarah Cratchit	Stacy Latham, Kara Emerson	Poultry Man	David-Michael Johnson
Tiny Tim	Alex Myers, Benjamin Mack	Mrs. Claus	Alison England
Peter Cratchit	Bradley Latham, John Zisa	Skaters	Laurie Welch, Randy Coyne

The Rockettes: Joyce Dwyer, Carol Harbich, Joan Peer Kelleher, Gerri Presky, Susan Boron, Dee Dee Knapp, Judy Little, Barbara Ann Cittadino, Phyllis Wujko, Eileen M. Collins, Pauline Achillas, Cynthia Miller, Susanne Doris, Carol Paracat, Pam Kelleher, Prudence Gray, Dottie Bell, Pam Stacy, Susan Theobald, Carol Beatty, Darlene Wendy, Lynn Sullivan, Elizabeth Chanin, Sonya Livingston, Stephanie James, Laraine Memola, Linda Riley, Phyllis Frew Ceroni, Laureen Repp, Setsuko Maruhashi, Susan Heart, Janice Cavargna, Mary Six Rupert, Katy Braff, Rosemary Noviello, Connie House-Cittadino, Mary Lee Dewitt,

Linda Deacon, Jennifer Jones, Beth Woods, Kiki Bennett, Stephanie Chase, Jereme Sheehan, Julie Branan, Eileen Woods, Maureen Stevens.

The New Yorkers: Gina Biancardi, Ann-Marie Blake, Alison England, Patrice Pickering, Laurie Stephenson, Amy Stoddard, Susan Streater, LeRoi Freeman, Malcolm Gets, Peter Gregus, David-Michael Johnson, David Koch, John Curtin-Michael, Steven Edward Moore.

Dancers: Joseph Bowerman, Richard Costa, Edward Henkel, Terry Lacy, Marty McDonough, Taylor Wicker, Travis Wright, Randy Coyne, Keith Davis, David Askler, Teresa DeRose, Andrea-Leigh Smith, Roie Ward, Laurie Welch, Laura Streets, Shelley Winters-Stein.

Elves: Bruce—Shari Weiser; Wiggle—John Edward Allen; Giggle—Michael J. Gilden; Jiggle—Scott Seidman; Squiggle—Lou Carry; Understudy—Elena Bertagnolli.

Orchestra: Joseph Church conductor; Stephen Bates associate conductor; Gilbert Bauer, Carmine Deleo, Howard Kaye, Joseph Kowalewski, Julius H. Kunstler, Nannette Levi, Samuel Marder, Holly Ovendown violin; Barbara Harrison, Andrea Andros viola; Frank Levy, Pamela Frame cello; Dean Crandall bass; Kenneth Emery flute; Gerard J. Niewood, Richard Oatts, Joseph Camilleri, Joshua Siegel, Kenneth Arzberger reeds; George Bartlett, Nancy Freimanis, French horn; Richard Raffio, Zachary Schnek, Norman Beatty trumpet; John Schnupp, David Jett, Mark Johansen trombone; John Bartlett tuba; Thomas J. Oldakowski drums; Mario DeCiutiis, Randall Max percussion; Anthony Cesarano guitar; Susanna Nason, Robert Goldstone piano; Jeanne Maier harp; Robert MacDonald, George Wesner, Robert Maidhoff organ.

Directed by Robert F. Jani; staging director, Frank Wagner; staging and choreography, Marilyn Clements, Violet Holmes, Linda Lemac; musical direction, Joseph Church; scenery, Charles Lisanby; costumes, Frank Spencer; costume coordinator, Donna Bailey; lighting, Ken Billington; creative coordinators, Donna Bailey, Phil Hettema; choral director, Sheldon Disrud; orchestrations, Elman Anderson, Robert M. Freedman, Michael Gibson, Don Harper, Arthur Harris, Bob Krogstad, Phillip J. Lang; production stage manager, Howard Kolins; stage managers, Peter Muste, Steven McCorkle, Mimi Apfel, Susan Green, Andy Feigin; press, Alyce Fischer, Drew Kerr.

The Music Hall's annual Christmas show with its famous Nativity pageant, last offered 11/13/87 for 152 performances under the title *The Magnificent Christmas Spectacular.*

SCENES: Overture, "We Wish You a Merry Christmas" (the Radio City Music Hall Orchestra). Scene 1: The Nutcracker, A Teddy Bear's Dream. Scene 2: *A Christmas Carol.* Scene 3: Christmas in New York (the New Yorkers and Company). Scene 4: Ice Skating in the Plaza. Scene 5: "The Twelve Days of Christmas." Scene 6: "They Can't Start Christmas Without Us" (Santa, Mrs. Claus, Elves). Scene 7: The Parade of the Wooden Soldiers (The Rockettes). Scene 8: Beginning of Santa's Journey. Scene 9: *The Night Before Christmas.* Scene 10: "The Christmas Song" (The New Yorkers); Scene 11: The Rockette Christmas Carousel (The Rockettes). Scene 12: The Living Nativity. Jubilant, "Joy to the World" (the Radio City Music Hall Orchestra, Company).

ORIGINAL MUSIC: "T'was the Night Before Christmas" by Tom Bahler; "They Can't Start Christmas Without Us" music by Stan Lebowsky, lyrics by Fred Tobias; "My First Real Christmas" music by Don Pippin, lyrics by Nan Mason; "Christmas in New York" by Billy Butt; "Christmas Is the Best Time of the Year" by Paul Johnson, arranged by Bob Krogstad. SPECIAL MUSICAL CREDITS: "Silent Night" arranged by Percy Faith; "The Twelve Days of Christmas" arranged by Tom Bahler and Don Dorsey; "The Christmas Song" by Mel Torme and Martin Wells, arranged by Bob Krogstad and Dick Bolks.

Circle in the Square. Schedule of two programs. **The Devil's Disciple** (113). Revival of the play by George Bernard Shaw. Opened November 13, 1988. (Closed February 19, 1989) **Ghetto** (33). By Joshua Sobol; English version by David Lan. Opened April 30, 1989. (Closed May 28, 1989) Produced by Circle in the Square Theater, Theodore Mann artistic director, Paul Libin producing director, at Circle in the Square Theater.

THE DEVIL'S DISCIPLE

Mrs. Dudgeon	Rosemary Murphy	Titus Dudgeon; Officer	Russell Leib
Essie	Marguerite Kelly	Mrs. Titus Dudgeon	Chandra Lee
Christy	Adam LeFevre	Richard Dudgeon	Victor Garber
Anthony Anderson	Remak Ramsay	Sergeant	Paul Ukena Jr.
Judith Anderson	Roxanne Hart	Maj. Swindon	Bill Moor
Lawyer Hawkins	Richard Clarke	Gen. Burgoyne	Philip Bosco

William Dudgeon; Officer; Burdenell......David Cryer

Mrs. William Dudgeon..................Carol Goodheart

Soldiers ....J. Grant Albrecht, Robert Emmet

Townspeople ....Connie Roderick, Tom Sminkey

Understudies: Mr. Garber—Robert Emmet; Mr. Bosco—Richard Clarke; Mr. Ramsay—David Cryer; Miss Murphy—Carol Goodheart; Messrs. Clarke, Moor—Russell Leib: Misses Hart, Kelly—Chandra Lee; Messrs. Cryer, Leib—Tom Sminkey; Messrs. Ukena, LeFevre—J. Grant Albrecht; Misses Goodheart, Lee—Connie Roderick.

Directed by Stephen Porter; scenery and costumes, Zack Brown; lighting, Curt Osterman; production stage manager, William Hare; stage manager, Bill Braden; press, Merle Debuskey, Leo Stern.

Time: 1777. Place: Websterbridge, New Hampshire. Act I, Scene 1: The Dudgeon house. Scene 2: Pastor Anderson's house. Act II: British headquarters.

The last major New York revival of *The Devil's Disciple* was by The BAM Theater Company 2/8/78 for 15 performances.

Philip Casnoff replaced Victor Garber 12/20/88; Lee Richardson replaced Philip Bosco 1/3/89; John Cunningham replaced Remak Ramsay 1/17/89.

GHETTO

Srulik ....Avner Eisenberg	Ooma; Dr. Weiner ....Alma Cuervo
Kittel ....Stephen McHattie	Rich Man..............................Richard M. Davidson
Hayyah....................................Helen Schneider	Judge....................................... David Rosenbaum
Dummy.............................Gordon Joseph Weiss	Luba ....Andrea Clark Libin
Gens...George Hearn	Yankel...Jon Rothstein
Hassid; Dr. Gottlieb.............................Jerry Matz	Yitzak Geivish.........................Matthew P. Mutrie
Weiskopf.....................................Donal Donnelly	Elia Geivish .... Jonathan Mann
Kruk..Jarlath Conroy	Dessler .... William Verderber
Haiken ....Marshall Coid	Averbuch ....Ahvi Spindell
Reed Player....................................David Hopkins	Levas ....Angelo Ragonesi
Guitar Player...............................Barry Mitterhoff	Woman..............................Julie Anne Eigenberg
Accordion Player........................William Swindler	German Soldiers.........Brian Maffitt, Spike McClure
Miriam..Julie Goell	

Directed by Gedalia Besser; scenery, Adrian Vaux; costumes, Edna Sobol; lighting, Kevin Rigdon; English lyrics, Jeremy Sams; musical direction and arrangements, William Schimmel; movement, Nir Ben Gal, Liat Dor; fight staging, B. H. Barry; production stage manager, William Hare.

True story of a theater troupe operating in the Nazi-occupied Jewish ghetto in Vilna, Lithuania in 1942 and 1943. A foreign (Israeli) play originally produced in Haifa in Hebrew in 1984, in West Germany in 1985 and later in American regional theater. This new English version was produced simultaneously in London at the National Theater, opening April 27.

*Rumors (256). By Neil Simon. Produced by Emanuel Azenberg at the Broadhurst Theater. Opened November 17, 1988.

Chris Gorman............................Christine Baranski	Ernie Cusack .... Andre Gregory
Ken Gorman.....................................Mark Nelson	Glenn Cooper .... Ken Howard
Claire Ganz.....................................Jessica Walter	Cassie Cooper.....................................Lisa Banes
Lenny Ganz.....................................Ron Leibman	Welch......................................Charles Brown
Cookie Cusack ....Joyce Van Patten	Pudney .... Cynthia Darlow

Standbys: Misses Baranski, Banes, Darlow—Kandis Chappell; Messrs. Nelson, Leibman, Brown—Gibby Brand; Misses Walter, Van Patten—Cynthia Darlow; Messrs. Gregory, Howard—Timothy Landfield.

Directed by Gene Saks; scenery, Tony Straiges; costumes, Joseph G. Aulisi; lighting, Tharon Musser; sound, Tom Morse; production stage manager, Peter Lawrence; stage manager, John Brigleb; press, Bill Evans & Associates, Sandy Manley, Jim Randolph.

Place: A house in Sneden's Landing, N.Y. Act I: An evening in June. Act II: A half-hour later.

Intricate pattern of farcical cover-ups among eight guests at an anniversary party at which the host has just made an unsuccessful attempt at suicide. Previously produced at the Old Globe Theater, San Diego.

Larry Linville replaced Ken Howard 12/26/88.

OUR TOWN—The cemetery scene in the Lincoln Center revival

Our Town (135). Revival of the play by Thornton Wilder. Produced by Lincoln Center Theater, Gregory Mosher director, Bernard Gersten executive producer, at the Lyceum Theater. Opened December 4, 1988. (Closed April 2, 1989)

Stage Manager	Spalding Gray	Man in Auditorium;	
Dr. Gibbs	James Rebhorn	Baseball Player	Steven Goldstein
Joe Crowell	Joey Shea	Lady in Box	Katharine Houghton
Howie Newsome	W. H. Macy	Simon Stimson	Jeff Weiss
Mrs. Gibbs	Frances Conroy	Mrs. Newsome	Mary McCann
Mrs. Webb	Roberta Maxwell	Mrs. Soames	Marcell Rosenblatt
George Gibbs	Eric Stoltz	Constable Warren	Tom Brennan
Rebecca Gibbs	Lydia Kelly	Si Crowell	Christopher Cunningham Jr.
Wally Webb	Shane Culkin	Baseball Players	Todd Weeks, Jordan Lage
Emily Webb	Penelope Ann Miller	Sam Craig	Roderick McLachlan
Prof. Willard	Bill Alton	Joe Stoddard	William Preston
Mr. Webb	Peter Maloney	Farmer McCarty	Patrick Tovatt
Woman in Balcony	Marilyn Hamlin	Mr. Greenough	Michael Barrett

Understudies: Mr. Preston—Bill Alton; Mr. Shea—Christopher Cunningham Jr.; Mr. Macy—Steven Goldstein; Messrs. Rebhorn, Alton, Maloney, Brennan—John Griesemer; Miss Conroy—Marilyn Hamlin; Misses Maxwell, Rosenblatt—Katharine Houghton; Messrs. Goldstein, McLachlan, Tovatt—Jordan Lage; Misses Miller, Hamlin, Houghton—Mary McCann; Mr. Weiss—Roderick McLachlan; Messrs. Culkin, Cunningham—Joey Shea; Mr. Gray—Patrick Tovatt; Miss Kelly—Amanda Weeden; Mr. Stoltz—Todd Weeks.

Directed by Gregory Mosher; scenery, Douglas Stein; costumes, Jane Greenwood; lighting, Kevin Rigdon; musical direction, Michael Barrett; production stage manager, Michael F. Ritchie; stage manager, Gary Natoli; press, Merle Debuskey, William Schelble.

Place: Grover's Corners, New Hampshire. The play was presented in three parts.

The last major New York revival of *Our Town* was the ANTA production on Broadway 11/27/69 for 36 performances.

Helen Hunt replaced Penelope Ann Miller 2/21/89; Don Ameche replaced Spalding Gray and Jason Gedrick replaced Eric Stoltz 3/21/89.

Legs Diamond (64). Musical based on the motion picture *The Rise and Fall of Legs Diamond*; book by Harvey Fierstein and Charles Suppon; music and lyrics by Peter Allen. Produced by James M. and James L. Nederlander, Arthur Rubin, The Entertainment Group and George M. Steinbrenner III in association with Jonathan Farkas and Marvin A. Krauss executive producer at the Mark Hellinger Theater. Opened December 26, 1988. (Closed February 19, 1989)

Jack Diamond	Peter Allen
Prison Guards	Stephen Bourneuf, Rick Manning
Madge	Brenda Braxton
Cigarette Girl	Deanna Dys
Bones	Christian Kauffmann
Augie	Raymond Serra
Kiki Roberts	Randall Edwards
Devane	Pat McNamara
Hotsy Totsy Announcer	Mike O'Carroll
Flo	Julie Wilson
Moran	Jim Fyfe
Arnold Rothstein	Joe Silver
Tropicabana Announcer	James Brandt
Champagne Girls	Carol Ann Baxter, Gwendolyn Miller
Showgirls	Colleen Dunn, Wendy Waring
Mourner	Ruth Gottschall
Burlesque Women	Gwendolyn Miller, Wendy Waring
Barber	Mike O'Carroll
Chinese Waiter	Norman Wendall Kauahi
Policeman	Paul Nunes
Jack Diamond's Secretary	Shelley Wald
F.B.I. Men	James Brandt, Rick Manning

Convicts: Adrian Bailey, Quin Baird, Frank Cava, Norman Wendall Kauahi, Bobby Moya, Paul Nunes, Keith Tyrone. Hotsy Totsy Girls: Carol Ann Baxter, Colleen Dunn, Deanna Dys, Gwendolyn Miller, Wendy Waring. Tuxedo Dancers: Stephen Bourneuf, Jonathan Cerullo, K. Craig Innes, Kevin Weldon. Latin Dancers: Adrian Bailey, Frank Cava, Norman Wendall Kauahi, Bobby Moya, Paul Nunes, Keith Tyrone. Gangsters: Quin Baird, Stephen Bourneuf, James Brandt, Jonathan Cerullo, Rick Manning, Bobby Moya, Paul Nunes, Mike O'Carroll. Taxi Dancers: Frank Cava, K. Craig Innes, Bobby Moya. Boys From Bay Ridge: Adrian Bailey, Rick Manning, Bobby Moya. A.R.'s Gang: Adrian Bailey, Quin Baird, Jonathan Cerullo, Rick Manning, Bobby Moya. Jack's Gang: Stephen Bourneuf, Frank Cava, K. Craig Innes, Norman Wendall Kauahi, Paul Nunes, Keith Tyrone.

Orchestra: James Sedlar 1st trumpet; James Hynes, Phil Granger trumpet; Porter Poindexter, James Miller trombone; Russ Rizner, French horn; John Purcell, Charles Millard clarinet; Lou Cortelezzi flute; Peter Angelo oboe; Joseph Grimaldi baritone saxophone; Ronald Melrose, Tim Stella synthesizer; Mark Berger bass; Larry Saltzman guitar; Glenn Rhian, Bruce Doctor drums; Bernard Zeller concert master; Kathy Livolsi, Al Cavaliere, Frank Wang violin; Susan Follari, Richard Spencer viola; Bruce Want, Marisol Espada cello.

Swings: Dan O'Grady, Jennifer Rymer, Steven Scionti. Understudies: Miss Wilson—Ruth Gottschall; Miss Edwards—Colleen Dunn; Messrs. Silver, McNamara—Mike O'Carroll; Mr. Kauffmann—Adrian Bailey; Mr. Fyfe—Frank Cava.

Directed by Robert Allan Ackerman; musical numbers choreographed by Alan Johnson; musical direction and vocal arrangements, Eric Stern; scenery, David Mitchell; costumes, Willa Kim; lighting, Jules Fisher; sound, Peter J. Fitzgerald; black art effects consultant, Ted Shapiro; orchestrations, Michael Starobin; dance music arrangements, Mark Hummel; production stage manager, Peter B. Mumford; stage manager, Gary M. Zabinski; press, Shirley Herz Associates, Glenna Freedman, Pete Sanders, Sam Rudy.

Highly fictionalized portrayal of the famous gangster Legs Diamond in New York in the Prohibition era.

ACT I

Overture ... Orchestra
Scene 1: Pennsylvania State Prison
"When I Get My Name in Lights" ... Jack, Convicts, Ensemble
Scene 2: Pennsylvania Station, New York City
Scene 3: The Hotsy Totsy Club and Grill
"Speakeasy" ... Ensemble
"Applause" ... Flo, Hotsy Totsy Girls
"Knockers" ... Jack, Hotsy Totsy Girls
Scene 4: The back room of the Hotsy Totsy Club
Scene 5: Hotsy Totsy Club alley
Scene 6: The stage of the Tropicabana
"I Was Made for Champagne" ... Kiki, Tropicabana Dancers

"Tropicabana Rhumba"..Jack, Kiki
Scene 7: Times Square
"Sure Thing Baby" ....Jack
Scene 8: The back room of the Hotsy Totsy Club
"Speakeasy Christmas"..Hotsy Totsy Dancers
"Charge It to A.R." ....Rothstein, Augie, Moran, Bones, Gangsters
Scene 9: Flo's office
"Only an Older Woman"..Jack, Flo
Scene 10: The Hotsy Totsy Club and Grill
"Taxi Dancer's Tango" ....Jack, Ensemble
Scene 11: Taxi Dancers' Dressing Room
Scene 12: Around New York
"Only Steal From Thieves"..Jack, Kiki, Gangsters
Scene 13: The Hotsy Totsy Club and Grill
"When I Get My Name in Lights" (Reprise)...Jack, Company

ACT II

Entr'acte.. Orchestra
Scene 1: A funeral parlor
"Cut of the Cards"..Jack, Company
Scene 2: The streets of New York
"Gangland Chase"...Jack, Gangsters
Scene 3: The Hotsy Totsy stage and the Tropicabana stage
"Now You See Me, Now You Don't" ....Jack, Kiki, Ensemble
Scene 4: The ladies' powder room of the Hotsy Totsy Club
"The Man Nobody Could Love".. Kiki, Flo, Madge
Scene 5: The back room of the Hotsy Totsy Club
Scene 6: The Hotsy Totsy stage
"The Music Went Out of My Life"...Flo
Scene 7: The Diamond Building
"Say It Isn't So" ....Jack, Company
Scene 8: The Hotsy Totsy Club and Grill
"All I Wanted Was the Dream"..Jack

Eastern Standard (92). Transfer from off Broadway of the play by Richard Greenberg. Produced by Jessica Levy in the Manhattan Theater Club production, Lynne Meadow artistic director, Barry Grove managing director, at the John Golden Theater. Opened January 5, 1989. (Closed March 25, 1989)

Stephen Wheeler ....Dylan Baker   Phoebe Kidde.............................Patricia Clarkson
Drew Paley ....Peter Frechette   Peter Kidde.....................................Kevin Conroy
Ellen...Barbara Garrick   May Logan.......................................Anne Meara

Understudies: Misses Clarkson, Garrick—Colette Kilroy; Messrs. Baker, Frechette, Conroy—Michael McKenzie.

Directed by Michael Engler; scenery, Philipp Jung; costumes, William Ivey Long; lighting, Donald Holder; sound, Jan Nebozenko; production stage manager, Pat Sosnow; stage manager, Tammy Taylor; press, David Powers, David Roggensack.

Time: Spring and summer, 1987. Act I: A restaurant, midtown Manhattan, late May. Act II, Scene 1: Stephen's summer house, a month later. Scene 2: Two weeks later. Scene 3: Two weeks later. Scene 4: The next morning. Scene 5: The next morning.

Sexual and social adventures of young achievers, as they try to rehabilitate a bag lady as part of their comedically-aimed search for the truth about their own lives and loves. Previously produced by Seattle Repertory Theater and in this production by Manhattan Theater Club off Broadway 10/27/88 for 46 performances; see its entry in the Plays Produced Off Broadway section of this volume.

A Best Play; see page 172.

*Black and Blue (144). Musical revue; musical numbers by various authors (see credits of authors of theater songs below). Produced by Mel Howard and Donald K. Donald in the Claudio Segovia-Hector Orezzoli production at the Minskoff Theater. Opened January 26, 1989.

Singers: Ruth Brown, Linda Hopkins, Carrie Smith.

Hoofers: Bunny Briggs, Ralph Brown, Lon Chaney, Jimmy Slyde, Dianne Walker.

Dancers: Rashamella Cumbo, Tanya Gibson, Germaine Goodson, Angela Hall, Kyme, Valerie Macklin, Deborah Mitchell, Valerie E. Smith, Frederick J. Boothe, Eugene Fleming, Ted Levy, Bernard Manners, Van Porter, Kevin Ramsey, Ken Roberson, Melvin Washington.

Younger Generation: Cyd Glover, Savion Glover, Dormeshia Sumbay.

Musicians: Martin Aubert guitar; Bill Easley, Haywood Henry clarinet, saxophone; Stephen Furtaldo, Virgil Jones, Emory Thompson trumpet; Roland Hanna piano; Al McKibbon bass; Leonard Oxley conductor, piano; Jerome Richardson alto saxophone; Grady Tate drums; Claude Williams violin; Britt Woodman trombone.

Standbys: Singers—Melba Joyce; Younger Generation—Tarik Winston.

Conceived and directed by Claudio Segovia and Hector Orezzoli; choreography, Cholly Atkins, Henry LeTang, Frankie Manning, Fayard Nicholas; scenery, costumes and lighting conception, Claudio Segovia, Hector Orezzoli; lighting design, Neil Peter Jampolis, Jane Reisman; musical supervision, arrangements and orchestrations, Sy Johnson; additional arrangements and orchestrations, Luther Henderson; sound, Abe Jacob; assistant choreographer, Dianne Walker; associate producer, Marilynn LeVine; production stage manager, Alan Hall; stage manager, Ruth E. Rinklin; press, P. R. Partners, Marilynn LeVine, Meg Gordean.

Celebration of American jazz and blues. A foreign show previously produced in Paris.

MUSICAL NUMBERS, ACT I: Blues ("I'm a Woman")—Linda Hopkins, Ruth Brown, Carrie Smith; Hoofers a Capella—Ralph Brown, Bernard Manners, Savion Glover, Bunny Briggs, Ted Levy, Jimmy Slyde, Lon Chaney; "Royal Garden Blues" (by Spencer and Clarence Williams)—Musicians; "St. Louis Blues"—Ruth Brown and musicians Roland Hanna, Haywood Henry, Britt Woodman, Emory Thompson, Grady Tate, Martin Aubert; "Everybody Loves My Baby" (choreography by Henry LeTang)—Dancers; "After You've Gone" (choreography by Cholly Atkins)—Hopkins, Manners, Male Dancers; "If I Can't Sell It, I'll Keep Sittin' on It" (by Andy Razaf)—Ruth Brown; "I Want a Big Butter and Egg Man" (choreography by Fayard Nicholas)—Smith, Eugene Fleming, Kevin Ramsey, Levy and musicians Hanna, Thompson.

Also "Rhythm Is Our Business" (by Sammy Cahn; choreography by Henry LeTang)—Younger Generation; "Mystery Song" (by Duke Ellington)—Tanya Gibson, Rashamella Cumbo, Valerie E. Smith; "Stompin' at the Savoy" (by Benny Goodman and Andy Razaf)—Slyde; "I've Got a Right to Sing the Blues" (by Harold Arlen and Ted Koehler)—Carrie Smith; "Black and Tan Fantasy" (by Duke Ellington; choreography by Frankie Manning)—Briggs, Dancers; "Come Sunday" (by Duke Ellington)—Hopkins; "Daybreak Express" (by Duke Ellington)—Musicians; "T'Ain't Nobody's Bizness If I Do" (by Porter Grainger)—Ruth Brown, Hopkins, Hanna; "That Rhythm Man" (by Fats Waller, Andy Razaf and Harry Brooks; choreography by Henry LeTang; arrangement and orchestration by Luther Henderson)—Dancers.

ACT II: "Swinging" to "Wednesday Night Hop" (choreography by Frankie Manning)—Dancers; "I'm Getting 'Long Alright"—Hopkins; "Memories of You" (by Eubie Blake and Andy Razaf; choreography by Cholly Atkins)—Dianne Walker, Manners, Ramsey; "Body and Soul" (by John Green, Edward Heyman, Robert Sour and Frank Eyton)—Ruth Brown; "I'm Confessing" (choreography by Cholly Atkins)—Kyme, Manners, Frederick J. Boothe, Levy, Ramsey and musicians Claude Williams, Aubert; "East St. Louis Toodle-oo" (by Duke Ellington)—Ralph Brown, Chaney; "Am I Blue"—Carrie Smith, Williams; "I Can't Give You Anything But Love" (by Jimmy McHugh and Dorothy Fields; choreography by Henry LeTang)—Angela Hall, Fleming, Dancers; "In a Sentimental Mood" (by Duke Ellington)—Briggs, Jerome Richardson; "Black and Blue" (by Andy Razaf, Fats Waller and Harry Brooks)—Ruth Brown, Hopkins, Carrie Smith, Slyde, Briggs; Finale (choreography by Henry LeTang; arrangements and orchestrations by Luther Henderson)—Younger Generation, Hoofers, Dancers.

*Born Yesterday (141). Revival of the play by Garson Kanin. Produced by Jay H. Fuchs, Columbia Artists Management, A. Joseph Tandet and the Cleveland Play House in association with Little Prince Productions, Ltd. at the 46th Street Theater. Opened January 29, 1989.

BORN YESTERDAY—Edward Asner and Madeline Kahn in a
scene from the Broadway revival of the play by Garson Kanin

Helen	Heather Ehlers	Harry Brock	Edward Asner
Paul Verrall	Daniel Hugh Kelly	Billie Dawn	Madeline Kahn
Bellhop; Bootblack	Gregory Jbara	Ed Devery	Franklin Cover
Bellhop; Barber; Waiter	Paul Hebron	Manicurist	Charlotte Booker
Eddie Brock	Joel Bernstein	Sen. Norval Hedges	John Wylie
Asst. Manager	Ron Johnston	Mrs. Hedges	Peggy Cosgrave

Standbys: Miss Kahn—Charlotte Booker; Messrs. Asner, Cover—Robert Murch; Misses Ehlers, Cosgrave, Booker—Pamela Pascoe. Understudies: Mr. Kelly—Paul Hebron; Mr. Wylie—Ron Johnston; Mr. Bernstein—Gregory Jbara.

Directed by Josephine R. Abady; supervised by John Tillinger; scenery, David Potts; costumes, Ann Roth; lighting, Jeff Davis; sound, Lia Vollack; associate producer, Martha Wilson; production stage manager, Don Walters; stage manager, Peggy Peterson; press, Jeffrey Richards Associates, Irene Gandy, Maria Somma.

Time: 1945. Place: Washington, D.C. Act I: September. Act II, Scene 1: About two months later. Scene 2: Later that night.

Born Yesterday was first produced on Broadway 2/4/46 for 1,642 performances and was named a Best Play of its season. This production, previously produced in regional theater at the Cleveland Play House and elsewhere, is its first major New York revival.

*Shirley Valentine (136). One-character play by Willy Russell; performed by Pauline Collins. Produced by The Really Useful Theater Company and Bob Swash at the Booth Theater. Opened February 16, 1989.

Standby: Miss Collins—Patricia Kilgarriff.

Directed by Simon Callow; design, Bruno Santini; lighting, Nick Chelton; production stage manager, Jeff Lee; stage manager, Michael McEowen; press, Philip Rinaldi.

Miss Collins plays Shirley Valentine, a Liverpool housewife who escapes from it all on a holiday in Greece. The play was presented in two parts. A foreign play previously produced in London.

A Best Play; see page 297.

Cafe Crown (45). Transfer from off Broadway of the revival of the play by Hy Kraft. Produced by LeFrak Entertainment, James M. Nederlander, Francine LeFrak, James L. Nederlander and Arthur Rubin in Joseph Papp's New York Shakespeare Festival production at the Brooks Atkinson Theater. Opened February 18, 1989. (Closed March 26, 1989)

Rubin	Jack Kenny	Beggar; Florist;	
Sam	Fyvush Finkel	Western Union Messenger	Sidney Armus
Jacobson	Bernie Passeltiner	Toplitz	George Guidall
Kaplan	Felix Fibich	Lester Freed	Steven Skybell
Mendel Polan	David Margulies	Norma Cole	Laura Sametz
Mrs. Perlman	Tresa Hughes	Ida Polan	Marilyn Cooper
Hymie	Bob Dishy	David Cole	Eli Wallach
Looie	Mitchell Jason	George Burton	Walter Bobbie
Walter	David Carroll	Lipsky	Carl Don
		Anna Cole	Anne Jackson

Understudies: Messrs. Margulies, Kenny, Passeltiner, Armus—Jack Aaron; Mr. Guidall—Sidney Armus; Miss Sametz—Susan Bruce; Misses Cooper, Hughes—Maggie Burke; Mr. Wallach—George Guidall; Miss Jackson—Tresa Hughes; Messrs. Carroll, Bobbie, Skybell—Jack Kenny; Messrs. Jason, Don, Fibich—Bernie Passeltiner; Messrs. Dishy, Finkel—Maurice Shrog.

Directed by Martin Charnin; scenery and costumes, Santo Loquasto; lighting, Richard Nelson; production stage manager, Thomas A. Kelly; stage manager, Lisa Buxbaum; press, Shirley Herz, Richard Kornberg.

Place: The Cafe Crown, Second Avenue and 12th Street in New York City. Act I: An autumn evening, 1940. Act II, Scene 1: Immediately after. Scene 2: Three weeks later.

This first major New York revival of *Cafe Crown* opened off Broadway at New York Shakespeare Festival 10/25/88 for 56 performances; see its entry in the Plays Produced Off Broadway section of this volume.

Hizzoner! (12). One-character play by Paul Shyre; performed by Tony Lo Bianco. Produced by Unicorn Entertainment, Inc., in association with Warner/Chappell Music, Inc. and Patricia Di Benedetto executive producer, at the Longacre Theater. Opened February 24, 1989. (Closed March 5, 1989)

Directed by John Going; scenery, Eldon Elder; costumes, Patrizia von Brandenstein; lighting, John McLain; sound, Abe Jacob; production stage manager, Michael A. Bartuccio; press, the Joshua Ellis Office, Chris Boneau.

Time: Mayor Fiorello H. LaGuardia's last day in office, 1945. Place: The office of the Mayor in City Hall, New York City. The play was presented in two parts.

Tony Lo Bianco as Mayor LaGuardia in a dramatic reminiscence of his flamboyant personality and distinguished career as mayor of New York City, 1933–1945. Previously produced in regional theater at Empire State Institute for the Performing Arts, Albany.

*Jerome Robbins' Broadway (109). Musical dance revue conceived, choreographed and directed by Jerome Robbins; music and lyrics by various authors and designs by various designers (see credits below). Produced by The Shubert Organization, Gerald Schoenfeld chairman, Bernard B. Jacobs president, Roger Berlind, Suntory International Corp., Byron Goldman and Emanuel Azenberg at the Imperial Theater. Opened February 26, 1989.

Co-director, Grover Dale; assistants to the choreographer, Cynthia Onrubia, Victor Castelli, Jerry Mitchell; musical direction, Paul Gemignani; production scenery, Robin Wagner; costume supervision, Joseph G. Aulisi; lighting, Jennifer Tipton; sound, Otts Munderloh; orchestrations, Sid Ramin, William D. Brohn; musical continuity, Scott Frankel; produced in association with Pace Theatrical Group; narrative continuity, Jason Alexander; production supervisor, Charles Blackwell; production stage manager, Beverley Randolph; stage manager, Jim Woolley; press, the Fred Nathan Company, Bert Fink.

Orchestra: Paul Gemignani conductor; Robert Chausow concert master; Dale Stuckenbruck, Ann Leathers, Martin Agee, Miohiso Takada, Carol Pool violin; Karl Bergen (principal), Sarah Adams viola; Lanny Paykin (principal), Roger Shell cello; Joseph Bongiorno bass; Les Scott, Alvin Hunt, John Moses, Richard Heckman, John Campo woodwind; Ronald Sell (principal), Richard Hagen, French horn; James Hynes (lead), Wilmer Wise (lead), Domnic Derasse, Lorraine Cohen trumpet; Jack Gale (principal), Bruce Bonvissuto, Dean Plank trombone; Michael Berkowitz drum set; Joseph Passaro percussion; Pamela Drews assistant conductor, keyboard.

A selection of dance numbers from Broadway shows for which Jerome Robbins did the choreography (and in some cases made other creative contributions, such as directing).

A Best Play; see page 377.

Kipling Houston replaced Robert La Fosse 4/22/89.

ACT I

Overture and Prologue

Overture songs: "I'm a Guy Who's Gotta Dance" (words and music by Hugh Martin) from *Look Ma, I'm Dancin'*; "Papa, Won't You Dance With Me?" (music by Jule Styne, lyrics by Sammy Cahn) from *High Button Shoes*; "Shall We Dance?" (music by Richard Rodgers, lyrics by Oscar Hammerstein II) from *The King and I*.

The Setter..Jason Alexander
Sung By..Michael Lynch, Debbie Shapiro, Company
Understudy: Mr. Alexander—Tom Robbins.

HIZZONER!—Tony Lo Bianco as Mayor Fiorello H. LaGuardia

From *On the Town* (1944): "New York, New York," "Sailors on the Town," "Ya Got Me"
        Book based on an idea by Jerome Robbins; book and lyrics by Betty Comden and Adolph Green; music by Leonard Bernstein; scenery, Oliver Smith; costumes, Alvin Colt.

Gaby	Robert La Fosse	Ozzie	Michael Kubala
Claire	Mary Ellen Stuart	Emcee	Jason Alexander
Chip	Scott Wise	Hildy	Debbie Shapiro
Dolores Dolores	Nancy Hess	1st Workman	David Lowenstein

        Sailors, Workmen, Dance Hall Hostesses, Passers-by, etc: Company.
        Dance Captains (all scenes): Susan Kikuchi, George Russell.
        Understudies: Mr. La Fosse—Christophe Caballero, Joey McKneely; Miss Shapiro—Donna Marie Elio; Mr. Kubala—Michael Scott Gregory, Michael Lynch; Miss Stuart—Nancy Hess, Faith Prince; Miss Hess—Pamela Khoury; Mr. Wise—Jack Noseworthy, Kelly Patterson; Messrs. Alexander, Lowenstein—Tom Robbins.
        Ensemble Understudies (all scenes): Richard Amaro, Jeffrey Lee Broadhurst, Mindy Cartwright, Camille de Ganon, Ramon Galindo, Gregorey Garrison, Carolyn Goor, Pamela Khoury, Greta Martin, Ellen Troy.

From *Billion Dollar Baby* (1945): "Charleston"
        Book and lyrics by Betty Comden and Adolph Green; music by Morton Gould; scenery, Oliver Smith; costumes, Irene Sharaff.

Cop	David Lowenstein	Collegiates	Elaine Wright, Angelo H. Fraboni
Doorman	Michael Lynch	Younger Generation	Christophe Caballero, Linda Talcott
Flappers	Barbara Yeager, Mary Ann Lamb, JoAnn M. Hunter	Older Generation	Barbara Hoon, Scott Fowler
Socialites	Jane Lanier, Nicholas Garr	Gangsters	Michael Scott Gregory, Scott Jovovich
Timid Girl	Susann Fletcher		
Good Time Charlie	Troy Myers	Bootleggers	Andrew Grose, Julio Monge

From *A Funny Thing Happened on the Way to the Forum* (1962): "Comedy Tonight"
        Book by Burt Shevelove and Larry Gelbart; music and lyrics by Stephen Sondheim; "Comedy Tonight" staged by Jerome Robbins; scenery and costumes, Tony Walton; dance music arrangement, Betty Walberg.

Pseudolus	Jason Alexander	2d Protean	Joey McKneely
1st Protean	Scott Wise	3d Protean	Michael Kubala

        Company: Charlotte d'Amboise, Dorothy Benham, Susann Fletcher, Michael Scott Gregory, Andrew Grose, Robert La Fosse, Mary Ann Lamb, David Lowenstein, Michael Lynch, Jack Noseworthy, Kelly Patterson, Luis Perez, Tom Robbins, Greg Schanuel, Debbie Shapiro.
        Understudies: Mr. Kubala—Michael Scott Gregory, David Lowenstein; Mr. Wise—Andrew Grose, Michael Lynch; Mr. McKneely—Jack Noseworthy, Kelly Patterson; Mr. Alexander—Tom Robbins.

From *High Button Shoes* (1947): "I Still Get Jealous"
        Book by Stephen Longstreet; music by Jule Styne; lyrics by Sammy Cahn; scenery, Oliver Smith; costumes, Miles White.

Ma	Faith Prince
Pa	Jason Alexander

        Understudies: Miss Prince—Nancy Hess, Mary Ellen Stuart; Mr. Alexander—Michael Kubala, Tom Robbins.

From *West Side Story* (1957): Suite of Dances
        Based on a conception of Jerome Robbins; book by Arthur Laurents; music by Leonard Bernstein; lyrics by Stephen Sondheim; scenery, Oliver Smith; costumes, Irene Sharaff; co-choreographer, Peter Gennaro; directed and choreographed by Jerome Robbins.

Tony	Robert La Fosse	Anita	Charlotte d'Amboise
Maria	Alexia Hess	Rosalia	Debbie Shapiro
Riff	Scott Wise	Graziella	Donna Di Meo
Bernardo	Nicholas Garr	"Somewhere" Soloist	Dorothy Benham

        The Jets: Joey McKneely (1st Jet), Christophe Caballero, Scott Fowler, Angelo H. Fraboni, Michael Scott Gregory, Andrew Grose, Eric A. Hoisington, Troy Myers.
        Jet Girls: Louise Hickey, Barbara Hoon, Mary Ann Lamb, Maria Neenan, Mary Ellen Stuart, Linda Talcott, Leslie Trayer, Alice Yearsley.

The Sharks: Jamie Cohen, Mark Esposito, Scott Jovovich, David Lowenstein, Michael Lynch, Julio Monge, Steve Ochoa, James Rivers.

Shark Girls: Irene Cho, Donna Marie Elio, Nancy Hess, JoAnn M. Hunter, Renee Stork, Andi Tyler, Elaine Wright, Barbara Yeager.

Understudies: Mr. McKneely—Jeffrey Lee Broadhurst, Christophe Caballero, Andrew Grose; Miss Di Meo—Camille de Ganon; Miss Shapiro—Donna Marie Elio; Mr. La Fosse—Scott Fowler, Angelo H. Fraboni; Mr. Wise—Andrew Grose, Kelly Patterson; Miss Hess—JoAnn M. Hunter, Ellen Troy; Miss Benham—Pamela Khoury; Miss d'Amboise—Barbara Yeager.

From *The King and I* (1951): "The Small House of Uncle Thomas"

Book and lyrics by Oscar Hammerstein II: music by Richard Rodgers: based on the novel *Anna and the King of Siam* by Margaret Landon; scenery, Jo Mielziner; costumes, Irene Sharaff; dance music arrangements, Trude Rittman.

Narrator	Barbara Yeager	Topsy	JoAnn M. Hunter
Eliza	Susan Kikuchi	Uncle Thomas	Barbara Hoon
King Simon	Joey McKneely	Angel; George	Irene Cho
Little Eva	Linda Talcott		

Royal Dancers: Christophe Caballero, Donna Di Meo, Mark Esposito, Eric A. Hoisington, Maria Neenan, Steve Ochoa, Renee Stork, Andi Tyler, Elaine Wright, Alice Yearsley.

Royal Singers: Dorothy Benham, Donna Marie Elio, Leslie Trayer, Nancy Hess, Louise Hickey, Mary Ellen Stuart.

Propmen: Jamie Cohen, Angelo H. Fraboni, Scott Fowler, Nicholas Garr, Scott Jovovich, James Rivera.

Understudies: Misses Talcott, Hoon, Cho—Mindy Cartwright; Miss Kikuchi—Irene Cho, JoAnn M. Hunter, Ellen Troy; Miss Hunter—Mindy Cartwright, Donna Di Meo, Greta Martin; Mr. McKneely, Miss Hoon—Ramon Galindo; Miss Yeager—Jane Lanier; Miss Cho—Ellen Troy.

From *Gypsy* (1959): "You Gotta Have a Gimmick"

Book by Arthur Laurents; music by Jule Styne; lyrics by Stephen Sondheim; suggested by the memoirs of Gypsy Rose Lee; scenery, Jo Mielziner; costumes, Raoul Pene du Bois.

Cigar	Jason Alexander	Mazeppa	Debbie Shapiro
Louise	Mary Ann Lamb	Electra	Susann Fletcher
Tessie	Faith Prince		

Understudies: Misses Shapiro, Fletcher—Donna Marie Elio; Miss Prince—Nancy Hess; Misses Prince, Shapiro—Pamela Khoury; Miss Lamb—Maria Neenan, Ellen Troy; Mr. Alexander—Tom Robbins; Miss Fletcher—Mary Ellen Stuart.

From *Peter Pan* (1954): "I'm Flying"

Book by James M. Barrie; music by Moose Charlap and Jule Styne; lyrics by Carolyn Leigh, Betty Comden and Adolph Green; new scenery by Robin Wagner; new costumes by Joseph G. Aulisi; flying by Foy.

Peter Pan	Charlotte d'Amboise	Michael	Linda Talcott
Wendy	Donna Di Meo	John	Steve Ochoa

Understudies: Miss d'Amboise, Mr. Ochoa—Jack Noseworthy; Miss Di Meo—Ellen Troy, Andi Tyler; Miss Talcott—Mindy Cartwright, Barbara Hoon.

From *High Button Shoes* (1947): "On a Sunday by the Sea"

Ballet music by Jule Styne; inspired by Mack Sennett comedies.

Floy	Jason Alexander	Uncle Willy	Michael Kubala
Pontdue	Troy Myers	Chief of Police	Michael Scott Gregory
Ma	Faith Prince	Life Guard	Tom Robbins
Fran	Barbara Yeager		

Cops: Mark Esposito, Angelo H. Fraboni, Andrew Grose, Eric A. Hoisington, Julio Monge, Greg Schanuel.

Bathing Beauties: Louise Hickey, Donna Di Meo, Susann Fletcher, JoAnn M. Hunter, Debbie Shapiro, Renee Stork, Leslie Trayer, Elaine Wright.

Twins: Alexia Hess and Maria Neenan; Scott Fowler and Scott Jovovich.

Crooks: Scott Wise, Nancy Hess, Linda Talcott.

Singers: Dorothy Benham, Christophe Caballero, Donna Marie Elio, Nicholas Garr, Barbara Hoon, David Lowenstein, Michael Lynch, Jack Noseworthy, Kelly Patterson, James Rivera, Mary Ellen Stuart, Leslie Trayer, Andi Tyler, Alice Yearsley.

Understudies: Mr. Gregory—Richard Amaro, Jeffrey Lee Broadhurst, Joey McKneely; Mr. Kubala—Jeffrey Lee Broadhurst, Gregorey Garrison; Twins—Carolyn Goor, Ellen Troy, Camille de Ganon; Mr. Robbins—Greg Schanuel; Mr. Alexander—Tom Robbins.

From *Miss Liberty* (1949), *Call Me Madam* (1950): "Mr. Monotony"

Music and lyrics by Irving Berlin; new costumes, Joseph G. Aulisi; dance music arrangement, Genevieve Pitot.

Singer	Debbie Shapiro	2d Dancer	Jane Lanier
1st Dancer	Luis Perez	3d Dancer	Robert La Fosse

Understudies: Miss Lanier—Charlotte d'Amboise, Camille de Ganon; Miss Shapiro—Donna Marie Elio; Mr. La Fosse—Scott Fowler, Kelly Patterson, Scott Jovovich; Mr. Perez—Angelo H. Fraboni.

From *Fiddler on the Roof* (1964)

Book by Joseph Stein; music by Jerry Bock; lyrics by Sheldon Harnick; based on Sholom Aleichem's stories by special arrangement of Arnold Perl; scenery, Boris Aronson; costumes, Patricia Zipprodt; dance music arrangement, Betty Walberg.

Tevye	Jason Alexander	Fruma-Sarah	Nancy Hess
Golde	Susann Fletcher	Lazar Wolf	Tom Robbins
Motel Kamzoil	Michael Lynch	Rabbi	Troy Myers
Tzeitel	Andi Tyler	Fiddler	Joey McKneely
Grandma Tzeitel	Barbara Hoon		

Bottle dancers: Christophe Caballero, Mark Esposito, Scott Jovovich, Greg Schanuel. Villagers, Wedding Guests: Company.

Understudies: Mr. Myers—Ramon Galindo; Mr. McKneely—Michael Scott Gregory; Mr. Lynch—Eric A. Hoisington; Mr. Robbins—Michael Kubala, David Lowenstein; Miss Fletcher—Pamela Khoury; Miss Hess—Pamela Khoury, Mary Ellen Stuart; Miss Tyler—Maria Neenan, Leslie Trayer; Miss Hoon—Jack Noseworthy, Linda Talcott; Mr. Alexander—Tom Robbins.

Finale from *On the Town* (1944) "Some Other Time," "New York, New York" (Reprise)

Setting for Broadway at Night, Robin Wagner.

Gaby	Robert La Fosse	Hildy	Debbie Shapiro
Chip	Scott Wise	Claire	Mary Ellen Stuart
Ozzie	Michael Kubala	Ivy	Alexia Hess

Three Sailors: Christophe Caballero, Kelly Patterson, Michael Scott Gregory; with the full company. Understudy: Miss Hess—Camille de Ganon.

*Lend Me a Tenor (104). By Ken Ludwig. Produced by Martin Starger and the Really Useful Theater Company, Inc. at the Royale Theater. Opened March 2, 1989.

Maggie	J. Smith-Cameron	Bellhop	Jeff Brooks
Max	Victor Garber	Diana	Caroline Lagerfelt
Saunders	Philip Bosco	Julia	Jane Connell
Tito Merelli	Ron Holgate	Radio Announcer	David Cryer
Maria	Tovah Feldshuh		

Standby: Messrs. Holgate, Bosco—David Cryer. Understudies: Messrs. Garber, Brooks—Michael Waldron. Misses Feldshuh, Connell—Jane Cronin; Misses Lagerfelt, Smith-Cameron—Eileen Dunn.

Directed by Jerry Zaks; scenery, Tony Walton; costumes, William Ivey Long; lighting, Paul Gallo; sound, Aural Fixation; music coordinator, Edward Strauss; production stage manager, Steven Beckler; stage manager, Clifford Schwartz; press, the Joshua Ellis Office, Adrian Bryan-Brown.

Time: 1934. Place: A hotel suite in Cleveland, Ohio. Act I, Scene 1: Early afternoon on a Saturday in September. Scene 2: Four hours later. Act II, Scene 1: That night, about 11 o'clock. Scene 2: Fifteen minutes later.

Comedy, crisis in an opera company when the star tenor cannot fulfill an engagement. An American play, previously produced in London and Paris (after a tryout at the American Stage Festival, Milford, N.H. 8/1/85), in its U.S. debut.

A Best Play; see page 327.

METAMORPHOSIS—Laura Esterman, Madeleine Potter, Mikhail Baryshnikov, Rene Auberjonois and Mitch Kreindel in Steven Berkoff's adaptation of Kafka

*Metamorphosis (72). By Steven Berkoff; adapted from a story by Franz Kafka. Produced by Lars Schmidt and Roger L. Stevens at the Ethel Barrymore Theater. Opened March 6, 1989. Recessed May 8, 1989 (scheduled to reopen June 11, 1989).

Gregor	Mikhail Baryshnikov	Greta	Madeleine Potter
Mr. Samsa	Rene Auberjonois	Chief Clerk	Mitch Kreindel
Mrs. Samsa	Laura Esterman	Lodger	T. J. Meyers

Understudies: Misses Potter, Esterman—Joanna Peled; Messrs. Auberjonois, Kreindel—T. J. Meyers; Mr. Meyers—Mitch Kreindel.

Directed by Steven Berkoff; musical direction and music performed by Larry Spivak; scenery, Duke Durfee; costumes, Jacques Schmidt; costume supervisor, Susan O'Donnell; lighting, Brian Nason; production stage manager, Patrick Horgan; stage manager, Brian Meister; press, David Powers.

Typical Kafka victim of bourgeois society (played by ballet star Baryshnikov in his dramatic acting debut) is transformed into a beetle. The play was presented without intermission. Previously produced in London and elsewhere.

Run for Your Wife! (52). By Ray Cooney. Produced by Don Taffner, Paul Elliott and Strada Entertainment Trust in the Theater of Comedy production at the Virginia Theater. Opened March 7, 1989. (Closed April 9, 1989)

John Smith	Ray Cooney	Bobby Franklyn	Gavin Reed
Detective Sgt. Troughton	Gareth Hunt	Reporter	Doug Stender
Barbara Smith	Hilary Labow	Mary Smith	Kay Walbye
Detective Sgt. Porterhouse	Dennis Ramsden	Stanley Gardner	Paxton Whitehead

Understudies: Messrs. Cooney, Ramsden, Reed—Doug Stender; Messrs. Whitehead, Hunt, Stender—Ian Stuart; Misses Labow, Walbye—Alexandra O'Karma.

Directed by Ray Cooney; scenery supervision, Michael Anania; costumes, Joseph G. Aulisi; lighting, Marilyn Rennagel; production stage manager, Amy Pell; stage manager, Travis Decastro; press, Jeffrey Richards Associates, Maria Somma.

Time: The present. Place: The Wimbledon flat of John and Mary Smith and, simultaneously, the Streatham flat of John and Barbara Smith. Act I: One sunny summer morning. Act II: Immediately following.

Happily married man with two households and two wives unaware of each other's existence. A foreign play previously produced in London and in U.S. regional theater.

*The Heidi Chronicles (96). Transfer from off Broadway of the play by Wendy Wasserstein. Produced by The Shubert Organization, Suntory International Corp. and James Walsh in association with Playwrights Horizons at the Plymouth Theater. Opened March 9, 1989.

Heidi Holland ....Joan Allen	Scoop Rosenbaum ....Peter Friedman
Susan Johnston..................................Ellen Parker	Jill; Debbie; Lisa................................Anne Lange
Chris Boxer; Mark; TV Attendant;	Fran; Molly; Betsy; April ....Joanne Camp
Waiter; Ray.................................. Drew McVety	Becky; Clara; Denise.......................Cynthia Nixon
Peter Patrone.................................... Boyd Gaines	

Understudies: Misses Allen, Parker—Laura Hicks; Misses Lange, Camp, Nixon—Amanda Carlin; Messrs. McVety, Gaines, Friedman—Stephen Stout.

Directed by Daniel Sullivan; scenery, Thomas Lynch; costumes, Jennifer von Mayrhauser; lighting, Pat Collins; sound, Scott Lehrer; projection design, Wendall Harrington; production stage manager, Roy Harris; stage manager, Mary Fran Loftus; press, the Fred Nathan Company, Marc P. Thibodeau.

Act I, Prologue: A lecture hall, New York, 1989. Scene 1: Chicago, 1965. Scene 2: Manchester, N.H., 1968. Scene 3: Ann Arbor, Mich., 1970. Scene 4: Chicago, 1974. Scene 5: New York, 1977. Act II (all scenes take place in New York), Prologue: A lecture hall, 1989. Scene 1: An apartment, 1980. Scene 2: A TV studio, 1982. Scene 3: A restaurant, 1984. Scene 4: The Plaza Hotel, 1986. Scene 5: A pediatrics ward, 1987. Scene 6: An apartment, 1989.

Comedy about a feminist and her friends and the divergence of individual attitudes and lives in this movement from 1965 to the present. Produced off Broadway at Playwrights Horizons 12/11/88 for 81 performances; see its entry in the Plays Produced Off Broadway section of this volume.

A Best Play; see page 257.

Chu Chem (44). Musical with book by Ted Allen; music by Mitch Leigh; lyrics by Jim Haines and Jack Wohl. Produced by The Mitch Leigh Company and William D. Rollnick at the Ritz Theater. Opened March 17, 1989. (Closed May 14, 1989)

The Oriental Company:

Prince..Kevin Gray	Shu-Wo; Propman; Villager..............Kenji Nakao
Elder ....Alvin Lum	Ho-Ke; Propman; Villager....................Jason Ma
Hong Ho....................................Chev Rodgers	Nu-Wo; Propman; Villager............Paul Nakauchi
Prince's Brother...........................Hechter Ubarry	Chueh-Wu; Propman; Guard ....Nephi Jay Wimmer
Daf-ah-Dil; Concubine; Villager............Zoie Lam	*The Westerners:*
Prompter..Timm Fujii	Chu Chem.....................................Mark Zeller
Na Mi; Concubine; Villager ....Simone Gee	Lotte ....Emily Zacharias
Lei-An; Concubine; Villager........... Keelee Sectoo	Yakob..Irving Burton

The Chu Chem Band: Don Jones keyboard 1; Brett Alan Sommer assistant musical director, Keyboard 2; Bill Meade wind synthesizer; Ray Kilday electric bass; Kevin Kuhn guitar synthesizer.

Standbys: Messrs. Zeller, Burton, Rodgers—Michael Ingram; Miss Zacharias—Mary Munger. Understudies: Messrs. Gray, Ubarry—Paul Nakauchi; Alvin Lum—Nephi Jay Wimmer; Mr. Fujii—Jason Ma; Miss Lam—Simone Gee; Misses Gee, Seetoo—Christine Toy; Messrs. Nakao, Ma, Nakauchi, Wimmer—David Stoll.

Directed by Albert Marre; musical and vocal direction, Don James; scenery, Robert Mitchell; costumes, Kenneth M. Yount; lighting, Jason Sturm; sound, Gary M. Stocker; orchestrations, Michael Gibson; production stage manager, Geraldine Teagarden; stage manager, Larry Smith; press, Shirley Herz Associates, Pete Sanders.

Time: Some 600 years ago. Place: China.

14th century Jews searching for a tribe of Israel which settled there 200 years before. Previously produced off off Broadway at Jewish Repertory Theater and in a 1966 version in Philadelphia.

ACT I

"Orient Yourself" ....Oriental Company
"What Happened, What?" .... Chu Chem, Yakob
"Welcome" ....Villagers
"You'll Have to Change" ....Lotte
"Love Is" ....Prince
"I'll Talk to Her" .... Chu Chem, Prince, Prince's Brother
"Shame on You" ....Chu Chem, Prince, Concubines
"It Must Be Good for Me" ....Lotte
"I'll Talk to Her" (Reprise) ....Chu Chem, Prince
"You'll Have to Change" (Reprise) ....Prince
"The River" .... Lotte, Prince, Propmen
"We Dwell in Our Hearts" ....Chu Chem, Lotte, Prince

ACT II

"Re-Orient Yourself" ....Oriental Company
"What Happened, What?" (Reprise) ....Yakob
"I Once Believed" ....Lotte
"It's Possible" ....Chu Chem
"Our Kind of War" ....Company
"Boom!" ....Hong Ho
Finale ....Company

The Wizard of Oz (39). Musical adapted by Michel M. Grilikhes. Produced by M. M. G. Arena Productions at Radio City Music Hall. Opened March 22, 1989. (Closed April 9, 1989)

Dorothy	Grace Greig	Hunk; Scarecrow	Joe McDonough
Aunt Em; Glinda	Linda Johnson	Hickory; Tin Woodsman	Joe Giuffre
Uncle Henry	John Sovec	Miss Gulch; Wicked Witch	Polly Seale
Zeke; Cowardly Lion	Guy Allen	Prof. Marvel; Wizard; Gate Keeper	Bart Williams

Directed and produced by Michel M. Grilikhes; choreography, Onna White; original music, Harold Arlen; original lyrics, E. Y. Harburg; original incidental music, Herbert Stothart; art direction, Jeremy Railton; scenery, Stephen Ehlers; costumes, Bill Campbell; dimensional sound, John Neal; music supervisor, Tom Worrall; associate choreographer, Jim Taylor; dance arrangements, Jackie Shaw O'Neill.

Musical spectacle aimed at arena presentation, based on the L. Frank Baum stories, acted out by the cast to pre-recorded dialogue and music, the latter excerpted from the 1939 motion picture.

Welcome to the Club (12). Musical with book by A. E. Hotchner; music by Cy Coleman; lyrics by Cy Coleman and A. E. Hotchner. Produced by Cy Coleman, A. E. Hotchner, William H. Kessler Jr. and Michael M. Weatherly in association with Raymond J. Greenwald at the Music Box. Opened April 13, 1989. (Closed April 22, 1989)

Arlene Meltzer	Marilyn Sokol	Kevin Bursteter	Scott Waara
Milton Meltzer	Avery Schreiber	Betty Bursteter	Jodi Benson
Gus Bottomly	Bill Buell	Carol Bates	Marcia Mitzman
Aaron Bates	Scott Wentworth	Eve Aiken	Terri White
Bruce Aiken	Samuel E. Wright	Winona Shook	Sharon Scruggs

Orchestra: David Pogue conductor; Donald Sosin assistant conductor; David Pogue, Donald Sosin, Lee Musiker keyboards; Ken Hitchcock reeds; Bob Rose guitar; David Finck bass; Marisol Espada, Arnold Schween cello; David Ratajczak percussion.

412 THE BEST PLAYS OF 1988–1989

Understudies: Misses White, Scruggs—Sally Mayes; Misses Sokol, Benson, Mitzman—Joanna Glushak; Messrs. Schreiber, Buell, Wright—Sal Mistretta; Messrs. Wentworth, Waara—Walter Hudson.

Directed by Peter Mark Schifter; musical numbers staged by Patricia Birch; musical direction, David Pogue; scenery, David Jenkins; costumes, William Ivey Long; lighting, Tharon Musser; sound, Otts Munderloh; orchestrations, Doug Katsaros; vocal arrangements, Cy Coleman, David Pogue; associate producer, Robert R. Larsen; production stage manager, Mary Porter Hall; stage manager, John C. McNamara; press, Jeffrey Richards Associates, Jillana Devine, Diane Judge.

Time: The present. Place: A section of a New York City jail exclusively reserved for alimony delinquents.

Comic reflections on divorce and marriage among a group jailed for non-payment of alimony. Previously produced in regional theater under the title *Let 'em Rot*.

ACT I

Overture

"A Place Called Alimony Jail"...Husbands, Wives
"Pay the Lawyer" ....Husbands
"Mrs. Meltzer Wants the Money Now!".. Arlene, Husbands
"That's a Woman"...Bates, Carol, Wives
"Piece of Cake"...Eve, Aiken
"Rio".. Meltzer, Wives, Gus
"It's Love! It's Love!" ....Gus, Husbands
"Holidays" ....Arlene
"Meyer Chickerman"..Meltzer
"The Trouble With You" .... Bates, Carol, Husbands, Wives
"Mother-in-Law"...Husbands
"At My Side" .... Aiken, Bursteter

ACT II

"Guilty" .... Winona
"Southern Comfort"... Winona, Bates, Wives, Husbands
"The Two of Us"...Aiken, Meltzer
"Miami Beach" ....Arlene, Aiken, Bursteter, Bates, Gus
"In the Name of Love" .... Carol
"Love Behind Bars"... Winona, Bates, Wives
"At My Side" (Reprise) ....Bursteter, Betty
"It Wouldn't Be You"..Husbands, Wives

*Barry Manilow at the Gershwin (36). One-man performance by Barry Manilow; conceived by Ernie Chambers, Jack Feldman, Roberta Kent, Barry Manilow and Bruce Sussman; written by Ken and Mitzie Welch, Roberta Kent and Barry Manilow. Produced by Garry C. Kief, James M. Nederlander, James L. Nederlander and Arthur Rubin at the Gershwin Theater. Opened April 18, 1989.

Directed by Kevin Carlisle; original production created and produced by Joe Gannon; musical direction, Bud Harner, Ron Pedley; design, Jeremy Railton; lighting, J. T. McDonald; stage manager, Jed DeFillipis; press, Solters/Roskin/Friedman, Keith Sherman, Susan DuBow.

Vocals: Marc Levine, John Pondel, Joe Melotti, Billy Kidd, Vanessa Brown, Dana Robbins, Debra Byrd.

Orchestra: Bud Harner drums; Ron Pedley, Joe Melotti, Billy Kidd keyboards; Marc Levine bass guitar, cello; John Pondel guitar; Vanessa Brown percussion; Dana Robbins woodwinds.

Concert-style production by and with Barry Manilow, who received a special Tony for a similar show in 1977.

*Starmites (40). Musical with book by Stuart Ross and Barry Keating; music and lyrics by Barry Keating. Produced by Hinks Shimberg, Mary Keil and Steven Warnick at Criterion Center Stage Right. Opened April 27, 1989.

On Earth:
Eleanor..Liz Larsen
Mother ....Sharon McNight
Innerspace:
Shak Graa ....Ariel Grabber
Spacepunk............................Brian Lane Green
Trinkulus.....................................Gabriel Barre
Starmites:
Ack Ack Ackerman.........................Bennett Cale
Herbie Harrison...................... Victor Trent Cook

Dazzle Razzledorf.....................Christopher Zelno
Diva... Sharon McNight
Bizarbara..Liz Larsen
Banshees:
Shotzi.....................................Mary Kate Law
Canibelle....................................Gwen Stewart
Balbraka................................... Freida Williams
Maligna .... Janet Aldrich
Droids ....John-Michael Flate, Ric Ryder

Musicians: Henry Aronson keyboards; Dianne Adams keyboards; Robert Kirshof guitars; Brian Hamm bass guitar; Jeffrey Potter percussion.

Understudies: Miss Larsen, Banshees, Droid—Wendy-Jo Vaughn; Miss McNight—Janet Aldrich; Messrs. Grabber, Green, Barre—John-Michael Flate; Messrs. Cale, Cook, Zelno—Ric Ryder.

Directed and staged by Larry Carpenter; choreography, Michele Assaf; musical direction and dance arrangements, Henry Aronson; scenery, Lowell Detweiler; costumes, Susan Hirschfeld; lighting, Jason Kantrowitz; sound, John Kilgore; orchestrations and sound effects, James McElwaine; associate musical direction and vocal arrangements, Dianne Adams; assistant choreographer, T. C. Charlton; associate producers, Peter Bogyo, John Burt, Severn Sandt; production stage manager, Zoya Wyeth; press, Shirley Herz, Glenna Freedman.

Time: Now. Place: Earth and Innerspace.

Rock musical about the science-fiction space adventures of a young woman coping with forces hostile to our solar system. Previously produced off off Broadway and in regional theater.

ACT I

Prologue: Eleanor's bedroom, Planet Earth
"Superhero Girl"..Eleanor
Scene 1: A sacrificial lab in Innerspace
"Starmites"...Starmites, Spacepunk
"Trink's Narration"...Trinkulus, Starmites
"Afraid of the Dark"................................Spacepunk, Starmites, Eleanor, Trinkulus
Scene 2: Shriekwood Forest
"Little Hero"...Eleanor
"Attack of Banshees" ....Banshees
Scene 3: Castle Nemesis: the Great Hall
"Hard To Be Diva"... Diva, Banshees
Scene 4: The castle mortuary
"Love Duet".. Spacepunk, Eleanor
Scene 5: Castle Nemesis: the Great Hall
"The Dance of Spousal Arousal"...Banshees, Bizarbara
Finaletto..Company

ACT II

Entr'acte.. Band
Scene 1: Castle Nemesis: the Great Hall
"Bizarbara's Wedding"..Bizarbara, Banshees
"Milady" ....Spacepunk, Starmites
Scene 2: The Chamber of Psychosorcery
"Beauty Within" .... Diva, Bizarbara
Scene 3: Castle Nemesis: the Great Hall
"The Cruelty Stomp"...Trinkulus, Company
"Reach Right Down"...Starmites, Diva, Banshees
Scene 4: A sacrificial lab in Innerspace
"Immolation"..Eleanor, Shak Graa, Spacepunk
"Starmites/Diva" (Reprise)...Diva, Starmites, Banshees
Epilogue: Eleanor's bedroom, Planet Earth
Finale ....Company

Largely New York (35). Play in pantomime "written" by Bill Irwin. Produced by James B. Freydberg, Kenneth Feld, Jerry L. Cohen, Max Weitzenhoffer, The John F. Kennedy Center for the Performing Arts and The Walt Disney Studios at the St. James Theater. Opened May 1, 1989.

Post-Modern Hoofer	Bill Irwin	Videographer	Dennis Diamond
Poppers	Leon Chesney, Steve Clemente	Video Assistant	Debra Elise Miller
Soloist	Margaret Eginton	Dean	Jeff Gordon

Ensemble: Michael Barber, Jon E. Brandenberg, Chris Quay Davis, Patti Dobrowolski, Raymond Houle, Amy Mack, Karen Omahen, Lori Vadino, Cindy Sue Williams, Toni Wisti, Christina Youngman.

Music: "Danced All Night" and "Three Questions" from *New Generation* performed by Wayne Horvitz.

Understudies: Miss Eginton—Christina Youngman; Messrs. Chesney, Clemente—John Christian; Mr. Gordon—Michael Barber; Mr. Diamond, Miss Miller—Mitchell Hamilton.

Directed by Bill Irwin; choreography, Bill Irwin, Kimi Okada; scenery, Douglas Stein; costumes, Rose Pederson; lighting, Nancy Schertler; sound, Bob Bielecki; video design, Dennis Diamond and Video Studios; original steps and routines, Margaret Eginton, Leon Chesney, Steve Clemente; executive producer, Robin Ullman; collaborator and production stage manager, Nancy Harrington; stage manager, Anna Jo Gender; press, the Fred Nathan Company, Marc P. Thibodeau.

Comedy, modern man coping with his technology-ridden environment, expressed in action without the spoken word. Previously produced in regional theater in Seattle and Washington. The play was presented without intermission.

PLAY WHICH CLOSED
PRIOR TO BROADWAY OPENING

Production which was organized by New York producers for Broadway presentation but which closed during its production and tryout period is listed below.

Senator Joe. Musical with libretto by Perry Arthur Kroeger; music by Tom O'Horgan. Produced by Adela Holzer and Chester Fox in previews at the Neil Simon Theater. Opened January 5, 1989. (Closed January 7, 1989)

CAST: Edward R. Murrow, Richard Nixon, Welch—Jeff Johnson; Eggene Celeste, Mamie Eisenhower, Fatty Deposit, Snake—Kristen Gray; Alger Hiss, Drew Pearson, Dean Acheson, David Schine, Jackie Gleason—Michael Rapposelli; Whittaker Chambers, Owen Lattimore, George Marshall, Julius Rosenberg, Ricky Ricardo—Tom Desrocher; Applause Girl, Dorothy Kenyon, Ethel Rosenberg, Lucy Ricardo—Michelle Fleisher; Applause Girl, Jean Kerr—Mary Robin Roth; Lena Horne, Flower Girl #2, Mrs. Voice of America—Cheryl Alexander.

Also Joe McCarthy—J. P. Dougherty; Chicken, Attorney, Office Boy #1, Enzyme, Lenin, Huck Finn, Ronald Reagan—Richard Coombs; Bess Truman—Elena Ferrante; Eleanor Roosevelt—Maggie-Meg Reed; Professor, Roy Cohn—Ric Ryder; Priest, Natasha, Major Domo—Michael Leslie; Statue of Liberty, Flower Girl #1—Mary Jo Limpert; Harry Truman, Stalin, Voice of America Man, Bobby Kennedy, Secretary Stevens—Aaron Mendelson; Office Boy #2—Raymond Patterson.

Directed by Tom O'Horgan; choreography, Wesley Fata; musical direction, Gordon Lowry Harrell; scenery, Bill Stabile; costumes, Randy Barcelo; lighting, John McLain; sound, Bernard Fox; original production art, Mark Kehoe, Dan Gosch; orchestrations, Jimmy Vivino; production stage manager, Jerry Bihm; stage manager, Bill McComb; press, Gifford/Wallace, Inc., Edwin Gifford, Marie Moschitta, Allison Shuker.

Time: The early 1950s. Place: In, about and around the minds of Joe McCarthy and those involved with him.

Reflections on the junior senator from Wisconsin, infamous for his witch-hunts of supposed Communists, and those who were a part of his times.

MUSICAL NUMBERS, ACT I: "The 50s," Prelude, "Cold War," "Hysteria," "Microfilm," "Black and Blue," "Where the War Left Us," "Dirt Between My Fingers," "Three First Ladies," "Communism," "Almighty American," "Dealing in Wheeling," "Charisma," "Rape of Liberty," "The Weakest Point," "The Briefcase," "What He Needs I Got," "Ism #1," "Take a Professor," "Ism #2," "Jeannie," "Was There Love," "Joe's Liver," "Cocktail Party," "Jungle of Lies," "Personal President."

ACT II: "What's My Lie," "The 50s" (Reprise), "The Wedding," "Slow as the Moon," "What's Up for You," "Book Burning," "Mamie and Bess Bicker," "I Knew a Man," "Twenty Years of Treason," "Have You No Shame," "Time Heals All Wounds," "See It Now," "Pussyfootin'," "Haunted Television," "Boozin' & Barfin'," "The Telephone," "The Army," "Make Up," "Ron and Bobby," "The Hearings," "Flashback," "Aftermath," "America," "Jungle of Lies."

PLAYS PRODUCED OFF BROADWAY

Some distinctions between off-Broadway and Broadway productions at one end of the scale and off-off-Broadway productions at the other were blurred in the New York Theater of the 1970s and 1980s. For the purposes of this *Best Plays* listing, the term "off Broadway" is used to distinguish a professional from a showcase (off-off-Broadway) production and signifies a show which opened for general audiences in a mid-Manhattan theater seating 499 or fewer and 1) employed an Equity cast, 2) planned a regular schedule of 8 performances a week in an open-ended run and 3) offered itself to public comment by critics at designated opening performances.

Occasional exceptions of inclusion (never of exclusion) are made to take in visiting troupes, borderline cases and nonqualifying productions which readers might expect to find in this list because they appear under an off-Broadway heading in other major sources of record.

Figures in parentheses following a play's title give number of performances. These figures do not include previews or extra non-profit performances.

Plays marked with an asterisk (*) were still running on June 1, 1989. Their number of performances is figured from opening night through May 31, 1989.

Certain programs of off-Broadway companies are exceptions to our rule of counting the number of performances from the date of the press coverage. When the official opening takes place late in the run of a play's regularly-priced public or subscription performances (after previews) we count the first performance of record, not the press date, as opening night—and in each such case in the listing we note the variance and give the press date.

In a listing of a show's numbers—dances, sketches, musical scenes, etc.— the titles of songs are identified wherever possible by their appearance in quotation marks (").

Most entries of off-Broadway productions which ran fewer than 20 performances are somewhat abbreviated, as are entries on running repertory programs repeated from previous years.

416

HOLDOVERS FROM PREVIOUS SEASONS

Plays which were running on June 1, 1988 are listed below. More detailed information about them appears in previous *Best Plays* volumes of appropriate date. Important cast changes since opening night are recorded in a section of this volume.

*The Fantasticks (12,106; longest continuous run of record in the American theater). Musical suggested by the play *Les Romanesques* by Edmond Rostand; book and lyrics by Tom Jones; music by Harvey Schmidt. Opened May 30, 1960.

*Vampire Lesbians of Sodom and Sleeping Beauty or Coma (1,614). Program of two plays by Charles Busch. Opened June 19, 1985.

*Nunsense (1,431). Musical with book, music and lyrics by Dan Goggin. Opened December 12, 1985.

*Driving Miss Daisy (854). By Alfred Uhry. Opened April 15, 1987.

*Steel Magnolias (817). By Robert Harling. Opened June 19, 1987.

Frankie and Johnny in the Clair de Lune (533). By Terrence McNally. Opened October 13, 1987. (Closed March 12, 1989)

*Perfect Crime (679). By Warren Manzi. Opened October 16, 1987.

A Shayna Maidel (501). By Barbara Lebow. Opened October 29, 1987. (Closed January 8, 1989)

Oil City Symphony (626). Musical revue written by the performers (Mike Craver, Mark Hardwick, Debra Monk, Mary Murfitt). Opened November 5, 1987. (Closed May 7, 1989)

*Tamara (578). By John Krizanc; conceived by Richard Rose and John Krizanc. Opened December 2, 1987. (Recessed January 18, 1988) Reopened February 2, 1988.

The Good and Faithful Servant (135). By Joe Orton. Opened February 10, 1988. (Closed June 5, 1988)

Without You I'm Nothing (214). One-woman show with Sandra Bernhard; written by Sandra Bernhard and John Boskovich. Opened March 31, 1988. (Closed October 2, 1988)

The Road to Mecca (172). By Athol Fugard. Opened April 12, 1988. (Closed September 11, 1988)

Ten Percent Revue (239). Musical revue with words and music by Tom Wilson Weinberg. Opened April 13, 1988. (Closed November 6, 1988)

Dandy Dick (54). Revival of the play by Arthur Wing Pinero. Opened May 11, 1988. (Closed June 26, 1988)

Three Ways Home (87). By Casey Kurtti. Opened May 11, 1988. (Closed July 24, 1988)

Bittersuite—One More Time (18). New edition of the musical revue with music by Elliot Weiss; lyrics by Michael Champagne. Opened May 16, 1988. (Closed June 12, 1988)

Kaye Ballard: Working 42d Street at Last! (29). One-woman show with Kaye Ballard; creative consultant, Ben Bagley. Opened May 16, 1988. (Closed June 12, 1988)

West Memphis Mojo (52). By Martin Jones. Opened May 21, 1988. (Closed July 7, 1988)

Romeo and Juliet (16). Revival of the play by William Shakespeare. Opened May 24, 1988. (Closed June 5, 1988)

The Wonder Years (23). Musical based on an idea by Leslie Eberhard; book by David Levy, David Holdgrive, Steve Liebman and Terry LaBolt; music and lyrics by David Levy. Opened May 25, 1988. (Closed June 12, 1988)

PLAYS PRODUCED JUNE 1, 1988–MAY 31, 1989

New York Shakespeare Festival. 1987–1988 season continued with **Zero Positive** (7). By Harry Kondoleon. Opened June 1, 1988. (Closed June 5, 1988) **The Death of Garcia Lorca**; (16). By Jose Antonio Real; translated by Julio Marzan. Opened June 28, 1988 as part of the First New York International Festival of the Arts. (Closed July 10, 1988) **Miracolo d'Amore** (47). Dance theater piece conceived by Martha Clarke; created with the company; music by Richard Peaslee. Produced in association with Spoleto Festival U.S.A. as part of the First New York International Festival of the Arts. Opened June 29, 1988. (Closed August 13, 1988) **Stranger Here Myself** (19). One-woman performance by Angelina Réaux; songs by Kurt Weill. Opened August 11, 1988. (Closed September 4, 1988) Produced by New York Shakespeare Festival, Joseph Papp producer, at the Public Theater (see note).

ALL PLAYS: Associate producer, Jason Steven Cohen; plays and musicals development, Gail Merrifield; press, Richard Kornberg, Barbara Carroll, Reva Cooper, Carol Fineman, Warren Anker.

ZERO POSITIVE

Himmer	David Pierce	Prentice	Richard McMillan
Jacob Blank	Edward Atienza	Patrick	Tony Shalhoub
Samantha	Frances Conroy	Debbie Fine	Beth Austin

Directed by Kenneth Elliott; original direction, Mark Linn-Baker; scenery, Adrianne Lobel; costumes, Susan Hilferty; lighting, Natasha Katz; production stage manager, Ruth Kreshka; stage manager, Lisa Ledwich.

Time: August 1987. Place: New York City. Act I, Scene 1: Sex with Johnny. Scene 2: Lust for life. Scene 3: The topless nurse. Act II, Scene 1: Curtain raiser. Scene 2: Denoument.

Eccentric reactions to mortality in the form of positive reactions to the AIDS virus test.

THE DEATH OF GARCIA LORCA

ACT I

The park in Madrid:
Federico Garcia Lorca .... Bernard White
The Poets:
Salvador Dali .... Al Rodriguez
Pablo Neruda .... Joseph Palmas
Gerardo Diego .... Rene Moreno
Luis Rosales................................. Cesar Evora
Jorge Guillen .... Jorge Luis Ramos
Rafael Alberti .... Roberto Medina
Vincente Alexandre .... Kevin Gray
Photographer .... Lionel Pina
Near orchard of San Vicente,
Lorca's family home:
Concha Montesinos .... Maria Christina Lozada
Mother of Federico................. Patricia Falkenhain
Angelina...................................... Margarita Irun
Little Girl in Black .... Sara Erde
Sgt. Ramacho.......................... Mario Arrambide
Falangists .... Kevin Gray, Al Rodriguez

Civil Guards .... Roberto Medina,
Tim Perez, Jorge Luis Ramos
Gabriel Perea Ruiz .... Joseph Palmas
The Imperial Cafe in Granada:
Falangist................................. Emilio Del Pozo
Local .... Mario Arrambide
Pepe .... Rene Moreno
Shoeshine Boy .... Sara Erde
Customers.......Jorge Luis Ramos, Joseph Palmas
Singer and Pianist.............. Consuelo Jean Routtu
Lt. Murillo...................................... Tim Perez
Ramon Ruiz Alonso................. Gonzalo Madurga
The house of the Rosales brothers:
Tia Luisa.................................. Judith Roberts
Esperanza .... Sara Erde
1910 Lorca .... Herbert Duarte
1920 Lorca .... Lionel Pina
Lorca as an Old Man .... Mario Arrambide

ACT II

House of Luis Rosales:
Miguel Rosales............................. Al Rodriguez
The office of Cmdr. Valdez:
Secretary.. Kevin Gray
Sergeant.. Tim Perez
Cmdr. Valdez........................... Emilio Del Pozo

Enrique .... Joseph Palmas
Don Manuel de Falla .... Mario Arrambide
The jail:
Joaquin Arcollas .... Roberto Medina
Dioscoro Galindo Gonzales......... Mario Arrambide
Rafael Galadi.............................. Rene Moreno

Musicians, New York 1929: Michael Ridley trumpet, James Alan Ford saxophone.

Directed by Carlos Giminez; scenery and costumes, Rafael Reyeros; lighting, Carlos Giminez; a project of Festival Latino 1988, Oscar Ciccone and Cecelia Vega directors; production stage manager, K. Siobhan Phelan; stage manager, Roylan Diaz.

The life and troubled times of the Spanish playwright and poet executed by Falangists during that country's civil war. A foreign (Venezuelan) play in its world premiere in English in this production.

MIRACOLO D'AMORE

Peter Becker
Rob Besserer
Felix Blaska
Marshall Coid
Larrio Ekson
Marie Fourcaut
Alexandra Ivanoff
David Jon

John Kelly
Francine Landes
Nina Martin
Adam Rogers
Paola Styron
Elisabeth Van Ingen
Nina Watt

Directed by Martha Clarke; scenery and costumes, Robert Israel; lighting, Paul Gallo; vocal director, Jeff Halpern; production stage manager, Steven Ehrenberg; stage manager, Elizabeth Sherman.

Imaginative performance piece presenting sexual conflicts in commedia dell'arte imagery.

STRANGER HERE MYSELF

Directed by Christopher Alden; scenery, Paul Steinberg; lighting, Anne Militello; musical direction, pianist, Christopher Berg; English translations, Michael Feingold; accordions, William Schimmel, William Swindler; percussion, Bill Ruyle; production stage manager, Jennifer Gilbert.

Lonely woman (portrayed by Angelina Réaux) in a seedy hotel room tells the story of the triumphs and discouragements of her life as a series of Kurt Weill songs.

MUSICAL NUMBERS, ACT I: "Epitaph" (words by Bertolt Brecht), "Fennimore's Song" (words by George Kaiser), "The Barbara Song" (words by Bertolt Brecht, translated by Marc Blitzstein), "Is It Him or Is It Me?" (words by Alan Jay Lerner), "Prologue" (words by Bertolt Brecht, translated by W. H. Auden and Chester Kallmann), "Berlin im Licht-Song" (Berlin in Lights), "Moon of Alabama" (words by Bertolt Brecht), "My Ship" (Childhood Dream, words by Ira Gershwin), "Song of the Big Shot" (words by Bertolt Brecht), "J'Attends un Navire" (I Wait for a Ship, words by Jacques Deval), "Lust" (words by Bertolt Brecht, translated by W. H. Auden and Chester Kallmann), "Je ne t'Aime Pas" (I Don't Love You, words by Maurice Magre), "Remember That I Care" (words by Langston Hughes).

ACT II: "I'm a Stranger Here Myself" (words by Ogden Nash), "Surabaya Johnny" (words by Bertolt Brecht), "Foolish Heart" (words by Ogden Nash), "Song of Mandalay" (words by Bertolt Brecht), "Nannas Lied" (words by Bertolt Brecht), "Lonely House" (words by Langston Hughes), "Le Train du Ciel" (The Heaven Train, words by Jacques Deval), "Solomon Song" (words by Bertolt Brecht, translated by Marc Blitzstein), "Youkali: Tango Habanera" (words by Roger Fernay), "Epitaph" (Reprise).

Note: In Joseph Papp's Public Theater there are many auditoria. *Zero Positive* played LuEsther Hall, *The Death of Garcia Lorca* played the Anspacher Theater, *Miracolo d'Amore* played the Estelle Newman Theater, *Stranger Here Myself* played the Susan Stein Shiva Theater.

Godspell (225). Revival of the musical based upon the gospel according to St. Matthew; conceived by John-Michael Tebelak; music by Stephen Schwartz. Produced by The Lamb's Theater Company, Carolyn Rossi Copeland producing director, at The Lamb's Theater. Opened June 12, 1988. (Closed December 31, 1988)

Trini Alvarado	Eddie Korbich
Anne Bobby	Mia Korf
Bill Damaschke	Robert McNeill
Laura Dean	Harold Perrineau Jr.
Angel Jemmott	Jeffrey Steefel

The Band: Steven M. Alper conductor, keyboards; Douglas Besterman assistant conductor, keyboards; Paul O'Keefe guitars; Bill Urmson bass; Bob George drums.

Understudy: Women—Marietta DePrima.

Directed by Don Scardino; musical direction, Steven M. Alper; scenery, Allison Campbell; costumes, David C. Woolard; lighting, Phil Monat; sound, T. Richard Fitzgerald; additional orchestrations, Steven M. Alper, Douglas Besterman; production stage manager, Fredric H. Orner; press, Ted Killmer.

Godspell was first produced off Broadway 5/17/71 for 2,124 performances and was transferred to Broadway 6/22/76 for an additional 527 performances. This is its first major New York revival.

The list of musical numbers in *Godspell* appears on page 349 of *The Best Plays of 1970-71*.

Playwrights Horizons. 1987–88 season concluded with **Right Behind the Flag** (15). By Kevin Heelan. Produced by Playwrights Horizons, Andre Bishop artistic director, Paul S. Daniels executive director, at Playwrights Horizons. Opened June 15, 1988. (Closed June 26, 1988)

Bernie	Kevin Spacey	Catherine	Amy Aquino
Frankie	W. T. Martin	Bartender; Timmerman	Paul McCrane
Vinnie	Joe Bellan	Cop	Richard Riehle
Joe	Herbert Rubens		

Directed by R. J. Cutler; scenery, Loy Arcenas; costumes, Candice Donnelly; lighting, Debra J. Kletter; sound, Lia Vollack; production stage manager, Suzanne Fry; press, Bob Ullman.

Time: The mid-1980s. Place: New York City. Act I, Scene 1: Sammy's barbershop, Columbus Avenue. Scene 2: Vinnie's appliance store. Scene 3: A bar on Columbus Avenue. Scene 4: Sammy's barbershop.

Scene 5: The bar. Scene 6: Sammy's barbershop. Act II, Scene 1: A different bar. Scene 2: A park bench. Scene 3: Bernie's apartment. Scene 4: Sammy's barbershop. Scene 5: Vinnie's appliance store.
Black comedy treatment of patriotism and the American dream.

Stages Trilingual Theater. Schedule of two programs. **Pavlovsky Marathon** (16). Program of three one-act plays by Eduardo Pavlovsky: *Slowmotion, Potestad* and *Pablo*. Opened June 15, 1988 as part of the First New York International Festival of the Arts. (Closed June 27, 1988) **English Mint/L'Amante Anglaise** (15). By Marguerite Duras. Opened June 30, 1988. (Closed July 10, 1988) Produced by Stages Trilingual Theater at the Cherry Lane Theater.

PAVLOVSKY MARATHON

Slowmotion
Dagomar...................................Tony Abatemarco
Amilcar...Hal Bokar
Rosa..Grace Zabriskie
    Translated and directed by Paul Verdier; lighting, Philip Allen; sound, Bill O'Shaughnessy.
    A boxing champion and his manager in the last stages of his career.

Potestad
El Hombre..............................Eduardo Pavlovsky
Tita ....Susana Evans
    Directed by Norman Brisky; music, Martin Pavlovsky; lighting, Philip Allen.

An adopted child is abducted from her father by a dictatorial government; performed in the Spanish language.

Pablo
L..Hal Bokar
V...Tony Maggio
    Translated and directed by Paul Verdier; lighting, Kevin Mahn; sound, Nathan Stein.
    Pinteresque discussion of Argentina's 1977 military dictatorship.

ALL PLAYS: Scenery, Jim Sweeters; stage manager, Sindy Slater; press, Peter Cromarty.
Foreign plays previously produced in Argentina and Los Angeles.

URBAN BLIGHT—John Rubinstein and Larry Fishburne in David Mamet's *Where Were You When It Went Down?* segment of the Manhattan Theater Club production

ENGLISH MINT/L'AMANTE ANGLAISE

Pierre Lannes......................................Hal Bokar   The Interrogator................................Paul Verdier
Claire Lannes ....Grace Zabriskie

Directed by Paul Verdier; scenery, Jim Sweeters; costumes, Emily Payne; lighting, Kevin Mahn; stage manger, Sindy Slater.

Thriller based on a housewife's murder of her housekeeper-cousin in France in 1949. A foreign play previously produced in France and in Los Angeles.

Circle Repertory Company. 1987–88 schedule concluded with **V&V Only** (26). By Jim Leonard. Produced by Circle Repertory Company, Tanya Berezin artistic director, Tim Hawkins managing director, B. Rodney Marriott associate artistic director, at Circle Repertory as part of the First New York International Festival of the Arts. Opened June 16, 1988. (Closed July 10, 1988)

Vito...Dick Boccelli   Raffiella..Tresa Hughes
Tommy....................................Robert Minicucci   Janey..Roxann Biggs
Donny...Brian Tarantina   Customer...Jordan Mott
Nick ....Erich Anderson   Steinway.. Ben Siegler
Antonio ....Allan Arbus

Understudies: Messrs. Boccelli, Arbus—Edward Seamon; Messrs. Tarantina, Anderson—John Viscardi; Messrs. Minicucci, Siegler—Jordan Mott; Miss Biggs—Catherine Parrinello; Mr. Mott—Forrest Williams.

Directed by Marshall W. Mason; scenery, John Lee Beatty; costumes, Susan Denison Geller; lighting, Dennis Parichy; sound, Chuck London/Stewart Werner; production stage manager, Denise Yaney; press, Gary W. Murphy.

Time: The present day. Place: A coffee shop in Little Italy/Soho. The play was presented in two parts.

Coffee shop owner and his friends in crisis in a redevelopment area. Previously produced by South Coast Repertory, Costa Mesa, Calif.

American Theater Exchange. Schedule of three transfers from regional theater. **Green Card** (9). By JoAnne Akalaitis, in the Mark Taper Forum Center Theater Group production, Gordon Davidson artistic director/producer, Stephen J. Albert managing director. Opened June 18, 1988. (Closed June 25, 1988) Repertory of two programs in the American Repertory Theater productions, Robert Brustein artistic director, Robert J. Orchard managing director, Richard Riddell associate director: **Six Characters in Search of an Author** (11), revival of the play by Luigi Pirandello, adapted by Robert Brustein and the Company, opened July 9, 1988; and **Big Time: Scenes From a Service Economy** (9), by Keith Reddin, opened July 16, 1988. (Repertory closed July 30, 1988). Produced by the Joyce Theater Foundation, Inc. and AT&T Onstage at the Joyce Theater as part of the First New York International Festival of the Arts.

GREEN CARD

Abraham Alvarez   Jim Ishida
Raye Birk   Josie Kim
Jesse Borrego   Dana Lee
Rosalind Chao   Alma Martinez
Pamela Dunlap   Jessie Nelson
George Galvan

Understudies: Women—Linda Callahan; Men—Miguel Sandoval.

Directed by JoAnne Akalaitis; scenery, Douglas Stein; costumes, Marianna Elliott; lighting, Frances Aronson; choreography, Carolyn Dyer; sound, Jon Gottlieb; slide projection, photography, Craig Collins; associate producer, Madeline Puzo; assistant directors, Linda Callahan, Elizabeth Diamond; production stage manager, Mireya Hepner; stage manager, Caryn Shick; press, Ellen Jacobs.

Act I: Prologue, Success Story, Customs and Costumes, Work, English, Natives, Immigration, California. Act II: Prologue, Religion, Colonialism, Culture, CIA, A Glossary, Testimony, Dead Letters, Dying in Your Dream, Waiting.

The immigrant's tale, from 1890s Ellis Island to modern Los Angeles. Previously produced at Mark Taper Forum.

SIX CHARACTERS IN SEARCH OF AN AUTHOR

The Company:		*The Characters:*	
Jack	John Grant-Phillips	Stepdaughter	Pamela Gien
Rooney	Tom Rooney	Mother	Priscilla Smith
Sandra	Sandra Shipley	Father	Alvin Epstein
Tommy	Thomas Derrah	Son	Benjamin Evett
Jeremy	Jeremy Geidt	Little Boy	Matthew Dundas
Peter	Peter Gerety	Little Girl	Dawn Kelly
Harry	Harry S. Murphy	Emilio Paz	Michael Balcanoff

Directed by Robert Brustein; original scenery and costume design, Michael H. Yeargan; lighting, Frank Butler; stage manager, Anne S. King.

Time and place: A rehearsal by the American Repertory Theater company at the Joyce Theater, New York. The play was presented without intermission.

Six Characters in Search of an Author was first produced on Broadway 10/30/22. It has been revived on Broadway 2/6/24 and 4/15/31 and off Broadway in the seasons of 1946–47 and 1955–56 and 3/8/63 for 529 performances. This production was first produced at American Repertory Theater, Cambridge, Mass.

BIG TIME: SCENES FROM A SERVICE ECONOMY

Paul	William Converse-Roberts	Peter	Peter Crombie
Fran	Cherry Jones	Ted	Thomas Derrah
Diane	Sandra Shipley	Hassan	Harry S. Murphy

Directed by Steven Schachter; scenery, Bill Clarke; costumes, Ellen McCartney; lighting, Thom Palm; sound, Stephen D. Santomenna; stage manager, Anne S. King.

Corrupt banker operates on an international scale.

Manhattan Theater Club. 1987–88 season concluded with **Urban Blight** (12). Musical revue based on an idea by John Tillinger; music by David Shire; lyrics by Richard Maltby Jr.; additional song by Edward Kleban; scenes contributed by various authors (see listing of credits below). Produced by Manhattan Theater Club, Lynne Meadow artistic director, Barry Grove managing director, at City Center Stage I. Opened June 19, 1988. (Closed July 1, 1988)

Larry Fishburne	Faith Prince
Nancy Giles	Rex Robbins
E. Katherine Kerr	John Rubinstein
Oliver Platt	

Musicians: Michael Skloff conductor, keyboard; Vince Fay bass; Jim Young drums; Peter Levin synthesizers.

Understudies: Darlene Bel Grayson, Roxie Lucas, Kenneth L. Marks, Thomas Young.

Directed by John Tillinger and Richard Maltby Jr.; scenery, Heidi Landesman; costumes, C. L. Hundley; lighting, Natasha Katz; musical supervision, Joel Silberman; conductor, Michael Skloff; musical staging, Charles Randolph-Wright; sound Daryl Bornstein; production stage manager, Ed Fitzgerald; stage manager, Daniel Bauer; press, Helene Davis, Leisha DeHart, Linda Feinberg.

The state of life in New York City, in song and sketch.

MUSICAL NUMBERS AND SKETCHES, ACT I: "Don't Fall for the Lights" (by Richard Maltby Jr. and David Shire; dialogue by Terrence McNally, A. R. Gurney and Richard Maltby Jr.)—Company; *Feeding the Baby* (by Shel Silverstein), Susan—Faith Prince, Ted—John Rubinstein, Baby—Oliver Platt; *Cardinal O'Connor* (by Christopher Durang), Cardinal O'Connor—Rex Robbins, Announcer—Rubinstein; *Fries and Shake* (by Larry Fishburne and Nancy Giles), Woman #1—Prince, Bill—Larry Fishburne, Ramona—Nancy Giles, Woman #2—E. Katherine Kerr; *Portrait #1:* "Life Story" (by Richard Maltby Jr. and David Shire), Woman—Prince; *White Walls* (by A. R. Gurney), Ed—Robbins, Mike—Platt; *Portrait #2:* "Miss Byrd" (by Richard Maltby Jr. and David Shire), Miss Byrd—Giles; *Transfiguration of Gerome* (by E. Katherine Kerr), Part I: Gerome—Kerr; *Subway Panhandlers* (by John Augustine), Man—Platt, Vietnam Vet—Fishburne, Man—Rubinstein, Rich Lady—Kerr; *Street Talk* (by Terrence McNally), Eubie—Fishburne, Charity Jones—Giles; *Transfiguration of Gerome* (by E. Katherine Kerr), Part II: Gerome—Kerr, Oliver—Platt; *Over There* (by George C. Wolfe), Jack—Rubinstein, Jill—Giles; *Woman Stand-Up* (by Christopher Durang), Woman (Cindy)—Prince; "Aerobicantata" (by Richard Maltby Jr. and David Shire), Men—Platt, Robbins, Rubenstein, Women—Giles, Prince.

ACT II: "Bill of Fare" (by Richard Maltby Jr. and David Shire), Waiter—Rubinstein, Patrons—Company; *Taxi From Hell* (by Ted Tally), Cabbie—Platt, Fare—Robbins; *Transfiguration of Gerome* (by E. Katherine Kerr), Part III: Gerome—Kerr, Nancy—Giles; *Speech to the Neighborhood Watch Committee* (by Arthur Miller), Barry Keefer—Rubinstein; *Transfiguration of Gerome* (by E. Katherine Kerr), Part IV: Gerome—Kerr, Oprah—Giles; *Smart Women/Brilliant Choices* (by Wendy Wasserstein), Woman—Prince, Man—Robbins; *Rope-a-Dope* (by Jules Feiffer), The Writer—Platt; *Portrait #3:* "There" (by Richard Maltby Jr. and David Shire), Jane—Kerr, George—Robbins; *Where Were You When It Went Down* (by David Mamet), A—Rubinstein, B—Fishburne; *Eliot's Coming* (by Charles Fuller), Kim—Giles; *Lonely Bohunks* (by John Bishop), Man—Platt, Woman—Kerr; *Bernard's Lament* (by Richard Wesley), Bernard—Fishburne; *Andre's Mother* (by Terrence McNally), Cal—Rubinstein, Penny—Prince, Arthur—Robbins, Andre's Mother—Kerr; "Self-Portrait" (by Edward Kleban), Man—Rubinstein; "Don't Fall for the Lights" (Reprise)—Company.

Stars in the Morning Sky (16). By Alexander Galin; English translation by Michael Stronin and Elise Thoron. Produced by Maly Productions, Inc., Ken Marsolais president, at the American Place Theater as part of the First New York International Festival of the Arts. Opened June 20, 1988. (Closed July 2, 1988)

Valentina	Galina Filimonova	Klara	Marina Gridasova
Nikolai	Sergei Kozyrev	Anna	Tatyana Shestakova
Maria	Natalya Akimova	Alexander	Vladimir Osipchuk
Lora	Irina Seleznyova		

Standbys: Misses Akimova, Seleznyova—Angelika Nevolina; Misses Gridasova, Filimonova—Natalia Fomenko.

Directed by Lev Dodin; co-director, Tatyana Shestakova; scenery, Alexei Porai-Koshitz; lighting, Oleg Kozlov; associate producer, Elizabeth D. White; produced in association with the U.S.S.R. Union of Theater Workers; production stage manager, Maureen F. Gibson; stage manager, Bonnie J. Baggesen; press, Burnham-Callaghan, Jacqueline Burnham.

Time: The eve of the 1980 Olympics. Place: An old derelict barracks which once served as an asylum for the mentally handicapped. The play was presented without intermission.

Prostitutes sent to a village near Moscow during the Olympics. A foreign play performed in the Russian language with simultaneous translation.

Lincoln Center Theater. 1987–88 season continued with **I'll Go On** (23). One-man play performed by Barry McGovern; adapted by Gerry Dukes and Barry McGovern from Samuel Beckett. Produced at the Mitzi E. Newhouse Theater by arrangement with Ken Marsolais and Patricia Daily, in the Gate Theater Dublin production, Michael Colgan director, as part of the First New York International Festival of the Arts. Opened June 22, 1988. (Closed July 17, 1988) **Road** (62). By Jim Cartwright. Co-produced at LaMama Annex

Theater with LaMama E.T.C., Ellen Stewart artistic director, Wickham Boyle executive director. Opened July 28, 1988. (Closed September 18, 1988)

I'LL GO ON

Directed by Colm O'Briain; design, Robert Ballagh; lighting, Rupert Murray; stage manager, Liz Small; press, Merle Debuskey, Mary Bryant.

Portrayal of bitterly eccentric characters from Samuel Beckett's novels *Molloy*, *Malone Dies*, and *The Unnamable*. The play was presented in two parts. A foreign play previously produced in Dublin, various centers in Europe and at Chicago's International Theater Festival.

ROAD

Scullery	Jack Wallace	Carol	Betsy Aidem
Louise; Clare	Joan Cusack	Eddie's Father; Professor; Jerry	Gerry Bamman
Louise's Brother; Brink; Joey	Kevin Bacon	Eddie; Skin-lad	Michael Wincott
Brenda; Molly; Helen	Jayne Haynes	(Other roles played by the Company)	

Understudies: Misses Cusak, Aidem—Debra Cole; Miss Haynes—Robin McKay; Messrs. Bacon, Wincott—Jake Weber.

Directed by Simon Curtis; scenery and costumes, Paul Brown; lighting, Kevin Rigdon; sound, Daniel Schreier; production stage manager, Jack Doulin; stage manager, Gary Natoli; press, Merle Debuskey, Bruce Campbell.

Time: Tonight. Place: A road in a small Lancashire town. The play was presented in two parts.

Episodes of life in a modern British slum, with the actors sharing the sets with members of the audience. A foreign play previously produced in London by the Royal Court Theater.

A Best Play; see page 131.

*New York Shakespeare Festival Shakespeare Marathon. Schedule of six revivals of plays by William Shakespeare (see note). **Much Ado About Nothing** (10 plus 5 partial performances). Opened July 14, 1988. (Closed July 31, 1988) **King John** (13). Opened August 18, 1988. (Closed September 4, 1988) Produced by New York Shakespeare Festival, Joseph Papp producer, in association with New York Telephone, with the cooperation of the City of New York, Edward I. Koch mayor, Mary Schmidt Campbell commissioner of cultural affairs, Henry J. Stern commissioner of parks and recreation, at the Delacorte Theater in Central Park.

Also **Coriolanus** (63). Opened November 22, 1988. (Closed January 15, 1989) **Love's Labor's Lost** (14). Opened February 22, 1989. (Closed March 5, 1989) **The Winter's Tale** (24). Opened March 21, 1989. (Closed April 9, 1989) ***Cymbeline** (1). Opened May 31, 1989. Produced by New York Shakespeare Festival, Joseph Papp producer, at the Public Theater (see note).

ALL PLAYS: Associate producer, Jason Steven Cohen; plays and musicals development, Gail Merrifield; press, Richard Kornberg, Barbara Carroll, Reva Cooper, Carol Fineman, Warren Anker, Amy Povich.

MUCH ADO ABOUT NOTHING

Leonato	Robert Gerringer	Margaret	Leslie Geraci
Messenger; Balthasar	Don Mayo	Ursula	Kate Wilkinson
Beatrice	Blythe Danner	Boy	Daniel Markel
Hero	Phoebe Cates	Dogberry	Jerry Stiller
Don Pedro	Brian Murray	Verges	MacIntyre Dixon
Benedick	Kevin Kline	Watch 1	Joe Zaloom
Don John	David Pierce	Watch 2	Steve Routman
Claudio	Don Reilly	Watch 3	William Preston

Antonio	George Hall	Friar Francis	Richard Woods
Conrade	Dan Butler	Sexton	David Landon
Borachio	Dylan Baker		

Ensemble: Augusta Allen-Jones, N. Richard Arif, Holly Baumgartner, Ethan T. Bowen, Andre Braugher, Brian Dykstra, Larry Green, Meghan Rose Krank, David Letwin, Michael Louden, Daniel Markel, Laura Sametz, Matt Servitto, Graham Winton.

Understudies: Mr. Gerringer—David Letwin; Miss Danner—Augusta Allen-Jones; Miss Cates—Meghan Rose Krank; Mr. Murray—David Landon; Mr. Kline— Andre Braugher; Mr. Pierce—Ethan T. Bowen; Mr. Reilly—Michael Louden; Mr. Butler—Graham Winton; Mr. Baker—Larry Green; Mr. Mayo—Matt Servitto; Miss Geraci—Laura Sametz; Miss Wilkinson—Holly Baumgardner; Mr. Stiller—MacIntyre Dixon; Mr. Dixon—William Preston; Messrs. Zaloom, Routman, Preston—Daniel Markel; Mr. Woods—N. Richard Arif; Mr. Landon—Brian Dykstra.

Directed by Gerald Freedman; scenery, John Ezell; costumes, Theoni V. Aldredge; lighting, Thomas R. Skelton; music, John Morris; choreography, Tina Paul; fights, B. H. Barry; production stage manager, Michael Chambers; stage manager, Pat Sosnow.

The last major New York revival of *Much Ado About Nothing* was by The Acting Company off Broadway 5/11/87 for 8 performances. The play was presented in two parts.

KING JOHN

King John	Kevin Conway	Citizen of Angiers; Abbot	Herb Downer
Prince Henry	Wade Raley	French Herald	Graham Winton
Arthur	Devon Michaels	English Herald;	
Pembroke	Michael Cumpsty	Archbishop of Canterbury	Andre Braugher
Salisbury	Christopher McHale	Archbishop of York	David Wheeler
Lord Bigot; Faulconbridge	Tom Dunlop	2d Monk	Larry Green
Hubert	Joe Morton	3d Monk	Ethan T. Bowen
Philip the Bastard	Jay O. Sanders	Executioner #1	Deryl Caitlyn
James Gurney; 1st Monk	Rob Labelle	Executioner #2	Gary Ruebsamen
King of France	Richard Venture	Queen Elinor	Jane White
Lewis	Michael Louden	Constance	Mariette Hartley
Duke of Austria	Jordan Lund	Blanch	Joyce O'Connor
Cardinal Pandulph	Moses Gunn	Lady Faulconbridge	Robin Moseley
Melun	Joseph Culliton	Ladies in Waiting	Alison Edwards, Laura Sametz

Soldiers, Monks, Attendants: Ron Bottitta, Teagle F. Bougere, Ethan T. Bowen, Andre Braugher, Deryl Caitlyn, Andrew Colteaux, Steven B. Dominguez, Brian Dykstra, Paul Eckstein, Larry Green, John Hickey, Rob Labelle, John J. Miskulin, Gary Ruebsamen, Matt Servitto, Rex Slate, David Wheeler, Graham Winton.

Understudies: Mr. Conway—Michael Cumpsty; Mr. Raley—John Hickey; Mr. Michaels—Wade Raley; Mr. Cumpsty—David Wheeler; Mr. McHale—Larry Green; Mr. Dunlop—Steven B. Dominguez; Mr. Morton—Andre Braugher; Mr. Sanders—John J. Miskulin; Mr. Venture—Joseph Culliton; Mr. Louden—Ron Bottitta; Mr. Lund—Deryl Caitlyn; Mr. Gunn—Teagle F. Bougere; Mr. Culliton—Andrew Colteaux; Mr. Downer—Ethan T. Bowen; Mr. Labelle—Rex Slate; Mr. Green—Matt Servitto; Mr. Bowen—Paul Eckstein; Miss White—Alison Edwards; Miss Hartley—Joyce O'Connor; Miss O'Connor—Laura Sametz; Miss Moseley—Alison Edwards; Mr. Winton—Brian Dykstra; Mr. Braugher—Gary Ruebsamen.

Directed by Stuart Vaughan; scenery, Bob Shaw; costumes, Lindsay W. Davis; lighting, John Gleason; music, Peter Golub; fights, B. H. Barry; production stage manager, Karen Armstrong; stage manager, John J. Toia.

Time: Beginning of the 13th century. Place: England and France. The play was presented in two parts.

The last major New York revival of *King John* was by New York Shakespeare Festival in Central Park 7/5/67 for 19 performances.

CORIOLANUS

Menenius Agrippa	Paul Hecht	Junius Brutus	Andre Braugher
Coriolanus	Christopher Walken	Tullus Aufidius	Keith David

Titus Lartius	Thomas Kopache	Volumnia	Irene Worth
Cominius	Moses Gunn	Virgilia	Ashley Crow
Sicinius Vellutus	Larry Bryggman	Valeria	Sharon Washington

Ensemble: Citizen, Senator, Soldier, 1st Officer—Ethan T. Bowen; 3d Citizen, Senator, Soldier—Deryl Caitlyn; Messenger, Citizen, Soldier, Senator—Albert Farrar; Citizen, Soldier—Tom McGowan; 2d Citizen, Senator, Soldier—Joseph C. Phillips; Citizen, Senator, Soldier, 2d Officer—Armand Schultz; 1st Citizen, Senator, Soldier—Roger Guenveur Smith; Citizen, Senator, Soldier—Matt Bradford Sullivan; Volscian Soldier, Volscian Lieutenant, Citizen—John Madden Towey.

Understudies: Mr. Walken—Andre Braugher; Mr. Bryggman—Armand Schultz.

Directed by Steven Berkoff; scenery, Loren Sherman; costumes, Martin Pakledinaz; lighting, Stephen Strawbridge; music composed and played by Larry Spivak; production stage manager, James Bernardi; stage manager, Buzz Cohen.

The last major New York revival of *Coriolanus* was by New York Shakespeare Festival at the Delacorte Theater 6/22/79 for 27 performances.

LOVE'S LABOR'S LOST

Ferdinand	Mark Moses	Boyet	John Horton
Longaville	Mark Hymen	Princess of France	Christine Dunford
Dumaine	Spike McClure	Maria	Kate Fuglei
Berowne	William Converse-Roberts	Katharine	Juliette Kurth
Anthony Dull	Steve Ryan	Rosaline	Roma Downey
Costard	Steve Routman	Forester	Brian Dykstra
Don Adriano de Armado	Richard Libertini	Sir Nathaniel	Ronn Carroll
Moth	P. J. Ochlan	Holofernes	Joseph Costa
Jaquenetta	Julia Gibson	Marcade	Davis Hall

Attendants: Peter Carlton Brown, Andrew Colteaux, Brian Dykstra, Michael Gerald.

Understudies: Messrs. Moses, McClure—Peter Carlton Brown; Mr. Ochlan—Max Casella; Messrs. Converse-Roberts, Hymen—Andrew Colteaux; Mr. Ryan—Brian Dykstra; Mr. Routman—Michael Gerald; Messrs. Costa, Carroll—Davis Hall.

Directed by Gerald Freedman; scenery, John Ezell; costumes, James Scott; lighting, Natasha Katz; music, John Morris; choreography, Tina Paul; production stage manager, Richard Constabile; stage manager, Michael Chambers.

Time: The 1930s. Place: Navarre. The play was presented in two parts.

The last major New York revival of *Love's Labor's Lost* was by Circle Repertory Company 10/11/84 for 38 performances.

THE WINTER'S TALE

Polixenes	Christopher Reeve	Cleomenes; Mariner;	
Leontes	Mandy Patinkin	Servant of Old Shepard	Albert Farrar
Hermione	Diane Venora	Dion	Peter Jay Fernandez
Camillo	James Olson	Old Shepherd	MacIntyre Dixon
Sicilian Lady; Mopsa	Kathleen McNenny	Clown	Tom McGowan
Mamillius	Jesse Bernstein	Autolycus	Rocco Sisto
Emilia; Dorcas	Bertina Johnson	Florizel	Graham Winton
Sicilian Lord; Time	Michael Cumpsty	Perdita	Jennifer Dundas
Antigonus	Graham Brown	Sicilian Gentleman	Dan Cordle
Paulina	Alfre Woodard	Harlequin	Rob Besserer
Jailer; Officer	Frank Raiter	Shepherdess (Bohemia)	Denise Faye

Players and Lords and Ladies (Sicilia): Rob Besserer, Cynthia Frieberg, Raymond Kurshal.

Understudies: Messrs. Reeve, Patinkin—Michael Cumpsty; Misses Venora, Woodard—Bertina Johnson; Messrs. Olson, Brown—Frank Raiter; Mr. Bernstein—Jonathan Gold; Miss Dundas—Kathleen McNenny; Messrs. McGowan, Winton, Fernandez, Farrar—Dan Cordle; Mr. Cumpsty—Peter Jay Fernandez.

THE WINTER'S TALE—Jennifer Dundas, Graham Winton, Mandy Patinkin, Alfre Woodard, James Olson, Christopher Reeve and Diane Venora in Shakespeare Marathon's 19th century transposition of the play

Directed by James Lapine; scenery, John Arnone; costumes, Franne Lee; lighting, Beverly Emmons; music, William Finn, Michael Starobin; musical direction, David Evans; choreography, Diane Martel; fights, B. H. Barry; production stage manager, Karen Armstrong; stage manager, Buzz Cohen.

Time: The late 18th century. Place: The Kingdoms of Sicilia and Bohemia. The play was presented in two parts.

The last major New York revival of *The Winter's Tale* was by BAM Theater Company off Broadway 2/12/80 for 27 performances.

CYMBELINE

Ghost Family:
Sicilius Leonatus..........................William Parry
Mother ....Mary Beth Peil
1st Brother ....Devon Michaels
2d Brother ....Eloise Watt
1st Gentleman; 1st Jailer ....Clement Fowler
2d Gentleman; British Lord ....Richard Hicks
Queen ....Joan MacIntosh
Imogen...Joan Cusack
Posthumus.................................Jeffrey Nordling
Lady to the Queen ....Wendy Lawless
Cymbeline................................George Bartenieff

Caius Lucius ....Earl Hindman
Soothsayer ....Rajika Puri
Belarius (Morgan).....................Frederick Neumann
Guiderius (Polydore)........................Jesse Borrego
Iachimo ....Michael Cumpsty
Philario; 2d Jailer ....John Madden Towey
Frenchman ....David Ossian
Gentleman; Roman Captain............Ethan T. Bowen
Gentleman; Messenger;
Court Attendant.........................David Neumann
Cornelius....................................Stefan Schnabel
Lady to Imogen......................Sharon Washington

Pisanio....................................Peter Francis James	Arviragus (Cadwal) ....Don Cheadle
Cloten...Wendell Pierce	1st British Captain.....................Teagle F. Bougere
1st Lord..Tom Fervoy	2d British Captain.......................Tom Dale Keever
2d Lord...Joe Zaloom	Jupiter...Jacob White

Soldiers: Teagle F. Bougere, Ethan T. Bowen, Tom Fervoy, Clement Fowler, Richard Hicks, Tom Dale Keever, Wendy Lawless, David Neumann, David Ossian, Wendell Pierce, Sharon Washington, Joe Zaloom.

Musicians: William Trigg percussion, Jill Jaffe viola.

Directed by JoAnne Akalaitis; scenery, George Tsypin; costumes, Ann Hould-Ward; lighting, Pat Collins; original music, Philip Glass; musical direction, Alan Johnson; projections, Stephanie Rudolph; fight direction, David Leong; choreography, Diane Martel; production stage manager, Steven Ehrenberg; stage manager, Pat Sosnow.

Time: In the midst of Celtic ruins—a romantic fantasy in Victorian England. Place: Britain, Italy, Wales.

Shakespeare's play transposed to the mid-19th century. The last major New York production of *Cymbeline* was by New York Shakespeare Festival 8/12/71 for 15 performances at the Delacorte Theater in Central Park.

Note: New York Shakespeare Festival's Shakespeare Marathon will continue through following seasons until all Shakespeare's plays have been presented. *A Midsummer Night's Dream*, *Julius Caesar* and *Romeo and Juliet* were presented last season (see their entries in the Plays Produced Off Broadway section of *The Best Plays of 1987–88*).

Note: In Joseph Papp's Public Theater there are many auditoria. *Coriolanus* and *The Winter's Tale* played the Anspacher Theater, *Love's Labor's Lost* and *Cymbeline* played the Estelle R. Newman Theater.

Roundabout Theater Company. 1987–88 season concluded with **The Mistress of the Inn** (55). Revival of the play by Carlo Goldoni; translated and adapted by Mark A. Michaels. Produced by Roundabout Theater Company, Gene Feist artistic director, Todd Haimes executive director, at the Christian C. Yegen Theater. Opened July 20, 1988. (Closed September 11, 1988)

Marchese di Forlipopoli.....................Edward Zang	Mirandolina.................................Tovah Feldshuh
Conte d'Albafiorita.............................George Ede	Il Cavaliere Servant........................Richard Levine
Fabrizio..Gabriel Barre	2d Servant......................................J. Peter Adler
Cavaliere di Ripafratta..........................Philip Kerr	

Directed by Robert Kalfin; scenery, Wolfgang Roth; costumes, Andrew B. Marlay; lighting, F. Mitchell Dana; sound, Philip Campanella; production stage manager, Roy W. Backes; press, the Joshua Ellis Office, Susanne Tighe.

Time: Spring 1753. Place: Mirandolina's Inn, Florence, Italy. Act I, Scene 1: Morning. Scene 2: Midday. Act II, Scene 1: Afternoon. Scene 2: Evening.

The last major New York revival of *The Mistress of the Inn* was by Civic Repertory Theater as *La Locandiera* 12/6/26 for 31 performances.

The Negro Ensemble Company. 1987–88 schedule concluded with **From the Mississippi Delta** (77). Return engagement of the play by Endesha Ida Mae Holland. Produced by The Negro Ensemble Company, Douglas Turner Ward producer, Leon B. Denmark producing director, at Theater Four. Opened August 19, 1988. (Closed October 23, 1988)

Woman One............................Gwen Roberts-Frost	Woman Three ....La Tanya Richardson
Woman Two ....Brenda Denmark	

Directed by Ed Smith; scenery, Steven Perry; costumes, Judy Dearing; lighting, William H. Grant III; sound, Jacqui Casto; production stage manager, Sandra L. Ross; press, Howard Atlee.

Time: The early 1950s through the mid-1980s. Synopsis: Memories; Calm, Balmy Days; Second Doctor Lady; The Delta Queen; The Water Meter; The Whole Town's Talking; The Funeral; From the Mississippi Delta; A Permit to Parade. The play was presented without intermission.

From the Mississippi Delta was produced last season off Broadway by The Negro Ensemble Company 11/18/87 for 48 performances.

Blues in the Night (45). Musical revue conceived by Sheldon Epps; musical numbers by various authors (see credits below). Produced by M Square Entertainment, Inc. and TV Asahi at the Minetta Lane Theater. Opened September 14, 1988. (Closed October 23, 1988)

Lady From the Road	Carol Woods	Girl With a Date	Leilani Jones
Woman of the World	Brenda Pressley	Man in the Saloon	Lawrence Hamilton

Blues in the Night Band: David Brunetti conductor, pianist; Keith Copeland drums; Fred Hunter bass; Virgil Jones trumpet; Bill Easley reeds.

Understudy: Mr. Hamilton—C. E. Smith.

Directed by Sheldon Epps; musical direction and additional arrangements, David Brunetti; scenery and costumes, Michael Pavelka; lighting, Susan A. White; sound, Charles Bugbee III; music supervisor arranger and orchestrator, Sy Johnson; assistant director, Patricia Wilcox; co-producers, Joshua Silver, Victoria Maxwell; associate producers, Colin Hooper, Betsy Lifton, Showpeople, Ltd.; production stage manager, Bruce H. Lumpkin; stage manager, Rob Babbitt; press, Peter Cromarty, David Gersten, Kevin Brockman.

Time: The late 1930s. Place: A cheap hotel. The play was presented in two parts.

Three women and a saloon singer, alone in their Chicago hotel rooms, run through "the memories and the music that get them through the night." Previously producd in other versions off Broadway 3/26/80 for 51 performances and on Broadway 6/2/82 for 53 performances; and in this version in 1987 in London, where it received an Olivier Award nomination as best musical.

ACT I

"Blue Blues" ....Company
    (by Bessie Smith)
"Four Walls (and One Dirty Window) Blues" .... Man, Lady
    (by Willard Robinson)
"I've Got a Date With a Dream" ....Woman, Girl
    (by Mack Gordon and Harry Revel)
"New Orleans Hop Scop Blues" .... Lady
    (by George W. Thomas)
"Stompin' at the Savoy" .... Woman
    (by Benny Goodman, Andy Razaf, Edgar Sampson and Chick Webb)
"Taking a Chance on Love" .... Girl
    (by Vernon Duke, John LaTouche and Ted Fetter)
"It Makes My Love Come Down" .... Women
    (by Bessie Smith)
"Lush Life" .... Woman
    (by Billy Strayhorn)
"I'm Just a Lucky So-and-So" ....Man
    (by Duke Ellington and Mack David)
"Take Me for a Buggy Ride" .... Lady
    (by Leola and Wesley Wilson)
"Wild Women Don't Have the Blues" ....Man
    (by Ida Cox)
"Lover Man" .... Lady
    (by Jimmy Davis, Jimmy Sherman and Roger Ramirez)
"Willow Weep for Me" .... Girl
    (by Ann Ronell)
"Kitchen Man" .... Lady
    (by Andy Razaf and Wesley Wilson)
"When Your Lover Has Gone" ....Woman, Girl
    (by A. E. Swan)
"Take It Right Back" .... Women

ACT II

Jam Session ("Wild Women Don't Have the Blues")..Band
"Blues in the Night"..Company
    (by Harold Arlen and Johnny Mercer)
"Dirty No-Gooder's Blues"..Lady
    (by Bessie Smith)
"When a Woman Loves a Man/Am I Blue"...Company
    (by Johnny Mercer, Gordon Jenkins and Bernard Hanighen/by Grand Clarke and Harry Akst)
"Rough and Ready Man".. Women
    (by Alberta Hunter)
"Reckless Blues".. Girl
    (by Bessie Smith)
"Wasted Life Blues"..Lady
    (by Bessie Smith)
"Baby Doll"..Man
    (by Bessie Smith)
"Nobody Knows You When You're Down and Out"..Company
    (by Jimmy Cox)
"I Gotta Right to Sing the Blues".. Women
    (by Harold Arlen and Ted Koehler)
"Four Walls" (Reprise)...Company

*Forbidden Broadway 1988 (later 1989) (296). Revised version of the revue with concept and parody lyrics by Gerard Alessandrini. Produced by Jonathan Scharer at Theater East. Opened September 15, 1988.

Toni DiBuono
Philip Fortenberry
Roxie Lucas

David B. McDonald
Michael McGrath

Understudies: Misses DiBuono, Lucas—Dorothy Kiara; Messrs. McDonald, McGrath—Phillip George.

Directed by Gerard Alessandrini; choreography, Roxie Lucas; costumes, Erika Dyson; production consultant, Pete Blue; associate producers, Arthur B. Brown, Chip Quigley; production stage manager, Jerry James; press, Glenna Freedman/Shirley Herz Associates.

Parodies of present and past stage material by Cole Porter, Stephen Sondheim, Richard Rodgers, Lorenz Hart and Oscar Hammerstein II, Alan Jay Lerner and Frederick Loewe, Jule Styne and Leo Robin, Jerry Bock and Sheldon Harnick, Frank Loesser, Andrew Lloyd Webber and Tim Rice, Charles Strouse and Martin Charnin, Kurt Weill and Bertolt Brecht, Leonard Bernstein, Jerry Herman, Jim Jacobs and Warren Casey, Allen Menken and Howard Ashman, Claude-Michel Schönberg, Alain Boublil and Herbert Kretzmer, Fats Waller, Noel Gay, Harold Karr and Matt Dubey and George M. Cohan.

Music and lyrics to "Forbidden Broadway 88," "Who Do They Know?" and "The Phantom of the Musical" by Gerard Alessandrini.

*Playwrights Horizons. Schedule of five programs. **Young Playwrights Festival** (27). Program of three one-act plays: *And the Air Didn't Answer* by Robert Kerr, *Seniority* by Eric Ziegenhagen and *Women and Wallace* by Jonathan Marc Sherman; presented in the Foundation of the Dramatists Guild production, Nancy Quinn producing director. Opened September 22, 1988. (Closed October 8, 1988) **Saved From Obscurity** (54). Dramatic monologue by Tom Mardirosian. Opened October 13, 1988. (Closed November 27, 1988) **The Heidi Chronicles** (81). By Wendy Wasserstein. Opened December 11, 1988. (Closed February 19, 1989 and transferred to Broadway; see its entry in the Plays Produced on Broadway section of this volume) **Gus and Al** (25). By Albert Innaurato. Opened February 27, 1989. (Closed March 19, 1989) ***Yankee Dawg You Die** (19). By Philip

Kan Gotanda. Opened May 14, 1989. Produced by Playwrights Horizons, Andre Bishop artistic director, Paul S. Daniels executive director, at Playwrights Horizons.

YOUNG PLAYWRIGHTS FESTIVAL

And the Air Didn't Answer

Dan Wilson........................... Robert Sean Leonard
Jennifer ....Jill Tasker
Mother.. Debra Monk
Renee.. Erica Gimpel
Father McLaughlin; Teacher; God;
    Scout Interviewer...................... Richard Council
Young Boy; Crusader; Abraham; Producer;
    Dante; Drunk in Park ....Jihmi Kennedy
Crusader; Isaac; Salesman; Alex Trebek; Virgil;
    Drunk in Park............................John Augustine
Directed by Christopher Durang; playwright advisor, Morgan Jenness; production stage manager, Stacey Fleischer. Comedy about a Catholic schoolboy in the throes of a crisis of faith.

Seniority

Debbie .... Bellina Logan
Fiona... Allison Dean
Ian..Jihmi Kennedy

Directed by Lisa Peterson; playwright advisor, Alfred Uhry; production stage manager, Paul Warren. Time: Autumn, midnight. Place: The living room of a house in a suburb. Emotional rivalries between two sisters.

Women and Wallace

Wallace Kirkman.............................Josh Hamilton
Mother ....Mary Joy
Grandmother................................Joan Copeland
Victoria ....Dana Behr
Psychiatrist ....Debra Monk
Sarah..Bellina Logan
Lili..Jill Tasker
Nina.. Joanna Going
Wendy..Erica Gimpel

Directed by Don Scardino; playwright advisor, Albert Innaurato; production stage manager, Roy Harris. Black comedy, a mother's suicide sends her son into a long period of mental and emotional distress.

ALL PLAYS: Scenery, Allen Moyer; costumes, Jess Goldstein; lighting, Nancy Schertier; sound, Lia Vollack; press, Shirley Herz Associates, Sam Rudy, David Roggensack.

These three plays by young authors (Robert Kerr 17, Eric Ziegenhagen 16, Jonathan Marc Sherman 18 at the time of submission) were selected from hundreds of entries in the Foundation of the Dramatists Guild's 7th annual playwriting contest for young people. The program was presented in two parts with the intermission following *Seniority*. In addition to the above full productions, *The Boiler Room* by Kevin Corrigan, directed by Lawrence Sacharow, Wendy Kesselman playwright advisor, was presented in 3 staged readings.

SAVED FROM OBSCURITY

Cast: Peter Appel, Frederica Meister, Tom Mardirosian, Hansford Rowe.

Directed by John Ferraro; scenery, Rick Dennis; costumes, Marilyn Keith; lighting, Jackie Manassee; sound, Frederick Wessler; production stage manager, Karen Armstrong; press, Philip Rinaldi.

An actor reviews the highlights of his New York career in supporting roles, with comments on real colleagues and productions he has encountered. The play was presented without intermission.

THE HEIDI CHRONICLES

Heidi Holland ....Joan Allan
Susan Johnston..................................Ellen Parker
Chris Boxer; Mark; TV Attendant; Walter;
    Ray... Drew McVety
Peter Patrone .... Boyd Gaines

Scoop Rosenbaum ....Peter Friedman
Jill; Debbie; Lisa...............................Anne Lange
Fran; Molly; Betsy; April ....Joanne Camp
Becky; Clara; Denise................ Sarah Jessica Parker

Directed by Daniel Sullivan; scenery, Thomas Lynch; costumes, Jennifer von Mayrhauser; lighting, Pat Collins; sound, Scott Lehrer; production stage manager, Roy Harris; press, Philip Rinaldi.

Act I, Prologue: A lecture hall, New York, 1988. Scene 1: Chicago, 1965. Scene 2: Manchester, N.H., 1967; Scene 3: Ann Arbor, Mich. 1970. Scene 4: Chicago, 1974. Scene 5: New York, 1977. Act II (all scenes take place in New York), Prologue: A lecture hall, 1988. Scene 1, An apartment, 1980. Scene 2, A TV studio, 1982. Scene 3: A restaurant, 1984. Scene 4: The Plaza Hotel, 1986. Scene 5: A pediatrics ward, 1987. Scene 6: An apartment, 1988.

Comedy about a feminist and her friends and the divergence of individual attitudes and lives from 1965 to the present.

A Best Play; see page 257.

GUS AND AL

Kafka; Sigmund Freud......................Charles Janasz	Natalie Bauer Lechner..........Cara Duff-MacCormick
Al...Mark Blum	Justine Mahler ....Christina Moore
Mrs. Briggs.....................................Helen Hanft	Alma Schindler ....Jennifer Van Dyck
Gustav Mahler...........................Sam Tsoutsouvas	Camillo..Bradley White

Understudies: Messrs. Janasz, Blum, Tsoutsouvas, White—Neal Lerner; Misses Hanft, Duff-MacCormick, Moore, Van Dyck—Kristine Nielsen.

Directed by David Warren; scenery, James Youmans; costumes, David C. Woolard; lighting, Robert Jared; sound, John Gromada; musical arrangements, Ted Sperling; production stage manager, Allison Sommers; stage manager, James Fitzsimmons.

Time and Place: Starting in Manhattan in 1989, changing to Vienna in 1901. The play was presented in two parts.

Disgruntled, critically-panned playwright named Albert Innaurato time-travels back to Mahler's era in search of consolation and new inspiration.

A Best Play; see page 307.

YANKEE DAWG YOU DIE

Vincent .... Sab Shimono
Bradley... Stan Egi

Directed by Sharon Ott; scenery and projection design, Kent Dorsey; costumes, Jess Goldstein; lighting, Dan Kotlowitz; music and sound design, Stephen Legrand, Eric Drew Feldman; production stage manager, Robin Rumpf; stage manager, Eric Osbun.

Time: The present. Place: Los Angeles. The play was presented in two parts.

Two Asian actors, one young and one elderly, differ in their approach to the world of theater and movies.

RECKLESS—Joyce Reehling and Robin Bartlett in the Circle Repertory Company production of the play by Craig Lucas

Circle Repertory Company 20th anniversary season. Schedule of five programs. **Reckless** (113). By Craig Lucas. Opened September 25, 1988. (Closed January 1, 1989) **Brilliant Traces** (41). By Cindy Lou Johnson. Opened February 5, 1989. (Closed March 12, 1989) **Dalton's Back** (30). By Keith Curran. Opened February 9, 1989. (Closed March 5, 1989) **Amulets Against the Dragon Forces** (39). By Paul Zindel. Opened April 5, 1989. (Closed May 7, 1989) And *Florida Crackers* scheduled to open 6/1/89. Produced by Circle Repertory Company, Tanya Berezin artistic director, Connie L. Alexis managing director, at Circle Repertory (*Brilliant Traces* at the Cherry Lane Theater).

RECKLESS

Rachel	Robin Bartlett	Roy; Tim Timko;	
Tom; Tom Jr	Michael Piontek	Talk Show Host	Kelly Connell
Lloyd	John Dossett	Trish; Woman Patient	Susan Blommaert
Pooty; Talk Show Guest	Welker White	Doctor One through Six	Joyce Reehling

Understudies: Miss Bartlett—Jane Loranger; Miss Blommaert—Jodi Manners; Kelly Connell—Robert Gladding; John Dossett—James Gregory Smith; Welker White—Carrena Lukas; Michael Piontek—Mark Torreso; Miss Reehling—Lynn Battaglia.

Directed by Norman René; scenery, Loy Arcenas; costumes, Walker Hicklin; lighting, Debra J. Kletter; sound, Chuck London/Stewart Werner; sign language consultant, Mona Bergman; production stage manager, Fred Reinglas; press, Gary W. Murphy.

A fantasy of self-discovery, as a wife and mother flees from the security of her home into the snowy Christmas night on an arduous adventure. The play was presented in two parts. Previously produced at the Ann Arbor Summer Festival and off off Broadway at The Production Company.

BRILLIANT TRACES

Henry Harry	Kevin Anderson
Rosannah DeLuce	Joan Cusack

Directed by Terry Kinney; scenery, John Lee Beatty; costumes, Laura Crow; lighting, Dennis Parichy; sound, Chuck London/Stewart Werner; fight coordinator, Rick Sordelet; production stage manager, Fred Reinglas.

Time: The present. Place: The state of Alaska, in the middle of nowhere. The play was presented without intermission.

Recluse's privacy is invaded by a runaway bride.

DALTON'S BACK

Dalton Possil	John Dossett	Mom	Lisa Emery
Teresa MacIntyre	Colleen Davenport	Hiram	Jayce Bartok
Dalty	Matt McGrath		

Understudies: Mr. Dossett—Dan Wantland; Miss Davenport—Stephanie Lessem; Mr. McGrath—Robert Gladding; Miss Emery—Lynn Battaglia; Mr. Bartok—Scott Constantine.

Directed by Mark Ramont; scenery, William Barclay; costumes, Susan Lyall; lighting, Dennis Parichy; sound, Robert J. Rick Jr.; production stage manager, Denise Yaney.

Time: The present. Place: Dalton's rooms. The play was presented in two parts.

Damage caused by abuse as a child endures into adulthood and threatens a romantic relationship.

AMULETS AGAINST THE DRAGON FORCES

Chris	Matt McGrath	Attendant #2; Joey	John Viscardi
Harold	Loren Dean	Richie	Robert Gladding
Floyd	John Spencer	Roochie	James Gregory Smith

Mrs. Boyd................................Deborah Hedwall   Rosemary......................................Carrena Lucas
Attendant #1; Leroy.................James Preston Bates

Directed by B. Rodney Marriott; scenery, David Potts; costumes, Walter Hicklin; lighting, Dennis Parichy; sound, Chuck London/Stewart Werner; original music, Norman L. Berman; fight director, Rick Sordelet; production stage manager, M. A. Howard.

Boy struggles to escape an oppressive existence in which his mother, a nurse, makes him come with her into the homes of her terminally ill patients. Previously produced at Coconut Grove Playhouse in a different version entitled *A Destiny With Half-Moon Street*.

Suds (81). Created and written by Melinda Gilb, Steve Gunderson and Bryan Scott; musical numbers by various authors (see credits below). Produced by Richard Redlin, Will Robertson, Bryan Scott and Norma and David Langworthy at the Criterion Center. Opened September 25, 1988. (Closed December 4, 1988)

Cindy..Christine Sevec   Dee Dee...Susan Mosher
Marge .... Melinda Gilb   Everyone Else............................ Steve Gunderson

Understudies: Misses Sevec, Gilb, Mosher—Jeanine Morick, Julie Waldman; Mr. Gunderson—Bob Stromberg.

Directed by Will Roberson; choreography, Javier Velasco; musical direction, William Doyle; scenery, Alan Okazaki; costumes, Gregg Barnes; lighting, Kent Dorsey; sound, Adam Wartnik; musical and vocal arrangements, Steve Gunderson; production stage manager, Mark Baltazar; stage manager, Laura Kravets; press, Jeffrey Richards Associates, Susan Chicoine.

Time: The early 1960s. Place: Anywhere, U.S.A. Act I: A laundromat. Act II: The same laundromat, next day.

Subtitled *The Rocking 60s Musical Soap Opera*, a collection of 51 songs from the 1960s in a story framework in which guardian angels come to the assistance of a despairing laundromat attendant. Previously produced at the Old Globe Theater, San Diego.

MUSICAL NUMBERS (in alphabetical order; songs marked with an asterisk * are by Burt Bacharach and Hal David; by two asterisks ** by Jeff Barry and Ellie Greenwich; by three asterisks *** by John Lennon and Paul McCartney): "A Little Bit of Soup" (by B. Russell), "(There's) Always Something There to Remind Me"*, "Anyone Who Had a Heart"*, "Are You Lonesome Tonight" (by R. Turk and L. Handman), "Baby It's You"*, "Be My Baby"***, "Big Man" (by G. Larson and B. Belland), "Birthday Party" (by J. Madera and D. White), "Chapel of Love"** (with Phil Spector), "Cindy's Birthday" (by H. Wynn and J. Hoover), "Color My World" (by J. Trent and T. Hatch), "Dedicated to the One I Love" (by L. Palling and R. Bass), "Do You Want to Know a Secret"***, "Don't Make Me Over"*, "Do Wah Diddy Diddy"***, "Easier Said Than Done" (by W. Linton and L. Huff), "The End of the World" (by S. Dee and A. Kert), "Happy Birthday Sweet Sixteen" (by Neil Sedaka), "Help Me Girl" (by L. Weiss and S. English), "How Can I Be Sure" (by F. Cavaliere and E. Brigati), "I Don't Wanna Be a Loser" (by R. Raleigh and M. Barkan), "I Got You (I Feel Good)" (by James Brown), "I Know a Place" (by T. Hatch), "I Will Follow Him" (by A. Altman, N. Gimbel and F. Pourcel), "I Say a Little Prayer"*.

Also "It's My Party" (by W. Gold, J. Gluck, H. Wiener and S. Gottlieb), "Johnny Angel" (by L. Pockriss and L. Duddy), "(The) Loco-Motion" (by Gerry Goffin and Carole King), "The Letter" (by W. Thompson), "Lollipops and Roses" (by T. Velona), "The Look of Love"**, "Mystery Date" (by J. Harvey), "Our Day Will Come" (by M. Garson and B. Hilliard), "Please Mr. Postman" (by F. Gorman, R. Bateman and B. Holland), "Respect" (by Otis Redding), "Reach Out in the Darkness" (by J. Post), "Round Every Corner" (by T. Hatch), "Secret Agent Man" (by J. Rivers), "Shout" (by R., B. and O. Isley), "Tell Him" (by B. Russell), "These Boots Are Made for Walking" (by L. Hazelwood), "Today I Met the Boy I'm Gonna Marry" (by T. Powers, Ellie Greenwich and Phil Spector), "Town Without Pity" (by D. Tomkin and N. Washington), "Walk on By"*, "We Can Work It Out"***, "Where the Boys Are" (by H. Greenfield and Neil Sedaka), "Wishing and Hoping"*, "Wonderful, Wonderful" (by S. Edwards and B. Raleigh), "You Can't Hurry Love" (by L. Dozier and B. and E. Holland), "You Don't Own Me" (by J. Madera and B. White), "You Don't Have to Say You Love Me" (by P. Donaggio, V. Pallavicini, V. Wickman and S. N. Bell).

SUDS—Christine Sevec, Steve Gunderson, Melinda Gilb and
Susan Mosher in the musical with songs from the 1960s

*Roundabout Theater Company. Schedule of five revivals. **Ghosts** (63). By Henrik
Ibsen; translated and adapted by Lars Johannesen. Opened October 5, 1988; see note. (Closed
November 27, 1988) **Enrico IV** (60). By Luigi Pirandello; translated by Robert
Cornthwaite. Opened December 21, 1988; see note. (Closed February 12, 1989) **The Mem-
ber of the Wedding** (70). By Carson McCullers. Opened March 8, 1989; see note.
(Closed May 7, 1989) ***Arms and the Man** (15). By George Bernard Shaw. Opened May
17, 1989; see note. Produced by Roundabout Theater Company, Gene Feist artistic director,
Todd Haimes executive director, at the Christian C. Yegen Theater. And *Privates on Parade*
scheduled to open 7/26/89.

GHOSTS

Mrs. Alving...........................Fionnula Flanagan	Jacob Engstrand...........................Edward Seamon
Oswald Alving.............................Raphael Sbarge	Regina Engstrand...........................Roma Downey
Pastor Manders ....David McCallum	

Directed by Stuart Vaughan; scenery, David Potts; costumes, Andrew B. Marlay; lighting, F. Mitchell Dana; sound, Philip Campanella; production stage manager, Kathy J. Faul; press, the Joshua Ellis Office, Susanne Tighe.

Time: Fall, 1881. Place: Mrs. Alving's home in Norway, Act I: Late afternoon. Act II, Scene 1: Early evening. Scene 2: The next morning.

The last major New York production of *Ghosts* was by the Mirror Theater off Broadway 5/15/84 for 16 performances.

ENRICO IV

Landolfo..................................Peter Francis James	Donna Matilde Spina.........................Diane Kagan
Arialdo...Joshua Worby	Frida .... Karen Chapman
Ordulfo.. Lazaro Perez	Dr. Dionisio Genoni ....Robert Stattel
Bertholdo... Richard Hicks	Barone Tito Belcredi ....Jack Ryland
Giovanni ....Frank Nastasi	Enrico IV .... Paul Hecht
Marchese Carlo di Nolli....................Brian Cousins	

Directed by J Ranelli; scenery, Marjorie Bradley Kellogg; costumes, Andrew B. Marlay; lighting, John Gleason; sound, Philip Campanella; production stage manager, Roy W. Backes.

Time: Summer, 1922. Place: Italy. Act I: Afternoon. Act II, Scene 1: Late afternoon. Scene 2: Evening.

This play about a nobleman's delusion of being a German emperor was first produced on Broadway 1/21/24 for 28 performances. It was revived off Broadway in the seasons of 1946–47 and 1947–48 and on Broadway as *Emperor Henry IV* 3/28/73 for 37 performances. This production is its first revival of record in the 1980s and the first under this title.

THE MEMBER OF THE WEDDING

Berenice Sadie Brown.......................... Esther Rolle	Mr. Addams....................................Drew Snyder
Frankie Addams .... Amelia Campbell	Mrs. West....................................Deborah Strang
John Henry West...............Calvin Lennon Armitage	Helen Fletcher..................................Donna Eskra
Jarvis Addams................................ David Whalen	Club Members..............Jeanne Bucci, Susan Honey
Janice...Jeri Leer	T.T. Williams..................................Lou Ferguson
Honey Camden Brown.................William Christian	Barney MacKean................... Steven Douglas Cook

Directed by Harold Scott; scenery, Thomas Cariello; costumes, Andrew B. Marlay; lighting, Shirley Prendergast; sound, Philip Campanella; production stage manager, Kathy J. Faul.

The Member of the Wedding was first produced on Broadway 1/5/50 for 501 performances and was named a Best Play of its season and won the Critics Award for best American play. Its only previous major New York revival was by New Phoenix Repertory Company on Broadway 1/2/75 for 12 performances.

ARMS AND THE MAN

Raina Petkoff ....Roma Downey	Petkoff ....MacIntyre Dixon
Catherine Petkoff ....Barbara Andres	Louka................................Catherine Christianson
Capt. Bluntschli.............................Daniel Gerroll	Sergius Saranoff.......................Christopher North
Nicola...Yusef Bulos	Major Plechanoff...........................Richard Buckley

Directed by Frank Hauser; scenery, Franco Colavecchia; costumes, A. Christina Giannini; lighting, F. Mitchell Dana; sound, Philip Campanella; production stage manager, Roy W. Backes.

Place: A small town in Bulgaria, near the Dragoman Pass. Act I: Raina's bedroom, evening, November 1885, immediately after the Battle of Slivnitza. Act II: The garden of the Petkoff House, forenoon, March 6, 1886, three days after the signing of the treaty. Act III: The Petkoff library, early afternoon the same day.

The last major New York revival of *Arms and the Man* was on Broadway by Circle in the Square 5/30/85 for 109 performances.

Note: Press date for *Ghosts* was 10/20/88, for *Enrico IV* was 1/18/89, for *The Member of the Wedding* was March 30, 1989, for *Arms and the Man* was 6/4/89.

The Taffetas (165). Musical conceived by Rick Lewis; musical numbers by various authors (see credits below). Produced by Arthur Whitelaw and James Shellenberger in association with Select Entertainment at the Cherry Lane Theater. Opened October 12, 1988 (Closed January 1, 1989 after 95 performances) Reopened February 1, 1989 at the Top of the Gate with Harold D. Cohen as an additional producer. (Closed April 9, 1989)

Donna..Jody Abrahams   Cheryl.......................................Melanie Mitchell
Kaye...Karen Curlee   Peggy.. Tia Speros

Musicians: Rick Lewis piano, Mike Osrowitz percussion, Alan Rubin bass.
Understudy: Misses Abrahams, Curlee, Mitchell, Speros—Jean Tait.
Directed by Steven Harris; staged and choreographed by Tina Paul; musical direction and vocal arrangements, Rick Lewis; scenery, Evelyn Sakash; costumes, David Graden; lighting, Ken Billington; associate producer, Adam Sternberg; production stage manager, Allison Sommers; press, Henry Luhrman Associates, Terry M. Lilly.
Musical sequences are titled as follows: Act I—Opening, For Lover and Dreamers, Swinging and Ringing With the Taffetas, Medley for Broken Hearts, Musical Surprises, A Taffeta Postcard; ACT II: Music! Music! Music!, Time Out With the Taffetas, Juke Box Heart Throbs, A Goodnight Wish.
Four singers "from Muncie, Indiana" making their TV debut on the old Dumont network create "A musical journey through the fabulous 1950s." Previously produced off off Broadway at Westbeth cabaret.

ACT I

"Sh-Boom" (by Feaster-Keyes-McRae-Edwards)..Company
"Love Is a Two-Way Street" (by N. Sherman-J. Keller) ....Company
"Mr. Sandman" (by Pat Ballard) ....Company
"The Three Bells" (by Jean Villard and Bert Reisfeld)...Company
"I'm Sorry" (by Self-Albritton)..Company
"Ricochet" (by Larry Coleman, Norman Gimbel and Joe Darion)...Donna
"I Cried"...Cheryl
"Cry" (by Kohlman) ....Peggy
"Smile" (by John Turner, Geoffrey Parsons and Charlie Chaplin) ....Company
"Tonight You Belong to Me" (by Billy Rose)...Peggy, Donna
"Achoo Cha-Cha (Gesundheit)" (by Patrick Welch-Michel Merlo)..Company
"Mockin' Bird Hill" (by V. Horton)..Kaye, Cheryl
"You Belong to Me" (by King-Stewart-Price) ....Company
"Happy Wanderer" (by Malen-Ridge)..Company
"Constantinople"...Company
"My Little Grass Shack" (by Bill Cogswell, Tommy Harrison and Johnny Noble)............................Peggy
"C'Est Si Bon" (by Seelen-Betti-Honeg)...Kaye
"Sweet Song of India" (by Kaye-Clayton) ....Company
"Arrivederci Roma" (by Sigman-Rasul-Giovanni)..Cheryl, Donna
"See the U.S.A. in Your Chevrolet" (by Leon Carr and Leo Corday).......................................Company
"Allegheny Moon" (by Hoffman-Manning) ....Cheryl
"Tennessee Waltz" (by Stewart-King)..Donna
"Old Cape Cod" (by Rathrock-Jeffrey-Yahus)..Kaye
"Nel Blue di Pinto di Blue (Volare)" (by Mondugno-Migliani-Parish)....................................Company
"Around the World" (by Harold Adamson and Victor Young) ....Company

ACT II

"Music! Music! Music!" (by B. Baum and S. Weiss)..Company
"You're Just in Love" (by Irving Berlin)..Company

"Love Letters in the Sand" ....Peggy
"L-O-V-E" ....Cheryl
"I-M-4-U" (by J. Melis and F. Marino)..Company
"Rag Mop" ....Company
"You, You, You" (by R. Mellin and L. Olias)..............................Peggy, Cheryl, Donna
"Puppy Love" (by Paul Anka) ....Kaye
"Doggy in the Window" (by B. Merrill)..Company
"The Hot Canary" (by R. Gilbert and P. Nero)..Company
"Tweedlee Dee" (by W. Scott)...Donna
"Oop Shoop"...Kaye
"Lollipop" (by B. Ross) ....Peggy
"Sincerely" (by Harvey Fuqua and Harvey Freed) ....Company
"Johnny Angel" (by L. Duddy and L. Pockriss)...Cheryl
"Mr. Lee" ....Donna
"Dedicated to the One I Love" (by Lowman Pauling and Ralph Bass) ....Peggy
"Where the Boys Are" (by Sedaka-Greenfield)..Kaye
"I'll Think of You" (by Noel Sherman and Clint Ballard Jr.)..........................Company
"Little Darlin'" (by Williams)...Company

New York Shakespeare Festival. Schedule of eight programs (see note). **What Did He See?** (50). By Richard Foreman; in the Ontological-Hysteric Theater production. Opened October 18, 1988. (Closed December 4, 1988) **Cafe Crown** (56). Revival of the play by Hy Kraft. Opened October 25, 1988. (Closed December 11, 1988 and moved to Broadway; see its entry in the Plays Produced on Broadway section of this volume) **For Dear Life** (16). By Susan Miller. Opened January 10, 1989. (Closed January 22, 1989) **Genesis** (8). Musical based on the medieval Mystery Plays; book and lyrics by A. J. Antoon and Robert Montgomery; music by Michael Ward. Opened January 17, 1989. (Closed January 22, 1989) **Songs of Paradise** (136). Musical in the Yiddish language based on the Biblical poetry of Itsik Manger; book by Miriam Hoffman and Rena Berkowicz Borow; music by Rosalie Gerut; in the Joseph Papp Yiddish Theater production. Opened January 23, 1989. (Closed May 21, 1989) **The Forbidden City** (70). By Bill Gunn. Opened April 6, 1989. (Closed June 4, 1989) **Temptation** (9). By Vaclav Havel; translated by Marie Winn. Opened April 9, 1989. (Closed April 16, 1989) And *Ubu*, adaptation of Alfred Jarry's play by Larry Sloan and Doug Wright, scheduled to open 6/25/89. Produced by New York Shakespeare Festival, Joseph Papp producer, at the Public Theater (see note).

ALL PLAYS: Associate producer, Jason Steven Cohen; plays and musicals development, Gail Merrifield; production manager, Andrew Mihok; press, Richard Kornberg, Barbara Carroll, Reva Cooper, Carol Fineman, Warren Anker.

WHAT DID HE SEE?

Cast: Lili Taylor, Rocco Sisto, Will Patton.
Directed and designed by Richard Foreman; lighting, Anne Militello; production stage manager, David Herskovits; assistant stage manager and Bear, Cass Rodeman.
Experimental and imaginative Foreman treatment of "a bizarre young man's dream to sail beyond the horizon," presented behind a plexiglass wall dividing audience and play.

CAFE CROWN

Kaminsky; Looie .... Mitchell Jason
Rubin ....Jack Kenny
Sam...Fyvush Finkel
Jacobson..................................Bernie Passeltiner
Kaplan ....Felix Fibich
Toplitz ....Harry Goz
Lester Freed................................... Steven Skybell
Norma Cole.....................................Laura Sametz
Ida Polan..................................... Marilyn Cooper
David Cole..Eli Wallach

Mendel Polan ....Joseph Leon
Mrs. Perlman ....Tresa Hughes
Walter..David Carroll
Beggar; Florist;
  Western Union Messenger ....Sidney Armus

George Burton................................Walter Bobbie
Lipsky..Carl Don
Anna Cole.....................................Anne Jackson

Standby: Mr. Wallach—George Guidall. Understudies: Misses Cooper, Jackson, Hughes—Rose Arrick; Messrs. Skybell, Bobbie—Jack Kenny.

Directed by Martin Charnin; scenery and costumes, Santo Loquasto; lighting, Richard Nelson; production stage manager, Alan R. Traynor; stage manager, Lisa Buxbaum.

Place: The Cafe Crown, Second Avenue and 12th Street, New York City. Act I: An autumn evening, 1940. Act II: Immediately after. Act III: Three weeks later.

Cafe Crown was first produced on Broadway 1/23/42 for 141 performances and was adapted by its author as a Broadway musical 4/17/64 for 3 performances. This is its first major New York revival.

GENESIS

Creation and the Fall of Lucifer
Lucifer ....Russ Thacker
  Angels: Bill Christopher-Myers, Mindy Cooper, Braden Danner, Raymond G. del Barrio, Melissa De Sousa, Ty Granaroli, David Patrick Kelly, Tina Paul, Christine Toy.

Creation and the Fall of Adam and Eve
Cherubim ....Christine Toy
Adam .... Stephen Bogardus, Ty Granaroli (Dancer)
Eve....................Mary Munger, Tina Paul (Dancer)
Satan ....Russ Thacker
  Angels: Mindy Cooper, Braden Danner, Raymond G. del Barrio, Melissa De Sousa.

Murder of Abel
Garcio...Russ Thacker
Cain ....David Patrick Kelly
Adam ....Stephen Bogardus
Abel ....Bill Christopher-Myers
Cherubim ....Christine Toy
Eve...Mary Munger

Noah's Ark
Noah......................................Stephen Bogardus
Nesta (Noah's Wife)..........................Mary Munger
Gossip Goodbody ....Tina Paul
Shem .... David Patrick Kelly
Miriam ....Christine Toy
Japhet................................Bill Christopher-Myers
Martha..Mindy Cooper
Ham..Russ Thacker
Mary...Melissa De Sousa
  Townspeople: Braden Danner, Raymond G. del Barrio, Ty Granaroli.

Abraham and Isaac
Abraham ....Stephen Bogardus
Sarah... Mary Munger
Isaac...Braden Danner
Cherubim.......................................Christine Toy

Orchestra: Michael Ward conductor, keyboards; Rich Maisel associate musical director, guitar, keyboards; Todd Isler percussion.

Understudies: Messrs. del Barrio, Granaroli—Patrick Cea; Misses Cooper, De Sousa—Nan Friedman; Miss Paul—Mindy Cooper.

Directed by A. J. Antoon; choreography, Lynne Taylor-Corbett; musical direction, Michael Ward; scenery and costumes, John Conklin; lighting, Jan Kroeze; sound, David A. Schnirman, Gene Ricciardi; production stage manager, Bonnie Panson; stage manager, Gregory Johnson.

Subtitled *Music and Miracles for a New Age*, Mystery-Play Bible stories. The show was presented in two parts.

FOR DEAR LIFE

Jake.. Tony Shalhoub
Maggie.. Bellina Logan
Catherine......................................Laila Robins
Dottie .... Christine Estabrook

Peter ....Joseph Lambie
Sam... Stephen Mailer
Emily...Jennifer Aniston

Directed by Norman René; scenery, Loy Arcenas; costumes, Walter Hicklin; lighting, Arden Fingerhut; dance, Theodore Pappas; fight staged by B. H. Barry.

Time: The Present. Act I: Jake and Catherine's apartment in New York City. Act II: The same. Act III: A country home.

Making a go of marriage while putting up with the major problems of the 1980s.

SONGS OF PARADISE

Adrienne Cooper
Rosalie Gerut
Avi Hoffman

David Kener
Eleanor Reissa

Directed by Avi Hoffman; musical direction, James Mironchik; scenery, Steven Perry; lighting, Anne Militello; music arrangements, Bevan Manson; musical staging, Eleanor Reissa; production stage manager, JoAnn Minsker; stage manager, Christine Wagner.

The story of Genesis in Yiddish with English translation, produced by Joseph Papp Yiddish Theater, Riverdale, N.Y., in association with YIVO Institute for Jewish Research.

ACT I

"Di Demerung" (The Twilight) .... Rosalie Gerut, Adrienne Cooper
Scene 1: Garden of Eden
    Odem (Adam) .... Avi Hoffman
    Khave (Eve) .... Eleanor Reissa
    Apple Tree .... David Kener
    "Khave and the Apple Tree" .... Reissa
    "Odem and Khave Duet" .... Reissa, Hoffman, Kener
Scene 2: Outside the Garden of Eden
    Khave .... Cooper
    Kain (Cain) .... Kener
    Heyvl (Abel) .... Hoffman
Scene 3: In the Land of Canaan
    Avrum (Abraham) .... Kener
    Sore (Sarah) .... Cooper
    Hoger (Hagar) .... Gerut
    Turks .... Cooper, Reissa, Hoffman
    "Avrum and Sore's Duet" .... Kener, Cooper
    "Hoger and the Turks" .... Gerut, Cooper, Reissa, Hoffman
    "Shir Hamaylesn" (Song of Blessings) .... Company
    "Hoger's Lament/Sore's Lullaby" .... Gerut, Cooper

ACT II

Scene 1: Rifke's Diner
    Waitress .... Gerut
    Customer .... Reissa
    Yankev (Jacob) .... Hoffman
    Eysev (Esau) .... Kener
Scene 2: The road to Aram
    Angels .... Reissa, Cooper, Kener
    Yankev .... Hoffman
    Rokhl (Rachel) .... Gerut
    "Yankev and Rokhl Duet" .... Gerut, Hoffman
Scene 3: Lovn's house
    Lovn (Laban) .... Kener
    Rokhl .... Gerut
    Yankev .... Hoffman
    Leye (Leah) .... Cooper
Scene 4: Zuleyka's boudoir
    Zuleyka .... Reissa
    Potifar .... Kener
    Yosef (Joseph) .... Hoffman
    "Yosef's Tango" .... Hoffman, Gerut, Cooper
Scene 5: Pharaoh's prison
    Finale: "The Farewell Song" .... Company

THE FORBIDDEN CITY

Nick Hoffenburg Jr.	Akili Prince	Loretta	Erika Alexander
Molly Hoffenburg	Gloria Foster	Smitty	Allie Woods Jr.
Nick Hoffenburg Sr.	Frankie R. Faison	Whistlin' Billy	Mansoor Najee-Ullah
Ivan Trumbull	P. Jay Sidney	David	Demetri Corbin
Cupid Trumbull	Cortez Nance Jr.	Hodge	William Cain
Abel Trumbull	Guy Davis		

Directed by Joseph Papp; scenery, Loren Sherman; costumes, Judy Dearing; lighting, Peter Kaczorowski; music supervision, Sam Waymon; production stage manager, James Bernardi; stage manager, Gwendolyn Gilliam.

Time: 1936. Place: Philadelphia. Act I, Scene 1: The Hoffenburg home, before sunrise and later that evening. Scene 2: A room in the Worcestershire Hotel. Act II: The Hoffenburg home, early the next morning.

Young man's struggle against his parental ties.

TEMPTATION

Dr. Libby Lorencova	Tanny McDonald	Director	Bill Moor
Dr. Kotrly	David Schechter	Special Secretary	Ron Karl West
Dr. Neuwirth	Joel McKinnon Miller	Vilma	Margaret Gibson
Marketa	Katherine Hiler	Mrs. Mulch	Sarah Melici
Dr. Henry Foustka	David Strathairn	Fistula	Bille Brown
Deputy Director	Larry Block	Lovers	Angel David, Annie Rae Etheridge
Petrushka	Marla Sucharetza	Dancer	Raymond G. del Barrio

Directed by Jiri Zizka; scenery, Jerry Rojo; costumes, Hiroshi Iwasaki; lighting, Jerold R. Forsyth; music, Adam Wernick; sound effects, Charles Cohen; projection design, Jeffrey S. Brown; tango choreography, Raymond G. del Barrio; production stage manager, Donald Christy; stage manager, Chris Sinclair.

Act I, Scene 1: The Institute, 9 a.m. Scene 2: Foustka's apartment, that evening. Scene 3: The garden of the Institute, later that night. Scene 4: Vilma's apartment, still later that night. Scene 5: The Institute, 9 a.m. the next morning. Act II, Scene 6: Foustka's apartment, that evening. Scene 7: The Institute, 9 a.m. the next morning. Scene 8: Vilma's apartment, that night. Scene 9: Foustka's apartment, later that night. Scene 10: The garden of the Institute, the next evening shortly before midnight.

Version of the Faust legend set in a modern totalitarian state. A foreign (Czechoslovakian) play whose author was in prison in his native land at the time of this U.S. premiere.

Note: In Joseph Papp's Public Theater there are many auditoria. *What Did He See?* and *Songs of Paradise* played the Susan Stein Shiva Theater, *Cafe Crown* played the Estelle R. Newman Theater, *Genesis* and *The Forbidden City* played LuEsther Hall, *For Dear Life* and *Temptation* played Martinson Hall.

Note: In addition to the programs listed above, New York Shakespeare Festival was in the midst of its Shakespeare Marathon, a six-year schedule of productions of all of Shakespeare's plays, which began 1/12/88 and continued this season at the Delacorte Theater in Central Park as well as the Public Theater; see the 1988–89 Shakespeare Marathon entries elsewhere in this Plays Produced Off Broadway section.

*The Cocktail Hour (258). By A. R. Gurney. Produced by Roger L. Stevens, Thomas Viertel, Steven Baruch and Richard Frankel at the Promenade Theater. Opened October 20, 1988.

Bradley	Keene Curtis	John	Bruce Davison
Ann	Nancy Marchand	Nina	Holland Taylor

Understudies: Mr. Curtis—Hansford Rowe; Mr. Davison—Richard Backus.

Directed by Jack O'Brien; scenery and costumes, Steven Rubin; lighting, Kent Dorsey; associate producer, Thomas Hall; production stage manager, Douglas Pagliotti; stage manager, Patrick Horrigan; press, David Powers, Mary Bryant.

Time: Early evening in early fall in the mid-1970s. Place: A city in upstate New York. The play was presented in two parts.

Playwright stirs up family emotions and conflicts by using his parents as leading characters in his next play. Previously produced at the Old Globe Theater, San Diego.

A Best Play; see page 148.

Richard Backus replaced Bruce Davison 4/11/89.

*Manhattan Theater Club. Schedule of seven programs. **Eastern Standard** (46). By Richard Greenberg. Opened October 27, 1988. (Closed December 4, 1988 and transferred to Broadway; see its entry in the Plays Produced on Broadway section of this volume) **Italian American Reconciliation** (57). By John Patrick Shanley. Opened October 30, 1988. (Closed December 18, 1988) **What the Butler Saw** (99). Revival of the play by Joe Orton. Opened March 8, 1989. (Closed May 10, 1989) ***Aristocrats** (42). By Brian Friel. Opened April 25, 1989. **Eleemosynary** (16). By Lee Blessing. Opened May 9, 1989. (Closed May 21, 1989) Also *The Lisbon Traviata* by Terrence McNally scheduled to open 6/20/89 and *The Loman Family Picnic* by Donald Margulies scheduled to open 6/6/89. Produced by Manhattan Theater Club, Lynne Meadow artistic director, Barry Grove managing director, at City Center, *Eastern Standard* and *What the Butler Saw* at Stage I, *Italian American Reconciliation*, and *Eleemosynary* at Stage II; and *Aristocrats* at Theater Four.

EASTERN STANDARD

Stephen Wheeler	Dylan Baker	Phoebe Kidde	Patricia Clarkson
Drew Paley	Peter Frechette	Peter Kidde	Kevin Conroy
Ellen	Barbara Garrick	May Logan	Anne Meara

Standbys: Miss Meara—Faith Geer; Misses Clarkson, Garrick—Collette Kilroy; Messrs. Baker, Frechette, Conroy—Michael McKenzie.

Directed by Michael Engler; scenery, Philipp Jung; costumes, Candice Donnelly; lighting, Dennis Parichy; sound, Daniel Moses Schreier; production stage manager, Pat Sosnow; stage manager, Tammy Taylor; press, Helene Davis, Linda Feinberg, Kim Moarefi.

Time: Spring and summer, 1987. Act I: A restaurant, midtown Manhattan, late May. Act II, Scene 1: Stephen's summer house, a month later. Scene 2: The same, two weeks later. Scene 3: The same, two weeks later. Scene 4: The same, the next morning. Scene 5: The same, the next morning.

Sexual and social adventures of young achievers, as they try to rehabilitate a bag lady as part of their comedically-aimed search for the truth about their own lives and loves. Previously produced by Seattle Repertory Theater.

A Best Play; see page 172.

ITALIAN AMERICAN RECONCILIATION

Aldo Scalicki	John Turturro	Aunt May	Helen Hanft
Huey Maximilian Bonfigliano	John Pankow	Janice	Jayne Haynes
Teresa	Laura San Giacomo		

Directed by John Patrick Shanley; scenery, Santo Loquasto; costumes, William Ivey Long; lighting, Peter Kaczorowski; sound, John Gromada; production stage manager, Ruth Kreshka.

Time: The spring. Place: Little Italy. The play was presented in two parts.

The bumpy ways of love, Italian-American style, as a pining husband attempts to restore his failed marriage.

WHAT THE BUTLER SAW

Dr. Prentice	Charles Keating	Nicholas Beckett	Bruce Norris
Geraldine Barclay	Joanne Whalley-Kilmer	Dr. Rance	Joseph Maher
Mrs. Prentice	Carole Shelley	Sgt. Match	Patrick Tull

Directed by John Tillinger; scenery, John Lee Beatty; costumes, Jane Greenwood; lighting, Ken Billington; sound, John Gromada; production stage manager, James Harker; stage manager, Camille Calman.

What the Butler Saw had its New York premiere off Broadway 5/4/70 for 224 performances and was named a Best Play of its season. It was revived off Broadway 7/3/81 for 12 performances. The present production was presented in two parts.

ARISTOCRATS

Willie Diver	John Christopher Jones	Eamon	John Pankow
Tom Hoffnung	Peter Crombie	Claire	Haviland Morris
Uncle George	Thomas Barbour	Judith	Kaiulani Lee
Casimir	Niall Buggy	Father	Joseph Warren
Alice	Margaret Colin	Anna's Voice	Roma Downey

Directed by Robin Lefèvre; scenery, John Lee Beatty; costumes, Jane Greenwood; lighting, Dennis Parichy; sound, John A. Leonard; production stage manager, Tom Aberger.

Time: Summer, mid-1970s. Place: Ballybeg Hall, the home of District Judge O'Donnell, overlooking the village of Ballybeg, County Donegal, Ireland. Act I: Early afternoon on a warm summer day. Act II: About an hour later. Act III: Early afternoon ten days later. The play was presented in two parts with the intermission following Act II.

Troubled reunion of a judge's family in Ireland in the 1970s symbolizes some of Ireland's national problems. A foreign play previously produced at the Abbey Theater, Dublin in 1979 and in London in 1988.

A Best Play; see page 352.

ELEEMOSYNARY

Dorothea	Eileen Heckart	Echo	Jennie Moreau
Artie	Joanna Gleason		

ELEEMOSYNARY—Joanna Gleason, Jennie Moreau and Eileen Heckart in the Manhattan Theater Club production of Lee Blessing's play

Directed by Lynne Meadow; scenery, John Lee Beatty; costumes, William Ivey Long; lighting, Dennis Parichy; production stage manager, Ruth Kreshka.

Three generations of strong-minded, feminist women reacting to each other. The play was presented without intermission.

American Place Theater. Schedule of three programs. **A Burning Beach** (13). By Eduardo Machado. Opened November 3, 1988. (Closed November 13, 1988) **The Unguided Missile** (9). By David Wolpe. Opened February 12, 1989. (Closed February 19, 1989) **The Blessing** (9). By Clare Coss. Opened May 21, 1989. (Closed May 28, 1989) Produced by American Place Theater, Wynn Handman director, at American Place Theater.

A BURNING BEACH

Marta	Lillian Garrett	Juan	George Lundoner
Ofelia	Ivonne Coll	Constance	Liann Pattison
Maria	Seret Scott	Un Hombre	Mateo Gomez

Directed by Rene Buch; scenery, Donald Eastman; costumes, Deborah Shaw; lighting, Anne Militello; sound, Daniel Moses Schreier; production stage manager, Rebecca Green; press, the Fred Nathan Company, Marc P. Thibodeau.

Emotional and political divisions within an aristocratic Cuban family during Jose Marti's revolutionary activities in 1895.

THE UNGUIDED MISSILE

Martha Mitchell	Estelle Parsons	Mike Madden; Todd Peterson;	
John Mitchell	Jerome Dempsey	Others	Barry Cullison
Photographer; Alan Webster; Others	Nick Searcy	Sherri Peterson	Lezlie Dalton
		Cathy; Dr. Kramer; Others	Mary Jo Salerno

Directed by Fred Kolo; scenery and lighting, Holger; costumes, Gail Cooper-Hecht; audio/visual producer, Matthew Heineman; production stage manager, Richard Hester.

The outspoken wife of the U.S. Attorney General during the events of Watergate.

THE BLESSING

Claudine	Louisa Horton	Restive	Anita Gillette
Kathleen	Beth Fowler	Nan	Kelly Bishop
Marilyn	Leila Boyd	Miss Mary	Anne Shropshire
Flora	Olga Merediz		

Directed by Roberta Sklar; scenery, Donald Eastman; costumes, Sally J. Lesser; lighting, Frances Aronson; sound, Daniel Moses Schreier; production stage manager, Richard Hester.

Time: Summer 1987. Place: Lerner Adult Home, the South Shore of Long Island. The play was presented in two parts.

Abrasive relationship of a mother, confined to a nursing home, and her lesbian daughter.

Lincoln Center Theater. Schedule of two revivals. **Waiting for Godot** (25). By Samuel Beckett; presented in the Mike Nichols production. Opened November 6, 1988. (Closed November 27, 1988) **Measure for Measure** (69). By William Shakespeare. Opened March 9, 1989. (Closed May 7, 1989) Produced by Lincoln Center Theater, Gregory Mosher director, Bernard Gersten executive producer, at the Mitzi E. Newhouse Theater.

WAITING FOR GODOT

Estragon......................................Robin Williams	Pozzo....................................F. Murray Abraham
Vladimir...Steve Martin	Boy...Lukas Haas
Lucky..Bill Irwin	

Understudies: Messrs. Williams, Martin—James Lally; Mr. Irwin—David Pierce; Mr. Abraham—Dan Butler; Mr. Haas—Atticus Brady.

Directed by Mike Nichols; scenery, Tony Walton; costumes, Ann Roth; lighting, Jennifer Tipton; sound, Tom Sorce; production stage manager, Bill Buxton; stage manager, Gwendolyn M. Gilliam; press, Merle Debuskey, Bill Evans, Bruce Campbell.

Act I: A road, evening. Act II: The next day, same time, same place.

The last major New York revival of *Waiting for Godot* was by The Acting Company 4/22/81 for 3 performances.

MEASURE FOR MEASURE

Vincentio...Len Cariou	Isabella..Kate Burton
Escalus...George Hall	Francisca................................... Marceline Hugot
Angelo.......................................Campbell Scott	Elbow .... Thomas Ikeda
Lucio................................... Reggie Montgomery	Froth......................................Ethyl Eichelberger
1st Gentleman; Varrius..................Marcus Giamatti	Justice; Friar Peter............................. Don Mayo
2d Gentleman; Abhorson ....Philip Moon	Secretary to Angelo.........................Koji Okamura
Mistress Overdone..............................Lois Smith	Juliet..............................Gabriella Diaz-Farrar
Pompey...Jack Weston	Boy.. Joel E. Chaiken
Claudio ....Bradley Whitford	Mariana ....Lorraine Toussaint
Provost...Deryl Caitlyn	Secretaries..................Robert Bella, Jonathan Baker
Father Thomas; Barnardine............ Mario Arrambide	

Officers: Jonathan Baker, Paul S. Eckstein, Jonathan Nichols, Ascanio Sharpé.

Understudies: Mr. Cariou—Mario Arrambide; Mr. Hall—Thomas Ikeda; Mr. Scott—Bradley Whitford; Mr. Montgomery—Ethyl Eichelberger; Messrs. Giamatti, Okamura—Robert Bella; Mr. Moon—Koji Okamura; Miss Smith—Marceline Hugot; Misses Diaz-Farrar, Toussaint—Kathryn Meisle; Mr. Weston—Don Mayo; Mr. Whitford—Jonathan Nichols; Messrs. Arrambide, Caitlyn—Marcus Giamatti; Misses Burton, Hugot— Gabriella Diaz-Farrar; Messrs. Ikeda, Eichelberger—Ascanio Sharpé; Mr. Mayo—Jonathan Baker; Mr. Chaiken—Adam Plotch; Officers—Philip Moon; Secretaries—Jonathan Baker.

Directed by Mark Lamos; scenery and costumes, John Conklin; lighting, Pat Collins; sound, David Budries; original music, Mel Marvin; stage manager, Wendy Chapin; press, Merle Debuskey, Bruce Campbell.

Place: Vienna. The play was presented in two parts.

The last major New York revival of *Measure for Measure* was by New York Shakespeare Festival at the Delacorte Theater in Central Park 6/30/85 for 25 performances.

Anthony Crivello replaced Mario Arrambide, Wayne Knight replaced Jack Weston, Lois Markle replaced Marceline Hugot, Marceline Hugot replaced Lois Smith, Kim Staunton replaced Lorraine Toussaint 4/11/89.

The Hired Man (33). Musical with book adapted by Melvyn Bragg from his novel; music by Howard Goodall. Produced by The Heritage Project, Inc., Brian Aschinger producer, at the 47th Street Theater. Opened November 10, 1988. (Closed December 18, 1988)

John ....Paul Avedisian	Landlady ....Robin Smith
Emily ....Carolyn Popp	Josh... David M. Beris
Jackson ....Ray Luetters	Chairman; Phographer; Alec.........Christopher Boyd
Isaac ....Ray Collins	Tom.. Keith D. Cooper
Seth...Nick Corley	Dan..Tom Freeman
May.. Corliss Preston	Beth......................................Aimee M. Luzier
Harry ....James O'Neill	Bob; Mr. Stephens.......................Bruce MacKillip
Sally...Gloria Boucher	Joe Sharp; Alf..................................Len Matheo
Blacklock...Bob Wilkens	Recruiting Officer...............................Larry Stotz
Pennington; Vicar .... Richard Lupino	

Understudies: Mr. Avedisian—Bruce MacKillip; Miss Popp—Marilyn Firment; Mr. Luetters—Tom Freeman; Mr. Collins—Christopher Boyd; Messrs. Corley, Boyd—David M. Beris; Misses Boucher, Smith—Aimee M. Luzier; Miss Preston—Gloria Boucher; Mr. O'Neill—Keith D. Cooper.

Orchestra: Ann Crawford piano; Madelyn Rubinstein, Frank Spitznagel, John Mulcahy keyboard; Jeff Gordon trumpet; Brian Allen string bass.

Directed by Brian Aschinger; musical staging, Rodney Griffin; musical direction, Ann Crawford; scenery, Tamara Kinkman; costumes, Patricia Adshead; lighting, Leon Di Leone; production stage manager, David Sitler; press, Jeffrey Richards Associates, Ben Morse.

American premiere of British musical about a farmhand trying to become a miner in order to support his family at the turn of the century. A foreign play previously produced throughout the United Kingdom.

ACT I

Scene 1: The hiring, 1896, Cockermouth, in the North of England
"Song of the Hired Man"..Company
"Fill It to the Top"..Isaac, Seth, John, Ensemble
"Now for the First Time" ....Emily, John
"Song of the Hired Man" (Reprise)...Workers
Scene 2: Work. Some months later, John and Emily's cottage at Crossbridge, Pennington's farm and surrounding farms
"Work Song: It's All Right for You"..Farmers, Workers
Scene 3: The Crossbridge cottage, a short time later
"Who Will You Marry Then?"...Emily, Sally
Time Passing..Instrumental Interlude
Scene 4: The Crossbridge cottage, 18 months later. The hunt.
"Get Up and Go, Lad"...Isaac, John, Ensemble
"I Wouldn't Be the First"...Emily, Jackson
Scene 5: After the hunt, Crossbridge cottage
"Fade Away"...John, Emily
Scene 6: The pub; the fight
"Hear Your Voice" ....Jackson
"What a Fool I've Been"..John
"If I Could"...Emily
"Song of the Hired Man (Reprise)/Men of Stone".................................Company

ACT II

Scene 1: Crossbridge, 16 years later; early summer 1914
"You Never See the Sun" ....May
Interlude: Jackson...Instrumental Ensemble
Scene 2: The cottage at the mining town of Whitehaven, a few months later
"What Would You Say to Your Son?" ....John
Scene 3: The union meeting
"Union Song: Men of Stone"..Seth, Blacklock, Men
Scene 4: Before the Great War
Interlude: Gathering of Soldiers...Instrumental Ensemble
"Farewell Song" ....Emily, John, Isaac, May, Ensemble
Scene 5: The war
"War Song: So Tell Your Children" ....Isaac, John, Jackson, Emily, May, Harry, Seth, Soldiers
Scene 6: 1919, the Crossbridge Club Walk
"Crossbridge Dance"... Isaac, Company
"No Choir of Angels"..Emily, John
Scene 7: Whitehaven: The cottage; the pit
"Hear Your Voice" (Reprise) ....Jackson
"If I Could" (Reprise)... Emily
Scene 8: Crossbridge: The re-hiring
Finale; "Song of the Hired Man" (Reprise)...................................Company

MEASURE FOR MEASURE—Len Cariou, Lorraine Toussaint
and Kate Burton in the Lincoln Center Theater revival

The Faithful Brethren of Pitt Street (8). By Philip Lamb. Produced by Jacob Salzman at the Orpheum Theater. Opened November 14, 1988. (Closed November 20, 1988)

Directed by Ethan Taubes; scenery and lighting, Jeffrey Schissler; costumes, Marianne Powell-Parker; sound, Aural Fixation; press, Henry Luhrman, Terry M. Lilly, David Lotz. With Michael Marcus, Sol Frieder, Carl J. Franco, Allen L. Rickman, David Hurst, Norman Kruger, Ward Saxton, Victor Arnold, Debra Stricklin.

Time: The present. Place: The stage of the Yiddish Art Theater. The play was presented in two parts.

Elderly arts lovers are conned into producing a student play with a new Yiddish theater group.

The Middle of Nowhere (24). Musical conceived and written by Tracy Friedman; based on songs by Randy Newman. Produced by Frank Basile, Lewis Friedman, Tom O. Meyerhoff and Albert Nocciolino at the Astor Place Theater. Opened November 20, 1988. (Closed December 11, 1988)

Joe	Roger Robinson	Girl	Diana Castle
G.I.	Vondie Curtis-Hall	Redneck	Tony Hoylen
Salesman	Michael Arkin		

The Back of the Bus Band: Jonny Bowden conductor, keyboards; Mark Belaire drums, percussion; Steve Gelfand electric bass, fretless bass; Dale Kleps alto sax, baritone sax, clarinet, wind synthesizer; Bob Loughlin electric guitar, acoustic guitar, banjo.

Standbys: Messrs. Robinson, Curtis-Hall—Rudy Roberson; Messrs. Arkin, Hoylen—Nick Searcy; Miss Castle—Christine Gaudet.

Directed and choreographed by Tracy Friedman; musical direction, Jonny Bowden; scenery, Loren Sherman; costumes, Juliet Polcsa, Loren Sherman; lighting, Phil Monat; sound, Christopher Bond; musical supervision, arrangements and orchestrations, Robby Merkin; associate choreographer, Richard Stafford; production stage manager, Ellen Raphael; press, the Joshua Ellis Office, Adrian Bryan-Brown, Jackie Green.

Time: 1969. Place: a bus depot somewhere on the back roads of Louisiana. The play was performed without intermission.

Stranded travellers fantasize a musical review with two dozen Randy Newman songs.

MUSICAL NUMBERS: "I Think It's Going to Rain Today," "Simon Smith," "Yellow Man," "Davy the Fat Boy," "Political Science," "Lonely at the Top," "Lover's Prayer," "Old Kentucky Home," "Tickle Me," "Maybe I'm Doing It Wrong," "They Just Got Married," "Short People."

Also "Song for the Dead," "Baltimore," "I'm Different," "It's Money That I Love," "Sigmund Freud's Impersonation," "Sail Away," "You Can Leave Your Hat On," "Old Man," "Marie," "Rednecks," "Mr. President," "Louisiana 1927."

Emerald City (17). By David Williamson. Produced off off Broadway by New York Theater Workshop, artistic director James C. Nicola, managing director Nancy Kassak Diekmann, at the Perry Street Theater. Opened November 30, 1988 in a limited engagement. (Closed December 18, 1988).

Colin	Daniel Gerroll	Mike	Dan Butler
Elaine	Doris Belack	Helen	Alice Haining
Kate	Gates McFadden	Malcolm	Jerry Lanning

Directed by R. J. Cutler; scenery, James Youmans; costumes, Michael Krass; lighting, Kenneth Posner; sound, John Gromada; production stage manager, Susan Hauser Weiss; press, Gary Murphy.

Time: Now. Place: Sydney, Australia. The play was presented in two parts.

A huckster and an idealist follow different but converging paths to success, in a comedy about achievers in the movie and publishing businesses. A foreign play previously produced in Sydney and elsewhere.

A Best Play (in our policy of citing specified special cases of OOB production); see page 196.

The Majestic Kid (54). By Mark Medoff. Produced by Golden Glow Unlimited, Ltd. at the Theater at St. Peter's Church. Opened December 1, 1988. (Closed January 15, 1989)

Aaron Weiss	Stuart Zagnit	Lisa Belmondo	Juliette Kurth
Judge William S. Hart Finlay	Michael Cullen	The Laredo Kid	Alex Wipf
A.J. Pollard	Kay Walbye	Grips	Eliza Berry, Rande Mele

Directed by Derek Wolshonak; scenery, Lewis Folden; costumes, Debra Stein; lighting, Scott Pinkney; music, Jan Scarbrough; lyrics, Mark Medoff, Jan Scarbrough; sound, The Sound Spa; stage manager, Sheri Kane; press, Peter Cromarty, David Gersten, Kevin Brockman.

Time: Not very long ago. Place: Our West. The play was presented in two parts.

Comic Western comparing 1980s morality with Western movies.

Sweethearts (54). Produced by Will You Remember Productions at the Actors' Playhouse. Opened December 7, 1988. (Closed January 22, 1989)

Jeanette MacDonald	Antoinette Mille
Nelson Eddy	Walter Adkins

Conductor/pianist, David Wolfson; costumes, Josie Garner; lighting, Paul Lindsay Butler; original musical arrangements, Don Chan; production stage manager, David G. O'Connell; press, Robert Ganshaw.

Subtitled "Nostalgic Musical Memories of Jeanette MacDonald and Nelson Eddy," a collection of their famous solos and duets loosely connected by an uncredited narrative of their careers. Previously produced at Pantages Center, Tacoma.

ACT I

Overture

"Beyond the Blue Horizon"..Jeanette

"My Own United States" ....Nelson

"Will You Remember"..Duet

"Marsovia"...Jeanette

Selections from *Naughty Marietta* ....Jeanette, Nelson
    "'Neath the Southern Moon," "I'm Falling in Love With Someone," "Tramp! Tramp! Tramp!", "Ah! Sweet Mystery of Life"

"San Francisco" ....Jeanette

"Shenandoah" ....Nelson

"Giannina Mia"..Jeanette

Selections from *Rose-Marie* ....Jeanette, Nelson
    "Rose-Marie," "Lak Jeem," "The Mounties," "Indian Love Call"

ACT II

Entr'acte

"Sweethearts" ....Duet

"Ciribiribin"..Jeanette

"While My Lady Sleeps" ....Nelson

"Farewell to Dreams"...Duet

"Will You Remember" (Reprise)..Duet

"Italian Street Song"...Jeanette

"Cuban Love Song"..Nelson

"The Rogue Song" ....Nelson

Selections from *New Moon*...Jeanette, Nelson
    "Wanting You," "Softly, as in a Morning Sunrise," "One Kiss," "Lover, Come Back to Me," "Stouthearted Men"

Finale ....Jeanette, Nelson

The Negro Ensemble Company. Schedule of two programs. **We.** Repertory of two plays by Charles Fuller: **Sally** (41) opened December 18, 1988 (matinee); **Prince** (41) opened December 18, 1988 (evening). (Repertory closed February 26, 1989) Produced by The Negro Ensemble Company, Douglas Turner Ward president, Leon B. Denmark producing director, at Theater Four.

PERFORMER	"SALLY"	"PRINCE"
Alvin Alexis	Yockum	Norman
Peggy Alston		Mary
Cynthia Bond	Young Slave Girl; Jonquil	
Carla Brothers		Tiche
Graham Brown		Stubbs
Rosanna Carter	Becky	Carrie
O. L. Duke	Vendross	
Carl Gordon	Sutton	Quash
Samuel L. Jackson	Prince	Prince
Pirie MacDonald		Dr. Bernard
William Mooney	General	Kellogg
Samuel Moses	Pell	Soldier 1
Raynor Scheine	Reporter	Proter
Larry Sharp	Lt. Cable	Duffy
Michele Shay	Sally	
Maureen Silliman		Hannah

Ed Wheeler	Washington	Burner
Hattie Winston		Lu
John Wooten		Soldier 2

BOTH PLAYS: Directed by Douglas Turner Ward; scenery, Charles McClennahan; costumes, Judy Dearing; lighting, Arthur Reese; sound, John T. Cherry; production stage manager, Wayne Elbert; press, Howard Atlee.

SALLY: Time—1862–63, winter. Place—Beaufort, S.C., various shifting locales of the Union Army on the march—battlefields, Union Army Headquarters, living quarters and campsites of ex-slaves. The play was presented in two parts.

In *Sally*, Part 1 of a five-part series of plays about American blacks in the 19th century after the Civil War, a black Union Army sergeant, Prince, is torn between his own colleagues and career and the newly-freed slaves trying to adjust to a new life which has almost as many problems as their former one.

PRINCE: Time—1864, fall and early winter. Place—Virginia, in the same Union Army and slave quarters as above. The play was presented in two parts.

In *Prince*, Part 2 of the *We* cycle, the sergeant has managed to remain in the Army successfully until past misdeeds catch up with him.

Phantasie (15). By Sybille Pearson. Produced by The Vineyard Theater, Doug Aibel artistic director, Barbara Zinn Krieger executive director, Jon Nakagawa managing director, at the Vineyard Theater. Opened January 17, 1989 (see note). (Closed January 29, 1989)

D	Diane Salinger	Lorraine; Maid; Mrs. Johnson;
Leah	Elzbieta Czyzewska	Dr. Croyers; Mom	Myra Taylor
Michael	Michael French	Desk Clerk; Man; Danny; Dr. Prager;
Valerie	Laurinda Barrett	Tenant; Pop	Ryan Cutrona

Directed by John Rubinstein; scenery, William Barclay; costumes, Deborah Shaw; lighting, Phil Monat; sound, Phil Lee; production stage manager, Shannon Graves; press, Bruce Cohen, Kathleen von Schmid.

Act I: The present, a hotel lobby in Boston; the past, various locations in D's life. Act II: Valerie's living room, past and present.

A young New York professional woman searches for her true identity.

Note: *Phantasie* was produced by The Vineyard Theater as an off-off-Broadway offering 12/22/88 and raised to full off-Broadway status 1/17/89.

*Bunnybear (134). By Nico Hartos. Produced by Nico Hartos and Vincent De Angelis in the Pyramid Group Theater Company production at the Peter Xantho Theater. Opened January 19, 1989.

Sandy	Laura Fay Lewis
Jack	Richard Flynn

Directed by Nico Hartos; scenery, D. C. Glenn-Marc Umile; lighting and sound, Winifred Powers; production stage manager, Hudson Plumb; press, Francine L. Trevens, Mike Kopelow.

Place: Jack and Sandy Hunter's one-bedroom apartment on the Upper West Side of Manhattan. Act I, Scene 1: Fall 1986, a Sunday afternoon. Scene 2: Monday, the next day, around 6 p.m. Scene 3: The same night, after Jack and Sandy return from a restaurant. Act II, Scene 1: Fall 1987. Scene 2: Two months later on a Friday, around 9 p.m. Scene 3: Several hours later that night. Scene 4: Two days later, early evening.

Quarrels between a husband and wife emotionally dominated by their pasts and family backgrounds.

*The Kathy and Mo Show: Parallel Lives (137). Two-character play written and performed by Mo Gaffney and Kathy Najimy. Produced by Kenneth F. Martel and Ellen M. Krass in the Martel Media Enterprises Production, in association with Home Box Office and Kenneth M. Weinstock, at the Westside Arts Theater. Opened January 31, 1989.

CHARACTERS: Kathy, Mo; Lady Anne, King Anne, Queen Anne; Madeline and Sylvia (A Field Trip); Lady and The Tramp; Kris and Jeff (San Diego State Coeds); Teri and Tina (Catholics); The Game Show Family; Junior and Eddie (Two Sensitive Guys From Queens); Karen Treadwell and Her Sister; Suzanna at 7 a.m.; Muffy and Tippy; Hank and Karen Sue; The Three Sisters; Evelyn and Evelyn; Bill and Janine (Futon Talk); Brooke and Elise, Rosy and Paul at the Ruby Slipper; Annette and Gina of Weehawken.

Directed by Paul Benedict; scenery, David Jenkins; costumes, Gregg Barnes; lighting, Frances Aronson; executive producer, James B. Freydberg; production stage manager, Brian A. Kaufman; stage manager, Kate Riddle; press, Peter Cromarty, Kevin Brockman, Dana Sherman.

Misses Gaffney and Najimy as a multitude of male and female characters, mostly satirical. The play was presented in two parts.

*Cantorial (122). By Ira Levin. Produced by Gordon/Oestreicher/Clyman Productions at Lamb's Theater. Opened February 14, 1989.

Warren Ives	Anthony Fusco	Donna Quinn	Joan Howe
Lesley Rosen	Lesly Kahn	William Ives	Robert Nichols
Morris Lipkind	Woody Romoff	Voice	Paul Zim
Philip Quinn	James DeMarse		

Understudies: Misses Kahn, Howe—Katherine Elizabeth Neuman; Messrs. Romoff, Nichols—David Howard.

Directed by Charles Maryan; scenery, Atkin Pace; costumes, Lana Fritz; lighting, Brian Nason; sound, Gary and Timmy Harris; production stage manager, Catherine A. Heusel; press, Shirley Herz Associates, Pete Sanders.

Time: The Present. Act I: Late summer, early fall. Act II: Late fall, early winter.

Young couple living in a former synagogue is haunted by the voice of a cantor. Previously produced off off Broadway by Jewish Repertory Theater.

*Other People's Money (121). By Jerry Sterner. Produced by Jeffrey Ash and Susan Quint Gallin in association with Dennis Grimaldi in the Hartford Stage Company production at the Minetta Lane Theater. Opened February 16, 1989.

William Coles	James Murtaugh	Bea Sullivan	Scotty Bloch
Andrew Jorgenson	Arch Johnson	Kate Sullivan	Mercedes Ruehl
Lawrence Garfinkle	Kevin Conway		

Directed by Gloria Muzio; scenery, David Jenkins; costumes, Jess Goldstein; lighting, F. Mitchell Dana; sound, David Budries; production stage manager, Stacey Fleischer; press, Shirley Herz Associates, Sam Rudy.

Time: The present. Place: New York and Rhode Island. The play was presented in two parts.

Anatomy of a Wall Street predator's takeover of a moribund New England manufacturing company. Previously produced by American Stage Company, Hartford, Conn.

A Best Play; see page 277.

Janet Zarich replaced Mercedes Ruehl 4/18/89.

Together Again for the First Time (30). Two-performer musical revue conceived by Barry Kleinbort and Colin Romoff; with Jo Sullivan and Emily Loesser. Produced by Martin R. Kaufman at the Kaufman Theater. Opened February 27, 1989. (Closed March 26, 1989)

Directed by Barry Kleinbort; musical staging, Donald Saddler; musical direction and arrangements, Colin Romoff; scenery, Phillip Baldwin; costumes, William Ivey Long; lighting, Ted Mather; sound, Sandor Margolin; bass, Douglas Romoff; stage manager, Elizabeth Heeden; press, Henry Luhrman Associates, Terry Lilly, David Lotz, Jim Randolph.

Jo Sullivan (Mrs. Frank Loesser) and her daughter Emily Loesser (in her stage debut) in a selection of songs, many of them from the great Broadway musicals.

ACT I: Prologue, Introductory Frank Loesser, What's Next, "I Love to Sing-A" (by Harold Arlen and E. Y. Harburg), "One More Kiss" (by Stephen Sondheim), "Mack the Knife" (by Kurt Weill and Marc Blitzstein), "I Wish It So" (by Marc Blitzstein), "Pack Up Your Sins" (by Irving Berlin), "What Is There to Say?" (by Vernon Duke and E.Y. Harburg), "The Glamorous Life" (by Stephen Sondheim), "Can't You Just See Yourself" (by Jule Styne and Sammy Cahn), What Was: The Broadway Musical.

ACT II: A Little Gershwin, "Can You Read My Mind" (by John Williams and Leslie Bricusse), "Sing Something Simple" (by Herman Hupfeld), "Every Time" (by Hugh Martin and Ralph Blane), "Everything I've Got" (by Richard Rodgers and Lorenz Hart), "Don't Let It Get You Down" (by Burton Lane and E. Y. Harburg), More of Loesser, Finale.

Reno in Rage and Rehab (89). One-woman performance by and with Reno. Produced by Ellen M. Krass and Home Box Office, James B. Freydberg executive producer, at the Actor's Playhouse. Opened March 13, 1989. (Closed May 28, 1989)

Directed by John Ferraro; lighting, Jackie Manassee; associate producer, Jacqueline Judd; press, Jeffrey Richards Associates.

Monologue of vignettes of modern living in New York City, presented without intermission. Previously produced off off Broadway at Performance Space 122.

The Night Hank Williams Died (64). By Larry L. King. Produced by Drew Dennett in the WPA Theater production, Kyle Renick artistic director, at the Orpheum Theater. Opened March 31, 1989. (Closed May 28, 1989)

Thurmond Stottle	Matt Mulhern	Moon Childers	Grady Smith
Gus Gilbert	Darren McGavin	Sheriff Royce Landon Jr.	Earl Hindman
Nellie Bess Powers Clark	Betsy Aidem	Mrs. Vida Powers	Phyllis Somerville

THE PHANTOM TOLLBOOTH—Martha Thompson and Ken Sawyer in the Acting Company production of Susan Nanus's stage adaptation of a children's book

454   THE BEST PLAYS OF 1988–1989

Understudies: Messrs. Mulhern, Hindman—Richard McWilliams; Miss Aidem—Tracy Thorne; Miss Somerville—Jill Parker Jones.

Directed by Christopher Ashley; scenery, Edward T. Gianfrancesco; costumes, Jess Goldstein; lighting, Graig Evans; sound, Aural Fixation; production stage manager, Greta Minsky; stage manager, John Frederick Sullivan; press, Jeffrey Richards Associates, Tony Armento.

Time: Summer, 1952. Place: Stanley, Texas. The play was presented in two parts.

Transfer from off off Broadway (WPA Theater) of play about a would-be song writer.

*Only Kidding! (55). By Jim Geoghan. Produced by Bruce Lazarus and Patrick Hogan at the Westside Arts Theater Upstairs. Opened April 14, 1989.

Jackie Dwayne	Larry Keith	Jerry Goldstein	Paul Provenza
Sheldon Kelinski	Howard Spiegel	Sal D'Angelo	Sam Zap
Tom Kelly	Andrew Hill Newman	Voice of Buddy King	Peter Waldren

Standbys: Messrs. Keith, Zap—Jerry Grayson; Messrs. Spiegel, Newman, Provenza—Robb Pruitt.

Directed by Larry Arrick; scenery, Karen Schulz; costumes, Jeffrey L. Ullman; lighting, Debra Dumas; sound, Paul Garrity; associate producer, Richard Vos; production stage manager, Zane Weiner; stage manager, Lori Culhane; press, Jeffrey Richards Associates, Jillana Devine.

Act I, Scene 1: A bungalow in the Catskills. Scene 2: A night club basement. Act II: The green room of "The Buddy King Show," three years later.

Comedy about standup comedy, the performers and those who write their material. Previously produced off off Broadway at American Jewish Theater.

Legends in Concert (22). Musical revue created by John Stuart. Produced by John Stuart at the Academy Theater. Opened May 10, 1989. (Closed May 28, 1989)

Jack Benny	Eddie Carroll	John Lennon	Randy Clark
Buddy Holly	George Trullinger	Judy Garland	Julie Sheppard
Liberace	Daryl Wagner	Nat King Cole	Donny Ray Evins
Al Jolson	Clive Baldwin	Elvis Presley	Tony Roi
Marilyn Monroe	Katie LaBourdette		

Singer/Dancers: Renee Chambers, Troy Christian, Vincent D'Elia, Elena Ferrante, Debby Kole, Gary La Rosa, Michael Roberts, Marrielle Monte.

Musicians: Bobby Baxmeyer, Paul Adamy, Towner Galaher, Cornelius Bumpus, Ronnie Buttacavoli, Mike Davis.

Directed by John Stuart; choreography, Inez Mourning; musical direction, Kerry McCoy; costumes, Betty Lurenz; lighting and production consultant, Dennis Condon; technical consultant, Ron Popp; multimedia design, Media Innovations/Joseph Jarred; technical director, Alan Murphy; lasers, Mark Fisher; production supervisor, Steve Yuhasz; associate producers, Don Saxon, Robert R. Blume, Malcolm Allen; press, the Joshua Ellis Office, Jackie Green, Adrian Bryan-Brown.

Nine show-biz "legends" (see list of characters above) impersonated in a concert-style revue. The show was presented in two parts.

Blame It on the Movies! (3). Musical revue compiled and conceived by Ron Abel, Billy Barnes and David Galligan from an original idea by Franklin R. Levy; original music and lyrics by Billy Barnes. Produced by Roger Berlind, Franklin R. Levy and Gregory Harrison at Criterion Center Stage Left. Opened May 16, 1989. (Closed May 17, 1989)

Sandy Edgerton	Peter Marc
Kathy Garrick	Dan O'Grady
Bill Hutton	Barbara Sharma
Christine Kellogg	Patty Tiffany

Band: John McDaniel piano, conductor; Norbert Goldberg drums; Steve Marzullo synthesizer; Scott Rosette bass; Kathryn Easter Harp.

Understudies: Ivy Austin, Pat Di Pasquale.

Directed by David Galligan; musical staging and choreography, Larry Hyman; musical direction and arrangements, Ron Abel; scenery, Fred Duer; costumes, Bonnie Stauch; lighting, Michael Gilliam; sound, Jon Gottlieb; production stage manager, Elsbeth M. Collins; stage manager, Andrea Iovino; press, the Joshua Ellis Office, Chris Boneau.

Part One: Blame It on the Movies, The Forties, The War Years, Foreign Film Tribute, Fox in Love. Part Two: Entr'acte, Saturday Matinee, Oscar Losers, A Tribute to the Hollywood Film Score: *A Place in the Sun Ballet*, Finale.

Compendium of memorable numbers from 40 years of movies, beginning from the 1930s.

*S. J. Perelman in Person (17). One-man performance written by Bob Shanks; based on the published works of S. J. Perelman; with Lewis J. Stadlen. Produced by Comco Productions, Inc. at the Cherry Lane Theater. Opened May 17, 1989.

Standby: Mr. Stadlen—Mitchell Greenberg.

Directed by Ann Shanks; scenery, Wes Peters; costumes, Leon I. Brauner; lighting, Mal Sturchio; production stage manager, Morgan Kennedy; press, Shirley Herz Associates, Glenna Freedman.

Time: The 1950s. Place: A study in New York City. The play was presented in two parts.

Lewis J. Stadlen impersonates the noted humorist, with the humorist sometimes taking off show biz celebrities like Groucho Marx and James Cagney.

*Laughing Matters (16). Revue of playlets by and with Linda Wallem and Peter Tolan; with music and lyrics by Peter Tolan. Produced by Zev Guber, Sanford H. Fisher and Beluga Entertainment Corporation at St. Peter's Church. Opened May 18, 1989.

Directed by Martin Charnin; scenery and lighting, Ray Recht; costumes coordinated by Jade Jobson (Miss Wallem's by Isaac Mizrahi, Mr. Tolan's by Giorgio Armani); production stage manager, Jonathan Dimock Secor; press, the Joshua Ellis Office, Jackie Green, Shannon Barr.

Satirical sketches of contemporary New York City, including Broadway shows and their authors. Previously produced OOB by Manhattan Punch Line in an earlier version.

ACT I

Inner Thoughts: Just before the curtain at St. Peter's now
Weird Interlude: A good table in a bad restaurant
    Bob's Friend .... Peter Tolan
    Bob's Other Friend .... Linda Wallem
Labor Relations: Mom-to-be's old bedroom in Naperville, just outside of Chicago
    Mom-to-be .... Wallem
    Pop-to-be .... Tolan
Nightmare on M Street: A personnel office in Washington, D.C., now
    Miss Femur .... Wallem
    Mr. Sheltie .... Tolan
The Gap: A corner booth very near the orchestra at the Rainbow Room
    Larry Bender .... Wallem
    Louise Bender .... Tolan
The Ten-Percent Solution: An 18th floor office at the most powerful talent agency on earth
    Bernie .... Tolan
    Darlingness .... Wallem
Bridge Over Troubled Daughters: A kitchen in Champagne-Urbana, 9 p.m. on a Saturday Night
    Martha .... Wallem
    Dennis .... Tolan

ACT II

John Loves Mary: A television studio in Los Angeles and elsewhere
Mary and Others .... Wallem
John and Others .... Tolan
"When You Live in New York," "Max" and "Next Season on Broadway"
Reunion: Outside the Metropolitan Tower on 57th Street, a rainy November afternoon
Inga.. Wallem
Vinnie .... Tolan
Back in Champaign-Urbana: Later that night, much later, much much later
Martha .... Wallem
Dennis .... Tolan
Inner Thoughts: Just after the final playlet at St. Peter's, now
Peter Tolan, Linda Wallem

*Showing Off (16). Cabaret revue with music, lyrics and sketches by Douglas Bernstein
and Denis Markell. Produced by Suzanne J. Schwartz and Jennifer Manocherian at Steve
McGraw's (formerly Palsson's). Opened May 18, 1989.

Douglas Bernstein   Donna Murphy
Veanne Cox   Mark Sawyer

Understudies: Messrs. Bernstein, Sawyer—Kristopher Antekeier; Misses Cox, Murphy—Laura Turnbull.
Directed and choreographed by Michael Leeds; musical direction and pianist, Stephen Flaherty; scenery and
props, Joseph Varga, Penny Holpit; costumes, Jeanne Button; lighting and sound, Josh Starbuck; associate
producer, Howard Deutsch; production stage manager, Robin Rogers; press, David Rothenberg.
Topical revue of excesses and eccentricities of modern life in New York City.

MUSICAL NUMBERS AND SKETCHES: "Showing Off"—Company; "72nd Street"—Company; Native
New Yorkers—Company; "I Don't Get It"—Mark Sawyer; "S.I.P."—Company; Showbiz Rabbi—Douglas
Bernstein; "They're Yours"—Donna Murphy, Veanne Cox; Mightier Than the Sword—Cox, Sawyer, Murphy;
"Michele"—Bernstein; "Raffi: The Concert Movie"—Company; "Rental Cruelty"—Murphy, Sawyer; "Joshua
Noveck"—Cox; "Ninas"—Company; "How Things Change"—Murphy; "Take de Picture"—Company; "Old
Fashioned Song"—Company.

The Acting Company. Schedule of three programs. Love's Labor's Lost (8). Revival
of the play by William Shakespeare. Opened May 22, 1989. (Closed May 26, 1989) Boy
Meets Girl (6). Revival of the play by Bella and Sam Spewack. Opened May 30, 1989.
(Closed June 3, 1989) The Phantom Tollbooth (2). By Susan Nanus; adapted from the
novel by Norton Juster; a Young Audience Project. Opened and closed June 4, 1989. Produced by The Acting Company, John Houseman founder, Margot Harley executive producer,
Gerald Gutierrez artistic director, at Marymount Manhattan Theater.

PERFORMER	"LOVE'S LABOR'S LOST"	"BOY MEETS GIRL"	"THE PHANTOM TOLLBOOTH"
Spencer Backwith	King Ferdinand	Rodney Bevan	Azaz; Whetherman
Anthony Cummings	Costard	Larry Toms	Wordsnatcher
Gayla Finer	Jaquenetta	Peggy; Nanny; 2d Nurse	Soundkeeper
Larry Green	Dumaine	Robert Law	Dr. Dischord
John Greenleaf	Moth	Rosetti	Senses Taker
Douglas Krizner	Don Adriano	J. Carlyle Benson	Terrible Trivium
Michael McCauley	Dull	Doctor; Announcer; Maj. Thompson	Wordsnatcher
Theresa McCarthy	Maria	1st Nurse	Dynne
Alison Stair Neet	(Princess of France; Rosaline)	Green	Princess of Reason

Laura Perrotta	(Princess of France; Rosaline)	Susie	Princess of Rhyme
David Rainey	Boyet	Slade	Mathemagician
Ken Sawyer	Longaville	Young Man; Studio Officer	Milo
Gary Sloan	Berowne		
Martha Thompson	Katharine	Miss Crews	Tock
John Tillotson	Holofernes	C. Elliot Friday	
Gregory Wallace	Marcade; Sir Nathaniel	Cutter	Humbug

(Parentheses indicate roles in which the performers alternated)

LOVE'S LABOR'S LOST: Directed by Paul Giovanni; scenery, Robert Klingelhoefer; costumes, Jess Goldstein; lighting, Stephen Strawbridge; dance consultation, Patricia Birch; songs and incidental music, Bruce Adolphe; staff repertory director, Jennifer McCray; production stage manager, C.A. Clark; stage manager, Richard Feldman; press, the Fred Nathan Company, Bert Fink.

Place: The park of the King of Navarre. The play was presented in two parts.

The last major New York production of *Love's Labor's Lost* was in New York Shakespeare Festival Marathon 2/22/89 for 14 performances; see its entry elsewhere in this section of this volume.

BOY MEETS GIRL: Voice of B.K.—Robin Williams; Voice of Hollywood—Kevin Kline.

Directed by Brian Murray; scenery, Derek McLane; costumes, Jennifer von Mayrhauser; lighting, Stephen Strawbridge; music, Bruce Pomahac; staff repertory director, Jennifer McCray; production stage manager, C.A. Clark; stage manager, Richard Feldman.

Time: 1935. Place: Hollywood. Act I: Mr. Friday's office at Royal Studios. Act II, Scene 1: Your own home, seven months later. Scene 2: Mr. Friday's office. Scene 3: The same, several hours later. Act III, Scene 1: A hospital corridor, three weeks later. Scene 2: Your own home. Scene 3: Mr. Friday's office. The play was presented in two parts with the intermission following Act II.

The last major New York revival of *Boy Meets Girl* was by the Phoenix Theater 4/13/76 for 10 performances.

THE PHANTOM TOLLBOOTH: Little Girl's Voice—Justine Cohen; Ensemble—David Rainey, Laura Perrotta, Alison Stair Neet, Larry Green, Theresa McCarthy, Gayla Finer, Michael MacCauley, Anthony Cummings, Douglas Krizner, John Greenleaf.

Directed by Jennifer McCray; scenery, Russell Parkman; costumes, Constance Romero; lighting, Stephen Strawbridge; dramaturgy, Susan Jones; sound, Scott Lehrer; music, Robert Waldman.

Adaptation of a children's novel weaving fantasy around names and numbers. Previously produced at Schimmel Center for the Arts, Pace University.

CAST REPLACEMENTS AND TOURING COMPANIES

Compiled by Stanley Green

The following is a list of the more important cast replacements in productions which opened in previous years, but were still playing in New York during a substantial part of the 1988–89 season; or were still on a first-class tour in 1988–89 (casts of first-class touring companies of previous seasons which were no longer playing in 1988–89 appear in previous *Best Plays* volumes of appropriate years).

The name of each major role is listed in *italics* beneath the title of the play in the first column. In the second column directly opposite appears the name of the actor who created the role in the original New York production (whose opening date appears in *italics* at the top of the column). Indented immediately beneath the original actor's name are the names of subsequent New York replacements, together with the date of replacement when available.

The third column gives information about first-class touring companies, including London companies (produced under the auspices of their original New York managements). When there is more than one roadshow company, #1, #2, etc., appear before the name of the performer who created the role in each company (and the city and date of each company's first performance appears in *italics* at the top of the column). Their subsequent replacements are also listed beneath their names, with dates when available.

ANYTHING GOES

	New York 10/13/87	*New Haven 10/19/88*
Reno Sweeney	Patti LuPone Linda Hart 6/28/88 Patti LuPone 7/5/88 Leslie Uggams 3/21/89	Leslie Uggams
Billy Crocker	Howard McGillin Gregg Edelman 5/16/89	Rex Smith
Moonface Martin	Bill McCutcheon	Rip Taylor
Elisha Whitney	Rex Everhart	Gordon Connell
Evangeline Harcourt	Anne Francine	Julie Kurnitz
Erma	Linda Hart Maryellen Scilla 4/89	Susan Terry

458

Lord Evelyn Oakleigh	Anthony Heald	Paul V. Ames
	Walter Bobbie 4/14/89	
Hope Harcourt	Kathleen Mahony-Bennett	Rebecca Baxter
	Nancy Opel 10/4/88	

BROADWAY BOUND

	New York 12/4/86
Kate	Linda Lavin
	Elizabeth Franz 8/25/87
	Joan Rivers 6/20/88
Eugene	Jonathan Silverman
	Evan Handler 7/7/87
	Adam Philipson 11/10/87
Stanley	Jason Alexander
	Mark Nelson 7/7/87
	David Nackman 4/18/88
	Peter Birkenhead 7/18/88
Blanche	Phillis Newman
	Carol Locatell 9/22/87
	Karen Ludwig 8/8/88
Ben	John Randolph
	Alan Manson 8/25/87

BURN THIS

	New York 10/14/87
Anna Mann	Joan Allen
	Lisa Emery 5/2/88
Pale	John Malkovich
	Eric Roberts 5/2/88
	Scott Glenn 8/27/88
Larry	Lou Liberatore
	Lonny Price 8/1/88

CABARET

	New York 10/22/87	*St. Louis 9/27/88*
Emcee	Joel Grey	Joel Grey
Sally Bowles	Alyson Reed	Nancy Ringham
Clifford Bradshaw	Gregg Edelman	Brian Sutherland
Fraulein Schneider	Regina Resnik	Marcia Lewis
Herr Schultz	Werner Klemperer	Michael Allinson
Ernst Ludwig	David Staller	Leslie Wolfe
Fraulein Kost	Nora Mae Lyng	Dorothy Stanley

CATS

	New York 10/7/82
Bustopher Jones	Stephen Hanan Paul Harman
Demeter	Wendy Edmead Beth Swearingen
Grizabella	Betty Buckley Loni Ackerman 9/5/88
Jennyanydots	Anna McNeely Marcy DeGonge
Mistoffelees	Timothy Scott Michael Barriskill
Mungojerrie	Rene Clemente Ray Roderick
Munkustrap	Harry Groener Robert Amirante
Rumpleteazer	Christine Langner Kristi Lynes
Skimbleshanks	Reed Jones Reed Jones
Victoria	Cynthia Onrubia Claudia Shell

Note: Only replacements during the 1988–89 season are listed above under the names of the original cast members. For previous replacements, see the following editions of *The Best Plays*: *1982–83* (p.437); *1983–84* (p.416); *1984–85* (p.414); *1986–87* (p.361); and *1987–88* (p.399).

A CHORUS LINE

	N.Y. Off Bway 4/15/75 *N.Y. Bway 7/25/75*
Zach	Robert LuPone Randy Clements 9/9/88 Robert LuPone 11/21/88
Richie	Ronald Dennis Bruce Anthony Davis Gordon Owens 2/20/89
Sheila	Carole Bishop Dana Moore Susan Danielle 3/27/89
Paul	Sammy Williams Wayne Meledandri Drew Geraci 6/10/88
Mark	Cameron Mason Andrew Grose
Diana	Priscilla Lopez Denise DiRenzo Arminae Azarian 2/13/89

Val	Pamela Blair 　Wanda Richert 11/88 　Diana Kavilis 2/20/89
Greg	Michel Stuart 　Bradley Jones 　Ron Navarre 3/23/89
Mike	Wayne Cilento 　Danny Herman 　Michael Gruber 1/16/89
Judy	Patricia Garland 　Cindi Klinger 　Angelique Ilo 4/24/89
Al	Don Percassi 　Tommy Re 　Stephen Bourneuf 3/27/89
Maggie	Kay Cole 　Dorothy (Tancredi)) Dybisz 　Michele Pigliavento 1/16/89 　Susan Santoro 4/21/89

Note: Only replacements during the 1988–89 season are listed above under the names of the original cast members. For previous replacements, see the following editions of *The Best Plays*: *1982–83* (p.437); *1983–84* (p.416); *1984–85* (p.414); *1985–86* (p.372); *1986–87* (p.361); and *1987–88* (p.400).

DRIVING MISS DAISY

	New York 4/15/87	*#1 Chicago 4/23/88* *#2 London 6/8/88* *#3 Philadelphia 9/21/88*
Daisy Werthan	Dana Ivey 　Frances Sternhagen 1/19/88	#1 Sada Thompson 　Ellen Burstyn 8/9/88 　Dorothy Loudon 10/26/88 #2 Wendy Hiller #3 Julie Harris
Hoke Coleburn	Morgan Freeman 　Earle Hyman 2/23/88	#1 Bill Cobbs #2 Clarke Peters #3 Brock Peters
Boolie Werthan	Ray Gill 　Anderson Matthews 11/8/88	#1 Matt DeCaro #2 Barry Foster #3 Stephen Root

THE FANTASTICKS

	New York 5/3/60
Matt	Kenneth Nelson 　Matthew Bennett 4/89
Louisa	Rita Gardner 　Kate Suber 11/15/88

Note: As of May 31, 1989, 33 actors had played the role of El Gallo, 26 had played Matt, and 31 had played Louisa. Only cast replacements during the 1988–89 season are listed above under the names of the original cast members. For previous replacements, see the following editions of *The Best Plays*: *1982–83* (p.442); *1983–84* (p.418); *1984–85* (p.415); *1985–86* (p.373); *1986–87* (p.361); *1987–88* (p.401).

FENCES

	New York 3/26/87	Los Angeles 9/28/88
Troy Maxson	James Earl Jones Billy Dee Williams 2/2/88	James Earl Jones
Rose	Mary Alice Lynne Thigpen 2/2/88	Lynne Thigpen
Cory	Courtney B. Vance Byron Keith Minns 2/2/88	Courtney B. Vance

FRANKIE AND JOHNNY IN THE CLAIR DE LUNE

	New York 10/13/87	Los Angeles 11/17/88
Frankie	Kathy Bates Carol Kane 5/24/88 Bonnie Franklin 9/13/88 Kathy Bates 1/3/89 Caroline Aaron 1/31/89	Kathy Bates
Johnny	Kenneth Welsh Bruce Weitz 5/24/88 Tony Musante 9/13/88 Tony Campisi 1/3/89 Bill Smitrovich 1/31/89	Kenneth Welsh

INTO THE WOODS

	New York 11/5/87	Ft. Lauderdale 11/22/88
Witch	Bernadette Peters Phylicia Rashad 4/14/88 Betsy Joslyn 7/5/88 Nancy Dussault 12/13/88 Bernadette Peters 5/23/89 Nancy Dussault 5/27/89	Cleo Laine Betsy Joslyn 5/89
Baker's Wife	Joanna Gleason Lauren Mitchell 6/28/88 Kay McClelland (alt.) 6/28/88 Mary Gordon Murray 7/19/88 Cynthia Sikes 11/15/88 Joanna Gleason 5/23/89 Kay McClelland 5/27/89	Mary Gordon Murray
Baker	Chip Zien	Ray Gill
Narrator	Tom Aldredge Dick Cavett 7/19/88 Tom Aldredge 9/13/88	Rex Robbins
Mysterious Man	Tom Aldredge Edmund Lyndeck 7/19/88 Tom Aldredge 9/13/88	Rex Robbins
Wolf; Cinderella's Prince	Robert Westenberg	Chuck Wagner
Jack's Mother	Barbara Bryne	Charlotte Rae Nora Mae Lyng 5/89

Little Red Riding-Hood	Danielle Ferland LuAnne Ponce 9/20/88	Tracy Katz
Cinderella	Kim Crosby	Kathleen Rowe McAllen Jill Geddes 3/89
Rapunzel	Pamela Winslow Marin Mazzie 3/7/89	Marguerite Lowell
Rapunzel's Prince	Chuck Wagner Dean Butler 3/7/89	Douglas Sills

LES MISERABLES

	New York 3/12/87	#1 Boston 12/5/87 #2 Los Angeles 5/21/88 #3 Tampa 11/28/88
Jean Valjean	Colm Wilkinson Garry Morris 11/30/87 Timothy Shew 5/30/88	#1 William Solo Craig Schulman 4/88 #2 William Solo Jean Bennett #3 Gary Barker
Javert	Terrence Mann Anthony Crivello 11/30/87 Norman Large 1/18/88 Anthony Crivello 3/14/88 Norman Large 7/19/88 Herndon Lackey 1/17/89	#1 Herndon Lackey #2 Jeff McCarthy #3 Peter Samuel
Fantine	Randy Graff Maureen Moore 7/19/88 Susan Dawn Carson	#1 Diane Fratantoni Ann Crumb Laurie Beechman 1/89 #2 Elinore O'Connell #3 Hollis Resnik
Enjolras	Michael Maguire Joseph Kolinski	#1 John Herrera #2 Greg Blanchard #3 Greg Zerkle
Marius	David Bryant Ray Walker Hugh Panaro	#1 Hugh Panaro #2 Reece Holland #3 Matthew Porretta
Cosette	Judy Kuhn Tracy Shayne	#1 Tamara Jenkins #2 Karen Fineman #3 Jacqueline Piro
Eponine	Frances Ruffelle Kelli James 9/15/87 Natalie Toro 7/88	#1 Renee Veneziale #2 Michaelle Nicastro #3 Michele Maika
Thenardier	Leo Burmester Ed Dixon	#1 Tom Robbins Neal Ben Ari 12/5/88 #2 Gary Beach #3 Paul Ainsley
Mme. Thenardier	Jennifer Butt	#1 Victoria Clark #2 Kay Cole #3 Linda Kerns

| *Gavroche* | Braden Danner
Danny Gerard | #1 Lantz Landry or Andrew
Renshaw
#2 Phillip Glasser or Josh C.
Williams
#3 Andrew Harrison Leeds or Sam
Brent Riegel |

M. BUTTERFLY

	New York 3/20/88	*London 4/20/89*
Rene Gallimard	John Lithgow David Dukes 8/22/88 John Rubinstein 2/20/89	Anthony Hopkins
Song Liling	B. D. Wong	G. G. Goei
Helga	Rose Gregorio Pamela Payton-Wright 9/5/88	Lynn Farleigh
Marc, etc.	John Getz Richard Poe 9/5/88	Ian Redford

Cris Groenendaal as The Phantom and Rebecca Luker as Christina
in the continuing Broadway production of *The Phantom of the Opera*

ME AND MY GIRL

	New York 8/10/86	San Francisco 10/6/87
Bill Snibson	Robert Lindsay Jim Dale 6/16/87 James Brennan 1/31/89	Tim Curry James Brennan 10/4/88 James Young 1/24/89
Sally Smith	Maryann Plunkett Ellen Foley 2/23/88	Donna Bullock Shari Cowart 10/4/88
Sir John Tremayne	George S. Irving Jay Garner 1/31/89	Barrie Ingham Gary Gage 10/4/88
Lady Jacqueline Carstone	Jane Summerhays Dee Hoty 2/23/88	Susan Cella
Maria Duchess of Dene	Jane Connell Sylvia O'Brien 1/31/89	Ursula Smith
Gerald Bolingbroke	Nick Ulett Edward Hibbert 10/87 Nick Ulett 4/18/88	Nick Ulett

THE PHANTOM OF THE OPERA

	New York 1/26/88	Los Angeles 5/31/89
The Phantom	Michael Crawford Timothy Nolen 10/10/88 Cris Groenendaal 3/20/89	Michael Crawford
Christine Daaé	Sarah Brightman Patti Cohenour 6/7/88 Dale Kristien (alt.) 7/88* Rebecca Luker (alt.) 3/89* Rebecca Luker 6/5/89 Katherine Buffaloe (alt.) (6/5/89)*	Dale Kristien Mary D'Arcy (alt.)*
Carlotta Giudicelli	Judy Kaye Marilyn Caskey 1/2/89	Leigh Munro
Raoul, Vicomte de Chagny	Steve Barton	Reece Holland

*Alternates play the role of Christine Monday and Wednesday evenings.

THE ROAD TO MECCA

	New York 4/12/88
Elsa Barlow	Amy Irving Kathy Bates 7/5/88

ROMANCE ROMANCE

	New York 5/1/88
Alfred Von Wilmers/Sam	Scott Bakula Barry Williams 10/4/88

A SHAYNA MAIDEL

New York 10/29/87

Luisa Weiss Pechenik Gordana Rashovich
  Tandy Cronyn 6/14/88
  Gordana Rashovich 9/6/88

SPEED-THE-PLOW

	New York 5/3/88	*#1 London 1/25/89* *#2 Chicago 3/1/89*
Bobby Gould	Joe Mantegna David Rasche 8/30/88	#1 Colin Stinton #2 William L. Peterson
Charlie Fox	Ron Silver Bob Balaban 8/30/88	#1 Alfred Molina #2 D. W. Moffett
Karen	Madonna Felicity Huffman 8/30/88	#1 Rebecca Pidgeon #2 Hope David

STEEL MAGNOLIAS

	New York 6/19/87	*#1 Ft. Lauderdale 1/17/89* *#2 London 3/7/89*
M'Lynn	Rosemary Prinz Maeve McGuire 5/89 Rosemary Prinz 7/89	#1 Barbara Rush #2 Rosemary Harris
Shelby	Betsy Aidem Stacy Ray 5/88 Cynthia Vance	#1 Tracy Shaffer #2 Joely Richardson
Truvy	Margo Martindale Suzy Hunt 5/89	#1 Margo Martindale #2 Maggie Steed
Annelle	Constance Shulman Dorrie Joiner	#1 Dawn Hopper #2 Janine Duvitski
Clairee	Kate Wilkinson Anna Minot	#1 June Lockhart Marion Ross #2 Stephanie Cole
Ouiser	Mary Fogarty Anne Pitoniak 5/88	#1 Carole Cook #2 Jean Boht

TAMARA

New York 12/2/87

Tamara de Lempicka Sara Botsford
  Christine Dunford 7/88

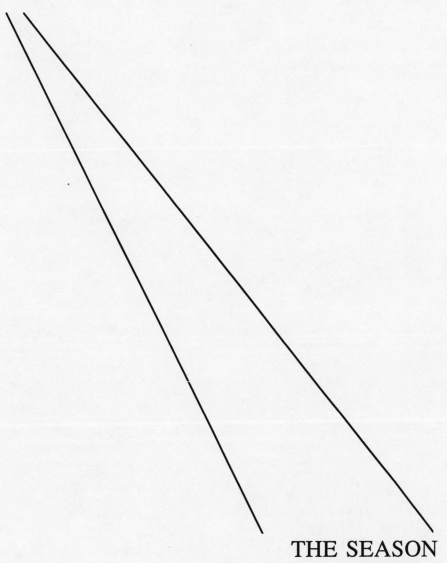

THE SEASON
OFF OFF BROADWAY

○
○
○

OFF OFF BROADWAY
○
By Mel Gussow
○
○
○

OFF OFF Broadway is, by definition, a nebulous environment for theater, but there are certain points of permanency. Two exemplars of survivability are LaMama and Theater for the New City, both of which have maintained open door policies for decades, and in so doing have encouraged both diversity and experimentation.

Ellen Stewart's LaMama remains a welcome home for visiting companies like Sarah Pia Anderson's production of Ibsen's *Rosmersholm* starring Suzanne Bertish, a notable revival that was first presented in London. At the same time, Miss Stewart presents virtuosic American artists like John Kelly. His one-man show *Ode to a Cube*, in which, among other oddities, he imitated the Mona Lisa, was one of the season's striking events.

Theater for the New City, under the artistic direction of Crystal Field and George Bartenieff, was as eclectic as ever. Among its high points this season were Theodora Skipitares's puppet musical *Empires and Appetites*, which charted the roles of food and famine through the ages; Leslie Mohn's *White Boned Demon*, a provocative study of Mme. Mao Zedong; and Romulus Linney's *Heathen Valley*. The Linney play, adapted by the author from his first novel, came to Theater for the New City after previous engagements in regional theaters (where it received the ATCA New Play Prize last season)—more and more a channel to off off Broadway, as well as to Broadway and off Broadway. *Heathen Valley*, cited here as an outstanding 1988–89 OOB production, deals challengingly with primitivism and theology in a remote area of the American South. It was given a suitably spare production by the author himself.

The Brooklyn Academy of Music's Next Wave Festival has become a state-of-the-performance-art gathering of individuals and companies in dance and music as well as theater, often combining all three disciplines. Featured this year were shows by two men who have worked as New Vaudeville partners, the juggler Michael Moschen and the clown Bob Berky. *Michael*

469

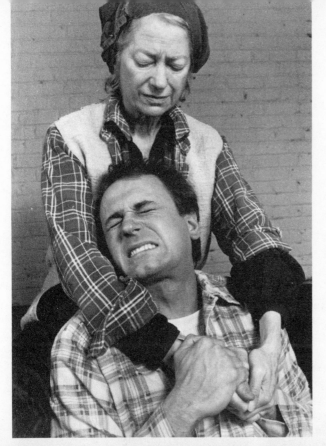

Left, Julie Follansbee and Scott Sowers in *Heathen Valley*—"deals challengingly with primitivism and theology in a remote area of the American South." *Below, Michael Moschen in Motion*—"combined sculpture in motion with feats of equipoise." *Opposite page,* Stephen Mellor, Mitch Markowitz (*in boat*) and Jan Leslie Harding in *Bad Penny*—"a sardonic serio-comedy about urban trauma."

Moschen in Motion cited here as an outstanding 1988–89 OOB production, was a particular delight, moving this extraordinary artist to a further rarefied plane, one on which he combined sculpture in motion with feats of equipoise. A disappointment in the Next Wave Festival was the long awaited full production of sections of the Lee Breuer-Bob Telson epic, *The Warrior Ant*.

The CSC continues to be re-emergent as a valuable classical company under the artistic direction of Carey Perloff. This season the work ranged from Miss Perloff's own production of Tony Harrison's *Phaedra Britannica* (with a superb performance by Bob Gunton) to *Rameau's Nephew*, an intellectual clown show adapted by the director Andrei Belgrader and Shelley Berc from the Diderot classic. The Pan Asian Repertory, led by Tisa Chang, provided its usual rewarding selection of new plays (including R. A. Shiomi's *Play Ball*) and a setting of *Three Sisters* on the Siberian-Mongolian border. For its final production of the season, Pan-Asian offered a novel experiment, a collaboration between its company actors and the avant-gardist Ping Chong. Mr. Chong's play *Noiresque: the Fallen Angel*, was a variation on *Alice in Wonderland*. Earlier in the season, at LaMama, Mr. Chong presented the more evocative *Skin: A State of Being*, a metaphorical flight to Xanadu.

The American Jewish Theater brought a popular regional play to New York, Mark Harelik's *The Immigrant: A Hamilton County Album*, in a new production starring Lonny Price as a new American in Texas. AJT also offered *Only Kidding*, Jim Geoghan's mirthful comedy about stand-up comics, a play that later moved into an extended run off Broadway. The Interart Theater unearthed Dennis Potter's early Gothic comedy *Brimstone and Treacle*, and The New Theater of Brooklyn gave a first New York staging to *No Limits to Love* by the late David Mercer.

Irish-American arts were doubly represented—by the Irish Arts Center (with the arresting feminist document, *Now and at the Hour of Our Death*, about political prisoners in Ireland) and by the new Irish Repertory Theater, which began its first season with *The Plough and the Stars* and ended with Thomas Murphy's *A Whistle in the Dark*, both revivals directed by Charlotte Moore.

Work at other off-off companies such as the WPA and the Hudson Guild was uneven, although the WPA was able to produce one deserved transfer to off Broadway, *The Night Hank Williams Died* by Larry L. King, a play in the shape of a country western ballad. Both the King play and Bruce Graham's apocalyptical comedy *Early One Evening at the Rainbow Bar and Grille* came to the WPA from regional theaters. The Hudson Guild presented the New York premiere of Thom Thomas's *Without Apologies*, a misguided sequel to *The Importance of Being Earnest*. In *Henry Lumper*, produced by Working Theater, Israel Horovitz relocated *Henry IV, Part 1* and *Part 2* in Gloucester, Mass. The Women's Project, divorced from the American Place Theater (its long-time home), offered Cassandra Medley's *Ma Rose*, a chronicle of several generations of a black family, and a co-production with Music-Theater Group of Eve Ensler's atmospheric *Ladies*, a collage about homeless women.

Everett Quinton, succeeding the late Charles Ludlam as head of the Ridiculous Theatrical Company, gave himself a flamboyant showcase with a one-man version of *A Tale of Two Cities*. Ethyl Eichelberger, a frequent past performer with the Ridiculous, was seen on several other stages—with the amusing *Fiasco* and the fiasco *Ariadne Obnoxious*.

This season saw the improvement of several younger companies, each certifying its niche off off Broadway. Primary Stages presented the local premiere of Lanie Robertson's *Nasty Little Secrets*, a play drawn from the life and death of Joe Orton, and followed that with David Ives's *Ancient History*, about the end of a romance that demonstrated the author's continuing nimbleness with language and theatrical technique. The New York Theater

Workshop had a noteworthy year with David Williamson's *Emerald City* (a Best Play), as well as Franz Xaver Kroetz's *The Nest*, a searing drama about the dangers of toxic waste; and Charles L. Mee Jr.'s fascinating, elliptical political comedy *The Investigation of the Murder in El Salvador*.

Because of its nomadic existence, En Garde Arts may be a pivotal off-off-Broadway company of its time. Under its founder and artistic director, Anne Hamburger, En Garde Arts stages plays in site-specific locations. The plays become the theatrical equivalent of museum installations, finding a home in city streets as well as storefronts and warehouses. This year the troupe was in residence in the historic Chelsea Hotel (with works dealing at least tangentially with life in that hotel) and, most adventurously, in Central Park. At three individual park locations, intrepid theatergoers watched plays unfold: Matthew Maguire's *Babel on Babylon*, Anna Cascio's *Minny and the James Boys* and Mac Wellman's *Bad Penny*. Though lasting only 30 minutes, *Bad Penny* is cited as an outstanding 1988–89 OOB production. A sardonic serio-comedy about urban trauma, the play was the best use to date of the site specific principle. It was performed on, around and in the Central Park lake. Sailing on that lake was the ominous Boatman of Bow Bridge. *Bad Penny* was given an evocative environmental production by Jim Simpson, with the talented cast headed by Jan Leslie Harding and Stephen Mellor.

Musically, off off Broadway was fairly unremarkable, except for Miss Skipitares's *Empires and Appetites*; the New York version of Melvyn Bragg's and Howard Goodall's musical, *The Hired Man*; and, especially, the York Theater Company's revival of *Sweeney Todd, the Demon Barber of Fleet Street* in a stunning environmental staging by Susan H. Schulman. Selling out its brief run at the York, the production was thereupon scheduled to be moved to Circle in the Square on Broadway. Bob Gunton, who gave a powerful portrayal in the title role, was one of several estimable actors who expanded their range on various off-off-Broadway stages this season. Others included Ethan Phillips and Dan Butler, who proved to be as versatile as they were prolific.

PLAYS PRODUCED
OFF OFF BROADWAY
AND ADDITIONAL PRODUCTIONS

Here is a comprehensive sampling of off-off-Broadway and other experimental or peripheral 1988–89 productions in New York, compiled by Camille Croce. There is no definitive "off-off-Broadway" area or qualification. To try to define or regiment it would be untrue to its fluid, exploratory purpose. The listing below of hundreds of works produced by more than 100 OOB groups and others is as inclusive as reliable sources will allow, however, and takes in all leading Manhattan-based, new-play-producing, English-language organizations.

The more active and established producing groups are identified in **bold face type**, in alphabetical order, with artistic policies and the names of the managing directors given whenever these are a matter of record. Each group's 1988–89 schedule is listed with play titles in CAPITAL LETTERS. Often these are works-in-progress with changing scripts, casts and directors, sometimes without an engagement of record (but an opening or early performance date is included when available).

Many of these off-off-Broadway groups have long since outgrown a merely experimental status and are offering programs which are the equal in professionalism and quality (and in some cases the superior) of anything in the New York theater, with special contractual arrangements like the showcase code, letters of agreement (allowing for longer runs and higher admission prices than usual) and, closer to the edge of the commercial theater, a so-called "mini-contract." In the list below, all available data on opening dates, performance numbers and major production and acting credits (almost all of them Equity members) is included in the entries of these special-arrangement offerings.

A large selection of lesser-known groups and other shows that made appearances off off Broadway during the season appears under the "Miscellaneous" heading at the end of this listing.

Amas Repertory Theater. Dedicated to bringing all people, regardless of race, creed, color or economic background, together through the creative arts. Rosetta LeNoire, founder and artistic director.

BLACKAMOOR (17). Book by Joseph George Caruso and Helen Kromer; music by Ulpio Minucci; lyrics by Helen Kromer. October 13, 1988. Director, Kent Paul; choreography and musical staging, Barry

474

McNabb; scenery, Steve Caldwell; lighting, Phil Monat; costumes, Jana Rosenblatt; musical director, Amy Engelstein. With Tony Clarke, Edouard Desoto, Brian Fisher, Guillermo Gonzalez, Ruthanna Graves, Carolyn Heafner, Lon Hurst, Christopher Innvar, David Jackson, Lorenzo, Evan Matthews, Herman Petras, Keelee Seetoo, Lynette Tompkins.

STEP INTO MY WORLD (24). Revue conceived, developed and directed by Ronald G. Russo; music and lyrics by Micki Grant. February 16, 1989. Choreography, Jeffrey Dobbs; lighting, Jeffrey Hubbell; costumes, Mary Ann Lach; musical director, George Caldwell. With Jennifer Bell, Jean Cheek, Ellen De Verne, Martron Gales, Evan Matthews, George Merritt, Kenn Miller, Ellen Sims, Darius Keith Williams, Deborah Woodson.

PRIZES (20). Book by Raffi Pehlivanian; music and lyrics by Charles DeForest. April 26, 1989. Director, Lee Minskoff; choreography, Margo Sappington; scenery, Jane Sablow; lighting, Beau Kennedy; costumes, Robert Griggs. With Nancy Groff, Allen Walker Lane, Heidi Mollenhauer, Luther Fontaine, Doug Okerson, Karen Ziemba, Martron Gales, Paul Hoover, Mary Stout, Darcy Thompson.

American Place Theater. In addition to the regular off-Broadway season, other special projects are presented. Wynn Handman, director, Mickey Rolfe, general manager.

American Humorists' Series. 13 performances each

CALVIN TRILLIN'S UNCLE SAM. Written and performed by Calvin Trillin. September 26, 1988. Production design, John M. Lucas.

A. WHITNEY BROWN'S THE BIG PICTURE (IN WORDS). Written and performed by A. Whitney Brown. March 28, 1989. Director, Wynn Handman; lighting, Brian MacDevitt.

American Theater of Actors. Dedicated to providing a creative atmosphere for new American playwrights, actors and directors. James Jennings, artistic director.

OTHELLO. By William Shakespeare. June 1, 1988. Directed by James Jennings; with Tom Major, Chessie Roberts, Edna Boyle, Scott Tuomey, Ric Fields, Andrea Fletcher, Shannon Whirry, Sam Inglese.

SCORPIONS IN THE CRADLE. By Marc Garcia. June 22, 1988. Director, James Jennings. With Karen Flannery, Patrick Shore, Linda Eskeland, Martin Widener.

THE NESTERS By Craig Sodaro. July 6, 1988. Director, Vince Tauro.

THE NIGHT WATCHMAN. By Steven David Schwab. July 6, 1988. Director, Loretta Palma. With F.R. Smith, Mat Sarter, Steven Solomon.

TWELFTH NIGHT. By William Shakespeare. July 6, 1988. Directed by Shep Pamplin.

Q Z Q. Written and directed by Donald L. Brooks. July 13, 1988.

BEACH HOUSE. By Eliza Miller. July 13, 1988. Director, Angela Foster. With Karen Flannery, Caroline Tenney, Catherine Brophy, Kristen Swanson.

NICKY. Written and directed by Kenthedo Robinson. July 13, 1988.

NIGHTLIFE. Written and directed by Rich Rubin. July 20, 1988.

ROWING THE STARS. Written and directed by James Jennings. July 27, 1988. With Linda Cherry, Randy Thoores, Danielle Gibbons, Christopher Jennings, Irving Butler, Gregory Burkart.

THE MERRY WIVES OF WINDSOR. By William Shakespeare. August 3, 1988. Directed by Michael Murnin.

ONE TO CARRY. By Albert Capa. August 10, 1988. Director, James Jennings. With Andrea Burandt, Evan Roberts, Jennifer Leigh Jennings.

COSMIC CRAZINESS. By Michael Racanelli. August 24, 1988. Director, John Sefakis.

SPRING STREET. By Edward and Mildred Lewis. August 24, 1988. Director, Donald Cox.

BETRAYALS OF MATTHEW HENSON. Written and directed by John Byrd. September 21, 1988. With Chessie Roberts, Bernadaire Lipscomb.

MOON OF THE GREEN GRASS. Written and directed by James Jennings. September 28, 1988. With Tom Major, Susan Talbot, Pat Fairly, Susan Chandler, Derek Webster.

PARKING LOT. By Peter Chelnik. October 5, 1988. Director, James Jennings.

GHOST TOWN. By Marc Garcia. November 2, 1988. Director, James Jennings. With David Hayden, Caroline Tenney, Sally Graudons, Matthew Caldwell.

HIDDEN AGENDA. By Mary Vasiliades. December 7, 1988. Director, Jaime Harris.

AT NEREYDA'S. By Raphael Diaz. December 7, 1988. Director, Bimbo Rivas.

I PLAYED THE PALACE. By Ken Sofronski. December 14, 1988. Director, John Sefakis.

THE OLD MERRY-GO-ROUND. By Harvey Parker. December 28, 1988. Director, Shep Pamplin.

GHOST TOWN. By Marc Garcia. January 11, 1989. Director, James Jennings. With Janet Kennedy, Pat Shore, Donna Avery, Joel Vic.

REMEMBERING THE FUTURE. By Larry Gray. January 11, 1989. Director, Gail Michaelson. With Robin Lilly, Don Sheehan.

SNATCH A FALLING STAR. By Craig Alpaugh. January 25, 1989. Director, Julie Blumberg.

THE SHAPE OF THINGS. By Walter Corwin. January 25, 1989. Director, Shep Pamplin. With Robin Lilly, Terence Reilly.

DAKOTA COWBOY. Written and directed by James Jennings. February 15, 1989. With Tom Major, Christina Styer, Heide Anderson, Simon Brooke, Christopher Jennings.

SLEEPER HOLD. By Stephen Jackson. February 15, 1989. Director, Phil Setrin.

CSC REPERTORY—Rajika Puri and Caroline Lagerfelt in *Phaedra Britannica*, a new version by Tony Harrison of Racine's *Phèdre*

THE SHEIK. Written and directed by Deloss Brown. February 22, 1989. With Anne Colby, Lloyd Garroway, Nancy Drake, Kathryn Singer, Mark Philpot.

DANNY ROCHA. By Kevin Kelly. February 22, 1989. Director, Douglas Matranga.

SPINSTERS. By Dan Calabrese. March 15, 1989. Director, Martin Teitel. With Mia Handler, Margaret A. Flanagan.

STUD POKER. By Charles Wilbert. March 16, 1989. Director, Roger Mrazek. With Tom Major, J. J. Clark, Simon Burke, Michele Miragliota.

SOUTH OF THE BORDER. By Roberto Monticello. March 22, 1989. Director, Nancy Robillard.

DAUGHTERS OF JERUSALEM WEEPING. Written and directed by James Crafford. March 29, 1989. With James Crafford, Bob Crafford, Jeremy Tow, Leslie Gerardo.

LATIN RETREAT. By Joseph Krawczyk. April 5, 1989. Director, James Jennings. With Will Buchanan, Robin Lilly, Joel Vic.

PRAIRIE FIRE. By Peter Chelnik. April 12, 1989. Director, James Jennings. With Bill Meizner, Lloyd Garroway, Jim Shanley, Robert Brush, Kelly McGary.

TAKEDOWN. By Eugene Barber. April 26, 1989. Director, Michael Murnin. With Tom Major, Wilbur Henry, Caroline Cole, Sally Graudons, Andrew Winkler, Lisa Juliano, Sam Inglese.

PARTNERS. Written and directed by Steve Silver. April 26, 1989.

DIAMOND LENS. Written and directed by Fred Panama. May 3, 1989.

CANARY IN A COAL MINE. By Doug Williams. May 17, 1989. Director, James Jennings. With F.R. Smith, John List, Debra Parker.

CAST IRON SMILE. By Nancy Bruff Gardner. May 24, 1989. Director, James Jennings. With Sally Graudons, Don Sheehan, Lorraine Marshall, Kerry Mortell, Tom Bruce, Lou Lagalante.

DON'T UNLOCK THE DOOR. By Craig Sodaro. May 24, 1989. Director, Vince Tauro. With Douglas Gibson, Mary Harper, Linda Cherry, Tim Douglas.

Circle Repertory Projects-in-Progress. Developmental programs for new plays. Tanya Berezin, artistic director, Connie L. Alexis, managing director.

AMULETS AGAINST THE DRAGON FORCES. By Paul Zindel. June 6, 1988. Director, B. Rodney Marriott.

POPE JOHN. By Patricia Goldstone. October 3, 1988. Director, Lee Costello.

THE MARRIAGE. By Terence Cannon. February 20, 1989. Director, Jonathan Hadary.

SUNSHINE. By William Mastrosimone. April 10, 1989. Director, Joe Brancato.

ARAB BRIDE. By James Ryan. May 22, 1989. Director, Mark Ramont.

CSC Repertory, Ltd. (Classic Stage Company). Aims to produce classics with a bold, contemporary sensibility. Carey Perloff, artistic director, Ellen Novack, managing director.

RAMEAU'S NEPHEW (30). By Denis Diderot, adapted and translated by Shelley Berc. October 19, 1988. Director, Andrei Belgrader; scenery, Anita Stewart; lighting, Robert Wierzel; costumes, Candice Donnelly. With Nicholas Kepros, Tony Shalhoub.

PHAEDRA BRITANNICA (28). By Tony Harrison, based on Jean Racine's *Phèdre*. December 14, 1988. Director, Carey Perloff; scenery, Donald Eastman; lighting, Frances Aronson; costumes, Gabriel Berry; music, Elizabeth Swados. With Caroline Lagerfelt, Bob Gunton, Jack Stehlin, Richard Riehle, Rajika Puri, John Wendes Taylor, Sakina Jaffrey, Meher Tatna, Michael Jayce, Winter Mead, Jill Williams.

DON JUAN OF SEVILLE (29). By Tirso de Molina, translated by Lynne Alvarez. April 2, 1989. Director, Carey Perloff; scenery, Donald Eastman; lighting, Frances Aronson; costumes, Gabriel Berry; music, Elizabeth Swados. With Jeffrey Nordling, Michael Perez, Robert Langdon Lloyd, Kim Yancey, Denise B. Mickelbury, Jack Stehlin, Ron Faber. (Co-produced by INTAR.)

Ensemble Studio Theater. Membership organization of playwrights, actors, directors and designers dedicated to supporting individual theater artists and developing new works for the stage. Over 250 projects each season, initiated by E.S.T. members. Curt Dempster, artistic director, Peter Shavitz, managing director.

MARATHON '88 (festival of one-act plays). BUSTER B AND OLIVIA by Shirley Kaplan, directed by Billy Hopkins; NEPTUNE'S HIPS by Richard Greenberg, directed by Christopher Ashley; SOMETHING ABOUT BASEBALL by Quincy Long, directed by Risa Bramon; A POSTER OF THE COSMOS by Lanford Wilson, directed by Jonathan Hogan; JULIET by Romulus Linney, directed by Peter Maloney; MANGO TEA by Paul Weitz, directed by Curt Dempster; HUMAN GRAVITY by Stuart Spencer, directed by Evan Yionoulis; DOOR TO CUBA by James Ryan, directed by Charles Richter; DIPHTHONG by Michael B. Kaplan, directed by Lisa Peterson; SLAUGHTER IN THE LAKE by Jose Rivera, directed by Joan Vail Thorne; THE MAN WHO CLIMBED THE PECAN TREES by Horton Foote, directed by Curt Dempster; SINGING JOY by Oyamo, directed by Peter Wallace. June 8–July 18, 1988. (Produced as part of the First New York International Festival of the Arts.)

OCTOBERFEST '88. Festival of 67 new plays by members, ranging from readings to rehearsed workshops. October 3–24, 1988.

THE PROMISE (21). By Jose Rivera. November 30, 1988. Director, David Esbjornson; scenery, Ann Sheffield; lighting, Greg MacPherson; costumes, Toni-Leslie James. With Donald Berman, Yusef Bulos, Ivonne Coll, Kate Gyllenhaal, Rene Moreno, Jaime Sanchez, Socorro Santiago.

THE MAGIC ACT (21). By Laurence Klavan. March 8, 1989. Director, Peter Zapp; scenery, Martha Fay; design concept, Brian Martin; lighting, David Higham; costumes, David Sawaryn. With Anne O'Sullivan, Rick Lawless, Cordelia Richards, Frederica Meister, Sam Schacht.

NEW VOICES '89 (staged readings of full-length plays): OPEN SPACES by Susan Kim, directed by D. S. Moynihan; YOKOHAMA DUTY by Quincy Long, directed by Kathleen Dimmick; GENERATIONS OF THE DEAD IN THE ABYSS OF CONEY ISLAND MADNESS by Michael Henry Brown, directed by L. Kenneth Richardson; SUNDAYS FOR MARY ELLEN MORGAN PINKERTON LOWE by Edward Napier, directed by Lisa Peterson; THE INDEPENDENCE OF EDDIE ROSE by William Yellow Robe Jr., directed by Jack Gelber. April 22–May 2, 1989.

Equity Library Theater. Primary mission is staging vital revivals. Jeffrey R. Costello, producing director.

THE MALE ANIMAL. By James Thurber and Elliott Nugent. September 29, 1988. Director, Geoffrey C. Shlaes; with Sandy Rowe, Robert Shampain, Robert McFarland, James Lish, Patricia Guinan, Regis Bowman, Jona Harvey.

FIORELLO! Book by Jerome Weidman and George Abbott; music by Jerry Bock; lyrics by Sheldon Harnick. October 27, 1988. Director, Bob Nigro; with Joe Dispenza, Felicia Farone, Mia Randall, Paul Laureano, Kathryn Kendall, Mark Goldbaum, Jane Wasser.

PEG O' MY HEART. By J. Hartley Manners. December 1, 1988. Director, D. J. Maloney; with Judith McIntyre, Tim Gail, Russell Goldberg, Yvette Edelhart, Marjorie Ann Miller, Stephen Gabis.

TOMFOOLERY. Musical revue by Tom Lehrer, adapted by Cameron Mackintosh and Robin Ray. January 5, 1989. Director, Pamela Hunt; with Don Bradford, Jack Doyle, Patricia Masters, John Remme.

FIFTH OF JULY. By Lanford Wilson. February 9, 1989. Director, Andrew Glant-Linden; with Jack L. Davis, Cate Damon, Laurence Overmire, Kevin Jeffries, Susanna Frazer, Rebecca Hoodwin, Joan Mann, Don Weingust.

LEAVE IT TO JANE. Book by Guy Bolton and P. G. Wodehouse; music and lyrics by Jerome Kern. March 9, 1989. Director, Lynnette Barkley; with Wendy Oliver, Peter Reardon, Nick Corley, Rob Donohoe, Susan Hartley, Marcus Powell.

THE THIRTEENTH CHAIR. By Bayard Veiller. April 13, 1989. Director, Maggie Jackson; with Malia Ondrejka, T. Ryder Smith, Maxine Taylor-Morris, Daniel Nalbach, Babs Hooyman, Hewitt Brooks.

GIGI. Book and lyrics by Alan Jay Lerner, based on Colette's novel; music by Frederick Loewe. May 11, 1989. Director, Gerard Alessandrini; with Russell Costen, Bob Cuccioli, Donna Ramundo, D'yan Forest, Pamela Shafer, Marylin Monaco, Lynette Bennett, Bernard Granville.

Hudson Guild Theater. Presents plays in their New York, American or world premieres. Geoffrey Sherman, producing director, Steve Ramay, associate director.

IN PERPETUITY THROUGHOUT THE UNIVERSE (28). By Eric Overmyer. June 11, 1988. Director, Stan Wojewodski Jr.; scenery, Christopher Barreca; lighting, Stephen Strawbridge; costumes, Robert Wojewodski. With Troy Evans, Arthur Hanket, Jennifer Harmon, Laura Innes, Tzi Ma, Carolyn McCormick.

TEA WITH MOMMY AND JACK (28). By Shela Walsh. October 19, 1988. Director, Lawrence Sacharow; scenery, Donald Eastman; lighting, Paul Wonsek; costumes, Marianne Powell-Parker; music, Peter Gordon. With David Groh, Sylvia Miles, Caris Corfman.

ALMOST PERFECT (35). By Jerry Mayer. November 30, 1988. Director, Geraldine Fitzgerald; scenery, James D. Sandefur; lighting, Phil Monat; costumes, Pamela Scofield. With Ethan Phillips, Mia Dillon, Bill Nelson, Ivar Brogger, Cathy Lee Crosby, Chevi Colton.

WITHOUT APOLOGIES (28). By Thom Thomas. February 1, 1989. Director, Edgar Lansbury; scenery, John Wulp; lighting, Paul Wonsek; costumes, Karen Hummel. With Laura Brutsman, Pauline Flanagan, Kurt Knudson, Edmund Lewis, Carrie Nye, Peter Pagan.

WALKERS (28). By Marion Isaac McClinton. March 29, 1989. Directors, Steven Ramay and Marion Isaac McClinton; scenery and lighting, Paul Wonsek; costumes, Elsa Ward. With Terry E. Bellamy, Iona Morris, Faye M. Price, Ron Dortch, John Henry Redwood, James A. Williams.

UP 'N' UNDER (28). By John Godber. May 24, 1989. Director, Geoffrey Sherman; scenery and lighting, Paul Wonsek; costumes, Pamela Scofield. With Ivar Brogger, Ray Collins, John Curless, Fredrick Hahn, Edmund Lewis, Elaine Rinehart.

INTAR Innovative cultural center for the Hispanic American community of New York focusing on the art of theater. Max Ferra, artistic director, James DiPaola, managing director.

ALMA (one-act). Book and lyrics by Ana Maria Simo, inspired by works of Quivedo; music by Fernando Rivas; director, Paul Zimet. WELCOME BACK TO SALAMANCA (one-act). Book and lyrics by Migdalia Cruz, loosely based on Cervantes's *The Cave of Salamanca*; music by Fernando Rivas; directed by George Ferencz. June 15, 1988. Scenery, Loy Arcenas; lighting, Beverly Emmons; costumes, Sally J. Lesser; musical director, Jeremy Kahn. With Irma-Estel LaGuerre, Nancy Sorel, Al DeCristo, Sheila Dabney, Alexis Reyes, John Seber, Steven Bland, Willie C. Barnes, Carlos Arevalo, Humberto Alabado.

SUEÑOS. (A co-production; See Mabou Mines entry.) DON JUAN OF SEVILLE. (A co-production; See CSC Repertory entry.)

Interart Theater. Committed to producing innovative work by women theater artists and to introducing New York audiences to a bold range of theater that is non-traditional in form or theme. Margot Lewitin, artistic director.

LITTLE WOMEN: THE TRAGEDY. By the Split Britches company. January 5, 1989. Scenery, Peggy Shaw and Joni Wong; lighting, Joni Wong; costumes, Susan Young. With Lois Weaver, Peggy Shaw, Debra Margolin.

BRIMSTONE AND TREACLE. By Dennis Potter. April 11, 1989. Director, Rosemary Hay; scenery, Christina Weppner; lighting, Frances Aronson; costumes, Martha Bromelmeier. With Shula Van Buren, Maggie Soboil, Frank Lazarus, Rudy Caporaso.

LaMama Experimental Theater Club (ETC). A busy workshop for experimental theater of all kinds. Ellen Stewart, founder and artistic director.

Schedule included:

I SHALL NEVER RETURN. Written and directed by Tadeusz Kantor. June 14, 1988. Choreography, Enrico Coffetti; sound, Tomasz Dobrowski. With Cricot 2 Theater Company. (Produced as part of the First New York International Festival of the Arts.)

ROAD. (A co-production; see its entry in the Plays Produced Off Broadway section of this volume.)

L'ANTICYCLONE DES ACORES. Conceived and directed by Luca Nicolaj. September 29, 1988.

A PROCESS. Written and directed by Gerald Thomas. October 6, 1988. Scenery and costumes, Daniela Thomas; lighting and sound, Gerald Thomas; music, Philip Glass and Jaques Morelenbaum. With Bete Coelho, Luis Damasceno, Oswaldo Barreto, Marco Stocco, Marcos Barreto, Megaly Bigg, Malu Pessin, Edilson Botelho, Zacharias Goulart, Simone Correa, Domingos Varela. (Presented in repertory with PRAGA and CARMEM COM FILTRO by Gerald Thomas.)

ODE TO A CUBE. One-man show by and with John Kelly. October 13, 1988. Lighting, Howard Thies.

SINODYSSEY. Written and directed by Ko Tin Lung. November 26, 1988. Music, Mica Nozawa and Brian Lee.

DON'T REMIND ME. By Georg Osterman. December 1, 1988. Director, Linda Chapman; music, Tom Judson.

ADULT ORGASM ESCAPES FROM THE ZOO. Monologue by Franca Rame and Dario Fo. January 5, 1989. With Denise Stoklos.

SKIN: A STATE OF BEING. Conceived and directed by Ping Chong. January 5, 1989.

THE BOOK AND THE STRANGER. Fables from the *Kalila Wa Dimna* adapted by Rinsala El-Khoury and Joumana Rizk. February 8, 1989. Directed by Joumana Rizk.

BLUE MOON. Written and directed by Steve Busa. February 2, 1989. Music, Stephen Peabody, Hannah Tennen and James Harry.

TRIPLETS IN UNIFORM. By Jeffrey Essmann. February 3, 1989. Director, David Warren; scenery, James Youmans; lighting, Howard Thies; costumes, Mary Beth Kilkelly; music, Michael-John LaChiusa. With Ann Mantel, Mary Shultz, Cornelia Kiss, Bob Koherr, Kim Sykes, Jeffrey Essmann, Kathy Kinney, Susan Finch.

MYTHOS OEDIPUS. Text and direction by Ellen Stewart (based on the Oedipus myth); music by Elizabeth Swados, Sheila Dabney, Genji Ito, David Sawyer and Michael Sirotta. DIONYSUS FILIUS DEI. Text and direction by Ellen Stewart, Greek translation by Eleni Petratos; vocal score by Elizabeth Swados; music by Sheila Dabney, Genji Ito and Michael Sirotta; choreography by Ellen Stewart and the company; scenery by David Adams, Mark Tambella, Watoku Ueno and Ellen Stewart; costumes by Sally J. Lesser; masks by Stephen Loebel. February 25, 1989. With the Great Jones Repertory Company.

THE OPTIMIST. By Emil Habibi. February 28, 1989. Director, Geula Jeffet-Attar.

WILD BILL FROM OLIVE HILL. By Bill Callihan. March 23, 1989.

THE NIGHT BEFORE THINKING. By Ahmed Yacoubi. March 30, 1989. Director, Ismael El-Kanater; music, Bachir Attar, Hassan Hakmoun and Radouane Laktib.

NEW CITIES. By Paul Zimet, in collaboration with the Talking Band. April 20, 1989. Director, Paul Zimet; choreography, Rocky Bornstein; scenery and lighting, Arden Fingerhut; costumes, Gabriel Berry; music, Ellen Maddow and Harry Mann. With the Talking Band (William Badgett, Ellen Maddow, Lizzie Olesker, Tina Shepard).

QUAIGH THEATER—James Rosin and Kricker James
in a scene from *Batting Practice* by Paul Gleason

QUASI-KINETICS. Theater-dance piece written and directed by Roger Babb. April 28, 1989. Choreography, Rocky Bornstein; scenery, Michael Fajans and Nick Fennel; music, Blue Gene Tyranny. With Paul Zimet, Mary Shultz, John Fleming, Nancy Alfaro, Rocky Bornstein, Susan Milani.

Lamb's Theater Company. Committed to developing and presenting new works in their most creative and delicate beginnings. Carolyn Rossi Copeland, producing director.

GIFTS OF THE MAGI. Book and lyrics by Mark St. Germain, based on the O. Henry story; music and lyrics by Randy Courts. November 30, 1988. Directed by Sonya Baehr; with Gabriel Barre, Jessica Beltz, Adam Bryant, Michael Calkins, Rebecca Renfroe, Scott Waara.

THE REVELATION OF JOHN (6). Adapted, directed and performed by Tom Key. March 12, 1989. Scenery, Michael C. Smith; lighting, Jeff Schissler.

CROSSIN' THE LINE (40). By Phil Bosakowski. May 8, 1989. Director, Sonya Baehr; scenery, Michael C. Smith; lighting, Dave Feldman; costumes, Debra Stein. With Brenda Thomas, Judy Malloy, Talia Paul, John Speredakos, Michael Francis Boyle, Josh Mosby.

Mabou Mines. Theater collaborative whose work is a synthesis of motivational acting, narrative acting and mixed-media performance. Collective artistic leadership.

FLOW MY TEARS, THE POLICEMAN SAID (21). By Philip K. Dick, adapted by Linda Hartinian. June 17, 1988. Director, Bill Raymond; choreography, Barbara Allen; scenery, Linda Hartinian; lighting, Anne Militello; costumes, Gabriel Berry; music, Tom Noonan; music for "Pizzeria Song," Bill Spencer; video, Paul Clay; sound, L. B. Dallas. With Honora Fergusson, Black-Eyed Susan, Greg Mehrten, Ann Shea, David Brisbin, Susan Berman, Paul Clay, David Pittu, Terry O'Reilly, Frederick Neumann, Ruth

Maleczech, Tracy Fowler, Nina Hellman, Gina Novish, Dahlia Schneider, Marni Task. (Produced as part of the First New York International Festival of the Arts.)

SUEÑOS (musical) (18+). Adapted and directed by Ruth Maleczech, from the writings of Sor Juana Inés de la Cruz, Eduardo Galeano and Homero Aridjis; music, Herschel Garfein; lyrics, Ruth Maleczech and George Emilio Sanchez; additional lyrics, Herschel Garfein. February 19, 1989. Choreography, Pat Hall Smith; scenery, Michael Deegan; lighting, Clay Shirky; costumes, Toni-Leslie James; murals, Eduardo Carrillo; musical director, Richard Pittman. With Lorraine Hunt, Irma-Estel LaGuerre, Tomas Milian. (Co-produced by INTAR, in association with Boston Musica Viva.)

Manhattan Punch Line. New York's only theater company devoted to comedy. Steve Kaplan, artistic director.

NEW VAUDEVILLE '88 (festival of new vaudeville performance art). Performers included: Wallem & Tolan, Tamara Jenkins, Tom Cayler, Brian O'Connor. October 8–18, 1988.

FIFTH ANNUAL FESTIVAL OF ONE-ACT COMEDIES: WONDERFUL PARTY by Howard Korder, directed by Val Hendrickson; THE GETTYSBURG SOUND BITE by Ted Tally, directed by Louis Scheeder; ONE MONDAY by Matt Cutugno, directed by Scott Rubsam; SEVEN MENUS by David Ives, directed by Fred Sanders; SEX LIVES OF SUPERHEROES by Stephen Gregg, directed by Paul Lazarus; THE NEWS FROM ST. PETERSBURG by Rich Orloff, directed by Adam Zahler; SEEING SOMEONE by Laurence Klavan, directed by Steve Kaplan; REQUIEM FOR A HEAVYWEIGHT by Mark O'Donnell, directed by Robin Saex; PILLOW TALK by Peter Tolan, directed by Jason McConnell Buzas; GOOD HONEST FOOD by Bill Bozzone, directed by Steve Kaplan. January 14–February 26, 1989. Scenery, James Wolk; lighting, Danianne Mizzy; costumes, Fontella Boone, Michael Schler. With Peter Basch, Brad Bellamy, Larry Block, Bill Cohen, Gary Cookson, Dan Desmond, Ellen Dolan, Steven Gilborn, Daniel Hagen, Tessie Hogan, Cady Huffman, Jack Kenny, Neal Lerner, Nicholas Levitin, Steven Marcus, Christiane McKenna, Barry Miller, Michael Piontek, Elaine Rinehart, Kathrin King Segal, Constance Shulman, Victor Slezak, Dan Strickler, Debra Stricklin, Ann Talman, Lois Taylor, Andrea Weber, Melissa Weil.

AN EVENING WITH WALLEM & TOLAN (28). Written and performed by Linda Wallem and Peter Tolan; music and lyrics, Peter Tolan. March 2, 1989. Director, Stephen Hollis; scenery, James Wolk; lighting, Danianne Mizzy; costumes, Paul Patropulos.

EQUAL 'WRIGHTS (one-act plays): THE AGREEMENT by Janet Neipris, directed by Steve Kaplan; MARATHONS by Terri Wagener, directed by Robin Saex; HOW IT HANGS by Grace McKeaney, directed by Melia Bensussen (12). May 5, 1989. Scenery, Matthew Moore and James Wolk; lighting, Brian MacDevitt; costumes, Michael Schler. With Caris Corfman, Beth Dixon, Michael French, Robin Groves, Miles Herter, Richmond Hoxie, Brian Keeler, Ilana Levine, Pat Nesbit, Susan Pellegrino, Peggity Price, Ellen Tobie, David Wasson.

FRIENDS (24). Written and directed by Lee Kalcheim. May 26, 1989. Scenery, Richard Meyer; lighting, Steve Rust. With Richard Lenz, David Spielberg.

Music-Theater Group. Pioneering in the development of new music-theater. Lyn Austin, producing director, Diane Wondisford, Mark Jones, associate producing directors.

Schedule included:

DANGEROUS GLEE CLUB (18). Conceived by Charles Moulton and Steve Elson; music by Steve Elson. February 14, 1989. Director and choreographer, Charles Moulton; lighting, Debra Dumas.

LADIES (28). By Eve Ensler; music by Joshua Schneider. March 28, 1989. Director, Paul Walker; scenery, Victoria Petrovich; lighting, Debra Dumas; costumes, Donna Zakowska. With Margaret Barker, Denise Delapenha, Alexandra Gersten, Allison Janney, Marcella Lowery, Isabell Monk, Novella Nelson, Ching Valdes/Aran, Beverly Wideman. (Co-produced by The Women's Project and Productions.)

Musical Theater Works. Developmental workshop where writers of musical theater learn by doing. Anthony J. Stimac, artistic director, Mark S. Herko, associate artistic director.

13 performances each

PASSIONATE EXTREMES. Chamber opera with libretto by Thayer Burch; music by George Quincy. October 5, 1988. Director, Mark S. Herko; scenery, James Noone; lighting, Ken Smith; costumes, Amanda J. Klein; musical director, Eric Barnes. With Ruthann Curry, Suellen Estey, James Hindman, Sarah Knapp, Steve Mattar, Pankchali Null, Alex Santoriello, Marianne Tatum.

KISS ME QUICK BEFORE THE LAVA REACHES THE VILLAGE. Book by Steve Hayes; music by Peter Ekstrom; lyrics and story by Steve Hayes and Peter Ekstrom. November 2, 1988. Director, Anthony J. Stimac; choreography, Frank Ventura; scenery, James Noone; lighting, Richard Latta; costumes, Amanda J. Klein; musical director, Albert Ahronheim. With Ray Wills, Maria Bostick, Donna English, Adinah Alexander, Mana Allen, David Barron, Bill Buell, Tom Farrell, Suzanne Hevner, Wade Howard, Skip Lackey, Kristine Nevins, Nicola Stimac, Bill Walters.

CRADLE SONG. Book and lyrics by Mary Bracken Phillips; music by Jan Mullaney. March 15, 1989. Director, Anthony J. Stimac; choreography, Janet Watson; scenery, Richard Ellis; lighting, Clarke W. Thornton; costumes, Amanda J. Klein; musical directors, Keith Levinson, Jan Mullaney. With Keith Charles, Mary Bracken Phillips, Carole Schweid, Paul E. Ukena Jr.

YOUNG RUBE. Book by George W. George and Matty Selman; music and lyrics by Matty Selman. April 19, 1989. Director, Mark S. Herko; choreography, Margie Castleman; scenery consultant, David Mitchell; lighting, Richard Latta; costumes, Amanda J. Klein; musical director, Bryan Louiselle. With Adinah Alexander, Maria Bostick, Kenneth Boys, Hal Hudson, Joan Jaffe, Skip Lackey, Gary Kirsch, Mike O'Carroll, Robert Polenz, Keith Savage, Don Stephenson, Miki Whittles.

New Dramatists. An organization devoted to playwrights; member writers may use the facilities for anything from private cold readings of their material to public script-in-hand readings. Joel Ruark, managing director, Jean Passanante, artistic director.

Public readings

COURAGE. Written and performed by John Pielmeier. June 1, 1988.
BOYS PLAY. By Jack Heifner. June 2, 1988. With Christopher Shaw, Andy McCutcheon.
SHORT PIECES. By John Pielmeier. June 3, 1988. Directed by Gloria Muzio; with Victor Slezak, Michael Morin, Walter Bobbie, Anne O'Sullivan.
THE ROWING MACHINE. By Willy Holtzman. September 26, 1988. Directed by John Pynchon Holms; with Marilyn McIntyre, Murray Rubinstein, Michael Burg.
TED AND EDNA. By Ana Marie Simo; music by Jeffrey Roy. September 29, 1988. Directed by Linda Chapman; with Laurie Franks, Al Carmines, Tom Donoghue, Ellie Ellsworth.
THE CEZANNE SYNDROME. By Normand Canac-Marquis; translated by Louison Danis. October 3, 1988. Directed by Liz Diamond; with Dierdre O'Connell, Anderson Matthews, Edward Baran.
SPACE. By David Spencer. October 10, 1988. Directed by Fritz Ertl; with Patrick Breen, Laura Innes, Mary Jay, Mark Truitt.
YOKOHAMA DUTY. By Quincy Long. October 11, 1988. Directed by Morgan Jenness; with Bruce Katzman, Tessie Hogan, Elizabeth Sung, Barton Heyman, Greg Germann, Frankie Faison, Richard Riehle.
IN LIVING COLOR. By Oyamo, Dianne McIntyre and Olu Dara. October 14, 1988. Choreographed by Dianne McIntyre; with Phillip Bond, Cheryl Freeman, Alexria Davis, Kathleen Sumler, Michael E. Stevens, Merle Holliman.
THE DUCK SISTERS. By Sheldon Rosen. October 19, 1988. Directed by Gordon Edelstein; with Phyllis Somerville, April Shawhan, Todd Randolph.
GIRL BAR. By Phyllis Nagy. November 1, 1988. Directed by Rosey Hay; with Margaret Klenck, Phyllis Somerville, Elizabeth Berridge, Erica Gimpelto, Helen Hunt.
THE SWEET DECEIT. By Joe Sutton. November 7, 1988. Directed by Michael Bloom; with Caroline Aaron, Richard Riehle, William D. Griffin, Fritz Sperberg, Karen Lee.

PECONG. By Steve Carter. November 16, 1988. Directed by Arthur French; with Miriam Burton, Copper Cunningham, Hazel Medina.

ALL THESE BLESSINGS. By June Jordan. November 18, 1988. Directed by Suzanne Bennett; with Nick Smith, Seret Scott, Robyn Hatcher, Randy Wilhelm.

THE TOWER. By Matthew Maguire. November 30, 1988. Directed by Jennifer McDowall; with Nicky Paraiso, Isabel Saez, Robyn Hatcher, Joyce Leigh Bowden, Graeme Malcolm.

BLEACHERS IN THE SUN. By Y York. December 5, 1988. Directed by Mark Lutwak; with Tom Wright, Ben Siegler, Elaine Rinehart, Jay O. Sanders, Brenda Thomas, Christopher McCann, Jennifer Leigh Warren, La Tanya Richardson, Dennis Green, Julia Glander.

THE CLOSER. By Willy Holtzman. January 25, 1989. Directed by R. J. Cutler; with Earl Hagan, Murray Rubinstein.

WHAT A MAN WEIGHS. By Sherry Kramer. February 6, 1989. Directed by Liz Diamond; with Caroline Aaron, Melissa Cooper, Anne O'Sullivan, Patrick O'Connell.

SPIELE '36. By Steve Carter. February 13, 1989. With Christopher Shaw, Bruce MacVittie, Kevin Geer, Joyce Leigh Bowden, Miles Grose, Steve Coats.

WHIRLIGIG. By Mac Wellman. February 14, 1989. Directed by Eric Mee; with Zivia Flomenhaft, Chuck Montgomery, Stuart Sherman.

STEEPLE CHASE. By John Pielmeier. February 21, 1989. With Adinah Alexander, Mia Dillon, Michael Morin, Bob Cuccioli, Michael Hardstark.

BAD PENNY. By Mac Wellman. March 1, 1989. With Stephen Mellor, Caris Corfman, Ray Xifo, Ryan Cutrona.

ACCELERANDO. By Lisa Loomer. March 7, 1989. Directed by Liz Diamond; with Jossie de Guzman, Marvin Einhorn, Bobo Lewis, Peter MacKenzie, Antonia Rey.

THE TEACHER'S REWARD. By Thomas G. Dunn. March 17, 1989. Directed by Liz Diamond; with John Connelly, Jeanette Horne.

WHOLE HEARTED. By Quincy Long. March 22, 1989. Directed by Kathleen Dimmick; with Bruce Katzman, Colette Kilroy, Billie Neal, Tessie Hogan, April Shawhan, Mark Lenard, Victor Raider-Wexler, Bill Youmans.

CAPTIVE. By Debbie Broadhead. April 12, 1989. Directed by Maria Gillen; with Sharon Brady, Chris Sena, Elizabeth DuVall, Benette Gilbert, Camryn Manheim, Julia Gibson.

CASANOVA. By Constance Congdon. April 20, 1989. Directed by Greg Leaming; with Yusef Bulos, Rocco Sisto, Caroline Aaron, Pamela Nyberg, Nesbitt Blaisdell, Joel Miller.

GERONIMO JONES. By Oyamo. May 1, 1989. Directed by Liz Diamond; with L. Peter Callender, Robert Jason, Miles Watson, Sheila Dabney.

THE MYSOGYNIST. By Michael Harding. May 9, 1989. Directed by R. J. Cutler; with Randy Danson, Tom Kopache.

MERE MORTALS and VARIATIONS ON THE DEATH OF TROTSKY by David Ives, directed by R.J. Cutler; MOM GOES TO THE PARTY by Y York, directed by Mark Lutwak; PROUD FLESH by James Nicholson, directed by Kim Sharp (one-acts). May 15, 1989.

FLOOR ABOVE THE ROOF (one-act). By Daniel Therriault. May 16, 1989. Directed by John Pynchon Holms; with Mark Smaltz, Randy Frazier, Isiah Whitlock Jr., Richard Fisk.

THE OLD LADY PLAY (one-act). By James Nicholson. May 17, 1989. Directed by Liz Diamond; with Phyllis Somerville, Bobo Lewis, Richmond Hoxie, Ellen Tobie.

INFINITY'S HOUSE. By Ellen McLaughlin. May 17, 1989. Directed by Richard Feldman; with David Adkins, Erik Knutsen, Mark Niebuhr, Gayle Cohen, Lisa Hamilton, Christopher Taylor.

...AND HOWL AT THE MOON. By James Nicholson. May 25, 1989. Directed by R. J. Cutler; with Bobo Lewis, David Adkins, Jeffrey Knauft, Michael Wells, Earl Hagan, John Scanlan, Deborah Hedwall.

New Federal Theater. Dedicated to presenting new playwrights and plays dealing with the black experience. Woodie King Jr., producer.

Schedule included:

JIKA (30). Written and directed by Maishe Maponya. June 30, 1988. Choreography, Welcome Msomi; scenery, Terry Chandler; lighting, William H. Grant III; costumes, Karen Perry. With Fana Kekana, Jerry Mofokeng. (Produced as part of the First New York International Festival of the Arts.)

GOOD BLACK... (36). By Rob Penny. October 19, 1988. Director, Claude Purdy; scenery, Ken Ellis; lighting, William H. Grant III; costumes, Karen Perry. With Dorothi Fox, Kenneth J. Green, Fern Howell, Amber Kain, Marcus Naylor, Alicia Rene Washington, Judi Ann Williams, Mel Winkler.

'TIS THE MORNING (36). By Ruth Beckford and Ron Stacker Thompson. January 12, 1989. Director, Ron Stacker Thompson; scenery, Kerry Sanders; lighting, Ernst Baxter; costumes, Rubee Taylor. With Ruth Beckford, Billy Hutton, Inez Norman, Margarette Robinson, Melvin Thompson.

A THRILL A MOMENT (36). Musical revue by William (Mickey) Stevenson. April 27, 1989. Director and choreographer, Edward Love; scenery, Richard Harmon; lighting, William H. Grant III, Jerry Forsyth; costumes, Fontella Boone; musical director, Grenoldo Frazier. With Adrian Bailey, Irene Datcher, Dwayne Grayman, Kelly Rice, Kiki Shepard, Gina Taylor, Allison Williams.

New York Shakespeare Festival Public Theater. Schedule of special projects, in addition to its regular off-Broadway productions. Joseph Papp, producer.

THE IMPERIALISTS AT THE CLUB CAVE CANEM (36). By Charles L. Mee Jr. June 17, 1988. Director, Erin B. Mee; scenery, Albert Webster; lighting, Josh Starbuck; costumes, Lissy Walker; music, Guy Yarden. With Kathleen Tolan.

FESTIVAL LATINO IN NEW YORK. Schedule included: DE LA CALLE by Jesus Gonzalez Davila, directed by Julio Castillo, with Roberto Sosa Martinez, Ana Mathilde, Alfredo Escobar, Luis De Icaza, Adalberto Parra; THE ISLAND (MOSQUITO) by Athol Fugard, John Kani and Winston Ntshona, Spanish translation and directed by Filander Funes, with Mario Balmaseda, Pedro Renteria, Juan Marcos Blanco; MADE IN LANUS by Nelly Fernandez Tiscornia, directed by Luis Brandoni, with Betiana Blum, Adrian Ghio, Marta Bianchi, Luis Brandoni; EL MARTIRIO DEL PASTORA by Samuel Rovinski, directed by Alfredo Catania, with Luis Fernando Gomez, Bernal Quesada, Gerardo Arce; MARIAMENEO, MARIAMENEO written and directed by Juan Sanchez, with Gaspar Campuzano, Francisco Sanchez, Marisa Collado, Ana Oliva; BANG BANG BLUES (work-in-progress) by Charles Gomez, directed by Jules Aaron, with Jane Galloway, Michael Canavan, Tony Plana, Al Rodriguez, Joseph Palmas, Gregory Itzin, Ada Maris, Mike Robelo, Joan Stuart-Morris. August 3–27, 1988.

JACKIE MASON: LONDON BOUND (6). January 24, 1989.

MANDY PATINKIN: DRESS CASUAL (cabaret). February 27, 1989.

New York Theater Workshop. Dedicated to the production of plays of intelligence and conscience and the development of new plays and emerging stage directors. James C. Nicola, artistic director, Nancy Kassak Diekmann, managing director.

L'ILLUSION (32). By Pierre Corneille, adapted by Tony Kushner. October 27, 1988. Director, Brian Kulick; scenery, Stephen Olson; lighting, Pat Dignan; costumes, Claudia Brown; music and sound, Mark Bennett. With Michael Galardi, Arthur Hanket, Neil Maffin, Victor Raider-Wexler, Socorro Santiago, Stephen Spinella, Regina Taylor, Isiah Whitlock Jr.

EMERALD CITY. By David Williamson. (A Best Play; see its entry in the Plays Produced Off Broadway section of this volume.)

In repertory:

THE NEST (13). By Franz Xaver Kroetz; director, Bartlett Sher; with Alma Cuervo, Matt Craven. MERCEDES (13). By Thomas Brasch; director, Cheryl Faver; with Sharon Brady, Larry Bazzell, Bruce Katzman. February 8, 1989. Scenery, Rob Murphy; lighting, Pat Dignan; costumes, Marina Draghici.

THE INVESTIGATION OF THE MURDER IN EL SALVADOR (39). By Charles L. Mee Jr. May 21, 1989. Director, David Schweizer; scenery, Tom Kamm; lighting, Anne Militello; costumes, Gabriel Berry; music, Peter Gordon. With Paul Schmidt, Thom Christopher, Kathleen Chalfant, Isiah Whitlock Jr., Leslie Nipkow, Greg Mehrten, Tom McDermott, Shona Tucker, Freddie Frankie.

The Open Eye: New Stagings. Goal is to gather a community of outstanding theater artists to collaborate on works for the stage for audiences of all ages and cultural backgrounds. Jean Erdman, founding director, Amie Brockway, artistic director.

ANGALAK (18). By Walt Vail. November 16, 1988. Director, Amie Brockway; choreography, Leslie Dillingham; scenery, Adrienne J. Brockway; lighting, Spencer Mosse. With Jose Andrews, Jane Lind, Allan Tung, Martha Gilpin, Mark Tankersley.

THE WALL INSIDE (19). By Thomas Cadwaleder Jones. March 4, 1989. Director, Kim T. Sharp; scenery, Adrienne J. Brockway; lighting, Donald A. Gingrasso. With Leland Gant, Dan Tubb, Oni Faida Lampley.

EYE ON DIRECTORS FESTIVAL (one-acts). Schedule included: THE STRONGER by August Strindberg, directed by Michelle Frenzer Cornell, with Roberta Shelton Cornell, Corinna May, Sherry Teitelbaum; FUGUE IN 30 MINUTES FLAT by Jameel Khaja and Doug La Brecque, music by Doug LaBrecque, with Sheila Head, Hilary James, Thomas Pasley; THE SICILIAN, OR, LOVE THE PAINTER by Molière, directed by Rebecca Kreinen, with David Amarel, Jeff Constan, Michael Fields, Dan Hazel, Brian MacReady, Stephen Moser, Sandra Scott, Lise Tribble; WAITING FOR LEPKE by Walt Vail, directed by David M. Nevarrez, with Roslyn Cohn, Stephen Gonya, Laurie Muir, Steve Robinson, Ben Schwartz; KATHLEEN NI HOULIHAN by William Butler Yeats, directed by Barbara Lynn Rice, with Ursula Burton, Rochelle DuBoff, Benjamin Henderson, Thomas Honeck, Mark Irish; WOMANCHILD by Melissa Carey, directed by Kim T. Sharp, with Patricia Denny, Elizabeth Gee, Laurie Muir, Kathleen O'Neill; BAGS by Anne McGravie, directed by Nan Siegmund, with Gloria Bogin, Susan Izatt, Joanne Joseph; BABY TALK by Chris Glaza Knudsen, directed by Sharone Stacy, with Scott Galbraith, Mary Schmidt; THE BLIND ONE-ARMED DEAF MUTE by Thomas Gueullette and GILES IN LOVE by Jan Potocki, directed by Sherry Teitelbaum, with Guy J. Ale, Brian Poteat, Stanley Allen Sherman, Andrea Sisniega. May 7-14, 1989.

Pan Asian Repertory Theater. Strives to provide opportunities for Asian American artists to perform under the highest professional standards and to create and promote plays by and about Asians and Asian Americans. Tisa Chang, artistic/producing director.

BOUTIQUE LIVING & DISPOSABLE ICONS (18). By Momoko Iko. June 24, 1988. Director, Tisa Chang; scenery, Jane Epperson; lighting, Clay Shirky; costumes, Eiko Yamaguchi. With Michi Kobi, Kitty Mei-Mei Chen, Norris M. Shimabuku, Ann M. Tsuji, Raul Aranas, Donald Li. (Produced as part of the First New York International Festival of the Arts.)

THREE SISTERS by Anton Chekhov, translated by Randall Jarrell. November 22, 1988. Directed by Margaret Booker; with Ginny Yang, Natsuko Ohama, Mary Lee-Aranas, Mia Korf, Mark W. Conklin, Ron Nakahara, Mel Duane Gionson, Donald Li, Philip Moon, Ernest H. Abuba, Michael G. Chin, Steve Park, Duyee Chang, Kati Kuroda.

PLAY BALL (18). By R. A. Shiomi. February 7, 1989. Director, Ernest H. Abuba; scenery, Atsushi Moriyasu; lighting, Victor En Yu Tan; costumes, Toni-Leslie James. With Ed Easton, James Jenner, Ron Nakahara, Steve Park, Norris M. Shimabuku, Kelley Hinman.

NOIRESQUE: THE FALLEN ANGEL (22). Conceived and directed by Ping Chong. May 4, 1989. Scenery, Ping Chong; lighting, Howard Thies; costumes, Matthew Yokobosky; sound, Brian Hallas. With Mel Duane Gionson, Kati Kuroda, Ron Nakahara, Norris M. Shimabuku, Mary Lee, Lauren Tom, Allan Tung.

The Puerto Rican Traveling Theater. Professional company presenting bilingual productions primarily of Puerto Rican and Hispanic playwrights, emphasizing subjects of relevance today. Miriam Colon, founder and producer.

THE GARDEN (24). Musical street play by Carlos Morton; Spanish translation, Manuel Martin; composer and musical director, Sergio Garcia-Marruz. August 2, 1988. With Jack Landron, Tony Mata, Irma-Estel LaGuerre, Carlos Carrasco.

HAPPY BIRTHDAY, MAMA (42). By Roberto Cossa; translated by Myra Gann. January 18, 1989. Director, Vicente Castro; scenery, Robert Klingelhoefer; lighting, Bill Simmons; costumes, Stephen Pardee. With Marta Vidal, Mateo Gomez, Nelson Landrieu, Eugenia Cross, Ruben Pia, Carmen Rosario.

QUINTUPLETS (42). By Luis Rafael Sanchez; translated by Alba Oms and Ivonne Coll. March 22, 1989. Director, Alba Oms; scenery, Robert Klingelhoefer; lighting, Bill Simmons; costumes, Laura Drawbaugh. With Ivonne Coll, Roberto Medina.

CONVERSATION AMONG THE RUINS (42). By Emilio Carballido. May 10, 1989. Director, Alejandra Gutierrez; scenery, Robert Klingelhoefer; lighting, Bill Simmons; costumes, Laura Drawbaugh. With Elizabeth Ruiz Clemens, Mark Morant, Teresa Yenque.

Quaigh Theater. Primarily a playwrights' theater, devoted to the new playwright, the established contemporary playwright and the modern (post-1920) playwright. Will Lieberson, artistic director.

BATTING PRACTICE. By Paul Gleason. November 15, 1988. Director, Will Lieberson; scenery, Kricker James; lighting and sound, Bob Mahnken. With Possum Badger, Kricker James, Les Miller, James Rosin.

The Ridiculous Theatrical Company. The late Charles Ludlam's comedic troupe devoted to productions of his original scripts and broad adaptations of the classics. Everett Quinton, artistic director, David Musselman, managing director.

Schedule included:

A TALE OF TWO CITIES. By Charles Dickens, adapted and performed by Everett Quinton. January 15, 1989. Director, Kate Stafford; scenery, Jan Bell, James Eckerle and Daphne Groos; lighting, Richard Currie; costumes, Susan Young.

SALOME by Oscar Wilde. April 21, 1989. Directed by Kestutis Nakas.

Second Stage Theater. Committed to producing plays believed to deserve another look, as well as new works. Robyn Goodman, Carole Rothman, artistic directors.

THE FILM SOCIETY (31). By Jon Robin Baitz. July 7, 1988. Director, John Tillinger; scenery, Santo Loquasto; lighting, Dennis Parichy; costumes, Candice Donnelly. With Nathan Lane, Laila Robins, Daniel Gerroll, William Glover, Margaret Hilton, Dillon Evans.

THE RIMERS OF ELDRITCH (44). By Lanford Wilson. November 8, 1988. Director, Mark Brokaw; scenery, Santo Loquasto; lighting, Jennifer Tipton; costumes, Ellen McCartney. With William Mesnik, Georgia Creighton, Mary Jay, Kaiulani Lee, Georgine Hall, Adam Storke, Gary Dean Ruebsamen, Suzy Hunt, Bill Mondy, Danielle du Clos, Barry Sherman, Stuart Rudin, Edward Cannan, Sharon Ernster, Jennie Moreau, Deborah Hedwall, Amy Ryan.

IN A PIG'S VALISE (57). Book and lyrics by Eric Overmyer; music by August Darnell. January 11, 1989. Director and choreographer, Graciela Daniele; scenery, Bob Shaw; lighting, Peggy Eisenhauer; costumes, Jeanne Button; musical director, Peter Schott. With Nathan Lane, Ada Maris, Jonathan Freeman, Thom Sesma, Reg E. Cathey, Charlie Lagond, Michael McCormick, Lauren Tom, Dian Sorel.

APPROACHING ZANZIBAR (54). By Tina Howe. April 8, 1989. Director, Carole Rothman; scenery, Heidi Landesman; lighting, Dennis Parichy; costumes, Susan Hilferty. With Harris Yulin, Jane Alexander, Clayton Barclay Jones, Angela Goethals, Jamie Ross, Maggie Burke, Damien Jackson, Aleta Mitchell, Bethel Leslie.

Soho Rep. Infrequently or never-before-performed plays by the world's greatest authors, with emphasis on language and theatricality. Marlene Swartz, Jerry Englebach, artistic directors.

THE BLITZSTEIN PROJECT: I'VE GOT THE TUNE and THE HARPIES (musical works of Marc Blitzstein) (24). Conceived, directed and additional text by Carol Corwen. September 14, 1988. Choreography, Barry R. Gallo; scenery, Jeffrey D. McDonald; lighting, Donald Holder; costumes, G. A. Howard; musical director, Donald Sosin. With Paul Binotto, Joanna Seaton, Loretta Giles, Helen Zelon, Daniel Baum, Don Mayo, Peter Schmitz, Jennifer Lee Andrews, Mary Eileen O'Donnell, Andre Montgomery, Mimi Higgins.

THE NEW WAVE OF QUEBEC (staged readings): LE CHIEN by Jean Marc Dalpe, translated by Maureen LaBonte and Jean Marc Dalpe, directed by Clinton Turner Davis; EVIDENCE TO THE CONTRARY by Helen Pedreault, translated by Linda Gaboriau, directed by Tom Szentgyorgyi; LILIES by Michel Marc Bouchard, translated by Linda Gaboriau, directed by David Briggs. January 29–February 12, 1989.

THE CEZANNE SYNDROME (24). By Normand Canac-Marquis; translated by Louison Danis. February 19, 1989. Director, Liz Diamond; scenery, Anne Servanton; lighting, Donald Holder; costumes, Sally J. Lesser. With David Strathairn, Caris Corfman, Edward Baran. (Produced as part of the New Wave of Quebec Festival.)

THE PHANTOM LADY (24). By Pedro Calderon de la Barca; translated by Edwin Honig. April 6, 1989. Director, Julian Webber; scenery, Stephen Olson; lighting, Donald Holder; costumes, Patricia Adshead; music, Jared Walker; fight director, Jim Manley. With Donald Berman, Gregor Paslawsky, Monique Fowler, Anne O'Sullivan, Brian P. Glover, Richard McMillan, Richard Karn, Valerie Charles, Jared Walker.

SOHO REP AFTER HOURS (late night performance series). Performers included: Valerie Charles, January 27–February 11, 1989; Deborah Margolin, April 7–28, 1989.

PAN ASIAN REPERTORY THEATER—James Jenner, Ron Nakahara and Norris M. Shimabuku in *Play Ball* by R. A. Shiomi

SCENES TO COME (staged readings): THE MALIGNANCY OF HENRIETTA LACKS written and directed by August Baker; MY DAUGHTER, THE SISTER by Matt Cutugno, directed by Rob Barron; A CONFESSION and LLOYD AND LEE by Steve Monroe, directed by Rob Barron and Steve Monroe; HOME FIRES by Molly Fowler and Karen L. de Balbian Verster, directed by Collette Berge; SMITTY'S NEWS by Conrad Bishop and Elizabeth Fuller, directed by Liz Diamond; BACKWARD ANTHOLOGY by Zoe Walker, directed by David Willinger; FILTHY TALK FOR TROUBLED TIMES by Neil LaBute, directed by Julian Webber; READY FOR THE RIVER by Neal Bell, directed by David Briggs. May 16–20, 1989.

NEW VOICES FOR THE AMERICAN MUSICAL: SEE HOW THEY RUN, book by Tom and Leah Greenwald, music and lyrics by Tom Greenwald; POE, book by R. Vincent Razor, music and lyrics by Brian Hobbs; THE CARE AND FEEDING OF THE YOUNG, music by Jimmy Roberts, lyrics by June Siegel; CROOKED LINES, book and lyrics by Mary Bracken Phillips, music by Jan Mullaney and Pepi Castro; HEROES, book and lyrics by Tom Toce, music by Douglas J. Cohen; CAPTAINS COURAGEOUS, book and lyrics by Patricia Cook, music by Frederick Freyer. May 21, 1989.

Theater Off Park. Concentrates on producing and developing new plays or musicals and revivals of obscure works by well-known writers, with an emphasis on social consciousness. Albert Harris, artistic director, Elizabeth M. Blitzer, managing director.

I COULD GO ON LIP-SYNCHING! By John Epperson and Justin Ross. November 10, 1988. Directed by Justin Ross. With John Epperson.

Theater for the New City. Developmental theater and new American experimental works. George Bartenieff, Crystal Field, artistic directors.

Schedule included:

A HISTORY OF FOOD: PART I, PART II AND A PREVIEW. Conceived, directed and designed by Theodora Skipitares; music by Pat Irwin; lyrics by Andrea Balis. June 9, 1988. Choreography, Gail Conrad; lighting, Craig Kennedy; shadow puppets, Stephen Kaplin. With Tom Costello, Victoria Klamp.

A CIRCLE (20). Written and directed by Bob Morris. June 20, 1988. Scenery, David Birn; lighting, Danianne Mizzy; costumes, Belinda Rachman. With Tim Gail, Jennifer Gatti. (Produced as part of the First New York International Festival of the Arts.)

THE CONEY ISLAND KID (13). Musical street play by Crystal Field, George Bartenieff and The TNC Company; music by Christopher Cherney; lyrics by Crystal Field. August 6, 1988. Director, Crystal Field; scenery, Anthony Angel; costumes, Brian Pride.

DREAMLAND. By Bina Sharif. August 25, 1988. Director, Rolf Johannsmeier; scenery, Norbert Kimmel; lighting, Zdenek Kriz; costumes, Gaetano Fazio. With Cameron Foord, Bina Sharif.

THE FIGHTER. By Daniel Keene. August 25, 1988. Director, Iris James; lighting, Maurice Peralta; music, Mark McSherry; lyrics, Daniel Keene. With Lindzee Smith, Rhonda Wilson, David Blackman.

BABBLING WITH JOE. By Agusto Machado. September 22, 1988.

MAINSTREAM. By Glyn Vincent. September 22, 1988.

FAMILY CREST. By Alan Roy. September 29, 1988.

WHY CAN'T WE TALK. Written and directed by Irving Burton. October 7, 1988. With the Speak Easy Players.

THE TRUE STORY (performance art). By Rucker and Russo. October 20, 1988.

DON JUAN IN N.Y.C. By Eduardo Machado; songs by Sergio Garcia-Marruz. November 10, 1988. Director, David Willinger; choreography, Michael Vasquez; scenery, Donald Eastman; lighting, Ron Burns; costumes, Tracy Oleinick; film, Tom Gladwell; incidental music, Saul Spangenberg. With Walter Krochmal, Jack Landron, Craig Bryant, Jim Lamb, Lisa Gluckin, Eugenia Cross, Irma-Estel LaGuerre, John Finch.

SAFE AS HOUSES. By Karen Walker. November 17, 1988. Director, Melia Bensussen.

GLAND MOTEL. By Ray Dobbins and the Bloolips. November 17, 1988. Director, Bette Bourne; lighting, Zdenek Kriz. With Bette Bourne, Precious Pearl, Hortence La Grand, Brenda Babe, La Belle Martyn.

AGAINST THE TIDE. Written and directed by Jamie Leo. December 8, 1988.

HEATHEN VALLEY. Written and directed by Romulus Linney. December 15, 1988. Scenery, Mark Marcante; lighting, Anne Militello. With Jim Ligon, Robert Hock, Scott Sowers, J. Joseph Houghton, Ann Sheehy, Julie Follansbee.

VKTMS: ORESTES IN SCENES. By Michael McClure. December 15, 1988. Director, Judith Malina.

WINNETOU'S SNAKE OIL SHOW FROM WIGWAM CITY. By Spiderwoman Theater. January 5, 1989.

BETTY BENDS THE BLUES. Written and composed by Ellen Maddow; directed by Paul Zimet; scenery, Janie Geiser; lighting, Carol Mullins; costumes, Gabriel Berry; with Ellen Maddow and Harry Mann. THE MALADY OF DEATH by Marguerite Duras; music by Blue Gene Tyranny; directed by Richard Armstrong; with Tina Shepard, Rosemary Quinn (The Talking Band). January 12, 1989.

WALKS OF INDIAN WOMEN. Multimedia work by Vira and Hortensia Colorado. February 23, 1989.

VOODOO ECONOMICS. By Larry Myers. February 23, 1989.

WHITE BONED DEMON. Written and directed by Leslie Mohn. February 23, 1989. Choreography, Alan Lindblad; scenery, Barbara Abramson and Gabriel Backlund; lighting, Vaclav Kucera; costumes, Mary Cricket Smith; music, James Harry and Chris Abajian. With Mark Amdahl, Daniel Boone, Andrea Dickerson, Bettina Geyer, Barbara Hiesiger, Lisa Hurst, Miriam Must, Stephen Peabody, Catherine Seitz, Zhang Xin.

BETWEEN THE ACTS. By Joan Schenkar. March 2, 1989.

SUN OF THE SLEEPLESS. By James Purdy. March 23, 1989.

BREAKAWAYS. By Bob Borsodi. March 30, 1989.

BROKEN BOHEMIAN HEARTS IN ALPHABET CITY (12). Cabaret conceived and directed by Jiri Schubert; written by Albert Oesterreicher and Ron Havern. April 21, 1989. Choreography, Nanna Nilsson; scenery, Anna Frisch; lighting, Zdenek Kriz; costumes, Brian Pride; musical director, Christopher Cherney. With Amy Coleman, Charles McKenna, Jeff Paul.

ONE DIRECTOR AGAINST HIS CAST. Musical by Crystal Field. April 21, 1989. Directors, Crystal Field and Mark Marcante; scenery, Myrna Duarte; lighting, Seth Orbach; costumes, Brian Pride; musical director, Arthur Abrams. With Guy Gsell, Jonathan Slaff, Crystal Field, Mark Marcante.

THE HEART OUTRIGHT (12). By Mark Medoff. May 11, 1989. Director, Mike Rutenberg; scenery, Peter R. Feuche; lighting, K. Robert Hoffman; costumes, Traci DiGesu. With David Andrews, Kim McCullum, Anjanette Comer, Kevin O'Connor.

THAT OLD COMEDY. By Walter Corwin. May 11, 1989.

EMPIRES AND APPETITES. Created, directed and designed by Theodora Skipitares; music by Pat Irwin; lyrics by Andrea Balis. May 11, 1989. Choreography, Gail Conrad; lighting, Pat Dignan. With Tom Costello, Trinket Monsod.

BRUNO'S DONUTS. By Sebastian Stuart. May 18, 1989. Director, Patrick Kerr. With Nancy Reed, Natasha Shulman, Crystal Field, Danny O'Shea, Steve Lott, Suzy Williams, Kirk Jackson, Chris Tanner, Tom Judson, Richard Spore, Mark Marcante.

The Vineyard Theater. A multi-art chamber theater dedicated to the development of new plays and musicals, music-theater collaborations and innovative revivals. Douglas Aibel, artistic director, Babraba Zinn Krieger, executive director, Jon Nakagawa, managing director.

THE GRANDMA PLAYS (33). By Todd Graff. September 17, 1988. Director, Steve Gomer; scenery, William Barclay; lighting, Phil Monat; costumes, Jennifer von Mayrhauser. With Renee Taylor, Elzbieta Czyzewska, Alma Cuervo, Francine Beers.

PHANTASIE (43). By Sybille Pearson. December 13, 1988. Director, John Rubinstein; scenery, William Barclay; lighting, Phil Monat; costumes, Deborah Shaw. With Laurinda Barrett, Ryan Cutrona, Elzbieta Czyzewska, Michael French, Diane Salinger, Myra Taylor.

The Women's Project and Productions. Nurtures, develops and produces plays written and, for the most part, directed by women. Julia Miles, founder and artistic director.

MAPPING THEATRICAL TERRITORIES (international festival focusing on heroic women). Schedule included: YOU STRIKE THE WOMAN, YOU STRIKE THE ROCK conceived and performed by the Vusisizwe Players (Poppy Tsira, Thobeka Maqutyana, Nomvula Qosha), directed by Phyllis Klotz; LETTERS TO A DAUGHTER FROM PRISON: INDIRA AND NEHRU by Lavonne Mueller, directed by Vijaya Mehta (staged reading); ANTIGONA FURIOSA by Griselda Gambaro (staged reading). June 21–July 3, 1988. (Produced as part of the First New York International Festival of the Arts.)

MA ROSE (21). By Cassandra Medley. October 11, 1988. Director, Irving Vincent; scenery, Phillip Baldwin; lighting, Pat Dignan; costumes, Judy Dearing. With Rosanna Carter, Herb Lovelle, Lizan Mitchell, La Tanya Richardson, Pawnee Sills.

NIEDECKER (21). By Kristine Thatcher. March 7, 1989. Director, Julianne Boyd; scenery, James Noone; lighting, Frances Aronson; costumes, Deborah Shaw. With Mary Diveny, Jane Fleiss, Frederick Neumann, Helen Stenborg.

LADIES. (Co-produced by the Music-Theater Group. See Music-Theater Group entry.)

O PIONEERS! (4). By Willa Cather, adapted by Darrah Cloud; music by Kim D. Sherman; lyrics by Darrah Cloud. April 14, 1989. Director, Kevin Kuhlke; scenery, John Wulp; lighting, Jeff Robbins; costumes, Mary Ellen Walter; musical director, Brian Russell. With Mary McDonnell, Randle Mell, Marsha June Robinson, Scott Rabinowitz, Kevin McDermott, Michael C. Hacker, Dorothy Longbrake, M. Elizabeth Kennedy, Dougald Park, Jennifer Rohn, Peter Lohnes, Christopher Noth, Angela Fie, Shona Curly, Kevin C. Loomis, Clayton Corzatte, C. R. Gardner, Jeffrey Zimmerman, Kathryn Mesney.

WPA Theater. Produces new American plays and neglected classics in the realistic idiom. Kyle Renick, artistic director, Edward T. Gianfrancesco, resident designer, Donna Lieberman, managing director.

MOROCCO (35). Written and directed by Allan Havis. July 10, 1988. Scenery, Bill Clarke; lighting, Craig Evans; costumes, Mimi Maxmen. With Sam Freed, George Guidall, Gordana Rashovich, Anthony Ruiz.

JUST SAY NO (34). By Larry Kramer. October 20, 1988. Director, David Esbjornson; scenery, Edward T. Gianfrancesco; lighting, Craig Evans; costumes, David C. Woolard. With Tonya Pinkins, David Margulies, Julie White, Keith Reddin, Richard Topol, Joseph Ragno, Richard Riehle, Kathleen Chalfant.

THE LADY IN QUESTION (16). By Charles Busch. November 18, 1988. Director, Kenneth Elliott; scenery, B. T. Whitehill; lighting, Vivien Leone; costumes, Robert Locke, Jennifer Arnold. With Mark Hamilton, Theresa Marlowe, Robert Carey, Arnie Kolodner, Andy Halliday, Kenneth Elliott, Charles Busch, Julie Halston, Meghan Robinson.

THE NIGHT HANK WILLIAMS DIED (49). By Larry L. King. January 24, 1989. Director, Christopher Ashley; scenery, Edward T. Gianfrancesco; lighting, Craig Evans; costumes, Jess Goldstein. With Matt Mulhern, Barton Heyman, Betsy Aidem, J. R. Horne, Steve Rankin, Phyllis Somerville.

EARLY ONE EVENING AT THE RAINBOW BAR AND GRILLE (35). By Bruce Graham. April 13, 1989. Director, Pamela Berlin; scenery, Edward T. Gianfrancesco; lighting, Craig Evans; costumes, Mimi Maxmen. With Dan Butler, Gregory Grove, Jay Patterson, Kent Broadhurst, Sharon Ernster, Julie White, William Wise.

York Theater Company. Specializing in producing new works, as well as in reviving great musicals. Janet Hayes Walker, producing director.

SING FOR YOUR SUPPER: A RODGERS AND HART MUSICAL CELEBRATION (19). October 14, 1988. Director and choreographer, Frank Wagner; scenery, James Morgan; lighting, Brian MacDevitt; musical director, James Stenborg. With Melodee Savage, Mark Martino, Karen Ziemba, Ira Hawkins, Jess Richards, Lynne Stuart.

MAX AND MAXIE (16). By James McLure. January 13, 1989. Director, D. Lynn Meyers; scenery and costumes, Eduardo Sicangco; lighting, Kirk Bookman and David Neville. With John Newton, Sandy Roveta, Robin Haynes.

SWEENEY TODD, THE DEMON BARBER OF FLEET STREET. Book by Hugh Wheeler, from Christopher Bond's adaptation; music and lyrics by Stephen Sondheim. March 31, 1989. Directed by Susan H. Schulman; with Bob Gunton, Beth Fowler, David Barron, Calvin Remsberg, Eddie Korbich, Gretchen Kingsley-Weihe, Jim Walton, Dawn Stone, Tony Gilbert, David E. Mallard, Ted Keegan, Mary Ellen Phillips, SuEllen Estey, Bill Nable.

THE LARK by Jean Anouilh, adapted by Lillian Hellman. May 19, 1989. Directed by Janet Hayes Walker; with Mel Boudrot, John Camera, Laura Carden, Ann Dowd, Lisa Fugard, Russell Lawyer, Michael McKenzie, John Newton, Tom Nichols, Dennis Parlato, Joel Swetow, Neil Vipond, Marie Wallace, Ralph David Westfall, Benjamin White.

Miscellaneous

In the additional listing of 1988–89 off-off-Broadway productions below, the names of the producing groups or theaters appear in CAPITAL LETTERS and the titles of the works in *italics*. This list consists largely of new or reconstituted works and excludes most revivals, especially of classics. It includes a few productions staged by groups which rented space from the more established organizations listed previously.

ACTOR'S OUTLET. *The Green Death* written and directed by Peter Mattaliano. October 13, 1988. With Nelson Avidon, Ralph Buckley, Frank Dahill, Janis Dardaris, Stephani Hardy, Suzy Hunt, Steve Robinson. *On the Prowl* (musical) by John Chibbaro and Claudia-JoAllmand. November 9, 1988. Directed by John Chibbaro. *The Dietrich Process* by Leo Rost. February 28, 1989. Directed by William Roudebushis.

ACTOR'S SPACE. *Shooting Stars* by Molly Newman. November, 1988. Directed by Richard Maynard; with Melissa Randel, Elizabeth Browning, Yvonne Campbell, Elizabeth C. Loftus, Karen Biderman.

AMERICAN JEWISH THEATER. *The Golden Leg* written and directed by David Glikin. September 8, 1988. With Joseph V. Francis, Robert Silver, Lucille Rivin, David Austin. *Only Kidding* by Jim Geoghan. October 25, 1988. Directed by Larry Arrick; with Larry Keith, Michael Jeter, Ethan Phillips, Paul Provenza, Sam Zap. *The Immigrant: A Hamilton County Album* by Mark Harelik, conceived by Mark Harelik and Randal Myler. February 7, 1989. Directed by John Driver; with Ann Hillary, Lonny Price, Nesbitt Blaisdell, Lisa Pelikan.

ARTS AT ST. ANN'S. *The Ritual of Solomon's Children* conceived and directed by W. S. Rendra; music by Tonny Prabowo. June 21, 1988. With Ken Zuraida, Nyai Dewi Pakis, Johnie Waromi, Ria Rondang Pardede, Adi Kurki, W. S. Rendra, Endang Talipaksa, Afrion, Tita Indriati, Otig Pakis, Amien Kamil (Teater Rendra). (Produced as part of the First New York International Festival of the Arts.) *Icarus* based on Pieter Brueghel's painting, "Landscape With the Fall of Icarus" by the Bread and Puppet Theater. December 2, 1988.

BEACON PROJECT. *Night Breath* by Dennis Clontz. April 5, 1989. Directed by Richard Bly; with Geraldine Singer, Elizabeth Huffman, Nancy Learmonth, Brian Markinson.

BILLIE HOLLIDAY THEATER. *Over Forty* (musical) book by Celeste; music and lyrics by Weldon Irvine. April 27, 1989. Directed by Mikell Pinkney; with Eunice Newkirk, Janyse M. Singleton, Marisa Francesca Turner, Lady Peachena.

BLUE HERON THEATER. *The Estate* written and directed by Ray Aranha. February 8, 1989. With George McGrath, Donald Lee Taylor, Jane Moore, Ennis Smith.

KAUFMAN THEATER—Lorraine Lanigan, David Proval and Stephen Hamilton in *My Unknown Son* by Daniel Curzon

BROOKLYN ACADEMY OF MUSIC. *Platee* (opera-ballet) libretto by Jacques Autreau; music by Jean-Philippe Rameau. October 13, 1988. With Piccolo Teatro dell'Opera. *Next Wave Festival*: works included *The Warrior Ant* conceived and directed by Lee Breuer, music by Bob Telson, with Frederick Neumann, Isabell Monk, Leslie Mohn, Ruth Maleczech; *Tango Varsoviano* (Warsaw Tango) written and directed by Alberto Felix, with Monica Lacoste, Adriana Diaz, Walter Gilmour, Cesar Repetto; *The Power Project* by Bob Berky and Mark Harrison in collaboration with the company, with Bob Berky, Wayne D. Doba, Diane Epstein, Rob O'Neill, Erin Cressida Wilson; *Michael Moschen in Motion* co-created by Michael Moschen, John Kahn and Joan Langue, music by David Van Tieghem, directed by Joan Langue, with Michael Moschen; *The Forest* (musical theater piece) by Robert Wilson and David Byrne, text by Heiner Muller and Darryl Pinckney. October 19–December 17, 1988. Majestic Theater: *Comet Messenger–Siegfried* written and directed by Hideki Noda, translated by Don Kenny. July 7, 1988. With Hideki Noda, Yasunori Danta, Katsuya Kobayashi. (Produced as part of the First New York International Festival of the Arts.)

CAFFÉ BONNELLE. *Ad Hock* (musical revue) music by Ralph Affoumado; lyrics by David Curtis and Alice Whitfield. January 15, 1989. Directed by Sue Lawless; with Philip Hernandez, Susan J. Jacks, Jana Robbins.

CATHEDRAL OF ST. JOHN THE DIVINE. *Gathering* and *Archpriest Avvakum: The Life Written by Himself* conceived and directed by Wlodzimierz Staniewski. June 14, 1988. With the Gardzienice Theater. (Produced as part of the First New York International Festival of the Arts.) *Manifest Destiny* (musical) by Raul S. Manglapus. September 21, 1988. Directed by Steve Pudenz.

CHOICES THEATER. *A Play Called Not and Now* by Gertrude Stein. March 10, 1989.

COURTYARD PLAYHOUSE. *Icetown* (one-acts): *Early Birds* and *Too Late* by John Jiler. May 7, 1989. With Kristen Childs, Richard Davidson, Alvin Moor, Kirk Baltz.

DANCE THEATER WORKSHOP. *The Summit* (performance art piece) by Jonathan and Barnaby Stone. August, 1988. With Lars Goran Persson, Jonathan Stone (Ralf Ralf). *The House of Horror* by and with Paul Zaloom. September 9, 1988. *Dark Shadows* adapted and directed by Brian Jucha. September, 1988. With Penny Boyer, Tina Shepard, Julian Stone. *The Story of Robert* and *The Reason for Breakfast* (performance art pieces) by and with Don McGashan and Harry Sinclair (Front Lawn). October 11, 1988. *The Song of Lawino* by Okot p'Bitek. December 23, 1988. Directed by Valeria Vasilevski; with Robin Wilson.

DON'T TELL MAMA. *AIDS Alive* (series of vignettes) by Lanie Robertson. July, 1988. With Kevin Madden, Nico Angelo, Tony Torres, Geoff Edholm, Tom Lutz. *Life Is Not Like the Movies* (musical revue) by Francesca Blumenthal. September, 1988. With Clint Clifford, Eileen Valentino, Andrea Green. *Damned If You Do* (revue) by Martin Schaeffer and Marc Malamed. November 5, 1988. Directed by Marc Malamed; with Robert Jensen, Pamela Prestyn, Sheri Matteo, Kim Lindsay, Marilyn O'Connell.

EN GARDE ARTS. *At the Chelsea* (performance art pieces): *Little House on the Prairie* by Stephen Balint; *A Quiet Evening with Sid and Nancy* by Penny Arcade; *The Room* by David Van Tieghem with Tina Dudek; *Embedded* by Ann Carlson; *A Way with Words: John Kelly as Dagmar Onassis Sings Like Joni Mitchell* by John Kelly; *Letters From Dead People* by Frank Maya. January 12–February 5, 1989. *In Central Park* (performance art pieces): *Babel on Babylon* by Matthew Maguire, *Minny and the James Boys* by Anna Cascio, *Bad Penny* by Mac Wellman. June 7, 1989.

FRANKLIN FURNACE. *Breakfast With the Moors Murderers* (performance piece) by Torture Chorus. January, 1989.

FREE THEATER PRODUCTIONS. Reading by Colleen Dewhurst. April 24, 1989.

GENE FRANKEL THEATER. *Empress of the Keyboard* (one-woman show) by and with Pamela Ross. April 7, 1989. Directed by Gene Frankel.

GOOD OMEN PRODUCTIONS. *The Legend of Sharon Shashanovah* by A. F. Horn. October 6, 1988. Directed by Sharon Gans; with Sharon Talbot, Jeremiah Sullivan, Irma St. Paule, Frank Nastasi, Christofer De Oni.

HARRY DE JUR PLAYHOUSE. *Apart From George* written and directed by Nick Ward. March 17, 1989. With Alan Bennion, Amelad Brown, Katrin Cartlidge, Matthew Scurfield. (Royal National Theater of Great Britain presented by Zebra Promotions.)

HUNTER PLAYHOUSE. *Ti Daro Quel Fior* by Marco Mete. June 29, 1988. With Compagnia dell'Atto. *La Nuotatrice Turca* written and directed by Francesco Caleffi. July 6, 1988. With Compagnia Opera Prima. (Produced as part of the First New York International Festival of the Arts.)

INTAR THEATER. *Walls of Chance* (musical) written and performed by Danny Curtis. May 11, 1989.

IRISH ARTS CENTER. *Bat the Father, Rabbit the Son* by and with Donal O'Kelly. November 3, 1988. Directed by Declan Hughes. *Now and at the Hour of Our Death* by Trouble and Strife Theater Company, inspired by Nell McCafferty's *The Armagh Women*. May 17, 1989. With Maeve Murphy, Finola Geraghty, Gaby Chiappe, Caroline Seymour.

JAPAN SOCIETY. *Water Station* written and directed by Shogo Ohta. June 19, 1988. With Tenkei Gekijo Group. (Produced as part of the First New York International Festival of the Arts.) *Kiyotsune: The Death of a Warrior* (Noh play with music), music by Ryo Noda. May 17, 1989.

JEAN COCTEAU REPERTORY. *Break of Noon* (Partage de Midi) by Paul Claudel, translated by Wallace Fowlie. September 17, 1988. Directed by Eve Adamson; with Joseph J. Menino, Craig Smith, Elise Stone, Harris Berlinsky. *Good* by C. P. Taylor. January 26, 1989. Directed by Robert Hupp; with Craig Smith, Harris Berlinsky, Jeanne Demers, Mark Schulte, Craig Cook.

JEWISH REPERTORY THEATER. *The Grand Tour* (musical) book by Michael Stewart and Mark Bramble; music and lyrics by Jerry Herman. June 16, 1988. Directed by Ran Avni; with Stuart Zagnit, Paul Ukena Jr., Steven Fickinger, Patricia Ben Peterson. *Cantorial* by Ira Levin. October 27, 1988. Directed by Charles Maryan; with Anthony Fusco, Lesly Kahn, Woody Romoff, James DeMarse, Joan Howe, Robert Nichols. *Chu Chem* by Ted Allan. December 27, 1988. Directed by Albert Marre; with Mark Zeller, Emily Zacharias, Irving Burton, Thom Sesma, Simone Gee, Zoie Lam, Chev Rodgers. *Bitter Friends* by Gordon Rayfield. February 9, 1989. Directed by Allen Coulter; with Sam Gray, Farryl Lovett, Bill Nelson, Dan Pinto, Ben

Siegler, Viola Harris, Yosi Sokolsky, Andrew Thain. *The Sunshine Boys* by Neil Simon. May 11, 1989. Directed by Marilyn Chris; with Lee Wallace, Bernie Passeltiner, Fred Einhorn, Miriam Burton, Edwin Bordo, Patrick Cognetta, Amy Gordon.

JOYCE THEATER. *Ariadne Obnoxious* conceived and directed by Ethyl Eichelberger. October 22, 1988. With Black-Eyed Susan, Ethyl Eichelberger.

JUDITH ANDERSON THEATER. *Resistance* by D. Keith Mano. June 2, 1988. Directed by Linda Laundra; with Don Chastain, Colin Fox, Laurie Kennedy, Michael Luciano, Thomas Nahrwold, Aideen O'Kelly, Patrick Rameau, Rachel West. *Madame Bovary* by Gustave Flaubert, adapted and directed by Paul Edwards. September 14, 1988. With Noelle Strong, Linda Key, Gita Donovan, Fern Dorsey, Mark W. Conklin.

KAUFMAN THEATER. *My Unknown Son* by Daniel Curzon. October 18, 1988. Directed by Sal Trapani; with David Proval, Lorraine Lanigan, Stephen Hamilton.

THE KITCHEN. *Sunspot* written and directed by John Jesurun. March 16, 1989. With Larry Tighe, Katrin Brinkmann, Black-Eyed Susan, Michael Tighe, Steve Buscemi, Jane Smith, Helena White, Sanghi Wager.

LIGHT OPERA OF MANHATTAN. *H.M.S. Pinafore* by W. S. Gilbert and Arthur Sullivan. September 21, 1988. *Sweethearts* by Victor Herbert. October 19, 1988. *Babes in Toyland* book by William Mount-Burke and Alice Hammerstein Mathias; music by Victor Herbert; lyrics by Alice Hammerstein Mathias. November 23, 1988. *The Student Prince* by Sigmund Romberg. January 11, 1989. *The Gondoliers* by W. S. Gilbert and Arthur Sullivan. February 22, 1989. *The Merry Widow* by Franz Lehar. March 22, 1989. *The New Moon* by Sigmund Romberg. April 19, 1989.

LINCOLN CENTER. *Serious Fun!* Schedule included *The Man Who Mistook His Wife for a Hat* (opera) libretto by Michael Morris and Christopher Rawlence, adapted by Michael Morris, Michael Nyman and Christopher Rawlence from Oliver Sack's book, music by Michael Nyman, directed by Michael Morris, with Frederick Westcott, John Duykers, Marni Nixon; *Fools Paradise* (performance art) by Ethyl Eichelberger and Geoff Hoyle; *All Talk, No Action* works by Paul Krassner, Karen Finley, Frank Maya, Allen Ginsberg and Philip Glass. July 14–August 4, 1988. *Lincoln Center Out-of-Doors Festival*. August, 1988.

MANHATTAN CLASS COMPANY. *Sharon and Billy* by Alan Bowne. October 20, 1988. Directed by W. D. Cantler; with Richard Grusin, Sonja Lanzener, Marisa Tomei, Mathew Vipond. *Fun* by James Bosley. October 30, 1988. Directed by Brian Mertes; with Amelia Campbell, Ken Marks, Maryann Urbano, Kelly Wolf. (*Sharon and Billy* and *Fun* played in repertory.) *Manhattan Class One-Act Festival: The Lost Colony* by Wendy MacLeod, directed by Michael Greif; *Red Sheets* by Erik Ehn, directed by Daniel Wilson; *Bikini Snow* by Anna Theresa Cascio, directed by Jimmy Bohr; *Dakota's Belly, Wyoming* by Eric Cressida Wilson, directed by Brian Mertes; *Catfish Loves Anna* by Constance Ray, directed by Kevin Kelley; *Prelude and Liebestod* by Terrence McNally, directed by Paul Benedict. February 26–April 1, 1989.

MOSAIC THEATER. *Sand* by Eric Bass. June 21, 1988. Directed by Richard Edelman; with Eric Bass, Martin Bachmann, Laura Fredericks. (Produced as part of the First New York International Festival of the Arts.)

NAT HORNE THEATER. *About Face Julyfest* (one-acts): *War and Things* by Lavonne Mueller, directed by Sheila Xonegos; *Shepards and Sheep* by Sean Burke, directed by Richard Corley; *Feeding the Moonfish* by Barbara Weichman, directed by Tom Kelley. July 19, 1989.

NEW ARTS THEATER. *Sleeping Dogs* by Neal Bell. March 21, 1989. Directed by Thomas Babe; with Richmond Hoxie, Christopher Fields, Leslie Lyles, Cynthia Kaplan, John P. Connolly, Jodie Markell, David Briggs, Richard Council.

NEW MEDIA REPERTORY. *Who Is Alice Daphne?* by Maryse Elot. December, 1988.

NEW PUNCTUATION ARMY. *Two for the Show* written and directed by Gayden Wren. June 29, 1988. With Thomas Gardner, David Sennett, Karen Pope.

NEW THEATER OF BROOKLYN. *Annulla, an Autobiography* written and directed by Emily Mann. October 27, 1988. With Linda Hunt, Karen Ludwig. *The Sunday Promenade* by Lars Forssell. February 23, 1989. Directed by Steve Stettler; with Jeff Rose, Trinity Thompson, Marty Lodge, Innes-Fergus McDade. *No Limits to Love* by David Mercer. April 27, 1989. Directed by Hilary Blecher; with Donna Davis, Richard Bekins, Robert Burke, Jeremiah Sullivan.

NEW YORK GILBERT AND SULLIVAN PLAYERS. *H.M.S. Pinafore.* November 22, 1988. Directed by Kristen Garver. *The Pirates of Penzance.* December 20, 1988. Directed by Albert Bergeret and Kristen Garver; with John Reed, Colby Thomas, Del-Bourree Bach, Michael Collins, Meredyth Rawlins, Gregory Mercer.

OPEN SPACE THEATER EXPERIMENT. *Knepp* by Jorge Goldenberg, translated by Judith Leverone. July 20, 1988. Directed by Susan Einhorn; with Ellen Barber, David Little, Annie Murray, Michael O'Gorman, Richard Riehle.

OPERA ENSEMBLE OF NEW YORK. *She Loves Me* (musical) book by Joe Masteroff; music by Jerry Bock; lyrics by Sheldon Harnick. May 3, 1989. Directed by John J. D. Sheehan.

PAUL MAZUR THEATER. *The Queen's Knight* by Frank Cossa. April 21, 1989. Directed by Ann Brebner; with Fred Burrell, Youssif Kamal, Susan Gosdick, Claywood Sempliner, Patrick Powers, Robin Connelly, Linda Shary.

PEARL THEATER COMPANY. *Berenice* by Jean Racine, translated by Earle Edgerton. November 4, 1988. Directed by Shepard Sobel; with Joel Swetow, Robin Leslie Brown, Stuart Lerch. *Hedda Gabler* by Henrik Ibsen, translated by Henry Beissel. January 13, 1989. Directed by Richard Fancy; with Joanne Camp, Stuart Lerch, James Nugent, Robin Leslie Brown.

PERFORMANCE SPACE 122. *How to Win Friends and Influence People* by and with Danny Mydlack. July, 1988. *Sex, Drugs and Rock 'n' Roll* by Eric Bogosian. August, 1988. *Fiasco* written and directed by Ethyl Eichelberger. August 11, 1988. With Ethyl Eichelberger, Helen Shumaker, Gerard Little, Katy Kierlam, Michael Osano. *Thup Thup Thup* by and with Jim Calder. October 8, 1988. *Shimmer* by and with John O'Keefe. January, 1989.

PRIMARY STAGES COMPANY. *Nasty Little Secrets* by Lanie Robertson. November 16, 1988. Directed by Stuart Ross; with Scott Renderer, Craig Fols, Colin Fox, John C. Vennema. *Ancient History* by David Ives. May 14, 1989. Directed by Jason McConnell Buzas; with Beth McDonald, Christopher Wells.

PROMENADE THEATER. *Love Letters* by A. R. Gurney. Presented on successive Mondays March 6–April 10, 1989 with different casts. Directed by John Tillinger; with Bruce Davison and Swoosie Kurtz; Stockard Channing and Bruce Davison; A. R. Gurney and Holland Taylor; Victor Garber and Dana Ivey; Swoosie Kurtz and Treat Williams; John Heard and Marsha Mason.

RAPP ARTS CENTER. *Tartuffe* by Molière, translated by Richard Wilbur. September, 1988. Directed by R. Jeffrey Cohen; with George McGrath, Raphael Nash, Jared Hammond, Maxine Prescott, Siri Wanamaker. *Fighting Light* by Greg Zittel. November 11, 1988. Directed by Matthew Penn; with Will Hare, Shelley Frew, Nanette Werness, Joel Anderson, Greg Natale.

RIVERWEST THEATER. *Lunatic and Lover* by Michael Meyer. August 16, 1988. Directed by Andy Jordan; with Richard Davidson, Joseph McKenna, Eileen Dunn, Diana LaMar. *Reaching Out* by Mary Ryzuk. November 1, 1988. Directed by Apollo Dukakis; with Christina Zorich, Victor Arnold, Marjorie Austrian, Gregory Henderson, Joseph Massa, Barbara Spiegel. *Chekhov in Love* by Tom Rothfield. May 9, 1989. Directed by Jaime Harris; with Evan Thompson, Patricia Randell.

SAMUEL BECKETT THEATER. *Judgment* by Barry Collins. September 29, 1988. Directed by John Russell Brown; with Matthew Conlon. *Ulysses in Nighttown* adapted by Marjorie Barkentin from James Joyce's *Ulysses.* January 19, 1989. Directed by Wayne Martens; with Leslie Block, Steve Coats, David Teschendorf, Kurt Ziskie, James Burke, Robert Molnar. *Red Devils* by Debbie Horsfield. April 28, 1989. Directed by Kirsten Sanderson; with Cynthia Rider, Halley DeVestern, Lillian Dean, Alicia Eve.

SOUPSTONE PROJECT. *Uncounted Blessings* (one-act plays): *Hidden in This Picture* by Aaron Sorkin, directed by David Saint; *Stacey Elizabeth Tries to Climb Out of Her Nightmare* by David Rush, directed by Avril Hordyk; *Forget Him* by Harvey Fierstein, directed by Neile Weissman. August, 1988. With Nathan Lane, Maggie Scott, Michael Rush, William Haynes, Tom Starace.

SOUTH STREET THEATER. *Guilty Conscience* by Richard Levinson and William Link. July 14, 1988. Directed by Vincent Bossone; with Steve Weiser, Julann Rosa, Tom Gebbie, Wendy Parks. *Paul Robeson* by Phillip Hayes Dean. August 10, 1988. Directed by Harold Scott; with Avery Brooks, Ernie Scott. *A Murder of Crows* by Ed Graczyk. September 14, 1988. Directed by Edward Stern; with Kim Hunter, Michael Higgins, Jay Devlin, Susan Greenhill, Terry Layman, Evelyn Page. *Ad Hock* music by Ralph Affoumado, lyrics by Alice Whitfield and David Curtis. November 6, 1988. Directed by Sue Lawless; with Alice Whitfield, Jan

MANHATTAN CLASS COMPANY—Matthew Vipond and
Marisa Tomei in a scene from *Sharon and Billy* by Alan Bowne

Neuberger, Mitchell Whitfield. *Faith* by Israel Horovitz, *Hope* by Terrence McNally and *Charity* by Leonard
Melfi (one-acts). December 18, 1988. Directed by Edward Berkeley; with Claiborne Cary, Rodney Scott
Hudson, Angela Nevard, John Rothman, Marilyn Sokol. *The Understanding* by William Mastrosimone. May
17, 1989. Directed by Joe Brancato.

TIME AND SPACE LIMITED. *Civil War Chronicles, Part V: Go Between Gettysburg* by Linda Mussman.
November 11, 1988.

TRIPLEX. *In Living Color* (musical dance play) by Oyamo; music by Olu Dara. February 23, 1989. Directed
and choreographed by Dianne McIntyre.

UBU REPERTORY THEATER. *You Have Come Back* by Fatima Gallaire-Bourega, translated by Jill
MacDougall. June 23, 1988. Directed by Francoise Kourilsky; with Frances Foster, Thomas C. Anderson,
Blanca Camacho, Carmen Rosario, Cherron Hoye, Laurine Towler, Rajika Puri, Rene Houtrides, Sharon
McGruder, Waguih Takla. (Produced as part of the First New York International Festival of the Arts.) *Alive by
Night* by Reine Barteve, translated by Alex Gross. May 10, 1989. Directed by Francoise Kourilsky; with T.
Scott Lilly, Joseph McKenna, Corliss Preston, Thomas Carson, Rene Houtrides.

UNDER ACME CABARET. *The Big Block Party* (musical revue) by Eric Blau. July 8, 1988. Directed by
Dinah Gravel.

VIETNAM VETERANS ENSEMBLE THEATER COMPANY. *Back in the World* by Stephen Mack Jones.
October 12, 1988. Directed by Thomas Bird; with Leo V. Finnie III, Norman Matlock, Howard Mungo,
Anthony Chisholm, Reg E. Cathey.

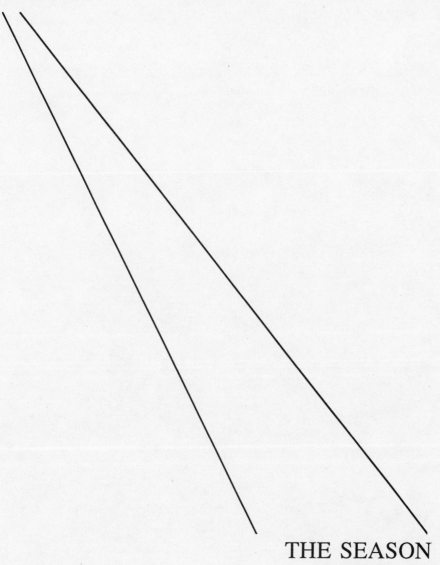

THE SEASON
AROUND
THE UNITED STATES

OUTSTANDING NEW PLAYS
CITED BY
AMERICAN THEATER CRITICS
ASSOCIATION

and

A DIRECTORY OF NEW-PLAY
PRODUCTIONS

THE American Theater Critics Association (ATCA) is the organization of 250 leading drama critics in all media in all sections of the United States. One of this group's stated purposes is "To increase public awareness of the theater as a *national* resource" (italics ours). To this end, ATCA has sited three outstanding new plays produced this season around the country, to be represented in our coverage of The Season Around the United States by excerpts from each of their scripts demonstrating literary style and quality. And one of these—August Wilson's *The Piano Lesson*—was designated the first-place play and received the fourth annual ATCA New Play Award of $1,000.

The process for selection of these outstanding plays is as follows: any ATCA member critic may nominate a play if it has been given a production in a professional house. It must be a finished play given a full production (not a reading or an airing as a play-in-progress). Nominated scripts were studied and discussed by an ATCA play-reading committee chaired by Dan Sullivan of the Los Angeles *Times* and comprising Ann Holmes of the Houston *Chronicle*, Damien Jaques of the Milwaukee *Journal*, Tom McCulloh of

Drama-Logue, Julius Novick of the *Village Voice* and Bernard Weiner of the San Francisco *Chronicle*. The committee members made their choices on the basis of script rather than production, thus placing very much the same emphasis as the editors of this volume in making the New York Best Play selections. There were no eligibility requirements except that a nominee be the first full professional production of a new work outside New York City within this volume's time frame of June 1, 1988 to May 31, 1989. If the timing of nominations and opening prevented some works from being considered this year, they will be eligible for consideration next year if they haven't since moved on to New York production. We offer our sincerest thanks and admiration to the ATCA members and their committee for the valuable insight into the 1988–89 theater season around the United States which their selections provide for this *Best Plays* record, in the form of the following excerpts from their scripts illustrating their style and the nature of their content, with brief introductions provided by the ATCA committee.

*Cited by American Theater Critics
as Outstanding New Plays
of 1988–89*

THE PIANO LESSON

A Play in Two Acts

BY AUGUST WILSON

Cast and credits appear on page 523

THE PIANO LESSON: This play is the fourth chapter in August Wilson's dramatic chronicle of black life in 20th century America, each episode set in a different decade. *Ma Rainey's Black Bottom* took place in the 1920s, *Fences* in the 1950s, *Joe Turner's Come and Gone* in the 1910s. *The Piano Lesson* happens in 1936 in Pittsburgh. Boy Willie ("*30 years old. He has an infectious grin and a boyishness that is apt for his name. He is brash and impulsive, talkative and somewhat crude in speech and manner*") and his quiet friend Lymon have come north in an old truck to sell a load of watermelons and to visit Boy Willie's widowed sister, Berneice. She is sure that her brother has got something up his sleeve, and she's right. In Berneice's parlor stands a curiously carved piano. Its totem faces were carved by their great-grandfather to please his master back in slavery days. A collector—and Boy Willie

503

knows one—would pay more than $1,000 for the instrument today. That would be enough for Boy Willie to establish himself as a landowner back home, the equal of any white man.

But Berneice won't hear of it. For her, the piano is sacred, even haunted. Didn't their father die because of it in 1911? It will stay where it is. As in most good plays, both brother and sister are right from their point of view, and neither intends to back off.

The following scene is from Act II, Scene 5. Doaker (*"a tall, thin man of 47, with severe features"*) is their uncle, a railroad man. He shares the house with Berneice. Avery is a born-again preacher who wants to marry Berneice, Maretha is Berneice's 12-year-old daughter.

BERNEICE: ..... I done told you to leave my house.

BOY WILLIE: I ain't in your house. I'm in Doaker's house. If he ask me to leave then I'll go on and leave. But consider me done left your part.

BERNEICE: Doaker, tell him to leave. Tell him to go.

DOAKER: Boy Willie ain't done nothing for me to put him out of the house. I told you if you can't get along just go on and don't have nothing to do with each other.

BOY WILLIE: I ain't thinking about Berneice.

He gets up and draws a line across the floor with his foot.

There! Now I'm out of your part of the house. I'm in Doaker's part. Consider me done left your part. Soon as Lymon come back with that rope, I'm gonna take that piano out of here and sell it.

BERNEICE: You ain't gonna touch that piano.

BOY WILLIE: Carry it out of here just as big and bold. Do like my daddy would have done come time to get Sutter's land.

BERNEICE: I got something to make you leave it over there.....

BOY WILLIE: It's got to come better than this thirty-two-twenty.

DOAKER: Why don't you all stop that. Boy Willie, go on and leave her alone. You know how Berneice get. Why you wanna sit there and pick with her?

BOY WILLIE: I ain't picking with her. I told her the truth. She the one talking about what she got. I just told her what she better have.

BERNEICE: That's all right. Doaker, leave him alone.

BOY WILLIE: She's trying to scare me. Hell, I ain't scared of dying. I look around and see people dying every day. You got to die to make room for somebody else. I had a dog that died. Wasn't nothing but a puppy. I picked it up and put it in a bag and carried it up there to Reverend C. L. Thompson's church. I carried it up there and prayed and asked Jesus to make it live like he did the man in the Bible. I prayed real hard. Knelt down and everything. Say ask in Jesus's name. Well, I must have called Jesus's name two hundred times. I called his name till my mouth got sore. I got up and looked in the bag, and the dog still dead. It ain't moved a muscle. I say, "Well, ain't nothing precious." And then I went out and killed me a cat. That's when I discovered the power of death. See, a nigger that ain't afraid to die is the worse kind of nigger for the white man. He can't hold that power over you. That's what I learned when I killed that cat. I got the power of death too. I can command him. I can call him up. The white man don't like to see that. He don't like for you to stand up and look him square in the eye and say, "I got it too." Then he got to deal with you square up.

BERNEICE: That's why I don't talk to him, Doaker. You try and talk to him, and that's the only kind of stuff that comes out of his mouth.

DOAKER: You say Avery gonna stop by after work?

BOY WILLIE: What Avery gonna do? Avery can't do nothing with me. I wish Avery would say something to me about this piano.

DOAKER: Berneice ain't said about that. Avery coming by to bless the house see if he can get rid of Sutter's ghost.

BOY WILLIE: Ain't nothing but a house full of ghosts down there at the church. What Avery look like chasing away somebody's ghost?

Maretha enters with the hot comb and hairdressing.

BERNEICE: Light that stove and set that comb over there to get hot. Get something to put around your shoulders.

BOY WILLIE: The Bible say an eye for an eye, a tooth for a tooth and a life for a life. Tit for tat. But you and Avery don't want to believe that. You gonna pass up that part cause it don't suit you. You gonna look over that part and

S. Epatha Merkerson as Berneice, Charles S. Dutton as Boy Willie
and Rocky Carroll as Lymon in August Wilson's *The Piano Lesson*

pretend it ain't in there. Everything else you gonna agree with. But if you gonna agree with part of it, you got to agree with all of it. You can't do nothing halfway. You gonna act like that part ain't in there. But you pull out the Bible and open it and see what it say. Ask Avery. He a preacher. He'll tell you it's in there. He the Good Shepherd. Unless he gonna shepherd you to heaven with half the Bible.

BERNEICE: Maretha, bring me that comb. Make sure it's hot.

Maretha brings the comb. Berneice begins to do her hair.

BOY WILLIE: I will say this for Avery. He done figured out a path to go through life. I don't agree with it. But he done fixed it so he can go right through it real smooth. Hell, he liable to end up with a million dollars that he done got from selling bread and wine.

MARETHA: OWWWWWWW!

BERNEICE: Be still, Maretha. If you was a boy I wouldn't be going through this.

BOY WILLIE: Don't you tell that girl that. Why you wanna tell her that?

BERNEICE: You ain't got nothing to do with this child.

BOY WILLIE: Telling her you wished she was a boy. How's that gonna make her feel?

BERNEICE: Boy Willie, go on and leave me alone.

DOAKER: Why don't you leave her alone? What you got to pick with her for? Why don't you go out and see what's out there in the streets? Have something to tell the fellows down home.

BOY WILLIE: I'm waiting on Lymon to get back with that truck. Why don't you go on out and see what's out there in the streets? You ain't go to work tomorrow. Talking about me ... why don't you go out there? It's Friday night.

DOAKER: I got to stay around here and keep youall from killing one another.

BOY WILLIE: You ain't got to worry about me. I'm gonna be here just as long as it takes Lymon to get back here with that truck. You ought to be talking to Berneice. Sitting up there telling Maretha she wished she was a boy. What kind of thing is that to tell a child? If you want to tell her something, tell her about that piano. You ain't even told her about that piano. Like that's something to be ashamed of. Like she supposed to go off and hide somewhere about that piano. You ought to mark down on the calendar the day that Papa Boy Charles brought that piano into the house. You ought to mark that day down and draw a circle around it ... and every year when it come up, throw a party. Have a celebration. If you did that she wouldn't have no problem in life. She could walk around here with her head held high. I'm talking about a big party. Invite everybody, mark that day down with special meaning. That way she know where she at in the world. You got her going out here thinking she wrong in the world. Like there ain't no part of it belong to her.

BERNEICE: Let me take care of my child. When you get one of your own, then you can teach it what you want to teach it.

Doaker exits into his room.

BOY WILLIE: What I want to bring a child into this world for? Why I wanna bring somebody else into all this for? I'll tell you this. If I was Rockefeller I'd have forty or fifty. I'd make one every day. Cause they gonna start out in life with all the advantages. I ain't got no advantages to offer nobody. Many is the time I looked at my daddy and seen him staring off at his hands. I got a little older, I know what he was thinking. He sitting there saying, "I got these big old hands, but what I'm gonna do with them? Best I can do is make a fifty-acre crop for Mr. Stovall. Both these big old hands capable of doing anything. I can take and build something with these hands. But where's the tools? All I got is these hands. Unless I go out here and kill me somebody and take what they got ... it's a long row to hoe for me to get something of my own. So what I'm gonna do with these big old hands?" What would you do? See now ... if he had his own land he wouldn't have felt that way. If he had something under his feet that belonged to him he could stand up taller. That's what I'm talking about. Hell, the land is there for everybody. All you got to do is figure out how to get you a piece. Ain't no mystery to life. You just got to go out and meet it square on. If you got a piece of land you'll find everything else fall right into place. You can stand right up next to the white man and talk about the price of cotton ... the weather, and anything else you want to talk about. If you teach that girl that she living at the bottom of life, she's gonna grow up and hate you.

BERNEICE: I'm gonna teach her the truth. That's just where she living. Only she ain't got to stay there. (*To Maretha.*) Turn your head over to the other side.

BOY WILLIE: This might be your bottom, but it ain't mine. I'm living at the top of life. I ain't gonna just take my life and throw it away at the bottom. I'm in the world like everybody else. The way I see it, everybody else got to come up a little taste to be where I am.

BERNEICE: You right at the bottom with the rest of us.

BOY WILLIE: I'll tell you this ... and ain't a living soul can put a come back on it. If you believe that's where you at then you gonna act that way. If you act that way then that's where you gonna be. It's as simple as that. Ain't no mystery to life. I don't know how you come to believe that stuff. Papa Boy Charles and Mama Ola wasn't living at the bottom of life. You ain't never heard them say nothing like that. They would have taken a strap to you if they heard you say something like that.

Doaker enters from his room.

Hey Doaker ... Berneice say the colored folks is living at the bottom of life. I try to tell her if she think that way, that's where she gonna be. You think you living at the bottom of life? Is that how you see yourself?

DOAKER: I'm just living the best way I know how. I ain't thinking about no top or no bottom.

BOY WILLIE: That's what I tried to tell Berneice. I don't know where she got that from. That sound like something Avery would say. Avery think cause the white man give him a turkey for Thanksgiving that makes him better than everybody else. That's gonna raise him out of the bottom of life. I don't need nobody to give me a turkey. I can get my own turkey. All you have to do is get out my way. I'll get me two or three turkeys.

BERNEICE: You can't even get a chicken, let alone two or three turkeys. All you got going for you is talk. You whole life that's all you ever had going for you. (*To Maretha.*) Straighten your head, Maretha. Don't be bending down like that. Hold your head up.

DOAKER: Why don't you go on and leave her alone.

BOY WILLIE: See now ... I'll tell you something about me. I done strung along and strung along. Going this way and that. Whatever way would lead me to a moment of peace. That's all I want. To be as easy with everything. But I wasn't born to that. I was born to a time of fire. The world ain't wanted no part of me. I could see that since I was about seven. The world say it's better off without me. See, Berneice accept that. She's trying to come up to where she can prove something to the world. I look around and say you all got to come up a little ways to be where I am. That's the way I see it. Hell, the world a better place cause of me. I don't see it like Berneice. I got a heart that beats here, and it beats just as loud as the next fellow's. Don't care if he black or white. Sometimes it beat louder. When it beat louder then everybody can hear it. Some people get scared of that. Like Berneice. Some people get scared to hear a nigger's heart beating. They think you ought to lay low with that heart. Make it beat quiet and go along with everything the way it is. But my mama ain't birthed me for nothing. So what I got to do? I got to mark my passing on the road. Just like you write on a tree, "Boy Willie was here." That's all I'm trying to do with that piano. Trying to put my mark on the road. Like my daddy done. My heart say for me to sell that piano and get me some land so I can make a life for myself to live in my own way. Other than that, I ain't thinking about nothing Berneice got to say.

THE PIANO LESSON *premiered as a work-in-progress at the O'Neill National Playwrights Conference in Waterford, Conn. in the summer of 1987 in a staged reading. It continued in production at the Yale Repertory Theater, New Haven, Conn. Nov. 23, 1987 and then at the Huntington Theater in Boston. This ATCA New Play Prize citation was made on the basis of its production at the Goodman Theater, Chicago, Jan. 16, 1989.*

GENERATIONS

A Play in Two Acts

BY DENNIS CLONTZ

Cast and credits appear on page 531

GENERATIONS: Time was when most generations existed under one roof—the new caring for the old with affection and understanding. But the golden years have become, in our era, an uneasy place to live out your life. The question has become, "What's to be done with aging parents?" In his play *Generations* Dennis Clontz examines this thorny question in a bucolic setting which gives an especially poignant aspect to his tale of retired Joshua, who has kidnapped his wife Rachel from the "home" where her doctors have placed her since she lost, except for rare instances, any connection with reality.

The scene is the mountain cabin where the Houser family spent the many happy summers of their youth. Joshua has primed the sons Joseph and Aron, and Aron's live-in girl friend Lilith, to be as they were when they were young, with Lilith standing in for the unexpected daughter Judith, for that is how Rachel thinks of them—she has no conception of the fact that they are grown and out of the nest. It is a game they play for her benefit and comfort.

JOSHUA (*sets down wood; gazes a moment at Joseph*): What's that in your hand, son?
JOSEPH: Oh, God, here we go again.

Kristina Coggins as Lilith and J. Downing as Joseph
in a scene from *Generations* by Dennis Clontz

JOSHUA: What did your mother and I tell you children would happen, if we caught any of you smoking or drinking before you were of age?

JOSEPH: Don't you think we're carrying this game just a little—

JOSHUA: Joseph. Come here.

JOSEPH: No, sir.

JOSHUA: Aron, bring your brother over here. (*Aron goes for Joseph. Joseph dodges him.*) Judith, help Aron.

> *Lilith moves in on Joseph, and she and Aron chase him about. The mood is playful, filled with laughter and ad libs. At last Joseph is caught and brought before Joshua.*

ARON: Whip him good, Dad.

JOSHUA: What do you have to say for yourself, young man?

JOSEPH: Judith made me do it.

JOSHUA: Uh-uh, don't lie.

JOSEPH: Well, she did! And Aron too. You gonna whip one of us, you gotta whip all of us.

JOSHUA: I don't think I whipped any of you except maybe once or twice your entire lives.

ARON: Now's your chance to make up for lost time.

JOSHUA: You ever whip Missy and Donald?

JOSEPH: Aron doesn't have any children, he's not married yet.

JOSHUA: Right. If—when you do, then?

ARON: I'll probably do like you: I'll lecture them to death.

JOSHUA: Lecture to—? Hmp. Your grandfather—don't think I ever told you kids much about him—but he was a blacksmith during the week. A minister on Sundays. He raised us with few words and a firm hand. And I mean a very firm hand. Sometimes wonder—if he had lived long enough to see any of you born—what kind of grandfather he would have made—if he would've approved—of my tenacious disposition towards lecturing. And you? What might you do? Whip or lecture?

JOSEPH: Not gonna have children.

Judith enters unnoticed with suitcase in hand.

JOSHUA: No?

JOSEPH: No reason to.

JOSHUA (*to Lilith*): What about you?

JOSEPH: Do we really have to go through this?

JOSHUA: Just curious.

JOSEPH: Look. Are you going to whip me or not?

JOSHUA: Not. Of course.

JUDITH: Spare the rod, spoil the child.

> *The others turn towards Judith in surprise. The following occurs quickly amid hugs and overlapping.*

JOSHUA: Honey!

JOSEPH (*delighted*): Oh, no!

ARON: Why didn't you tell me you were planning on—?

JUDITH (*to Joseph*): Look at you.

JOSEPH: Looking pretty good, huh?

JUDITH (*taking in the cabin and environment*): And this place.

JOSHUA: Seventeen years.

JUDITH: Since we've all been—?

JOSEPH (*dragging Lilith towards Judith*): I want you to meet—

JOSHUA: 1972.

JUDITH: God.

JOSEPH: —Lilith.

LILITH: I've heard so much about—

JUDITH (*to Joseph*): You married?

JOSEPH: Live-in wench.

ARON: How did you manage to get here? You said—

JOSEPH: She flew, what do you think? Rented a beaut of a car and—

JUDITH (*to Aron*): Priorities.

JOSHUA: An anniversary barbecue wouldn't have seemed right without you being—

JUDITH: Anni—? Oh, my God! I forgot! It's—(*Glances at Aron.*) That's why—

ARON: I didn't put it together myself either.

JUDITH: Where's Mom?

ARON: Inside.

JUDITH: Alone? Are you crazy? (*She starts for the cabin.*)

ARON: Judith—

JOSHUA: Honey—

ARON: Wait!

JUDITH: I just want to—

ARON: You can't. I mean—not just yet.

JUDITH (*to Joshua*): Why not?

JOSEPH (*under his breath, turning away*): Oh, Jesus.

JOSHUA: Honey—Joseph, Lilith and Aron—they all came up together. And, ah—Rachel made—certain assumptions. About—

     Indicates Lilith.

JUDITH: What kind of assumptions?

JOSHUA: There's a very precarious balance at play here. The slightest upset—we could lose her again.

JUDITH (*referring to Lilith*): —that she's—me?

JOSEPH: And it's 1972.

JUDITH: 1972? Then Momma is—she's able to—?

ARON: You should see her, it's like she's—you know—like Mom. Like old times. Except—two and two isn't quite four.

JOSHUA: You okay, honey?

JUDITH: Just—winded. Who am I then? If *she's* me. (*Sharply, to Aron.*) You said you could handle the situation.

ARON: I am. The best I can.

JOSEPH: What situation?

ARON: When you telephoned me, you said you couldn't—

JUDITH: I changed my mind.

ARON: So don't blame me!

JOSHUA: Blame me. After all—that is what parents are for, isn't it?

JUDITH: That so?

JOSHUA: Not that it begins that way. You start off—first few years—what between electric sockets, stairs and the medicine cabinet—

JOSEPH: Oh, God, another lecture.

JOSHUA: —With the sole mission of preventing the kid from self-destructing. Then, somewhere around four or five, all your energy goes into trying to keep that child from totally destroying the home and the entire neighborhood.

ARON: Ain't that the truth.

JOSHUA (*zeroing in on Aron*): Then, from eight to twelve, it gets abstract. Things like morality, character. Right and wrong—(*Then on Joseph.*) Finally, once they're adolescents, or idle-escents as the case may be—you fight like hell to keep them from becoming too much of an individual. You don't realize all the stages until you see them grown.

JUDITH: And you scare them half to death?

JOSHUA: When, finally, you have to ask yourself: did I make the right choices? Are they complete enough? Strong enough? Did I fail them? Somewhere, somehow—helped—After all the dirty diapers, the tears, the cuts and bruises. After the thirty, forty pairs of shoes they've outgrown—they stand before you. Like a judgement. And you've got to ask: did I do enough?

ARON: You did fine, Dad.

JOSHUA: Your mother loves it here, Aron.

ARON: It shows. She seems real happy.

JOSHUA: She is—damn. We should move to Oregon. California—southern California, it's changed. Back in forty-four, when I first came out there, in the service, met your mother, she was working out at Lockheed. We'd go to the San Fernando Valley for a country outing. I mean—you hit Canoga Park, Tarzana—you were talking rural. And San Diego. God, San Diego was nothing but a sleepy little hamlet.

JUDITH: I never knew that—she worked.

JOSHUA: Same building that Marilyn Monroe worked before Monroe became a star. War effort. Deadly with a rivet gun, your mother was. And cute. Not beautiful like Monroe or Bacall, when Bacall was young. But cute, huggable. Like Doris Day. Still is—hmp! Rachel hasn't changed a bit in all those years. Shame the same can't be said for California. It's dying. More it grows, the more it becomes a goddamn wasteland.

JOSEPH (*under his breath*): Jesus.

JOSHUA: What?

JOSEPH: Nothing.

JOSHUA: No. You got something to say, say it. You've been muttering under your breath from the day you were born.

JOSEPH: Yeah. Sure.

JOSHUA: It's God's truth. (*To the others.*) Dr. Kruger, Parkview Hospital, delivered him, hmm? Took him right out of Rachel, raised him up the feet, and gave him a healthy swat on the butt. Did he bawl? Did he cry? No, sir—you muttered under your breath. Unnerved Kruger something fierce. Man almost gave up obstetrics after that. Time you stop muttering, Joseph, and speak your mind.

JOSEPH: No reason to.

JOSHUA: I do wish you'd do something about that damn beer. For Rachel.

LILITH (*takes beer*): I'll put it in a Coke can.

JOSEPH: Fine. Whatever will keep the family happy. (*Lilith goes inside the cabin; watching her go, Joseph comes to look upon Judith.*) Who the hell *is* she suppose to be, huh, Dad? Looks like this barbecue has a few loose ends to it. You wanna be my girl friend?

ARON: You're too young for girl friends.

JOSEPH: Too young for beer; too young for women. Hell, why do I even exist?

JUDITH: Maybe you don't.

JOSEPH: That would definitely put us in the same boat, wouldn't it?

ARON: Trudy.

JOSEPH: Huh?

ARON: She could be Trudy.

JOSEPH (*laughs*): Oh, what tangled webs we weave.

JUDITH: I'll pass on the opportunity. (*She starts for the cabin, realizes she can't really go inside. Joshua starts to say something to her.*) No, I, ah—just. A few minutes alone, okay?

> *She exits around the side of the cabin.*

JOSEPH: Judith? Judy? Boy, you really know how to insult a person.

ARON: Just a thought. Trudy came up with the family the last time we—. "Last year."

JOSEPH: And you banged her down by the bluff.

ARON: Huh?

JOSEPH: Talk about vivid memories. Trudy kept asking: "Do you have one of those thing-a-bobs?" And Aron—he's tearing apart his wallet looking for a thing-a-bob.

ARON: You sneaky little pervert.

JOSEPH: But you lost it, didn't you, Aron? No thing-a-bob.

ARON: Enough already.

JOSEPH: God, you were pathetic.

ARON: So forget it.

JOSEPH: Can't. (*Tapping his head.*) It's burned up here with a red hot branding iron. Cause up till then, I'd never seen two people really "doing it." Oh, I had *heard* Mom and Dad on the weekends. (*To Joshua.*) Judith turned me on to that little ritual.

JOSHUA (*more surprised than angered.*) You little sons of bitches.

JOSEPH: But actually see it. Uh-uh. And then Trudy started beating her fists against Aron, saying, "Goddamn it, you came, didn't you, didn't you?"

ARON: Shut up.

JOSEPH: High point of my childhood, watching my big brother, my idol, knock up some high school cheerleader. Really should keep track of your thing-a-bobs. Might keep you from lying. The marriage was another lie.

JOSHUA: You stop it right now.

JOSEPH: It's like Dad lamenting the loss of California.

JOSHUA: I don't know what your beef is, but you're not spoiling this—

JOSEPH: Oh, com'on! Man, you made your money off real estate and development—you've got no right to bitch about it being a wasteland. You did in southern California the same way Aron did in a cheerleader—Jesus. Excuse me—(*Pulls up his pants legs.*)—but it's getting kind of deep around here. If it wasn't for Mom—

> *Lilith comes out onto the porch with a Coke can. Joseph mimics wading as he crosses to take the can from her.*

Hold on, there. It's not safe to come off that porch without hip boots. It's deep and getting deeper. Thanks, Sis. Ain't she a hell of a sister?

> *He kisses her full on the mouth.*

LILITH (*struggling against him.*): Don't start anything, please.

JOSEPH: No? Never.

> *Lilith goes back inside.*

JOSHUA: You finished with your tantrum?

JOSEPH: I'm taking a run down to the store. (*Starts off.*)

JOSHUA: Joseph? Today is special to your mother. Don't ruin it.

JOSEPH: You want to have a fun-filled barbecue, fine. Just don't try to make it too "golden"—Goddamn cabin looks like shit.

> *He exits.*

JOSHUA: Why is there so much hate in that boy?

ARON: It's not hate, Dad. I just think he never forgave any of us for being merely human. We lead him to expect so much more.

JOSHUA: He's right. Look at this place—is that the truth—about Trudy and you? Our first summer here—Rachel and I, once you kids were asleep. We'd take our sleeping bag down by the bluff. Some wine sometimes. Watch the stars—make love.

ARON: Yeah?

JOSHUA: Sometimes.

ARON: My very own parents. Geez.

GENERATIONS *premiered Feb. 4, 1989 at the Colony Studio Theater in Los Angeles.*

THE DOWNSIDE

A Play in Three Acts

BY RICHARD DRESSER

Cast and credits appear on page 537

THE DOWNSIDE: Richard Dresser's play is a high-rise comedy about the way we work now. The scene is the sleek offices of Mark and Maxwell, a pharmaceutical company. The marketing department has been given exactly one month to plot the launch of a new anti-stress drug, Maxolan-3000. Naturally, everyone is highly stressed: a poor launch could lead to a "re-structuring" of the department. There's also a tiny problem with the chemical formulation of Maxolan-3000. It makes people delusional.

Think of the play as *How to Succeed in Business Without Really Trying* crossed with *An Enemy of the People*. In the following scene, at the end of Act I, Scene 2, the office purge has begun. Its first victim seems to be Carl, whose only qualification for a corporate career is that he looks good in a suit. Here the gang says farewell to Carl at the annual Christmas party. As usual, Carl—his second talent—doesn't understand the situation. Meanwhile Dave, their boss, keeps checking in by speaker-phone.

ROXANNE: I think we better get this thing going. With the snowstorm I don't know how long people will stay.
Handing Carl the present.

Carl?

CARL: For me? Wow, I'm really touched.

Carl turns and sees the sign "Farewell Carl."

DIANE: It's the least we could do.

JEFF: And believe me, we wanted to do the least for you. Only kidding, Carl.

CARL: I bet Stan is behind this.

ROXANNE: Why Stan?

CARL: He's the only one I told about my ski trip to Utah. I sure didn't expect such a sendoff.

Carl opens the present, a briefcase.

Thanks a lot. Really. This is, boy, I don't know ... I've never had friends like this ...

Ben enters.

Thanks, Ben. I know you're part of this—

BEN: Part of what?

CARL: My going away party.

J. Smith-Cameron and Mark Blum in a scene from Richard Dresser's *The Downside* as produced at the Long Wharf Theater, New Haven

BEN: Where are you going?

CARL: Skiing in Utah.

BEN: That's nice, Carl. But you can give me the fucking briefcase.

> *Ben grabs the briefcase.*

JEFF: Ben!

CARL: It's mine! They gave it to me!

BEN: Yeah, well I'm the one that got fired! I want the present!

DIANE: You got fired?

ALAN: Ben is through at this company. We wish you all the best, Ben.

JEFF: My God, Ben, I thought you got promoted—

ROXANNE: When did this happen?

BEN: Fuck it. You know what I'm saying? Just fuck it.

ALAN (*raising his glass*): Fuck it.

JEFF (*to Ben*): Man, I feel so bad for you. I was just thinking how great it was about the promotion.

CARL (*grabbing the briefcase*): It had my name on the card, Ben—

ROXANNE (*grabbing it back, then tossing it to Ben*): The present is not for you, Carl, O.K.?

CARL (*grabbing it back from Ben*): But I wanted—

DIANE (*grabbing it from Carl and handing it to Ben*): Shut up, Carl. Ben, I don't know what to say.

> *Ben is clutching the briefcase. We hear Dave's voice from the speaker.*

DAVE: Happy holidays, everyone.

ALAN (*turning to the speaker*): Dave! Good to see you!

DAVE: Central switchboard put me through. I just wanted to wish everyone all the best for the holidays. I know how hard you've been working—

BEN (*giving the speaker the finger*): Merry Christmas, Dave! My wife sends her best, too!

DAVE: Thanks, Jeff. I've just been sitting here on the plane brainstorming—

> *We hear commotion in the background on the speaker.*

My flight is getting in to Newark in a couple of hours, and I'll be coming straight to the office, so Alan, if we could meet—

ALAN: There's a helluva storm here, Dave. We're all going home a little early—

> *In the background on the speaker we hear voices screaming in Spanish.*

DAVE (*utterly calm*): That's O.K., there seems to be a bit of hijacking in progress so I'll have to sign off. I'll call you at home, Alan, and for all the rest of you, enjoy your holidays and keep up the good work. Let's be thankful for all we have during this joyful holiday season—

A gunshot and a scream, then the speaker goes dead.
ALAN: Dave? Dave, are you O.K.?
The others crowd around the speaker and stare at it with concern.
Blackout.

THE DOWNSIDE *had its premiere at the Long Wharf Theater, New Haven, Conn. Oct. 16, 1987. This ATCA citation was made on the basis of its production at the Cricket Theater, Minneapolis, Sept. 14, 1988.*

A DIRECTORY OF NEW-PLAY PRODUCTIONS

Compiled by Sheridan Sweet

Professional 1988–89 productions of new plays by leading companies around the United States that supplied information on casts and credits of first productions at Sheridan Sweet's request, plus a few reported by other reliable sources, are listed below in alphabetical order of the locations of the producing organizations. Date given is opening date, included whenever a record was obtainable from the producing management. All League of Resident Theaters (LORT) and other Equity groups were queried for this comprehensive Directory. Those not listed here either did not produce new or newly-revised scripts in 1988–89 or had not responded by press time. Most of the productions listed—but not all—are American or world premieres. Some are new revisions, second looks (as in the case of some ATCA selections) or scripts produced previously but not previously reported in Best Plays.

Albany: Capital Repertory Company

(Producing directors, Bruce Bouchard, Peter H. Clough)

SAINT FLORENCE. By Elizabeth Diggs. October 1, 1988. Director, Jules Aaron; scenery, Rick Dennis; lighting, Victor En Yu Tan; costumes, James Scott; sound, Kevin Bartlett; choreography, Constance Valis Hill.

Sidney Herbert	Robin Chadwick
Parthe Nightingale	Carole Monferdini
Nurse Pearl	Susan Pope
Nurse Zoe	Pat Timm
Fanny Nightingale	Jane Welch
Florence Nightingale	Claire Beckman

Nurse Gale; Lady Canning;
   Sister Ann.....................Darcy Pulliam

W.E.N. Nightingale; Dr. John Hall... James Pritchett

Henry	William Gurr

Mary Stanley;
   Nurse in Dream...............Emily Arnold McCully
Walter Hamilton.............................Edmund Lewis
Richard Monckton Milnes;
   Dr. Cumming....................................Jim Abele
Charles; A Soldier...................K. Scott Coopwood
Gilbert; An Orderly..........................David Howell

Time: 1830–1860. Place: England and the Crimea. One intermission.

Albany: Empire State Institute for the Performing Arts

(Literary manager, James Farrell)

Staged Readings:

DRAGONS, A MUSICAL. By Sheldon Harnick. June 17, 1988. Director, Billie Allen.

AFTER THE DANCING IN JERICHO. By P.J. Barry. July 1, 1988. Director, Ed Lange.

ACADEMY THEATER—Frank Wittow, Ruth Reid and
Carol Mitchell-Leon in *The Keepers* by Barbara Lebow

Atlanta: Academy Theater

(Producing artistic director, Frank Wittow)

THE KEEPERS. By Barbara Lebow. November 3,
1988. Director, Barbara Lebow; scenery, Michael
Halpern; lighting, Paul R. Ackerman; costumes,
Chris Cook; sound, Michael Keck.

Nathanial Brockett............................Frank Wittow
Octavia Brockett...................................Ruth Reid
Angeline Brockett....................Carol Mitchell-Leon
    Time: 1855. Place: A lighthouse on a rock island
off the coast of Maine. One intermission.

THE REALISTS. By Murphy Guyer. February 9,
1989. Director, Murphy Guyer; scenery, Patricia
Martin; lighting, Jeffrey Nealer; costumes, Chris
Cook; sound, Mike Mitten.

Scott..Haynes Brooke
Jenny ....Shawna McKellar
Jennifer...Ruth Reid
Scotty ....Clark Taylor
Old Man ....Kevin Crysler
    Time: The future. Place: An American City.

Genesis Series, New Play Program:

SAMANTHA. By Linda Anderson. October 20,
1988. Director, Gregory Blum.
BAIT SHOP. By Ed Brock Jr. May 4, 1989.
Director, Haynes Brooke.

Atlanta: Alliance Theater Company

(Artistic director, Robert Farley)

DOUBLE DOUBLE. By Eric Elise and Roger Rees. October 19, 1988. Director, Munson Hicks; scenery, John Falabella; costumes, Susan E. Mickey; Lighting, Michael Stauffer. With Michele Farr, Francois Giroday. One intermission.

Bristol, Pa.: Bristol Riverside Theater

(Artistic director, Susan D. Atkinson)

HAPPY ENDING. By Garson Kanin. November 3, 1988. Director, Garson Kanin; scenery, Joseph A. Varga; costumes, Debra Stein; lighting, Scott Pinkney; sound, Arnold S. Goldman.
Quentin Drew .... Peter Donat
Peg Malone.................................... Marian Seldes
Jenny Fantucci................................Cecelia Peck
Spencer Drew .... Geoffrey Lower
One intermission.

WINTERTIME. By John Liam Joyce. January 26, 1989. Directed by Susan D. Atkinson; scenery, Nels Anderson; lighting, John Culbert.
Boots Donnelly.............................Churchill Clark
Danny Donnelly.............................Norman Large
Meg Donnelly Ryan..........................Lucy Martin
One intermission.

Buffalo: Studio Arena Theater

(Artistic director, David Frank; managing director, Raymond Bonnard)

ABINGDON SQUARE. By Maria Irene Fornes (new version). November 4, 1988. Director, Maria Irene Fornes.

PlayWorks (Staged Readings):

EDEN CREEK. By Dwight Watson. May 8, 1989. Director, Susan Shaughnessy. With Melinda Adamczyk, Margo Davis, Kim Dallaire, Darlene Pickering Hummert, Pamela Rose, Joyce Stilson.

AMERICAN LIFE AND CASUALTY. By Stuart Flack. May 15, 1989. Director, Ross Wasserman. With Stuart Roth, Michael Russo, Brian LaTulip, Anne Gayley, Susan Shaughnessy.
FELLOW AMERICANS. By E. M. Schlosser. May 22, 1989. Director, Ross Wasserman. With Keith Elkins, John Kiousis, Donald Savage, Richard Hummert, Bryan Hayes, Anne Gayley, Nancy Doherty, Michael Karr, Stuart Roth.

Cambridge, Mass.: American Repertory Theater

(Artistic director, Robert Brustein)

MASTERGATE. By Larry Gelbart. February 8, 1989. Director, Michael Engler; scenery, Philipp Jung; costumes, Candice Donnelly; lighting, James F. Ingalls.
With Jerome Kilty, Jeremy Geidt, Thomas Derrah, Benjamin Evett, Alvin Epstein, Harry S. Murphy,

Steve Hofvendahl, Daniel Von Bargen, Joseph Daly, David Asher, Cherry Jones, Bari Hochwald, Deanna Dunmyer, Sean Runnette, Christopher Colt.

Chicago: Goodman Theater

(Artistic director, Robert Falls; producing director, Roche Schulfer)

THE PIANO LESSON. By August Wilson. January 16, 1989. Director, Lloyd Richards; scenery, E. David Cosier Jr.; costumes, Constance Romero; lighting, Christopher Akerlind; sound, J. Scott Servheen; musical direction and original music, Dwight Andrews.

Doaker	Paul Butler
Boy Willie	Charles S. Dutton
Lymon	Rocky Carroll
Berneice	S. Epatha Merkerson
Avery	Tommy Hollis
Wining Boy	Lou Myers
Grace	Tonya Pinkins

And with Tressa-Janae Thomas.

Time: 1936. Place: Pittsburgh, the house of Doaker Charles, where he lives with his niece Berneice. One intermission. (ATCA New Play Prize winner; see introduction to this section.)

SMOOCH MUSIC. By David Cale; music by Roy Nathanson. March 8, 1989. With David Cale.

THE SPEED OF DARKNESS. By Steve Tesich. April 14, 1989. Director, Robert Falls; scenery, Thomas Lynch; lighting, Michael S. Philippi; costumes, Nan Cibula; sound and original music, Rob Milburn.

Joe	Bill Raymond
Anne	Lee Guthrie
Mary	Brigitte Bako
Lou	Stephen Lang
Eddie	Andy Hirsch

Time: The present. Place: South Dakota. One intermission.

MILL FIRE. By Sally Nemeth. April 25, 1989. Director, David Petrarca; scenery, Linda Buchanan; lighting, Robert Christen; costumes, Laura Cunningham; sound, Rob Milburn.

Widows	Martha Lavey, Mary Ann Thebus, Jacqueline Williams
Marlene	Kelly Coffield
Champ	James Krag
Sunny	Kate Buddeke
Bo	B. J. Jones
Jemison	Paul Mabon
Minister, OSHA Investigator	Timothy Grimm

Time: July, 1978. Place: Birmingham, Ala. One intermission.

Chicago: Steppenwolf Theater Company

(Artistic director, Randall Arney; managing director, Stephen B. Eich)

KILLERS. By John Clive. June 13, 1988. Director, Randall Arney; scenery and lighting, Kevin Rigdon; costumes, Erin Quigley; sound, Richard Woodbury; original music, Ralph Carney.

Charles Blackwell	Robert Brueler
Earl	Nathan Davis
Lou	Jim True
Husband	Ted Levine
Faye	Laurie Metcalfe

One intermission.

THE GRAPES OF WRATH. Adapted from the novel by John Steinbeck and directed by Frank Galati. September 18, 1988. Scenery and lighting, Kevin Rigdon; costumes, Kevin Rigdon, Erin Quigley; sound, Rob Milburn; original music, Michael Smith; choreography, Peter Amster.

With John D. Allison, Elizabeth K. Austin, Robert Breuler, P. J. Brown, Cheryl Lynn Bruce, Keith Byron-Kirk, Ron Crawford, Darryl D. Davis, Nathan Davis, Relioues De Var, Jim Donovan, Howard Elfman, Louise Freistadt, Jessica Grossman, Tim Hopper, Tom Irwin, Tonia Jackson, Terry Kinney, Nancy Lollar, Dana Lubotsky, Terrance MacNamara, Ramsay Midwood, James Noah, Lucina Paquet, Rondi Reed, John C. Reilly, Christian Robinson, Paul G. Scherrer, Theodore Schult, Eric Simonson, Gary Sinise, L. J. Slavin, Lois Smith, Michael Smith, Rick Snyder, Miriam Sturm, Skipp Sudduth, Yvonne Suhor, Jim True, Elsa Wenzel, Alan Wilder.

Time: 1938. Place: Oklahoma. One intermission.

Cincinnati: Cincinnati Playhouse in the Park

(Artistic director, Worth Gardner; managing director, Kathleen Panoff)

INVENTION FOR FATHERS AND SONS. By Alan Brody. March 30, 1989. Director, Jay E. Raphael; scenery, Charles Caldwell; lighting, Kirk Bookman; costumes, Rebecca Senske; original music, Worth Gardner.

With Len Stanger, Ross Bickel, Gordon MacDonald, Catherine Wolf, Jacquelyn Riggs, Regina Pugh, Elaine Grollman, Herman O. Arbeit.

Cleveland: Cleveland Play House

(Artistic director, Josephine R. Abady)

ON THE WATERFRONT. By Budd Schulberg and Stanley Silverman; adapted from Budd Schulberg's novel. October 18, 1988. Director, Josephine R. Abady.

With Grant Snow, Kelly Curtis.

THE CEMETERY CLUB. By Ivan Menchell. May 16, 1989. Director, Josephine R. Abady; scenery, David Potts; costumes, Jane Greenwood, David

Charles; lighting, Dennis Parichy; sound, Lia Vollack.

Ida ....Elizabeth Franz
Lucille..Nanette Fabray
Doris...Doris Belack
Sam...................................... Eugene Troobnick
Mildred..Joyce Krempel
One intermission.

Costa Mesa, Calif.: South Coast Repertory

(Producing artistic director, David Emmes; artistic director, Martin Benson)

Mainstage:

AT LONG LAST LEO. By Mark Stein. October 28, 1988. Director, Steven Albrezzi; scenery, Cliff Faulkner; lighting, Peter Maradudin; costumes, Walker Hicklin; music consultant, Jimmy Vann.
Dad... Tom Troupe
Mom .... Priscilla Pointer
Sheila .... Anni Long
Bartholomew..............Peter Hamilton, John Wilson
Leo... Michael Kaufman
Gloria ....Annie LaRussa
One intermission.

ABUNDANCE. By Beth Henley. April 21, 1989. Director, Ron Lagomarsino; scenery, Adrianne Lobel; lighting Paulie Jenkins; costumes, Robert Wojewodski; music and sound, Michael Roth.
Bess Johnson....................................O-Lan Jones
Macon Hill ....Belita Moreno
Jack Flan... Bruce Wright
William Curtis ....Jimmie Ray Weeks
Elmore Crome.................................John Walcutt
Time: The late 1860s and the 25 years that follow.
Place: The Wyoming Territory and later St. Louis, Mo.

DRAGON LADY. By Robert Daseler. May 2, 1989.

Director, Jerry Patch; scenery, Cliff Faulkner; lighting, Tom Ruzika; costumes, Susan Denison Geller; original music and sound, Eric Allaman.
Alex...Richard Doyle
Margo .... Robin Pearson Rose
Paul...Hal Landon Jr.
Nan.. Julie Fulton
Time and Place: A contemporary Southern California suburb. One intermission.

Second Stage:

THE GEOGRAPHY OF LUCK. By Marlane Meyer. May 16, 1989. Director, Roberta Levitow.

California Play Festival Staged Readings:

SOILED EYES OF A GHOST. By Erin Cressida Wilson. May 13, 1989. Director, Peter Brosius. With Shawn Modrell, Joe Spano, Janni Bren, James LeGros.
ONCE IN ARDEN. By Richard Hellesen. May 15, 1989. Director, Martin Benson. With Nan Martin, James W. Winker, Gregory Itzin, I. M. Hobson, Mitchell Ryan.
THE LAND OF PLENTY. By Sam Garcia Jr. May 19, 1989. Director, Jose Cruz Gonzalez. With Don Took, Hal Bokar, George Galvan, Art Koustik, Robert Crow, Danny de la Paz, Jennifer Flackett.

THE BALLAD OF YACHIYO. By Philip Kan Gotanda. May 20, 1989. Director, Lee Shallat. With Denice Kumagai, Francois Chau, Diane Kobayashi, Yuki Okamura, Diane Takei, Keone Young.

Hispanic Playwrights Project:

Public Readings/Mainstage
BROKEN BOUGH. By Lynnette Serrano-Bonaparte. August 12, 1988.
PARTING GESTURES. By Rafael Lima. August 13, 1988.
BANG BANG BLUES. By Charles Gomez. August 13, 1988.
Workshop Readings/Second Stage
SIMPLY MARIA. By Josefina Lopez
IMAGENES. By Bernardo Solano.

THE IMMACULATE SALVATION AUTO BODY PARTS STORE. By Rafael Melendez.
Year-Round Lab
MOMIO. By Freddy Fraguada. June 1988.
BUSCANDO AMERICA. By Roy Conboy. July 1988.

Newscripts (Staged Readings):
LOST ELECTRA. By Bruce Rodgers. November 14, 1988. Director, Martin Benson.
ABOUT TO BEGIN. By Jerome Kilty. December 12, 1988. Director, Margaret Booker.
SEARCH AND DESTROY. By Howard Korder. February 6, 1989. Director, David Chambers.
ROMANTICS. By Jeremy Lawrence. March 27, 1989. Director, Eli Simon.

Dallas: Theater 3

(Founding artistic director, Norma Young; executive producer-director, Jac Alder)

A QUARREL OF SPARROWS. By James Duff. October 15, 1988. Director, Jac Alder; scenery, Cheryl Denson; lighting, Ken Hudson; costumes, Christopher Kovarik.
August Ainsworth......................Laurence O'Dwyer
Rosanna Ainsworth ....Norma Young
Paul Palmer ....John Evans
Angela Mercer ....Jo Haden
Lynn Waters................................John Figlmiller
Place: The country residence of August Ainsworth

on the South Fork of Long Island near Sag Harbor. One intermission.

Staged Readings:
AND THE MEN SHALL ALSO GATHER. By Jeff Stetson.
CRAZY FROM THE HEART. By Edit Villarreal.
BANG BANG BLUES. By Charles Gomez.
COOKIE AND LEROY. By Walter Allen Bennett.

Denver: Denver Center Theater Company

(Artistic director, Donovan Marley)

DARKSIDE. By Ken Jones. January 10, 1989. Director, Jared Sakren; scenery, John Dexter; lighting, Daniel L. Murray; costumes, Patricia Ann Whitelock; sound, Matthew Morgan.
Capcom; Camera Man........... Stephen Lee Anderson
William C. Griffin ....Michael X. Martin
Gerald R. Smith.............................Robert Eustace
Edward Scott Stone............................Craig Ryder
Beth Griffin......................................Cara Wilder
Gigi Stone...............................Laura Ann Worthen
Bob Hughes; Reporter.......................Scott Putman
Photographer.....................................Ann Patricio
Time: The early autumn of 1973. Place: The moon and various locations on earth.

EXCLUSIVE CIRCLES. By Kendrew Lascelles. March 7, 1989. Director, Bruce K. Sevy; scenery, John Dexter; lighting, Daniel L. Murray; costumes, Janet S. Morris.

Nel (du Plessis) Davis ....Kay Doubleday
Kline Davis.....................................Jamie Horton
Millicent Dabini...........................Lydia Hannibal
Bosman du Plessis.....................Kendrew Lascelles
Hannie..Ann Patricio
Time: The recent past. Place: Durban, South Africa.

CHILD OF LUCK. By Donald Freed. May 8, 1989. Director, Laird Williamson; scenery and costumes, Andrew Y. Yelusich; lighting, Charles McLeod; sound, Thomas Ciufo.
With Jamie Horton, Archie Smith, James J. Lawless, Jeffrey W. Nickelson, Percy Howard Lyle Jr., Kendrew Lascelles, Jim Baker, DeAnn Mears, Kay Doubleday, John Clark, Carole Elmore, Mitchell Hudson, Merrill Key, Blayne Lemke, Ken Allen Robertson, Steve Wilson.
One intermission.

GOODSPEED OPERA HOUSE—Cheryl Freeman, Noreen Crayton
and Tina Fabrique (*in front row*) in the new musical *Abyssinia*

Detroit: Attic Theater

(Artistic director, Lavinia Moyer; managing director, Bruce Makous)

WOODY GUTHRIE'S AMERICAN SONG. Songs
and writings by Woody Guthrie. Adapted and directed
by Peter Glazer; scenery, Philipp Jung; lighting,
David Noling; costumes, Deborah Shaw; musical
direction, Jeff Waxman.

1st Young Man............................Scott Wakefield

2d Young Man...............................David Lutken
Man..Tom McKeon
Young Woman..............................Mimi Bessette
Woman...............................Liz Trevor Corrigan
    Time: Now and in the 1930s and 1940s. Place:
America. One intermission.

East Haddam, Conn: Goodspeed Opera House

(Executive producer, Michael P. Price; associate artistic director, Dan Siretta)

ABYSSINIA (musical). Book by James Racheff and
Ted Kociolek; lyrics by James Racheff; music by Ted
Kociolek. June 8, 1988. Direction and musical
staging, Tazewell Thompson; musical direction and
arrangements, Daryl Waters; technical director,
Daniel Renn; scenery, James Leonard Joy; lighting,
Alen Lee Hughes; costumes, Amanda J. Klein.
Abyssinia Jackson.........................Noreen Crayton
Mother Vera....................................Tina Fabrique

Patience Jackson...........................Cheryl Freeman
Mothers of the Church:
    Selma......................................LaDonna Mabry
    Corine ....Mary Bond Davis
    Mavis......................................Kimberly Harris
Lilly Noreen..............................Vanessa Williams
Minister.......................................Lehman Beneby
Gang of Boys:
    Marcus............................ Stanley Wayne Mathis

Leon ....Demetri Corbin
Jesse .... Scott Leonard Fortune
Members of the Congregation:
  Brother Samuels.........................Rufus Bonds Jr.
  Mother Samuels......................Vanessa Williams

Deacon Daniels..............................David Toney
Trembling Sally................................ Fanni Green
  Time: The past. Place: Rural Oklahoma. One intermission.

Evanston, Ill.: Northlight Theater

(Artistic director, Russell Vandenbroucke; managing director, Susan Medak)

TALKING TO MYSELF. Adapted and directed by Paul Sills from Studs Terkel's book. September 7, 1988. Scenery, Carol Bleackley; lighting, Rita Pietraszek; costumes, Jessica Hahn.

  With Dennis Cockrum, Christopher Holloway, Eddie Jemison, Warren Leming, Rachel MacKinnon, Joann Shapiro, Peter Van Wagner.

  One intermission.

PASTEL REFUGEES (musical). Book by Greg Fleming and Jeff Berkson; music and lyrics by Jeff Berkson. April 12, 1989. Director, Doug Finlayson;

musical director, Steve Rashid; scenery, Linda Buchanan; lighting, Ken Bowen; costumes, Fran Maggio.
Dov ....Jonathan Mozes
Chris...Sarah Hummon
Mickey.......................................Nancy J. Seifried
Lonnie...Darius de Haas
Rich...Peter Van Wagner
Carla...Sybil Walker
  Time: The present. Place: Group room of a hospital in-patient unit. One intermission.

Fort Worth: Hip Pocket Theater

(Producer, Diane Simons; artistic director, Johnny Simons)

WIDOWS. By Ariel Dorfman. July 22, 1988. Director, Susan Chapek; scenery, Wenhai Ma; lighting, Dennis Runge; costumes, Diane Simons; composer, Bob Price.
Alexandra...Susan Neely
Yanina ....Suzanne Turner
Alonso..Zelmer Phillips
Alexis...Costa Caglage
Fidelia...Maurie Taylor
Sofie Ruentes...................................Jude Johnson
Captain ....Douglas Balentine
Lieutenant..Jerry Betsill

Emmanuel..Pat Dias
Cecilia...Miriam Angress
Father Gabriel .... Dick Harris
Journalist..Libby Villari

YOUNG DOWDS. By Johnny Simons. April 28, 1989. Director, Johnny Simons; lighting, Paul Chadwick, Douglas Balentine; costumes, Diane Simons; music, Douglas Balentine.
June Dowdy....................................Lake Simons
Jane Dowdy....................................Marzee Baker
Dodson...Dylan Griffin

Fort Worth: Stage West

(Artistic and managing director, Jerry Russell)

HOUSEWIVES: A TRILOGY. By Anne Clayton. July 29, 1988. Director, Jerry Russell; scenery and lighting, Michael O'Brien; costumes, Jim Covault.

It's A Wonderful Life
Vera...Bonnie Pemberton
Zeus ....Barry Dale
Vince......................................Stephen Cummins
Richard..Doug Jackson
Phil...Buckley Sachs
Buffy ....Suzi McLaughlin

Chorus ....Mary Catherine Keaton-Jordon,
                          Joe Delane, Janice Jeffrey
Mom's Voice
Marla ....Joyce Ingle
Marla Jean................................. Suzi McLaughlin
Mary Kaye ....Bonnie Pemberton
Necessary Existence in Suburbia
Swoozie....................................Bonnie Pemberton
Joan .... Suzi McLaughlin

Time: The present. Place: Three kitchens. Two intermissions.

MOONSHADOW. By Richard Hellesen. January 18, 1989. Director, Jerry Russell; scenery, Bob Lavallee; lighting, Jay Isham.
Ellen..Jane Milburn

Jeff ....Todd Anderson
Laurel...Laura Becker
Jack ....Jim Covault
Mark...David Poynter
  Time: July 20, 1969, Sunday. Place: A house in Castalia, Ill., a small town east of Springfield. One intermission.

Gloucester, Mass.: Gloucester Stage Company

(Artistic director, Israel Horovitz)

Staged Readings:
DEATH QUILT. By Leslie Harrell.
THE CHROMA LINE. By Larry Blamire.

BETTER DAYS. By Richard Dresser.
A BLUE AND GOLD MISTAKE. By Raymond Pape.

Hartford, Conn.: Hartford Stage Company

(Artistic director, Mark Lamos; managing director, David Hawkanson)

THE PAPER GRAMOPHONE. By Alexander Chervinsky. February 11, 1989. Based on a screen play by Alexander Chervinsky; adapted by Yuri Yeremin and Alexander Chervinsky; English translation by Mary-Helen Ayres. Director, Yuri Yeremin; scenery and costumes, Michael Yeargan; lighting, Ken Tabachnick; sound, David Budries.
Lidia Ivanovna...........................Kathleen Chalfant
Victoria..Ann Dowd
Semyon...Ray Virta
Oscar Borisovich................................Jack Bittner
Student...Evan Blackford
  Time: Winter and spring, 1947. Place: A small town in the Soviet Union. One intermission.

PEER GYNT. By Henrik Ibsen; new translation by Gerry Bamman and Irene B. Berman. March 30, 1989. Director, Mark Lamos; scenery, John Conklin; lighting, Pat Collins; costumes, Merrily Murray-Walsh; sound, David Budries; original music, Mel Marvin.
Peer Gynt ....Richard Thomas
Ase..Patricia Conolly
Crones .... Helen Harrelson, Nancy Wolfe
Aslak; Herr Trumpeterstrale;
  1st Mate ....Thomas Schall
Bridegroom; Mads Moen; Ugly Brat.......... Barry Lee

Master of Ceremonies; Monsieur Ballon; Thief;
  Strange Passenger ....Paul Kandel
Groom's Father; Oldest Troll;
  Button Molder........................ Wyman Pendleton
Groom's Mother.......................... Helen Harrelson
Solveig...Tara Hugo
Helga; Solveig's Sister................. Christine Shaker
Solveig's Father; Old Man of Dovre;
  King of the Trolls; Herr von Eberkopf;
  Sheriff .... Stephen Rowe
Ingrid; Woman in Green; Tumbleweed;
  Dead Leaves................................... Leslie Geraci
Herd Girls ....Adina Porter, Christine Shaker,
                                        Harriette H. Holmes
Troll Witches............Helen Harrelson, Nancy Wolfe
Voice; Master Cotton; Statue of Memnon;
  Ship's Captain; Broken Straws........ Terrence Caza
Slaves ....David Scott Meikle, Benjamin Rayner
Slave Master; Fellah; Minister;
  Scrawny Person......................... Philip Goodwin
Fence; Hussein; Bo'sun ....Gregg Daniel
Anitra; Dew Drops...........................Adina Porter
Begriffenfeldt; Cook....................... Peter Von Berg
Asylum Guards .... Ken Festa, Paul Kandel,
                                        Thomas Schall
Ship's Watch................................... Tim Murray
Moaning Wind.................................Nancy Wolfe

Horse Cave, Ky.: Horse Cave Theater

(Director, Warren Hammack)

THE AWAKENING. By Sallie Bingham. July 14, 1988.

Houston: Alley Theater

(Artistic director, Gregory Boyd)

THE MERRY WIVES OF WINDSOR, TEXAS (A Western with music, from Shakespeare). Conceived and adapted by John L. Haber; music and lyrics by Tommy Thompson, Jack Herrick, Bland Simpson and Jim Wann. December 1, 1988. Director, Thomas Bullard; musical director, Jack Herrick; musical staging, Marcia Milgrom Dodge; scenery, Charles S. Kading; lighting, John E. Ore; costumes, Donna Kress; sound, Daniel Van Pelt.

Colonel John Falstaff, a Confederate War
   Veteran......................................Paul C. Thomas
His Band of Renegades:
   Capt. Pistol....................................Jack Herrick
   Corp. Nym...................................Clay Buckner
   Pvt. Bardolph.......................Tommy Thompson
   Robin...Chris Frank
Master Fenton ....John Foley
Windsor, Texas:
   Master George Page ....Jim McQueen
   Mistress Margaret Page......................Beth Dixon
   Miss Anne Page............................ Susan Welby
   Master Frank Ford ....Brandon Smith
   Mistress Alice Ford.........................Donna Davis
   Lucas ....Jim Jorgensen

Chester .... Greg Schrader
Preacher Hugh Evans................... Robert Graham
Robert Shallow ....Timothy Arrington
Master Abraham Slender....................Jeff Bennett
Peter Simple.........................Jonathan Fishman
Dr. Caius ....Charles Sanders
Mistress Quickly .... Bonnie Gallup
John Rugby................................... Tom Santos
Host...James Black
Townspeople: Don Arthur, Jill Brennan, Lisa McEwen, Mary Ryan.

HEAVEN'S HARD. By Jordan Budde. February 23, 1989. Director, Allen R. Belknap; scenery, Keith Belli; lighting, John E. Ore; costumes, Lauren K. Lambie; sound, Daniel Van Pelt; original music, Brian Hurley.

Bo Barton....................................Conan McCarty
Arly Barton ....Mary Doyle
Betty Barton ....Nora Chester
Cody Barton ....Calista Flockhart
   Time: The present. Place: A small town in East Texas. One intermission.

ALLEY THEATER—*In foreground,* Paul C. Thomas as Falstaff and Beth Dixon as Mistress Page in *The Merry Wives of Windor, Texas*

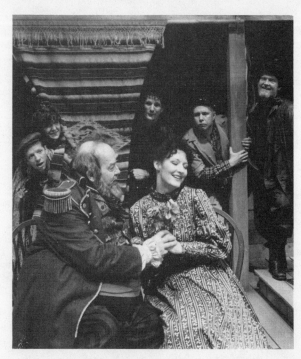

Kansas City, Mo.: Missouri Repertory Theater

(Artistic director, George Keathley)

Second Stage (Staged Readings):

THE SWEET BY AND BY. By Frank Higgins. January 12, 1989. Director, George Keathley. With Rebecca Taylor, Sarah Lahey, Nora Denney, Barbara Houston, Jeffrey Guyton, William Murphy, Scott Schwemmer.

FLORIDA CRACKERS. By William S. Leavengood. February 14, 1989. Director, John Bishop. With Andy Sherman, Scott Rymer, Scott Cordes, Sarah Peacock, Kenneth M. Boehr, Cyndi Coyne, Don Richard.

La Jolla, Calif.: La Jolla Playhouse

(Artistic director, Des McAnuff; managing director, Alan Lezey)

TWO ROOMS. By Lee Blessing. June 26, 1988. Director, Des McAnuff; scenery, Marjorie Bradley Kellogg; costumes, Susan Hilferty; lighting, Peter A. Kaczorowski; music and sound, Michael S. Roth.
    With Amanda Plummer, Brent Jennings, Jo Henderson, Jon De Vries.

80 DAYS (musical). Book by Snoo Wilson; music and lyrics by Ray Davies. August 28, 1988. Director, Des McAnuff; scenery, Douglas W. Schmidt; costumes, Susan Hilferty; lighting, David F. Segal; sound, John Kilgore; musical supervision, Danny Troob; musical direction, Jonny Bowden;

orchestrations, Robby Merkin; vocal arrangements, Danny Troob, Jonny Bowden; incidental music, Ada Janik.
    With Brooks Almy, Don Amendolia, Matthew Eaton Bennett, Stephen Bogardus, Yamil Borges, Jay Garner, Randy Graff, Ernest Harada, Scott Harlan, Paul Kandel, Timothy Landfield, Scotch Ellis Loring, Deborah Nichimura, Lannyl Stephens, Cynthia Vance, Matthew Wright, Risa Benson, Kevin Connell, Karen Gedissman, Mindy Hull, Sylvia MacCalla, Jim Morlino, Andrew Weems, Christopher Zelno.

Lancaster, Pa.: Fulton Opera House

(Executive director, Deidre W. Jacobson; artistic director, Kathleen A. Collins)

THE MULE AND THE MILKY WAY. By Susan Kander. February 9, 1989. Director, Carol M. Tanzman; scenery, Robert Klingelhoefer; lighting, Bill Simmons; costumes, Beth Dunkelberger.
Manda......................................Gabrielle Carteris
Sal...Jo Twiss

Mac ....Frank Hankey
Louis ....Steve Harper
Bill...Carleton Carpenter
    Time: Early May through early July. Place: A family farm in Iowa. One intermission.

Lansing, Mich.: BoarsHead: Michigan Public Theater

(Artistic director, John Peakes)

SISTERS. By Andrew Jones. October 21, 1988. Director, Judith L. Gentry; designer, Kyle Euckert; lighting and sound, James E. Peters; costumes, Kate Hudson.
Dorothy Gottfried...........................Rebecca Borter
Annabelle Schneider........................Carmen Decker
Otto John Gottfried.............................John Peakes
Ben Pike...Kyle Euckert
Herman Galt...................................Buck Schirner

Place: Sierra Shadows Estates Mobile Home Park in a small, central California city. One intermission.

Winterfare '89. New Play Festival.
January 26–March 5, 1989:

THEATER TRIP. By Jules Tasca. Director, Suann Pollock; designer, Kyle Euckert; properties designer, Louise Phetteplace; lighting and sound, James E. Peters; costumes, Kate Hudson.

Man..Buck Schirner
Woman ....Barbara Garren
Author ....Kyle Euckert
   One intermission.

SWEET-TALKER. By Larry Atlas. Director, Kent R. Brown; production designer, Kyle Euckert; properties designer, Louise Phetteplace; lighting and sound, James E. Peters; costumes, Cathi Jones.
Dan ....Robert Kurcz
John ....Michael Page
Barbara....................................Laural Merlington
Jean ....Evelyn Orbach

Staged Readings:

JOE MOMMA. By Ron Mark. Director, John Peakes.
MOON SHADOW. By Richard Hellesen. Director, Jonathan Gillespie.
BAR STORIES. By Nancy Minckler. Director, Jonathan Gillespie.
AND THE HOME OF THE BRAVE. By Rodney Vaccaro. Director, Jonathan Gillespie.

Los Angeles: The Colony Studio Theater

(Executive directors, Mark and Kathryn Fuller)

GENERATIONS. By Dennis Clontz. February 4, 1989. Director, Robert O'Reilly; scenery, J. Downing; lighting, Matthew O'Donnell.
Joseph...J. Downing
Lilith.......................................Kristina Coggins
Aron.......................................Richard Lineback
Joshua...Russ Marin
Judith..Judith Heinz
Rachel..Kathryn Fuller
   Time: The present. Place: Houser family cabin in the Oregon mountains. One intermission. (An ATCA selection; see introduction to this section.)

Los Angeles: Los Angeles Theater Center

(Artistic producing director, Bill Bushnell)

KINGFISH. By Marlane Meyer. September 2, 1988. Director, David Schweizer; scenery, Douglas D. Smith; lighting, Marianne Schneller; costumes, Susan Nininger; sound, Jon Gottlieb; music, Steve Moshier.
Wylie... Buck Henry
Kingfish...Philip Littell
Hal...Merritt Butrick
Finney ....Sam Anderson
Edward; Mack............................Tony Abatemarco
Wanda....................................Jacque Lynn Colton
   One intermission.

THE MODEL APARTMENT. By Donald Margulies. November 4, 1989. Director, Robert Levitow; scenery, John Iacovelli; lighting, Liz Stillwell; costumes, Ann Bruice; sound, Jon Gottlieb.
Lola...Erica Yohn
Max...Milton Selzer
Debby; Deborah..............................Chloe Webb
Neil..Zero Hubbard
   Time: The present. Place: The model apartment in a condominium development in Florida.

STONE WEDDING. By Milcha Sanchez-Scott. November 23, 1988. Director, Jose Luis Valenzuela; scenery, Gronk; lighting, Margaret Anne Dunn; costumes, David Velasquez; sound, Jon Gottlieb; music, Marcos Loya.
Daniel..E. J. Castillo
Tree ....Evelina Fernandez
Huitzilopochtli................................ Marcos Loya
Father Stephan.................................Julio Medina
Lorenza...Angela Moya
Sister Mary Katherine......................Susan Powell
Pete .... Marco Rodriquez
Jr.; Rick .... Valente Rodriguez
Yvonne..Lupe Ontiveros
   One intermission.

STARS IN THE MORNING SKY. By Alexander Galin; translated by Elise Thoron. December 9, 1988. Director, Bill Bushnell; scenery and lighting, Douglas D. Smith; costumes, Marianne Elliott; sound, Jon Gottlieb.
Lora...Nora Heflin
Valentina ....Madge Sinclair
Anna...................................... Deirdre O'Connell
Alexander..............................Gregory Wagrowski
Nikolai...Robert Beltran
Maria .... Neith Hunter
Klara...Sharon Barr

Time: The Olympics, summer, 1980. Place: A village, 101 kilometers outside of Moscow. One intermission.

DEMON WINE. By Thomas Babe. February 3, 1989. Director, David Schwizer; scenery, Timian Alsaker; lighting, Marianne Schneller; costumes, Susan Nininger; sound, Jon Gottlieb; original music, Steve Moshier.

Jimmy	Bill Pullman
Curly	Tom Waits
Vinnie	Philip Baker Hall
Fast Mail; Smith	Jan Munroe
Mary	Carol Kane
Bill	Bud Cort
Wanda	Vanessa Marquez
Gangsters	Delbert Highlands, Kevin Symons

Place: Gotham. One intermission.

MINAMATA. By Reza Abdoh and Mira-Lani Oglesby. April 7, 1989. Director, Reza Abdoh; scenery and costumes, Timian Alsaker; lighting, Timian Alsaker and Douglas D. Smith; sound, Jon Gottlieb; choreography, Rene Olivas Gubernick.

Mack; Pregnant Woman	Tony Abatemarco
Old Woman; Dying Man's Wife	Semina DeLaurentis
Expert Witness	Tom Fitzpatrick
Bunzo's Mother; Fisherman	Karole Foreman
Mercy; Alice's Mother	Maureen Kelly
Old Woman; Dying Man's Wife	Emily Kuroda
Del; Alice's Father	Mark Christopher Lawrence
Ruth; Magician	Allyson Rice
Alice; Fisherman	Ken Roht
Lawyer; Dying Man	Mark Rosenblatt
Bunzo; Musician	Andy Taylor

Los Angeles: Mark Taper Forum

(Artistic director/producer, Gordon Davidson; managing director, Stephen J. Albert)

NOTHING SACRED. By George F. Walker; based on the novel *Fathers and Sons* by Ivan Turgenev. August 28, 1988. Director, Michael Lindsay-Hogg; scenery, Eugene Lee; lighting, Natasha Katz; costumes, Robert Blackman; original music, Nathan Birnbaum.

Bailiff	Ned Bellamy
Gregor	Douglas Roberts
Arkady	Corey Parker
Bazarov	Tom Hulce
Nikolai (Petrovich) Kirsanov	Raye Birk
Piotr	Ford Rainey
Fenichka	Mary Kohnert
Pavel (Petrovich) Kirsanov	Franklyn Seales
Sitnikov	Gregory Cooke
Anna	Margaret Gibson
Sergei	Walter Olkewicz

Ensemble: David Giella, Karl Wiedergott, John Warner Williams.

Time: Early summer, 1859. Place: Russia. One intermission.

DUTCH LANDSCAPE. By Jon Robin Baitz. January 8, 1989. Director, Gordon Davidson; scenery, Heidi Landesman; lighting, Tharon Musser; costumes, Ann Bruice; music, Rick Baitz; sound, Jon Gottlieb.

Larry Cole	Philip Reeves
Rose Asch	Penny Fuller
Alex Asch	Todd Merrill
Daniel Asch	Raphael Sbarge
Edna Tululu	Olivia Virgil Harper
Philip Asch	Stephen Joyce

Heine Van Broughe	Dakin Matthews

Time: New Year's Eve, 1977. Place: A rebuilt farmhouse perched in the Natal Hills outside Durban, South Africa. One intermission.

MAKING NOISE QUIETLY. By Robert Holman. February 10, 1989. Director, Dennis Erdman; scenery, John Iacovelli; lighting, Paulie Jenkins; costumes, Marianna Elliott; sound, Stephen Shaffer. One intermission.

Being Friends

Oliver Bell	Daniel J. O'Connor
Eric Faber	Robert Petkoff

Time: July 1944. Place: The corner of a field in Kent.

Lost

May Appleton	Jeanne Hepple
Geoffrey Church	Evan MacKenzie

Time: June 1982. Place: A terraced house in Redcar, England during the Falklands War.

Making Noise Quietly

Helene Ensslin	Elizabeth Hoffman
Alan Tadd	Christopher Grove
Sam	Chris Demetral

Time: August 1986. Place: A wood in the Black Forest, Germany.

SANSEI. Created and performed by Hiroshima. March 12, 1989. Director, Robert Egan; scenery, Mark Wendland; lighting, Jeff Ravitz; costumes, Lydia Tanji.

D.K.	Marc Hayashi
Danny	Nelson Mashita

Johnny ....Lane Nishikawa
June...Natsuko Ohama
  One intermission.

STAND-UP TRAGEDY. By Bill Cain. May 20, 1989. Director, Ron Link; scenery, Yael Pardess; lighting, Michael Gilliam; costumes, Carol Brolaski; sound, Jon Gottlieb.

Father Ed Larkin .... Vaughn Armstrong
Marco Ruiz....................................Anthony Barrile
Freddy...Marcus Chong
Tom Griffin ....Jack Coleman
Luis...Marvin Columbus
Bob Kenter.....................................John C. Cooke
Lee Cortez ....Michael DeLorenzo
Pierce Brennan................................... Dan Gerrity
Henry Fernandez....................................Ray Oriel
Carlos Cruz...................................Lance Slaughter
  Time: 1980s. Place: A small Catholic school for Hispanic boys on New York's Lower East Side. One intermission.

Taper, Too:

THE DAY YOU'LL LOVE ME. By Jose Ignacio Cabrujas; translated by Eduardo Machado. January 6, 1989. Director, Lillian Garrett; scenery, Deborah Raymond, Dorian Vernacchio; lighting, Liz Stillwell; costumes, Susan Denison Geller; sound, Philip G. Allen; dance sequence, Gary Mascaro.

Maria Luisa..................................Wanda De Jesus
Pio ....Miguel Sandoval
Elvira...Rose Portillo
Matilde...Maritza Rivera
Placido .... Marc Tubert
Le Pera...Geno Silva
Gardel.....................................John Castellanos
  Time: 1935. Place: Caracas. One intermission.

Los Angeles: Odyssey Theater Ensemble

(Artistic director, Ron Sossi)

McCARTHY. By Jeff Goldsmith. July 9, 1988. Director, Frank Condon; scenery, Christa Bartels; lighting, Doc Ballard; costumes, Martha Ferrara; sound, Vincent Landay.

G. David Schine........................Christopher Babson
Sen. Welker; Reporter; Col. Aaron Coleman;
  Francis Carr; Others...................... Don Boughton
Sen. Benton; William Mandell;
  Others ....Stephen Bradley
Sen. Joseph McCarthy .... Victor Brandt
Army Secretary Stevens; Sen. Hickenlooper;
  Republican Senators; Others..............Jack Bridges
Sen. Hennings; Sen. Jackson, Convention
  Announcer; Others....................Christopher Carroll
Sen. Green; Joseph Welch;
  Others ....C. Thomas Cunliffe
Sen. Lodge; Salt Lake City Commentator;
  Reporter; Others............................Scot Douglas
Sen. Lucas; Maj. Irving Peress; Others.. Brian Dunne
Roy M. Cohn...............................Robert Fieldsteel
Sen. Flanders; President of the Senate;
  Others .... Jack Frankel
Bobby Kennedy; Reporter; Others...........Steve Holt
Reporter; Announcers; News Room Director;
  Others .... Miles Mason
Sen. Mundt; Republican Official;
  Others ....Thomas Murphy
Sen. Millard Tydings; Brig. Gen. Ralph Zwicker;
  Others ....Peter Henry Schroeder
Jean Kerr .... Catherine Theobald

Time: 1950–1954. Place: United States of America. One intermission.

SPRING AWAKENING. By Frank Wedekind; translated by Rick Foster. January 1, 1989. Director, Michael Arabian; scenery, Don Llewellyn, Saeed Jedjazi; lighting, Marianne Schneller; costumes, Betty Berberian; sound, Steve Barr; mask design, Lisa Cooperman.

Thea.. Nell Buttolph
Herr Gabor; Principal Sunprick ....Michael Covert
Ernst Robel; Diethelm.......................Clay Crosby
Frau Bergmann; Hungergut;
  Dr. Cutitoff .... Rebecca Donner
Martha.. Sala Iwamatsu
Hans Rilow ....Randy Kaplan
Lammermeier; Helmuth;
  Gorillagrease ....Stephan Klein
Gerhardt; Pudgycudgel ....Sam Loewenberg
Ilse ....Lara Lyon
Moritz Stiefel ....Jon Mathews
Masked Man; Bonebreak ....Jillian McWhirter
George Zirschnitz; Flypaper;
  Gaston...............................Alejandro Membreno
Wendla Bergmann...............................Lycia Naff
Otto; Pastor Baldgut............................Tony Patin
Frau Gabor ....Julie Pop
Herr Stiefel; Dr. Fizzwater;
  Slitherquick .... Ian Romeyn
Ina Meuller.............................. Catherine Selfridge

ON LOS ANGELES STAGES—*Above,* Orson Bean and Craig Zehms in the musical *Symmes's Hole* by Randy Dreyfus at Odyssey Theater Ensemble; *below,* Ray Oriel, Lance Slaughter, Michael DeLorenzo (*obscured*), John C. Cooke, Marcus Chong, Anthony Barrile and Dan Gerrity in *Stand-Up Tragedy* by Bill Cain at Mark Taper Forum

Melchior Gabor.................................Scott Warner
Robert; Ruprecht; Tonguebeat......J. Michael Warren
Time: May through November. One intermission.

SYMMES' HOLE (musical). By Randy Dreyfus.
May 6, 1989. Director, Carol Corwen; musical
director, David Holladay; choreographer, Mark Reina;
scenery, Don Llewellyn; lighting, Doc Ballard;
costumes, Neal San Teguns.
James McBride.....................................Orson Bean

John Cleves Symmes.....................Albert Macklin
Smoot...Kevin Pariseau
Frye..Thom McCleister
Chubb...Tom Dugan
Benjamin Lockwood;
    Jeremiah N. Reynolds.....................Craig Zehms
Maryanne.......................................Lori Michael
    Time: 1812–1859. Place: America. One
intermission.

Louisville, Ky.: Actors Theater of Louisville

(Producing director, Jon Jory)

Humana Festival of New Plays.
March 1–April 8, 1989:

In the Victor Jory Theater—Scenery, Paul Owen;
lighting, Victor En Yu Tan; costumes, Michael
Krass; sound, Mark Hendren.
THE BUG. By Richard Strand. Director, Jules Aaron.
Linda Taylor.....................................Suzanna Hay
Dennis Post.....................................Keith Reddin
Kimberly Miles...........................Julianne Moore
David Rajeski..............................Keith Langsdale
Mark Kropp....................................Mark Mineart
    Time: The present. Place: At the adminstrative
office of Jericho, Inc., a computer automation firm.
One intermission.
BLOOD ISSUE. By Harry Crews. Director, Jon
Jory.
George...............................John Dennis Johnston
Joe...George Gerdes
Ethel.....................................Nancy Niles Sexton
Pete...Bob Burrus
Mabel...Anne Pitoniak
Gaye Nell.....................................Dawn Didawick
George Jr.......................................Alan Pottinger
Buster...Danny Campbell
    Time: The present. Place: South Georgia. One
intermission.
BONE-THE-FISH. By Arthur Kopit. Director, James
Simpson.
Al...Joseph Ragno
Lou...Barbara Eda-Young
Jerry...Bruce Adler
Ramon..Richard Perez
Zalinka.......................................Julianne Moore
Tim..Steven Ramsey
Physician....................................Keith Langsdale
    Time: The present. Place: Los Angeles. One

intermission.

In the Pamela Brown Auditorium—Scenery, Paul
Owen; lighting, Ralph Dressler; costumes, Lewis D.
Rampino; sound, Mark Hendren.
AUTUMN ELEGY. By Charlene Redick. Director,
Gloria Muzio.
Manson Litchfield..........................Gwyllum Evans
Cecelia Litchfield........................Carmen Mathews
Claude Sevier..Ray Fry
Anne Marie Carrigan.........................Barbara Gulan
    One intermission.
STAINED GLASS. By William F. Buckley Jr.
Director, Steven Schachter
Count Axel Wintergrin.................William McNulty
Blackford Oakes............................William Carden
Countess Wintergrin.........................Adale O'Brien
Erika Chadinoff................................Barbara Gulan
Dean Acheson...........................Donald Symington
Allen Dulles....................................William Swan
Rufus.....................................Edward James Hyland
Roland Himmelfarb.................Mark Sawyer-Dailey
Jurgen Wagner............................James MacDonald
Andy Grossinger...................John Dennis Johnston
Alfred North Whitehead.....................George Gerdes
Bolgin...Andy Backer
    Time: Autumn, 1952. Place: A village in West
Germany. One intermission.

Staged Reading:

INCIDENT AT SAN BAJO. By Brad Korbesmeyer.
April 1, 1989. Director, Frazier W. Marsh. With
John Dennis Johnston, Mary Boucher, Anne
Pitoniak, Ed Hyland, Joanne Manley, Jonathan Fried,
George Gerdes.

Lowell, Mass.: Merrimack Repertory Theater

(Producing director, Daniel L. Schay)

TO FORGIVE, DIVINE. By Jack Neary. February 6, 1989. Director, Jack Neary; scenery, Leslie Taylor; costumes, Jane Alois Stein; lighting, John Ambrosone.
Margaret Crowley...........................Jennifer Hugus

Milly Mullin................................Betty Lee Bogue
Jerry Dolan..Sam Rush
Katie Cachenko...............................Josie McElroy
Ralph Cachenko.....................Matthew Kimbrough
Two intermissions.

Malvern, Pa.: The People's Light and Theater Company

(Producing director, Danny Fruchter)

ZIG ZAG ZELDA. By Drury Pifer. May, 1989. Director, Drury Pifer; scenery and lighting, James F. Pyne Jr.; costumes, P. Chelsea Harriman; sound, Drury Pifer.
Victor; Scott .... Peter DeLaurier
Brenda; Zelda ....Ceal Phelan

THE TEMPTATION OF MADDIE GRAHAM. By Phyllis Purscell. May, 1989. Director, Joan Vail Thorne; scenery and lighting, James F. Pyne Jr.;

costumes, P. Chelsea Harriman; sound, Charles T. Brastow.
Maddie Graham ....Joan Stanley
Director; Roommate; Waiter; Doctor;
  Agent; Frank; Pursesnatcher.................Tom Teti
Sarah Turner.......................................Dody Fogel
Evie Watson......................................Carla Belver
Time: The present. Place: New York City. One intermission.

Memphis: Playhouse on the Square

(Executive director, Jackie Nichols; artistic director, Ken Zimmerman)

REMEMBERING THE FUTURE. By Larry Gray. February 16, 1989. Director, Anthony Isbell; scenery, Michael J. Dempsey; lighting, Andrea C. Hoffman; costumes, Curtis C.
Carmen ....Juliene B. Burgess

Russ ....S. A. Weakley
Time: Three years ago and the present. Place: Carmen's mother's house, Louisiana. One intermission.

Millburn, N.J.: Paper Mill Playhouse

(Executive producer, Angelo del Rossi)

BEYOND A REASONABLE DOUBT. By Nathan Mayer. February 15, 1989. Director, Thomas Gruenewald; scenery, Michael Anania; lighting, Marilyn Rennagel; costumes, Alice Hughes; sound, David R. Paterson.
Kenneth Hayes....................................David Groh
Ruth Ballard................................Karen Valentine
Jail Guard ....Richard Pruitt
Time: An afternoon in July. One intermission.

Laboratory Production:

RHYTHM RANCH: A B-WESTERN MUSICAL. Book and lyrics, Hal Hackady; music, Fred Stark. February 27, 1989. Director and choreographer,

Pamela Hunt; musical director, Ted Kociolek; scenery, Michael Anania; lighting, Valerie Lau-Kee; costumes, Alice Hughes.
Sam Graybeal ....Steven F. Hall
Babe Blandish .... Donna Kane
Cactus.....................................Charles C. Welch
Utah; Natchez ....Timmy Fauvell
Lucy ....Kaye Ballard
Dixie...Ron Bohmer
Brandy..Diana Castle
Tulsa Del Rio.......................................Ken Land
Tumbleweeds.............Patti Allison, Dorie Herndon, Denise Nolin
Joey Blandish...................................Buddy Smith

Staged Readings:

TIES THAT BIND. By Rob Melnyk. January 20, 1989. Director, Jane Dentinger.

THE LAND OF LITTLE HORSES. By Rebecca Gilman. March 6, 1989. Director, Jane Dentinger.

ARTHUR, THE MUSICAL. Book and lyrics, David Crane and Marta Kauffman; music, Michael Skloff. April 17, 1989. Director, Richard Maltby Jr.

Milwaukee: Milwaukee Repertory Theater

(Artistic director, John Dillon; managing director, Sara O'Connor)

PRECIOUS MEMORIES. By Romulus Linney. October 23, 1988. Director, John Dillon; scenery, Loy Arcenas; lighting, Allen Lee Hughes; costumes, John Carver Sullivan; musical director, Edward Morgan.

Elmer	James Pickering
Annie	Amy Malloy
Judy	Catherine Lynn Davis
Benjamin Pitman	Tom McDermott
Barbara	Rose Pickering
Avery	Norman Moses
Leena	Marie Mathay
Shelby	Mark Corkins
Crutch Holston	Richard Halverson
Oats Pyatt	Jason Fitz-Gerald

Time: 1921. Place: Maynard, N.C., a small mill town in the foothills of the Appalachian mountains.

AND WHAT OF THE NIGHT? By Maria Irene Fornes. March 4, 1989. Director, Maria Irene Fornes; scenery, John Story; lighting, LeRoy Stoner; costumes, Cecilia Mason.

Charlie

Nadine	Marilyn Frank
Charlie	Steven J. Gefroh
Pete	Daniel Mooney
Leah	Marie Mathay
Rainbow	Kelly Maurer
Birdie	Catherine Lynn Davis
Joe	Steven Folstein

Panhandlers: Nomi Bence, Larry Dean Birkett, Terrance P. Flynn, Steven Folstein, Cynthia Hewett, Heather L. Kendall, Amy Malloy, Joan Rater, Holly Smith

Time: 1958. Place: A place that is economically depressed.

Lust

Ray	Daniel Mooney
Joseph	Kenneth Albers
Helena	Marie Mathay
Jim; Boy	Larry Dean Birkett
She; Birdie	Catherine Lynn Davis
Lorraine	Kelly Maurer
Wang	Steven J. Gefroh
Girl	Amy Malloy
Wing	Marilyn Frank
Crows	Steven Folstein, Terrance P. Flynn

Time: 1978–1989. Place: In a major city.

Springtime

Greta	Catherine Lynn Davis
Rainbow	Kelly Maurer
Ray	Daniel Mooney

Time: Spring of 1978. Place: The courtyard of a mental institution and Rainbow's bedroom.

Hunger

Charlie	Kenneth Albers
Birdie	Catherine Lynn Davis
Ray	Daniel Mooney
Reba	Marilyn Frank
Angel	Thomas Van Voorhees

Time: 1988. Place: A warehouse in a major city.

Minneapolis: The Cricket Theater

(Artistic director, William Partlan)

THE DOWNSIDE. By Richard Dresser. September 14, 1988. Director, William Partlan; scenery and costumes, Vera Mednikov; lighting, Tina Charney; composer and sound design, Mark Bloom.

Roxanne	Cheryl Ronning
Diane	Sally Wingert
Jeff	Christopher Bloch
Ben	Bill Schoppert
Alan	Richard Erickson
Voice of Dave	Dave Moore
Carl	Peter Moore
Stan	Kurt Schweickhardt
Gary	Allan Hickle-Edwards

Time: A month in December and January. Place: The marketing department of Mark & Maxwell, a pharmaceutical company in New Jersey. Two intermissions. (An ATCA selection; see introduction to this section.)

DIAMOND CUT DIAMOND. By Jeff Wanshel. March 15, 1989. Director, William Partlan; scenery, G. W. Mercier; lighting, Tina Charney; costumes, Lynn Farrington; original music, James Conely.

With David Fox-Brenton, Mark Benninghofen, Richard Anson, Shirley Venard, Bernadette Sullivan, Sally Wingert, Craig Benson, Richard Long, Fred

Major, Terry Edward Moore.

ALL GOD'S DANGERS. By Theodore Rosengarten, Michael Hadley and Jennifer Hadley. May 31, 1989. Director, William Partlan; scenery, Skip Mercier; lighting, Tina Charney.

Nate Shaw..................................... Cleavon Little
    Place: Rural Alabama.

Minneapolis: Tyrone Guthrie Theater

(Artistic director, Garland Wright)

FRANKENSTEIN—PLAYING WITH FIRE. By Barbara Field; adapted from the novel by Mary Shelley. July 8, 1988. Director, Michael Maggio; scenery, John Arnone; costumes, Jack Edwards; lighting, Marcus Dillard; sound, John Calder.
Frankenstein................................ Stephen Pelinski
The Creature................................ Peter Syvertsen
Victor .... Curzon Dobell
Adam.......................................John Carroll Lynch
Elizabeth .... Olivia Birkelund
Prof. Krempe.................................. Michael Tezla
    One intermission.

PRAVDA. By Howard Brenton and David Hare. January 13, 1989. Director, Robert Falls; scenery and props, John Arnone; costumes, Jane Greenwood; lighting, James F. Ingalls; composer and sound designer, Rob Milburn; fight coordinator, Michael Tezla.
Andrew May..........................Michael Countryman
Rebecca Foley .... Amy Morton
Harry Morrison; Compositor.............. Edgar Meyer
Hamish McLennan; Hannon Spot.......... Alan Wilder
Bill Smiley....................................Peter Thoemke
Moira Patterson .... Brenda Wehle
Sir Stamford Foley; Bingo Winner .... Richard Dix
Youth Opportunities Worker .... Rana Haugen

Lambert LeRoux .... Daniel Davis
Donna Leroux; Cindy........................ Sherri Bustad
Michael Quince....................... Richard S. Iglewski
Eaton Sylvester................................ Tim Hopper
Dennis Payne; Ian Ape-Warden....John Carroll Lynch
Elliot Fruit-Norton ....Richard Ooms
Waiter ....Jerry Newhouse
Reporter.......................................Nathaniel Fuller
Bishop of Putney..............................John Lewin
Lord Silk ....Michael Tezla
Cliveden Whicker-Baskett.....................Paul Drake
Mac Wellington; Doug Fenton.......Stephen Yoakum
Larry Punt.......................................Tom Fervoy
Jack Bond....................................John Bottoms
Leander Scroop.................David Anthony Brinkley
Cartoonist..Bruce Bohne
Princess Jill................................Claudia Wilkens
Bert...Emil Herrera
    Newsvendors: Mark Benninghofen, Keith Joachim, Emil Herrera. Journalists, Maintenance Engineers, Barmaids, Dogtrack Derelicts, Bingo Girls: Timothy J. Hasenstein, Mark Kramschuster, Beth Lisowski, Don Martin, Pete Renner, Heather Sampon, Sam Selvaggio, Peter Skyervold, John Townsend, Chas. Truog, Bob Werner, Daniel Wolfe.
    One intermission.

Montclair, N.J.: Whole Theater

(Producing artistic director, Olympia Dukakis)

BETTER LIVING. By George F. Walker. November 1, 1988. Director, Max Mayer; scenery, Lewis Folden; lighting, Rachel Budin; costumes, Donna Marie Larsen.
Jack..Rick Weatherwax
Junior ....Ralph Marrero
Gail...Dorrie Joiner
Nora .... Olympia Dukakis
Mary Ann.................................Alexandra Gersten

Elizabeth.....................................Jane Kaczmarek
Tom..Louis Zorich
    Place: Working class area of a big city. One intermission.

DUBLINERS. Adapted from James Joyce by Dear Knows Company. January 13, 1939. Director, Paul Walker; score, Leslie Steinweiss.

GEORGE STREET PLAYHOUSE—Audra Lindley and
James Whitmore in a scene from *The Eighties* by Tom Cole

SPARE PARTS. By Elizabeth Page. February 7,
1989. Director, Susan Einhorn; scenery, Ursula
Belden; lighting, Ann Wrightson; costumes, David
Murin; sound, Phil Lee.

Henry...Don R. McManus
Lois..Kristin Griffith
Jax ....Randy Danson
Selma ....Margo Skinner
Perry...Mark Shannon

Time: The present. Place: Hartford and New Haven,
Conn. One intermission.

FRATERNITY. By Jeff Stetson. March 14, 1989.

Director, Clinton Turner Davis; scenery, Jack
Chandler; lighting, William H. Grant III; costumes,
Alvin B. Perry.

Rev. Benjamin Franklin Wilcox............Ray Aranha
Lawrence "Turk" Maddox ...Helmar Augustus Cooper
Preston Greystone...........................Will Carpenter
Turner Greystone...............................Nick Smith
Charles Lincoln...............................Lloyd Hollar
Paul Stanton...................................Basil Wallace
Brandon Carrington..........................Eric A. Payne

Time: The present. Place: A city in the South. One
intermission.

New Brunswick, N.J.: Crossroads Theater Company

(Producing artistic director, Rick Khan)

TO GLEAM IT AROUND, TO SHOW MY SHINE.
By Bonnie Lee Moss Rattner. October 1, 1988.
Director, Rick Khan; scenery, Dan Proett; lighting,
Shirley Prendergast; costumes, Judy Dearing; sound,
Rob Gorton.

Janie May Crawford......................Denise Nicholas
Nanny Crawford...........................Minnie Gentry
Phoeby Watson.............................Novella Nelson
Joe Starks..Adam Wade

Vergible Woods..............................Kevin Jackson
Sam Watson; Ed Dockery..............Noble Lee Lester
Hezekiah; Lias .... Marvin Jefferson
Amos Hicks;
Sop-De-Bottom ....Helmar Augustus Cooper
Daisy Blunt; Poony ....Louise Gorham
Lige Moss; Bootyny; Johnny Taylor....Cedric Turner
Lulu Moss; Nunky ....Myla Churchill

Time: Early 1900s. Place: In Eatonville, Fla., the first incorporated all-colored town. One intermission.

THE MOJO AND THE SAYSO. By Aishah Rahman. November 12, 1988. Director, George Ferencz; scenery, Bill Stabile; lighting, Blu; costumes, Sally J. Lesser, sound, Rob Gorton.

Awilda ....Stephanie Berry
Blood.. Victor Mack
Acts...Matthew Idason
Pastor ....Gregory Daniel

Time: Now, Sunday. Place: The living room of the Benjamins' home. One intermission.

SPOOKS. By Don Evans. April 29, 1989. Director, Seret Scott; scenery, Dan Proett; lighting, William H. Grant III; costumes, Beth Ribblett; sound, Rob Gorton.

Howard ....Reuben Green
Karen ....Myra Taylor
Son...Lex Monson
Lucinda..Lizan Mitchell
The Ghost......................................W.C. Warner

Time: The present. Place: Virginia. One intermission.

New Brunswick, N.J.: George Street Playhouse

(Producing director, Gregory S. Hurst)

TALES OF TINSELTOWN (musical). Book and lyrics by Michael Colby; music by Paul Katz. January 6, 1989. Director, Larry Carpenter; musical direction, Steve Alper; choreographer, Baayork Lee; orchestrations, Larry Hochman; scenery, Loren Sherman; lighting, Marcia Madeira; costumes, Lindsay W. Davis; sound, Jim Landis.

Adele DeRale.................................Laura Kenyon
Ellie Ash..............................Patricia Ben Peterson
Elmo Green.....................................Evan Pappas
Norman G. Neinshtein ....Robert Dorfman
Lulu Beauveen....................................Janice Lynde
Tony Toscanini.................................Nat Chandler
Betha Powell...............................Kathryn Kendall
Danny Burke ....Mark Bove

Time: 1935. Place: Hollywood. The action flashes forward and back through the years 1932–1936. One intermission.

THE EIGHTIES. By Tom Cole. February 8, 1989. Director, Lamont Johnson; scenery, Atkin Pace; lighting, Donald Holder; costumes, Barbara Forbes.

He ....James Whitmore
She...Audra Lindley

Place: A condominium kitchen. One intermission.

Staged Readings:

PENDRAGON. By Laurie Hutzler. February 28, 1989. Director, Wendy Liscow. With Dion Graham, Cheryl Hulteen, Matt Walton, Ellen Hulkower, Bob Bender, Jeff Hasler.

THE BEST MAN. By Doug McGrath. May 11, 1989. Director, Wendy Liscow. With Brian Ready, Lelan Orser, Melissa Christopher, Steve Podenz, Will Osborne, Virginia Robinson, Heidi Carty.

REMEMBER THE ALIMONY. By Stephen Young. June 7, 1989. Director, Susan Kerner. With Ron Siebert, Terri Cavanaugh, Eleanor Reissa, Susan Greenhill.

New Haven, Conn.: Long Wharf Theater

(Artistic director, Arvin Brown; executive director, M. Edgar Rosenblum)

LOVE LETTERS. By A. R. Gurney. November 3, 1988. Director, John Tillinger; lighting, Judy Rasmuson.

Andrew Makepeace Ladd III ....John Rubinstein
Melissa Gardner ....Joanna Gleason

One intermission.

SOME SWEET DAY. By Nancy Fales Garrett. March 14, 1989. Director, Seret Scott; scenery, Michael H. Yeargan; lighting, Pat Collins; costumes, David Murin.

Vernard Morgan Jr. ....Terry Alexander
Ben Morgan....................................Damien Leake
Raymond Morgan.............................Herb Lovelle
Vernard Morgan Sr............................ Mike Hodge
Shug...Yvette Hawkins
Elizabeth Morgan McKee................. Rosanna Carter
Annie Mae Morgan......................Cynthia Belgrave
Elijah Morgan...................................Clebert Ford
Judy Miller.....................................Cynthia Mace
Mr. Abercrombie...........................Jack R. Marks

Place: The Morgan residence, Perry, S.C. Two intermissions.

REBEL ARMIES DEEP INTO CHAD. By Mark
Lee. April 7, 1989. Director, John Tillinger; scenery,
John Lee Beatty; lighting, Marc B. Weiss; costumes,
Candice Donnelly.
Dove..Alan Scarfe
Neal...Joe Urla
Mary.................................Pamela Tucker-White
Christina..Gail Grate
  Time: Early 1980s. Place: A rented cottage north
of Nairobi, Kenya. One intermission.

Workshop Productions:
FORGIVING TYPHOID MARY. By Mark St.
Germain. January 3, 1989.
SONGS FROM DISTANT LANDS. By Corinne
Jacker. January 24, 1989.
MINOR DEMONS by Bruce Graham. February 14,
1989.
A DANCE LESSON by David Wiltse. March 7,
1989.

New Haven, Conn.: Yale Repertory Theater

(Artistic director, Lloyd Richards)

THE WARRIOR ANT (musical). Book by Lee
Breuer; music by Bob Telson; lyrics by Lee Breuer.
October 10, 1988. Director, Lee Breuer.

MOON OVER MIAMI. By John Guare. February
22, 1989. Director, Andrei Belgrader; scenery, Judy
Gailen; costumes, Candice Donnelly; lighting, Scott
Zielinski; sound, G. Thomas Clark, Ann Johnson;
musical direction, incidental music and arrangements,
Lawrence Yurman; words and music, John Guare;
music for "Osvaldo's Song," Galt MacDermot.
  With Oliver Platt, Susan Kellermann, Richard
Spore, Stanley Tucci, Frances Barney, Dana
Morosini, Jacquelyn Mari Roberts, Ali Sharaf, Mary
Walden, Lewis J. Stadlen, Laurel Cronin, Lawrence
Yurman, Sam Stoneburner, Walker Jones, Roger
Bechtel, Dennis Reid, Richard Riehle, Tony
Shalhoub, Robert Russell, Mary Mara, Jim
MacLaren, Julie Hagerty, John R. Conway, Martin
Blanco, Robin Selfridge, Ann Whitney.

COBB. By Lee Blessing. March 24, 1989. Director,
Lloyd Richards; scenery, Rob Greenberg; costumes,
Joel O. Taylor; lighting, Ashley York Kennedy;
sound, G. Thomas Clark; incidental music by Scott
Davenport Richards.
Mr. Cobb.......................................Josef Sommer
The Peach ....James E. Reynolds
Ty ....Chris Cooper
Oscar Charleston ....Delroy Lindo
  No intermission.

Winterfest 9 (Jan. 10–Feb. 4, 1989):
PHAEDRA AND HIPPOLYTUS. By Elizabeth
Egloff. Director, Christopher Grabowski.
THE BEACH. By Anthony Giardina. Director, Amy
Saltz.
STARTING MONDAY. By Anne Commire.
Director, Peter Mark Schifter.
INTERROGATING THE NUDE. By Doug Wright.
Director, Gitta Honegger.

Norfolk, Va.: Virginia Stage Company

(Artistic director, Charles Towers; managing director, Dan Martin)

FOSSEY. By Lois Meredith. January 3, 1989.
Director, Pamela Berlin; scenery, Michael Ganio;
lighting, Judy Rasmuson; costumes, Candice Cain;
composer and sound, Dary John Mizelle.

Dian Fossey ....Lois Meredith
  Time: December 27, 1985. Place: Dian Fossey's
cabin, Karisoke Research Center in the Virunga
Mountains, Rwanda, Africa. One intermission.

Omaha: The Omaha Magic Theater

(Artistic director, Jo Ann Schmidman)

Play Event Series (Staged Readings):
MY FOETUS LIVED ON AMBOY STREET. By
Ronald Tavel. October 28, 1988.
ALARMS. By Susan Yankowitz. November 11,
1988.

THREE FRONT. By Rochelle Owens. November
25, 1988.
THE HEART THAT EATS ITSELF. By Rosalyn
Drexler. December 9, 1988.

Pasadena: The Pasadena Playhouse

(Artistic director, Susan Dietz; managing director, Lars Hansen)

ACCOMPLICE. By Rupert Holmes. February 5, 1989. Director, Art Wolff; scenery, David Jenkins; lighting, Martin Aronstein; costumes, Kathleen Detoro; sound, Jon Gottlieb.

With Michael McKean, Natalia Nogulich, Harry Shearer, Pamela Brull.

Time: Early 1970's. Place: The moorland cottage of Derek and Janet Taylor and a suite at the Connaught Hotel. One intermission.

Discovery Series I (Staged Readings):

NOBLE ADJUSTMENT. Written and directed by D. L. Coburn. July 11, 1988. With Joe Spano, Ian Patrick Williams, Matt Landers, Audra Lindley, Randee Heller, Eloise Coopersmith.

MICHAEL BYERS INSIGHT OUT (one-man musical). By Kristi Kane. August 22, 1988. Director, Craig Noel.

Discovery Series II (Staged Readings):

TENNESSEE JAR. By John Lewter. December 19, 1988. Director, Michael Cooper. With Kathy Bates, Dirk Blocker, Carol Hickey, Stephanie Faracy, Wil Wheaton, Michael Gough.

THE EIGHTIES. By Tom Cole. January 9, 1989. Director, Lamont Johnson. With Audra Lindley, James Whitmore.

ALFRED STIEGLITZ LOVES O'KEEFE. By Lanie Robertson. April 17, 1989. With Amanda McBroom.

AD WARS. By Vince McKewin. May 22, 1989. Director, Jenny Sullivan. With John Cypher, Teryn Jenkins, Helen Shaver, Rick Holden, Leo Rossi, Rhonda Dorton, James Komack, David Meyers.

Philadelphia: America Music Theater Festival

1,000 AIRPLANES ON THE ROOF (musical monodrama). By David Henry Hwang; music by Philip Glass. September 22, 1988. Director, Philip Glass; projections, Jerome Sirlin; lighting, Robert Wierzel; musical direction, Martin Goldray; sound, Kurt Munkacsi.

With Jody Long and Patrick O'Connell alternating performances.

BETSEY BROWN (musical). Book by Ntozake Shangé and Emily Mann; adapted by Ntozake Shangé from her novel; music by Baikida Carroll; lyrics by Ntozake Shange, Emily Mann and Baikida Carroll. March 30, 1989. Director, Emily Mann; musical staging, Edward Love; music supervision, Daryl Waters; scenery Marjorie Bradley Kellogg; costumes, Jennifer von Mayrhauser; lighting, Craig Miller; sound, Ronald F. Lorman; orchestrations, G. Harrell.

Betsy Brown	Michelle Thomas
Allard	Amir Williams
Margot	Mesha Millington
Charlie	Marc Hardy

Greer	Tim Strong
Jane	Alisa Gyse
Vida	Ann Duquesnay
Mr. Jeff	Vondie Curtis-Hall
Eugene	Sean Grant
Regina	Carol Lynn Maillard
Roscoe	Marion J. Caffey
Carrie	Kecia Lewis-Evans
Mrs. Maureen	Cookie Watkins

One intermission.

POWER FAILURE (music drama). Libretto by Rinde Eckert; score by Paul Dresher. May 4, 1989. Director, Tom O'Horgan; scenery and costumes, Michael Olich; lighting, Larry Neff; sound, Jay Cloidt.

Charles Smithson	John Duykers
Merle Townsend	Rinde Eckert
Ruth Lehmann	Stephanie Friedman
Judith Niles	Sara Ganz

One intermission.

Philadelphia: Philadelphia Drama Guild

(Producing director, Gregory Poggi)

ROCKY AND DIEGO. By Roger Cornish. April 21, 1989. Director, John Henry Davis; scenery, John Jensen; lighting, F. Mitchell Dana; costumes, Karen Roston; sound, Robert Biasetti.

McCARTER THEATER—Jerry Mayer and Kimberly King
in a scene from *Dividing the Estate* by Horton Foote

Nelson Rockefeller .... Robert Sean Leonard	Jenny Murphy................................ Amy Hoffman
Diego Rivera............................... Marco St. John	Abby Rockefeller................................Julia Meade
May Bliss.. Hannah Cox	Frida Kahlo Rivera..............................Mary Testa
Workmen.......................Brad Rickel, Mark Silence	Time: Spring of 1933. Place: In and around New
Todd ....John Carpenter	York City. One intermission.
Joel Rack.................................. Allen Fitzpatrick	

Philadelphia: Philadelphia Festival Theater for New Plays

(Artistic director, Carol Rocamora)

A PEEP INTO THE TWENTIETH CENTURY. By Christopher Davis; based on his novel. October 20, 1988. Director, James J. Christy; scenery, Philip A. Graneto; costumes, Vickie Esposito; lighting, Curt Senie; sound, Jeff Chestek.

Rev. Hannibal Show......................Jeffrey Hayenga	
Rupert Weber ....Ben Siegler	
Cpl. Kernahan .... Giovanni Moscardino	
Sgt. Fred McDade.........................Pirie MacDonald	
George Taggart .... Tom Teti	
Dr. Stephen Clark ....James McCrane	
Marcus Bush ....Tim Moyer	
Warden Hiram Buxton.................... James Schlatter	
Jack Fisch....................... Andrew William Bradley	

One intermission.

THE RABBIT FOOT. By Leslie Lee. December 1,

1988. Director, Walter Dallas; scenery, Jim Youmans; lighting, Curt Senie; costumes, Vickie Esposito; sound, Conny M. Lockwood; musical direction, Walter Dallas.

Singin' Willie Ford......................... Willie Woods	
Big Bertha Mae ....Erma Campbell	
Holly Day.......................Denise Burse-Mickelbury	
Johnny Hopper............................Ruben S. Hudson	
Berlinda .... Elain Graham	
Reggie.. Michael Beach	
Viola... Frances Foster	

Time: Summer of 1920. Place: Rural Mississippi. One intermission.

A PIECE OF MY HEART. By Shirley Lauro. March 5, 1989. Director, Walton Jones; scenery, Rosario Provenza; costumes, Barbara Bell; lighting,

Donald Holder; sound, Conny M. Lockwood.
Marylou ....D'Jamin Bartlett
Whitney ....Peggity Price
Steele...Saundra McClain
Martha ....Suzy Hunt
Sissy .... Robin Groves
Leeann ....Freda Foh Shen
Man..Tom Stechschulte
One intermission.

MOON OVER THE BREWERY. By Bruce Graham.
April 13, 1989. Director, James J. Christy; scenery,
James Wolk; costumes, Vickie Esposito; lighting,
Karl Haas; sound, Conny M. Lockwood.
Amanda Lipsky............................Eevin Hartsough

Randolph ....Jeffrey Hayenga
Warren Zimmerman ....Matthew Lorcicchio
Miriam Lipsky.................................Debra Monk
One intermission.

AMORPHOUS GEORGE. By Glen Merzer. May 4,
1989. Director, W. H. Macy; scenery, James Wolk;
costumes, Vickie Esposito; lighting, Karl Haas;
sound, Conny M. Lockwood.
Nora..Susan Woods
Vic ....Fred Sanders
Will...Jack Kenny
Sharon...Mary McCann
George................................. Michael Countryman

Philadelphia: The Philadelphia Theater Company

(Artistic director, Sara Garonzik; managing director, Ira Schlosser)

ELAINE'S DAUGHTER. By Mayo Simon. October
26, 1988. Director, Jules Aaron; scenery, Nancy
Thun; costumes, Frankie Feher; lighting, Karl Haas.
Elaine ....Marilyn Rockafellow
Beth...Jill Holden
Tom .... David Bottrell
Gus ....Herbert Rubens
Eliot.. Bill Winkler
One intermission.

Stages '88, June 14–19, 1988, Workshop
Presentations:

TEARS OF RAGE. By Doris Baizley. Director,
Harold Scott.
YESTERDAY'S HERO. By Michael Grady.
Director, Lynn M. Thompson.
CATCH! By Jason Katims. Director, Jan Silverman.

Readings:

THE RULE OF THREE'S. By Jeffrey Hatcher.
GHOST ON THE RIVER. By Ellen Byron.

Philadelphia: Walnut Studio Theater

(Executive director, Bernard Havard)

THE ARCHER'S TALE. By Esmond Knight.
February 7, 1989. Director, Toby Robertson;
lighting, De Vida Jenkins.
Archer...Kenneth Gilbert

WITH ALBERT EINSTEIN. By Lou Greenstein and
Don Auspitz. February 28, 1989. Director, Deborah

Baer Quinn; scenery, Judi Guralnick; lighting, Bob
Scheeler.
Albert Einstein................................Don Auspitz
Voice #1; Voice #4.........................Douglas Wing
Voice #2...Aldona Page
Voice #3......................................Barbara Kristal
Voice #5.......................................Renate Potjan
Voice #6......................................Lou Greenstein

Philadelphia: The Wilma Theater

(Artistic/producing directors, Jiri Zizka, Blanka Zizka)

THE CONCERT AT SAINT OVIDE FAIR. By
Antonio Buero Vallejo; translated and adapted by
Marion Peter Holt. September 27, 1988. Director,
Blanka Zizka; scenery and costumes, Hiroshi

Iwasaki; lighting, Jerold R. Forsyth; sound and
original music, Adam Wernick; projections, Jeff
Brown.
    With Mark Zeisler, Lauren Pierson, Charles

Antalosky, Michael Lewis, Robert MacCallum, Donna Browne, Michael Lee Sharp, Robert Hubbard, Douglas Wing, Michael P. Toner, Peter Wray, Charles Isdell.

INCOMMUNICADO. By Tom Dulack. February 28, 1989. Director, Blanka Zizka; scenery, Andrei Efremoff; lighting, Jerold R. Forsyth; costumes, Lara Ratnikoff; original music, Adam Wernick.

Ezra Pound.......................................David Hurst
MP.......................................Anthony Chisholm
Till...Reginal Flowers
Lawyer...Peter Wray
Doctor...David Simson
Time: Spring, summer and fall, 1945. Place: A military detention camp near Pisa, Italy. One intermission.

Princeton, N.J.: McCarter Theater

(Artistic director, Nagle Jackson; managing director, John Herochik)

SMOKE ON THE MOUNTAIN. By Constance Ray. July 21, 1988. Director, Alan Bailey.
Mervin Oglethorpe....................Kevin Chamberlin
June Sanders.................................Constance Ray
Burl Sanders...............................William Mesnik
Vera Sanders.....................................Linda Miles
Stanley Sanders...............................Dan Manning
Denise Sanders.........................Courtenay Collins
Dennis Sanders...............................Robert Olsen
    Time: 1938. Place: Mt. Pleasant, North Carolina, the home of Pleasant Pickles. One intermission.

DIVIDING THE ESTATE. By Horton Foote. March 28, 1989. Director, Jamie Brown; scenery, Jeff Modereger; lighting, Phil Monat; costumes, Pam Scofield.
Doug...............................Thomas Martell Brimm
Emily...Julie Corby
Irene.....................................Debora Jeanne Culpin
Son of Gordon...............................Edmund Davys
Lewis...Jay Doyle
Sissie...Ginger Finney
Stella...Jane Hoffman
Lucille..Annette Hunt
Mary Jo.......................................Kimberly King

Lucy...Mary Martello
Bob..Jerry Mayer
Cathleen...Thea Perkins
Mildred...Beatrice Winde
    Time: The Present. Place: Harrison, Tex. One intermission.

New Play Readings, 1988–89 (Staged Readings):
SOLITARY DANCERS. By Jan Paetrow. October 17, 1988.
ABSOLUTE SQUARE. By Susan Reinhard. October 24, 1988.
BANKRUPT DAYS. By Matt Cutugno.
A KIND OF MADNESS. By Nikki Harmon. November 21, 1988.
DESSERT AT WAFFLE HOUSE, BREAKFAST ANYTIME. By Christopher Kyle. April 3, 1989.
NATURAL PHENOMENA. By Harvey Huddleston. April 3, 1989.
MARTIAN GOTHIC. By Don Nigro. April 17, 1989.
RETURN TO THE RIVER. By Charles Dumas. May 1, 1989.

Providence, R.I.: Trinity Repertory Company

BOY GIRL BOY GIRL. By Barbara Blumenthal. May 31, 1989. Director, Neal Baron; scenery, Robert D. Soule; lighting, Colleen Kingdon; costumes, Marilyn Salvatore.

With Michael Cobb, David Kennett, Geraldine Librandi, Brian McEleney, Anne Scurria, Sarah Clossey.

Roanoke, Va.: Mill Mountain Theater

(Literary manager, Jo Weinstein; associate director, Ernest Zulia)

O. HENRY'S CHRISTMAS CAROL (musical). Book, lyrics and music by Milton Granger. December 9, 1988.

TWO BEERS AND A HOOK SHOT. By Kent R. Brown. December 14, 1988.

Fall Festival of New Works. Oct. 21–Nov. 5, 1988:

THE HILL-MATHESON AFFAIR. By Robert Clyman. Director, Mary Leigh Best; scenery and lighting, John Sailer; costumes, Monica Weinzapfel.
With Tom Honer, Jerry McMechan, Roger Mangels, Robert S. Barmettler, Elizabeth Tunstall, Ernest Zulia.

A CHRISTIAN BURIAL. By Jo Weinstein. Director, Jere Lee Hodgin.
With Hugh Hodgin, Ann Owen Pierce, Jewell Robinson, Tom Mason.

THE PROPOSAL. Written and directed by Milton Granger.
With Lenora Atkins, Jayne Levesque Vest, Debra Nichols, Tami Desiree Bick, Pamela Fiocca, Jean Harper Vernon.

COUNTDOWN. By Christopher Yavelow. Director, Milton Granger.
With Lawrence Evans, Linda Granger, Angela Case.

Rochester, N.Y.: GeVa Theater

(Producing artistic director, Howard J. Millman; managing director, William B. Duncan)

Staged Readings:

A PIECE OF MY HEART. By Shirley Lauro. September 26, 1988.

ESTABLISHED PRICE. By Dennis McIntyre. November 7, 1988.
THE AGENT. By James McClure. January 23, 1989.

Rockville Center, N.Y.: Long Island Stage

(Artistic director, Clinton J. Atkinson)

AFTERSHOCKS. By Doug Haverty. February 28, 1989. Director, Clinton J. Atkinson; scenery, Jim Youmans; lighting, John Hickey; costumes, Don Newcomb.

Daphne May Potatski......................Marilyn Chris
Olive McKay..............................Ruth Livingston
Beth White..Jane Hoppe
Time: The present. Place: A mobile home located in Valencia, Calif., just north of Hollywood. One intermission.

Sacramento: Sacramento Theater Company

(Producing director, Mark Cuddy)

AWAY. By Michael Gow. April 28, 1989. Director, Mark Cuddy; scenery, Jeff Hunt; lighting, Maurice Vercoutere; costumes, Debra Bruneaux.
Roy..David de Berry
Coral ....Jan Akers Wagner
Jim..Tim McDonough
Gwen ....Janice Fuller
Harry..Norm Armour
Vic ....Kirsten Giroux
Meg..Karen Pollard
Tom...John Plummer

St. Louis, Mo.: The Repertory Theater of St. Louis

(Artistic director, Steven Woolf; managing director, Mark D. Bernstein)

OFFSHORE SIGNALS. By Roger Cornish. December 20, 1988. Director, Edward Stern; scenery, David Potts; lighting, Peter E. Sargent; costumes, Dorothy L. Marshall.
Latino; Cordell Hull; Clive Goforth.......Alan Clarey
Schmuel ....Henry Stram
Breckenridge Long ....John MacKay
Patricia Kirk................................Susan Pellegrino

REPERTORY THEATER OF ST. LOUIS—John MacKay
and Steven Dennis in *Offshore Signals* by Roger Cornish

Robert Harris..................................Steven Dennis
Clifford Churchwright................Ronald Wendschuh
Rabbi Stephen Wise ....Peter Johl
Secretary; Mrs. Essex;
    Wren Officer.............. BettyAnn Leeseberg-Lange
Cosgrove Essex; Franklin Delano
    Roosevelt....................................Joneal Joplin
    Time: 1943. Place: In and around Washington,
D.C. One intermission.

Lab Project:

IMPASSIONED EMBRACES. By John Pielmeier.
January 27, 1989. Director, Susan Gregg.
THIN AIR: TALES FROM A REVOLUTION. By
Lynne Alvarez. March 31, 1989. Director, Susan
Gregg.

St. Paul: Actors Theater of St. Paul

(Artistic director, Michael Andrew Miner)

FOUR OUR FATHERS. By Jon Klein. November
11, 1988. Director, Michael Andrew Miner; scenery
and lighting, Nayna Ramey; costumes, Rich
Hamson.
Eddie..James Harris
Christopher.......................................John Seibert
Father Jensen.............................D. Scott Glasser
Pee Jay...Tim Dana
Harding .... Walter Stanley
Manda .... Annie Enneking
Sarah .... Terry Heck
Paxton .... David M. Kwiat
Rosalee...Norma Fire

LAST SUMMER IN CHULIMSK. By Alexander
Vampilov. April 21, 1989. Director, Valerie Fokin;
scenery, costumes and lighting, Vladimir
Makushenk, Olga Tvardovskaya.
Valentina .... Karen Samuelson
Ilya.. Sami Ali
Zina...Terry Heck
Mechetkin...................................D. Scott Glasser
Anna..Norma Fire
Afanasi...David Kwiat
Pomigalov .... Chuck Hilton
Vladimir ....Bruce Bohne
Pavel...John Seibert
    One intermission.

San Diego: Old Globe Theater

(Artistic director, Jack O'Brien)

THE COCKTAIL HOUR. By A. R. Gurney. June 2, 1988. Director, Jack O'Brien; scenery and costumes, Steven Rubin; lighting, Kent Dorsey; sound, Corey L. Fayman.

Bradley	Keene Curtis
Ann	Nancy Marchand
John	Bruce Davison
Nina	Holland Taylor

Time: Early fall in the mid-1970s. Place: A city in upstate New York. One intermission.

WHITE LINEN (musical). Book and lyrics by Stephen Metcalfe; music by Douglas Michilinda and Stephen Metcalfe. July 13, 1988. Director, Jack O'Brien; scenery, Douglas W. Schmidt; costumes, Steven Rubin; lighting, Robert Peterson; sound, Michael Holten; musical direction, Bruce K. Sevy; vocal and musical arrangements and incidental music, Bill Elliott; fight choreography, Steven Rankin.

With Dann Florek, Kenneth Marshall, Julian Gamble, John Walcutt, Thomas S. Oleniacz, Patrick T. O'Brien, Henry J. Jordan, Damon T. Bryant, Alice McMasters, David R. Conner, Kate Frank, Helen Hudson, Deena Burke, Melissa McCracken, Roxanne Petermeier, Keith Devaney, John Padilla, Matt Edwards, Joseph Hulser.

One intermission.

RUMORS. By Neil Simon. September 22, 1988. Director, Gene Saks; scenery, Tony Straiges; lighting, Tharon Musser; costumes, Joseph G. Aulisi.

Cassie Cooper	Lisa Banes
Chris Gorman	Christine Baranski
Welch	Charles Brown
Pudney	Cynthia Darlow
Ernie Cusack	Andre Gregory
Glenn Cooper	Ken Howard
Lenny Ganz	Ron Leibman
Ken Gorman	Mark Nelson
Cookie Cusack	Joyce Van Patten
Claire Ganz	Jessica Walter

Place: A house in Sneden's Landing, N.Y. One intermission.

UP IN SARATOGA. By Terrence McNally. March 9, 1989. Director, Jack O'Brien; scenery, Douglas W. Schmidt; lighting, David F. Segal; costumes, Robert Wojewodski; composer, Bob James; sound, Tony Tait.

Miss Effie Remington	Finn Carter
Mrs. Felicity Vanderpool	Dorothy Constantine
Mrs. Lucy Carter	Marietta DePrima
Mr. Noah Remington	William Duff-Griffin
Mr. Cyrus Vanderpool	Mitchell Edmonds
Mr. Frank Littlefield	Matthew Edwards
Mr. Cornelius Wethertree	Jack Fletcher
Sir Mortimer Muttonleg	Laurence Guittard
Hon. William Carter	Richard Kneeland
Muffins	Vicki Lewis
Gyp	Sterling Macer
Mrs. Olivia Alston	Lauren Mitchell
Mr. Frederick Augustus Carter	Mark Neely
Miss Virginia Vanderpool	Mary-Louise Parker
Mr. Jack Benedict	Ethan Phillips
Miss Dorothy Livingston	Laura Rearwin
Mr. Robert Sackett	Jon Tenney
Miss Lily Ogden	Mary Kay Wulf

Time: Late spring and midsummer of 1893. One intermission.

Play Discovery Program (Staged Readings):

THE BEST MAN. By Douglas McGrath.
PARADISE. By Mark Lee.
BREAKING LEGS. By Tom Dulack.
CRAZY FROM THE HEART. By Edit Villarreal.
MY LIFE A LOADED GUN. By Velina Hasu Houston.

Santa Monica, Calif.: Santa Monica Playhouse

(Artistic directors, Evelyn Rudi, Chris De Carlo)

DEAR GABBY, THE CONFESSIONS OF AN OVER-ACHIEVER. By Evelyn Rudie. June 1, 1988. Director, Chris DeCarlo; scenery, Timothy Chadwick; lighting, James Cooper; costumes, Ashley Hayes, Cheryl Moffatt.

Alex	Alex Cohen
Liz	Liz Dean
Shana	Shana Feste
Obi	Obi Ndefo
Jennifer	Jennifer Pastiloff
Chloë	Chloë
Heather	Heather Ross
Abby	Abby Shafran
Aisha	Aisha Waglé

Time: The present. Place: The rooms in Alex's head.

DOUBLE STANDER'ED (one-act plays) by Jay Randy Stander. July 8, 1988. Director, Barry Nedler; scenery, Timothy Chadwick; lighting, James Cooper; music, Steven Corn.

Urban Rock

Riley ....Gary Matanky
Neff... Matti Leshem
Place: Riley's living room on an upper floor of an urban apartment building.

Empathy

Alice..Lisa Figueroa
George ....Dalton Younger
Thelma Nexter ....Rhonda Ossipoff

Fred Nexter.....................................J. W. Fletcher
Marv Henderfarb ....Dan Perrett
Emily Henderfarb.............................Eugenia Ives
Place: George and Alice's backyard and bathroom, Saturday and Sunday.

THE PET SHOW. By Mitch Giannunzio. March 17, 1989. Director, Lawrence Osgood; scenery, Timothy Chadwick; lighting, James Cooper; sound, Lynn Yamaha.

Charlotte... Bibi Besch
John...Kenneth Tigar
Rachel......................................Barbara Whinnery
Time: November. Place: An apartment in a large American city. One intermission.

Sarasota: Asolo Performing Arts Center

(Artistic director, John Ulmer)

QUARRY. By Ronald Bazarini. March 24, 1989. Director, Garry Allan Breul; scenery, Rick Cannon; lighting, Martin Petlock, Rick Cannon; costumes, Howard Tsvi Kaplan.

Noel ....Jeff Herbst
Oliver ....David Peshek
Claudette .... Robert Patteri

Manila...Lea Floden
Warren......................................Todd C. Johnson
Hilda.. Liz Vago
Time: March, 1948. Place: In Noel's apartment/studio in the French Quarter of New Orleans. One intermission.

Seattle: A Contemporary Theater

(Artistic director, Jeff Steitzer)

A CHORUS OF DISAPPROVAL. By Alan Ayckbourn. July 14, 1988. Director, Jeff Steitzer; music, Todd Moeller; scenery, Michael Olich; costumes, Laura Crow; lighting, Rick Paulsen.

Guy Jones..............................R. Hamilton Wright
Dafydd ap Llewellyn ....John Aylward
Hannah Llewellyn ....Marianne Owen
Bridget Baines...................................Karen Meyer
Mr. Ames...................................... Todd Moeller
Enid Washbrook....................................Jo Vetter
Rebecca Huntley-Pike ....Susan Ludlow-Corzatte
Fay Hubbard.................................Linda Edmond
Ian Hubbard....................................Robert Nadir

Jarvis Huntley-Pike...............................Rick Tutor
Ted Washbrook ....Kurt Beattie
Crispin Usher ....Morgan Strickland
Linda Washbrook...........................Shelli Shulkin
One intermission.

GOD'S COUNTRY. By Steven Dietz. August 18, 1988. Director, David Ira Goldstein; scenery, Shelley Henze Schermer; sound, Jim Ragland.

With John Aylward, Kurt Beattie, Gordon Carpenter, Anne Christianson, Linda Emond, Matthew Flemming, John Gilbert, Rex McDowell, Marianne Owen, Ben Prager, Michael Winters.

Seattle: The Empty Space Theater

(Artistic director, M. Burke Walker; managing director, Melissa Hines)

THE BIG BAD WOLF AND HOW HE GOT THAT WAY. By Greg Palmer. January 4, 1989. Director and choreographer, Steve Tomkins; scenery and

lighting, Richard Devin; costumes, Bill Forrester; music, John Engerman.
Pig #1; Mayor .... David Pichette

Pig #2; Pete Peep......................Eric Ray Anderson
Pig #3; Townsperson......................Rex McDowell
Talking Animal Fairy; Townsperson;
  Ramona....................................Jayne Muirhead
Mrs. Watkins; Pianist........................Mary Levine

Fred Watkins; Trombonist; Pianist........Andy Shaw
Little Red Riding Hood;
  Townsperson...........................Peggy O'Connell
Granny.......................................Brian Thompson
Wolf.....................................G. Valmont Thomas

Seattle: The Group Theater

(Artistic director, Ruben Sierra; acting managing director, Marla Miller Heck)

OUR MOTHERS' STORIES. By Nikki Nojima Louis. May 10, 1989. Director, Jacqueline Moscou; scenery and lighting, Darren McCroom; costumes, Kathleen Maki; music, Joseph Seserko.

With Phyllis Brisson, Debra Grober, Nikki Nojima Louis, Angela Maetas, Kibibi Monie.

Time: Our past. Place: Somewhere in Washington State. One intermission.

STEALING (musical). Book and lyrics by Ted Sod; music by Suzanne Grant and Pamela Gerke. June 1, 1989. Director, Rita Giomi; choreography, Nancy Cranbourne; musical director, Suzanne Grant; scenery, Jeffrey A. Frkonja; lighting, Rex Carleton; costumes, Heather Hudson.
Jay Benedict....................................Mark Anders
Bernadette Yvonne Chappel..........Cynthena Sanders
Emily Cross..................................Rachel Coloff
Darryl Drayton...............................Mark Conley
Irene Rifkin.....................................Joanne Klein
Maxine Thomasello.................Fristie Dale Sanders

Victor Thomasello.....................Floyd Van Buskirk
  Time: The present. Place: New York City. One intermission.

Workshop Productions:

IRA FREDERICK ALDRIDGE. By William Hairston.
INDEPENDENCE OF EDDIE ROSE. By William S. Yellow Robe Jr.

Staged Readings:

FRATERNITY. By Jeff Stetson.
BREAKING THE COCOON OF IGNORANCE. By Selaelo Maredi.
A DAY AND A LIFE. By Anne L. Peters.
ORIGAMI. By D. A. Tsufura.
BUSCANDO AMERICA/SEEKING AMERICA. By Roy Conboy.
THE SAVIOR. By Carlos Morton.

Seattle: Intiman Theater

(Artistic director, Elizabeth Huddle)

THE LAST UNICORN (musical). Book and lyrics by Peter S. Beagle; music by Elaine Lang and June Richards. August 17, 1988. Director, Elizabeth Huddle; choreography, Kent Stowell; design, Robert Dahlstrom; musical direction and arrangements, Larry Delinger; sound, Maribeth Back.
Prince Lir..Mark Anders
Butterfly; Mabruk; Cat................Suzanne Bouchard
Mayor; King Haggard.....................Richard Farrell
Mommy Fortuna...............................Tamu Gray
Molly Grue................................Gretchen Orsland
Capt. Cully.....................................Daniel Renner

Guard...David Baldwin
Girl; Princess..............................Karen Kay Cody
Rukh; Drinn; Skull.....................Clayton Corzatte
Jack Jingly.......................................James Kearny
Schmendrick..................................David Pichette
Singing Ensemble.................................Jan Zabel
Unicorn; Lady Amalthea................Linnette Hitchin
Tree Ballet.....................................Julie Tobiason
Harpy; Bull Ballets;
  Dance Ensemble.....................Kabby Mitchell III
Bull Ballet;Dance Ensemble........Christopher Kenny,
                                        Christopher Smidt

Seattle: Seattle Repertory Theater

(Artistic director, Daniel Sullivan; managing director, Benjamin Moore)

LARGELY NEW YORK. By Bill Irwin and friends. January 6, 1989. Director, Bill Irwin; choreographer,

Kimi Okada; scenery, Douglas Stein; lighting, Nancy Schertler; costumes, Rose Pederson.

SEATTLE REPERTORY THEATER—John Procaccino and Jeannie Carson in *Truffles in the Soup* by Daniel Sullivan and the resident acting company

Post-Modern Hoofer.............................Bill Irwin
Poppers.................Leon Chesney, Steve Clemente
Soloist.....................................Margaret Eginton
Videographer ....Kevin O'Hara
Video Assistant................................Debra Miller
Dean...Jeff Gordon
 Ensemble: Christy Bain, Mike Barber, Jon E. Brandenberg, Maggie Carney, Patti Dobrowolski, Raymond Houle, Amy Mack, Victoria Millard, Paul T. Mitri, Karen Omahen, Nick Plakias, Susan Riddiford, Christian Swenson, Lori Vadino, Cindy Williams.

TRUFFLES IN THE SOUP. By Daniel Sullivan and the Seattle Repertory Theater Acting Company. April 26, 1989. Director, Daniel Sullivan; scenery, Douglas W. Schmidt; lighting, Pat Collins; costumes, Ann Hould-Ward.
Truffles ....John Procaccino
Dolores ....Jeannie Carson
Vinnie..Wendell Wright

Brighella...John Aylward
Ralph Lombardi ....Woody Eney
Sylvester Lombardi.................R. Hamilton Wright
Benito Pantaloni...................William Biff McGuire
Clarice Pantaloni ....Marianne Owen
Louise Pantaloni ....Priscilla Hake Lauris
Beatrice Rasponi........................Barbara Dirickson
Angelo ....Stephen Pelinski
Neighbors ....Ed Caldwell, James Kelly
 Time: The present. Place: The City. One intermission.

The Other Season (Workshop Productions):

SUNSHINE. By William Mastrosimone. March 17, 1989. Director, Joe Brancato; scenery, Randall Richards; lighting, Jeff Robbins; costumes, Rose Pederson; sound, Steven M. Klein.
Sunshine...Maggie Baird
Robby...Joseph McNally
Nelson..................................... Christopher Curry
 Time: Now.

STRANGERS ON EARTH. By Mark O'Donnell. March 31, 1989. Director, Douglas Hughes; scenery, Randall Richards; lighting, Jeff Robins; costumes, Rose Pederson; sound, Steven M. Klein.

Hank Knox .... Mark Chamberlin
Priscilla Fairburn .... Sarah Brooke
Margaret Gaminski .... Katie Forgette
Pony Crocker .... Joseph McNally
Mutt Vespucci .... George Catalano

O PIONEERS. By Darrah Cloud. April 14, 1989. Director, Kevin Kuhlke; music director, Brian Russell; scenery, John Wulp; lighting, Jeff Robins; costumes, Mary Ellen Walter; sound, Steven M. Klein.

Alexandra.................................Mary McDonnell
Carl Linstrum....................................Randle Mell
Angelique; Ilsa................... Marsha June Robinson

Amedee; Man in Dream .... Scott Rabinowitz
Marcel; Finn............................ Kevin McDermott
Joe Tovesky; Nelse...................Michael C. Hacker
Young Marie ....Dorothy Longbrake
Annie Lee; Old Mrs. Lee........M. Elizabeth Kennedy
Lou... Peter Lohnes
Frank Shabata...........................Christopher Noth
Signa .... Angela Fie
Millie...Shona Curly
Oscar.......................................Kevin C. Loomis
Ivar..Clayton Corzatte
Father...C. R. Gardner
Young Emil ....Jeffrey Zimmerman
Mother ....Kathryn Mesney
Emil ....Dougald Park
Marie ....Jennifer Rohn
Time: 1890s and 16 years later. Place: Hanover, Nev. One intermission.

Stockbridge, Mass.: Berkshire Theater Festival

(Artistic director, Richard Dunlap; managing director, Carol Dougherty)

TUSITALA. By James Prideaux. August 3, 1988. Director, George Schaefer; scenery, Ed Wittstein; costumes, Noel Taylor; lighting, Jeff Davis; sound, Lia Vollack.

La Faele/Warrior ....William Hao
Sosimo ....Frank Camacho
Louis Stevenson ....Tom Tammi
Lloyd.. Robert Sedgwick

Fanny..Julie Harris
Belle ....Linda Purl
Aunt Maggie ....Brenda Forbes
Kapele...Patrick Munoz
Cedarcrantz................................Jeremiah Sullivan
Native Girl..Kriss Hughes
One intermission.

Teaneck, N.J.: American Stage Company

(Producing directors, Theodore Rawlins, James R. Singer)

FOREVER PLAID (musical). By Stuart Ross. December 7, 1988. Musical direction and arrangements, James Raitt.
With Jason Graae, Dirk Lombard, Don Kehr, John Caraccioli.

HOME GAMES. By Tom Ziegler. January 18, 1989. Director, Roderick Cook.
With John Braden, Kymberly Dakin, Robert Sedgwick.

THE BLUEBIRD OF HAPPINESS. By N. Richard Nash. February 22, 1989. Director, N. Richard Nash; scenery, James Morgan; costumes, Debra Stein; lighting, Kenneth Posner; sound, Richard Sirois.
Annie Jacobs ....Pauline Lepor
Simon Farber.............................Tyagi Schwartz
Bessie Farber ....Rose Arrick
Philip Farber ....Don Peoples
Ben Farber..................................Jeffrey Hayenga
One intermission.

Washington, D.C.: Arena Stage

(Producing director, Zelda Fichandler)

BRIAR PATCH. By Deborah Pryor. January 13, 1989. Director, Max Mayer; scenery, David M. Glenn; lighting, Christopher Townsend; costumes,

Betty Siegel.
Inez Macbeth ....Marissa Copeland
Edgar Macbeth ....John Leonard Thompson

Flowers...David Marks   Druden Leigh Hunt ....Bob Kirsh
Butcher Lee Harrell.....................Sarah C. Marshall   Officer Avon....................................Sandra Bowie

Washington, D.C.: Kreeger Theater

THE FOOL SHOW. By Geoff Hoyle. February 1, 1989. Directed by Geoff Hoyle; collaborator, Randall Kline; scenic artist, Macrina Toussaint; technical direction and lighting design, Craig Blackley. With Geoff Hoyle. One intermission.

Waterford, Conn.: The O'Neill Theater Center's National Playwrights Conference

(Artistic director, Lloyd Richards)

July 3–31, 1988 (Staged Readings):

DEMON WINE. By Thomas Babe.
GAS. By Robert Berger.
THE HILL-MATHESON AFFAIR. By Robert Clyman.
STARTING MONDAY. By Anne Commire.
THE BEACH. By Anthony Giardina.
TO MY LOVING SON. By Nancy Gilsenan.
BIRDSEND. By Keith Huff.
BROTHER CHAMP. By Michael Kassin.
BLACK HOLES. By Leslie Lyles.
SUFFERING FOOLS. By Douglas Post.
FORGIVING TYPHOID MARY. By Mark St. Germain.
AND THE MEN SHALL ALSO GATHER. By Jeff Stetson.
SODBUSTERS. By Craig Volk.
A SLICE OF PIE. By Jeff Wanshel.
INTERROGATING THE NUDE. By Doug Wright.

Williamstown, Mass.: Williamstown Theater Festival

(Executive director, George Morfogen; artistic directors, Peter Hunt, Austin Pendleton)

THE LEGEND OF OEDIPUS. By Kenneth Cavander. June 23, 1988. Director, Nikos Psacharopoulos; scenery, John Conklin; lighting, Pat Collins; costumes, Merrily Murray-Walsh.

Oedipus...Joe Morton
Jocasta ....Joan Van Ark
Polyneices ....Michael Cumpsty
Eteocles... Rob Knepper
Antigone ....Jane Kaczmarek
Ismene ....Jean Hackett
Creon..Daniel Davis
Halmon......................................Tony Goldwyn
Dionysos...................................Richard Kneeland
Apollo..Lewis J. Stadlen
Teiresias .... George Morfogen
Pythoness ....Myra Taylor
Chief Priest......................................Tom Tammi
Priests................Michael Baratta, Thomas Hildreth
Theseus ....Douglas Kritzner
Shepherd; Old Man .... Emery Battis
Storyteller...................................Randall Duk Kim
Theban Sentry...........................Wayne Alexander
Theban Guard..................................Paul Giamatti
Messenger from Corinth ....John Hickey
Evadne..................................... Vanessa Marshall
    Place: In and around Thebes, Athens and Delphi. One intermission.

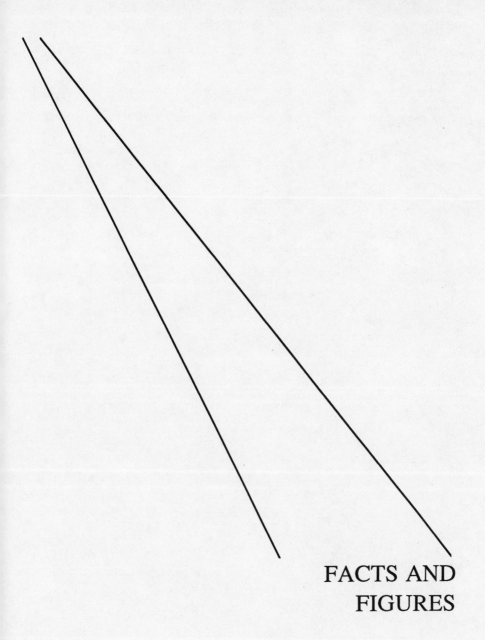

FACTS AND
FIGURES

LONG RUNS ON BROADWAY

The following shows have run 500 or more continuous performances in a single production, usually the first, not including previews or extra non-profit performances, allowing for vacation layoffs and special one-booking engagements, but not including return engagements after a show has gone on tour. In all cases, the numbers were obtained directly from the show's production offices. Where there are title similarities, the production is identified as follows: (p) straight play version, (m) musical version, (r) revival.

THROUGH MAY 31, 1989

(PLAYS MARKED WITH ASTERISK WERE STILL PLAYING JUNE 1, 1989)

Plays	Number Performances	Plays	Number Performances
*A Chorus Line	5,756	Ain't Misbehavin'	1,604
†*Oh! Calcutta! (r)	5,856	*Me and My Girl	1,595
42nd Street	3,486	Mary, Mary	1,572
Grease	3,388	Evita	1,567
Fiddler on the Roof	3,242	The Voice of the Turtle	1,557
Life With Father	3,224	Barefoot in the Park	1,530
Tobacco Road	3,182	Brighton Beach Memoirs	1,530
Hello, Dolly!	2,844	Dreamgirls	1,522
*Cats	2,777	Mame (m)	1,508
My Fair Lady	2,717	Same Time, Next Year	1,453
Annie	2,377	Arsenic and Old Lace	1,444
Man of La Mancha	2,328	The Sound of Music	1,443
Abie's Irish Rose	2,327	How to Succeed in Business	
Oklahoma!	2,212	Without Really Trying	1,417
Pippin	1,944	Hellzapoppin	1,404
South Pacific	1,925	The Music Man	1,375
The Magic Show	1,920	Funny Girl	1,348
Deathtrap	1,793	Mummenschanz	1,326
Gemini	1,788	Angel Street	1,295
Harvey	1,775	Lightnin'	1,291
Dancin'	1,774	Promises, Promises	1,281
La Cage aux Folles	1,761	The King and I	1,246
Hair	1,750	Cactus Flower	1,234
The Wiz	1,672	Sleuth	1,222
Born Yesterday	1,642	Torch Song Trilogy	1,222
The Best Little Whorehouse in Texas	1,639	1776	1,217

---

† *Oh! Calcutta!* plays more than Broadway's regular 8 performances weekly from time to time, so that it has played more performances than *A Chorus Line* to date, though *A Chorus Line* has been in continuous run more than a year longer.

Plays	Number Performances	Plays	Number Performances
Equus	1,209	La Plume de Ma Tante	835
Sugar Babies	1,208	Three Men on a Horse	835
Guys and Dolls	1,200	The Subject Was Roses	832
Amadeus	1,181	Inherit the Wind	806
Cabaret	1,165	No Time for Sergeants	796
Mister Roberts	1,157	Fiorello!	795
Annie Get Your Gun	1,147	Where's Charley?	792
The Seven Year Itch	1,141	The Ladder	789
Butterflies Are Free	1,128	Forty Carats	780
Pins and Needles	1,108	The Prisoner of Second Avenue	780
Plaza Suite	1,097	Oliver!	774
They're Playing Our Song	1,082	The Pirates of Penzance (1980 r)	772
Kiss Me, Kate	1,070	Woman of the Year	770
Don't Bother Me, I Can't Cope	1,065	Sophisticated Ladies	767
The Pajama Game	1,063	My One and Only	767
Shenandoah	1,050	Bubbling Brown Sugar	766
The Teahouse of the August Moon	1,027	State of the Union	765
Damn Yankees	1,019	Starlight Express	761
Never Too Late	1,007	The First Year	760
Big River	1,005	Broadway Bound	756
Any Wednesday	982	You Know I Can't Hear You When the Water's Running	755
A Funny Thing Happened on the Way to the Forum	964	Two for the Seesaw	750
The Odd Couple	964	Joseph and the Amazing Technicolor Dreamcoat (r)	747
Anna Lucasta	957	Death of a Salesman	742
Kiss and Tell	956	For Colored Girls, etc.	742
Dracula (r)	925	Sons o' Fun	742
Bells Are Ringing	924	Candide (mr)	740
The Moon Is Blue	924	Gentlemen Prefer Blondes	740
Beatlemania	920	The Man Who Came to Dinner	739
The Elephant Man	916	Nine	739
Luv	901	Call Me Mister	734
Chicago (m)	898	West Side Story	732
Applause	896	High Button Shoes	727
Can-Can	892	Finian's Rainbow	725
Carousel	890	Claudia	722
I'm Not Rappaport	890	The Gold Diggers	720
Hats Off to Ice	889	Jesus Christ Superstar	720
Fanny	888	Carnival	719
Children of a Lesser God	887	The Diary of Anne Frank	717
Follow the Girls	882	I Remember Mama	714
Camelot	873	Tea and Sympathy	712
I Love My Wife	872	Junior Miss	710
*Les Misérables	868	Last of the Red Hot Lovers	706
The Bat	867	Company	705
My Sister Eileen	864	Seventh Heaven	704
No, No, Nanette (r)	861	Gypsy (m)	702
Song of Norway	860	The Miracle Worker	700
Chapter Two	857	That Championship Season	700
A Streetcar Named Desire	855	Da	697
Barnum	854	The King and I (r)	696
Comedy in Music	849	Cat on a Hot Tin Roof	694
Raisin	847	Li'l Abner	693
You Can't Take It With You	837		

Plays	Number Performances
The Children's Hour	691
Purlie	688
Dead End	687
The Lion and the Mouse	686
White Cargo	686
Dear Ruth	683
East Is West	680
Come Blow Your Horn	677
The Most Happy Fella	676
*Anything Goes (r)	675
The Doughgirls	671
The Impossible Years	670
Irene	670
Boy Meets Girl	669
The Tap Dance Kid	669
Beyond the Fringe	667
Who's Afraid of Virginia Woolf?	664
Blithe Spirit	657
A Trip to Chinatown	657
The Women	657
*Into the Woods	655
Bloomer Girl	654
The Fifth Season	654
Rain	648
Witness for the Prosecution	645
Call Me Madam	644
Janie	642
The Green Pastures	640
Auntie Mame (p)	639
A Man for All Seasons	637
The Fourposter	632
The Music Master	627
Two Gentlemen of Verona (m)	627
The Tenth Man	623
Is Zat So?	618
Anniversary Waltz	615
The Happy Time (p)	614
Separate Rooms	613
Affairs of State	610
Oh! Calcutta!	610
Star and Garter	609
The Mystery of Edwin Drood	608
The Student Prince	608
Sweet Charity	608
Bye Bye Birdie	607
Irene (r)	604
Sunday in the Park With George	604
Adonis	603
Broadway	603
Peg o' My Heart	603
Street Scene (p)	601
Kiki	600
Flower Drum Song	600
A Little Night Music	600

Plays	Number Performances
Agnes of God	599
Don't Drink the Water	598
Wish You Were Here	598
A Society Circus	596
Absurd Person Singular	592
A Day in Hollywood/A Night in the Ukraine	588
The Me Nobody Knows	586
The Two Mrs. Carrolls	585
Kismet (m)	583
Detective Story	581
Brigadoon	581
No Strings	580
Brother Rat	577
Blossom Time	576
Pump Boys and Dinettes	573
Show Boat	572
The Show-Off	571
Sally	570
Golden Boy (m)	568
One Touch of Venus	567
The Real Thing	566
Happy Birthday	564
Look Homeward, Angel	564
Morning's at Seven (r)	564
*The Phantom of the Opera	563
The Glass Menagerie	561
I Do! I Do!	560
*Sarafina!	560
Wonderful Town	559
Rose Marie	557
Strictly Dishonorable	557
Sweeney Todd, the Demon Barber of Fleet Street	557
A Majority of One	556
The Great White Hope	556
Toys in the Attic	556
Sunrise at Campobello	556
Jamaica	555
Stop the World—I Want to Get Off	555
Florodora	553
Noises Off	553
Ziegfeld Follies (1943)	553
Dial "M" for Murder	552
Good News	551
Peter Pan (r)	551
Let's Face It	547
Milk and Honey	543
Within the Law	541
Pal Joey (r)	540
What Makes Sammy Run?	540
The Sunshine Boys	538
What a Life	538
Crimes of the Heart	535

Plays	Number Performances	Plays	Number Performances
The Unsinkable Molly Brown	532	Half a Sixpence	511
The Red Mill (r)	531	The Vagabond King	511
A Raisin in the Sun	530	The New Moon	509
Godspell	527	The World of Suzie Wong	508
Fences	526	The Rothschilds	507
The Solid Gold Cadillac	526	On Your Toes (r)	505
Biloxi Blues	524	Sugar	505
Irma La Douce	524	Shuffle Along	504
The Boomerang	522	Up in Central Park	504
Follies	521	Carmen Jones	503
Rosalinda	521	The Member of the Wedding	501
The Best Man	520	Panama Hattie	501
Chauve-Souris	520	Personal Appearance	501
Blackbirds of 1928	518	Bird in Hand	500
The Gin Game	517	Room Service	500
Sunny	517	Sailor, Beware!	500
Victoria Regina	517	Tomorrow the World	500
Fifth of July	511		

LONG RUNS OFF BROADWAY

Plays	Number Performances	Plays	Number Performances
*The Fantasticks	12,106	*Driving Miss Daisy	854
The Threepenny Opera	2,611	The Mad Show	871
Forbidden Broadway	2,332	Scrambled Feet	831
Little Shop of Horrors	2,209	The Effect of Gamma Rays on Man-in-the-Moon Marigolds	819
Godspell	2,124	*Steel Magnolias	817
Jacques Brel	1,847	A View From the Bridge (r)	780
Vanities	1,785	The Boy Friend (r)	763
*Vampire Lesbians of Sodom	1,614	True West	762
You're a Good Man Charlie Brown	1,597	Dime a Dozen	728
*Nunsense	1,431	Isn't It Romantic	733
The Blacks	1,408	The Pocket Watch	725
One Mo' Time	1,372	The Connection	722
Let My People Come	1,327	The Passion of Dracula	714
The Hot 1 Baltimore	1,166	Adaptation & Next	707
I'm Getting My Act Together and Taking It on the Road	1,165	Oh! Calcutta!	704
Little Mary Sunshine	1,143	Scuba Duba	692
El Grande de Coca-Cola	1,114	The Foreigner	686
One Flew Over the Cuckoo's Nest (r)	1,025	The Knack	685
The Boys in the Band	1,000	*Perfect Crime	679
Fool for Love	1,000	The Club	674
Cloud 9	971	The Balcony	672
Sister Mary Ignatius Explains It All for You & The Actor's Nightmare	947	Penn & Teller	666
Your Own Thing	933	America Hurrah	634
Curley McDimple	931	Oil City Symphony	626
Leave It to Jane (r)	928	Hogan's Goat	607
		Beehive	600

Plays	*Number Performances*
The Trojan Women	600
The Dining Room	583
Krapp's Last Tape & The Zoo Story	582
The Dumbwaiter & The Collection	578
*Tamara	578
Dames at Sea	575
The Crucible (r)	571
The Iceman Cometh (r)	565
The Hostage (r)	545

Plays	*Number Performances*
What's a Nice Country Like You Doing in a State Like This?	543
Frankie and Johnny in the Claire de Lune	533
Six Characters in Search of an Author (r)	529
The Dirtiest Show in Town	509
Happy Ending & Day of Absence	504
Greater Tuna	501
A Shayna Maidel	501
The Boys From Syracuse (r)	500

NEW YORK DRAMA CRITICS AWARDS, 1935–36 TO 1988–89

Listed below are the New York Drama Critics Circle Awards from 1935–36 through 1987–88 classified as follows: (1) Best American Play, (2) Best Foreign Play, (3) Best Musical, (4) Best, regardless of category (this category was established by new voting rules in 1962–63 and did not exist prior to that year).

1935–36—(1) Winterset
1936–37—(1) High Tor
1937–38—(1) Of Mice and Men, (2) Shadow and Substance
1938–39—(1) No award, (2) The White Steed
1939–40—(1) The Time of Your Life
1940–41—(1) Watch on the Rhine, (2) The Corn Is Green
1941–42—(1) No award, (2) Blithe Spirit
1942–43—(1) The Patriots
1943–44—(2) Jacobowsky and the Colonel
1944–45—(1) The Glass Menagerie
1945–46—(3) Carousel
1946–47—(1) All My Sons, (2) No Exit, (3) Brigadoon
1947–48—(1) A Streetcar Named Desire, (2) The Winslow Boy
1948–49—(1) Death of a Salesman, (2) The Madwoman of Chaillot, (3) South Pacific
1949–50—(1) The Member of the Wedding, (2) The Cocktail Party, (3) The Consul
1950–51—(1) Darkness at Noon, (2) The Lady's Not for Burning, (3) Guys and Dolls
1951–52—(1) I Am a Camera, (2) Venus Observed, (3) Pal Joey (Special citation to Don Juan in Hell)
1952–53—(1) Picnic, (2) The Love of Four Colonels, (3) Wonderful Town
1953–54—(1) Teahouse of the August Moon, (2) Ondine, (3) The Golden Apple

1954–55—(1) Cat on a Hot Tin Roof, (2) Witness for the Prosecution, (3) The Saint of Bleecker Street
1955–56—(1) The Diary of Anne Frank, (2) Tiger at the Gates, (3) My Fair Lady
1956–57—(1) Long Day's Journey Into Night, (2) The Waltz of the Toreadors, (3) The Most Happy Fella
1957–58—(1) Look Homeward, Angel, (2) Look Back in Anger, (3) The Music Man
1958–59—(1) A Raisin in the Sun, (2) The Visit, (3) La Plume de Ma Tante
1959–60—(1) Toys in the Attic, (2) Five Finger Exercise, (3) Fiorello!
1960–61—(1) All the Way Home, (2) A Taste of Honey, (3) Carnival
1961–62—(1) The Night of the Iguana, (2) A Man for All Seasons, (3) How to Succeed in Business Without Really Trying
1962–63—(4) Who's Afraid of Virginia Woolf? (Special citation to Beyond the Fringe)
1963–64—(4) Luther, (3) Hello, Dolly! (Special citation to The Trojan Women)
1964–65—(4) The Subject Was Roses, (3) Fiddler on the Roof
1965–66—(4) The Persecution and Assassination of Marat as Performed by the Inmates of the Asylum of Charenton Under the Direction of the Marquis de Sade, (3) Man of La Mancha

1966–67—(4) The Homecoming, (3) Cabaret
1967–68—(4) Rosencrantz and Guildenstern Are
Dead, (3) Your Own Thing
1968–69—(4) The Great White Hope, (3) 1776
1969–70—(4) Borstal Boy, (1) The Effect of Gamma
Rays on Man-in-the-Moon Marigolds, (3)
Company
1970–71—(4) Home, (1) The House of Blue Leaves,
(3) Follies
1971–72—(4) That Championship Season, (2) The
Screens, (3) Two Gentlemen of Verona
(Special citations to Sticks and Bones and
Old Times)
1972–73—(4) The Changing Room, (1) The Hot l
Baltimore, (3) A Little Night Music
1973–74—(4) The Contractor, (1) Short Eyes, (3)
Candide
1974–75—(4) Equus, (1) The Taking of Miss Janie,
(3) A Chorus Line
1975–76—(4) Travesties, (1) Streamers, (3) Pacific
Overtures
1976–77—(4) Otherwise Engaged, (1) American
Buffalo, (3) Annie
1977–78—(4) Da, (3) Ain't Misbehavin'
1978–79—(4) The Elephant Man, (3) Sweeney Todd,
the Demon Barber of Fleet Street
1979–80—(4) Talley's Folly, (2) Betrayal, (3) Evita
(Special Citation to Peter Brook's Le

Centre International de Créations
Théâtrales for its repertory)
1980–81—(4) A Lesson From Aloes, (1) Crimes of
the Heart (Special citations to Lena
Horne: The Lady and Her Music and the
New York Shakespeare Festival
production of The Pirates of Penzance)
1981–82—(4) The Life & Adventures of Nicholas
Nickleby, (1) A Soldier's Play
1982–83—(4) Brighton Beach Memoirs, (2) Plenty,
(3) Little Shop of Horrors (special
citation to Young Playwrights Festival)
1983–84—(4) The Real Thing, (1) Glengarry Glen
Ross, (3) Sunday in the Park With
George (Special citation to Samuel
Beckett for the body of his work)
1984–85—(4) Ma Rainey's Black Bottom
1985–86—(4) A Lie of the Mind, (2) Benefactors
(Special citation to The Search for Signs
of Intelligent Life in the Universe)
1986–87—(4) Fences, (2) Les Liaisons Dangereuses,
(3) Les Misérables
1987–88—(4) Joe Turner's Come and Gone, (2) The
Road to Mecca, (3) Into the Woods
1988–89—(4) The Heidi Chronicles, (2) Aristocrats
(Special citation to Bill Irwin for Largely
New York)

NEW YORK DRAMA CRITICS CIRCLE VOTING, 1988–89

The New York Drama Critics Circle voted Wendy Wasserstein's *The Heidi Chronicles* the best play of the season on the first ballot by a majority of 10 of the 18 members voting their first choices, as follows: *The Heidi Chronicles* 10 (Clive Barnes, New York *Post*; John Beaufort, *Christian Science Monitor*; Sylviane Gold and Edwin Wilson, *Wall Street Journal*; Richard Hummler, *Variety*; Michael Kuchwara, Associated Press; Edith Oliver, *The New Yorker*; William Raidy, Newhouse Chain; Douglas Watt, *Daily News*; Linda Winer, *Newsday*), *Eastern Standard* 2 (Jacques Le Sourd, Gannett Newspapers; Julius Novick, *Village Voice*), *The Film Society* 2 (Howard Kissel, *Daily News*; Mimi Kramer, *The New Yorker*), *Other People's Money* 2 (Don Nelsen, *Daily News*; John Simon, *New York*) and 1 each for *Ghetto* (Michael Feingold, *Village Voice*) and *Spoils of War* (William A. Henry III, *Time*).

An American play having been named best regardless of category, the Circle then proceeded to name Brian Friel's *Aristocrats* the best foreign play of the season on the multiple-choice second ballot, after the first ballot of first choices failed to produce a majority. The first-ballot result was *Aristocrats* 8 (Beaufort, Henry, Hummler, Le Sourd, Kuchwara, Novick, Oliver, Wilson),

Shirley Valentine 5 (Barnes, Kissel, Nelsen, Raidy, Watt) and one each for *Emerald City* (Simon), *Ghetto* (Feingold), *I'll Go On* (Winer) and *No Limits to Love* (Kramer), with Gold abstaining. The Circle then proceeded under its rules to a second ballot of weighted choices (first 3 points, second 2, third 1) on which *Aristocrats* won with 32 points, more than enough required for a winner (three times the number of members voting, divided by 2, plus 1—i.e., 27), against *Shirley Valentine* 20, *I'll Go On* 11, *Ghetto* 10, *Emerald City* 4, *I Shall Never Return* 3, *No Limits to Love* 3 and *Run for Your Wife* 2.

The critics voted 15-1 not to give an award for best musical this year, but they voted a special award to Bill Irwin for his show *Largely New York*. Two of the members (Simon and Watt) voted by proxy, two (Jack Kroll, Allan Wallach) were absent and not voting. Prior to the voting meeting May 15 the New York *Times* critics had resigned from the Circle under an order by the paper's executive editor to all *Times* critics to withdraw from such "consensual procedures."

CHOICES OF SOME OTHER CRITICS

Critic	Best Play	Best Musical
John A. Gambling WOR–AM	The Heidi Chronicles	Jerome Robbins' Broadway
Susan Granger WMCA	The Heidi Chronicles	Jerome Robbins' Broadway
Stewart Klein WNYW–TV	The Heidi Chronicles	Abstain
Joanna Langfeld LBS Radio Network	The Heidi Chronicles	Jerome Robbins' Broadway
Jim McLaughlin CBS This Morning	The Heidi Chronicles	Jerome Robbins' Broadway
Richard Scholem WGSM–Radio	The Heidi Chronicles, Other People's Money	Jerome Robbins' Broadway
Richard Shepard WNEW–Radio	Amidst the Floating Monsters	Jerome Robbins' Broadway
Joel Siegel WABC–TV	The Heidi Chronicles	Jerome Robbins' Broadway
Liz Smith Syndicated Columnist	Other People's Money	Jerome Robbins' Broadway
Leida Snow WINS Radio	Only Kidding	Jerome Robbins' Broadway
Nancy Vreeland *Dance* Magazine	Largely New York	Jerome Robbins' Broadway
Allan Wallach *Newsday*	The Heidi Chronicles	Jerome Robbins' Broadway

PULITZER PRIZE WINNERS, 1916–17 TO 1988–89

1916–17—No award
1917–18—Why Marry?, by Jesse Lynch Williams
1918–19—No award
1919–20—Beyond the Horizon, by Eugene O'Neill
1920–21—Miss Lulu Bett, by Zona Gale
1921–22—Anna Christie, by Eugene O'Neill
1922–23—Icebound, by Owen Davis
1923–24—Hell-Bent fer Heaven, by Hatcher Hughes
1924–25—They Knew What They Wanted, by
    Sidney Howard
1925–26—Craig's Wife, by George Kelly
1926–27—In Abraham's Bosom, by Paul Green
1927–28—Strange Interlude, by Eugene O'Neill
1928–29—Street Scene, by Elmer Rice
1929–30—The Green Pastures, by Marc Connelly
1930–31—Alison's House, by Susan Glaspell
1931–32—Of Thee I Sing, by George S. Kaufman,
    Morrie Ryskind, Ira and George Gershwin
1932–33—Both Your Houses, by Maxwell Anderson
1933–34—Men in White, by Sidney Kingsley
1934–35—The Old Maid, by Zoë Akins
1935–36—Idiot's Delight, by Robert E. Sherwood
1936–37—You Can't Take It With You, by Moss
    Hart and George S. Kaufman
1937–38—Our Town, by Thornton Wilder
1938–39—Abe Lincoln in Illinois, by Robert E.
    Sherwood
1939–40—The Time of Your Life, by William
    Saroyan
1940–41—There Shall Be No Night, by Robert E.
    Sherwood
1941–42—No award
1942–43—The Skin of Our Teeth, by Thornton
    Wilder
1943–44—No award
1944–45—Harvey, by Mary Chase
1945–46—State of the Union, by Howard Lindsay
    and Russel Crouse
1946–47—No award
1947–48—A Streetcar Named Desire, by Tennessee
    Williams
1948–49—Death of a Salesman, by Arthur Miller
1949–50—South Pacific, by Richard Rodgers, Oscar
    Hammerstein II and Joshua Logan
1950–51—No award
1951–52—The Shrike, by Joseph Kramm
1952–53—Picnic, by William Inge
1953–54—The Teahouse of the August Moon, by
    John Patrick
1954–55—Cat on a Hot Tin Roof, by Tennessee
    Williams

1955–56—The Diary of Anne Frank, by Frances
    Goodrich and Albert Hackett
1956–57—Long Day's Journey Into Night, by
    Eugene O'Neill
1957–58—Look Homeward, Angel, by Ketti Frings
1958–59—J.B., by Archibald MacLeish
1959–60—Fiorello!, by Jerome Weidman, George
    Abbott, Sheldon Harnick and Jerry Bock
1960–61—All the Way Home, by Tad Mosel
1961–62—How to Succeed in Business Without
    Really Trying, by Abe Burrows, Willie
    Gilbert, Jack Weinstock and Frank
    Loesser
1962–63—No award
1963–64—No award
1964–65—The Subject Was Roses, by Frank D.
    Gilroy
1965–66—No award
1966–67—A Delicate Balance, by Edward Albee
1967–68—No award
1968–69—The Great White Hope, by Howard
    Sackler
1969–70—No Place To Be Somebody, by Charles
    Gordone
1970–71—The Effect of Gamma Rays on Man-in-
    the-Moon Marigolds, by Paul Zindel
1971–72—No award
1972–73—That Championship Season, by Jason
    Miller
1973–74—No award
1974–75—Seascape, by Edward Albee
1975–76—A Chorus Line, by Michael Bennett,
    James Kirkwood, Nicholas Dante, Marvin
    Hamlisch and Edward Kleban
1976–77—The Shadow Box, by Michael Cristofer
1977–78—The Gin Game, by D.L. Coburn
1978–79—Buried Child, by Sam Shepard
1979–80—Talley's Folly, by Lanford Wilson
1980–81—Crimes of the Heart, by Beth Henley
1981–82—A Soldier's Play, by Charles Fuller
1982–83—'night, Mother, by Marsha Norman
1983–84—Glengarry Glen Ross, by David Mamet
1984–85—Sunday in the Park With George, by
    James Lapine and Stephen Sondheim
1985–86—No award
1986–87—Fences, by August Wilson
1987–88—Driving Miss Daisy, by Alfred Uhry
1988–89—The Heidi Chronicles, by Wendy
    Wasserstein

Santo Loquasto's Tony Award-winning setting for *Cafe Crown,* also
cited by *Best Plays* as the outstanding straight-play design of the season

THE TONY AWARDS, 1988–89

The American Theater Wing's Antoinette Perry (Tony) Awards are presented annually in recognition of distinguished artistic achievement in the
Broadway theater. The League of American Theaters and Producers and the
American Theater Wing present the Tony Awards, founded by the Wing in
1947. Legitimate theater productions opening in eligible Broadway theaters
during the eligibility season of the current year—May 5, 1988 to May 3,
1989—are considered for Tony nominations.

The Tony Awards Administration Committee appoints the Tony Awards
Nominating Committee which makes the actual nominations. The Administra-
tion Committee decided to eliminate two of the 19 Tony categories for this
season: Best Book of a Musical and Best Score of a Musical. The 1988–89
Nominating Committee consisted of Schuyler Chapin, Alvin Colt, Jean Dal-
rymple, Leonard Fleischer, Leonard Harris, Mary Henderson, Rosetta
LeNoire, R. Z. Manna, Eve Merriam and Jeffrey Sweet, associate editor of
Best Plays.

The Tony Awards are voted by the members of the governing boards of the four theater artists' organizations: Actors' Equity Association, the Dramatists Guild, the Society of Stage Directors and Choreographers and the United Scenic Artists, plus the members of the first and second-night theater press, the board of directors of the American Theater Wing and the membership of the League of American Theaters and Producers. Because of fluctuation within these boards, the size of the Tony electorate varies from year to year. In the 1988–89 season, there were 750 qualified Tony voters.

The list of 1988–89 nominees follows, with winners in each category listed in **bold face type**.

BEST PLAY (award goes to both author and producer). *Largely New York* by Bill Irwin, produced by James B. Freydberg, Kenneth Feld, Jerry L. Cohen, Max Weitzenhoffer, John F. Kennedy Center for the Performing Arts and Walt Disney Studio; *Lend Me a Tenor* by Ken Ludwig, produced by Martin Starger and The Really Useful Theater Company; *Shirley Valentine* by Willy Russell, produced by The Really Useful Theater Company and Bob Swash; *The Heidi Chronicles* by **Wendy Wasserstein**, produced by **The Shubert Organization, Suntory International Corp., James Walsh** and **Playwrights Horizons**.

BEST MUSICAL (award goes to the producer). *Black and Blue* produced by Mel Howard and Donald K. Donald; *Jerome Robbins' Broadway* produced by **The Shubert Organization, Roger Berlind, Suntory International Corp., Byron Goldman** and **Emanuel Azenberg**; *Starmites* produced by Hinks Shimberg, Mary Keil and Steven Warnick.

BEST LEADING ACTOR IN A PLAY. Mikhail Baryshnikov in *Metamorphosis*, **Philip Bosco** in *Lend Me a Tenor*, Victor Garber in *Lend Me a Tenor*, Bill Irwin in *Largely New York*.

BEST LEADING ACTRESS IN A PLAY. Joan Allen in *The Heidi Chronicles*, **Pauline Collins** in *Shirley Valentine*, Madeline Kahn in *Born Yesterday*, Kate Nelligan in *Spoils of War*.

BEST LEADING ACTOR IN A MUSICAL. **Jason Alexander** in *Jerome Robbins' Broadway*, Gabriel Barre in *Starmites*, Brian Lane Green in *Starmites*, Robert La Fosse in *Jerome Robbins' Broadway*.

BEST LEADING ACTRESS IN A MUSICAL. **Ruth Brown** in *Black and Blue*, Charlotte d'Amboise in *Jerome Robbins' Broadway*, Linda Hopkins in *Black and Blue*, Sharon McNight in *Starmites*.

BEST FEATURED ACTOR IN A PLAY. Peter Frechette in *Eastern Standard*. **Boyd Gaines** in *The Heidi Chronicles*, Eric Stoltz in *Our Town*, Gordon Joseph Weiss in *Ghetto*.

BEST FEATURED ACTRESS IN A PLAY. **Christine Baranski** in *Rumors*, Joanne Camp in *The Heidi Chronicles*, Tovah Feldshuh in *Lend Me a Tenor*, Penelope Ann Miller in *Our Town*.

BEST FEATURED ACTOR IN A MUSICAL. Bunny Briggs in *Black and Blue*, Savion Glover in *Black and Blue*, Scott Wentworth in *Welcome to the Club*, **Scott Wise** in *Jerome Robbins' Broadway*.

BEST FEATURED ACTRESS IN A MUSICAL. Jane Lanier in *Jerome Robbins' Broadway*, Faith Prince in *Jerome Robbins' Broadway*, **Debbie Shapiro** in *Jerome Robbins' Broadway*, Julie Wilson in *Legs Diamond*.

BEST DIRECTION OF A PLAY. Bill Irwin for *Largely New York*, Gregory Mosher for *Our Town*, Daniel Sullivan for *The Heidi Chronicles*, **Jerry Zaks** for *Lend Me a Tenor*.

BEST DIRECTION OF A MUSICAL. Larry Carpenter for *Starmites*, **Jerome Robbins** for *Jerome Robbins' Broadway*, Peter Mark Schifter for *Welcome to the Club*, Claudio Segovia and Hector Orezzoli for *Black and Blue*.

BEST SCENIC DESIGN. **Santo Loquasto** for *Cafe Crown*, Thomas Lynch for *The Heidi Chronicles*, Claudio Segovia and Hector Orezzoli for *Black and Blue*, Tony Walton for *Lend Me a Tenor*.

BEST COSTUME DESIGN. Jane Greenwood for *Our Town*, Willa Kim for *Legs Diamond*, William Ivey Long for *Lend Me a Tenor*, **Claudio Segovia** and **Hector Orezzoli** for *Black and Blue*.

BEST LIGHTING DESIGN. Neil Peter Jampolis and Jane Reisman for *Black and Blue*, Brian Nason for

Metamorphosis, Nancy Schertler for *Largely New York*, **Jennifer Tipton** for *Jerome Robbins' Broadway*.

BEST CHOREOGRAPHY. Michele Assaf for *Starmites*, **Cholly Atkins, Henry LeTang, Frankie Manning** and **Fayard Nicholas** for *Black and Blue*, Bill Irwin and Kimi Okada for *Largely New York*, Alan Johnson for *Legs Diamond*.

BEST REVIVAL OF A PLAY OR MUSICAL. *Ah, Wilderness!* produced by Ken Marsolais, Alexander H. Cohen, The Kennedy Center for the Performing Arts, Yale Repertory Theater, Richard Norton, Irma Oestreicher and Elizabeth D. White; *Ain't Misbehavin'* produced by The Shubert Organization, Emanuel Azenberg, Dasha Epstein and Roger Berlind; *Cafe Crown* produced by LeFrak Entertainment, James M. Nederlander, Francine LeFrak, James L. Nederlander and Arthur Rubin; **Our Town** produced by **Lincoln Center Theater, Gregory Mosher** and **Bernard Gersten**.

SPECIAL TONY AWARD. Hartford Stage Company, Hartford, Conn.

TONY AWARD WINNERS, 1947–1989

Listed below are the Antoinette Perry (Tony) Award winners in the categories of Best Play and Best Musical from the time these awards were established (1947) until the present.

1947—No play or musical award
1948—Mister Roberts; no musical award
1949—Death of a Salesman; Kiss Me, Kate
1950—The Cocktail Party; South Pacific
1951—The Rose Tattoo; Guys and Dolls
1952—The Fourposter; The King and I
1953—The Crucible; Wonderful Town
1954—The Teahouse of the August Moon; Kismet
1955—The Desperate Hours; The Pajama Game
1956—The Diary of Anne Frank; Damn Yankees
1957—Long Day's Journey Into Night; My Fair Lady
1958—Sunrise at Campobello; The Music Man
1959—J.B.; Redhead
1960—The Miracle Worker; Fiorello! and The Sound of Music (tie)
1961—Becket; Bye Bye Birdie
1962—A Man for All Seasons; How to Succeed in Business Without Really Trying
1963—Who's Afraid of Virginia Woolf?; A Funny Thing Happened on the Way to the Forum
1964—Luther; Hello, Dolly!
1965—The Subject Was Roses; Fiddler on the Roof
1966—The Persecution and Assassination of Marat as Performed by the Inmates of the Asylum of Charenton Under the Direction of the Marquis de Sade; Man of La Mancha
1967—The Homecoming; Cabaret

1968—Rosencrantz and Guildenstern Are Dead; Hallelujah, Baby!
1969—The Great White Hope; 1776
1970—Borstal Boy; Applause
1971—Sleuth; Company
1972—Sticks and Bones; Two Gentlemen of Verona
1973—That Championship Season; A Little Night Music
1974—The River Niger; Raisin
1975—Equus; The Wiz
1976—Travesties; A Chorus Line
1977—The Shadow Box; Annie
1978—Da; Ain't Misbehavin'
1979—The Elephant Man; Sweeney Todd, the Demon Barber of Fleet Street
1980—Children of a Lesser God; Evita
1981—Amadeus; 42nd Street
1982—The Life & Adventures of Nicholas Nickleby; Nine
1983—Torch Song Trilogy; Cats
1984—The Real Thing; La Cage aux Folles
1985—Biloxi Blues; Big River
1986—I'm Not Rappaport; The Mystery of Edwin Drood
1987—Fences; Les Misérables
1988—M. Butterfly; The Phantom of the Opera
1989—The Heidi Chronicles; Jerome Robbins' Broadway

THE OBIE AWARDS, 1988-89

The *Village Voice* Off-Broadway (Obie) Awards are given each year for excellence in various categories of off-Broadway (and frequently off-off-Broadway) shows, with close distinctions between these two areas ignored. The 34th annual Obies for the 1988-89 season were voted by a panel of *Village Voice* critics (Eileen Blumenthal, Michael Feingold, Robert Massa, Erika Munk, Julius Novick, Gordon Rogoff, Alisa Solomon and Ross Wetzsteon, chairman) plus Martha Coigney and Margo Jefferson as guest judges.

SUSTAINED ACHIEVEMENT. **Irene Worth**

PERFORMANCE. **Mark Blum** for *Gus and Al*, **Niall Buggy** for *Aristocrats*, **William Converse-Roberts** for *Love's Labor's Lost*, **Fyvush Finkel** for *Cafe Crown*, **Gloria Foster** for *The Forbidden City*, **Paul Hecht** for *Enrico IV*, **Nancy Marchand** for *The Cocktail Hour*, **Tim McDonnell** for *Diary of a Madman*, **Will Patton** for *What Did He See?*, **Lonny Price** for *The Immigrant*, **Everett Quinton** for *A Tale of Two Cities*, **Rocco Sisto** for *The Winter's Tale*, **Kathy Najimy** and **Mo Gaffney** for *The Kathy and Mo Show*.

DIRECTION. **Ingmar Bergman** for *Hamlet*, **Peter Stein** for *Falstaff*.

SUSTAINED EXCELLENCE. Direction, **Rene Buch**. Set Design, **Donald Eastman**. Costume Design, **Gabriel Berry, Susan Young**.

CITATIONS. **Leo Bassi** for *Nero's Last Folly*; **Dance Theater Workshop**; **The Dramatists Guild** for the Young Playwrights Festival; **Janie Geiser** for *Stories From Here*; **Rachel Rosenthal** for *Rachel's Brain*; **Tamamatsu Yoshida** for *The Warrior Ant*; **Paul Zaloom** for *The House of Horror*.

GRANTS. Cash, **Cucaracha Workhouse Theater, The Living Theater, Playwriting Workshop, Intar Hispanic Playwrights-in-Residence Laboratory, The Frank Silvera Writers Workshop**.

ADDITIONAL PRIZES AND AWARDS, 1988-89

The following is a list of major prizes and awards for achievement in the theater this season. In all cases the names and/or titles of the winners appear in **bold face type**.

4th ANNUAL ATCA NEW-PLAY AWARD. For an outstanding new play in cross-country theater, voted by a committee of the American Theater Critics Association. *The Piano Lesson* by August Wilson.

1988 ELIZABETH HULL-KATE WARRINER AWARD. To the playwright whose work dealt with controversial subjects involving the fields of political, religious or social mores of the time, selected by the Dramatists Guild Council. **Wendy Wasserstein** for *The Heidi Chronicles*.

8th ANNUAL WILLIAM INGE AWARD. For lifetime achievement in the American Theater. **Horton Foote**.

5th ANNUAL GEORGE AND ELISABETH MARTON AWARD. To recognize and encourage a new American playwright selected by a committee of the Foundation of the Dramatists Guild. **Lee Blessing** for *A Walk in the Woods*.

11th ANNUAL SUSAN SMITH BLACKBURN PRIZE. To a woman who deserves recognition for having written a work of outstanding quality for the English-speaking theater. **Wendy Wasserstein** for *The Heidi Chronicles*.

34th ANNUAL DRAMA DESK AWARDS. For outstanding achievement, voted by an association of New York drama reporters, editors and critics. Plays—New play, *The Heidi Chronicles* by Wendy

Wasserstein; Director, **Jerry Zaks** for *Lend Me a Tenor*; Actor, **Philip Bosco** in *Lend Me a Tenor*; Actress, **Pauline Collins** in *Shirley Valentine*; Featured actor, **Peter Frechette** in *Eastern Standard*; Featured actress, **Tovah Feldshuh** in *Lend Me a Tenor*. Musicals—New musical, *Jerome Robbins' Broadway*; Actor, **Jason Alexander** for *Jerome Robbins' Broadway*; Actress, **Toni DiBuono** in *Forbidden Broadway*. Revival, *Our Town*. Unique theatrical experience, **Bill Irwin's** *Largely New York*. Design—Scenery, **Santo Loquasto** for *Cafe Crown* and *Italian American Reconciliation*; Costumes, **William Ivey Long** for *Lend Me a Tenor*; Lighting, **Jennifer Tipton** for *Long Day's Journey Into Night, Waiting for Godot* and *Jerome Robbins' Broadway*.

Special awards—**Bernard Gersten** and **Gregory Mosher** for revitalizing Lincoln Center Theater; **John McGlinn** for his dedication to preserving great musical theater scores; **Manhattan Theater Club** for setting high standards, encouraging new playwrights and importing unusual plays from abroad; **Paul Gemignani** in recognition of consistently outstanding musical direction and commitment to the theater; **Jerome Robbins** for an imperishable legacy of great American musicals.

OUTER CRITICS CIRCLE AWARDS. For outstanding achievement in the 1988–89 New York theater season, voted by critics of out-of-town and foreign periodicals. Broadway production of a play, *The Heidi Chronicles*. Actor in a play, **Kevin Conway** in *Other People's Money*. Actress in a play, **Pauline Collins** in *Shirley Valentine*. Off-Broadway play, *Other People's Money*. Director, **Jerry Zaks** for *Lend Me a Tenor*. Broadway musical, *Jerome Robbins' Broadway*. Actress in a musical, **Ruth Brown** in *Black and Blue*. Actor in a musical, **Jason Alexander** in *Jerome Robbins' Broadway*. Revival, *Our Town*. Striking debut of an actor, **Peter Frechette** in *Eastern Standard*. Striking debut of an actress, **Toni DiBuono** in *Forbidden Broadway*. Scenery, costume and lighting design, *Lend Me a Tenor*. John Gassner Playwright Award, **Jerry Sterner** for *Other People's Money*.

Special Awards: **Mikhail Baryshnikov** for acting in *Metamorphosis*; Ensemble acting, the cast of *Lend Me a Tenor*; **Jewish Repertory Theater** for its 1988–89 productions (*Cantorial* and *Chu Chem*).

11th ANNUAL KENNEDY CENTER HONORS. For distinguished achievement by individuals who have made significant contributions to American culture through the arts. **Alvin Ailey, George Burns, Myrna Loy, Alexander Schneider, Roger L. Stevens.**

GEORGE OPPENHEIMER/NEWSDAY AWARD. For the best new American playwright whose work is produced in New York City or on Long Island. **James Grimsley** for *Mr. Universe*.

1989 ALAN SCHNEIDER AWARD. For a director who has exhibited exceptional talent through work in a specific community or region, selected by a panel of professionals comprising John Dillon, Michael Kahn, Mary B. Robinson and Peter Zeisler. **Kyle Donnelly.**

53d ANNUAL DRAMA LEAGUE AWARDS. Distinguished performance, **Pauline Collins**. Musical theater, **Mandy Patinkin**. Unique contribution, **Joseph Papp.**

1989 THEATER WORLD AWARDS. For outstanding new talent in Broadway and off-Broadway productions during the 1988–89 season, selected by a committee comprising Clive Barnes, Douglas Watt and John Willis. **Dylan Baker** and **Peter Frechette** of *Eastern Standard*, **Joan Cusack** of *Road* and *Brilliant Traces*, **Loren Dean** of *Amulets Against the Dragon Forces*, **Sally Mayes** of *Welcome to the Club*, **Sharon McNight** of *Starmites*, **Jennie Moreau** of *Eleemosynary*, **Paul Provenza** and **Howard Spiegel** of *Only Kidding*, **Kyra Sedgwick** of *Ah, Wilderness!*, **Eric Stoltz** of *Our Town*, **Joanne Whalley-Kilmer** of *What the Butler Saw*.

Special awards: **Mikhail Baryshnikov** and **Pauline Collins** for their outstanding Broadway debuts in *Metamorphosis* and *Shirley Valentine*.

JOSEPH KESSELRING FUND AWARD. For playwrights, selected by a committee of the National Arts Club comprising T. E. Hambleton, Edwin Wilson and Lanford Wilson. **Diane Ney** for *The Jeremiah*. Honorable mention to **Frank Hogan** and **Jose Rivera.**

5th ANNUAL NEW YORK DANCE AND PERFORMANCE AWARDS. For choreographers and performance artists who presented new work in New York during the 1987–88 season, selected by a committee of 23 persons active in those fields. Choreographer/creator awards: **Ann Carlson, William Forsythe, Ann Hamilton, John Kelly, Tere O'Connor, Otrabanda** (Robert Babb, Rocky Bornstein, Michael Fajans, Nick Fennel, Gene Tyranny), **Elizabeth Streb, Wim Vandekeybus** and **Maximalist** (Thierry de Mey, Peter Vermeersch). Performer awards: **Lance Gries, Kate Johnson, Joseph Lennon, Norwood Pennewell, Keith Sabado, Ron Vawter**. Composer awards: **James Baker, Jeff Halpern, Gene Tyranny**. Visual design awards: **David Ferri, Janie Geiser, Carol Mullins,**

Stan Pressner. Special awards: **Bessie Schönberg, Act Up** (Aids Coalition to Unleash Power).

1988 MR. ABBOTT AWARD. For lifetime achievement in the theater, sponsored by the Stage Directors and Choreographers Workshop Foundation. **Agnes de Mille.**

COMMON WEALTH AWARD. For excellence of achievement and high potential for future contributions to the dramatic arts. **Jennifer Tipton.**

1989 ZEISLER AWARD. For distinguished achievement in the nonprofit professional theater. **Ruth Maleczech.**

THEATER HALL OF FAME. Annual election by members of the profession of nominees selected by vote of the members of the American Theater Critics Association. **George Balanchine, Ruby Dee, Dorothy Fields, Herbert Fields, Max Gordon, Danny Kaye, Siobhan McKenna, Mike Nichols, Elliot Norton** and **Eli Wallach.**

1988 JUJAMCYN THEATERS AWARD. Honoring an American Regional theater that has made an outstanding contribution to the development of creative talent for the theater. **The Second Stage Theater.**

AMERICAN THEATER WING DESIGN AWARDS. For designs originating in the U.S., voted by a committee comprising Tish Dace, Henry Hewes, Edward F. Kook, Julius Novick and Patricia McKay. Scene design, **Jerome Sirlin** for *1,000 Airplanes on the Roof.* Lighting design, **Jennifer Tipton** for *Jerome Robbins' Broadway, Long Day's Journey Into Night, The Rimers of Eldritch* and *Waiting for Godot.* Noteworthy Unusual Effect, **Alison Yerxa** for The Ant in *The Warrior Ant.*

45th ANNUAL CLARENCE DERWENT AWARDS. For the most promising male and female actors on the metropolitan scene during the 1988–89 season. **Mercedes Ruehl** in *Other People's Money* and **John Pankow** in *Aristocrats.*

JOSEPH JEFFERSON AWARDS. 20th annual citations for achievement in Chicago theater. Plays—Production, *Passion Play* at the Goodman Theater. Director, **Frank Galati** for *Passion Play.* Actor in a principal role, **Bill Cobbs** in *Driving Miss Daisy.* Actress in a principal role, **Gcina Mhlope** in *Have You Seen Zandile?.* Actor in a supporting role, **Jim True** in *Killers.* Actress in a supporting role, **Irma P. Hall** in *Have You Seen Zandile?.* Ensemble acting, *The Common Pursuit.* Musicals—Production, *La Cage aux Folles* at Candlelight Dinner Theater. Director, **Robert Falls** for *Pal Joey.* Actor in a

principal role, **James Harms** in *La Cage aux Folles.* Actress in a principal role, **Carlin Glynn** in *Pal Joey.* Actor in a supporting role, **Gordon McClure** in *La Cage aux Folles.* Actress in a supporting role, **Shannon Cochran** in *Pal Joey.* Cameo performance, **Barbara E. Robertson** in *Pal Joey.* Original music, **Robert Waldman** for *Driving Miss Daisy.* Choreography, **Ann Reinking** and **Chet Walker** for *Pal Joey.* Musical direction, **Kevin Stites** for *Pal Joey*, **Nick Venden** for *La Cage aux Folles.* Revues—Director, **Andre De Shields** for *The Colored Museum.* Actor in a principal role, **Terrence A. Carson** in *The Colored Museum.* Actress in a principal role, **Sybil Walker** in *The Colored Museum.* Design—Scenery, **Thomas Lynch** for *Pal Joey.* Costumes, **Martin Pakledinaz** for *Pal Joey.* Lighting, **Kevin Rigdon** for *Passion Play.* Sound, **Rob Milburn** for *Passion Play.*

16th annual awards of the Joseph Jefferson Citations Wing for excellence in non-Equity Chicago theater April 1, 1988–March 31, 1989. Production, *Anyone Can Whistle* and *Noises Off* at Pegasus Players. Performance, **Colette Hawley** in *Anyone Can Whistle*, **Pamela Webster** in *Noises Off*, **Harry J. Lennix** in *Caught in the Act*, **Neil Gray Giuntoli** in *The Crate Dweller.* Ensemble, *Noises Off.* Direction, **Victoria Bussert** for *Anyone Can Whistle*, **Michael Leavitt** for *Noises Off*, **Meryl Friedman** for *The Jungle Book.* Musical direction, **Jeff Lewis** for *Anyone Can Whistle.* Original incidental music, **Jacquie Krupka** and **Willie Steele** for *The Jungle Book.* New work, *Exploits of a Living Newspaper* by Writing Committee of Blind Parrot Production. Scene design, **Russ Borski** for *Anyone Can Whistle*, **Russ Jones** *Noises Off.* Costume design, **Laura Cunningham** and **Margaret Fitzsimmons-Morettini** for *The Jungle Book.* Special Honors Citations: **Pegasus Productions** "for its commitment to community outreach programming that involves the young, the elderly, the handicapped, the homeless and the disenfranchised;" **Midtown Bank** in recognition of its support of the Chicago theater community.

20th ANNUAL LOS ANGELES CRITICS CIRCLE AWARDS. For distinguished achievement in Los Angeles theater during 1988. Production—*The Crucible* produced by South Coast Repertory; *El Salvador* produced by Diane Wade; *Fences* produced by Carol Shorenstein Hayes in association with Yale Repertory Theater. Direction—**Martin Benson** for *The Crucible*, **Victor Pappas** for *South Central Rain*, **Jeff Seymour** for *El Salvador.* Writing—**Jules Feiffer** for *Carnal Knowledge*, **Rafael Lima** for *El Salvador*, **August Wilson** for

Fences. Leading performance—**Danny Aiello** in *Hurlyburly*, **Kathy Bates** in *Frankie and Johnny in the Clair de Lune*, **James Earl Jones** in *Fences*, **James Morrison** in *El Salvador*, **Lynne Thigpen** in *Fences*, **Chloe Webb** in *The Model Apartment*, **Paxton Whitehead** in *How the Other Half Loves*. Featured performance—**Kandis Chappell** in *The Crucible*, **Vincent J. Isaac** in *Distant Fires*, **Scott Lincoln** in *South Central Rain*, **Deirdre O'Connell** in *Stars in the Morning Sky*. Creation performance—**Jude Narita** in *Coming Into Passion/Song for a Sunset*. Ensemble performance—*Lies and Legends*. Scene design—**Don Llewellyn** for *Distant Fires*, **Deborah Raymond** and **Dorian Vernacchio** for *Breaking the Silence*. Costume design—**Andreane Neofitou** for *Les Misérables*, **Shigeru Yaji** for *The School for Scandal*. Lighting design—**Margaret Anne Dunn** for *Stone Wedding*, **David Hersey** for *Les Misérables*, **Tom Ruzika** for *The Crucible*. Original music—**Claude Michel Schönberg** for *Les Misérables*. Margaret Harford Award—**The Actor's Gang**. Lifetime Achievement Award—**Martin Magner**.

7th ANNUAL ELLIOT NORTON AWARD. To that person who, during the previous year, has made an outstanding contribution to theater in Boston. **Jacques Cartier** for direction of Molière's *Don Juan*. Specially commended: **Michael Goodson, Ruth Maleczech, Tina Packer**. Citations: **Robert Merowitz, Allen Koenig**.

5th ANNUAL HELEN HAYES AWARDS. In recognition of excellence in the Washington, D.C. theater. Resident shows—Production of a play, *Six Characters in Search of an Author* by Arena Stage; Production of a musical, *The Cocoanuts* by Arena Stage; New play, *The Night Hank Williams Died* by Larry L. King; Lead Actress, **Jennifer Mendenhall** in *Aunt Dan and Lemon*; Lead actor, **Michael Willis** in *The Boys Next Door*; Supporting actress, **Sarah C. Marshall** in *Baby With the Bathwater*; Supporting actor, **Edward Gero** in *Macbeth*; Lead actress in a musical, **Kim Criswell** in *Side by Side by Sondheim*; Lead actor in a musical, **Charles Janasz** in *The Cocoanuts*; Director, **Liviu Ciulei** for *Six Characters in Search of an Author*; Lighting design, **Allen Lee Hughes** for *Six Characters in Search of an Author*; Costume design, **William Pucilowsky** for *The Constant Wife*; Scene design, **Russell Metheny** for *Eleemosynary*. Non-resident shows—Production, *The Search for Signs of Intelligent Life in the Universe*; Lead actor, **Victor Garber** in *Wenceslas Square*; Lead Actress, **Lily Tomlin** in *The Search for Signs of Intelligent Life in the Universe*; Director, **Jane Wagner** for *The Search*

for Signs of Intelligent Life in the Universe; Supporting performer, **Bruce Norris** in *Wenceslas Square*.

13th ANNUAL CARBONELL AWARDS. South Florida critics' choices for the year's bests. Road shows—Production, *42nd Street*; Director/actor **Ray Cooney** for *Two Into One*; Actress, **Chita Rivera** for *Can-Can*; Supporting actor, **Barry Lee** for *Big River*; Supporting actress, **Pamela Dillon** for *Two Into One*. Regional plays—Production, *Biloxi Blues*; Director, **Kenneth Kay** for *Biloxi Blues*; Actor, **William Hindman** in *Papa*; Actress, **Jackie Lowe** in *Lady Day at Emerson's Bar and Grill*; Supporting actor, **Dan Leonard** in *Criminal Minds*; Supporting actress, **Nancy Barnett** in *On the Verge*. Regional musicals—Production, *The Best Little Whorehouse in Texas*; Director, **Bob Bogdanoff** for *The Best Little Whorehouse in Texas*; Choreographer, **Scott Shettleroe** for *My One and Only*; Musical director, **Mace Graham** for *The Best Little Whorehouse in Texas*; Actor, **Greg Phelps** in *My One and Only*; Actress, **Julie Prosser** in *Baby*; Supporting actor, **Don Whisted** in *The Best Little Whorehouse in Texas*; Supporting actress, **Mona Jones** in *Mayor*. Regional technical—Scenery, **Fred Kolo** for *The Rink*; Lighting, **Robert D. Clark** for *Teibele and Her Demon*; Costumes, **Jeffrey B. Phipps** for *Mrs. Warren's Profession*. George Abbott Award "for outstanding achievement in the arts," **Ruth Foreman**.

1987–88 DENVER DRAMA CRITICS CIRCLE AWARDS. For the best of the Denver season. New play, *Lady I and Lady II Talk Like Pigeons, They Dooo...They Dooo* by Arnold Rabin. Production of a musical, *Beehive*. Production of a play, *The Price*. Touring production, *Me and My Girl*. Best seasons—For a theater company, **Colorado Shakespeare Festival**; For an actor, **Terry Burnsed**; For an actress, **Sandra Ellis Lafferty**. Performances—Ensemble, *The Fifth of July*; Actor in a leading role, **Merrill Key** in *As Is*; Actress in a leading role, **Karen Erickson** in *Entertaining Mr. Sloane*; Actor in a musical, **Gregory Price** in *La Cage aux Folles*; Actress in a musical, **Leslie Hendrix** in *Guys and Dolls*; Supporting actor, **Guy Raymond** in *The Price*; Supporting actress, **Suzanne L. Fountain** in *The Glass Menagerie*. Director, **Frank Georgianana** for *The Price*. Scenery, **Andrew V. Yelusich** for *The Price*. Costumes, **Zina Lee Armstrong** for *Amadeus*. Lighting, **Sheree Goecke** for *Biedermann and the Firebugs*. Sound, **Lia Vollack** for *Hamlet*. Choreography, *42nd Street*.

5th ANNUAL SAN DIEGO THEATER CRITICS CIRCLE AWARDS. For outstanding achievement during the 1987–88 season. Outstanding new play, *The Cocktail Hour* by A. R. Gurney. Outstanding new musical, *80 Days* by Snoo Wilson and Ray Davies. Outstanding production, *Red Noses*. Outstanding road show, *Joe Turner's Come and Gone*. Score, **Gina Leishman** for *Red Noses*. Director, **John Hirsch** for *Coriolanus*. Lead actor, **Byron Jennings** in *Coriolanus*. Leading actress, **Rosina Widdowson-Reynolds** in *Private Lives*.

Supporting actor, **Dakin Matthews** in *Coriolanus*. Supporting actress, **Shuko Akune** in *Tea*. Scenery, **John Arnone** for *Lulu*. Costumes, **Robert Wojewodski** for *Love's Labor's Lost*. Lighting, **Kent Dorsey** for *Coriolanus*. Sound, **Michael Holten** and **Conrad Susa** for *Coriolanus*. Choreography, **Javier Velasco** for *Suds*.

Special awards: **William B. Eaton** for the "exceptional professionalism" of years of service with the Old Globe Theater; **Scripteasers** for 40 years of service to and support of aspiring playwrights.

1988–1989 PUBLICATION OF RECENTLY-PRODUCED PLAYS

Accidental Death of an Anarchist. Dario Fo. Methuen (paperback).

Another Antigone. A.R. Gurney. Nelson Doubleday.

Big Time (Scenes from a Service Economy). Keith Reddin. Broadway Play Publishing (paperback).

Drinking in America. Eric Bogosian. Vintage/Random House (paperback).

Esther: A Vaudeville Megillah. Elizabeth Swados. Broadway Play Publishing (paperback).

Frankie and Johnny in the Clair de Lune. Terrence McNally. Nelson Doubleday.

Ghetto. Joshua Sobol. Nick Hern Books (paperback).

I'm Not Rappaport. Herb Gardner. Grove Press (paperback).

In Perpetuity Throughout the Universe. Eric Overmyer. Broadway Play Publishing (paperback).

Joe Turner's Come and Gone. August Wilson. New American Library (paperback).

Just Say No: A Play About a Farce. Larry Kramer. Broadway Play Publishing (paperback).

Laughing Wild. Christopher Durang. Nelson Doubleday.

Lettice and Lovage/Yonadab. Peter Schaffer. Penguin (paperback).

M. Butterfly. David Henry Hwang. New American Library (paperback).

Mountain Language. Harold Pinter. Grove Press (paperback).

National Anthems. Dennis McIntyre. Grove Press (paperback).

Place With the Pigs, A. Athol Fugard. Faber and Faber (paperback).

Playboy of the West Indies. Mustapha Matura. Broadway Play Publishing (paperback).

Real Estate. Louise Page. Samuel French (paperback).

Roots in a Parched Ground/Lily Dale/The Widow Claire. Horton Foote. Grove Press (also paperback).

Safe Sex. Harvey Fierstein. Atheneum (also paperback)

Shayna Maidel, A. Barbara Lebow. New American Library (paperback).

Shirley Valentine/One For the Road. Willy Russell. Atheneum (paperback).

Smile (libretto). Howard Ashman and Marvin Hamlisch. Samuel French.

Speed-the-Plow. David Mamet. Grove Press (also paperback).

Tamara. John Krizang. Stoddard (paperback).

Temptation. Vaclav Havel. Grove Press (paperback).
Three Postcards (libretto). Craig Lucas and Craig Carnelia. Dramatists Play Service (paperback and spiral bound).
Uncle Vanya. Anton Chekhov, adapted by David Mamet. Grove Press (paperback).
Walk in the Woods, A. Lee Blessing. New American Library (paperback).
What's Wrong With This Picture? Donald Margulies. Broadway Play Publishing (paperback).

A SELECTED LIST OF OTHER PLAYS PUBLISHED IN 1988–89

Adrienne Kennedy in One Act. Adrienne Kennedy. University of Minnesota Press.
American Clock, The. Arthur Miller. Grove Press
Andromache. Jean Racine. Applause (paperback).
Bacchides. Plautus. Aris & Phillips (paperback).
Best Short Plays of 1988, The. Ramon Delgado, editor. Applause (paperback).
Complete Beyond the Fringe, The. Alan Bennett et al. Methuen (paperback).
Brecht: Plays One. Bertolt Brecht. Methuen (paperback).
Brecht: Plays Two. Bertolt Brecht. Methuen (paperback).
Brecht: Plays Three: Bertolt Brecht. Methuen (paperback).
Coastal Disturbances: Four Plays by Tina Howe. Tina Howe. Theater Communications Group. (also paperback).
Complete Plays of Oscar Wilde, The. Oscar Wilde. Methuen (paperback).
Eugene O'Neill: The Unfinished Plays. Eugene O'Neill. Continuum.
Famous American Plays of the 1930s. Harold Clurman. Dell (paperback).
Famous American Plays of the 1940s. Henry Hewes. Dell (paperback).
Famous American Plays of the 1950s. Lee Strasberg. Dell (paperback).
Famous American Plays of the 1960s. Harold Clurman. Dell (paperback).
Famous American Plays of the 1970s. Ted Hoffman. Dell (paperback).
Famous American Plays of the 1980s. Robert Marx. Dell (paperback).
Five Plays by Gorky. Maxim Gorky. Methuen (paperback).
Four Plays by Marsha Norman. Marsha Norman. Theater Communications Group (paperback).
Knight of the Burning Pestle, The. Francis Beaumont. Manchester University Press (paperback).
Lulu. Peter Barnes. Methuen (paperback).
Madman and the Nun, The and Crazy Locomotive, The: Three Plays. Stanislow Ignacy Witkiewicz. Applause (paperback).
Marivaux: Plays. Pierre Marivaux. Methuen (paperback).
More Stately Mansions. Eugene O'Neill. Oxford.
Marionettes, The. William Faulkner. University Press of Virginia.
New French Plays. David Bradby and Claude Schumacher, selectors. Methuen (paperback).

New Inn, The: Revels Plays Edition. Ben Jonson. Manchester University Press (paperback).
O'Neill: Complete Plays. Eugene O'Neill. Three-volume boxed set. Viking.
Selected Plays of Dion Boucicault. Chosen and introduced by Andrew Parkin. Catholic
    University Press (paperback).
Stars in the Morning Sky: New Soviet Plays. Michael Glenny, introducer. Nick Hern Books
    (paperback).
Three Theban Plays (Humanities). Sophocles. Aris & Phillips (paperback).
Totem Voices: Plays from the Black World Repertory. Paul Carter Harrison, editor. Grove
    Press (also paperback).

NECROLOGY

MAY 1988–MAY 1989

PERFORMERS

Abba, Marta (87)—June 24, 1988
Ames, Angela (32)—November 27, 1988
Adkins, J. Thomas (62)—July 13, 1988
Allison, May (98)—March 27, 1989
Andrews, Harry (77)—March 7, 1989
Aragon, Jesse (32)—November 8, 1988
Arundell, Dennis (90)—Winter, 1988
Averino, Olga (93)—January 17, 1989
Bailey, John (73)—February 18, 1989
Baird, Eugenie (63)—June 12, 1988
Ball, Lucille (77)—April 26, 1989
Barbee, Ruby (84)—December 21, 1988
Barnett, Nate (48)—May 29, 1988
Barrier, Ernestine (81)—February 13, 1989
Barrington, Michael (63)—June 5, 1988
Barry, Edwina (102)—July 7, 1988
Barry, Joan (87)—April 10, 1989
Barsi, Judith (11)—July 27, 1988
Bazlen, Brigid (44)—May 25, 1989
Beam, Alvin (51)—January 15, 1989
Benson, Joe (73)—March 27, 1989
Beres, Mark (29)—January 19, 1989
Blier, Bernard (73)—March 29, 1989
Boatner, Joseph (70)—May 8, 1989
Bond, Greg (35)—June 10, 1988
Boswell, Vet (77)—November 12, 1988
Bowman, Priscilla (60)—July 24, 1988
Boyle, Robert (39)—May 16, 1989
Brandon, Jane Hopkins (60)—July 4, 1988
Brown, Pamela (64)—January 26, 1989
Brown, Tally (64)—May 6, 1989
Brubach, Robert (33)—December 25, 1988
Burke, James E. Jr. (68)—October 1, 1988
Burke, Rick (26)—February 19, 1989

Burt, Wilson E. (76)—March 20, 1989
Calder, Len (40)—February 14, 1989
Carradine, John (82)—November 27, 1988
Carter, Chelle (35)—July 1, 1988
Carter, John (77)—July 22, 1988
Carter, William (53)—July 28, 1988
Cassavetes, John (59)—February 3, 1989
Castang, Veronica (50)—November 5, 1988
Castellano, Richard (55)—December 10, 1988
Challee, William (84)—March 18, 1989
Chamberlin, Jayne (47)—August 29, 1988
Clark, Dort (71)—March 30, 1989
Coley, Thomas (76)—May 23, 1989
Colin, Jean (83)—March 7, 1989
Comstock, Betsy (65)—February 21, 1989
Condos, Nick (73)—July 9, 1988
Connelly, Christopher (47)—December 7, 1988
Connor, Whitfield (71)—July 16, 1988
Cook, Nathan (38)—June 11, 1988
Coonan, Sheila M. (66)—March 28, 1989
Cooper, Dorothy J. (82)—December 7, 1988
Cortez, Mildred (72)—May 16, 1989
Cortland, Nicholas (47)—August 21, 1988
Costa, Bob (66)—February 19, 1989
Coulouris, George (85)—April 25, 1989
Covan, Willie (92)—May 7, 1989
Cuevas, David (33)—August 16, 1988
Curtis, Billy (79)—November 9, 1988
D'Angelo, Salvatore J. (68)—March 19, 1989
Daniels, Billy (73)—October 7, 1988
Dansereau, Muriel Tannehill (96)—May 13, 1989
Darget, Chantal (54)—July 6, 1988

575

Davenport, Jasmine (33)—August 9, 1988
Davis, Onnie (51)—June 14, 1988
Dawn, Hazel (98)—August 29, 1988
Day, Dennis (71)—June 22, 1988
Day, Gloria—May 14, 1989
Daye, Billy E. (55)—March 7, 1989
DeAngelus, Alfred (70)—January 4, 1989
DeBlon, Jack (58)—July 25, 1988
Deene, Lally (68)—September 20, 1988
Dell, Gabriel (68)—July 3, 1988
DeSales, Francis (76)—September 25, 1988
DeVol, Grayce—February 1, 1989
Dexter, Marie (71)—June 18, 1988
Dickens, Homer (63)—February 5, 1989
Dittman, Kean Gus (57)—January, 1989
Doherty, Charla (41)—May 29, 1988
Doner, Kitty (92)—August 26, 1988
Dorning, Robert (75)—February 20, 1989
Duggan, Elizabeth (56)—June 7, 1988
Dunn, Benny (75)—April 16, 1989
Dunstan, Wayne (60)—July 28, 1988
Edwards, Jimmy (68)—July 7, 1988
Eldridge, Florence (87)—August 1, 1988
Enters, Angna (82)—February 25, 1989
Errigo, Billy (37)—August 24, 1988
Evans, Maurice (87)—March 12, 1989
Evans, Peter (38)—May 20, 1989
Farley, Morgan (90)—October 11, 1988
Farmer, Mary Virginia (90)—May 19, 1988
Farrell, Jack (52)—June 27, 1988
Felligrini, Gene (44)—May 10, 1988
Fender, Michael Doyle (47)—September, 1988
Fennelly, Catherine R. (95)—June 10, 1988
Field, Sean (60's)—March 6, 1989
Finley, Evelyn (73)—April 7, 1989
Fischer, Geoffrey (51)—November 4, 1988
Fisher, Jerry (55)—July 15, 1988
Fleisig, Alan L.—January 10, 1989
Flood, Gerald (61)—April 12, 1989
Flowers, Wayland (48)—October 11, 1988
Fonseca, Larry (52)—November 14, 1988
Ford, Ross (65)—June 22, 1988
Forrest, William H. (86)—January 26, 1989

Fowle, Frank III (43)—January 19, 1989
Foy, Madeline (80)—July 5, 1988
Franklin, Carolyn (43)—April 24, 1989
Frey, Leonard (49)—August 24, 1988
Friebus, Florida (79)—May 27, 1988
Frobe, Gert (75)—September 4, 1988
Frome, Milton (78)—March 21, 1989
Gamer, Henry (75)—February 15, 1989
Gammill, Noreen (90)—December 20, 1988
Ganzer, John (33)—December 3, 1988
Geer, Lenny (75)—January 9, 1989
Geise, Sugar (71)—October 30, 1988
Gelfer, Steven (39)—December 26, 1988
Gifford, Alan (78)—March 29, 1989
Gil, Gilbert (74)—August 25, 1988
Gittens, Chriss (86)—August 21, 1988
Gorman, Bobby (59)—October 11, 1988
Graham, Geordie (88)—October 11, 1988
Grandin, Ethel (94)—September 28, 1988
Groman, Janice (51)—September 2, 1988
Hackney, Doris (64)—November 30, 1988
Hagerman, Thomas (55)—October 15, 1988
Hall, Alice May (96)—June 13, 1988
Halpern, Dina (79)—February 17, 1989
Harburg, Edelanine (88)—March 26, 1989
Harris, Fox (52) December 27, 1988
Hawthorne, Maggie (39)—October 2, 1988
Hawtrey, Charles (73)—October 27, 1988
Hayes, Grace (93)—February 1, 1989
Heinemann, Richard (76)—July 27, 1988
Heller, Jackie (86)—July 15, 1988
Henderson, Bill (51)—Spring 1989
Henderson, Jo (54)—August 6, 1988
Henshaw, Wandalie (54)—April 29, 1989
Hohman, Charles L. (68)—February 16, 1989
Holland, Anthony (60)—July 10, 1988
Holt, Jason (39)—March 6, 1989
Horney, Brigitte (77)—July 27, 1988
Hovey, Serge (69)—May 5, 1989
Hulburd, Nelda Marshall (85)—January 26, 1989
Ilson, William—June 20, 1988
Irvine, Kiana R. (91)—May 7, 1989
Jacobson, Henrietta (82)—October 9, 1988
Jaffe, Allen (60)—March 18, 1989
James, Emrys (59)—February 5, 1989

Janiss, Vivi (mid-60's)—September 7, 1988

Johnstone, Peggy (89)—December 25, 1988

Jonew, Duane (51)—July 22, 1988

Jordan, Dorothy (82)—December 7, 1988

Karina, Lea (75)—December 22, 1988

Katz, Michael M. (32)—September 14, 1988

Kavanaugh, Richard (47)—August 6, 1988

Kenner, Warren (64)—March 21, 1989

Kinnear, Roy (54)—September 20, 1988

Kirkpatrick, May Elizabeth (87)—November 27, 1988

Klein, Herb (72)—July 17, 1988

Kornfeld, Emily (73)—April 21, 1989

Kotecki, Dennis (33)—April 20, 1989

Kramer, Mandel J. (72)—January 29, 1989

LaCaresse, Arthur A. (78)—February 24, 1989

Lafont, Pauline (26)—November 21, 1988

Lampkin, Charles (76)—April 17, 1989

LeFevre, Alphus (76)—December 9, 1988

Leigh, George (78)—December 11, 1988

Leonard, Jack (73)—June 1988

Liazza, Stella de Mette (97)—May 17, 1989

Liepa, Maris (52)—March 25, 1989

Lillie, Beatrice (94)—January 20, 1989

Lindsay, Phillip (64)—October 22, 1988

Lland, Michael (64)—January 20, 1989

Lloyd, Jimmy (69)—August 25, 1988

Loder, John (90)—December 1988

Logan, Nedda Harrigan (89)—April 1, 1989

London, Chet (57)—September 15, 1988

Long, John F. (46)—April 2, 1989

Low, Carl (71)—October 19, 1988

Luckham, Cyril (81)—February 7, 1989

Lummis, Dayton (84)—June 23, 1988

Mack, Marion (87)—May 1, 1989

Manley, James Carl (37)—September 7, 1988

Mansfield, Marian (83)—November 16, 1988

Maris, Monica (43)—November 16, 1988

Martin-Harvey, Muriel (97)—December 15, 1988

Mauch, Mary Elchlepp (70)—July 15, 1988

Maura, Luis (38)—May 14, 1988

McClary, Bill (44)—January 6, 1989

McClelland, Allan (71)—Winter 1989

McGuire, Tucker (75)—Summer 1988

McIlwraith, David H.—April 15, 1989

McMillan, Kenneth (56)—January 8, 1989

Meeker, Ralph (67)—August 5, 1988

Melville, Sam (52)—March 9, 1989

Meyer, James (41)—December 26, 1988

Milanov, Zinka (83)—May 30, 1989

Milford, Kim (37)—December 13, 1988

Millar, Ainslie (69)—Spring 1989

Miller, Joan (78)—August 31, 1988

Mills, Herbert (77)—April 12, 1989

Mintz, Eli (83)—June 8, 1988

Mitchell, Ewing Young (77)—September 2, 1988

Moberly, Robert (49)—October 17, 1988

Morin, Alberto (86)—April 7, 1989

Morris, Mary (72)—October 14, 1988

Murphy, Timothy Patrick (29)—December 6, 1988

Murray, Colin (86)—April 15, 1989

Murray, Ken (85)—October 12, 1988

Napier, Alan (85)—August 8, 1988

Navarre, Michael (33)—May 28, 1988

Neidorf, Ross Lee (34)—March 4, 1989

Neighbors, David—April 17, 1989

Nelson, Christine (60)—August 15, 1988

Neuss, Wolfgang (63)—April 5, 1989

Niclas, Emmy (90's)—May 28, 1988

Nissen, Greta (82)—May 15, 1988

Norden, Christine (63)—September 21, 1988

Oakes, Betty (60)—July 27, 1988

O'Day, Nell (79)—January 3, 1989

O'Down, Frank (38)—June 4, 1988

O'Hanlon, George (76)—February 11, 1989

Oliver, Virgil (72)—June 3, 1988

Orrin, Dale Linx (36)—May 8, 1989

Ozeray, Madeleine (79)—March 29, 1989

Papkin, Mary Ellen (86)—March 4, 1989

Parenti, Franco (67)—May 28, 1989

Prado, Raul (78)—April 8, 1989

Prokofiev, Lina (91)—January 3, 1989

Quertermous, Charlie (41)—April 17, 1989

Quinn, Louis (73)—September 15, 1988
Radner, Gilda (42)—May 19, 1989
Raines, Ella (66)—May 30, 1988
Ramsey, Anne (59)—August 11, 1988
Ray, James (57)—December 3, 1988
Raymond, Helen (85)—Spring 1989
Rechtzeit, Jack 85)—July 24, 1988
Regan, Danny (65)—August 15, 1988
Rehfuss, Heinz (71)—June 27, 1988
Rhoad, Herbert (44)—December 18, 1988
Rich, Irene (96)—April 21, 1989
Riley,Jay Flash (72)—September 20, 1988
Robinson, Rad (77)—September 20, 1988
Ross, Lanny (82)—April 25, 1989
Rowe, Frances (75)—July 31, 1988
Russ, Reim (34)—May 1988
Sauers, Patricia (49)—March 25, 1989
Seefried, Irmgard (69)—November 24, 1988
Seymour, Anne (79)—December 8, 1988
Sfat, Dina Kutner (50)—March 20, 1989
Shaw, Victoria (53)—August 17, 1988
Sherman, Hiram (81)—April 11, 1989
Sherman, Madeline Fairbanks (82)—January 26, 1989
Sherwood, Lydia (82)—April 20, 1989
Sherwood, Madeleine H. (89)—April 4, 1989
Sigler, Scott (32)—September 28, 1988
Silva, Trinidad Jr. (38)—July 31, 1988
Silver, Joe (66)—February 27, 1989
Smith, Charles (68)—December 26, 1988
Smith, Elizabeth Stevens (70)—June 11, 1988
Smith, Fatman (67)—March 10, 1989
Smith, Tucker (52)—December 22, 1988
Sobel, Jack (91)—August 13, 1988
Spekter, Edythe Schneider (68)—March 14, 1989
Spinell, Joe (51)—January 13, 1989
Squire, William (72)—May 3, 1989
Starrett, Jack (52)—March 27, 1989
Stockton, Peggy (52)—September 12, 1988
Stuart, Jerri Rogers—February 6, 1989
Sylvester, James (42)—December 16, 1988
Tate, John (38)—April 15, 1989

Taylor, Valerie (85)—October 24, 1988
Terry, Don (86)—October 6, 1988
Thomas, Ann (75)—April 28, 1989
Thompkins, Toney (33)—May 11, 1988
Thornton, George Morris (67)—April 16, 1989
Todd, Lori Mattis (45)—April 9, 1989
Uhley, Patricia (68)—November 9, 1988
Vail, Lillian (96)—April 1, 1989
Vanel, Charles (96)—April 15, 1989
Varden, Norma (90)—January 19, 1989
Vincent, Romo (80)—January 16, 1989
Von Stroheim, Valerie (91)—October 22, 1988
Vorster, Gordon (64)—Winter 1988
Walsh, Martin J. (41)—July 7, 1988
Washbourne, Mona (84)—November 15, 1988
Washington, Vernon (64)—June 7, 1988
Waskul, Robert R. (34)—December 3, 1988
Watkins, June (73)—May 26, 1989
Watson, Douglass (67)—May 1, 1989
Watts, Arthur (80)—October 10, 1988
Webber, Robert (64)—May 19, 1989
West, Lockwood (83)—March 28, 1989
Wetmore, Joan (77)—February 13, 1989
White, John Sylvester (68)—September 11, 1988
Whitley, Keith (33)—May 9, 1989
Willes, Jean (65)—January 3, 1989
Williams, Clark (83)—February 13, 1989
Williams, Guy (65)—May 6, 1989
Willman, Noel (70)—December 24, 1988
Wilson, Trey (40)—January 16, 1989
Woodbury, Joan (73)—February 22, 1989
Woodland, Norman (83)—April 3, 1989
Worth, Maggie (58)—October 20, 1988
Wrather, Bonita Granville (65)—October 11, 1988
Wyckoff, Michael (69)—July 30, 1988
Zang, Edward (54)—March 14, 1989

PLAYWRIGHTS

Bernard, Thomas (58)—February 12, 1989
Bernstein,Robert(69)—December19, 1988
Bettenbender, John I. (67)—June 24, 1988

Braswell, John (51)—February 16, 1989
Carroll, Sidney (75)—November 3, 1988
Cary, Falkland (92)—April 7, 1989
Casey, Warren (53)—November 8, 1988
Chodorov, Edward (84)—October 9, 1988
Collins, Kathleen (46)—September 18, 1988
Cyr, Paul J. (37)—March 12, 1989
Driver, Donald (65)—June 27, 1988
Dyne, Michael (70)—May 17, 1989
Fletcher, Bramwell (84)—June 22, 1988
Franken, Rose (92)—June 22, 1988
Gallagher, Larry (41)—September 27, 1988
Geddes, Virgil (92)—May 24, 1989
Giantvalley, Scott (39)—March 2, 1989
Gress, Elsa (69)—July 19, 1988
Gunn, Bill (59)—April 5, 1989
Hocquenghem, Guy (42)—August 28, 1988
Howard, DuMont (34)—November 6, 1988
Jacobson, Doris (74)—July 23, 1988
John, Errol (64)—July 10, 1988
Johnson, Michael (36)—June 13, 1988
Kirkwood, James (64)—April 22, 1989
Koltes, Bernard-Marke (41)—April 15, 1989
Leach, Wilford (59)—June 18, 1988
Logan, Joshua (79)—July 12, 1988
Lynch, Liam (52)—April 25, 1989
Meyers, Timothy Francis (44)—March 14, 1989
Morgan, Brian G. (43)—February 5, 1989
Parker, Stewart (47)—November 2, 1988
Philips, Judson (85)—March 7, 1989
Pinero, Miguel (41)—June 16, 1988
Rella, Ettore (81)—October 16, 1988
Roos, Joanna (88)—May 13, 1989
Schehade, Georges (81)—January 18, 1989
Shafer, Roxanne (57)—February 22, 1989
Shulman, Max (69)—August 28, 1988
Tiller, Ted (75)—September 24, 1988
Tiscornia, Nelly Fernandez (60)—October 4, 1988
Vehr, Bill (48)—August 2, 1988
Whitmore, George (43)—April 19, 1989

COMPOSERS, LYRICISTS

Atwood, Hubbard M. (70)—September 21, 1988
Baker, David (60)—July 16, 1988
Benjamin, Claude (81)—May 2, 1989
Blatt, Jerry (47)—January 19, 1989
Calvi, Pino (58)—January 4, 1989
Capizzi, Leonard J. (47)—October 12, 1988
Che, Chico (43)—March 29, 1989
Cook, Ray (42)—March 20, 1989
Green, Johnny (80)—May 15, 1989
Hamblen, Stuart (80)—March 8, 1989
Harris, Bill (63)—December 6, 1988
Henderson, Horace (83)—August 29, 1988
Heywood, Eddie (73)—January 2, 1989
Hoffman, Jack (72)—January 16, 1989
Jary, Michael (81)—July 12, 1988
Leclerc, Feliz (74)—August 8, 1988
Lynn, George (73)—March 16, 1989
Murray, Lyn (79)—May 29, 1989
Newman, Lionel (73)—February 3, 1989
Nisbet, Robert (tt)—December 16, 1988
Paige, Richard E. (83)—August 15, 1988
Raposo, Joe (51)—February 5, 1989
Reichner, S. Bickley (84)—April 8, 1989
Scelsi, Giacinto (83)—July 26, 1988
Sims, Harry (80)—February 9, 1989
Smith, Julia (78)—April 27, 1989
Sorabji, Kaikhosru (96)—October 15, 1988
Sorozabal, Pablo (91)—December 26, 1988
Stein, Ronald (58)—August 15, 1988
Stuckey, Nat (54)—August 24, 1988
Vejvoda, Jaromir (86)—November 13, 1988

PRODUCERS, DIRECTORS, CHOREOGRAPHERS

Albery, Donald (74)—September 14, 1988
Aron, Jean-Paul (61)—August 20, 1988
Ashcroft, Ronnie (65)—December 14, 1988
Ashton, Frederick (83)—August 18, 1988

Ball, Elmer M. Jr. (52)—November 29, 1988

Ballantyne, Colin Sandergrove (79)—July 1, 1988

Barr, Richard (71)—January 8, 1989

Bernd, John Jeffrey (35)—August 28, 1988

Bigelow, Paul (83)—May 18, 1988

Brookner, Howard (34)—April 27, 1989

Carpenter, Freddie (80)—January 19, 1989

Cayatte, Andre (80)—February 6, 1989

Chabert, Robert (89)—July 17, 1988

Chaison, William (44)—January 13, 1989

Christensen, Harold (84)—February 20, 1989

Chwat, Jacques (53)—August 8, 1988

Crinkely, Richmond D. (49)—January 29, 1989

DaCosta, Morton (74)—January 29, 1989

Daniels, Marc (77)—April 23, 1989

DeFelice, Harold (38)—July 4, 1988

Dennick, Robin (32)—September 12, 1988

Dentler, Mary Ann (96)—December 14, 1988

Dudley, Terence (69)—December 25, 1988

Duncan, Jeff (59)—May 26, 1989

Durante, Vito (64)—May 6, 1989

Ehre, Ida (88)—February 16, 1989

Feldman, Edward H. (68)—November 30, 1988

Field, Ron (55)—February 6, 1989

Forella, Ronn (50)—January 18, 1989

Frank, Mary K. (77)—November 20, 1988

Frank, Melvin (75)—October 13, 1988

Glover, Guy (79)—Summer 1988

Hager, Louis Busch (58)—December 16, 1988

Hammond, Sally (53)—June 8, 1988

Heilweil, David (71)—February 15, 1989

Hemsley, Winston DeWitt (42)—May 9, 1989

Hickox, Douglas (59)—July 25, 1988

Holley, Robert Bruce (59)—November 11, 1988

Hope, Harry (52)—November 6, 1988

Houseman, John (86)—October 31, 1988

Howard, Ted (77)—December 22, 1988

Jeffrey, Howard (53)—November 2, 1988

Jurriens, Henny (40)—April 9, 1989

Kaufman, Colette C.C. (49)—May 28, 1988

Kessler, Ken M. Jr. (68)—January 31, 1989

Koster, Henry (83)—September 21, 1988

LeBorg, Reginald (86)—March 25, 1989

Lipton, Michael Charles (50)—November 7, 1988

Lynn, Amy (73)—August 6, 1988

Macdonald, Craig (48)—February 24, 1989

Manou, Rallou (73)—October 15, 1988

Mansfield, Irving (80)—August 25, 1988

Moore, Jack (62)—June 23, 1988

Morency, Jean Daniel (51)—July 20, 1988

Olsen, Kenneth M. (60)—February 21, 1989

Peckham, Charles S. (56)—April 1, 1989

Psacharopoulos, Nikos (60)—January 12, 1989

Quinn, Douglas (33)—June 5, 1988

Rawley, Ernest (83)—January 16, 1989

Rodham, Robert D. (48)—July 14, 1988

Scarborough, Danny (41)—May 1989

Silverman, Mark (36)—February 3, 1989

Stone, Edward (34)—December 1, 1988

Swallo, Wendy (57)—April 7, 1989

Tasker, John (55)—June 18, 1988

Thompson, Edmonstone F. Jr. (44)—July 31, 1988

Tuttle, Frank Pay (86)—May 8, 1989

Von Fritsch, Gunther (84)—August 27, 1988

Warren, Jerry (mid-60's)—August 21, 1988

Wolff, Lothar (79)—October 2, 1989

Zegart, Arthur (72)—February 2, 1989

DESIGNERS

Allen, Reg (71)—March 30, 1989

Bailey, Brian (30)—March 2, 1989

Butler, Lawrence W. (80)—October 19, 1988

Dali, Salvador (84)—January 23, 1989

Deskey, Donald (94)—April 29, 1989

Dohanos, Peter S. (57)—December 27, 1988

Dulong, Richard (36)—May 10, 1988

Grimes, Stephen (61)—September 12, 1988

Gundelfinger, Alan M. (88)—January 26, 1989

Hoffman, Matthew J. III (45)—September 10, 1988

Howland, Robert Lantz (40)—August 5, 1988

Irving, Laurence (91)—October 23, 1988

LeCain, Errol (47)—January 3, 1989

Lonergan, Arthur (83)—January 23, 1989

McCoy, Maria (46)—April 11, 1989

Ponnell, Jean-Pierre (56)—August 11, 1988

Ricci, Armondo T. (93)—October 14, 1988

Rogers, Ben (83)—August 23, 1988

Roth, Wolfgang (78)—November 11, 1988

Ryman, Herbert Dickens (78)—February 10, 1989

Scott, Walter (82)—February 2, 1989

Shrum, John Howard (61)—September 10, 1988

Starr, Melvin (69)—May 30, 1988

Suppon, Charles (40)—Spring 1989

Troast, George (78)—October 10, 1988

CRITICS

Allen, Tom (50)—September 30, 1988

Bahrenberg, Bruce (57)—March 4, 1989

Ball, John (77)—October 15, 1988

Bellamy, Peter (74)—January 6, 1989

Belser, Lee (73)—November 26, 1988

Cedrone, Clara—October 7, 1988

Davis, Gerald (54)—June 22, 1988

Fidler, Jimmie (89)—August 9, 1988

Frederick, Robert B. (69)—August 17, 1988

Graham, Sheilah (84)—November 17, 1988

Green, Ted (76)—August 4, 1988

Gross, Roland (80)—February 11, 1989

Halliwell, Leslie (59)—January 21, 1989

Kogran, Herman (74)—March 8, 1989

McCord, Bert (74)—October 28, 1988

McGovern, Bernard (47)—November 4, 1988

Michelson, Herv (57)—August 12, 1988

Mila, Massimo (78)—December 26, 1988

Nesbitt, James R. (55)—September 26, 1988

Ottaway, Robert (68)—July 14, 1988

Perrotti, Gary Edward (35)—July 18, 1988

Rosenthal, Stuart (41)—Spring 1989

Sauvage, Leo (75)—October 30, 1988

Schack, William (90)—November 19, 1988

Schlaerth, J. Don (60)—July 9, 1988

Young, L. Masco (66)—January 11, 1989

CONDUCTORS

Allen, Bob (75)—April 24, 1989

Austin, Arthur (77)—May 9, 1989

Belasco, Leon (86)—June 1, 1988

Bleyer, Archie (79)—March 20, 1989

Bradway, Wendell E. (76)—February 22, 1989

Cox, Ainslee (52)—September 5, 1988

Dell'Isola, Savatore (88)—March 13, 1989

Dorati, Antal (82)—November 13, 1988

Drybread, Claude S. (77)—March 8, 1989

Dunbar, Rudolph (81)—June 10, 1988

Hodge, Leslie (75)—December 6, 1988

Ingalls, Philip E.—August 27, 1988

Jaroff, Serge (89)—October 5, 1988

Jones, W. Ifor (88)—November 11, 1988

Julian, Dan (82)—April 27, 1989

LaMont, Jimmy (75)—September 9, 1988

Mauldin, Randolph (47)—April 16, 1989

Meltzer, Andrew (40)—June 22, 1988

Patane, Guiseppe (57)—May 30, 1989

Saffir, Kurt (59)—November 1, 1988

Safren, Irving Israel (85)—November 1, 1988

Sebastian, Georges (85)—April 12, 1989

Van Straten, Alfred (82)—December 4, 1988

Vera, Joe (73)—October 5, 1988

Voorhees, Donald (85)—January 10, 1989

Washington, Bernie (83)—March 5, 1989

MUSICIANS

Alexander, Ashley (52)—August 18, 1988

Alexander, Elmer (66)—October 9, 1988

Allen, Thomas Sylvester (57)—August 30, 1988

Beverly, Edna Mae (75)—February 21, 1989

Bliss, John (32)—June 7, 1988

Bolotine, Leonid (87)—November 23, 1988

Brauer, Edward G. (77)—March 24, 1989

Brennan, Marguerite (95)—March 28, 1989

Broadbent, George (83)—July 16, 1988

Bronstein, Raphael (93)—November 4, 1988

Brown, Lawrence (81)—September 5, 1988

Burns, Kenneth C. (69)—February 4, 1989

Burns, Mabel L. (105)—March 10, 1989

Byrnes, Robert E. (76)—April 26, 1989

Calhoun, Joe (77)—July 23, 1988

Chambers, James (68)—January 1, 1989

Civil, Alan (59)—March 19, 1989

Clinch, Paul (41)—November 8, 1988

Cobb, Arnett (70)—March 24, 1989

Cohen, Irvin Leonard (73)—November 9, 1988

Colantuoni, Harry (36)—June 16, 1988

Comfort, Joe (71)—October 29, 1988

Compinsky, Manuel (87)—January 8, 1989

Cory, Armand (60)—December 31, 1988

Covington, Glenn (61)—September 18, 1988

Crook, Herman (89)—June 10, 1988

Cunningham, Bradley (63)—November 25, 1988

Daniels, Peter (65)—February 8, 1989

Davis, Jesse Ed (43)—June 22, 1988

DeGroote, Steven (36)—May 22, 1989

Duffy, Terry (67)—Summer 1988

Eldridge, Roy (78)—February 26, 1989

Ellis, Van Zandt (44)—June 24, 1988

Eyle, Feliz (89)—July 5, 1988

Frank, Mary Ganley (70)—July 15, 1988

Gerbeck, Raymond (66)—November 16, 1988

Geruschat, Carl (57)—May 19, 1989

Gimpel, Jakob (82)—March 12, 1989

Gregor, Marty (89)—November 21, 1988

Grimes, Lloyd (72)—March 4, 1989

Hammond, Vernon (78)—July 29, 1988

Handley, Gertrude (85)—November 16, 1988

Hart, David (37)—May 25, 1988

Haynes, Arminius N. (102)—October 6, 1988

Heard, J.C. (71)—September 27, 1988

Hodge, Van (34)—April 22, 1989

Kelly, Rex (74)—February 24, 1989

Koski, Edward (72)—March 13, 1989

Krasnopolsky, Michael (94)—August 8, 1988

LaFurn, Gerry (59)—November 9, 1988

Leeson, Cecil (86)—April 14, 1989

Lewenthal, Raymond (62)—November 21, 1988

Lovett, Samuel (94)—January 23, 1989

Maher, Joseph L. (89)—November 11, 1988

Martin, Ronald S. (82)—November 13, 1988

Mastropaolo, Charles (69)—February 7, 1989

McCallum, John Jr. (36)—January 23, 1989

Miller, Randall V. (80)—February 18, 1989

Mitchell, Howard (77)—June 22, 1988

Moon, Joseph (76)—December 16, 1988

Morton, Gertrude (80)—January 14, 1989

Moss, Wilmont (90)—September 15, 1988

Murphy, Edward A. (82)—March 5, 1989

Nash, James D. (74)—August 24, 1988

Navarra, Andre (77)—July 30, 1988

Newborn, Phineas, Jr. (57)—May 26, 1989

Panitz, Murray W. (63)—April 13, 1989

Paul, Emmanuel (84)—May 23, 1988

Perez, Jose (78)—October 16, 1988

Reitz, Robert (78)—September 18, 1988

Root, Bill—June 30, 1988

Roseveare, Jim (48)—December 11, 1988

Rouse, Charlie (64)—November 30, 1988

Rudin, Nat (78)—February 25, 1989

Schmidt, Henry W. (90)—July 27, 1988

Schmidt, Otto (70)—September 1, 1988

Schubert, Laraine (47)—July 20, 1988

Shaw, Woody Herman (44)—May 9, 1989

Simon, Sam (83)—May 23, 1988
Smith, Dalton (53)—April 26, 1989
Springs, Laddie (88)—July 14, 1988
Stanco, Giselda (87)—August 7, 1988
Staub, Frank L. (81)—August 24, 1988
Stipher, Adrian C. (80)—November 26, 1988
Tarras, Dave (95)—February 13, 1989
Temerson, Leon (83)—June 13, 1988
Thomas, David—June 6, 1988
Tipton, Billy (74)—January 21, 1989
Towlen, Gary (45)—June 22, 1988
Tunnell, John (52)—Fall 1988
Urban, Bela (76)—September 4, 1988
Vinson, Eddie (70)—July 2, 1988
Wahrer, Steve (47)—January 21, 1989
Watson, Douglas C. (81)—April 25, 1989
Webb, Mary (82)—Spring 1989
Wells, Gertrude (88)—November 25, 1988
Whyte, Duncan (78)—Winter 1989
Woodyard, Sam (63)—September 20, 1988

OTHERS

Adajian, Pearl Elmast (90)—March 29, 1989
    Owner, Adajian's, Hartford
Addams, Charles (76)—September 29, 1988
    Cartoonist
Allen, Alfred Reginald (83)—July 3, 1988
    Theater executive
Barnes, William E. Jr. (56)—March 9, 1989
    Agent
Bennett, Alvin S. (62)—March 15, 1989
    Liberty Records
Berk, Tony (28)—July 21, 1988
    Stage manager
Berlin, Ellin (85)—July 29, 1988
    Wife of Irving Berlin
Bond, James (89)—February 14, 1989
    Ornithologist, 007's namesake
Borow, Willard (70)—October 9, 1988
    Philadelphia theater muralist
Bowers, Frank O. (55)—August 24, 1988
    Wig master

Brand, Harry (92)—February 22, 1989
    Publicist
Bruno, Dominic (71)—June 30, 1988
    Nightclub owner
Carcione, Joe (73)—August 2, 1988
    TV Greengrocer
Carse, John G.—Spring 1989
    Glasgow theater director
Clarke, T.E.B. (81)—February 11, 1989
    British screen writer
Clough, Goldie Stanto (87)—April 3, 1989
    Ziegfeld's secretary
Coates, Helen Grace (89)—February 27, 1989
    Leonard Bernstein's secretary
Cohen, Aaron (34)—September 8, 1988
    Agent
Collins, Charles E. (46)—July 29, 1988
    Stage manager
Como, William (63)—January 1, 1989
    Editor-in-chief, *Dance Magazine*
Corbett, J. Ralph (91)—October 3, 1988
    Cincinnati art patron
Courtney, Cress (74)—September 11, 1988
    Agent
Curtis, Joseph W. (68)—July 11, 1988
    Joshua Logan's assistant
De Mave, Helen McKay—December 10, 1988
    John Golden's assistant
de Mendelssohn-Bartholdy, George H. (75)—September 7, 1988
    Vox Records
du Maurier, Daphne (81)—April 19, 1989
    Author
Dunn, Nicholas (31)—June 23, 1988
    Stage manager
Durden, Wally (63)—October 18, 1988
    Beverly Hills Hotel
Evans, Richard W. (63)—November 2, 1988
    Stage manager
Fineman, Joel (42)—March 25, 1989
    Shakespeare scholar
Fischer, Jerry (73)—August 15, 1988
    Mercury Records
Fowler, David (52)—March 11, 1989
    Arts administration

Frosch, Aaron (64)—April 29, 1989
Lawyer
Furse, Russell L. (88)—December 17,
1988
Co-founder TV Academy
Geiringer, Karl (89)—January 10, 1989
Musicologist
Goeld, Seymour (71)—May 30, 1988
Caesar's Palace
Golden, Gertrude (75)—September 15,
1988
Publicist
Goldstraub, Mark Neil (37)—December
14, 1988
Publicist
Gordon, Max (86)—May 11, 1989
Village Vanguard
Griffith, William (60)—November 12,
1988
Ballet teacher
Grossinger, Paul (73)—April 7, 1989
Grossinger's Hotel
Gurian, Manning (74)—August 3, 1988
Publicist
Heider, Wally (66)—March 24, 1989
Hindsight Records
Hill, Rosemary (61)—May 1989
Stage manager
Holbrook, Jay C. (35)—June 19, 1988
Baltimore Opera
Household, Geoffrey (87)—October 4,
1988
Author
Josephson, Barney (86)—September 29,
1988
Cafe Society
Kafkalis, Nikos (45)—October 8, 1988
Stage manager
Kaltenbach, Jerry (51)—November 15,
1988
Ohio State Fair
Kandel, Emmanuel (78)—July 27, 1988
Bonded Services
Karp, Oscar (74)—July 29, 1988
Oscar's Restaurant
Kaufman, Les (80)—January 9, 1989
Publicist

Kimbrough, Emily (90)—February 11,
1989
Author
Kingsley, Lee Goode (80)—January 30,
1989
New York Philharmonic
Kozak, Roman (40)—October 13, 1988
Billboard
La Chappelle, Gilbert (37)—August 21,
1988
Makeup artist
L'Amour, Louis (80)—June 10, 1988
Author
Larsen, Jens Peter (86)—August 22, 1988
Musicologist
Lee, Jennie (84)—November 17, 1988
British arts administrator
Lenny, Jack (81)—March 12, 1989
Theatrical manager
LeVeque, Edward (92)—January 28, 1989
Keystone Kop
Lieber, Perry (93)—December 12, 1988
Publicist
Lipton, Harry (73)—May 29, 1988
Agent
Luhrman, Henry (47)—April 11, 1989
Publicist
Lurie, Jerome D. (71)—August 17, 1988
Lawyer
Marshall, Betty Voigt (70)—January 22,
1989
Newsweek
Martus, Ida (93)—March 23, 1989
Theater for schools
McCaffrey, Eddie (79)—July 7, 1988
Variety
McNellis, Maggie (71)—May 24, 1989
Radio personality
Melnitz, William W. (88)—January 12,
1989
UCLA College of Fine Arts
Metz, Ernest St. John (67)—August 9, 1988
Vocal coach
Morrison, Herb (83)—January 10, 1989
Hindenburg crash reporter
Parlett, Thomas Ward (43)—April 2, 1989
Theatrical manager

Pearson, Ben (74)—July 5, 1988
  Agent
Peckerman, Joseph (41)—August 13, 1988
  Lawyer
Pierson, Frank (55)—November 11, 1988
  St. Louis theater
Pior, Frank (68)—February 7, 1989
  Dance instructor
Pope, Generoso P. Jr. (61)—October 2,
  1988
  National Enquirer
Powers, Michael Francis (51)—Sept. 19,
  1988
  Agent
Prude, Walter Foy (78)—August 29, 1988
  Hurok manager
Regner, Elmer (86)—March 8, 1989
  Milwaukee theater
Reilly, Jack (89)—July 3, 1988
  Director, special events
Rendell, Henry M. (75)—December 8,
  1988
  Old Vic wardrobe
Resnick, Irving (72)—January 18, 1989
  Caesar's Palace
Reynolds, Paul R. (83)—June 10, 1988
  Agent
Rice, Alfred (81)—March 29, 1989
  Lawyer
Riolo, Anthony (46)—March 28, 1989
  Ballet executive
Rivkin, Joe (81)—February 3, 1989
  Agent
Roberts, Christopher (37)—April 29, 1989
  Theatrical manager
Robinson, Max (49)—December 20, 1988
  TV anchorman
Roginski, Ed (44)—July 28, 1988
  Hollywood Reporter
Rosen, Charles (70)—October 1988
  Miami show business

Rosenbaum, Hattie (82)—December 24, 1988
  Manager
Roud, Richard (59)—January 15, 1989
  New York Film Festival
Schoenfeld, Joe (81)—November 22, 1988
  Daily Variety
Shuttleworth, William (25)—June 1, 1988
  Publicist
Silverstein, Leo (73)—November 14, 1988
  Agent
Slaff, George (83)—March 24, 1989
  Lawyer
Soper, John D. (40)—September 20, 1988
  Translator
Spanognoletti, Dominic T. (67)—Jan. 11,
  1989
  Lawyer
Stavens, Gary (36)—September 30, 1988
  Makeup artist
Stevens, Lee (56)—February 2, 1989
  Agent
Sugarman, Elias E. (87)—May 31, 1988
  Billboard
Sully, Joe—August 2, 1988
  Agent
Taktsis, Costas (51)—August 28, 1988
  Author
Tubbs, Vincent (73)—January 15, 1989
  Publicist
Vinson, Clyde M. (60)—February 5, 1989
  Teacher
Wall, Sam (75)—January 8, 1989
  Publicist
Weiner, Richard (36)—August 28, 1988
  Agent
Weiner, Robert L. (53)—March 4, 1989
  Theater manager
Werner, Eric (87)—July 28, 1988
  Musicologist
Wood, Michael (76)—Winter 1989
  Royal Ballet of Britain

THE BEST PLAYS, 1894–1988

Listed in alphabetical order below are all those works selected as Best Plays in previous volumes of the *Best Plays* series. Opposite each title is given the volume in which the play appears, its opening date and its total number of performances. Two separate opening-date and performance-number entries signify two separate engagements off Broadway and on Broadway when the original production was transferred from one area to the other, usually in an off-to-on direction. Those plays marked with an asterisk (*) were still playing on June 1, 1989 and their number of performances was figured through May 31, 1989. Adaptors and translators are indicated by (ad) and (tr), the symbols (b), (m) and (l) stand for the author of the book, music and lyrics in the case of musicals and (c) signifies the credit for the show's conception.

NOTE: A season-by-season listing, rather than an alphabetical one, of the 500 Best Plays in the first 50 volumes, starting with the yearbook for the season of 1919–1920, appears in *The Best Plays of 1968–69*.

PLAY	VOLUME	OPENED	PERFS
ABE LINCOLN IN ILLINOIS—Robert E. Sherwood	38–39	Oct. 15, 1938	472
ABRAHAM LINCOLN—John Drinkwater	19–20	Dec. 15, 1919	193
ACCENT ON YOUTH—Samson Raphaelson	34–35	Dec. 25, 1934	229
ADAM AND EVA—Guy Bolton, George Middleton	19–20	Sept. 13, 1919	312
ADAPTATION—Elaine May; and NEXT–Terrence McNally	68–69	Feb. 10, 1969	707
AFFAIRS OF STATE—Louis Verneuil	50–51	Sept. 25, 1950	610
AFTER THE FALL—Arthur Miller	63–64	Jan. 23, 1964	208
AFTER THE RAIN—John Bowen	67–68	Oct. 9, 1967	64
AGNES OF GOD—John Pielmeier	81–82	Mar. 30, 1982	486
AH, WILDERNESS!—Eugene O'Neill	33–34	Oct. 2, 1933	289
AIN'T SUPPOSED TO DIE A NATURAL DEATH—(b, m, l) Melvin Van Peebles	71–72	Oct. 7, 1971	325
ALIEN CORN—Sidney Howard	32–33	Feb. 20, 1933	98
ALISON'S HOUSE—Susan Glaspell	30–31	Dec. 1, 1930	41
ALL MY SONS—Arthur Miller	46–47	Jan. 29, 1947	328
ALL OVER TOWN—Murray Schisgal	74–75	Dec. 12, 1974	233
ALL THE WAY HOME—Tad Mosel, based on James Agee's novel *A Death in the Family*	60–61	Nov. 30, 1960	333
ALLEGRO—(b, l) Oscar Hammerstein II, (m) Richard Rodgers	47–48	Oct. 10, 1947	315
AMADEUS—Peter Shaffer	80–81	Dec. 17, 1980	1,181
AMBUSH—Arthur Richman	21–22	Oct. 10, 1921	98
AMERICA HURRAH—Jean-Claude van Itallie	66–67	Nov. 6, 1966	634
AMERICAN BUFFALO—David Mamet	76–77	Feb. 16, 1977	135

592   THE BEST PLAYS OF 1988–1989

PLAY	VOLUME	OPENED	PERFS
ENTER MADAME—Gilda Varesi, Dolly Byrne	20–21	Aug. 16, 1920	350
ENTERTAINER, THE—John Osborne	57–58	Feb. 12, 1958	97
EPITAPH FOR GEORGE DILLON—John Osborne, Anthony Creighton	58–59	Nov. 4, 1958	23
EQUUS—Peter Shaffer	74–75	Oct. 24, 1974	1,209
ESCAPE—John Galsworthy	27–28	Oct. 26, 1927	173
ETHAN FROME—Owen and Donald Davis, based on Edith Wharton's novel	35–36	Jan. 21, 1936	120
EVE OF ST. MARK, THE—Maxwell Anderson	42–43	Oct. 7, 1942	307
EXCURSION—Victor Wolfson	36–37	Apr. 9, 1937	116
EXECUTION OF JUSTICE—Emily Mann	85–86	Mar. 13, 1986	12
EXTREMITIES—William Mastrosimone	82–83	Dec. 22, 1982	325
FALL GUY, THE—James Gleason, George Abbott	24–25	Mar. 10, 1925	176
FAMILY BUSINESS—Dick Goldberg	77–78	Apr. 12, 1978	438
FAMILY PORTRAIT—Lenore Coffee, William Joyce Cowen	38–39	May 8, 1939	111
FAMOUS MRS. FAIR, THE—James Forbes	19–20	Dec. 22, 1919	344
FAR COUNTRY, A—Henry Denker	60–61	Apr. 4, 1961	271
FARMER TAKES A WIFE, THE—Frank B. Elser, Marc Connelly, based on Walter D. Edmonds's novel *Rome Haul*	34–35	Oct. 30, 1934	104
FATAL WEAKNESS, THE—George Kelly	46–47	Nov. 19, 1946	119
FENCES—August Wilson	86–87	Mar. 26, 1987	526
FIDDLER ON THE ROOF—(b) Joseph Stein, (l) Sheldon Harnick, (m) Jerry Bock, based on Sholom Aleichem's stories	64–65	Sept. 22, 1964	3,242
5TH OF JULY, THE—Lanford Wilson (also called *Fifth of July*)	77–78	Apr. 27, 1978	159
FIND YOUR WAY HOME—John Hopkins	73–74	Jan. 2, 1974	135
FINISHING TOUCHES—Jean Kerr	72–73	Feb. 8, 1973	164
FIORELLO!—(b) Jerome Weidman, George Abbott, (l) Sheldon Harnick, (m) Jerry Bock	59–60	Nov. 23, 1959	795
FIREBRAND, THE—Edwin Justus Mayer	24–25	Oct. 15, 1924	269
First Lady—Katharine Dayton, George S. Kaufman	35–36	Nov. 26, 1935	246
FIRST MONDAY IN OCTOBER—Jerome Lawrence, Robert E. Lee	78–79	Oct. 3, 1978	79
FIRST MRS. FRASER, THE—St. John Ervine	29–30	Dec. 28, 1929	352
FIRST YEAR, THE—Frank Craven	20–21	Oct. 20, 1920	760
FIVE FINGER EXERCISE—Peter Shaffer	59–60	Dec. 2, 1959	337
FIVE-STAR FINAL—Louis Weitzenkorn	30–31	Dec. 30, 1930	175
FLIGHT TO THE WEST—Elmer Rice	40–41	Dec. 30, 1940	136
FLOATING LIGHT BULB, THE—Woody Allen	80–81	Apr. 27, 1981	65
FLOWERING PEACH, THE—Clifford Odets	54–55	Dec. 28, 1954	135
FOLLIES—(b) James Goldman, (m, l) Stephen Sondheim	70–71	Apr. 4, 1971	521
FOOL, THE—Channing Pollock	22–23	Oct. 23, 1922	373
FOOL FOR LOVE—Sam Shepard	83–84	May 26, 1983	1,000
FOOLISH NOTION—Philip Barry	44–45	Mar. 3, 1945	104
FOREIGNER, THE—Larry Shue	84–85	Nov. 1, 1984	686

INDEX

INDEX

Play titles **appear in** bold face. *Bold face italic* page numbers refer to those pages where complete cast and credit listings for New York productions may be found.

609

656   INDEX

ABOUT THE EDITORS

Otis L. Guernsey Jr., editor of the Best Plays yearbook, began his long association with the theater at Yale University, where he wrote three plays that were presented by student groups. For nineteen years he was associated with the *New York Herald Tribune*, beginning as copy boy and then graduating to reporter, film and drama critic, and drama editor. He became a freelance writer in 1960, authoring two original film stories. He now edits the *Dramatists Guild Quarterly* and is a national popular lecturer on the modern theater. He is a former member of the New York Film Critics (past chairman) and the New York Drama Critics Circle. Mr. Guernsey has also been a member of the panel of critics who selected the Tony Award nominees and served as a member of the advisory committee of the Bicentennial program at Kennedy Center, Washington, D.C. He is a charter member of the newly formed national critics' organization, the American Theater Critics Association. Mr. Guernsey's collected annual SEASON IN NEW YORK reports have been drawn from twenty-two volumes of BEST PLAYS and now form a continuing detailed history and critical appraisal of the New York Stage in his monumental work: CURTAIN TIMES: The New York Theater 1965–1987 (Applause Books).

Jeffrey Sweet's plays, including *The Value of Names, Ties* and *Porch*, have been presented off Broadway, on television, and in dozens of institutional theaters, earning him the NEA Fellowship in Literature, the Outer Critics Circle Award, the Heideman Award and two Society of Midland Authors Awards. He also wrote an oral history of the Second City troupe called *Something Wonderful Right Away*, and has been a regular contributor to the *Dramatists Guild Quarterly* since 1970. He is an alumnus of the O'Neill Center's National Critics Institute, to which he has often returned as a guest lecturer, and studied with Clive Barnes at NYU. He has also taught or run workshops for SUNY at Purchase, HB Studios, New Dramatists (of which he is a member) and the Goodman Theater. He and his wife Sheridan live in Manhattan with their son Jonathan.